Our American Sisters

Second Edition

OUR AMERICAN SISTERS
Women in
American Life and Thought

Jean E. Friedman
Dutchess Community College
State University of New York

William G. Shade
Lehigh University

Allyn and Bacon, Inc.
Boston London Sydney Toronto

Library of Congress Cataloging in Publication Data

Friedman, Jean E   comp.
  Our American sisters.

  Bibliography: p.
  1. Women—United States—History—Addresses, essays, lectures. 2. Women—United States—Social conditions—Addresses, essays, lectures. I. Shade, William G., joint comp. II. Title.
HQ1420.F74   1976   301.41'2'0973   76-21252

ISBN 0-205-05578-8

WOMEN.SJ

HQ
1410
C93
1976

Contents

Preface

Since 1970, when we began working on the first edition of *Our American Sisters,* we have been impressed by the immense outpouring of high quality scholarship that has come to characterize the field of women's history. We became aware of how quickly our book was becoming dated. With the help of numerous professors in the field of women's history who have commented on the first edition, and with the consistent support of our editor Robert Patterson, we have tried to bring *Our American Sisters* up to date.

We have expanded and revised this edition to incorporate the best scholarship that has appeared since 1970, while retaining the strengths of the first edition. The chronological organization and ten of the essays of the first edition appear again. Fourteen new essays have been included from journals such as *American Quarterly, The Journal of Social History,* and *Feminist Studies.* We have made an effort to maintain a balance of material devoted to each period of American history, and essays have been added to fill gaps in the conceptual structure of the book. This edition has more material on American attitudes toward women and on working-class women. The editors' introductions to each historical era have been expanded to touch upon important material not covered in the essays and to provide the student with an inclusive bibliography of recent writings relating to each period. There is also a general bibliography of easily obtainable books, primarily paperbacks, to orient the beginning student to the subject.

In addition to those friends whom we thanked in the first edition and who have continued to sustain our efforts, such as Mary Jo Hill and Joe Dowling, we have developed new debts with this edition. Women scholars all over the country have given needed encouragement and support, but none has been a happier acquaintance than Dorothy Lipson. The readers for Allyn and Bacon saved us from many errors and were most helpful, especially Sharon Hartman Strom. Among our colleagues and friends, Larry Leder, Carroll Pursell, Mary Lou Shade, Elsa Dixler, Judy Kohl, and Bonnie Polgardy helped us out in one way or another.

J.E.F.

W.G.S.

Introduction

A decade ago one of the leading historians in the United States warned his colleagues that their traditional approaches to American history seriously perverted the subject. At the time, David Potter was referring to the way in which historians have ignored women and belittled their role in American history. Major generalizations about the American character have totally ignored women, and when historians have commented upon women, their views have been wildly inconsistent. In part this situation was a product of ignorance. Only a handful of relevant monographs existed in the 1960s, and the treatment of women in general studies was woefully inadequate. Few aspects of the history of women in America had drawn serious attention. As late as 1969 Gerda Lerner could write, "The striking fact about the historiography of women is the general neglect of the subject by historians."

By the mid-1970s the situation changed dramatically. The emergence of the movement for women's liberation in the 1960s heightened women's consciousness of their position in American society and led to demands for college courses that would enable women to regain their history. By 1975 approximately ninety colleges offered interdisciplinary majors in Women's Studies; of the over 4,000 courses on women, there were approximately 300 on the history of American women. At the same time, historians—many of whom were feminists—revealed a new concern for the subject. The number of texts and monographs has grown geometrically. Scholarly journals are increasingly open to studies concerning women. Rarely does an issue of the *American Quarterly, Journal of Social History,* or *Journal of Interdisciplinary History* fail to include at least one relevant article, and new journals such as *Feminist Studies, Women's Studies,* and *Signs* are devoted entirely to the subject. Conferences on the history of women have been sponsored across the country. The programs of the annual meetings of major historical organizations feature growing numbers of sessions on women. By almost any measure, the history of women is now attracting unparalleled interest.

The origins of this dramatic change in the historical treatment of women can be found in the shift in attitudes toward women in American society, in the rise of women's professional aspirations and their place in the history profession, and in a renewed interest in social history and historical sociology. Although all historians of women are not feminists—feminist history is not simply propaganda for the movement—the revival of interest in the history of women is intimately linked to the revival of feminism in the past decade.

Earlier in this century, the passage of the Nineteenth Amendment sparked a good deal of professional interest in the history of American women, and a number of major books on the subject appeared during the interwar period. Feminism was probably in better repute in the 1920s than at any time in American history. During that decade the birth rate fell precipitously, and increasing numbers of women entered graduate schools. The proportion of women earning M.A.'s and Ph.D.'s rose dramatically to a high point in 1930 and then declined slightly during the Great Depression. The number of women college professors grew, and women played a relatively more important role within the history profession than they do today. At the time that this generation of women was entering the history profession, several influential historians evidenced heightened interest in the role of women in history, as part of their rebellion against the legalistic and narrowly political focus of their predecessors.

The fascination of Progressive historians with social and economic aspects of history and their tendency to view American history in terms of the conflict between conservatives and reformers led at least two of the most important and widely read male historians of this era to study the role of women in American history. In 1922, Arthur Schlesinger, in *New Viewpoints in American History,* included an essay on women that protested "the pall of silence" cast over the subject. Later in the decade Charles and Mary Beard co-authored the extremely influential, *The Rise of American Civilization,* which devoted a large amount of space to women, emphasizing their economic importance. During the interwar years men and women influenced by the Progressive school integrated discussions of women's roles into studies of social history and produced a number of classic monographs on women in America.

Although historians trained in the 1920s and 1930s maintained their concern for the history of women, by 1940 a reversal of earlier trends became apparent. The feminists, whose story Schlesinger thought "one of the noblest chapters in the history of American democracy," fell into increasing public disrepute. The birth rate rose dramatically as the post–World War II generation of women appeared dominated by what sociologist Jesse Bernard has called the "Motherhood Mania." The percentage of women completing M.A. and Ph.D. degrees declined as the birth rate climbed. Not only did the attitude of women toward competition in the academic world change, but the attitudes of academic men toward women changed for the worse. During this strange interlude, attention to the history of women faded; even areas of American life in which women had traditionally played important roles went unstudied. When families in America were once again growing and the role of the homemaker was exalted in the media, the historical study of the family languished. The study of political, diplomatic, and economic elites characterized the historiography of these years.

Since the early 1960s the fortunes of the history of women have changed as each of the trends that characterized the preceding decades was reversed. Feminism and feminist issues have gained renewed popularity. In the late 1950s, the birth rate once again began to fall. Each year the number of young women choosing to continue their education increased. Although the proportion of women holding Ph.D.'s in history has not yet reached the level of the 1920s, it has risen dramatically since the nadir of the 1950s. At the same time the attitudes of male colleagues born since the late 1930s represent a distinct improvement over those of the previous generation. Finally, the 1960s witnessed a revival of interest in social history and the processes of social change that has broadened the concept of legitimate subjects of history. The "new" social history, which studies sexual behavior and sex roles, the effects of demographic change, religious and ethnic conflict, and marriage and the family, has suddenly "rediscovered" women everywhere in the American past.

Before the present revival of women's history, most historians writing on women focused narrowly upon the history of the feminist movement and what Schlesinger called women's "contributions to American national progress." Since this approach characterized the writings of the feminist chroniclers, it was only natural that the Progressive historians, who were sympathetic to the feminist cause and concerned with reform, carried these views over into professional history. But a more comprehensive approach to the history of women is necessary if we are to recapture the wealth and texture of women's lives in the American past.

A general consideration of the current scholarship suggested to us a rather crude taxonomy which has served to organize the essays in this book. We have divided American history into four chronological periods of rather unequal length, but which nonetheless seem to present a sense of surface continuity in relation to the history of American women. Each section is preceded by an introduction that outlines the major unifying themes of the period and relates the essays to these themes. Within each period we have attempted to include material bearing on the three most distinctive aspects of the history of American women: society's definition of the nature of women and their proper roles; the actual conditions of women and the social and economic functions that they performed; and women's response to their special intellectual, socioeconomic, and political problems. Finally, several essays have been included to show the differential effects of changes in these areas on subgroups of women, in order to take into account the effects of region, class, race, religion, and ethnicity. It is our hope that this relatively simple organizational structure will highlight the importance of the essays and facilitate the integration of this excellent recent scholarship into a more comprehensive framework for the study of the American past.

I

Women in Colonial America

From the settlement of Jamestown until the outbreak of the American Revolution, the colonists struggled to establish a stable society based upon the English model. In each new settlement they rebuilt familiar social, political, and economic institutions and endeavored to reaffirm the ideals and values of English civilization. Sometimes immediately, but more often gradually, the new environment and the absence of central authority altered institutions and attitudes. Colonial society slowly evolved into one quite different from the Mother Country; by the mid-eighteenth century, the transplanted Englishman became a "new man," an American. The effects of this process upon the status of women highlight their anomalous position in American history.

The first mainland colonies were founded as business ventures. It was not until societies were established in the New World that a significant number of women crossed the Atlantic. Throughout the colonial period men outnumbered women. This basic demographic fact accounted for the earlier age at which colonial women married and the greater "liberties and privileges" that they enjoyed in relation to European women.[1] Isolation and a limited labor supply enhanced the woman's value to the family. "The wife and mother in the rude settlement on or near the frontier was more than a housekeeper; she was an indispensable part of the apparatus of survival."[2] Elsewhere in an economy dominated by farms and small shops, women worked side-by-side with men, and often ran large plantations or carried on the family business following the death of a husband or father. Necessity determined that few jobs were deemed inappropriate for colonial women; they were blacksmiths and barbers, tanners and tavern keepers.

The first three selections of part I, which deal with the day-to-day lives of colonial women, reveal why foreign observers generally believed women in America occupied a higher status than their European counterparts. The community placed strong emphasis on the social role of the family and closely surveyed the moral life of its members. But as Edmund Morgan shows in "The Puritans and Sex," the colonists were neither unrealistic nor "puritanical" about sexual matters, as has often been charged. They were well aware that "sexual intercourse was a human necessity" and believed that "marriage was the proper place for it." Although they were unable to contain all sexual impulses wholly within the bounds of marriage—Morgan reminds us that "illicit sexual intercourse was common"—the Puritan magistrates encouraged early marriage and took every means to ensure "peaceful cohabitation." Adultery was severely punished, but divorces and annullments were *relatively* easy to obtain. Perhaps the most interesting aspect of the Puritan attitude toward sexual intercourse was the degree to which the magistrates acknowledged and respected sexual needs of women as well as of men. John Demos extends Morgan's analysis in his study of Plymouth Colony, *A Little Commonwealth*, which shows that the court records of the Plymouth Colony contain only minor traces of a double standard. Demos' study of decision making in the family also reveals that in their day-to-day lives women stood more nearly equal to their husbands than has generally been supposed.

Clearly the family was an essential element of the colonial community. Women shared responsibility for religious, social, and economic functions, and the roles of husband and wife were less neatly compartmentalized than they were in the nineteenth century. The cooperation and intimacy between husbands and wives that characterized colonial marriages sometimes led women outside the home into business and political affairs. As Julia Cherry Spruill shows in the selection from her book, *Women's Life and Work in the Southern Colonies*, colonial women often shared their husband's careers, mending political fences or fomenting revolution. Spruill discusses the remarkable exploits of Margaret Brent, executrix of the estate of Governor Leonard Calvert and one of the "most prominent personages" in Maryland, "whose business and public activities fill many pages of court records and suggest a career which the most ambitious modern feminists might envy."

By the eighteenth century in America, common social practice, specific legislation, and the development of equity law freed married women from complete domination by their husbands and gave them a certain amount of legal autonomy unknown under the common law of England. However, colonial society was basically masculine in orientation. Attitudes toward women during the period remained traditional, differing little from those of contemporary Europeans. The belief in the inferiority of women was universal. Although American women were far better off than their English sisters and although in some areas their legal position improved during the colonial period, women, particularly those who were married, suffered under numerous legal and social restrictions.[3]

If some women participated in public affairs, the lives of most women were generally circumscribed within the family where wives were expected to be subservient to their husbands. Political rights were almost completely restricted to men as heads of families. Access to the professions was closed to women on the grounds that they should "refrain from such things as proper for men whose minds are stronger."[4] Although colonial Americans considered piety a major feminine grace, only a few denominations allowed women to preach. In general they followed the admonition of St. Paul that "women keep silent in the churches." In "The Case of the American Jezebels," Lyle Koehler discusses Anne Hutchinson, the most famous woman preacher of the colonial era. By focusing on women's frustration with the limitations imposed upon them by traditional roles and by the magistrates' fears of the socially destructive consequences of women's departure from their proper sphere, Koehler provides an entirely new perspective on the Antinomian controversy of the 1630s in Massachusetts Bay.[5] Colonial Americans "viewed the whole of society as an intricate series of ranks, a profusion of finely graded positions of authority and subordination, which neither male nor female could circumvent."[6] Thus, violation of sexual norms induced a spectre of moral and civil anarchy threatening the entire social order and undermining the very basis of civilization as they knew it.

During the Revolution, American women aided the patriot cause in a variety of ways.[7] Women rose up to oppose the Stamp Act, the hated tea tax, and the Coercive Acts. There were Daughters of Liberty as well as Sons of Liberty. During the war Ester De Berdt Reed and Sara Bache, Benjamin Franklin's daughter, headed an effort to supply troops with badly needed clothing. Many lesser known women moved into the growing textile industry. Although the American Revolution produced no great heroine, "Molly Pitcher" and Margaret Corbin were noted for their courage during battle, and Deborah Sampson Gannett served in the Continental Army disguised as Robert Shurtleff. The Revolution, however, brought little change in women's status or in men's attitudes toward women. At the close of the Revolution, the brilliant and witty Abigail Adams chided her husband, saying, "I cannot say that I think you are very generous to the ladies; for whilst you are proclaiming peace and goodwill to men, emancipating all nations, you insist upon retaining an absolute power over all wives."[8]

The education of women mirrored society's attitudes. Illiteracy among women was rampant; perhaps as many as two-thirds of the women in sixteenth-century New England were unable to write their name. In the seventeenth century, women's literacy improved, but even at the end of the colonial period "female illiteracy remained quite common and women were always at a distinct disadvantage in obtaining basic education."[9] Women who managed to attend school found opportunities limited. In the lower grades boys and girls attended school together, but beyond that point the colleges that trained men for the professions and the grammar schools that prepared men for the colleges were closed to women as a matter of course. Even when coeducation became more popular at the end of the eighteenth century, its advocates like Richard Rush emphasized the need for educated mothers to raise children, rather than stressing the intellectual contributions of women. Linda K. Kerber's essay, "Daughters of Columbia," traces the post-revolutionary debate over the proposals of Rush, Charles Brockden Brown, and Judith Sargent Murray, the author of the Constantia letters, for the education of women. Kerber shows that traditional conceptions of a woman's proper sphere persisted even in the optimistic atmosphere of the new republic, and that seemingly radical proposals for education of women were limited.

Although the birth rate was declining and women were gaining greater control over their sexual lives, the position of women in American society was deteriorating as the eighteenth century drew to a close.[10] The close relationship between husband and wife described by Demos continued to exist on the frontier and in rural areas where men and women, of necessity, shared responsibilities for home and family. But in the urban areas and among the upper classes the roles of men and women were becoming more clearly differentiated and the first signs of the so-called Victorian morality appeared. The increasing differentiation of sex roles and the acceptance of English ideals of the relations of the sexes was related to the appearance of sharper class distinctions and growing economic specialization, which separated the functions of men and women physically and psychologically. "In the creation of a middle class, essentially urban style of life, women who early had shared in the direction of farms and the rigors of pioneer existence, were expected to preside gracefully over drawing rooms."[11]

In the South, the idealization of white womanhood was intertwined with the growth of slavery and anxieties about miscegenation. Spruill notes that "In the Southern colonies the eighteenth century saw a decline in the vigor and self-reliance of women in wealthier families and a lessening of their influence in public matters." The selection from Winthrop Jordan's *White Man's Burden* reveals the interrelationship between racial attitudes and sexual myths in early America and hints at the deep effect that the degradation of blacks had upon whites. As do Morgan and Demos, Jordan portrays a much freer climate of discussion of sex and a much more open acceptance of sexuality in the early part of the colonial period. But with the entrenchment of slavery, sexual relations became warped and a double standard emerged in a distinctive form that irreparably scarred Southern women of both races.[12]

Little is known about the lives of the large number of Afro-American women brought into the colonies as slaves, but certain ideas can be inferred from the work of writers such as Jordan.[13] Although their status undoubtedly evolved from servant to slave for life, along with that of Afro-American men, one of the first references to slavery in colonial records concerns a woman in Massachusetts who in 1639 refused to allow her master to mate her with a Negro man on the grounds that such was "beyond her slavery. . . ."[14] Early in the eighteenth century, the law of slavery was codified and conditions became increasingly severe. Miscegenation, which had been widespread during the previous century, was banned. As the century wore on, manumission grew increasingly difficult. Due to the nature of the tasks to which they were assigned, slave women were probably more easily assimilated into their new life than were African men, and they may have adjusted more easily to the rigors of slavery.[15] There are, however, numerous instances of resistance by women for whom the harshness of their lives was compounded by physical and sexual abuse. The Revolution led to the abolition of slavery in the Northern states, but had little positive effect on the status of the vast majority of blacks enslaved below the Mason–Dixon line.

NOTES

1. Roger Thompson, *Women in Stuart England and America: A Comparative Study* (London: Routledge and Kegan Paul, 1974); Daniel Scott Smith, "The Demographic History of Colonial New England," *Journal of Economic History* 32 (March 1972): 165–83.

2. Carl Degler, *Out of Our Past: The Forces that Shaped Modern America* (New York: Harper & Row, 1970), pp. 55–56.

3. Mary Sumner Benson, *Women in Eighteenth Century America* (New York: Columbia University Press, 1935).

4. John Winthrop, *Journal,* in *Up From the Pedestal: Selected Writings in the History of American Feminism,* Aileen Kraditor, ed. (Chicago: Quadrangle Books, 1968), p. 30.

5. Two other interesting essays show how attention to women's history can enlighten traditional subjects of interest: *see* John Demos, "Underlying Themes in the Witchcraft of Seventeenth Century New England," *American Historical Review,* 75 (June 1970): 1311–26; and Cedric B. Cowing, "Sex and Preaching in the Great Awakening," *American Quarterly* (Fall 1968): 624–44.

6. Mary P. Ryan, *Womanhood in America from Colonial Times to the Present* (New York: New Viewpoints, 1975), p. 40. See also Ben Barker-Benfield, "Ann Hutchinson and the Puritan Attitude toward Women," *Feminist Studies* 2 (1972): 65–96.

7. Elizabeth Cometti, "Women in the American Revolution," *The New Quarterly* 20 (September 1947): 329–46.

8. Quoted in Arthur Schlesinger, *New Viewpoints in American History* (New York: Macmillan, 1922), p. 131. On the limits of Abigail Adams's feminism, *see* Linda Grant DePauw, "The American Revolution and the Rights of Women: The Feminist Theory of Abigail Adams." (Unpublished paper delivered at the Organization of American Historians Meeting, Boston, 1975.)

9. Kenneth A. Lockridge, *Literacy in Colonial New England: An Enquiry into the Social Context of Literacy in the Early Modern West* (New York: W.W. Norton and Co., 1974), p. 4.

10. Daniel Scott Smith, "Family Limitation, Sexual Control and Domestic Feminism in Victorian America," in *Clio's Consciousness Raised,* Mary Hartman and Lois W. Banner, eds. (New York: Harper & Row, 1974), argues that the lower birth rate, greater longevity, and Victorian sexual ethics of the nineteenth century improved women's position.

11. Page Smith, *Daughters of the Promised Land* (Boston: Little, Brown, and Co., 1970), p. 68. Smith refers to this shift of attitudes as "The Great Repression."

12. For a modern, white, Southern woman's poignant discussion of this subject, *see* Lillian Smith, *Killers of the Dream* (New York: W.W. Norton and Co., 1949). The long-term effects on black women of the sexual mythology connected with slavery and the subsequent caste system can be seen in Allison Davis and John Dollard, *Children of Bondage* (New York: Harper & Row, 1964); and William H. Greer and Price M. Cobbs, *Black Rage* (New York: Basic Books, 1968).

13. *See also* these excellent recent studies: Gerald W. Mullin, *Flight and Rebellion: Slave Resistance in Eighteenth-Century Virginia* (New York: Oxford University Press, 1972); and Peter H. Wood, *Black Majority: Negroes in Colonial South Carolina from 1670 through the Stono Rebellion* (New York: Alfred A. Knopf, 1974).

14. Carl Degler, "Slavery and the Genesis of American Race Prejudice," *Comparative Studies in Society and History* 2 (October 1959): 49–66. For a decade in the seventeenth century, Maryland enslaved white women who married black slaves.

15. Mullin, *Flight and Rebellion,* pp. 103–05.

1

The Puritans and Sex

Edmund S. Morgan

Henry Adams once observed that Americans have "ostentatiously ignored" sex. He could think of only two American writers who touched
upon the subject with any degree of boldness—Walt Whitman and Bret
Harte. Since the time when Adams made this penetrating observation,
American writers have been making up for lost time in a way that
would make Bret Harte, if not Whitman, blush. And yet there is still
more truth than falsehood in Adams's statement. Americans, by comparison with Europeans or Asiatics, are squeamish when confronted
with the facts of life. My purpose is not to account for this squeamish-
ness, but simply to point out that the Puritans, those bogeymen of the
modern intellectual, are not responsible for it.

At the outset, consider the Puritans' attitude toward marriage and
the role of sex in marriage. The popular assumption might be that the
Puritans frowned on marriage and tried to hush up the physical aspect
of it as much as possible, but listen to what they themselves had to say.
Samuel Willard, minister of the Old South Church in the latter part of
the seventeenth century and author of the most complete textbook of
Puritan divinity, more than once expressed his horror at "that Popish
conceit of the Excellency of Virginity."[1] Another minister, John Cotton, wrote that

> Women are Creatures without which there is no comfortable Living for
> man: it is true of them what is wont to be said of Governments, *That bad*
> *ones are better than none:* They are a sort of Blasphemers then who

From *The New England Quarterly* 15 (December 1942): 591–607. Reprinted with permission
of the author.

dispise and decry them, and call them *a necessary Evil,* for they are *a necessary Good.*[2]

These sentiments did not arise from an interpretation of marriage as a spiritual partnership, in which sexual intercourse was a minor or incidental matter. Cotton gave his opinion of "Platonic love" when he recalled the case of

> one who immediately upon marriage, without ever approaching the *Nuptial Bed,* indented with the *Bride,* that by mutual consent they might both live such a life, and according did sequestring themselves according to the custom of those times, from the rest of mankind, and afterwards from one another too, in their retired Cells, giving themselves up to a Contemplative life; and this is recorded as an instance of no little or ordinary Vertue; but I must be pardoned in it, if I can account it no other than an effort of blind zeal, for they are the dictates of a blind mind they follow therein, and not of that Holy Spirit, which saith *It is not good that man should be alone.*[3]

Here is as healthy an attitude as one could hope to find anywhere. Cotton certainly cannot be accused of ignoring human nature. Nor was he an isolated example among the Puritans. Another minister stated plainly that "the Use of the Marriage Bed" is "founded in mans Nature," and that consequently any withdrawal from sexual intercourse upon the part of husband or wife "Denies all reliefe in Wedlock vnto Human necessity: and sends it for supply vnto Beastiality when God gives not the gift of Continency."[4] In other words, sexual intercourse was a human necessity and marriage the only proper supply for it. These were the views of the New England clergy, the acknowledged leaders of the community, the most Puritanical of the Puritans. As proof that their congregations concurred with them one may cite the case in which the members of the First Church of Boston expelled James Mattock because, among other offenses, "he denied Coniugall fellowship vnto his wife for the space of 2 years together vpon pretense of taking Revenge upon himself for his abusing of her before marryage."[5] So strongly did the Puritans insist upon the sexual character of marriage that one New Englander considered himself slandered when it was reported, "that he Brock his deceased wife's hart with Greife, that he wold be absent from her 3 weeks together when he was at home, and wold never come nere her, and such Like."[6]

There was just one limitation which the Puritans placed upon sexual relations in marriage: sex must not interfere with religion. Man's chief end was to glorify God, and all earthly delights must promote that end, not hinder it. Love for a wife was carried too far when it led a man to neglect his God:

> ... sometimes a man hath a good affection to Religion, but the love of his
> wife carries him away, a man may bee so transported to his wife, that hee
> dare not bee forward in Religion, lest hee displease his wife, and so the
> wife, lest shee displease her husband, and this is an inordinate love, when it
> exceeds measure [7]

Sexual pleasures, in this respect, were treated like other kinds of
pleasure. On a day of fast, when all comforts were supposed to be
foregone in behalf of religious contemplation, not only were tasty food
and drink to be abandoned but sexual intercourse, too. On other
occasions, when food, drink, and recreation were allowable, sexual
intercourse was allowable too, though of course only between persons
who were married to each other. The Puritans were not ascetics; they
never wished to prevent the enjoyment of earthly delights. They merely
demanded that the pleasures of the flesh be subordinated to the greater
glory of God: husband and wife must not become "so transported with
affection, that they look at no higher end than marriage it self." "Let
such as have wives," said the ministers, "look at them not for their own
ends, but to be fitted for Gods service, and bring them nearer to
God."[8]

Toward sexual intercourse outside marriage the Puritans were as
frankly hostile as they were favorable to it in marriage. They passed
laws to punish adultery with death, and fornication with whipping. Yet
they had no misconceptions as to the capacity of human beings to obey
such laws. Although the laws were commands of God, it was only
natural—since the fall of Adam—for human beings to break them.
Breaches must be punished lest the community suffer the wrath of
God, but no offense, sexual or otherwise, could be occasion for surprise
or for hushed tones of voice. How calmly the inhabitants of seventeenth-century New England could contemplate rape or attempted rape
is evident in the following testimony offered before the Middlesex
County Court of Massachusetts:

> The examination of Edward Wire taken the 7th of october and alsoe
> Zachery Johnson, who sayeth that Edward Wires mayd being sent into the
> towne about busenes meeting with a man that dogd hir from about Joseph
> Kettles house to goody marches. She came into William Johnsones and
> desired Zachery Johnson to goe home with her for that the man dogd hir.
> accordingly he went with her and being then as far as Samuell Phips his
> house the man over tooke them. which man caled himselfe by the name of
> peter grant would have led the mayd but she oposed itt three times: and
> coming to Edward Wires house the said grant would have kist hir but she
> refused itt: wire being at prayer grant dragd the mayd between the said
> wiers and Nathanill frothinghams house. hee then flung the mayd downe
> in the streete and got atop hir; Johnson seeing it hee caled vppon the

fellow to be sivill and not abuse the mayd then Edward wire came forth and ran to the said grant and took hold of him asking him what he did to his mayd, the said grant asked whether she was his wife for he did nothing to his wife: the said grant swearing he would be the death of the said wire. when he came of the mayd; he swore he would bring ten men to pul down his house and soe ran away and they followed him as far as good[y] phipses house where they mett with John Terry and George Chin with clubs in there hands and soe they went away together. Zachy Johnson going to Constable Heamans, and wire going home. there came John Terry to his house to ask for beer and grant was in the streete but afterward departed into the towne, both Johnson and Wire both aferme that when grant was vppon the mayd she cryed out severall times.

Deborah hadlocke being examined sayth that she mett with the man that cals himselfe peeter grant about good prichards that he dogd hir and followed hir to hir masters and there threw hir downe and lay vppon hir but had not the use of hir body but swore several othes that he would ly with hir and gett hir with child before she got home.

Grant being present denys all saying he was drunk and did not know what he did.[9]

The Puritans became inured to sexual offenses, because there were so many. The impression which one gets from reading the records of seventeenth-century New England courts is that illicit sexual intercourse was fairly common. The testimony given in cases of fornication and adultery—by far the most numerous class of criminal cases in the records—suggests that many of the early New Englanders possessed a high degree of virility and very few inhibitions. Besides the case of Peter Grant, take the testimony of Elizabeth Knight about the manner of Richard Nevars's advances toward her:

The last publique day of Thanksgiving (in the year 1674) in the evening as I was milking Richard Nevars came to me, and offered me abuse in putting his hand, under my coates, but I turning aside with much adoe, saved my self, and when I was settled to milking he agen took me by the shoulder and pulled me backward almost, but I clapped one hand on the Ground and held fast the Cows teatt with the other hand, and cryed out, and then came to mee Jonathan Abbot one of my Masters Servants, whome the said Never asked wherefore he came, the said Abbot said to look after you, what you doe unto the Maid, but the said Never bid Abbot goe about his businesse but I bade the lad to stay.[10]

One reason for the abundance of sexual offenses was the number of men in the colonies who were unable to gratify their sexual desires in marriage.[11] Many of the first settlers had wives in England. They had come to the new world to make a fortune, expecting either to bring their families after them or to return to England with some of the riches of America. Although these men left their wives behind, they brought their sexual appetites with them and in spite of laws which required them to return to their families, they continued to stay, and more continued to arrive, as indictments against them throughout the seventeenth century clearly indicate.

Servants formed another group of men, and of women too, who could not ordinarily find supply for human necessity within the bounds of marriage. Most servants lived in the homes of their masters and could not marry without their consent, a consent which was not likely to be given unless the prospective husband or wife also belonged to the master's household. This situation will be better understood if it is recalled that most servants at this time were engaged by contract for a stated period. They were, in the language of the time, "covenant servants," who had agreed to stay with their masters for a number of years in return for a specified recompense, such as transportation to New England or education in some trade (the latter, of course, were known more specifically as apprentices). Even hired servants who worked for wages were usually single, for as soon as a man had enough money to buy or build a house of his own and to get married, he would set up in farming or trade for himself. It must be emphasized, however, that anyone who was not in business for himself was necessarily a servant. The economic organization of seventeenth-century New England had no place for the independent proletarian workman with a family of his own. All production was carried on in the household by the master of the family and his servants, so that most men were either servants or masters of servants; and the former, of course, were more numerous than the latter. Probably most of the inhabitants of Puritan New England could remember a time when they had been servants.

Theoretically no servant had a right to a private life. His time, day or night, belonged to his master, and both religion and law required that he obey his master scrupulously.[12] But neither religion nor law could restrain the sexual impulses of youth, and if those impulses could not be expressed in marriage, they had to be given vent outside marriage. Servants had little difficulty in finding the occasions. Though they might be kept at work all day, it was easy enough to slip away at night. Once out of the house, there were several ways of meeting with a maid. The simplest way was to go to her bedchamber, if she was so fortunate as to have a private one of her own. Thus Jock, Mr. Solomon Phipps's Negro man, confessed in court

> that on the sixteenth day of May 1682, in the morning, betweene 12 and one of the clock, he did force open the back doores of the House of Laurence Hammond in Charlestowne, and came in to the House, and went up into the garret to Marie the Negro.

He doth likewise acknowledge that one night the last week he forced into the House the same way, and went up to the Negro Woman Marie and that the like he hath done at severall other times before.[13]

Joshua Fletcher took a more romantic way of visiting his lady:

> Joshua Fletcher . . . doth confesse and acknowledge that three severall nights, after bedtime, he went into Mr Fishes Dwelling house at Chelmsford, at an open window by a ladder that he brought with him. the said windo opening into a chamber, whose was the lodging place of Gresill Juell servant to mr. Fiske. and there he kept company with the said mayd. she sometimes having her cloathes on, and one time he found her in her bed.[14]

Sometimes a maidservant might entertain callers in the parlor while the family were sleeping upstairs. John Knight described what was perhaps a common experience for masters. The crying of his child awakened him in the middle of the night, and he called to his maid, one Sarah Crouch, who was supposed to be sleeping with the child. Receiving no answer, he arose and

> went downe the stayres, and at the stair foot, the latch of doore was pulled in. I called severall times and at the last said if shee would not open the dore, I would breake it open, and when she opened the doore shee was all undressed and Sarah Largin with her undressed, also the said Sarah went out of doores and Dropped some of her clothes as shee went out. I enquired of Sarah Crouch what men they were, which was with them. Shee made mee no answer for some space of time, but at last shee told me Peeter Brigs was with them, I asked her whether Thomas Jones was not there, but shee would give mee no answer.[15]

In the temperate climate of New England it was not always necessary to seek out a maid at her home. Rachel Smith was seduced in an open field "about nine of the clock at night, being darke, neither moone nor starrs shineing." She was walking through the field when she met a man who

> asked her where shee lived, and what her name was and shee told him. and then shee asked his name, and he told her Saijing that he was old Good-man Shepards man. Also shee saith he gave her strong liquors, and told her that it was not the first time he had been with maydes after his master was in bed.[16]

Sometimes, of course, it was not necessary for a servant to go outside his master's house in order to satisfy his sexual urges. Many cases of fornication are on record between servants living in the same house. Even where servants had no private bedroom, even where the whole family slept in a single room it was not impossible to make love. In fact many love affairs must have had their consummation upon a bed in which other people were sleeping. Take for example the case of Sarah Lepingwell. When Sarah was brought into court for having an illegitimate child, she related that one night when her master's brother, Thomas Hawes, was visiting the family, she went to bed early. Later, after Hawes had gone to bed, he called to her to get him a pipe of tobacco. After refusing for some time,

> at the last I arose and did lite his pipe and cam and lay doune one my one bead and smoaked about half the pip and siting vp in my bead to giue him his pip my bead being a trundell bead at the sid of his bead he reached beyond the pip and Cauth me by the wrist and pulled me on the side of his bead but I biding him let me goe he bid me hold my peas the folks wold here me and if it be replyed come why did you not call out I Ansar I was posesed with fear of my mastar least my master shold think I did it only to bring a scandall on his brothar and thinking thay wold all beare witnes agaynst me but the thing is true that he did then begete me with child at that tim and the Child is Thomas Hauses and noe mans but his.

In his defense Hawes offered the testimony of another man who was sleeping "on the same side of the bed," but the jury nevertheless accepted Sarah's story.[17]

The fact that Sarah was intimidated by her master's brother suggests that maidservants may have been subject to sexual abuse by their masters. The records show that sometimes masters did take advantage of their position to force unwanted attentions upon their female servants. The case of Elizabeth Dickerman is a good example. She complained to the Middlesex County Court,

> against her master John Harris senior for profiring abus to her by way of forsing her to be naught with him: . . . he has tould her that if she tould her dame: what cariag he did show to her shee had as good be hanged and shee replyed then shee would run away and he sayd run the way is befor you: . . . she says if she should liwe ther shee shall be in fear of her lif.[18]

The court accepted Elizabeth's complaint and ordered her master to be whipped twenty stripes.

So numerous did cases of fornication and adultery become in seventeenth-century New England that the problem of caring for the children of extra-marital unions was a serious one. The Puritans solved it, but in such a way as to increase rather than decrease the temptation to sin. In 1668 the General Court of Massachusetts ordered:

> that where any man is legally convicted to be the Father of a Bastard childe, he shall be at the care and charge to maintain and bring up the

same, by such assistance of the Mother as nature requireth, and as the Court from time to time (according to circumstances) shall see meet to Order: and in case the Father of a Bastard, by confession or other manifest proof, upon trial of the case, do not appear to the Courts satisfaction, then the Man charged by the Woman to be the Father, shee holding constant in it, (especially being put upon the real discovery of the truth of it in the time of her Travail) shall be the reputed Father, and accordingly be liable to the charge of maintenance as aforesaid (though not to other punishment) notwithstanding his denial, unless the circumstances of the case and pleas be such, on the behalf of the man charged, as that the Court that have the cognizance thereon shall see reason to acquit him, and otherwise dispose of the Childe and education thereof.[19]

As a result of this law a girl could give way to temptation without the fear of having to care for an illegitimate child by herself. Furthermore, she could, by a little simple lying, spare her lover the expense of supporting the child. When Elizabeth Wells bore a child, less than a year after this statute was passed, she laid it to James Tufts, her master's son. Goodman Tufts affirmed that Andrew Robinson, servant to Goodman Dexter, was the real father, and he brought the following testimony as evidence:

> Wee Elizabeth Jefts aged 15 ears and Mary tufts aged 14 ears doe testyfie that their being one at our hous sumtime the last winter who sayed that thear was a new law made concerning bastards that If aney man wear aqused with a bastard and the woman which had aqused him did stand vnto it in her labor that he should bee the reputed father of it and should mayntaine it Elizabeth Wells hearing of the sayd law she sayed vnto vs that If shee should bee with Child shee would bee sure to lay it vn to won who was rich enough abell to mayntayne it wheather it wear his or no and shee farder sayed Elizabeth Jefts would not you doe so likewise If it weare your case and I sayed no by no means for right must tacke place: and the sayd Elizabeth wells sayed If it wear my Caus I think I should doe so.[20]

A tragic unsigned letter that somehow found its way into the files of the Middlesex County Court gives more direct evidence of the practice which Elizabeth Wells professed:

> der loue i remember my loue to you hoping your welfar and i hop to imbras the but now i rit to you to let you nowe that i am a child by you and i wil ether kil it or lay it to an other and you shal have no blame at al for I haue had many children and none have none of them. . . . [i.e., none of their fathers is supporting any of them.][21]

In face of the wholesale violation of the sexual codes to which all these cases give testimony, the Puritans could not maintain the severe penalties which their laws provided. Although cases of adultery occurred every year, the death penalty is not known to have been applied more than three times. The usual punishment was a whipping or a fine, or both, and perhaps a branding, combined with a symbolical execution in the form of standing on the gallows for an hour with a rope about the neck. Fornication met with a lighter whipping or a lighter fine, while rape was treated in the same way as adultery. Though the Puritans established a code of laws which demanded perfection—which demanded, in other words, strict obedience to the will of God, they nevertheless knew that frail human beings could never live up to the code. When fornication, adultery, rape, or even buggery and sodomy appeared, they were not surprised, nor were they so severe with the offenders as their codes of law would lead one to believe. Sodomy, to be sure, they usually punished with death; but rape, adultery, and fornication they regarded as pardonable human weaknesses, all the more likely to appear in a religious community, where the normal course of sin was stopped by wholesome laws. Governor Bradford, in recounting the details of an epidemic of sexual misdemeanors in Plymouth, wrote resignedly:

> it may be in this case as it is with waters when their streames are stopped or damned up, when they gett passage they flow with more violence, and make more noys and disturbance, then when they are suffered to rune quietly in their owne chanels. So wickednes being here more stopped by strict laws, and the same more nerly looked unto, so as it cannot rune in a comone road of liberty as it would, and is inclined, it searches every wher, and at last breaks out wher it getts vente.[22]

The estimate of human capacities here expressed led the Puritans not only to deal leniently with sexual offenses but also to take every precaution to prevent such offenses, rather than wait for the necessity of punishment. One precaution was to see that children got married as soon as possible. The wrong way to promote virtue, the Puritans thought, was to "ensnare" children in vows of virginity, as the Catholics did. As a result of such vows, children, "not being able to contain," would be guilty of "unnatural pollutions, and other filthy practices in secret: and too oft of horrid Murthers of the fruit of their bodies," said Thomas Cobbett.[23] The way to avoid fornication and perversion was for parents to provide suitable husbands and wives for their children:

> Lot was to blame that looked not out seasonably for some fit matches for his two daughters, which had formerly minded marriage (witness the contract between them and two men in *Sodom* called therefore for his Sons in Law, which had married his daughters, Gen. 19. 14.) for they

seeing no man like to come into them in a conjugall way . . . then they plotted that incestuous course, whereby their Father was so highly dishonoured. . . .[24]

As marriage was the way to prevent fornication, successful marriage was the way to prevent adultery. The Puritans did not wait for adultery to appear; instead, they took every means possible to make husbands and wives live together and respect each other. If a husband deserted his wife and remained within the jurisdiction of a Puritan government, he was promptly sent back to her. Where the wife had been left in England, the offense did not always come to light until the wayward husband had committed fornication or bigamy, and of course there must have been many offenses which never came to light. But where both husband and wife lived in New England, neither had much chance of leaving the other without being returned by order of the county court at its next sitting. When John Smith of Medfield left his wife and went to live with Patience Rawlins, he was sent home poorer by ten pounds and richer by thirty stripes. Similarly Mary Drury, who deserted her husband on the pretense that he was impotent, failed to convince the court that he actually was so, and had to return to him as well as to pay a fine of five pounds. The wife of Phillip Pointing received lighter treatment: when the court thought that she had overstayed her leave in Boston, they simply ordered her "to depart the Towne and goe to Tanton to her husband." The courts, moreover, were not satisfied with mere cohabitation; they insisted that it be peaceful cohabitation. Husbands and wives were forbidden by law to strike one another, and the law was enforced on numerous occasions. But the courts did not stop there. Henry Flood was required to give bond for good behavior because he had abused his wife simply by "ill words calling her whore and cursing of her." The wife of Christopher Collins was presented for railing at her husband and calling him "Gurley gutted divill." Apparently in this case the court thought that Mistress Collins was right, for although the fact was proved by two witnesses, she was discharged. On another occasion the court favored the husband: Jacob Pudeator, fined for striking and kicking his wife, had the sentence moderated when the court was informed that she was a woman "of great provocation."[25]

Wherever there was strong suspicion that an illicit relation might arise between two persons, the authorities removed the temptation by forbidding the two to come together. As early as November, 1630, the Court of Assistants of Massachusetts prohibited a Mr. Clark from "cohabitacion and frequent keepeing company with Mrs. Freeman, vnder paine of such punishment as the Court shall thinke meete to inflict." Mr. Clark and Mr. Freeman were both bound "in XX £ apeece that Mr. Clearke shall make his personall appearance att the nexte Court to be holden in March nexte, and in the meane tyme to carry himselfe in good behaviour towards all people and espetially towards Mrs. Freeman, concerneing whome there is stronge suspicion of incontinency." Forty-five years later the Suffolk County Court took the same kind of measure to protect the husbands of Dorchester from the temptations offered by the daughter of Robert Spurr. Spurr was presented by the grand jury

> for entertaining persons at his house at unseasonable times both by day and night to the greife of theire wives and Relations &c The Court having heard what was alleaged and testified against him do Sentence him to bee admonish't and to pay Fees of Court and charge him upon his perill not to entertain any married men to keepe company with his daughter especially James Minott and Joseph Belcher.

In like manner Walter Hickson was forbidden to keep company with Mary Bedwell, "And if at any time hereafter hee bee taken in company of the saide Mary Bedwell without other company to bee forthwith apprehended by the Constable and to be whip't with ten stripes." Elizabeth Wheeler and Joanna Peirce were admonished "for theire disorderly carriage in the house of Thomas Watts being married women and founde sitting in other mens Laps with theire Armes about theire Necks." How little confidence the Puritans had in human nature is even more clearly displayed by another case, in which Edmond Maddock and his wife were brought to court "to answere to all such matters as shalbe objected against them concerning Haarkwoody and Ezekiell Euerells being at their house at unseasonable tyme of the night and her being up with them after her husband was gone to bed." Haarkwoody and Everell had been found "by the Constable Henry Bridghame about tenn of the Clock at night sitting by the fyre at the house of Edmond Maddocks with his wyfe a suspicious weoman her husband being on sleepe [sic] on the bedd." A similar distrust of human ability to resist temptation is evident in the following order of the Connecticut Particular Court:

> James Hallett is to returne from the Correction house to his master Barclyt, who is to keepe him to hard labor, and course dyet during the pleasure of the Court provided that Barclet is first to remove his daughter from his family, before the sayd James enter therein.

These precautions, as we have already see, did not eliminate fornication, adultery, or other sexual offenses, but they doubtless reduced the number from what it would otherwise have been.[26]

In sum, the Puritan attitude toward sex, though directed by a belief in absolute, God-given moral values, never neglected human nature. The rules of conduct which the Puritans regarded as divinely ordained had been formulated for men, not for angels and not for beasts. God had created mankind in two sexes: He had ordained marriage as desirable for all, and sexual intercourse as essential to marriage. On the other hand, He had forbidden sexual intercourse outside of marriage. These were the moral principles which the Puritans sought to enforce in New England. But in their enforcement they took cognizance of human nature. They knew well enough that human beings since the fall of Adam were incapable of obeying perfectly the laws of God. Consequently, in the endeavor to enforce those laws they treated offenders with patience and understanding, and concentrated their efforts on prevention more than on punishment. The result was not a society in which most of us would care to live, for the methods of prevention often caused serious interference with personal liberty. It must nevertheless be admitted that in matters of sex the Puritans showed none of the blind zeal or narrow-minded bigotry which is too often supposed to have been characteristic of them. The more one learns about these people, the less do they appear to have resembled the sad and sour portraits which their modern critics have drawn of them.

NOTES

1. Samuel Willard, *A Compleat Body of Divinity* (Boston, 1726), 125 and 608–613.

2. John Cotton, *A Meet Help* (Boston, 1699), 14–15.

3. *A Meet Help,* 16.

4. Edward Taylor, *Commonplace Book* (manuscript in the library of the Massachusetts Historical Society).

5. Records of the First Church in Boston (manuscript copy in the library of the Massachusetts Historical Society), 12.

6. Middlesex County Court Files, folder 42.

7. John Cotton, *A Practical Commentary . . . upon the First Epistle Generall of John* (London, 1656), 126.

8. *A Practical Commentary,* 126.

9. Middlesex Files, folder 48.

10. Middlesex Files, folder 71.

11. Another reason was suggested by Charles Francis Adams in his scholarly article, "Some Phases of Sexual Morality and Church Discipline in Colonial New England," *Proceedings* of the Massachusetts Historical Society, xxvi, 477–516.

12. On the position of servants in early New England see *More Books*, xvii (September, 1942), 311–328.

13. Middlesex Files, folder 99.

14. Middlesex Files, folder 47.

15. Middlesex Files, folder 52.

16. Middlesex Files, folder 44.

17. Middlesex Files, folder 47.

18. Middlesex Files, folder 94.

19. William H. Whitmore, editor, *The Colonial Laws of Massachusetts.* Reprinted from the Edition of 1660 (Boston, 1889), 257.

20. Middlesex Files, folder 52.

21. Middlesex Files, folder 30.

22. William Bradford, *History of Plymouth Plantation* (Boston, 1912), II, 309.

23. Thomas Cobbett, *A Fruitfull and Usefull Discourse touching the Honour due from Children to Parents and the Duty of Parents towards their Children* (London, 1656), 174.

24. Cobbett, 177.

25. Samuel E. Morison and Zechariah Chafee, editors, *Records of the Suffolk County Court, 1671–1680. Publications of the Colonial Society of Massachusetts,* xxix and xxx, 121, 410, 524, 837–841, and 1158; George F. Dow, editor, *Records and Files of the Quarterly Courts of Essex County, Massacusetts* (Salem, 1911–21), I, 274; and v, 377.

26. *Records of the Suffolk County Court,* 442–443 and 676; John Noble, editor, *Records of the Court of Assistants of the Colony of Massachusetts Bay* (Boston, 1901–28), II, 8; *Records of the Particular Court of Connecticut,* Collections of the Connecticut Historical Society, xxii, 20; and a photostat in the library of the Massachusetts Historical Society, dated March 29, 1653.

2

Husbands and Wives

John Demos

No aspect of the Puritan household was more vital than the relationship of husband and wife. But the study of this relationship raises at once certain larger questions of sex differentiation: What were the relative positions of men and women in Plymouth Colony? What attributes, and what overall valuation, were thought appropriate to each sex?

We know in a general way that male dominance was an accepted principle all over the Western World in the seventeenth century. The fundamental Puritan sentiment on this matter was expressed by Milton in a famous line in *Paradise Lost:* "he for God only, she for God in him " and there is no reason to suspect that the people of Plymouth would have put it any differently. The world of public affairs was nowhere open to women—in Plymouth only males were eligible to become "freemen." Within the family the husband was always regarded as the "head"—and the Old Colony provided no exceptions to this pattern. Moreover, the culture at large maintained a deep and primitive kind of suspicion of women, solely on account of their sex. Some basic taint of corruption was thought to be inherent in the feminine constitution—a belief rationalized, of course, by the story of Eve's initial treachery in the Garden of Eden. It was no coincidence that in both the Old and the New World witches were mostly women. Only two allegations of witchcraft turn up in the official records of Plymouth,[1] but other bits of evidence point in the same general direction. There are, for example, the quoted words of a mother beginning an emotional plea to her son: "if you would beleive a woman beleive mee. . . ."[2] And why *not* believe a woman?

The views of the Pilgrim pastor John Robinson are also interesting in this connection. He opposed, in the first place, any tendency to regard women as "necessary evils" and greatly regretted the currency of such opinions among "not only heathen poets . . . but also wanton Christians." The Lord had created both man and woman of an equal perfection, and "neither is she, since the creation more degenerated than he from the primitive goodness."[3] Still, in marriage some principles of authority were essential, since "differences will arise and be seen, and so the one must give way, and apply unto the other; this, God and nature layeth upon the woman, rather than upon the man." Hence the proper attitude of a wife towards her husband was "a reverend subjection."[4]

However, in a later discussion of the same matter Robinson developed a more complex line of argument which stressed certain attributes of inferiority assumed to be inherently feminine. Women, he wrote, were under two different kinds of subjection. The first was framed "in innocency" and implied no "grief" or "wrong" whatsoever. It reflected simply the woman's character as "the weaker vessel"—weaker, most obviously, with respect to intelligence or "understanding." For this was a gift "which God hath . . . afforded [the man], and means of obtaining it, above the woman, that he might guide and go before her."[5] Robinson also recognized that some men abused their position of authority and oppressed their wives most unfairly. But *even so*—and this was his central point—resistance was not admissible. Here he affirmed the second kind of subjection laid upon woman, a subjection undeniably "grievous" but justified by her "being first in transgression." In this way—by invoking the specter of Eve corrupting Adam in paradise—Robinson arrived in the end at a position which closely approximated the popular assumption of woman's basic moral weakness.

Yet within this general framework of masculine superiority there were a number of rather contrary indications. They seem especially evident in certain areas of the law. Richard B. Morris has written a most interesting essay on this matter, arguing the improved legal status of colonial women by comparison to what still obtained in the mother country.[6] Many of his conclusions seem to make a good fit with conditions in Plymouth Colony. The baseline here is the common law tradition of England, which at this time accorded to women only the most marginal sort of recognition. The married woman, indeed, was largely subsumed under the legal personality of her husband; she was virtually without rights to own property, make contracts, or sue for damages on her own account. But in the New World this situation was perceptibly altered.

Consider, for example, the evidence bearing on the property rights of Plymouth Colony wives. The law explicitly recognized their part in the accumulation of a family's estate, by the procedures it established for the treatment of widows. It was a basic principle of inheritance in this period—on both sides of the Atlantic—that a widow should have the use or profits of one-third of the land owned by her husband at the time of his death and full title to one-third of his movable property. But at least in Plymouth, and perhaps in other colonies as well, this expressed more than the widow's need for an adequate living allowance. For the laws also prescribed that "if any man do make an irrational and unrighteous Will, whereby he deprives his Wife of her reasonable allowance for her subsistencey," the Court may "relieve her out of the estate, notwithstanding by Will it were otherwise disposed; especially in such case where the Wife brought with her good part of the Estate in Marriage, or hath by her diligence and industry done her part in the getting of the Estate, and was otherwise well deserving."[7] Occasionally the Court saw fit to alter the terms of a will on this account. In 1663, for example, it awarded to widow Naomi Silvester a larger share of her late husband's estate than the "inconsiderable pte" he had left her, since she had been "a frugall and laborious woman in the procuring of the said estate."[8] In short, the widow's customary "thirds" was not a mere dole; it was her *due.*

But there is more still. In seventeenth-century England women were denied the right to make contracts, save in certain very exceptional instances. In Plymouth Colony, by contrast, one finds the Court sustaining certain kinds of contracts involving women on a fairly regular basis. The most common case of this type was the agreement of a widow and a new husband, made *before* marriage, about the future disposition of their respective properties. The contract drawn up by John Phillips of Marshfield and widow Faith Doty of Plymouth in 1667 was fairly standard. It stipulated that "the said Faith Dotey is to enjoy all her house and land, goods and cattles, that shee is now possessed of, to her owne proper use, to dispose of them att her owne free will from time to time, and att any time, as shee shall see cause." Moreover this principle of separate control extended beyond the realm of personal property. Phillips and widow Doty each had young children by their previous marriages, and their agreement was "that the children of both the said pties shall remaine att the free and proper and onely dispose of theire owne naturall parents, as they shall see good to dispose of them."[9] Any woman entering marriage on terms such as these would seem virtually an equal partner, at least from a legal standpoint. Much rarer, but no less significant, were contracts made by women *after* marriage. When Dorothy Clarke wished to be free of her husband Nathaniel in 1686, the Court refused a divorce but allowed a separation. Their estate was then carefully divided up by contract to which the wife was formally a party.[10] Once again, no clear precedents for this procedure can be found in contemporary English law.

The specific terms of some wills also help to confirm the rights of women to a limited kind of ownership even within marriage. No husband ever included his wife's clothing, for example, among the property to be disposed of after his death. And consider, on the other side, a will like that of Mistress Sarah Jenny, drawn up at Plymouth in 1655. Her husband had died just a few months earlier, and she wished simply to "Despose of som smale thinges that is my owne proper goods leaveing my husbands will to take place according to the true Intent and meaning thereof."[11] The "smale thinges" included not only her wardrobe, but also a bed, some books, a mare, some cattle and sheep. Unfortunately, married women did not usually leave wills of their own (unless they had been previously widowed); and it is necessary to infer that in most cases there was some sort of informal arrangement for the transfer of their personal possessions. One final indication of these same patterns comes from wills which made bequests to a husband and wife separately. Thus, for example, Richard Scalis of Scituate conferred most of his personal possessions on the families of two married daughters, carefully specifying which items should go to the daughters themselves and which to their husbands.[12] Thomas Rickard, also of Scituate, had no family of his own and chose therefore to distribute his property among a variety of friends. Once again spouses were treated separately: "I give unto Thomas Pincin my bedd and Rugg one paire of sheets and pilloty . . . I give and bequeath unto Joane the wife of the aforsaid Thomas Pincin my bason and fouer sheets . . . I give and bequeath unto Joane Stanlacke my Chest . . . unto Richard Stanlacke my Chest . . . unto Richard Stanlacke my best briches and Dublit and ould Coate."[13]

The questions of property rights and of the overall distribution of authority within a marriage do not necessarily coïncide; and modern sociologists interested in the latter subject usually emphasize the process of decision-making.[14] Of course, their use of live samples gives them a very great advantage; they can ask their informants, through questionnaires or interviews, which spouse decides where to go on vacation, what kind of car to buy, how to discipline the children, when to have company in, and so forth. The historian simply cannot draw out this kind of detail, nor can he contrive any substantial equivalent.

But he is able sometimes to make a beginning in this direction; for example, the records of Plymouth do throw light on two sorts of family decisions of the very greatest importance. One of these involves the transfer of land, and illustrates further the whole trend toward an expansion of the rights of married women to hold property. The point finds tangible expression in a law passed by the General Court in 1646: "It is enacted &c. That the Assistants or any of them shall have full power to take the acknowledgment of a bargaine and sale of houses and lands . . . And that the wyfe hereafter come in & consent and acknowledg the sale also; but that all bargaines and sales of houses and lands made before this day to remayne firm to the buyer notwithstanding the wife did not acknowledge the same."[15] The words "come in" merit special attention: the authorities wished to confront the wife personally (and even, perhaps, privately?) in order to minimize the possibility that her husband might exert undue pressure in securing her agreement to a sale.

The second area of decision-making in which both spouses shared an important *joint* responsibility was the "putting out" of children into foster families. For this there was no statute prescribing a set line of procedure, but the various written documents from specific cases make the point clearly enough. Thus in 1660 "An Agreement appointed to bee Recorded" affirmed that "Richard Berry of Yarmouth with his wifes Concent and other frinds; hath given unto Gorge Crispe of Eastham and his; wife theire son Samuell Berry; to bee att the ordering and Disposing of the said Gorge and his wife as if hee were theire owne Child."[16] The practice of formally declaring the wife's consent is evident in all such instances, when both parents were living. Another piece of legal evidence describes an actual deathbed scene in which the same issue had to be faced. It is the testimony of a mother confirming the adoption of her son, and it is worth quoting in some detail. "These prsents Witnesse that the 20th of march 1657–8 Judith the wife of William Peaks acknowlidged that her former husband Lawrance Lichfeild lying on his Death bedd sent for John Allin and Ann his wife and Desired to give and bequeath unto them his youngest son Josias Lichfeild if they would accept of him and take him as theire Child; then they Desired to know how long they should have him and the said Lawrance said for ever; but the mother of the child was not willing then; but in a short time after willingly Concented to her husbands will in the thinge."[17] That the wife finally agreed is less important here than the way in which her initial reluctance sufficed to block the child's adoption, in spite of the clear wishes of her husband.

Another reflection of this pattern of mutual responsibility appears in certain types of business activity—for instance, the management of inns and taverns ("ordinaries" in the language of the day). All such establishments were licensed by the General Court; hence their history can be followed, to a limited degree, in the official Colony Records. It is interesting to learn that one man's license was revoked because he had recently "buryed his wife, and in that respect not being soe capeable of keeping a publicke house."[18] In other cases the evidence is less explicit but still revealing. For many years James Cole ran the principal ordinary in the town of Plymouth, and from time to time the Court found it necessary to censure and punish certain violations of proper decorum that occurred there. In some of these cases Cole's wife Mary was directly implicated. In March 1669 a substantial fine was imposed "for that the said Mary Cole suffered divers psons after named to stay drinking on the Lords day . . . in the time of publicke wor-shipp."[19] Indeed the role of women in all aspects of this episode is striking, since two of the four drinking customers, the "divers psons after named," turned out to be female. Perhaps, then, women had considerable freedom to move on roughly the same terms with men even into some of the darker byways of Old Colony life.

The Court occasionally granted liquor licenses directly to women. Husbands were not mentioned, though it is of course possible that all of the women involved were widows. In some cases the terms of these permits suggest retail houses rather than regular inns or taverns. Thus in 1663 "Mistris Lydia Garrett" of Scituate was licensed to "sell liquors, alwaies provided . . . that shee sell none but to house keepers, and not lesse than a gallon att a time;"[20] and the agreement with another Scituate lady, Margaret Muffee, twenty years later, was quite similar.[21] But meanwhile in Middlebury one "Mistress Mary Combe" seems to have operated an ordinary of the standard type.[22] Can we proceed from these specific data on liquor licensing to some more general conclusion about the participation of women in the whole field of economic production and exchange? Unfortunately there is little additional hard evidence on one side or the other. The Court Records do not often mention other types of business activity, with the single exception of milling; and no woman was ever named in connection with this particular enterprise. A few more wills could be cited—for instance, the one made by Elizabeth Poole, a wealthy spinster in Taunton, leaving "my pte in the Iron workes" to a favorite nephew.[23] But this does not add up to very much. The economy of Plymouth was, after all, essentially simple—indeed "underdeveloped"—in most important respects. Farming claimed the energies of all but a tiny portion of the populace; there was relatively little opportunity for anyone, man or woman, to develop a more commercial orientation. It is known that in the next century women played quite a significant role in the business life of many parts of New England,[24] and one can view this pattern as simply the full development of possibilities that were latent even among the first generations of settlers. But there is no way to fashion an extended chain of proof.

Much of what has been said so far belongs to the general category of the rights and privileges of the respective partners to a marriage. But what of their duties, their basic responsibilities to one another? Here, surely, is another area of major importance in any assessment of the character of married life. The writings of John Robinson help us to make a start with these questions, and especially to recover the framework of ideals within which most couples of Plymouth Colony must have tried to hammer out a meaningful day-to-day relationship. We have noted already that Robinson prescribed "subjection" as the basic duty of a wife to her husband. No woman deserved praise, "how well endowed soever otherwise, except she frame, and compose herself, what may be, unto her husband, in conformity of manners."[25] From the man, by contrast, two things were particularly required: "love . . . and wisdom." His love for his wife must be "like Christ's to his church: holy for quality, and great for quantity," and it must stand firm even where "her failings and faults be great." His wisdom was essential to the role of family "head"; without it neither spouse was likely to find the way to true piety, and eventually to salvation.

It is a long descent from the spiritual counsel of John Robinson to the details of domestic conflict as noted in the Colony Records. But the Records are really the only available source of information about the workings of actual marriages in this period. They are, to be sure, a negative type of source; that is, they reveal only those cases which seemed sufficiently deviant and sufficiently important to warrant the attention of the authorities. But it is possible by a kind of reverse inference to use them to reconstruct the norms which the community at large particularly wished to protect. This effort serves to isolate three basic obligations in which both husband and wife were thought to share.

There was, first and most simply, the obligation of regular and exclusive cohabitation. No married person was permitted to live apart from his spouse except in very unusual and temporary circumstances (as when a sailor was gone to sea). The Court stood ready as a last resort to force separated couples to come together again, though it was not often necessary to deal with the problem in such an official way. One of the few recorded cases of this type occurred in 1659. The defendant was a certain Goodwife Spring, married to a resident of Watertown in the Bay Colony and formerly the wife and widow of

Thomas Hatch of Scituate. She had, it seems, returned to Scituate some three or four years earlier, and had been living "from her husband" ever since. The Court ordered that "shee either repaire to her husband with all convenient speed, . . . or . . . give a reason why shee doth not." [26] Exactly how this matter turned out cannot be determined, but it seems likely that the ultimate sanction was banishment from the Colony. The government of Massachusetts Bay is known to have imposed this penalty in a number of similar cases. None of the extant records describe such action being taken at Plymouth, but presumably the possibility was always there.

Moreover, the willful desertion of one spouse by the other over a period of several years was one of the few legitimate grounds for divorce. In 1670, for example, the Court granted the divorce plea of James Skiffe "haveing received sufficient testimony that the late wife of James Skiffe hath unlawfully forsaken her lawfull husband . . . and is gone to Roanoke, in or att Verginnia, and there hath taken another man for to be her husband."[27] Of course, bigamy was always sufficient reason in itself for terminating a marriage. Thus in 1680 Elizabeth Stevens obtained a divorce from her husband when it was proved that he had three other wives already, one each in Boston, Barbadoes, and a town in England not specified.[28]

But it was not enough that married persons should simply live together on a regular basis; their relationship must be relatively peaceful and harmonious. Once again the Court reserved the right to interfere in cases where the situation had become especially difficult. Occasionally both husband and wife were judged to be at fault, as when George and Anna Barlow were "severly reproved for theire most ungodly liveing in contension one with the other, and admonished to live otherwise." [29] But much more often one or the other was singled out for the Court's particular attention. One man was punished for "abusing his wife by kiking her of from a stoole into the fier,"[30] and another for "drawing his wife in an uncivell manor on the snow."[31] A more serious case was that of John Dunham, convicted of "abusive carriage towards his wife in continuall tiranising over her, and in pticulare for his late abusive and uncivill carryage in endeavoring to beate her in a deboist manor." [32] The Court ordered a whipping as just punishment for these cruelties, but the sentence was then suspended at the request of Dunham's wife. Sometimes the situation was reversed and the woman was the guilty party. In 1655, for example, Joan Miller of Taunton was charged with "beating and reviling her husband, and egging her children to healp her, bidding them knock him in the head, and wishing his victuals might coak him."[33] A few years later the wife of Samuel Halloway (also of

Taunton) was admonished for "carryage towards her husband . . . soe turbulend and wild, both in words and actions, as hee could not live with her but in danger of his life or limbs."[34]

It would serve no real purpose to cite more of these unhappy episodes—and it might indeed create an erroneous impression that marital conflict was particularly endemic among the people of the Old Colony. But two general observations are in order. First, the Court's chief aim in this type of case was to restore the couple in question to something approaching tranquility. The assumption was that a little force applied from the outside might be useful, whether it came in the form of an "admonition" or in some kind of actual punishment. Only once did the Court have to recognize that the situation might be so bad as to make a final reconciliation impossible. This happened in 1665 when John Williams, Jr., of Scituate, was charged with a long series of "abusive and harsh carriages" toward his wife Elizabeth, "in speciall his sequestration of himselfe from the marriage bed, and his accusation of her to bee a whore, and that especially in reference unto a child lately borne of his said wife by him denied to bee legittimate."[35] The case was frequently before the Court during the next two years, and eventually all hope of a settlement was abandoned. When Williams persisted in his "abuses," and when too he had "himself . . . [declared] his insufficency for converse with weomen,"[36] a formal separation was allowed—though not a full divorce. In fact, it may be that his impotence, not his habitual cruelty, was the decisive factor in finally persuading the Court to go this far. For in another case, some years later, a separation was granted on the former grounds alone.[37]

The second noteworthy aspect of all these situations is the equality they seem to imply between the sexes. In some societies and indeed in many parts of Europe at this time, a wife was quite literally at the mercy of her husband—his prerogatives extended even to the random use of physical violence. But clearly this was not the situation at Plymouth. It is, for example, instructive to break down these charges of "abusive carriage" according to sex: one finds that wives were accused just about as often as husbands. Consider, too, those cases of conflict in which the chief parties were of opposite sex but not married to one another. Once again the women seem to have held their own. Thus we have, on the one side, Samuel Norman punished for "strikeing Lydia, the wife of Henery Taylor,"[38] and John Dunham for "abusive speeches and carriages"[39] toward Sarah, wife of Benjamin Eaton; and, on the other side, the complaint of Abraham Jackson against "Rose, the wife of Thomas Morton, . . . that the said Rose, as hee came from worke, did abuse him by calling of him lying rascall and rogue."[40] In short, this does *not* seem to have been a society characterized by a really pervasive, and operational, norm of male dominance. There is no evidence at all of habitual patterns of deference in the relations between the sexes. John Robinson, and many others, too, may have assumed that woman was "the weaker vessel" and that "subjection" was her natural role. But as so often happens with respect to such matters, actual behavior was another story altogether.

The third of the major obligations incumbent on the married pair was a normal and exclusive sexual union. As previously indicated, impotence in the husband was one of the few circumstances that might warrant a divorce. The reasoning behind this is nowhere made explicit, but most likely it reflected the felt necessity that a marriage produce children. It is worth noting in this connection some of the words used in a divorce hearing of 1686 which centered on the issue of a man's impotence. He was, according to his wife, "always unable to perform the act of generation."[41] The latter phrase implies a particular view of the nature and significance of the sexual act, one which must have been widely held in this culture. Of course, there were other infertile marriages in the same period which held together. But perhaps the cause of the problem had to be obvious—as with impotence—for the people involved to consider divorce. Where the sexual function appeared normal in both spouses, there was always the hope that the Lord might one day grant the blessing of children. Doubtless for some couples this way of thinking meant year after year of deep personal disappointment.

The problem of adultery was more common—and, in a general sense, more troublesome. For adultery loomed as the most serious possible distortion of the whole sexual and reproductive side of marriage. John Robinson called it "that most foul and filthy sin, . . . the disease of marriage," and concluded that divorce was its necessary "medicine."[42] In fact, most of the divorces granted in the Old Colony stemmed from this one cause alone. But adultery was not only a strong *prima facie* reason for divorce; it was also an act that would bring heavy punishment to the guilty parties. The law decreed that "whosoever shall Commit Adultery with a Married Woman or one Betrothed to another Man, both of them shall be severely punished, by whipping two several times . . . and likewise to wear two Capital Letters A.D. cut out in cloth and sewed on their uppermost Garments . . . and if at any time they shall be found without the said Letters so worne . . . to be forthwith taken and publickly whipt, and so from time to time as often as they are found not to wear them."[43]

But quite apart from the severity of the prescribed punishments, this statute is interesting for its definition of adultery by reference to a married (or bethrothed) *woman.* Here, for the first time, we find some indication of difference in the conduct expected of men and women.

The picture can be filled out somewhat by examining the specific cases of adultery prosecuted before the General Court down through the years. To be sure, the man involved in any given instance was judged together with the woman, and when convicted their punishments were the same. But there is another point to consider as well. All of the adulterous couples mentioned in the records can be classified in one of two categories: a married woman and a married man, or a married woman and a single man. There was, on the other hand, no case involving a married man and a single woman. This pattern seems to imply that the chief concern, the essential element of sin, was the woman's infidelity to her husband. A married man would be punished for his part in this aspect of the affair—rather than for any wrong done to his own wife.

However, this does not mean that a man's infidelities were wholly beyond reproach. The records, for example, include one divorce plea in which the wife adduced as her chief complaint "an act of uncleanes" by her husband with another woman.[44] There was no move to prosecute and punish the husband—apparently since the other woman was unmarried. But the divorce was granted, and the wife received a most favorable settlement. We can, then, conclude the following. The adultery of a wife was treated as both a violation of her marriage (hence grounds for divorce) *and* an offense against the community (hence cause for legal prosecution). But for comparable behavior by husbands only the former consideration applied. In this somewhat limited sense the people of Plymouth Colony do seem to have maintained a "double standard" of sexual morality.

Before concluding this discussion of married life in the Old Colony and moving on to other matters, one important area of omission should at least be noted. Very little as been said here of love, affection, understanding—a whole range of positive feelings and impulses— between husbands and wives. Indeed the need to rely so heavily on Court Records has tended to weight the balance quite conspicuously on the side of conflict and failure. The fact is that the sum total of actions of divorce, prosecutions for adultery, "admonitions" against habitual quarreling, does not seem terribly large. In order to make a proper assessment of their meaning several contingent factors must be recognized; the long span of time they cover, the steady growth of the Colony's population (to something like 10,000 by the end of the century),[45] the extensive jurisdiction of the Court over many areas of domestic life. Given this overall context, it is clear that the vast majority of Plymouth Colony families never once required the attention of the authorities. Elements of disharmony were, at the least, controlled and confined within certain limits.

But again, can the issue be approached in a more directly affirmative way? Just how and how much, did feelings of warmth and love fit into the marriages of the Old Colony? Unfortunately our source materials have almost nothing to say in response to such questions. But this is only to be expected in the case of legal documents, physical remains, and so forth. The wills often refer to "my loveing wife"—but it would be foolish to read anything into such obvious set phrases. The records of Court cases are completely mute on this score. Other studies of "Puritan" ideals about marriage and the family have drawn heavily on literary materials—and this, of course, is the biggest gap in the sources that have come down from Plymouth Colony. Perhaps, though, a certain degree of extrapolation is permissible here; and if so, we must imagine that love was quite central to these marriages. If, as Morgan has shown, this was the case in Massachusetts Bay, surely it was also true for the people of Plymouth.[46]

There are, finally, just a few scraps of concrete evidence on this point. As previously noted, John Robinson wrote lavishly about the importance of love to a marriage—though he associated it chiefly with the role of the husband. And the wills should be drawn in once again, especially those clauses in which a man left specific instructions regarding the care of his widow. Sometimes the curtain of legal terms and style seems to rise for a moment and behind it one glimpses a deep tenderness and concern. There is, for example, the will written by Walter Briggs in 1676. Briggs's instructions in this regard embraced all of the usual matters—rooms, bedding, cooking utensils, "lyberty to make use of ye two gardens." And he ended with a particular request that his executors "allow my said wife a gentle horse or mare to ride to meeting or any other occasion she may have, & that Jemy, ye neger, catch it for her."[47] Surely this kind of thoughtfulness reflected a larger instinct of love—one which, nourished in life, would not cease to be effective even in the fact of death itself.

NOTES

1. The first occurred in 1661, in Marshfield. A girl named Dinah Silvester accused the wife of William Holmes of being a witch, and of going about in the shape of a bear in order to do mischief. The upshot, however, was a suit for defamation

against Dinah. The Court convicted her and obliged her to make a public apology to Goodwife Holmes. *Plymouth Colony Records*, III, 205, 207, 211. The second case (at Scituate, in 1677) resulted in the formal indictment of one Mary Ingham—who, it was said, had bewitched a girl named Mehitable Woodworth. But after suitable deliberations, the jury decided on an acquittal. *Plymouth Colony Records*, V, 223–24.

2. From a series of depositions bearing on the estate of Samuel Ryder, published in *Mayflower Descendant*, XI, 52. The case is discussed in greater detail below, pp. 165–66.

3. *The Works of John Robinson*, ed. Robert Ashton (Boston, 1851), I, 236.

4. *Ibid.*, 239–40.

5. *Ibid.*, 240.

6. Richard B. Morris, *Studies in the History of American Law* (New York, 1930), Chapter III, "Women's Rights in Early American Law."

7. Brigham *The Compact with the Charter and Laws of the Colony of New Plymouth*, 281.

8. *Plymouth Colony Records*, IV, 46.

9. *Ibid.*, 1643–64. For another agreement of this type, see *Mayflower Descendant*, XVII, 49 (the marriage contract of Ephraim Morton and Mistress Mary Harlow). The same procedures can be viewed, retrospectively, in the wills of men who had been married to women previously widowed. Thus when Thomas Boardman of Yarmouth died in 1689 the following notation was placed near the end of his will: "the estate of my wife brought me upon marriage be at her dispose and not to be Invintoried with my estate." *Mayflower Descendant*, X, 102. See also the will of Dolar Davis, *Mayflower Descendant*, XXIV, 73.

10. *Mayflower Descendant*, VI, 191–92.

11. *Mayflower Descendant*, VIII, 171.

12. *Mayflower Descendant*, XIII, 94–96.

13. *Mayflower Descendant*, IX, 155.

14. See, for example, Robert O. Blood, Jr., and Donald M. Wolfe, *Husbands and Wives* (Glencoe, Ill., 1960), esp. ch. 2.

15. Brigham, *The Compact with the Charter and Laws of the Colony of New Plymouth*, 86.

16. *Mayflower Descendant*, XV, 34.

17. *Mayflower Descendant*, XII, 134.

18. *Plymouth Colony Records*, IV, 54.

19. *Plymouth Colony Records*, V, 15.

20. *Plymouth Colony Records*, IV, 44.

21. *Plymouth Colony Records*, VI, 187.

22. *Ibid.*, 141.

23. *Mayflower Descendant*, XIV, 26.

24. Elizabeth Anthony Dexter, *Colonial Women of Affairs* (Boston, 1911).

25. *The Works of John Robinson*, I, 20.

26. *Plymouth Colony Records*, III, 174.

27. *Plymouth Colony Records*, V, 33.

28. *Plymouth Colony Records*, VI, 44–45.

29. *Plymouth Colony Records*, IV, 10.

30. *Plymouth Colony Records*, V, 61.

31. *Plymouth Colony Records*, IV, 47.

32. *Ibid.*, 103–4.

33. *Plymouth Colony Records*, III, 75.

34. *Plymouth Colony Records*, V, 29.

35. *Plymouth Colony Records*, IV, 93.

36. *Ibid.*, 125.

37. *Plymouth Colony Records*, VI, 191.

38. *Plymouth Colony Records*, V, 39.

39. *Ibid.*, 40.

40. *Plymouth Colony Records*, IV, 11.

41. *Plymouth Colony Records*, VI, 191.

42. *The Works of John Robinson*, I, 241.

43. Brigham, *The Compact with the Charter and Laws of the Colony of New Plymouth*, 245–46.

44. *Plymouth Colony Records*, III, 221.

45. There are three separate investigations dealing with this question: Bowen, *Early Rehoboth*, I, 15–24; Joseph B. Felt, "Population of Plymouth Colony," in American Statistical Association *Collections*, I, Pt. ii (Boston, 1845), 143–44; and Bradford, *Of Plymouth Plantation*, xi.

46. See Edmund Morgan, *The Puritan Family* (New York, 1966), esp. 46 ff.

47. *Plymouth Colony Records*, VI, 134–35.

3

Participation in Public Affairs

Julia Cherry Spruill

Wifehood and motherhood ... were held before the colonial woman as the purpose of her being, and home as the sphere of all her actions. Her mission in life was, first, to get a husband and then to keep him pleased, and her duties were bearing and rearing children and caring for her household. Her education, directed to these ends, consisted of instructions in morality, training in household occupations, and, among the upper class, the acquirement of the social amenities. But while home-making was the one occupation for which women were trained and was probably the sole business of a large majority, it did not absorb all the energies of some women and was by no means the only employment required of others. Quite a few gentlewomen interested themselves in affairs beyond their households, and a much larger number than is generally known were forced by necessity into performing services outside their own families.

Women, it will be remembered, had an active part in founding the southern colonies. Not only did wives accompany their husbands to the New World and share with them the hardships and responsibilities of subduing the wilderness, but single women came on their own ventures, bringing in new settlers, and establishing plantations.[1] It is true that women were desired as colonists chiefly to provide comfortable homes for the masculine settlers and to bear children to increase the population, but while performing these functions the more energetic were active also in public affairs. In the early records appear the names of a

From *Women's Life and Work in the Southern Colonies* (Chapel Hill: The University of North Carolina Press, 1938). Reprinted by permission.

number who distinguished themselves in matters of common concern and of some who, while not deliberately championing the principle of political rights for their sex, were drawn into the public arena by their exertions in behalf of friends or relatives or in the protection of their own private estates.

Among the "women of figure" at Jamestown at an early date was the wife of Thomas Nuice, whose strenuous efforts in relieving the needs of the poor and suffering inhabitants of the little colony during the war and famine of 1622 were commended to the Virginia Company in London and inscribed in the public documents.[2] Another notable Virginia dame was remembered for her courage and independence during the same evil times. The historian Stith relates that during the fearful days following the Indian massacre the authorities, "much frightened at this lamentable and unexpected Disaster," decided to abandon the outlying plantations and assemble all the inhabitants into five or six of the most defensible places. It was impossible, naturally, on sudden notice for the planters to transfer their cattle and other goods, and several of the most daring, unwilling to leave their plantations to be pillaged by the Indians, refused to move themselves and their people. Among them was Mistress Alice Proctor, a widow described as "a proper, civil, and modest Gentlewoman," who "with an heroic spirit" defended her plantation against the assaults of the Indians for over a month. Later she continued in her refusal to obey the order of the council to abandon her house for a safer place at Jamestown until the officers threatened to burn it down.[3]

A Virginia matron who at an early period left her housekeeping to interfere in political matters was Elizabeth Pott, wife of John Pott, one of Virginia's earliest physicians. Dr. Pott was acting governor of Virginia in 1629 and was later chief agitator against unpopular Governor Harvey. Soon after the arrival of Harvey in Virginia, Dr. Pott was charged with cattle stealing and tried before the general court. He was found guilty, but the question of his punishment was referred to the king of England. Mistress Pott, in defiance of authorities, boarded a vessel and traveled all the way to London to defend her husband before the king. There she pleaded his cause so earnestly that she secured a pardon for him.[4]

A few decades later, women were among the most zealous participants in the popular uprising known as Bacon's Rebellion. The wife of Anthony Haviland, one of the first to help gather the people together, was sent posthaste up and down the country as Bacon's emissary to carry his "declaration papers." Sarah Drummond, wife of William Drummond, Bacon's leading adviser, by her fiery speeches denouncing and defying Governor Berkeley, spurred the wavering to action. Sarah

Grendon, wife of Colonel Thomas Grendon, was charged with being "a great encourager and assister in the late horrid Rebellion" and was the only woman excepted from the pardon in the act of indemnity and free pardon passed by the Assembly in February, 1677.[5]

Another instigator of rebellion was Lydia, wife of Major Edmund Chiesman, an insurgent who after Bacon's death was condemned to death by Berkeley. One of the chroniclers of the time gives this dramatic account of Mistress Chiesman's gallant defence of her husband: "When that the Major was brought into the Governours presence, and by him demanded, what made him to ingage in Bacon's designes? Before that the Major could frame an answer to the Governours demand; his Wife steps in and tould his honour that it was her provocations that made her husband joyne in the case that Bacon contended for; ading; that if he had not bin enfluenced by her instigations, he had never don that which he had done. Therefore (upon her bended knees) she desired of his honour, that since what her husband had done, was by her meanes, and so, by consequence, she most guilty, that she might be hanged and he pardoned. Though the Governour did know, that what she had saide, was neare to the truth, yet he said little to her request. . . ."[6] Mistress Chiesman's courageous shouldering of responsibility did not save her husband, for he escaped the gallows only by dying in prison before the governor's vengeance could be executed.

Other gentlewomen, wives of Berkeley's supporters, were impressed by the rebels into service in a unique manner. An Cotton, one of the leading chroniclers of the rebellion, gives this account of Bacon's extraordinary tactics: "He was no sooner arrived at Towne [Jamestown] but by several small partyes of Horse (2 or 3 in a party, for more he could not spare) he fetcheth into his little Leagure, all the prime mens wives, whose Husbands were with the Governour, (as coll. Bacon's Lady, Madm. Bray, Madm. Page, Mdm. Ballard, and others) which the next morning he presents to the view of their husbands and ffriends in towne, upon the top of the small worke hee had cast up in the night; where he caused them to tarey till hee had finished his defence against his enemies shott. . . ."[7] Another annalist wrote of Bacon's placing the gentlewomen atop his breastworks: "The poor Gentlwomen were mightily astonished at this project; neither were their husbands voide of amazements at this subtill invention. If Mr. Fuller thought it strange, that the Divells black guard should be enrouled Gods shoulders, they made it no less wonderful, that their innocent and harmless wives should thus be entred a white garde to the Devill. This action was a method in war, that they were not well acquainted with (no not those the best inform'd in military affaires) that before they could com to pearce their enemies sides, they must be obliged to dart their weapons through their wives brest."[8] Naturally Berkeley's supporters refused to fire upon their wives. So, concluded the narrator, "these Ladyes white Aprons" proved to be of greater protection to Bacon and his men than all his fortifications.

Lady Berkeley was not among the "white aprons." Neither was she at home attending to household occupations. According to a letter written by Mistress Bacon to her sister, June 29, 1676, the governor had sent his lady to England with "great complaints" against Bacon, relying upon her, apparently, to represent to those in authority his side of the troublous events.[9]

Though the complaints carried by Dame Berkeley were first to reach the ears of the king, those of Bacon's female followers later also crossed the Atlantic and helped to bring royal censure and reproof upon the governor. When, after Bacon's sudden death and the subsequent disorganization of his supporters Berkeley regained power, he charged the chief of his opponents with treason, confiscated their estates, and had twenty-three hanged. Among these was William Drummond, husband of the spirited Sarah. Mistress Drummond did not bow in calm resignation to the governor's orders. Determined to justify her husband and proclaim Berkeley's harshness as well as to regain her property, she sent a petition to the Lords for Trade and Plantations, explaining that her husband had been sentenced to die by martial law and executed, though he had never borne arms or any military office, and that the governor had seized his plantation and goods and forced her and her five children to fly from their habitation. Her case was reported to the king, who ordered that her property be restored and announced that her husband had been put to death contrary to the laws of the kingdom.[10]

In Maryland as in Virginia, women took part in political and religious struggles and were active in other public matters. An account of the quarrel and battle between Governor Stone and the Puritan Party in 1655 mentions women among the participants. It tells of the Puritans' capture of the governor and all his company and relates that the victors condemned ten to death, executed four, and would have executed all had it not been for the incessant pleading of some good women, which saved some, and the petitions of the soldiers, which saved others.[11] The Puritans, endeavoring to prevent stories of their brutality from getting abroad and determined to have only favorable accounts of their actions presented before Cromwell, immediately sent dispatches to England and attempted to keep their prisoners incommunicado. But the governor's wife, Virlinda, who had not been allowed to see her wounded husband, was determined that he and his followers should not suffer from the misrepresentation of Puritan messengers.

She wrote at once to Lord Baltimore, describing the armed conflict and explaining the issues from the governor's point of view. Her letter shows not merely a keen interest in her husband's predicament but also an understanding of the whole political situation.[12] Another Maryland matron to plead her husband's cause before his enemies could "make their owne tale" in England was Barbara Smith, wife of Captain Richard Smith of Calvert County. During the Revolution of 1689, when her husband was imprisoned for refusing to take part with the insurgents, Mistress Smith hurried to England to lay his case before the authorities there.[13]

The outstanding woman in early Maryland, however, was not a devoted wife, but, as she appears repeatedly in the records, "Mistresse Margarett Brent, Spinster." This remarkable woman was not only the most conspicuous of her sex, but was one of the most prominent personages in the colony, whose business and public activities fill many pages of court records and suggest a career which the most ambitious of modern feminists might envy. Margaret Brent was of distinguished family and apparently a person of means, but as a Catholic she suffered persecution in England. Dissatisfied, probably, with the disabilities of her family under the English laws and encouraged by Lord Baltimore's extraordinary offers of land and privileges in Maryland, she decided to emigrate, and, with her brothers Giles and Fulke and her sister Mary, arrived in the province in November, 1638.

Though accompanied by their brothers, the Mistresses Brent came on their own ventures, bringing in servants, patenting large tracts of land in their own rights, and establishing plantations. As owners of manorial estates, they had the right to hold courts-baron, where controversies relating to manor lands were tried and tenants did fealty for their lands, and courts-leet, where residents on their manors were tried for criminal offences. One of the few surviving records of a court-baron is of that held at St. Gabriel's Manor by the steward of Mistress Mary Brent, where the tenant appeared, "did fealty to the Lady," and took possession of thirty-seven acres according to the custom of the manor.[14] Whether Mistress Margaret exercised such feudal rights over her tenants does not appear, but the many references to her in the minutes of the provincial court bear witness to her diligence and perseverance in prosecuting her debtors. Between the years 1642 and 1650 her name occurs no less than one hundred and thirty-four times in the court records, and during these eight years there was hardly a court at which she did not have at least one case. Occasionally she appeared as defendant, but oftener as plaintiff, and, it is interesting to know, a majority of these cases were decided in her favor.

Her successful handling of her own affairs probably accounts for her being called upon often to act on behalf of her friends and members of her family. When her brother Fulke returned to England, he gave her a power of attorney to conduct his affairs, and on several occasions she acted for her other brother, Giles.[15] As guardian of the little Indian princess, Mary Kittamaquund, daughter of the Piscataway Emperor, she brought suits and collected debts due her, and she also acted as agent for other gentlewomen.[16] Because she so frequently transacted business for others by power of attorney, it has been mistakenly assumed that she was an attorney at law, but no evidence appears to show that she made any claim to membership in the legal profession.

During the first eight years of her residence in Maryland, Mistress Brent's energies were exerted largely in the conduct of private business, but rapidly moving events following the civil wars thrust her into a position of great public responsibility and for a time placed in her hands the destiny of the whole colony. Leonard Calvert, the governor, went to England in April, 1643, to consult with his brother, Lord Baltimore, about affairs in the province and, on his return in September, 1644, found the colony on the verge of an insurrection. Led by William Claiborne and Richard Ingle, a band of rebels soon took possession of Kent Island, invaded the western shore, and established themselves at St. Mary's. Governor Calvert with a large number of the councillors fled to Virginia, leaving Maryland in a state of anarchy. Toward the end of 1646 he returned with a small force of Virginians and Maryland refugees, entered St. Mary's, and established his authority over the province. But he had hardly restored order when on June 9, 1647, he died, leaving Maryland once more without a strong hand to direct her affairs.[17] On his deathbed, by a nuncupative will, he named Thomas Greene to succeed him as governor and appointed Margaret Brent his executrix with the enigmatical instruction, "Take all and pay all."[18]

With her appointment as executrix of Governor Calvert, Margaret Brent's public career began. She was summoned into court to answer numerous suits for his debts and found it necessary to start legal proceedings for sums due his estate. The most urgent matter before her was the satisfaction of debts due the soldiers of Fort Inigoes. Governor Calvert had brought these volunteers from Virginia to help regain the government from the rebels, and, in order to secure their much needed services, had pledged his entire estate and that of the Lord Proprietor to pay them. Before his executrix could complete her inventory, the captain of the fort, on behalf of the soldiers, demanded their back wages and secured an attachment upon the whole Calvert estate.[19]

Mistress Brent now found herself confronted by a grave and critical situation. Leonard Calvert's estate was inadequate to meet the demands upon it. The price of corn was soaring higher and higher and famine threatened. Enemies of the existing government were just outside the borders of the province, awaiting an opportunity for a new invasion, and the hungry soldiers in the fort, frightened by the rise in prices and the scarcity of food, became unruly and threatened mutiny. Realizing the necessity for prompt and decisive measures, she demanded and obtained a power to act as attorney for the Lord Proprietor and quieted the clamorous soldiers by promising to send to Virginia for corn and by selling enough of the proprietary's cattle to pay them. Thus she rescued the struggling little colony from certain disaster and very probably saved it from all the evils of another civil war.

One of Maryland's historians, commenting upon her courageous handling of the situation, suggests that Leonard Calvert might have done better had he reversed his testamentary dispositions and made Margaret Brent governor and Thomas Greene executor.[20] But it was not a day of political rights for women, as Mistress Margaret soon discovered. On January 21, 1647, probably in order to be in a better position to look after the Calvert interests, she went before the assembly and demanded a seat, thereby unconsciously distinguishing herself as the first woman in America to claim the right to vote. The minutes of the proceedings for the day state: "Came Mrs Margarett Brent and requested to have vote in the howse for herselfe and voyce also for that att the last Court 3d: Jan: it was ordered that the said Mrs. Brent was to be looked upon and received as his Lordships Attorney. The Governor denyed that the sd Mrs Brent should have any vote in the howse."[21] She did not submit quietly to this decision, however, for, according to the record, she protested against all the proceedings in the assembly unless she might be present and vote.

The members of the assembly, while unwilling to allow a woman within the sacred precincts of their ordained sphere, nevertheless appreciated her public services and commended her to the Lord Proprietor. Lord Baltimore, ignorant of the succession of disturbances in his colony and hearing of the bold manner in which Margaret Brent had taken matters into her own hands and disposed of his cattle, wrote to the assembly, complaining of her highhandedness. In answer, the assembly wrote him a long letter describing the calamities and disorders they had suffered and concluding with this earnest justification of their country-woman: ". . . as for Mrs Brents undertaking and medling with your Lordships Estate here (whether she procured it with her own and others importunity or no) we do Verily Believe and in Conscience report that it was better for the Collonys safety at that time in her hands than in any mans else in the whole Province after your Brothers death for the Soldiers would never have treated any other with that Civility and respect and though they were even ready at times to run into mutiny yet she still pacified them till at the last things were brought to that straight that she must be admitted and declared your Lordships Attorney by an order of Court (the Copy whereof is herewith inclosed) or else all must go to ruin Again and then the second mischief had been doubtless far greater than the former so that if there hath not been any sinister use made of your Lordships Estate by her from what it was intended and engaged for by Mr Calvert before his death, as we verily Believe she hath not, then we conceive from that time she rather deserved favour and thanks from your Honour for her so much Concurring to the Public Safety then to be liable to all those bitter invectives you have been pleased to express against her."[22] Lord Baltimore was not moved by this spirited defence to withdraw his accusations or to express any appreciation of Mistress Brent's services, but continued distrustful and hostile.

Margaret Brent's fall from grace, however, was not due altogether to her selling the proprietary cattle. She and her family were the victims of a new policy which the proprietor was observing in order to meet the change in English politics. A shrewd politician, Lord Baltimore warily watched the undercurrents of popular feeling in England, determined to gain the good will of those in power and thereby save his proprietary estates by whatever means he found expedient. Perceiving the rise of the Puritans to power in Parliament, he sought to conciliate them by showing disfavor to prominent Catholics and granting concessions to Protestants in Maryland.[23] Deprived of the Maryland proprietor's favor, the Brents moved down to Westmoreland County in Virginia, where they patented land and established a plantation, giving it the significant name "Peace." Though Mistress Margaret continued active in the conduct of business for other people and for herself, she was no longer prominent in political affairs and after about 1650 her name disappears from the public records.

The idea of a woman's conducting business enterprises and having a hand in public matters was not new to the early colonists. It was customary for English women of the aristocracy to be interested in national affairs and for those of the lower classes to be engaged in what today we call gainful occupations. Family letters and other records present gentlewomen as active participants on both sides of the political and religious struggles of the first half of the seventeenth century.[24] Among the nobility, the management of the family estate was often left to the care of the wife while the husband was detained at court, was devoting himself to politics, science or religion, or was abroad for business or pleasure. The wife of the English husbandman looked after the farm during his absence and at his death frequently took over its entire management. Poorer women labored for wages in the fields at almost every kind of farm work. Women of means sometimes carried on enterprises requiring considerable capital, and wives of shopkeepers and tradesmen, whose places of business were ordinarily in the home, commonly assisted their husbands in their shops. Women also practiced medicine and surgery and had almost a complete monopoly in the field of obstetrics.[25]

But with the advance of the seventeenth century, English women of the upper classes came to be less concerned with business and other affairs. The great increase in wealth and the vogue for frivolous entertainments following the Restoration discouraged the exercise of initiative, energy, and independence in the conduct of practical affairs and brought about a rapid deterioration in the physique, the morale, and the general efficiency of upper-class women.[26] Their whole education in the eighteenth century stressed sex differences, encouraged the development of passive rather than active qualities, opposed robustness of mind and body as vulgar, and emphasized the importance of ornamental rather than utilitarian accomplishments. In the southern colonies also the eighteenth century saw a decline in the vigor and self-reliance of women in wealthier families and a lessening of their influence in public matters. Because of the rural character of their lives and the general influence of the frontier, American ladies were less idle and artificial than those in England, but compared with the daring and independent matrons of the preceding century, they appear somewhat effeminate and timid.

In the back settlements and on the frontier, women continued to be valued for their strength and valor, and though their exploits seldom got into the records, they were probably busy with many matters beyond their cabins. The early records of Georgia tell of the important part played by Mary Musgrove [later Matthews], daughter of an Indian mother and an English father, and wife of a Carolina trader.[27] Finding that she could speak the Creek language as well as English and that she had a great influence over the Indians and was a skillful diplomat, Oglethorpe secured her services as interpreter and adviser on Indian affairs, agreeing to allow her an annual stipend of one hundred pounds. That he relied upon her advice is evident in many references to her like the following in the secretary's journal: "Matthews Wife has always been in great Esteem with the General, and not without good Reason; for being half Indian by Extract, she has a very great influence upon many of them particularly the Creek Nation, our next neighbours . . . and the General would advise with her in many Things, for his better dealing with the Indians; taking her generally for his Interpreter, and using her very kindly on all Occasions."[28]

Mary was a person of means as well as influence. She owned broad acres of valuable land and had many Indian traders under her command. When food was scarce, she supplied the hungry colonists with provisions and at her own expense furnished Indian warriors to serve Oglethorpe. When trouble threatened with the neighboring Spanish colony of Florida, Oglethorpe sent her to the border to establish a trading post on the Altamaha River, from which she could watch the Spaniards and acquaint him with their movements and at the same time treat with the Indians and keep them on friendly terms with the Georgia colonists. When hostilities began, she rallied her war Indians to Oglethorpe's side and sent her traders to the conflict. Until her marriage with Thomas Bosomworth, an avaricious and unscrupulous English clergyman, who attempted to use her influence over the Indians and in the colony to acquire wealth and power for himself, she continued to be of incalculable help to Oglethorpe and the colonists.[29] One of Georgia's historians writes of her services: "Her assistance was invaluable, and her aid, not only in concluding treaties but also in securing warriors from the Creek confederacy during the conflict between Georgia and Florida, indispensable. Promptly did she respond on all occasions to any request made of her. . . . She was certainly of great use to him [Oglethorpe] and to the colony."[30]

Other women in pioneer communities probably played important rôles which were not committed to record, and, as will be shown in following chapters, many throughout the colonies were occupied with making a living. But those who enjoyed the advantages of wealth and refinement came more and more to be content to be "shining ornaments" in their families. A comparison of petitions presented by the undaunted dames of the first years of the colonies with the requests of the more modest ladies of the next century reveals a consciousness of sex and an unnatural prudishness in the latter not observable in their pioneer grandmothers. Sarah Drummond, Virlinda Stone, and Margaret Brent stated their requests confidently and boldly, professed no ignorance of politics, and made no attempt to excuse their interference in public matters. Their petitions disclose no doubts regarding their ability to understand and explain the political issues of the time or their right to interpose in matters of public concern. The women of the later period appear disinclined to admit any interest in public policy and anxious lest their private requests be mistaken for an unwomanly meddling in politics. One petitioner, for instance, soliciting Governor Martin of North Carolina regarding some requirements made of her husband, was very careful to preface her entreaty with this modest declaration: "It is not for me, unacquainted as I am with the politics and laws, to say with what propriety this was done."[31] A petition of some ladies of Wilmington, North Carolina, asking the governor to rescind an order regarding the removal of the wives and children of Tories from the state, declares apologetically, "It is not the province of our sex to reason deeply upon the policy of the order," and justifies their "earnest supplication" on the grounds that it was prompted by the distress of the innocent and helpless.[32]

These petitioners had evidently been carefully educated in the eighteenth century ideals of female character. They had doubtless read in their *Spectators* that participating in politics was "repugnant to the softness, the modesty, and those other endearing qualities . . . natural to the fair sex," and agreed that gentlewomen should "distinguish themselves as tender mothers and faithful wives rather than as furious partisans."[33] In many admonitions like the following from one of their textbooks on behavior, they had been warned against presuming to understand political matters: "It [politics] is a subject entirely above your sphere. I would not willingly resign any of the privileges that properly belong to our sex; but, I hope, I shall have all the sensible part of it on my side, when I affirm that the conduct and management of state affairs is a thing with which we have no concern. Perhaps our natural abilities are not equal to such an arduous task; at any rate, our education, as it is now conducted, is too slight and superficial to render us competent judges of these matters; and I have always thought it as ridiculous for a woman to put herself in a passion about political disputes, as it would be for a man to spend his time haranguing upon the colour of a silk, or the water of a diamond."[34]

During the Revolution, women emerged for a time from their circumscribed sphere. Moralists who had maintained that woman's interests should be confined to her family, as soon as serious national difficulties threatened, sought to arouse her patriotism and began to apprise her of her public duty. Journalists who previously had commended the sex for their retiring modesty, now praised the more daring female patriots for their display of zeal. Women who joined themselves into associations and gave public demonstrations of their patriotism were applauded loudly and even had their names printed in the papers.[35] The lively protests of the ladies of the famous Edenton tea party, which provoked the customary ridicule from male wits in England, were commended by neighboring journalists.[36] The voluntary association of "the young ladies of the best families of Mecklenburg County" in North Carolina and their public declarations not to receive the addresses of any gentleman who had failed to do his military duty were acclaimed by the newspapers as significant and exemplary proceedings,[37] and similar resolutions adopted by the ladies of Rowan County were entered into the minutes of the Committee of Safety as "worthy the imitation of every young lady in America."[38] Enthusiastic matrons plunged into the conflict and wrote fiery articles for the newspapers inciting their countrywomen to action. One of these ardent patriots wrote that when she reflected on the American grievances she was ready to start up with sword in hand to fight by the side of her husband.[39] Other correspondents urged their countrywomen not to be "tame spectators" and reminded them that "much, very much depends on the public virtue the ladies will exert at this critical juncture."[40]

But the Revolution had no permanent effect on the status of women. The author of the Declaration of Independence believed that woman's place was the home and hoped that American women would be "too wise to wrinkle their foreheads with politics."[41] The popular phrases, "rights of man," and "all men are created free and equal," so often on the lips of men and women of the period, were generally applied to men only. Glancing into the future, we find the founders of the republic no more ready to permit their wives and daughters to have a hand in public affairs than were the founders of the colonies.

In church affairs as in those of government, while women were generally supposed to be meek and quiet onlookers, they were sometimes persons of influence. The Anglican Church, the established form of worship in all the southern colonies, held strictly to the Pauline doctrine regarding woman, maintaining her inferiority and subjection in the creation and her exclusion from all church offices. Representative of the views of orthodox divines, were those of the author of *The Ladies Calling*. While regarding woman as the "weaker vessel," he allowed her a soul "of as Divine an Original" and as "endless a Duration" as that of man. Indeed, "in respect to their eternal well-being," he believed God gave women advantages over men, for he implanted in them "some native propensions" toward virtue and "closelier fenced them in" from temptations and "those wider excursions, for which the customary liberties of the other Sex afford a more open way." Piety was a virtue enjoined especially on woman and irreligion was more odious in her than in man. But, though possessing "peculiar aptness" toward piety, she should not presume to lift her voice in the church. The silence enjoined upon the sex by the apostle, he declared, was based "not only on the inferiority of the Woman in regard of the creation and first sin . . . but also on the presumption that they needed instruction."[42] Nonconformists, though holding somewhat different views of her natural tendency toward virtue, agreed that woman should not presume to understand theology, pass judgment on the sermons, or teach in the church. But they all expected her to understand the fundamental principles of religion well enough to teach them to her children and servants, and, if her husband were an unbeliever, to reclaim him by persuasive arguments as well as by her good example. Also, though she had no voice in church business, it was taken for granted that she was a more faithful attendant at divine services than her husband, and a generous contributor. . . .

NOTES

1. See Spruill, *Women's Life and Work in the Southern Colonies*, p. 11.

2. *Records of the Virginia Company of London*, II, 383.

3. William Stith, *History of Virginia*, pp. 235–36; *William and Mary Quarterly*, XV, 39.

4. *Ibid.*, XIV, 99.

5. *Ibid.*, XV, 41.

6. "Narrative of the Indian and Civil Wars in Virginia, in the Years 1675 and 1676." *Force Tracts*, I (No. 11), 34.

7. "An Account of Our Late Troubles in Virginia," *Force Tracts*, I (No. 9), 8.

8. "Narrative of the Indian and Civil Wars in Virginia," *Force Tracts*, I, (No. 11), 22.

9. *William and Mary Quarterly*, IX, 5.

10. *Virginia Magazine*, XXII, 235–36; Neill, *Virginia Carolorum*, p. 380.

11. John Langford, "Refutation of Babylon's Fall," *Narratives of Early Maryland*, p. 264.

12. The whole of her letter is given in the *Narratives of Maryland*, pp. 265–67.

13. *Archives of Maryland*, VIII, 153; *Maryland Magazine*, II, 374.

14. *Archives of Maryland*, IV, 417.

15. *Ibid.*, IV, 192, 228, 357, 477, 481; X, 28, 49.

16. *Ibid.*, IV, 259, 264, 265, 487–88.

17. William Hand Browne, *Maryland: A History of a Palatinate* (Boston and New York, 1884), pp. 58–64.

18. *Archives of Maryland*, IV, 314.

19. *Ibid.*, p. 338.

20. Browne, *op. cit.*, p. 64.

21. *Archives of Maryland*, I, 215.

22. *Ibid.*, I, 216–17.

23. Matthew Page Andrews, *History of Maryland: Province and State* (New York, 1929), p. 93.

24. Alice Clark, *Working Life of Women in the Seventeenth Century* (London and New York, 1919), pp. 23–28.

25. *Ibid.*, pp. 14–23, 29–35, 44–92, 150–289.

26. *Ibid.,* pp. 35–41.

27. After Musgrove's death, Mary married Jacob Matthews, and as a third husband married Rev. Thomas Bosomworth.

28. *Colonial Records of Georgia,* IV, 518.

29. Merton Coulter, "Mary Musgrove, Queen of the Creeks," *Georgia Historical Quarterly,* XI, 1–30.

30. Charles C. Jones, *History of Georgia* (2 vols. Boston and New York, 1883), I, 384.

31. *State Records of North Carolina,* XVI, 389–90.

32. *Ibid.,* pp. 467–79.

33. Nos. 57, 81, 342.

34. *The Polite Lady,* pp. 266–67.

35. Articles of this type appear in the *Virginia Gazette,* December 24, 1767, February 18, 1768, July 27, 1769, January 20 and 27, 1774, June 9 and November 3, 1774; *South Carolina Gazette,* April 3, 1775; *South Carolina Gazette and Country Journal,* January 7, 1766, August 2, 1774; *Georgia Gazette,* January 6, 1768; (Fayetteville) *North Carolina Gazette,* September 14, 1789.

36. *Virginia Gazette,* November 3, 1774. Postscript.

37. *South Carolina and American General Gazette,* February 9, 1776.

38. *Colonial Records of North Carolina,* X, 594.

39. *Virginia Gazette,* September 21, 1776.

40. *Ibid.,* September 15, 1774.

41. *Writings of Thomas Jefferson* (ed., Ford), V, 390–91. Also Randolph, *Domestic Life of Thomas Jefferson,* p. 158.

42. (2d ed., 1673), pp. 8–9, 81, 101.

4

The Case of the American Jezebels:
Anne Hutchinson and Female Agitation
during the Years of
Antinomian Turmoil, 1636-1640

Lyle Koehler

Between 1636 and 1638 Massachusetts boiled with controversy, and for more than three centuries scholars have attempted to define and redefine the nature, causes, and implications of that controversy. Commentators have described the rebellious Antinomians as "heretics of the worst and most dangerous sort" who were guilty of holding "absurd, licentious, and destructive" opinions,[1] as "a mob scrambling after God, and like all mobs quickly dispersed once their leaders were dealt with,"[2] and as the innocent victims of "inexcusable severity and unnecessary virulence."[3] Other narrators have called the most famous Antinomian, Anne Hutchinson, a "charismatic healer, with the gift of fluent and inspired speech,"[4] another St. Joan of Arc,[5] a rebel with a confused, bewildered mind,[6] and a woman "whose stern and masculine mind . . . triumphed over the tender affections of a wife and mother."[7]

Almost without exception, these critics and defenders of Ms. Hutchinson and the Antinomians have dealt specifically with Antinomianism as a religious movement and too little with it as a social movement.[8] Emery Battis has traced the occupational status of 190

From the *William and Mary Quarterly* 31 (January 1974). Reprinted by permission.

Mr. Koehler wishes to acknowledge the valuable assistance and encouragement of Karin Rabe, who participated in the analysis of the appeal of Antinomianism to women and sharpened many nuances of expression.

Antinomians and Antinomian sympathizers to examine the secular as well as the religious aspects of the controversy, but his work suffers from one major oversight: only three of his rebels are female.[9] As Richard S. Dunn has rightly observed, "The role of women in colonial life continues to be neglected,"[10] and only one colonial specialist, Michael J. Colacurcio, has been much concerned with women as Antinomians. Colacurcio has argued that sexual tensions were central to the Antinomian controversy, but it is not his primary concern to describe the nature of those tensions. Rather, he focuses on Anne Hutchinson as a "type" of Hawthorne's scarlet lady, Hester Prynne.[11] Dunn's appeal, "We need another view of Ms. Hutchinson,"[12] still entices.

That Anne Hutchinson and many other Puritan women should at stressful times rebel, either by explicit statement or by implicit example, against the role they were expected to fulfill in society is readily understandable, since that role, in both old and New England, was extremely limiting. The model English woman was weak, submissive, charitable, virtuous, and modest. Her mental and physical activity was limited to keeping the home in order, cooking, and bearing and rearing children, although she might occasionally serve the community as a nurse or midwife. She was urged to avoid books and intellectual exercise, for such activity might overtax her weak mind, and to serve her husband willingly, since she was by nature his inferior.[13] In accordance with the Apostle Paul's doctrine, she was to hold her tongue in church and be careful not "to teach, nor to usurp authority over the man, but to be in silence."[14]

In their letters, lectures, and historical accounts many of the Bay Colony men and some of the women showed approval of modest, obedient, and submissive females. Governor John Winthrop's wife Margaret was careful to leave such important domestic matters as place of residence to her husband's discretion, even when she had a preference of her own. She was ashamed because she felt that she had "no thinge with in or with out" worthy of him and signed her letters to him "your faythfull and obedient wife" or "your lovinge and obedient wife." Lucy Downing, Winthrop's sister, signed her chatty letters to her brother, "Your sister to commaund." Elizabeth, the wife of Winthrop's son John, described herself in a letter to her husband as "thy eaver loveing and kinde wife to comande in whatsoeaver thou plesest so long as the Lord shall bee plesed to geve me life and strenge."[15]

Winthrop himself was harshly critical of female intellect. In 1645 he wrote that Ann Hopkins, wife of the governor of Connecticut, had lost her understanding and reason by giving herself solely to reading and writing. The Massachusetts statesman commented that if she "had attended her household affairs, and such things as belong to women, and not gone out of her way and calling to meddle in such things as are proper for men, whose minds are stronger, etc. she had kept her wits, and might have improved them usefully and honorably in the place God had set her." Earlier he had denounced Anne Hutchinson as "a woman of a haughty and fierce carriage, of a nimble wit and active spirit, and a very voluble tongue, more bold then a man, though in understanding and judgement, inferiour to many women."[16]

Winthrop echoed the expectations of the male-dominated society in which he lived, in much the same way as the New England propagandist William Wood and Anne Hutchinson's ministerial accusers did. In 1634 Wood praised the Indian women's "mild carriage and obedience to their husbands," despite his realization that Indian men were guilty of "churlishness and inhumane behavior" toward their wives. Reverend John Cotton arrived in Boston in 1633 and soon requested that women desiring church membership be examined in private since a public confession was "against the apostle's rule and not fit for a women's modesty." At a public lecture less than a year later Cotton explained that the apostle directed women to wear veils in church only when "the custom of the place" considered veils "a sign of the women's subjection." Cambridge minister Thomas Shepard, one of Anne Hutchinson's most severe critics, commended his own wife for her "incomparable meekness of spirit, toward myself especially," while Hugh Peter, a Salem pastor and another of Ms. Hutchinson's accusers, urged his daughter to respect her feminine meekness as "Womans Ornament."[17]

The female role definition that the Massachusetts ministers and magistrates perpetuated severely limited the assertiveness, the accomplishment, the independence, and the intellectual activity of Puritan women. Bay Colony women who might resent such a role definition before 1636 had no ideological rationale around which they could organize the expression of their frustration—whatever their consciousness of the causes of that frustration. With the marked increase of Antinomian sentiment in Boston and Anne Hutchinson's powerful example of resistance, the distressed females were able—as this article will attempt to demonstrate—to channel their frustration into a viable theological form and to rebel openly against the perpetuators of the spiritual and secular status quo. Paradoxically enough, the values that Antinomians embraced minimized the importance of individual action, for they believed that salvation could be demonstrated only by the individual feeling God's grace within.

The process of salvation and the role of the individual in that process was, for the Puritan divines, a matter less well defined. The question of the relative importance of good works (i.e., individual effort) and grace (i.e., God's effort) in preparing man for salvation had concerned English Puritans from their earliest origins, and clergymen of old and New England attempted to walk a broad, although unsure, middle ground between the extremes of Antinomianism and Arminianism. But in 1636 Anne Hutchinson's former mentor and the new teacher of the Boston church, John Cotton, disrupted the fragile theological balance and led the young colony into controversy when he "warned his listeners away from the specious comfort of preparation and re-emphasized the covenant of grace as something in which God acted alone and unassisted."[18] Cotton further explained that a person could become conscious of the dwelling of the Holy Spirit within his soul and directed the Boston congregation "not to be afraid of the word *Revelation*."[19] The church elders, fearing that Cotton's "Revelation" might be dangerously construed to invalidate biblical law requested a clarification of his position.

While the elders debated with Cotton the religious issues arising out of his pronouncements, members of Cotton's congregation responded more practically and enthusiastically to the notion of personal revelation by ardently soliciting converts to an emerging, loosely-knit ideology which the divines called pejoratively Antinomianism, Opinionism, or Familism.[20] According to Thomas Weld, fledgling Antinomians visited new migrants to Boston, "especially, men of note, worth, and activity, fit instruments to advance their designe." Antinomian principles were defended at military trainings, in town meetings, and before the court judges. Winthrop charged the Opinionists with causing great disturbance in the church, the state, and the family, and wailed, "All things are turned upside down among us."[21]

The individual hungry for power could, as long as he perceived his deep inner feeling of God's grace to be authentic, use that feeling to consecrate his personal rebellion against the contemporary authorities. Some Boston merchants used it to attack the accretion of political power in the hands of a rural-dominated General Court based on land instead of capital. Some "ignorant and unlettered" men used it to express contempt for the arrogance of "black-coates that have been at the Ninneversity."[22] Some women, as we will see, used it to castigate the authority of the magistrates as guardians of the state, the ministers as guardians of the church, and their husbands as guardians of the home. As the most outspoken of these women, Anne Hutchinson diffused her opinions among all social classes by means of contacts made in the course of her profession of midwifery and in the biweekly teaching sessions she held at her home. Weld believed that Ms. Hutchinson's lectures were responsible for distributing "the venome of these [Antinomian] opinions into the very veines and vitalls of the People in the Country."[23]

Many women identified with Ms. Hutchinson's rebellious intellectual stance and her aggressive spirit. Edward Johnson wrote that "the weaker Sex" set her up as "a Priest" and "thronged" after her. John Underhill reported he daily heard a "clamor" that "New England men usurp over their wives, and keep them in servile subjection." Winthrop blamed Anne for causing "divisions between husband and wife . . . till the weaker give place to the stronger, otherwise it turnes to open contention," and Weld charged the Antinomians with using the yielding, flexible, and tender women as "an Eve, to catch their husbands also." One anonymous English pamphleteer found in Antinomianism a movement "somewhat like the Trojan horse for rarity" because "it was covered with womens aprons, and bolstered out with the judgement and deep discerning of the godly and reverent."[24]

From late 1636 through early 1637 female resistance in the Boston church reached its highest pitch. At one point, when pastor John Wilson rose to preach, Ms. Hutchinson left the congregation and many women followed her out of the meetinghouse. These women "pretended many excuses for their going out," an action which made it impossible for the authorities to convict them of contempt for Wilson. Other rebels did, however, challenge Wilson's words as he spoke them, causing Weld to comment, "Now the faithfull Ministers of Christ must have dung cast on their faces, and be no better than Legall Preachers, Baals Priests, Popish Factors, Scribes, Pharisees, and Opposers of Christ himselfe."[25]

Included among these church rebels were two particularly active women, Jane (Mrs. Richard) Hawkins and milliner William Dyer's wife Mary, both of whom Winthrop found obnoxious. The governor considered the youthful Ms. Dyer to be "of a very proud spirit," "much addicted to revelations," and "notoriously infected with Mrs. Hutchinson's errors." Ms. Dyer weathered Winthrop's wrath and followed Anne to Rhode Island, but her "addictions" were not without serious consequence. Twenty-two years later she would return to Boston and be hanged as a Quaker.[26] The other of Hutchinson's close female associates, Jane Hawkins, dispensed fertility potions to barren women and occasionally fell into a trance-like state in which she spoke Latin. Winthrop therefore denounced her as "notorious for familiarity with the devill," and the General Court, sharing his apprehension, on March 12, 1638, forbade her to question "matters of religion" or "to meddle" in "surgery, or phisick, drinks, plaisters, or oyles." Ms. Hawkins apparently disobeyed this order, for three years later the Court banished her from the colony under the penalty of a severe whipping or such other punishment as the judges thought fit.[27]

Other women, both rich and poor, involved themselves in the Antinomian struggle. William Coddington's spouse, like her merchant husband, was "taken with the familistical opinions."[28] Mary Dummer, the wife of wealthy landowner and Assistant Richard Dummer, convinced her husband to move from Newbury to Boston so that she might be closer to Ms. Hutchinson.[29] Mary Oliver, a poor Salem calenderer's wife, reportedly exceeded Anne "for ability of speech, and appearance of zeal and devotion" and, according to Winthrop, might "have done hurt, but that she was poor and had little acquaintance [with theology]." Ms. Oliver held the "dangerous" opinions that the church was managed by the "heads of the people, both magistrates and ministers, met together," instead of the people themselves, and that anyone professing faith in Christ ought to be admitted to the church and the sacraments. Between 1638 and 1650 she appeared before the magistrates six times for remarks contemptuous of ministerial and magisterial authority and experienced the stocks, the lash, the placement of a cleft stick on her tongue, and imprisonment. One of the Salem magistrates became so frustrated with Ms. Oliver's refusal to respect his authority that he seized her and put her in the stocks without a trial. She sued him for false arrest and collected a minimal ten shillings in damages. Her victory was short-lived, however, and before she left Massachusetts in 1650 she had managed to secure herself some reputation as a witch.[30]

Mary Oliver and the other female rebels could easily identify with the Antinomian ideology because its theological emphasis on the inability of the individual to achieve salvation echoed the inability of women to achieve recognition on a sociopolitical level. As the woman realized that she could receive wealth, power, and status only through the man, her father or her husband, so the Antinomian realized that he or she could receive grace only through God's beneficence. Thus, women could have found it appealing that in Antinomianism *both* men and women were relegated vis-à-vis God to the status that women occupied in Puritan society vis-à-vis men, that is, to the status of malleable inferiors in the hands of a higher being. All power, then, emanated from God, raw and pure, respecting no sex, rather than from male authority figures striving to interpret the Divine Word. Fortified by a consciousness of the Holy Spirit's inward dwelling, the Antinomians could rest secure and self-confident in the belief that they were mystic participants in the transcendent power of the Almighty, a power far beyond anything mere magistrates and ministers might muster. Antinomianism could not secure for women such practical earthly powers as sizable estates, professional success, and participation in the church and civil government, but it provided compensation by reducing the significance of these powers for the men. Viewed from this perspective, Antinomianism extended the feminine experience of humility to both sexes, which in turn paradoxically created the possibility of feminine pride, as Anne Hutchinson's dynamic example in her examinations and trials amply demonstrated.

Anne Hutchinson's example caused the divines much frustration. They were chagrined to find that she was not content simply to repeat to the "simple Weomen"[31] the sermons of John Wilson, but that she also chose to interpret and even question the content of those sermons. When she charged that the Bay Colony ministers did not teach a covenant of grace as "clearly" as Cotton and her brother-in-law, John Wheelwright, she was summoned in 1636 to appear before a convocation of the clergy. At this convocation and in succeeding examinations, the ministers found particularly galling her implicit assertion that she had the intellectual ability necessary to judge the truth of their theology. Such an assertion threatened their self-image as the intellectual leaders of the community and the spokesmen for a male-dominated society. The ministers and magistrates therefore sharply criticized Anne for not fulfilling her ordained womanly role. In September 1637 a synod of elders resolved that women might meet "to pray and edify one another," but when one woman "in a prophetical way" resolved questions of doctrine and expounded Scripture, then the meeting was "disorderly." At Anne's examination on November 7 and 8, Winthrop began the interrogation by charging that she criticized the ministers and maintained a "meeting and an assembly in your house that hath been condemned by the general assembly as a thing not tolerable nor comely in the sight of God nor fitting for your sex." Later in the interrogation, Winthrop accused her of disobeying her "parents," the magistrates, in violation of the Fifth Commandment, and paternalistically told her, "We do not mean to discourse with those of your sex." Hugh Peter also indicated that he felt Anne was not fulfilling the properly submissive, nonintellectual feminine role. He ridiculed her choice of a female preacher of the Isle of Ely as a model for her own behavior and told her to consider "that you have stept out of you place, *you have rather bine a Husband than a Wife and a preacher than a Hearer; and a Magistrate than a Subject.*"[32]

When attacked for behavior inappropriate to her sex, Ms. Hutchinson did not hesitate to demonstrate that she was the intellectual equal of her accusers. She tried to trap Winthrop when he charged her with dishonoring her "parents": "But put the case Sir that I do fear the Lord and my parents, may not I entertain them that fear the Lord because my parents will not give me leave?" To provide a biblical justification for her teaching activities, she cited Titus's rule (2:3–4) "that the elder women should instruct the younger." Winthrop ordered her to take that rule "in the sense that elder women must instruct the younger about their business, and to love their husbands." But Anne disagreed with this interpretation, saying, "I do not conceive but that it is meant for some publick times." Winthrop rejoined, "We must . . . restrain you from maintaining this course," and she qualified, "If you have a rule for it from God's word you may." Her resistance infuriated the governor, who exclaimed, "We are your judges, and not you ours." When Winthrop tried to lure her into admitting that she taught men, in violation of Paul's proscription, Anne replied that she throught herself justified in teaching a man who asked her for instruction, and added sarcastically, "Do you think it not lawful for me to teach women and why do you call me to teach the court?"[33]

Anne soon realized that sarcastic remarks would not persuade the court of the legitimacy of her theological claims. Alternatively, therefore, she affected a kind of modesty to cozen the authorities at the same time that she expressed a kind of primitive feminism through double-entendre statements and attacked the legitimacy of Paul's idea of the nonspeaking, nonintellectual female churchmember. When the Court charged her with "prophesying," Anne responded, "The men of *Berea* are commended for examining *Pauls* Doctrine; wee do no more [in our meetings] but read the notes of our teachers Sermons, and then reason of them by searching the Scriptures."[34] Such a statement was on one level an "innocent" plea to the divines that the women were only following biblical prescription. On another level it was an attack on the ministers for presuming to have the final word on biblical interpretation. On yet a third level, since she focused on "Pauls Doctrine" and reminded men that they should take another look at that teaching, her statement was a suggestion that ministerial attitudes toward women ought to be reexamined.

At another point Anne responded to Winthrop's criticism with a similar statement having meaning on three levels. The governor had accused her of traducing the ministers and magistrates and, when summoned to answer this charge, of saying that "the fear of man was a snare and therefore she would not be affeared of them." She replied, "They say I said the fear of man is a snare, why should I be afraid. When I came unto them, they urging many things unto me and I being backward to answer at first, at length this scripture came into my mind

29th Prov. 15. The fear of man bringeth a snare, but who putteth his trust in the Lord shall be safe."[35] Once again, her response was phrased as an "innocent" plea to God to assuage her fears, while at the same time it implied that God was on her side in opposition to the ministers and magistrates. Her statement also told women that if they trusted in God they need not fear men, for such fear trapped them into being "backward" about reacting in situations of confrontation with men.

Anne, although aware of the "backwardness" of women as a group, did not look to intensified group activity as a remedy for woman's down-trodden status. Her feminism consisted essentially of the subjective recognition of her own strength and gifts and the apparent belief that other women could come to the same recognition. A strong, heroic example of female self-assertiveness was necessary to the development of this recognition of one's own personal strength. Anne chose the woman preacher of the Isle of Ely as her particular heroic model; she did, Hugh Peter chided, "exceedingly magnifie" that woman "to be a Womane of 1000 hardly any like to her." Anne could thus dissociate herself from the "divers worthy and godly Weomen" of Massachusetts and confidently deride them as being no better than "soe many Jewes," unconverted by the light of Christ.[36] Other Bay Colony women who wished to reach beyond the conventional, stereotypic behavior of "worthy and godly Weomen" attached themselves to the emphatic example of Anne and to God's ultimate power in order to resist the constraints which they felt as Puritan women.

Fearful that Ms. Hutchinson's example might be imitated by other women, the divines wished to catch her in a major theological error and subject her to public punishment. Their efforts were not immediately successful. Throughout her 1637 examination Anne managed to parry the verbal thrusts of the ministers and magistrates by replying to their many questions with questions of her own, forcing them to justify their positions from the Bible, pointing out their logical inconsistencies, and using innuendo to cast aspersions upon their authoritarianism. With crucial assistance from a sympathetic John Cotton, she left the ministers with no charge to pin upon her. She was winning the debate when, in an apparently incautious moment, she gave the authorities the kind of declaration for which they had been hoping. Raising herself to the position of judge over her accusers, she asserted, "I know that for this you goe about to doe to me, God will ruine you and your posterity, and this whole State." Asked how she knew this, she explained, "By an immediate revelation."[37] With this statement Anne proved her heresy to the ministers and they then took steps to expose her in excommunication proceedings conducted before the Boston church. The divines hoped to expel a heretic from their midst, to reestablish support for the

Puritan way, to prevent unrest in the state and the family, and to shore up their own anxious egos in the process.

The predisposition of the ministers to defame Ms. Hutchinson before the congregation caused them to ignore what she was actually saying in her excommunication trial. Although she did describe a relationship with Christ closer than anything Cotton had envisioned, she did not believe that she had experienced Christ's Second Coming in her own life. Such a claim would have denied the resurrection of the body at the Last Judgment and would have clearly stamped her as a Familist.[38] Ms. Hutchinson's accusers, ignoring Thomas Leverett's reminder that she had expressed belief in the resurrection, argued that if the resurrection did not exist, biblical law would have no validity nor the marriage covenant any legal or utilitarian value. The result would be a kind of world no Puritan could tolerate, a world where the basest desires would be fulfilled and "foule, groce, filthye and abominable" sexual promiscuity would be rampant. Cotton, smarting from a psychological slap Anne had given him earlier in the excommunication proceedings[39] and in danger of losing the respect of the other ministers, admonished her with the words "though I have not herd, nayther do I thinke, you have bine unfaythfull to your Husband in his Marriage Covenant, *yet that will follow upon it.*" By referring to "his" marriage covenant Cotton did not even accord Anne equal participation in the making of that covenant. The Boston teacher concluded his admonition with a criticism of Anne's pride: *"I have often feared the highth of your Spirit and being puft up with your owne parts."*[40]

Both the introduction of the sexual issue into the trial and Cotton's denunciation of Ms. Hutchinson must have had the effect of curbing dissent from the congregation. Few Puritans would want to defend Anne in public when such a defense could be construed as supporting promiscuity. Since Cotton had earlier been sympathetic to the Antinomian cause and had tried to save Anne at her 1637 examination, his vigorous condemnation of her must have confused her following. Cotton even went so far as to exempt the male Antinomians from any real blame for the controversy when he characterized Antinomianism as a women's delusion. He urged that women, like children, ought to be watched, reproved Hutchinson's sons for not controlling her theological ventures, and called those sons "Vipers . . . [who] *Eate through the very Bowells of your Mother,* to her Ruine." Cotton warned the Boston women "to looke to your selves and to take heed that you reaceve nothinge for Truth which hath not the stamp of the Word of God [as interpreted by the ministers] . . . for you see she [Anne] is but a Woman and *many unsound and dayngerous principles are held by her.*" Thomas Shepard agreed that intellectual activity did not suit women and warned the congregation that Anne was likely "to seduce and draw away many, Espetially simple Weomen of her owne sex."[41]

The female churchmembers, who would have had good reason to resent the clergy's approach, could not legitimately object to the excommunication proceedings because of Paul's injunction against women speaking in church. Lacking a clearly-defined feminist consciousness and filled with "backward" fear, the women could not refuse to respect that injunction, even though, or perhaps because, Anne had been presented to the congregation as the epitome of despicableness, as a woman of simple intellect, and as a liar, puffed up with pride and verging on sexual promiscuity. This caricature of Anne did not, however, prevent five men, including her brother-in-law Richard Scott and Mary Oliver's husband Thomas, from objecting to her admonition and excommunication. Cotton refused to consider the points these men raised and dismissed their objections as rising out of their own self-interest or their natural affection for Anne.[42]

In Anne's excommunication proceedings the ministers demonstrated that they had found the means necessary to deal effectively with this rebellious woman and a somewhat hostile congregation. At her examination and her excommunication trial Anne attempted to place the ministers on the defensive by questioning them and forcing them to justify their positions while she explained little. She achieved some success in the 1637 trial, but before her fellow churchmembers she found it difficult to undercut the misrepresentation of her beliefs and the attack on her character. Perhaps fearing the banishment which had been so quickly imposed on her associate, John Wheelwright, she recanted, but even in her recantation she would not totally compromise her position. She expressed sorrow for her errors of expression but admitted no errors in judgment and assumed no appearance of humiliation. When Wilson commanded her *as a Leper to withdraw your selfe out of the Congregation,*" Anne rose, walked to the meetinghouse door, accepted Mary Dyer's offered hand, and turned to impugn her accusers' power: "The Lord judgeth not as man judgeth, better to be cast out of the Church then to deny Christ."[43]

During the year and a half following Ms. Hutchinson's excommunication, the Massachusetts ministers and magistrates prosecuted several other female rebels. In April 1638 the Boston church cast out Judith Smith, the maidservant of Anne's brother-in-law, Edward Hutchinson, for her "obstinate persisting" in "sundry Errors." On October 10 of the same year the Assistants ordered Katherine Finch to be whipped for "speaking against the magistrates, against the Churches, and against the

Elders." Less than a year later Ms. Finch again appeared before the Assistants, this time for not carrying herself "dutifully to her husband," and was released upon promise of reformation. In September 1639 the Boston church excommunicated Philip(a?) Hammond "as a slaunderer and revyler both of the Church and Common Weale." Ms. Hammond, after her husband's death, had resumed her maiden name, operated a business in Boston, and argued in her shop and at public meetings "that Mrs. Hutchinson neyther deserved the Censure which was putt upon her in the Church, nor in the Common Weale." The Boston church also excommunicated two other women for partially imitating Anne Hutchinson's example: Sarah Keayne was found guilty in 1646 of "irregular prophesying in mixed assemblies," and Joan Hogg nine years later was punished "for her disorderly singing and her idleness, and for saying she is commanded of Christ so to do."[44]

The Salem authorities followed Boston's example in dealing with overly assertive women. In late 1638 the Salem church excommunicated four of Roger Williams's former followers: Jane (Mrs. Joshua) Verin, Mary Oliver, servant Margery Holliman, and widow Margery Reeves. These women had consistently refused to worship with the congregation, and the latter two had denied that the churches of the Bay Colony were true churches.[45] Yet another woman, Dorothy Talby, who was subject to a different kind of frustration, troubled the Essex County magistrates by mimicking Anne Hutchinson's proclamation of "immediate revelation" to justify her personal rebellion. In October 1637 the county court ordered her chained to a post "for frequent laying hands on her husband to the danger of his life, and contemning the authority of the court," and later ordered her whipped for "misdemeanors against her husband." Later, according to Winthrop, she claimed a "revelation from heaven" instructing her to kill her husband and children and then broke the neck of her three-year-old daughter, Difficult. At her execution on December 6, 1638, Ms. Talby continued her defiance by refusing to keep her face covered and expressing a desire to be beheaded, as "it was less painful and less shameful."[46]

Dorothy Talby was one of an increasing number of women to appear before the General Court and the Court of Assistants, an increase which seemed to reflect both a greater rebelliousness in women and a hardening of magisterial attitudes. In the first five years of Puritan settlement only 1.7 percent of the persons convicted of criminal offenses by the Deputies and the Assistants were women. During and after the years of the Antinomian controversy the percentage of female offenders was significantly higher—6.7 percent from 1635 to 1639 and 9.4 percent from 1640 to 1644. If Charles E. Banks's enumeration of 3,505 passengers from ship lists is representative of the more than 20,000 persons who came to Massachusetts between 1630 and 1639, it can be assumed that the number of women did not increase proportionately to the number of men. Banks's ship lists reveal that 829 males and 542 females came to Massachusetts between 1630 and 1634, a number which increased in the next five years to 1,279 males and 855 females. The percentage of females increased only .6 percent, from 39.5 percent between 1630 and 1634 to 40.1 percent between 1635 and 1639.[47] These comparative figures suggest that by 1640 the magistrates could no longer afford to dismiss with verbal chastisement females found guilty of drunkenness, cursing, or pre-marital fornication.[48]

The magistrates not only used the threat of a humiliating court-room appearance and possible punishment to keep female rebels quiet but also levied very stringent penalties on male Antinomian offenders. Anne Hutchinson's son-in-law William Collins was sentenced to pay a £100 fine for charging the Massachusetts churches and ministers with being anti-Christian and calling the king of England the king of Baby-lon. Anne's son Francis, who had accompanied Collins to Boston in 1641, objected to the popular rumor that he would not sit at the same table with his excommunicated mother and, feeling that the Boston church was responsible, called that church "a strumpet." The church excommunicated Francis and the Assistants fined him £40, but neither he nor Collins would pay the stipulated amounts (even when those fines were reduced to £40 and £20) and therefore spent some time in jail.[49]

Besides prosecuting Antinomian sympathizers in church and court, the Massachusetts ministers and magistrates carefully watched new ministers, lest they deliver "some points savoring of familism,"[50] and justified the emergent orthodox position in their sermons and publica-tions. Of these publications, which were directed at audiences both in New and old England, John Cotton's *Singing of Psalmes a Gospel-Ordinance* most significantly asserted the traditional feminine role-response. The Boston teacher, apparently with Ms. Hutchinson in mind, told his readers that "the woman is more subject to error than a man" and continued, "It is not permitted to a woman to speak in the Church by way of propounding questions though under pretence of desire to learn for her own satisfaction; but rather it is required she should ask her husband at home. For under pretence of questioning for learning sake, she might so propound her question as to teach her teachers; or if not so, yet to open a door to some of her own weak and erroneous apprehensions, or at least soon exceed the bounds of womanly mod-esty." Cotton explained that a woman could speak in church only when she wished to confess a sin or to participate in singing hymns.[51]

Other Bay Colony leaders popularized the idea that the intellectual woman was influenced by Satan and was therefore unable to perform the necessary functions of womanhood. Weld described Mary Dyer's abortive birth as "a woman child, a fish, a beast, and a fowle, all woven together in one, and without an head," and wrote of Anne Hutchinson's probable hydatidiform mole as "30. monstrous births . . . none at all of them (as farre as I could ever learne) of humane shape."[52] According to Winthrop's even more garish account of Mary Dyer's child, the still-born baby had a face and ears growing upon the shoulders, a breast and back full of sharp prickles, female sex organs on the rear and buttocks in front, three clawed feet, no forehead, four horns above the eyes, and two great holes upon the back.[53] Wheelwright wrote from his new home in Exeter to attack the governor's farfetched description of these births. That clergyman called Winthrop's monsters "a monstrous conception of his brain, a spurious issue of his intellect," and told that governor that he should know better *then to delude the world with untruths.* [For] I question not his learning, etc. but I admire his certainty or rather impudence: did the man obtestricate [obstetricate]?"[54]

Despite Wheelwright's effort, Weld's opinion that "as she had vented mishapen opinions, so she must bring forth deformed monsters" impressed the people of the Bay Colony, a people who believed that catastrophic occurrences were evidences of God's displeasure. Some Massachusetts residents viewed the births as the products of both the women's "mishapen opinions" and their supposed promiscuity. Edward Johnson and Roger Clap lamented the "phantasticall madnesse" of those who would hold "silly women laden with their lusts" in higher esteem than "those honoured of Christ, indued with power and authority from him to Preach." A rumor reached England that Henry Vane had crossed the Atlantic in 1637 with Ms. Dyer and Ms. Hutchinson and had "debauched both, and both were delivered of monsters."[55] It was also widely rumored that three of the Antinomian women, Anne Hutchinson, Jane Hawkins, and Mary Oliver, had sold their souls to Satan and become witches. Anne in particular "gave cause of suspicion of witchcraft" after she easily converted to Antinomianism one new male arrival in Rhode Island.[56]

The promotion of the belief that the Antinomian female leaders were witches filled with aberrant lusts and unable to live as proper women was accompanied by an attack on the masculinity of some of the Antinomian men. Although Anne's husband, William, had been a prosperous landowner, a merchant, a deputy to the General Court, and a Boston selectman, Winthrop described him as a "man of very mild temper and weak parts, and wholly guided by his wife." Clap also felt that William Hutchinson and the other Antinomian men were deficient in intellect and judgment. He expressed surprise that any of the men in the movement had "strong parts."[57]

While Massachusetts gossip focused on disordered Antinomian births, lusty Antinomian women, and weak Antinomian men, Winthrop and Cotton tried to convince their English and New England readers that public opinion had been solidly behind Ms. Hutchinson's excommunication. Winthrop contended that "diverse women" objected to this rebel's example and would have borne witness against her "if their modesty had not restrained them." Cotton supported the governor's claim by construing the relative silence at Anne's church trial to mean that the "whole body of the Church (except her own son) consented with one accord, to the publick censure of her, by admonition first, and excommunication after." By asserting this falsehood and ignoring Leverett's admission that many churchmembers wished to stay Anne's excommunication, Cotton made it appear that any person who complained about her censure was contradicting the near-unanimous opinion of the congregation.[58]

The effort to discredit the Antinomians and Antinomian sentiment in the Bay Colony was quite successful. By the late 1640s Antinomianism, in a practical sense, was no longer threatening; the ministers and magistrates had managed to preserve a theological system they found congenial. "*Sanctification* came to be in some Request again; and there were *Notes* and *Marks* given of a good Estate."[59] The position of Massachusetts women within the religious system remained essentially unchanged, while in Rhode Island and nearby Providence Plantations the status of women was somewhat improved. In Providence and Portsmouth the men listened to the wishes of the women and protected the "liberty" of women to teach, preach, and attend services of their choosing. When Joshua Verin, one of the original settlers at Providence, restrained his wife Jane from attending religious services at Roger Williams's home, a town meeting considered the matter. John Greene argued before the townsmen that if men were allowed to restrain their wives, "all the women in the country would cry out." William Arnold rejoined that God had ordered the wife to be subject to her husband and that such a commandment should not be broken merely to please women. According to Winthrop, the townsmen "would have censured Verin, [but] Arnold told them, that it was against their own order, for Verin did that he did out of conscience; and their order was, that no man should be censured for his conscience." Winthrop neglected to record that the town meeting did disfranchise Verin until he declared that he would not restrain his wife's "libertie of conscience," nor did Winthrop mention that Verin had "trodden" his wife "under foot tyrannically and brutishly," endangering her life. After his censure, Verin returned to Salem, and Roger Williams urged Winthrop to prevent this "boisterous and desperate" young man from hauling "his wife with ropes to Salem, where she must needs be troubled and troublesome."[60]

After Anne Hutchinson's arrival and throughout the remainder of the century, women taught and preached in public in Rhode Island. Johnson wrote that in 1638 "there were some of the female sexe who (deeming the Apostle Paul to be too strict in not permitting a room [woman] to preach in the publique Congregation) taught notwithstanding . . . having their call to this office from an ardent desire of being famous." According to Johnson, Anne Hutchinson, "the grand Mistresse of them all, . . . ordinarily prated every Sabbath day, till others, who thirsted after honour in the same way with her selfe, drew away her Auditors."[61] This prating was more purposive than Johnson might have been willing to admit, for Anne soon involved herself in a new controversy, this one springing out of the resentment of many of the poorer inhabitants of the settlement toward Judge (Governor) William Coddington's autocratic rule, his land allotment policy, and his efforts to establish a church resembling closely the Massachusetts example.[62] Allying herself with Samuel Gorton, a religious freethinker and a defender of justice for all men, "rich or poore, ignorant or learned," Anne began to attack the legitimacy of *any* magistracy. Together, she and Gorton managed to foment the rebellion of April 28, 1639, in which the Portsmouth inhabitants formed a new body politic, ejected Coddington from power, and chose William Hutchinson to replace him. William, however, also did not believe in magistracy and soon refused to occupy the office of judge. Coddington, who had fled south with his followers to found Newport, then claimed the judgeship by default, was recognized by the Massachusetts authorities, and proceeded to administer the affairs of Rhode Island.[63] Gorton and at least eleven others responded to Coddington's resumption of power by plotting armed rebellion against him and were ultimately banished from the colony. Anne broke with the Gortonists over that issue, and she and William joined the Newport settlement.[64]

William Hutchinson died at Newport in 1640, and for much of that year Anne was silent. By 1641, however, she had come out of mourning and, according to Winthrop, turned anabaptist. She and "divers" others supported passive resistance to authority, "denied all magistracy among Christians, and maintained that there were no churches since those founded by the apostles and evangelists, nor could any be."[65] Such opinions achieved enough popularity in Rhode Island to contribute to the dissolution of the church at Newport,[66] although not enough to remove Coddington from power. Disgruntled and fearing that Massachusetts would seize the Rhode Island settlements, Anne sought refuge in the colony of New Netherland in 1642, but her stay there was not long. In August 1643 she, William Collins, two of her sons, and three of her daughters were killed by Indians who had quarreled with her Dutch neighbors.[67]

The Massachusetts clergy rejoiced. Not only had God destroyed the "American Jesabel,"[68] but the Lord's vengeance had descended upon her sons and daughters, the poisoned seed. Peter Bulkeley spoke for all the Massachusetts ministers when he concluded, "Let her damned heresies shee fell into . . and the just vengeance of God, by which shee perished, terrifie all her seduced followers from having any more to doe with her leaven."[69] But her "seduced followers" were horrified only at the reaction of the Puritan clergy. Anne's sister, Katherine Scott, commented that the Bay Colony authorities "are drunke with the blod of the saints," and Anne's former Portsmouth neighbor, Randall Holden, blamed those same authorities for forcing Anne first to Rhode Island and ultimately to her death. He reminded them of her partially successful struggle against authority: "you know . . . your great and terrible word magistrate is no more in its original, than masterly or masterless which hath no great lustre in our ordinary acceptation."[70]

Impervious to such protests, the Bay Colony divines considered Anne Hutchinson's death to be the symbolic death of Antinomianism. To these divines she had been the incarnation of the Antinomian evil, and their accounts of the Antinomian stress in Boston accented *her* beliefs, *her* activities, and *her* rebelliousness. The ministers were not as concerned with the important roles played by Coddington, Wheelwright, Vane, and the other male Antinomian leaders because none of these men threatened the power and status structure of society in the concrete way that Anne Hutchinson did. Anne was clearly not, as the ministers might have wished, a submissive quiet dove, content to labor simply in the kitchen and the childbed. She was witty, aggressive, and intellectual. She had no qualms about castigating in public the men who occupied the most authoritative positions. She claimed the right to define rational, theological matters for herself and by her example spurred other women to express a similar demand. Far from bewildered, she thwarted her accusers with her intellectual ability. Perceiving her as a threat to the family, the state, the religion, and the status hierarchy, the Puritan authorities directed their antagonism against Anne's character and her sex. By doing so, they managed to salve the psychological wounds inflicted by this woman who trod so sharply upon their male status and their ministerial and magisterial authority. Their method had a practical aspect as well; it helped restore respect for the ministry and curb potential dissent.

Anne's ability to attract large numbers of women as supporters caused the ministers and magistrates some worry but little surprise, since they believed that women were easily deluded. They chided Anne for choosing a female preacher as a role model and refused to attribute any merit to her at times subtle, at times caustic intellectual ability. They could see only the work of Satan in Anne's aggressiveness and not the more human desire for equal opportunity and treatment which this rebel never hesitated to assert by example in the intellectual skirmishes she had with her accusers throughout her trials. The double oppression of life in a male-dominated society, combined with biological bondage to her own amazing fertility, could not destroy her self-respect. Because of the theologically based society in which she lived, it was easy for her to ally herself with God and to express her self-confidence in religious debates with the leading intellectual authorities. Neither Anne's rebellion nor the rebellion of her female followers was directed self-consciously against their collective female situation or toward its improvement. Specific feminist campaigns for the franchise, divorce reform, female property ownership after marriage, and the like would be developments of a much later era. For Anne Hutchinson and her female associates Antinomianism was simply an ideology through which the resentments they intuitively felt could be focused and actively expressed.

NOTES

1. John A. Albro, ed., *The Works of Thomas Shepard,* I (New York, 1967 [orig. publ. n.p., 1853]), cxvi–cxvii.

2. Darrett B. Rutman, *Winthrop's Boston: Portrait of a Puritan Town, 1630–1649* (Chapel Hill, N. C., 1965), 121.

3. John Stetson Barry, *The History of Massachusetts. The Colonial Period* (Boston, 1855), 261.

4. Andrew Sinclair, *The Emancipation of the American Woman* (New York, 1966), 23.

5. Edith Curtis, *Anne Hutchinson: A Biography* (Cambridge, Mass., 1930), 72–73.

6. Emery Battis, *Saints and Sectaries: Anne Hutchinson and the Antinomian Controversy in the Massachusetts Bay Colony* (Chapel Hill, N. C., 1962), 9, 50–56, 90, admits that Ms. Hutchinson had a "prodigious memory and keen mind," but he believes that she was "wracked with unbearable doubt" as a result of her inability to find a male "mental director." Her husband could not fulfill this need, for he "seems to have lacked the power to provide adequate support and direction for his wife." Ms. Hutchinson's rebellion, according to Battis, grew out of this need for

male guidance and was accentuated by the fact that she was experiencing menopause and felt that "her own inadequacy was at least in part responsible" for the death of two of her children. Of these many reasons for Ms. Hutchinson's restlessness Battis substantiates only his conclusion that she was undergoing menopause. His argument is weakened, however, by anthropological research which ties the psychological distress of menopause to the loss of self-esteem that middle-aged women experience in societies where their status deteriorates at menopause. See Joan Solomon, "Menopause: A Rite of Passage," *Ms.*, I (Dec. 1972), 18. Puritan New England was clearly not such a society, for elderly women could serve as deaconesses and, since they were free from the materialistic proclivities of youth, could furnish venerable examples for younger women. See Benjamin Colman, *The Duty and Honour of Aged Women. A Sermon on the Death of Madam Abigail Foster* (Boston, 1711), 11–30.

7.   Peter Oliver, *The Puritan Commonwealth. An Historical Review of the Puritan Government in Massachusetts in its Civil and Ecclesiastical Relations* . . . (Boston, 1856), 181.

8.   Anne Hutchinson and the Antinomians have been treated sympathetically in Charles Francis Adams, *Three Episodes of Massachusetts History* (Boston, 1892); Brooks Adams, *The Emancipation of Massachusetts* (Boston, 1887); Winnifred King Rugg, *Unafraid: A Life of Anne Hutchinson* (Boston, 1930); Theda Kenyon, *Scarlet Anne* (New York, 1939); Vernon Louis Parrington, *Main Currents in American Thought: The Colonial Mind* (New York, 1927); Eleanor Flexner, *Century of Struggle: The Woman's Rights Movement in the United States* (Cambridge, Mass., 1959); Elisabeth Anthony Dexter, *Colonial Women of Affairs: A Study of Women in Business and the Professions before 1776* (Boston, 1924); Sinclair, *Emancipation of American Woman;* Rufus M. Jones, *The Quakers in the American Colonies* (New York, 1911); Curtis, *Anne Hutchinson;* Barry, *History of Massachusetts.* Critics of Anne and the Antinomians include Henry Martyn Dexter, *As to Roger Williams, and His "Banishment" from the Massachusetts Plantation; with a Few Further Words Concerning the Baptists, the Quakers, and Religious Liberty* (Boston, 1873); George E. Ellis, "Life of Anne Hutchinson with a Sketch of the Antinomian Controversy in Massachusetts," in Jared Sparks, ed., *The Library of American Biography*, 2d Ser., VI (Boston, 1849); John Gorham Palfrey, *A Compendious History of the First Century of New England* . . . (Boston, 1872); Thomas Jefferson Wertenbaker, *The First Americans, 1607–1690* (New York, 1927); Oliver, *Puritan Commonwealth;* Rutman, *Winthrop's Boston.* More balanced treatments are Edmund S. Morgan, *The Puritan Dilemma: The Story of John Winthrop* (Boston, 1958), and Battis, *Saints and Sectaries.*

9.   Battis, *Saints and Sectaries,* 249–307. The three women whom Battis lists as Antinomians are Anne Hutchinson, Jane Hawkins, and Mary Dyer.

10.   "The Social History of Early New England," *American Quarterly*, XXIV (1972), 677.

11.   "Footsteps of Anne Hutchinson: The Context of *The Scarlet Letter*," *ELH*, XXXIX (1972), 459–494.

12.   Dunn, "Social History of Early New England," *Amer. Qtly.*, XXIV (1972), 677.

13.   Studies of early 17th-century English attitudes about women appear in Georgiana Hill, *Women in English Life from Mediaeval to Modern Times* (London, 1896); M. Phillips and W. S. Tomkinson, *English Women in Life and Letters*

(London, 1926); Gamaliel Bradford, *Elizabethan Women* (Boston, 1936); Doris Mary Stenton, *The English Woman in History* (London, 1957).

14. I Tim. 2:11–12. St. Paul told the Corinthians: "Let your women keep silence in the churches; for it is not permitted unto them to speak; but they are commanded to be under obedience, as also saith the law. And if they will learn any thing, let them ask their husbands at home; for it is a shame for women to speak in the church" (I Cor. 14:34–35).

15. Margaret Winthrop to John Winthrop, 1624–1630, *The Winthrop Papers* (Boston, 1929–1944), I, 354–355; II, 165, 199; Lucy Downing to John Winthrop, 1636–1640, Massachusetts Historical Society, *Collections*, 5th Ser., I (Boston, 1871), 20, 25, 27; Elizabeth Winthrop to John Winthrop, ca. June 1636, *Winthrop Papers*, III, 267.

16. James Kendall Hosmer, ed., *Winthrop's Journal: "History of New England," 1630–1649*, Original Narratives of Early American History (New York, 1908), II, 225; John Winthrop, *A Short Story of the Rise, reign, and ruine of the Antinomians, Familists and Libertines* in David D. Hall, ed., *The Antinomian Controversy, 1636–1638: A Documentary History* (Middletown, Conn., 1968), 263.

17. William Wood, *New Englands Prospect* . . . (London, 1634), 121–122; Hosmer, ed., *Winthrop's Journal*, I, 107, 120; Michael McGiffert, ed., *God's Plot: The Paradoxes of Puritan Piety, Being the Autobiography and Journal of Thomas Shepard* (Amherst, Mass., 1972), 70; Hugh Peter, *A Dying Fathers Last Legacy to An Only Child: Or, Mr. Hugh Peter's Advice to His Daughter* . . . (Boston, 1717), 22.

18. Morgan, *Puritan Dilemma*, 137. McGiffert's introduction to Shepard's autobiography and journal contains a discussion of the Puritans' problems with assurance. See McGiffert, ed., *God's Plot*, 1–32. Puritan attitudes toward the preparation process are treated comprehensively and perceptively in Norman Pettit, *The Heart Prepared: Grace and Conversion in Puritan Spiritual Life* (New Haven, Conn., 1966).

19. John Cotton, *A Treatise of the Covenant of Grace, as it is despensed to the Elect Seed, effectually unto Salvation* (London, 1671), 177. Cotton's subsequent debate with the other ministers appears in Hall, ed., *Antinomian Controversy*, 24–151.

20. The Familists or Family of Love, a sect which originated in Holland about 1540 and spread to England, gained a largely undeserved reputation for practicing promiscuity. Antinomianism was associated in the Puritan mind with the licentious orgies that accompanied the enthusiasm of John Agricola in 16th-century Germany. Opinionism was a term often used for any theology that the divines disliked. James Hastings, ed., *Encyclopaedia of Religion and Ethics* (New York, 1908–1926), I, 581–582; V, 319; IX, 102.

21. Thomas Weld, "The Preface," to Winthrop, *Short Story*, in Hall, ed., *Antinomian Controversy*, 204, 208–209; Winthrop, *Short Story*, ibid., 253.

22. J. Franklin Jameson, ed., *Johnson's Wonder-Working Providence, 1628–1651*, Original Narratives of Early American History (New York, 1910), 127.

23. Weld, "Preface," to Winthrop, *Short Story*, in Hall, ed., *Antinomian Controversy*, 207.

24. Jameson, ed., *Johnson's Wonder-Working Providence*, 132; John Underhill, *Newes from America; or A New and Experimentall Discoverie of New England* . . .

(London, 1638), reprinted in Mass. Hist. Soc., *Colls.*, 3d Ser., VI (Boston, 1837), 5; Winthrop, *Short Story*, in Hall, ed., *Antinomian Controversy*, 253; Weld, "Preface," to Winthrop, *Short Story, ibid.*, 205–206; *Good News from New England: with An exact Relation of the first planting that Countrey* (1648), reprinted in Mass. Hist. Soc., *Colls.*, 4th Ser., I (1852), 206.

25. John Cotton, *The Way of Congregational Churches Cleared,* in Hall, ed., *Antinomian Controversy*, 423, and Weld, "Preface," to Winthrop, *Short Story, ibid.*, 209.

26. Hosmer, ed., *Winthrop's Journal,* I, 266; Winthrop, *Short Story,* in Hall, ed., *Antinomian Controversy*, 281; Horatio Rogers, "Mary Dyer Did Hang Like a Flag," in Jessamyn West, ed., *The Quaker Reader* (New York, 1962), 168–175.

27. Jameson, ed., *Johnson's Wonder-Working Providence,* 132; Winthrop, *Short Story,* in Hall, ed., *Antinomian Controversy*, 281; Nathaniel B. Shurtleff, ed., *Records of the Governor and Company of the Massachusetts Bay in New England, 1628–1641* (Boston, 1853), I, 224, 329.

28. Hosmer, ed., *Winthrop's Journal,* I, 270.

29. "The Rev. John Eliot's Record of Church Members, Roxbury, Massachusetts," in *A Report of the Boston Commissioners, Containing the Roxbury Land and Church Records* (Boston, 1881), 77.

30. Hosmer, ed., *Winthrop's Journal,* I, 285–286; George Francis Dow, ed., *Records and Files of the Quarterly Courts of Essex County, Massachusetts, 1636–1656,* I (Salem, Mass., 1911), 12, 138, 180, 182–183, 186; John Noble, ed., *Records of the Court of Assistants of the Colony of the Massachusetts Bay, 1630–1644,* II (Boston, 1904), 80, hereafter cited as *Assistants Records;* Sidney Perley, *History of Salem, Massachusetts, 1638–1670,* II (Salem, Mass., 1926), 50; Thomas Hutchinson, *The Witchcraft Delusion of 1692* (Boston, 1870), 6.

31. "A Report of the Trial of Mrs. Anne Hutchinson before the Church in Boston," in Hall, ed., *Antinomian Controversy*, 365.

32. Hosmer, ed., *Winthrop's Journal,* I, 234; "The Examination of Mrs. Anne Hutchinson at the Court at Newtown," in Hall, ed., *Antinomian Controversy,* 312–314, 318; "Trial of Anne Hutchinson before Boston church," *ibid.,* 380, 382–383.

33. "Examination of Mrs. Hutchinson at Newtown," in Hall, ed., *Antinomian Controversy*, 313–316.

34. Winthrop, *Short Story, ibid.,* 268.

35. "Examination of Mrs. Hutchinson at Newtown," *ibid.,* 330.

36. "Trial of Anne Hutchinson before Boston church," *ibid.,* 380. That Ms. Hutchinson chose a woman preacher as a model for her rebellious behavior, instead of the more popular "Spirit-mystic" and "apostle of Ely," William Sedgwick, indicates that Anne had some level of feminist self-awareness and suggests that she was not greatly in need of specifically male guidance. Cotton expressed the view that she was far from satisfied with his guidance. "Mistris *Hutchinson* seldome resorted to mee," he wrote, "and when she did come to me, it was seldome or never (that I can tell of) that she tarried long. I rather think, she was loath to resort much to me, or, to conferre long with me, lest she might seeme to learne somewhat from me." Cotton, *Congregational Churches Cleared, ibid.,* 434. Cotton's testimony may not be completely accurate, as he was writing to wash the Antinomian stain off his own hands.

Little is known about Anne Hutchinson's role-model, the woman of Ely. Thomas Edwards, a contemporary Puritan divine, remarked that "there are also some women preachers in our times, who keep constant lectures, preaching weekly to many men and women. In Lincolnshire, in Holland and those parts [i.e., the parts about Holland in Lincolnshire] there is a woman preacher who preaches (it's certain), and 'tis reported also she baptizeth, but that's not so certain. *In the Isle of Ely (that land of errors and sectaries) is a woman preacher also.*" See his *Gangraena* ... (London, 1646), Pt. ii, 29, quoted in Battis, *Saints and Sectaries,* 43n.

37. Winthrop, *Short Story,* in Hall, ed., *Antinomian Controversy,* 273, and "Examination of Mrs. Hutchinson at Newtown," *ibid.,* 337.

38. A good discussion of the theological issues surrounding resurrection is provided in Jesper Rosenmeier, "New England's Perfection: The Image of Adam and the Image of Christ in the Antinomian Crisis, 1634 to 1638," *William and Mary Quarterly,* 3d Ser., XXVII (1970), 435–459. Rosenmeier depicts Ms. Hutchinson too explicitly as a Familist without supplying sufficient evidence.

39. Ms. Hutchinson had responded to an argument of Cotton's with the rejoinder, "I desire to hear God speak this and not man." "Trial of Anne Hutchinson before Boston church," in Hall, ed., *Antinomian Controversy,* 358, 362, 355.

40. *Ibid.,* 372. See Battis, *Saints and Sectaries,* 52n.

41. "Trial of Anne Hutchinson before Boston church," in Hall, ed., *Antinomian Controversy,* 369, 370, 365.

42. *Ibid.,* 385–387, 366–368.

43. *Ibid.,* 378, 388, and Winthrop, *Short Story, ibid.,* 307.

44. Richard D. Pierce, ed., *The Records of the First Church in Boston, 1630–1868,* I, in Colonial Society of Massachusetts, *Publications,* XXXIX (Boston, 1961), 22, 25; *Assistants Records,* II, 78, 82; Emil Oberholzer, Jr., *Delinquent Saints: Disciplinary Action in the Early Congregational Churches of Massachusetts* (New York, 1956), 85; "The Diaries of John Hull," American Antiquarian Society, *Archaelogia Americana,* III (Worcester, Mass., 1857), 192n.

45. Joseph B. Felt, *Annals of Salem, Massachusetts,* II (Salem, Mass., 1845), 573, 576, and Charles Henry Pope, *The Pioneers of Massachusetts* (Boston, 1900), 382.

46. Dow, ed., *Essex County Court Records,* I, 6, 9; *Assistants Records,* II, 78; "A Description and History of Salem by the Rev. William Bentley," Mass. Hist. Soc., *Colls.,* 1st Ser., VI (Boston, 1799), 252; Hosmer, ed., *Winthrop's Journal,* I, 282–283; Felt, *Annals of Salem,* II, 420. The attitude of Dorothy Talby's husband may have contributed to the release of her violent inclinations, for on July 1, 1639, he was censured by the Salem church for "much pride and unnaturalness to his wife." Perley, *History of Salem,* II, 52.

47. The author has calculated the percentage of female offenders from the *Assistants Records* and the percentage of male and female arrivals in New England from the ship lists in Charles Edward Banks, *The Planters of the Commonwealth: A Study of the Emigrants and Emigrations in Colonial Times* ... (Boston, 1930). The increase in female offenders may not seem very significant at first glance. However, if the sex distribution of the Massachusetts population remained stable between 1630 and 1644, which is a big assumption, a z-score comparison of the 1630 to 1634 and the 1635 to 1639 populations yields a result statistically significant at the 5% level. A comparison of the 1630 to 1634 and the 1640 to the 1644 populations yields an even more astounding result which is significant at the 1% level. There is a

1% statistical probability that the increase in female offenders from 1630 to 1644 is due only to chance.

48. Before 1641 the Deputies and Assistants did not prosecute women for fornication or lascivious behavior unless those women were considered "whores" or "sluts." Premarital sexual activity was believed to be sinful, but the male was considered the active, initiatory agent and the female the passive, yielding participant. As a result of this guiding conceptualization, only 2 women but 17 men were convicted of fornication or enticement to fornication between 1630 and 1639. After the assertiveness of many women in the Antinomian unrest had proven to the authorities that women must be held more accountable for their actions, the magistrates began to prosecute both male and female fornicators, including for the first time women who had become pregnant and then married the fathers of their children. Between 1640 and 1644 18 men and 10 women were punished for premarital sexual activities. *Assistants Records*, II, *passim*; Shurtleff, ed., *Mass. Bay Records*, I, II, *passim.*

49. *Assistants Records*, II, 109; Hosmer, ed., *Winthrop's Journal*, II, 38–40; John Cotton to Francis Hutchinson, Mass. Hist. Soc., *Colls.*, 2d Ser., X (1823), 186. In 1633 the Assistants fined Capt. John Stone £100 for assaulting Justice Roger Ludlow and calling him a "just ass." Four years later Robert Anderson was fined £50 for "contempt," but no other reviler of authority was fined more than £20. *Assistants Records*, II, 35, 66.

50. In 1639 the authorities criticized the Rev. Hanserd Knowles for holding "some of Mrs. Hutchinson's opinions" and two years later forced the Rev. Jonathan Burr to renounce certain errors which, wrote Winthrop, "savor[ed] of familism." Hosmer, ed., *Winthrop's Journal*, I, 295; II, 22–23.

51. "Psalm-Singing a Godly Exercise" [*Singing of Psalmes a Gosepl-Ordinance* . . . (London, 1650)], in Edmund Clarence Stedman and Ellen MacKay Hutchinson, eds., *A Library of American Literature From the Earliest Settlement to the Present Time*, I (New York, 1891), 266.

52. Weld, "Preface," to Winthrop, *Short Story*, in Hall, ed., *Antinomian Controversy*, 214. Dr. Paul A. Younge's diagnosis of Ms. Hutchinson's "30. monstrous births" as an hydatidiform mole, a uterine growth which frequently accompanies menopause, is adopted in Battis, *Saints and Sectaries*, 346.

53. Winthrop, *Short Story*, in Hall, ed., *Antinomian Controversy*, 280–281.

54. Charles H. Bell, ed., *John Wheelwright: His Writings, Including His Fast-Day Sermon, 1637, and His Mercurius Americanus, 1645; with a Paper upon the Genuineness of the Indian Deed of 1629, and a Memoir* (Boston, 1876), 195–196.

55. Weld, "Preface," to Winthrop, *Short Story*, in Hall, ed., *Antinomian Controversy*, 214; Jameson, ed., *Johnson's Wonder-Working Providence*, 28; "Roger Clap's Memoirs," in Alexander Young, ed., *Chronicles of the First Planters of the Colony of Massachusetts Bay, from 1623–1636* (Boston, 1846), 360; "From Majr. Scott's mouth," Mass. Hist. Soc., *Proceedings*, 1st Ser., XIII (1873–1875), 132. John Josselyn, a British traveler, wrote that he was surprised to find "a grave and sober person" who told him about Mary Dyer's "monster" on his first visit to Massachusetts in 1639. See his *An Account of Two Voyages to New-England* . . . (London, 1675), 27–28.

56. Hosmer, ed., *Winthrop's Journal*, II, 8.

57. *Ibid.*, I, 299, and "Clap's Memoirs," in Young, ed., *First Planters of Massachusetts*, 360.

58. Winthrop, *Short Story,* in Hall, ed., *Antinomian Controversy,* 307, and Cotton, *Congregational Churches Cleared, ibid.,* 420.

59. George H. Moore, "Giles Firmin and His Various Writings," *Historical Magazine,* 2d Ser., III (1868), 150, quoting Giles Firmin, Πανομογια, *a brief review of Mr. Davis's Vindication: giving no satisfaction . . .* (London, 1693).

60. Hosmer, ed., *Winthrop's Journal,* I, 286–287; John Russell Bartlett, ed., *Records of the Colony of Rhode Island and Providence Plantations, in New England, 1636–1663,* I (Providence, R. I., 1856), 16; Roger Williams to John Winthrop, May 22, 1638, in John R. Bartlett, ed., *The Complete Writings of Roger Williams* (New York, 1963 [orig. publ. Providence, R. I., 1874]), 95–96; Williams to Winthrop, Oct. 1638, *ibid.,* 124.

61. Jameson, ed., *Johnson's Wonder-Working Providence,* 186.

62. Howard M. Chapin, *Documentary History of Rhode Island,* II (Providence, R. I., 1916), 68, 84. Coddington controlled the dispensation of land titles because the original deed to Rhode Island was issued in his name.

63. Edward Winslow, *Hypocrisie Unmasked: A true Relation of the Proceedings of the Governour and Company of the Massachusetts against Samuel Gorton . . .* (London, 1646), 44, 54–55, 67; Hosmer, ed., *Winthrop's Journal,* I, 297, 299; Chapin, *History of Rhode Island,* II, 56–57; William Coddington to John Winthrop, Dec. 9, 1639, *Winthrop Papers,* IV, 160–161; Robert Baylie, *A Dissuasive from the Errours of the Time . . .* (London, 1645), 150.

64. Chapin, *History of Rhode Island,* II, 68, and Winslow, *Hypocrisie Unmasked,* 53, 83.

65. Hosmer, ed., *Winthrop's Journal,* II, 39.

66. Thomas Lechford, *Plain Dealing: or, Newes from New-England . . .* (London, 1642), reprinted in Mass. Hist. Soc., *Colls.,* 3d Ser., III (Boston, 1833), 96.

67. "Letter of Randall Holden, Sept. 15th, 1643," *ibid.,* I (1825), 13, and Samuel Niles, "A Summary Historical Narrative of the Wars in New-England with the French and Indians, in the several Parts of the Country," *ibid.,* VI (1837), 201.

68. Winthrop, *Short Story,* in Hall, ed., *Antinomian Controversy,* 310.

69. Perry Miller, *The New England Mind: The Seventeenth Century* (New York, 1939), 391. Increase Mather saw the hand of God at work again when Anne's son Edward died from Indian wounds in 1675. "It seems to be an observable providence," Mather observed, "that so many of that family die by the hands of the uncircumcised." "Diary of Increase Mather, 1674–87," Mass. Hist. Soc., *Procs.,* 2d Ser., XIII (1900), 400.

70. Katherine Scott to John Winthrop, Jr., 1658, Mass. Hist. Soc., *Colls.,* 5th Ser., I (1871), 96–97, and "Letter of Randall Holden, Sept. 15th, 1643," *ibid.,* 3d Ser., I (1825), 13–15.

5

Daughters of Columbia:
Educating Women for the Republic, 1787-1805

Linda K. Kerber

"I expect to see our young women forming a new era in female history," wrote Judith Sargent Murray in 1798.[1] Her optimism was part of a general sense that all possibilities were open in the post-Revolutionary world; as Benjamin Rush put it, the first act of the republican drama had only begun. The experience of war had given words like "independence" and "self-reliance" personal as well as political overtones; among the things that ordinary folk had learned from wartime had been that the world could, as the song had it, turn upside down. The rich could quickly become poor, wives might suddenly have to manage family businesses; women might even, as the famous Deborah Gannett had done, shoulder a gun. Political theory taught that republics rested on the virtue of their citizens; revolutionary experience taught that it was useful to be prepared for a wide range of unusual possibilities.[2]

A desire to explore the possibilities republicanism now opened to women was expressed by a handful of articulate, urban, middle-class men and women. While only a very few writers—Charles Brockden Brown, Judith Sargent Murray, Benjamin Rush—devoted extensive attention to women and what they might become, many essayists explored the subject in the periodical literature. In the fashion of the day, they concealed their identity under pseudonyms like "Cordelia," "Constantia," or, simply, "A Lady." These expressions came largely from Boston, New York, and Philadelphia: cities which were the centers of publishing. The vitality of Philadelphia, as political and social capital, is well known; the presence of so many national legislators in the city, turning up as they did at dances and dinner parties, was no doubt intellectually invigorating, and not least for the women of Philadelphia. In an informal way, women shared many of the political excitements of the city. Philadelphia was the home of the Young Ladies' Academy, founded in 1786, with explicitly fresh ideas about women's education, and an enrollment of more than a hundred within two years; Benjamin Rush would deliver his "Thoughts upon Female Education" there. The first attempt at a magazine expressly addressed to women was made by the Philadelphia *Lady's Magazine and Repository.* Two of the most intense anonymous writers—"Sophia" and "Nitidia"—wrote for Philadelphia newspapers. And after the government moved to Washington, Joseph Dennie's *Port Folio* solicited "the assistance of the ladies," and published essays by Gertrude Meredith, Sarah Hall, and Emily Hopkinson. Boston and New York were not far behind in displaying similar interests: in New York, Noah Webster's *American Magazine* included in its prospectus a specific appeal for female contributors; the *Boston Weekly Magazine* was careful to publish the speeches at the annual "Exhibition" of Susanna Rowson's Young Ladies' Academy.

Most jouranlists' comments on the role and functions of women in the republic merged, almost imperceptibly, into discussions of the sort of education proper for young girls. A pervasive Lockean environmentalism was displayed; what people were was assumed to be dependent on how they were educated. "Train up the child in the way he should grow, and when he is old he will not depart from it"; the biblical injunction was repeatedly quoted, and not quoted idly. When Americans spoke of what was best for the child they were also speaking— implicitly or explicitly—of their hopes for the adult. Charles Brockden Brown, for example, is careful to provide his readers with brief accounts of his heroines' early education. When we seek to learn the recipe for Murray's "new era in female history" we find ourselves reading comments on two related themes: how young women are to be "trained up," and what is to be expected of them when they are old.

If the republic were to fulfill the generous claims it made for the liberty and competence of its citizens, the education of young women would have to be an education for independence rather than for an upwardly mobile marriage. The periodicals are full of attacks on fashion, taking it for an emblem of superficiality and dependence. The Philadelphia *Lady's Magazine* criticized a father who prepared his daughters for the marriage market: "You boast of having given your daughters an education which will enable them 'to shine in the first circles.' . . . They sing indifferently; they play the harpsichord indifferently; they are mistresses of every common game at cards . . . they . . . have just as much knowledge of dress as to deform their persons by an awkward imitation of every new fashion which appears. . . . Placed in a situation of difficulty, they have neither a head to dictate, nor a hand to help in any domestic concern."[3] Teaching young girls to dress well was part of the larger message that their primary lifetime goal must be marriage; in this context, fashion became a feature of sexual politics. "I have sometimes been led," remarked Benjamin Rush, "to ascribe the invention of ridiculous and expensive fashions in female dress entirely to the gentlemen in order to divert the ladies from improving their minds and thereby to secure a more arbitrary and unlimited authority over them."[4] In the marriage market, beauty, flirtatiousness, and charm were at a premium; intelligence, good judgment, and competence (in short, the republican virtues) were at a discount. The republic did not need fashion plates; it needed citizens— women as well as men—of self-discipline and of strong mind. The contradiction between the counsel given to young women and their own self-interest, as well as the best interests of the republic, seemed obvious. The marriage market undercut the republic.[5]

Those who addressed themselves to the problem of the proper education for young women used the word "independence" frequently. Sometimes it was used in a theoretical fashion: How, it was asked, can women's minds be free if they are taught that their sphere is limited to clothing, music, and needlework? Often the context of independence is economic and political: it seemed appropriate that in a republic women should have greater control over their own lives. "The *dependence* for which women are uniformly educated" was deplored; it was pointed out that the unhappily married woman would quickly discover that she had "neither liberty nor property."[6]

The idea that political independence should be echoed by a self-reliance which would make women as well as men economically independent appears in its most developed form in a series of essays Judith Sargent Murray published in the *Massachusetts Magazine* between 1792 and 1794, and collected under the title *The Gleaner* in 1798. Murray insisted that instruction in a manual trade was especially appropriate in a republic, and decried the antiegalitarian habit of assuming that a genteel and impractical education was superior to a vocational one. She was critical of fathers who permitted their sons to grow up without knowing a useful skill; she was even more critical of parents who "pointed their daughters" toward marriage and dependence. This made girls' education contingent on a single event; it offered them a single image of the future. "I would give my daughters every accomplishment which I thought proper," Murray wrote, "and to crown all, I would early accustom them to habits of industry and order. They should be taught with precision the art economical; they should be enabled to procure for themselves the necessaries of life; independence should be placed within their grasp." Repeatedly Murray counseled that women should be made to feel competent at something: "A woman *should reverence herself.*"[7]

Murray scattered through the *Gleaner* essays and brief fictional versions of self-respecting women, in the characters of Margaretta, Mrs. Virgilius, and Penelope Airy. In his full-length novel *Ormond*, published in 1799, Charles Brockden Brown imagined a considerably more developed version of a competent woman. Constantia Dudley is eminently rational. When her father is embezzled of his fortune she, "her cheerfulness unimpaired," sells "every superfluous garb and trinket," her music and her books; she supports the family by needlework. Constantia never flinches; she can take whatever ill fortune brings, whether it is yellow fever or the poverty that forces her to conclude that the only alternative to starvation is cornmeal mush three times a day for three months. Through it all, she resists proposals of marriage, because even in adversity she scorns to become emotionally dependent without love.[8]

Everything Constantia does places her in sharp contrast to Helena Cleves, who also "was endowed with every feminine and fascinating quality." Helena has had a genteel education; she can paint, and sing, and play the clavichord, but it is all fashionable gloss to camouflage a lack of real mental accomplishment and self-discipline. What Brown called "exterior accomplishments" were acceptable so long as life held no surprises, but when Helena meets disaster, she is unprepared to maintain her independence and her self-respect. She falls into economic dependence upon a "kinswoman"; she succumbs to the "specious but delusive" reasoning or Ormond, and becomes his mistress. He takes advantage of her dependence, all the while seeking in Constantia a rational woman worthy of his intelligence; eventually, in despair, Helena kills herself.[9]

The argument that an appropriate education would steel girls to face adversity is related to the conviction that all citizens of a republic should be self-reliant. But the argument can be made independent of explicit republican ideology. It may well represent the common sense of a revolutionary era in which the unexpected was very likely to happen; in which large numbers of people had lived through reversals of fortune, encounters with strangers, physical dislocation. Constantia's friend Martinette de Beauvais has lived in Marseilles, Verona, Vienna, and Philadelphia; she had dressed like a man and fought in the American Revolution; after that she was one of the "hundreds" of women who took up arms for the French.[10] Constantia admires and sympathizes with her friend; nothing in the novel is clearer than that women who are not ready to maintain their independence in a crisis, as Constantia and Martinette do, risk sinking, like Helena, into prostitution and death.

The model republican woman was competent and confident. She could ignore the vagaries of fashion; she was rational, benevolent, independent, self-reliant. Writers who spoke to this point prepared lists of what we would now call role models: heroines of the past offered as assurance that women could indeed be people of accomplishment. There were women of the ancient world, like Cornelia, the mother of the Gracchi; rulers like Elizabeth of England and the Empress Catherine of Russia; a handful of Frenchwomen: Mme. de Genlis, Mme. Maintenon, and Mme. Dacier; and a long list of British intellectuals: Lady Mary Wortley Montagu, Hannah More, Elizabeth Carter, Mrs. Knowles (the Quaker who had bested Dr. Johnson in debate), Mary Wollstonecraft, and the Whig historian Catharine Macaulay.[11] Such women were rumored to exist in America; they were given fictional embodiment by Murray and Brown. Those who believed in these republican models demanded that their presence be recognized and endorsed, and that a new generation of young women be urged to make them patterns for their own behavior. To create more such women became a major educational challenge.

Writers were fond of pointing out that the inadequacies of American women could be ascribed to early upbringing and environmental influences. "Will it be said that the judgment of a male of two years old, is more sage than that of a female of the same age?" asked Judith Sargent Murray. "But . . . as their years increased, the sister must be wholly domesticated, while the brother is led by the hand through all the flowery paths of science." The *Universal Asylum* published a long and thoughtful essay by "A Lady" which argued that "in the nursery, strength is equal in the male and female." When a boy went to school, he immediately met both intellectual and physical challenge; his teachers instructed him in science and language, his friends dared him to fight, to run after a hoop, to jump a rope. Girls, on the other hand, were "committed to illiterate teachers, . . . cooped up in a room, confined to needlework, deprived of exercise." Thomas Cooper defined the problem clearly: "We first keep their minds and then their persons in subjection," he wrote. "We educate women from infancy to marriage, in such a way as to debilitate both their corporeal and their mental powers. All the accomplishments we teach them are directed not to their future benefit in life but to the amusement of the male sex; and having for a series of years, with much assiduity, and sometimes at much expense, incapacitated them for any serious occupation, we say they are not fit to govern themselves."[12]

Schemes for the education of the "rising generation" proliferated in the early republic, including a number of projects for the education of women. Some, like those discussed in the well-known essays of Benjamin Rush and Noah Webster, were theoretical; others took the form of admitting girls to boys' academies or establishing new schools for girls. There were not as many as Judith Sargent Murray implied when she said: "Female academies are everywhere establishing," but she was not alone in seeing schools like Susanna Rowson's Young Ladies' Academy and the Young Ladies' Academy of Philadelphia as harbingers of a trend. One pamphlet address, written in support of the Philadelphia Academy, expressed the hope that it would become "a great national seminary" and insisted that although "stubborn prejudices still exist . . . we must (if open to conviction) be convinced that *females* are fully capable of sounding the most profound depths, and of attaining to the most sublime excellence in every part of science."[13]

Certainly there was a wide range of opinion on the content and scope of female education in the early republic. Samuel Harrison Smith's essay on the subject, which won the American Philosophical Society's 1797 prize for the best plan for a national system of education, began by proposing "that every male child, without exception, be educated."[14] At the other extreme was Timothy Dwight, the future president of Yale, who opened his academy at Greenfield Hill to girls and taught them the same subjects he taught to boys, at the same time and in the same rooms.[15] But Dwight was the exception. Most proposals for the education of young women agreed that the curriculum should be more advanced than that of the primary schools but somewhat less than that offered by colleges and even conventional boys' academies. Noah Webster thought women should learn speaking and writing, arithmetic, geography, belles-lettres; "A Reformer" in the *Weekly Magazine* advocated a similar program, to which practical instruction in nursing and cooking were added. Judith Sargent Murray thought women should be able to converse elegantly and correctly, pronounce French, read history (as a narrative substitute for novels, rather than for its own interest or value), and learn some simple geography and astronomy.[16] The best-known proposal was Benjamin Rush's; he too prescribed reading, grammar, penmanship, "figures and bookkeeping," geography. He added "the first principles of natural philosophy," vocal music (because it soothed cares and was good for the lungs) but not instrumental music (because, except for the most talented, it seemed a waste of valuable time), and history (again, as an antidote to novel reading).

Rush offered his model curriculum in a speech to the Board of Visitors of the Young Ladies' Academy of Philadelphia, later published and widely reprinted under the title "Thoughts upon Female Education Accommodated to the Present State of Society, Manners and Government in the United States of America." The academy claimed to be the first female academy chartered in the United States; when Rush spoke, on July 28, 1787, he was offering practical advice to a new school. Rush linked the academy to the greater cause of demonstrating the possibilities of women's minds. Those who were skeptical of education for women, Rush declared, were the same who opposed "the general diffusion of knowledge among the citizens of our republics." Rush argued that "female education should be accommodated to the state of society, manners, and government of the country in which it is conducted." An appropriate education for American women would be condensed, because they married earlier than their European counterparts; it would include bookkeeping, because American women could expect to be "the stewards and guardians of their husbands' property," and executrices of their husbands' wills. It would qualify them for "a general intercourse with the world" by an acquaintance with geography and chronology. If education is preparation for life, then the life styles of American women required a newly tailored educational program. [17]

The curriculum of the Young Ladies' Academy (which one of the Board of Visitors called "abundantly sufficient to complete the female mind") included reading, writing, arithmetic, English grammar, composition, rhetoric, and geography. It did not include the natural philosophy Rush hoped for (although Rush did deliver a dozen lectures on "The Application of the Principles of Natural Philosophy, and Chemistry, to Domestic and Culinary Purposes"); it did not include advanced mathematics or the classics. [18]

In 1794 the Young Ladies' Academy published a collection of its graduation addresses; one is struck by the scattered observations of valedictorians and salutatorians that reading, writing, and arithmetic were not enough. Priscilla Mason remarked in her 1793 graduation address that while it was unusual for a woman to address "a promiscuous assembly," there was no impropriety in women's becoming accomplished orators. What had prevented them, she argued, was that "our high and mighty Lords . . . have denied us the means of knowledge, and then reproached us for the want of it. . . . They doom'd the sex to servile or frivolous employments, on purpose to degrade their minds, that they themselves might hold unrivall'd, the power and pre-eminence they had usurped." Academies like hers enabled women to increase their knowledge, but the forums in which they might use it were still unavailable: "The Church, the Bar, and the Senate are shut against us."[19]

So long as the propriety of cultivating women's minds remained a matter for argument, it was hard to press a claim to public competence; Priscilla Mason was an exception. Rush had concluded his advice to the Young Ladies' Academy by challenging his audience to demonstrate "that the cultivation of reason in women is alike friendly to the order of nature and the private as well as the public happiness." But meeting even so mild a challenge was difficult; "bluestocking" was not a term of praise in the early republic. "Tell me," wrote the Philadelphian Gertrude Meredith angrily, ". . . do you imagine, from your knowledge of the young men in this city, that ladies are valued according to their mental acquirements? I can assure you that they are not, and I am very confident that they never will be, while men indulge themselves in expressions of contempt for one because she has a *bare elbow,* for another because she . . . never made a *good pun, nor smart repartee. . . .* [Would they] not titter . . . at her expense, if a woman made a Latin quotation, or spoke with enthusiasm of Classical learning?"[20] When Gertrude Meredith visited Baltimore, she found that her mildly satirical essays for the *Port Folio* had transformed her into a formidable figure: "Mrs. Cole says she should not have been more distressed at visiting Mrs. Macaulay the authoress than myself as she had heard I *was so sensible,* but she was very glad to find I was so free and easy. You must allow," she concluded dryly, "that this compliment was elegantly turned." A similar complaint was made by an essayist whom we know only as "Sophia":

> A woman who is conscious of possessing, more intellectual power than is requisite in superintending the pantry, and in adjusting the ceremonials of a feast, and who believes she, in conforming to the will of the giver, in improving the gift, is by the wits of the other sex denominated a learned lady. She is represented as disgustingly slovenly in her person, indecent in her habits, imperious to her husband, and negligent of her children. And the odious scarecrow is employed, exactly as the farmer employs his unsightly bundle of rags and straw, to terrify the simple birds, from picking up the precious grain, which he wishes to monopolize. After all this, what man in his sober senses can be astonished, to find the majority of women as they really are, frivolous and volatile; incapable of estimating their own dignity, and indifferent to the best interests of society. . . ?[21]

These women were not creating their own paranoid images of discouragement. The same newspapers for which they wrote often printed other articles insisting that intellectual accomplishment is inappropriate in a woman, that the intellectual woman is not only invading a male province, but must herself somehow be masculine. "Women of masculine minds," wrote the Boston minister John Sylvester John Gardiner, "have generally masculine manners, and a robustness of person ill calculated to inspire the tender passion." Noah Webster's *American Magazine*, which in its prospectus had made a special appeal to women writers and readers, published the unsigned comment: "If we picture to ourselves a woman . . . firm in resolve, unshaken in conduct, unmoved by the delicacies of situation, by the fashions of the times, . . . we immediately change the idea of the sex, and . . . we see under the form of a woman the virtues and qualities of a man." Even the *Lady's Magazine*, which had promised to demonstrate that "the FEMALES of Philadelphia are by no means deficient in *those talents*, which have immortalized the names of a *Montagu*, a *Craven*, a *More*, and a *Seward*, in their inimitable writings," published a cautionary tale, whose moral was that although "learning in men was the road to preferment . . . consequences very opposite were the result of the same quality in women." Amelia is a clergyman's only daughter; she is taught Latin and Greek, with the result that she becomes "negligent of her dress," and "pride and pedantry grew up with learning in her breast." Eventually she is avoided by both sexes, and becomes emblematic of the fabled "white-washed jackdaw (who, aiming at a station from which nature had placed him at a distance, found himself deserted by his own species, and driven out of every society)." For conclusion there was an explicit moral: "This story was intended (at a time when the press overflows with the productions of female pens) . . . to admonish them, that . . . because a few have gained applause by studying the dead languages, all womankind should [not] assume their Dictionaries and Lexicons; else . . . (as the Ladies made rapid advances towards manhood) we might in a few years behold a sweepstakes rode by women, or a second battle at Odiham, fought with superior skill, by Mesdames Humphries and Mendoza."[22]

The prediction that accomplishment would unsex women was coupled with the warning that educated women would abandon their proper sphere; the female pedant and the careful housekeeper were never found in the same person. The most usable cautionary emblem for this seems to have been Mary Wollstonecraft, whose life and work linked criticism of women's status with free love and political radicalism. Mary Wollstonecraft's *Vindication of the Rights of Women* was her generation's most coherent statement of what women deserved and what they might become. The influence of any book is difficult to trace, and although we know that her book was reprinted in Philadelphia shortly after its publication in 1792, it would be inaccurate to credit Wollstonecraft with responsibility for raising in America questions relating to the status of women. It seems far more likely that she verbalized effectively what a larger public was already thinking or was willing to hear; "In very many of her sentiments," remarked the Philadelphia Quaker Elizabeth Drinker, "she, as some of our friends say, *speaks my mind.*"[23]

Wollstonecraft's primary target was Rousseau, whose definition of woman's sphere was a limited one: "The empire of women," Rousseau had written, "is the empire of softness, of address, of complacency; her commands are caresses; her menaces are tears." Wollstonecraft perceived that to define women in this way was to condemn them to "a state of perpetual childhood"; she deplored the "false system of education" which made women "only anxious to inspire love, when they ought to cherish a nobler ambition, and by their abilities and virtues exact respect." Women's duties were different from those of men, but they similarly demanded the exercise of virtue and reason; women would be better wives and mothers if they were taught that they need not depend on frivolity and ignorance. Wollstonecraft ventured the suggestion that women might study medicine, politics, and business, but whatever they did, they should not be denied civil and political rights, they should not have to rely on marriage for assurance of economic support, they should not "remain immured in their families groping in the dark."[24]

If, in some quarters, Mary Wollstonecraft's work was greeted as the common sense of the matter, in others it was met with hostility. The *Vindication* was a popular subject of satire, especially when, after the author's death in childbirth in 1797, William Godwin published a *Memoir* revealing that she had lived with other men, and with Godwin himself before her pregnancy and their marriage. Critics were then freed to discount her call for reform as the self-serving demand of a woman of easy virtue, as Benjamin Silliman did throughout his *Letters of Shahcoolen.* Timothy Dwight, who had taken the lead in offering young women education on a par with young men, shuddered at Wollstonecraft and held "the female philosopher" up to ridicule in "Morpheus," a political satire which ran for eight installments in the *New-England Palladium.*[25] Dwight called Wollstonecraft "an unchaste woman," "a sentimental lover," "a strumpet"; as Silliman had done, he linked her radical politics to free love. " 'Away with all monopolies,' " Dwight has her say. " 'I hate these exclusive rights; these privileged orders. I am for having everything free, and open to all; like the air which we breathe. . . .' "

" 'Love, particularly, I suppose, Madam [?]' "

" 'Yes, brute, love, if you please, and everything else.' "[26] Even Charles Brockden Brown's feminist tract *Alcuin* concluded with a long gloss on the same theme: to permit any change in women's status was to imply the acceptance of free love. Alcuin, who has been playing the conservative skeptic, concludes that once it is established that marriage "has no other criterion than custom," it becomes simply "a mode of sexual intercourse." His friend Mrs. Carter protests energetically that free love is not at all what she wanted; " 'because I demand an equality of conditions among beings that equally partake of the same divine reason, would you rashly infer that I was an enemy to the institution of marriage itself?' " Brown lets her have the last word, but he does not make Alcuin change his mind.[27]

Dwight had one final charge to make against Wollstonecraft; he attacked her plea that women emerge from the confines of their families. " 'Who will make our puddings, Madam?' " his protagonist asks. When she responds: " 'Make them yourself,' " he presses harder: " 'Who shall nurse us when we are sick?' " and, finally, " 'Who shall nurse our children?' " The last question reduces the fictional Mary to blushes and silence.[28]

It would not, however, reduce Rush, or Murray, or Brown, to blushes and silence. (Nor, I think, would it have so affected the real Mary Wollstonecraft.) They had neither predicted that women would cease their housewifely duties nor demanded that women should. Priscilla Mason's demand that hitherto male professions be opened to women was highly unusual, and even she apologized for it before she left the podium. There were, it is true, some other hints that women might claim the privileges and duties of male citizens of the republic. In *Alcuin*, Mrs. Carter explains her intense political disappointment through the first two chapters, arguing that Americans had been false to their own revolutionary promises in denying political status to women. "If a stranger questions me concerning the nature of our government, I answer, that in this happy climate all men are free: the people are the source of all authority; from them it flows, and to them, in due season, it returns . . . our liberty consists in the choice of our governors: all, as reason requires, have a part in this choice, yet not without a few exceptions . . . females . . . minors . . . the poor . . . slaves. . . . I am tired of explaining this charming system of equality and independence." St. George Tucker, commenting on Blackstone, acknowledged that women were taxed without representation; like "aliens . . . children under the age of discretion, idiots, and lunatics," American women had neither political nor civil rights. "I fear there is little reason for a compliment to our laws for their respect and favour to the female sex," Tucker concluded. As Tucker had done, John Adams acknowledged that women's experience of the republic was different from men's; he hesitantly admitted that the republic claimed the right "to govern women without their consent." For a brief period from 1790 to

1807, New Jersey law granted the franchise to "all free inhabitants," and on occasion women exercised that right; it is conceivable that New Jersey might have stood as a precedent for other states. Instead, New Jersey's legislature rewrote its election law; the argument for political competence was taken no further.[29]

All of these were hesitant suggestions introduced into a hostile intellectual milieu in which female learning was equated with pedantry and masculinity. To resist those assumptions was to undertake a great deal; it was a task for which no one was ready; indeed, it is impossible to say that anyone really wanted to try. Instead, the reformers would have been quick to reply, with Brown's Mrs. Carter, that they had no intention of abandoning marriage; that they had every intention of making puddings and nursing babies; that the education they demanded was primarily to enable women to function more effectively within their traditional sphere, and only secondarily to fulfill demands like Priscilla Mason's that they emerge from it. People were complaining that American women were boring, frivolous, spending excessive amounts of money for impractical fashions; very well, a vigorously educated woman would be less likely to bore her husband, less likely to be a spendthrift, better able to cope with adverse fortune. Judith Sargent Murray versified an equation:

> Where'er the maiden Industry *appears,*
> *A thrifty contour every object wears;*
> *And when fair* order *with the nymph combines,*
> *Adjusts, directs, and every plan designs,*
> *Then* Independence *fills her peerless seat,*
> *And lo! the matchless trio is complete.*

Murray repeatedly made the point that the happiness of the nation depended on the happiness of families; and that the "felicity of families" is dependent on the presence of women who are "properly methodical, and economical in their distributions and expenditures of time." She denied that "the present enlarged plan of female education" was incompatible with traditional notions of women's duties: she predicted that the "daughters of Columbia" would be free of *"invidious and rancorous passions"* and "even the semblance of pedantry"; "when they become wives and mothers, they will fill with honour the parts allotted them."[30]

Rarely, in the literature of the early Republic, do we find any objection to the notion that women belong in the home; what emerges is the argument that the Revolution had enlarged the significance of what women did in their homes. Benjamin Rush's phrasing of this point is instructive; when he defined the goals of republican women, he was careful not to include a claim to political power: "The equal share that every citizen has in the liberty and the possible share he may have in the government of our country make it necessary that our ladies should be qualified to a certain degree by a peculiar and suitable education, *to concur in instructing their sons in the principles of liberty and government.*" The Young Ladies' Academy promised "not wholly to engross the mind" of each pupil, "but to allow her to prepare for the duties in life to which she may be destined." Miss P.W. Jackson, graduating from Mrs. Rowson's Academy, explained what she had learned of the goals of the educated woman: "A woman who is skilled in every useful art, who practices every domestic virtue . . . may, by her precept and example, inspire her brothers, her husband, or her sons, with such a love of virtue, such just ideas of the true value of civil liberty . . . that future heroes and statesmen, who arrive at the summit of military or political fame, shall *exaltingly declare, it is to my mother I owe this elevation.*" By their household management, by their refusal to countenance vice, crime, or cruelty in their suitors and husbands, women had the power to direct the moral development of the male citizens of the republic. The influence women had on children, especially on their sons, gave them ultimate responsibility for the future of the new nation.[31]

This constellation of ideas, and the republican rhetoric which made it convincing, appears at great length in the Columbia College commencement oration of 1795. Its title was "Female Influence"; behind the flowery rhetoric lurks a social and political message:

> Let us then figure to ourselves the accomplished woman, surrounded by a sprightly band, from the babe that imbibes the nutritive fluid, to the generous youth just ripening into manhood, and the lovely virgin. . . . Let us contemplate the mother distributing the mental nourishment to the fond smiling circle, by means proportionate to their different powers of reception, watching the gradual openings of their minds, and studying their various turns of temper. . . . Religion, fairest offspring of the skies, smiles auspicious on her endeavours; the Genius of Liberty hovers triumphant over the glorious scene. . . . Yes, ye fair, the reformation of a world is in your power. . . . Reflect on the result of your efforts. Contemplate the rising glory of confederated America. Consider that your exertions can best secure, increase, and perpetuate it. The solidity and stability of the liberties of your country rest with you; since Liberty is never sure, 'till Virtue reigns triumphant. . . . Already may we see the lovely daughters of Columbia asserting the importance and the honour of their sex. It rests with you to make this retreat [from the corruptions of Europe] doubly peaceful, doubly happy, by banishing from it those crimes and corrup-

tions, which have never yet failed of giving rise to tyranny, or anarchy. While you thus keep our country virtuous, you maintain its independence. . . .[32]

Defined this way, the educated woman ceased to threaten the sanctity of marriage; the bluestocking need not be masculine. In this awkward—and in the 1790s still only vaguely expressed—fashion, the traditional womanly virtues were endowed with political purpose. A pivotal political role was assigned to the least political inhabitants of the Republic. Ironically, the same women who were denied political identity were counted on to maintain the republican quality of the new nation. "Let the ladies of a country be educated properly," Rush said, "and they will not only make and administer its laws, but form its manners and character."[33]

When Americans addressed themselves to the matter of the role of women, they found that those who admired bluestockings and those who feared them could agree on one thing: in a world where moral influences were fast dissipating, women as a group seemed to represent moral stability. Few in the early republic demanded, in a sustained way, substantial revisions in women's political or legal status; few spoke to the nascent class of unskilled women workers. But many took pride in the assertion that properly educated republican women would stay in the home and, from that vantage point, would shape the characters of their sons and husbands in the direction of benevolence, self-restraint, and responsible independence. They refuted charges of free love and masculinization; in doing so they created a justification for woman as household goddess so deeply felt that one must be permitted to suspect that many women of their generation were *refusing* to be household goddesses.[34] They began to make the argument for intelligent household management that Catharine Beecher, a generation later, would enshrine in her *Treatise on Domestic Economy* as woman's highest goal. The Daughters of Columbia became, in effect, the Mothers of the Victorians. Whether Judith Sargent Murray, Charles Brockden Brown, or Benjamin Rush would have approved the ultimate results of their work is hard to say.

NOTES

1. *The Gleaner,* III (Boston, 1798), 189.
2. Montesquieu's comment that republics differed from other political systems

by the reliance they placed on virtue is explored in Howard Mumford Jones, *O Strange New World* (New York, 1964), p. 431.

3. August 1792, pp. 121–123.

4. "Thoughts upon Female Education, Accommodated to the Present State of Society, Manners, and Government in the United States of America" (Philadelphia and Boston, 1787). Reprinted in Frederick Rudolph, ed., *Essays on Education in the Early Republic* (Cambridge, Mass., 1865), p. 39.

5. "The greater proportion of young women are trained up by thoughtless parents, in ease and luxury, with no other dependence for their future support than the precarious chance of establishing themselves by marriage: for this purpose (the men best know why) elaborate attention is paid to external attractions and accomplishments, to the neglect of more useful and solid acquirements. . . . [Marriage is the] *sole* method of procuring for themselves an establishment." *New York Magazine*, August 1797, p. 406. For comment on the marriage market, see letter signed "A Matrimonial Republican" in Philadelphia *Lady's Magazine*, July 1792, pp. 64–67; "Legal Prostitution, Or Modern Marriage," Boston *Independent Chronicle*, October 28, 1793. For criticism of fashion, see *American Magazine*, December 1787, p. 39; July 1788, p. 594; *American Museum*, August 1788, p. 119; *Massachusetts Mercury*, August 16, 1793; January 16, 1795.

6. *New York Magazine*, August 1797, p. 406; Philadelphia *Universal Asylum and Columbian Magazine*, July 1791, p. 11.

7. Murray, *Gleaner*, I, 168, 193.

8. Charles Brockden Brown, *Ormond; Or the Secret Witness*, ed. by Ernest Marchand (New York, 1799; reprinted 1937, 1962), p. 19.

9. *Ibid.*, pp. 98–99.

10. "It was obvious to suppose that a woman thus fearless and sagacious had not been inactive at a period like the present, which called forth talents and courage without distinction of sex, and had been particularly distinguished by female enterprise and heroism." *Ibid.*, p. 170.

11. For examples of such lists, see: Murray, *Gleaner*, III, 200–219; John Blair Linn, *The Powers of Genius: A Poem in Three Parts* (Philadelphia, 1802); Philadelphia *Weekly Magazine*, August 4, 11, 1798; *Port Folio*, February 12, 1803; September 27, 1806; Philadelphia *Minerva*, March 14, 1795. For the admiration expressed by Abigail Adams and Mercy Otis Warren for Catharine Macaulay, see Abigail Adams to Isaac Smith, Jr., April 20, 1771; Abigail Adams to Catharine Sawbridge Macaulay, n.d., 1774; Mercy Otis Warren to Abigail Adams, January 28, 1775; in L. H. Butterfield, ed., *Adams Family Correspondence*, I (Cambridge, Mass., 1963), 76–77, 177–179, 181–183. For the circle of English "bluestockings," in the 1780s, see M. G. Jones, *Hannah More* (Cambridge, 1952), pp. 41–76.

12. *Massachusetts Magazine*, II (March 1790), 133; *Universal Asylum and Columbian Magazine*, July 1791, p. 9; Thomas Cooper, "Propositions Respecting the Foundation of Civil Government," in *Political Arithmetic* (Philadelphia [?], 1798), p. 27. See also *Boston Weekly Magazine*, May 21, 1803, pp. 121–122; *American Museum*, January 1787, p. 59; Philadelphia *Lady's Magazine*, June 1792.

13. J. A. Neale, "An Essay on the Genius and Education of the Fair Sex," Philadelphia *Minerva*, April 4, March 21, 1795.

14. *Remarks on Education: Illustrating the Close Connection between Virtue and Wisdom* (Philadelphia, 1798), reprinted in Rudolph, *Essays on Education*, p. 211.

Smith did acknowledge that female instruction was important, but commented that concepts of what it should be were so varied that he feared to make any proposals, and despaired of including women in the scheme he was then devising. "It is sufficient, perhaps, for the present, that the improvement of women is marked by a rapid progress and that a prospect opens equal to their most ambitious desires" (p. 217). The other prizewinner, Samuel Knox, proposed to admit girls to the primary schools in his system, but not to the academies or colleges. Knox's essay, "An Essay on the Best System of Liberal Education," may be found in Rudolph, *Essays on Education*, pp. 271–372.

15. Charles E. Cunningham, *Timothy Dwight: 1752–1817: A Biography* (New York, 1942), pp. 154–163.

16. Noah Webster, "Importance of Female Education," in *American Magazine,* May 1788, pp. 368, 369. This essay was part of his pamphlet *On the Education of Youth in America* (Boston, 1790), conveniently reprinted in Rudolph, *Essays on Education,* pp. 41–78. *Weekly Magazine,* April 7, 1798; Murray, *The Gleaner,* I, 70–71.

17. Benjamin Rush, "Thoughts upon Female Education," in Rudolph, *Essays on Education,* pp. 25–40. See also the comments of the Reverend James Sproat, a member of the Board of Visitors, June 10, 1789, in *The Rise and Progress of the Young Ladies' Academy of Philadelphia; Containing an Account of a Number of Public Examinations and Commencements; the Charter and Bye-Laws; Likewise, a Number of Orations delivered by the Young Ladies, and several by the Trustees of Said Institution* (Philadelphia, 1794), p. 24.

18. Benjamin Say, "Address," December 4, 1789, in *Rise and Progress of the Young Ladies' Academy,* p. 33; Benjamin Rush, *Syllabus of Lectures, Containing the Application of the Principles of Natural Philosophy* . . . (Philadelphia, 1787). Rush, of course, was waging his own crusade against the classics as inappropriate in a republic; he argued elsewhere that to omit Latin and Greek would have the beneficial effect of diminishing "the present immense disparity which subsists between the sexes, in the degrees of their education and knowledge." When his contemporaries omitted the classics from the female curriculum it was usually because they thought women's minds were not up to it. Rush, "Observations upon the Study of the Latin and Greek Languages," in *Essays, Literary, Moral and Philosophical* (Philadelphia, 1798), p. 44.

19. Priscilla Mason, "Oration," May 15, 1793, in *Rise and Progress of the Young Ladies' Academy,* pp. 90–95. See also the valedictory oration by Molly Wallace, June 12, 1792, *ibid.,* pp. 73–79.

20. Letter signed M.G., "American Lounger," *Port Folio,* April 7, 1804.

21. Gertrude Meredith to David Meredith, May 3, 1804, Meredith Papers, Historical Society of Pennsylvania; Philadelphia *Evening Fireside,* April 6, 1805.

22. *New-England Palladium,* September 18, 1801; *American Magazine,* February 1788, p. 134; *Lady's Magazine,* January 1793, pp. 68–72. (The "battle at Odiham" refers to a famous bare-knuckle prize fight, one of the earliest major events in the history of boxing, fought in 1788 by Daniel Mendoza and Richard Humphries in Hampshire, England.) Other attacks on female pedantry, which express the fear that intellectual women will be masculine, are found in the *American Magazine,* March 1788, pp. 244–245 ("To be lovely you must be content to be women . . . and leave the masculine virtues, and the profound researches of study to the province of the other sex"); *New-England Palladium,* September 4, 18, December 4,

1801, March 5, 9, 1802; Benjamin Silliman, *Letters of Shahcoolen, a Hindu Philosophy, Residing in Philadelphia; To His Friend, El Hassan, an Inhabitant of Delhi* (Boston, 1802), pp. 23–24, 62; *American Museum*, December 1788, p. 491; *Boston Weekly Magazine*, March 24, 1804, p. 86 ("Warlike women, learned women, and women who are politicians, equally abandon the circle which nature and institutions have traced round their sex; they convert themselves into men").

23. *Extracts from the Journal of Elizabeth Drinker, from 1759 to 1807, A.D.*, ed. by Henry D. Biddle (Philadelphia, 1889), p. 285. The entry is dated April 22, 1796.

24. Mary Wollstonecraft, *A Vindication of the Rights of Woman, With Strictures on Political and Moral Subjects* (New York, 1891), pp. 23, 149–156.

25. *New-England Palladium*, November 24, 27, December 8, 11, 15, 1801; March 2, 5, 9, 1802. Identification of Dwight as author is made by Robert Edson Lee, "Timothy Dwight and the Boston *Palladium*," *New England Quarterly*, XXXV (1962), 229–239.

26. *New-England Palladium*, March 9, 1802.

27. Charles Brockden Brown and Lee R. Edwards, *Alcuin: A Dialogue* (New York, 1971), pp. 44–88.

28. *New-England Palladium*, March 9, 1802.

29. Brown, *Alcuin*, pp. 32–33; St. George Tucker, *Blackstone's Commentaries: With Notes of Reference, to the Constitution and Laws, of the Federal Government of the United States, and of the Commonwealth of Virginia*, II (Philadelphia, 1803), 145, 445; John Adams to James Sullivan, May 26, 1776, in *The Works of John Adams*, ed. by Charles Francis Adams, IX (1856), 375–379; Edward Raymond Turner, "Women's Suffrage in New Jersey: 1790–1807," *Smith College Studies in History*, I (1916), 165–187. Opposition to woman suffrage apparently surfaced after women voted as a bloc in an unsuccessful attempt to influence the outcome of an Essex County election in 1797.

30. *Gleaner*, I, 161, 12, 29, 191, 190.

31. Rush, "Thoughts upon Female Education," in Rudolph, *Essays on Education*, p. 28 (my italics); "On Female Education," *Port Folio*, May 1809, p. 388; *Boston Weekly Magazine*, October 29, 1803.

32. *New York Magazine*, May 1795, pp. 301–305.

33. Rush, "Thoughts upon Female Education," in Rudolph, *Essays on Education*, p. 36.

34. See, for example, *Boston Weekly Magazine*, December 18, 1802; *Weekly Magazine*, March 3, 1798; *Port Folio*, February 12, 1803, March 3, 1804, April 20, 1805.

6

Fruits of Passion:
The Dynamics of Interracial Sex

Winthrop D. Jordan

When Europeans met Africans in America the result was slavery, revolt, the sociability of daily life, and, inevitably, sexual union. The blending of black and white began almost with the first contact of the two peoples and has far outlasted the institution of chattel slavery.

The tensions which arose may be viewed in several interrelated ways. The Englishmen who came to America brought with them not merely a prevalent social mood but also certain specific sexual standards and certain more or less definite ideas about African sexuality. Many of them came with more or less explicit intentions as to the proper character of the communities they wished to establish in the wilderness. These intentions were not always, or perhaps ever, fully realized; they were deflected—again sometimes more, sometimes less— by conditions in the New World. One of the most important deflectors was the development of a racial slavery which itself became one of the New World's "conditions," though of course the character of this condition was not everywhere the same. The Negro was encountered in very different contexts in the various English colonies. Particularly important in making for differences in the Englishman's reaction to interracial sex was the demographic pattern which developed during the first quarter of the eighteenth century; variations in the numbers of the

From *The White Man's Burden* (New York: Oxford University Press, 1974), derived from *White Over Black: American Attitudes toward the Negro,* 1550–1812 (Chapel Hill: The University of North Carolina Press and The Institute of Early American History and Culture, 1968). Reprinted by permission of The North Carolina Press.

races and of the sexes in the English colonies may be shown to be almost determinative in shaping certain attitudes.

REGIONAL STYLES IN
RACIAL INTERMIXTURE

Miscegenation was extensive in all the English colonies, a fact made evident to contemporaries by the presence of large numbers of mulattoes. It is impossible to ascertain how much intermixture there actually was, though it seems likely there was more during the eighteenth century than at any time since. Although miscegenation was probably most common among the lower orders, white men of every social rank slept with black women. Almost everyone who wrote anything about America commented upon this fact of life.

No one thought intermixture was a good thing. Rather, English colonials were caught in the push and pull of an irreconcilable conflict between desire and aversion for interracial sexual union. The prerequisite for this conflict is so obvious as to be too easily overlooked: desire and aversion rested on the bedrock fact that white men perceived Negroes as being *both alike and different* from themselves. Without perception of similarity, no desire and no widespread gratification was possible. Without perception of difference, on the other hand, no aversion to miscegenation nor tension concerning it could have arisen. Without perception of difference, of course, the term *miscegenation* had no meaning. Given these simultaneous feelings of desire and aversion, it seems probable that of the two the latter is more demanding of explanation. The sexual drive of human beings has always, in the long run, overridden even the strongest sense of difference between two groups of human beings and, in some individuals, has even overridden the far stronger sense which men have of the difference between themselves and animals. What demands explanation, in short, is why there was *any* aversion among the white colonists to sexual union with blacks.

In most colonies virtually all the offspring of interracial unions were illegitimate, though legally sanctified interracial marriage did occur, especially though not exclusively in New England. Miscegenation in colonial America, as has been true since, typically involved fornication between white men and black women, though the inverse combination was common, far more so than is generally supposed. Probably a majority of interracial marriages in New England involved Negro men and white women of "the meaner sort." In the plantation colonies, although there were occasional instances of white women marrying black men, legitimization of this relationship was unusual.

Public feeling against miscegenation was strong enough to force itself over the hurdles of the legislative process into the statute books of many English continental colonies. As early as the 1660's the Maryland and Virginia assemblies had begun to lash out at miscegenation in language dripping with distaste and indignation. By the turn of the century it was clear in many continental colonies that the English settlers felt genuine revulsion for interracial sexual union, at least in principle. Two northern and all the plantation colonies legally prohibited miscegenation. Though there were exceptions, the weight of community opinion was set against the sexual union of white and black, as the long-standing statutory prohibitions indicated. In significant contrast, none of the British West Indian assemblies prohibited extramarital miscegenation.

In the West Indian colonies especially, and less markedly in South Carolina, the pattern of miscegenation was far more inflexible than in the other English settlements. White women in the islands did not sleep with black men, let alone marry them. Nor did white men actually marry Negroes or mulattoes. Yet white men commonly, almost customarily, took Negro women to bed with little pretense at concealing the fact. Edward Long of Jamaica described the situation: "He who should presume to shew any displeasure against such a thing as simple fornication, would for his pains be accounted a simple blockhead; since not one in twenty can be persuaded, that there is either sin; or shame in cohabiting with his slave." Negro concubinage was an integral part of island life, tightly interwoven into the social fabric.

It is scarcely necessary to resort to speculation about the influence of tropical climate in order to explain this situation, for life in the islands was in large degree shaped by the enormous disproportion of Negroes to white settlers and characterized by brutal nakedness of planter domination over the slaves. In the West Indian islands and to less extent South Carolina, racial slavery consisted of unsheathed dominion by relatively small numbers of white men over enormous numbers of Negroes, and it was in these colonies that Negro men were most stringently barred from sexual relations with white women. Sexually, as well as in every other way, Negroes were utterly subordinated. White men extended their dominion over their Negroes to the bed, where the sex act itself served as ritualistic re-enactment of the daily pattern of social dominance.

Congruent to these regional differences in slavery and interracial relationships were the bedrock demographic facts which so powerfully influenced, perhaps even determined, the kind of society which emerged in each colony. With blacks overwhelmingly outnumbering whites in the various islands (ten to one in Jamaica), and with whites outnumbering Negroes everywhere on the continent except South Carolina, it was inevitable that radically dissimilar social styles should have developed in the two areas. As a French traveler perceptively characterized this dissimilarity in 1777: "In the colonies of the Antilles, most of the colonists are people who have left their homeland with the intention of rebuilding their fortunes. Far from settling in the islands, they look upon them merely as a land of exile, never as a place where they plan to live, prosper, and die. On the other hand, the Anglo-American colonists are permanent, born in the country and attached to it; they have no motherland save the one they live in; and, although London formerly was so considered, they have clearly proved that they held it in less esteem than they did the prosperity, tranquility, and freedom of their own country." The West Indian planters were lost not so much in the Caribbean as in a sea of blacks. They found it impossible to re-create English culture as they had known it. They were corrupted by living in a police state, though not themselves the objects of its discipline. The business of the islands was business, the production of agricultural staples; the islands were not where one really lived, but where one made one's money. By contrast, the American colonists on the continent maintained their hold upon their English background, modifying it less for accommodating slavery than for winning the new land. Unlike the West Indian planters, they felt no need to be constantly running back to England to reassure themselves that they belonged to civilization. Because they were conscious of having attained a large measure of success in transplanting their own society, they vehemently rejected any trespass upon it by a people so alien as the Negroes. The islanders could hardly resent trespass on something which they did not have.

It was precisely this difference which made the Negro seem so much more alien on the continent than on the islands, and miscegenation accordingly less common. For a West Indian to have declared, with Judge Samuel Sewall of Boston, that Negroes "cannot mix with us and become members of society, . . . never embody with us and grow up into orderly Families, to the Peopling of the Land" would have been false by reason of the extensive blending of the races in the islands and meaningless because the "peopling" of the islands had already been accomplished—by Africans. Americans on the continent stood poised for a destiny of conquering a vast wilderness, while Englishmen in the little crowded islands looked forward down a precipice of slave rebellion, or at best a slippery slope of peaceful but inevitable defeat. Certainly the bustling communities on the continent had good reason to feel that they had successfully established a beachhead of English civilization in America. They possessed optimism, self-confidence, and a well-defined sense of Englishness, a sense which came automatically to bear when they were confronted with peoples who seemed appreciably dissimilar. When large numbers of very dissimilar people threatened the identity of the continental colonists, their response was rejection of those people in the mind and a tendency to perceive them as being more dissimilar than ever. For the sense of dissimilarity fed on itself: once the cycle was started, the differences between white Americans and "others," which first sparked anxiety and rejection, loomed progressively larger and generated further anxiety and rejection.

Certainly many Americans on the continent became convinced that the American people were not intended to be Negroes. Benjamin Franklin, who was as fully attuned to American destiny as anyone, nervously expressed the idea that the continent should belong to "White People." "I could wish their Numbers were increased. Why increase the Sons of Africa, by Planting them in America, where we have so fair an Opportunity, by excluding all Blacks and Tawneys, of increasing the lovely White and Red? But perhaps I am partial to the Complexion of my Country," he concluded with his usual self-conscious good sense, "for such Kind of Partiality is natural to Mankind." Franklin was expressing an important feeling, one which a famous Virginian, William Byrd, expressed more directly: "They import so many Negros hither, that I fear this Colony will some time or other be confirmed by the Name of New Guinea."

It was more than a matter of colonial Americans not wanting to give their country over to Africans. Miscegenation probably did not seem so much a matter of long-term discoloration as an immediate failure to live up to immemorial standards. Here again, the intentions which drove English overseas expansion were of crucial importance. The colonists' conviction that they must sustain their civilized condition wherever they went rendered miscegenation a negation of the underlying plan of settlement in America. Simply because most blacks were chattel slaves, racial amalgamation was stamped as irredeemably illicit; it was irretrievably associated with loss of control over the baser passions, with weakening of traditional family ties, and with breakdown of proper social ordering. Judge Sewall's "orderly Families" were rendered a mockery by fathers taking slave wenches to bed.

At the same time it would be a mistake to suppose that the *status* of Negroes in itself aroused white aversion to intermixture; the physical difference was of crucial importance. Without that difference there could never have developed well-formulated conceptions about sexual relations between Africans and Europeans in America. Although perhaps there was some feeling that the laws which prevented racial intermingling helped prevent blacks, as one astute foreign observer put it, "from forming too great opinions of themselves," the underlying reason for their passage was that these mixtures were "disagreeable" to white men.

MASCULINE AND FEMININE MODES IN CAROLINA AND AMERICA

On the face of things it seems paradoxical that the one region on the continent which had become demographically most like a new Guinea should have been the one in which white men seemed least anxious about interracial sexual activity. While permanent unions between persons of the two races normally were quiet or secretive affairs elsewhere on the continent, in South Carolina and particularly in Charleston they were not. It was the only city worthy of the name in the plantation colonies. It was an elegant, gay, extravagant city, where men took advantage of certain of their opportunities in more overt, more relaxed, and probably more enterprising fashion than in the colonies to the north. They possessed an abundance of black women. The result may best be described by a visiting merchant from Jamaica (where the atmosphere surrounding interracial sex was so utterly different from New England), who wrote from Charleston in 1773: "I know of but one Gentleman who professedly keeps a Mulatto Mistress and he is very much pointed at: There are swarms of Negroes about the Town and many Mulattoes, and by the Dress of the Girls, who mostly imitate their Mistresses, I have no doubt of their Conversations with the whites, but they are carried on with more privacy than in our W. India Islands." "As I travell'd further North," the Jamaican visitor continued concerning his trip from Charleston to North Carolina, "there were fewer Negroes about the Houses, and these taken less notice of, and before I finish'd my Journey North, I found an empty House, the late Tenant of which had been oblig'd by the Church Wardens to decamp on Account of his having kept a Black Woman. Dont suppose Fornication is out of Fashion here," he added reassuringly about North Carolina, "more than in other Places, No! the difference only is, that the White Girls monopolize it."

Here was an important regional difference in social "fashion." Charleston was the only English city on the continent where it was at all possible to jest publicly concerning miscegenation. In 1736 the

South-Carolina Gazette published some frank advice to the bachelors and widowers of Charleston: "that if they are in a Strait for Women, to wait for the next Shipping from the Coast of Guinny. Those African Ladies are of a strong, robust Constitution: not easily jaded out, able to serve them by Night as well as Day. When they are Sick, they are not costly, when dead, their funeral Charges are but . . . an old Matt, one Bottle Rum, and a lb. Sugar [.] The cheapness of a Commo-di-ty becomes more taking when it fully Answers the end, or T___l." Next week another writer replied in obvious determination not to be out-done in indelicacy of expression: "In my Opinion, our Country-Women are full as capable for Service either night or day as any African Ladies whatsoever. . . . In all Companies wheresoever I have been, my Country-Women have always the praise for their Activity of Hipps and humoring a Jest to the Life in what Posture soever their Partners may fancy, which makes me still hope that they'll have the Preference before the black Ladies in the Esteem of the Widowers and Batchelors at C___town." Next week the *Gazette* published still another verse.

If these contributions to the *South-Carolina Gazette* were a trifle raw by the standards of a modern family newspaper, they reflected more than eighteenth-century literary frankness about sex. Newspapers elsewhere on the continent did not publish similar discussions of interracial sex, though everywhere (including Boston) they published some none-too-delicate pieces concerning sexual matters. Only in Charleston was it possible to debate publicly, "Is sex with Negroes right?"

This distinctiveness was owing partly to South Carolina's distinctive economic and social history. The preponderance of slaves in the low country tended to give white men a queasy sense that perhaps they were marooned, a feeling that their society was irrevocably committed to Negro slavery and that somehow their mere Englishness had lost its savor in the shuffle for plantation prosperity. The effect of this uneasi-ness was to make men feel like both fleeing and embracing Negro slavery all at once: hence the common annual flights from the planta-tions to Charleston and from South Carolina to northern cities and England, the negation of cherished traditional liberties in the slave codes, the importation of more and more slaves, the continual efforts to encourage white immigration, and not least, the simultaneous em-bracing of Negro women and rejection of the ensuing offspring. Caught as they were in powerful crosscurrents, it is no wonder that white men in Charleston joked nervously about their sexual abandon.

For white women the situation was different, and here again the Charleston area seems to have been characterized by attitudes somewhere midway between those of the West Indies and further north. In the islands, where English settlers were most thoroughly committed to a Negro slave society and where strenuous attempts to attract more white settlers had been unavailing, white women were, quite literally, the repositories of white civilization. White men tended to place them protectively upon a pedestal and then run off to gratify their passions elsewhere. For their part white women, though they might propagate children, inevitably held themselves aloof from the world of lust and passion, a world which reeked of infidelity and Negro slaves. Under no circumstances would they have attempted, any more than they would have been allowed, to clamber down from their pedestal to seek pleasures of their own across the racial line. In fact white women in the West Indies tended to adhere rigidly to the double sexual standard which characterized English sexual mores and to refrain more than in the continental colonies from infidelity with white men. The oppressive presence of slavery itself tended to inhibit the white woman's capacity for emotional, sexual, and intellectual commitment. She served principally an ornamentive function, for everything resembling work was done by Negro slaves. Visitors to the islands were almost universally agreed in describing her life as one of indolence and lassitude, though some were impressed by a formal, superficial gaiety. Her choices were to withdraw from the world or to create an unreal one of her own.

The white women of the Charleston area were less tightly hemmed in. Nevertheless, they rarely if ever established liaisons with Negro men, as happened in the South Carolina back country. Some visitors to the city were struck by their desiccated formality, which seems now to betray the strains imposed by the prevailing pattern of miscegenation. One traveler from Philadelphia described his unfavorable impressions in Charleston by first lamenting that the "superabundance of Negroes" had "destroyed the activity of whites," who "stand with their hands in their pockets, overlooking their negroes." In his letter of 1809 (known only as published much later in the century with some Victorian censorship at the end), he went on to say,

> These, however, are not one tenth of the curses slavery has brought on the Southern States. Nothing has surprised me more than the cold, melancholy reserve of the females, of the best families, in South Carolina and Georgia. Old and young, single and married, all have that dull frigid insipidity, and reserve, which is attributed to solitary old maids. Even in their own houses they scarce utter anything to a stranger but yes or no, and one is perpetually puzzled to know whether it proceeds from awkwardness or dislike. Those who have been at some of their Balls [in Charleston] say that the ladies hardly even speak or smile, but dance with as much gravity, as if they were performing some ceremony of devotion. On the contrary,

the negro wenches are all sprightliness and gayety; and if report be not a defamer—

The dissipation of the white gentleman was as much a tragedy for his white lady as for him. A biracial environment warped her affective life in two directions at once, for she was made to feel that sensual involvement with the opposite sex burned bright and hot with unquenchable passion and at the same time that any such involvement was utterly repulsive.

If women were particularly affected by the situation in South Carolina, white persons of both sexes in *all* the English colonies were affected in a more general way by the tensions involved in miscegenation. Though these tensions operated in white men rather differently than in white women, it seems almost self-evident that the emergent attitudes toward Negroes possessed a unity which transcended differences between the two sexes. Put another way, out of a pattern of interracial sexual relationships which normally placed white men and white women in very different roles, there arose a common core of belief and mythology concerning the Negro which belonged to neither sex but to white American culture as a whole. The emergence of common beliefs out of divergent experiences was of course principally a function of the homogenizing effect of culture upon individual experience, but it is important to bear in mind that the *functional* significance of beliefs about the Negro may have been very different for white women than for white men even when the beliefs themselves were identical. Since the English and colonial American cultures were dominated by males, however, sexually-oriented beliefs about the Negro in America deprived principally from the psychological needs of men and were to a considerable extent shaped by specifically masculine modes of thought and behavior. This is not to say the American attitudes toward the Negro were *male* attitudes but merely that when one talks about *American* attitudes toward anything (the frontier, the city, money, freedom, the Negro) one is using a shorthand for attitudes common to both sexes but predominantly male in genesis and tone.

NEGRO SEXUALITY AND SLAVE INSURRECTION

As for these ideas or beliefs about the Negro, many seem startlingly modern. Least surprising, perhaps, was the common assumption that black women were especially passionate, an idea which found literary or at least literate expression especially in the *South-Carolina Gazette* and in West Indian books. The Negro woman was the sunkissed embodiment of ardency:

> Next comes a warmer race, from sable sprung,
> To love each thought, . . . to lust each nerve is strung;
>
>   .   .   .
>
> These sooty dames, well vers'd in Venus's school,
> Make love an art, and boast they kiss by rule.

If such amiable assessments found their way into public print, one can imagine what tavern bantering must have been like.

Plainly white men were doing more than reporting pleasant facts. For by calling the Negro woman passionate they were offering the best possible justification for their own passions. Not only did the black woman's warmth constitute a logical explanation for the white man's infidelity, but, much more important, it helped shift responsibility from himself to her. If she was *that* lascivious—well, a man could scarcely be blamed for succumbing against overwhelming odds.

Attitudes toward the Negro male were more complex and potentially far more explosive. The notion that black men were particularly virile, promiscuous, and lusty was of course not new in the eighteenth century, but the English colonists in America showed signs of adding a half-conscious and revealingly specific corollary: they sometimes suggested that black men lusted after white women. There was probably some objective basis for the charge, since sexual intercourse with a white woman must in part have been for black men an act of retribution against the white man. For different reasons there was also good basis for the common feeling that only the most depraved white woman would consent to sleep with a Negro, since white women of the lowest class had the least to lose in flouting the maxims of society and the most reason to hate them. No matter how firmly based in fact, however, the image of the sexually aggressive Negro was rooted even more firmly in deep strata of irrationality. For it is apparent that white men projected their own desires onto Negroes: their own passion for black women was not fully acceptable to society or the self and hence not readily admissible. Sexual desires could be effectively denied and the accompanying anxiety and guilt in some measure eased, however, by imputing them to others. It is not we, but others, who are guilty. It is not we who lust, but they. Not only this, but white men anxious over their own sexual inadequacy were touched by a racking fear and jealousy. Perhaps the Negro better performed his nocturnal offices than the white man. Perhaps, indeed, the white man's woman really wanted the Negro more than she wanted him.

Significantly, these tensions tended to bubble to the surface especially at times of interracial crisis when the colonists' control over their Negroes appeared in jeopardy. During many scares over slave conspiracies, for instance, reports circulated that the Negroes had plotted killing all white persons except the young women, whom they "intended to reserve for themselves." In fact these charges were ill-founded at best, for there is no evidence that any Negroes in revolt ever seized any white women for their "own use," even though rebellious slaves certainly had opportunity to do so during the successful insurrections in the West Indies and also at Stono in South Carolina.

From these indications it seems more than likely that fears of Negro sexual aggression during periods of alarm over insurrection did not represent direct response to actual overt threat, but rather a complex of reactions in the white man. Any group faced with a real threat of serious proportions is inclined to sense, even on a conscious level, a sexual element in the opponents' aggressiveness—as many have identified Communism with free love. Any black insurrection, furthermore, threatened the white man's dominance, including his valuable sexual dominance, and hence the awful prospect of being overthrown was bound to assume a sexual cast. And finally, white men anxious and guilty over their own sexual aggressiveness were quick to impute it to others, especially at a time of interracial crisis. One has only to imagine the emotions flooding through some planter who had been more or less regularly sleeping with some of his slave wenches when he suddenly learned of a conspiracy among their male counterparts; it was virtually inevitable that his thoughts turn in a torrent of guilt to the "safety" of his wife.

DISMEMBERMENT, PHYSIOLOGY, AND SEXUAL PERCEPTIONS

The white man's fears of Negro sexual aggression were equally apparent in the use of castration as a punishment in the colonies. This weapon of desperation was not employed by angry mobs in the manner which became familiar after Emancipation. Castration was dignified by specific legislative sanction as a lawful punishment in Antigua, the Carolinas, Bermuda, Virginia, Pennsylvania, and New Jersey. It was sometimes prescribed for such offenses as striking a white person or running away: employed in this way, castration was a not irrational method of slave control, closely akin to the Jamaica law which authorized severing one foot of a runaway. Yet castration was not simply another of the many brands of hideous cruelty which graced the colonial criminal codes: it was reserved for Negroes and occasionally Indians. In some colonies, laws authorizing castration were worded so as to apply to all blacks whether free or slave. As a legal punishment castration was a peculiarly American experiment, for there was no basis for it in English law. Indeed officials in England were shocked and outraged at the idea, calling castration "inhumane and contrary to all Christian Laws," "a punishment never inflicted by any Law [in any of] H.M. Dominions." Some Americans thought the practice necessary to restrain a lecherous and barbarous people; Englishmen thought the barbarity was on the other side.

Castration of blacks clearly indicated a need in white men to persuade themselves that they were really masters and in all ways masterful, and it illustrated dramatically the ease with which white men slipped over into treating their Negroes like their bulls and stallions whose "spirit" could be subdued by emasculation. In some colonies, moreover, the specifically sexual aspect of castration was so obvious as to underline how much of the white man's insecurity about blacks was fundamentally sexual. The Pennsylvania and New Jersey laws passed early in the eighteenth century (and quickly disallowed by authorities in England) prescribed castration of Negroes as punishment for one offense only, attempted rape of a white woman. Still more strikingly, Virginia's provision for castration of Negroes, which had been on the books for many years and permitted castration for a variety of serious offenses, was repealed in 1769 for humanitarian reasons, but the repealing statute specifically declared that it might still be inflicted for one particular offense—rape or attempted rape of a white woman.

The concept of the Negro's aggressive sexuality was reinforced by what was thought to be an anatomical peculiarity of the Negro male. He was said to possess an especially large penis. The idea was considerably older even than the exegesis on Ham's offense against his father offered by West African travelers. Indeed the idea without question predated the settlement of America and possibly even the Portuguese explorations of the West African coast. Several fifteenth-century map makers decorated parts of Africa with little naked figures which gave the idea graphic expression, and in due course, in the seventeenth century, English accounts of West Africa were carefully noting the "extraordinary greatness" of the Negroes' "members." By the final quarter of the eighteenth century the idea that the Negro's penis was larger than the white man's had become something of a commonplace in European scientific circles. Whether it was a commonplace in popular circles in the English colonies is more difficult to ascertain, since it was scarcely the sort of assertion likely to find its way into print even if a great many people talked about it. Certainly the idea was not unheard of, for as an officer in the First Pennsylvania Regiment commented pointedly in his journal about the Negro boys waiting on Virginia dinner tables: "I am surprized this does not hurt the feelings of this fair Sex to see these young boys of about Fourteen and Fifteen years Old to Attend them. these whole nakedness Expos'd and I can Assure you It would Surprize a person to see these d___d black boys how well they are hung."

Partly because their relationships with blacks were structured by daily contact, Negroes seemed more highly sexed to the colonists than did the American Indians. The magnitude of the differentiation they made between the two aboriginal peoples on this score was so great as to suggest that it reflected not merely the immediate circumstances in which the colonists found themselves but the entirety of English historical experience since the beginning of expansion overseas. Far from finding Indians lusty and lascivious, they discovered them to be notably deficient in ardor and virility. (Eventually and almost inevitably a European commentator announced that the Indian's penis was smaller than the European's.) And the colonists developed no image of the Indian as a potential rapist: their descriptions of Indian attacks did not include the Indians "reserving the young women for themselves." In fact the entire interracial sexual complex did not pertain to the Indian. In the more settled portions of the colonies, Englishmen did not normally take Indian women to bed, but neither did an aura of tension pervade the sexual union of red and white. Of the various laws which penalized illicit miscegenation, none applied to Indians, and only North Carolina's (and Virginia's for a very brief period) prohibited intermarriage. On the contrary, several colonists were willing to allow, even advocate, intermarriage with the Indians—an unheard of proposition concerning Negroes.

MULATTO OFFSPRING IN A BIRACIAL SOCIETY

Inevitably, miscegenation resulted in children. Somehow they had to be accommodated to a system of racial slavery whose strictest logic their existence violated. How were mulattoes to be treated? Were they to be free or slave, acknowledged or denied, white or black? The ways in which American colonials answered these questions are profoundly revealing. The question arose, of course, in the cultural matrix of purpose, accomplishment, self-conception, and social circumstances of settlement in the New World. Inevitably the fruits of interracial sex grew differently in different contexts of self-identification.

As far as the continental colonies were concerned, it is easy to detect a pattern which has since become so familiar to Americans that they rarely pause to think about it or to question its logic and inevitability. The word *mulatto* is not frequently used in the United States. For social purposes a mulatto is termed a "Negro." Americans lump together both socially and legally all persons with perceptible admixture of African ancestry, thus making social definition without regard to genetic logic; white blood becomes socially advantageous only in overwhelming proportion. This peculiar bifurcation seems to have existed almost from the beginning of English contact with Africans. The word *mulatto*, borrowed from the Spanish, was in English usage from about 1600 and was probably first used in Virginia records in 1666. Thereafter laws dealing with Negro slaves began to add "and mulattoes," presumably to make clear that mixed blood did not confer exemption from slavery. From the first, every English continental colony lumped mulattoes with Negroes in their slave codes and in statutes governing the conduct of free Negroes: the law was clear that mulattoes and Negroes were not to be distinguished for different treatment.

In addition to the statutory homogenization of all persons of African ancestry, mulattoes do not seem to have been accorded higher status than Negroes in actual practice. Whatever the case in other countries or in later centuries, mulattoes seem generally to have been treated no better than unmixed Africans. The diaries, letters, travel accounts, and newspapers of the period do not indicate any pronounced tendency to distinguish mulattoes from Negroes, any feeling that their status was higher and demanded different treatment. These sources give no indication, for instance, that mulattoes were preferred as house servants or concubines. There was a relatively high proportion of mulattoes among manumitted slaves, but probably this was owing to the desire of some masters to liberate their own offspring.

The existence of a rigid barrier between whites and those of African ancestry necessarily required a means by which the barrier could on occasion be passed. Some accommodation had to be made for those persons with so little African blood that they appeared to be white, for one simply could not go around calling apparently white persons Negroes. Once the stain was washed out visibly it was useless as a means of identification. Thus there developed the silent mechanism of "passing." Such a device would have been unnecessary if those of mixed ancestry and appearance had been regarded as midway between white and black. It was the existence of a broad chasm which necessitated the sudden leap which passing represented.

It is possible to find direct evidence of successful passing, but unfortunately there is no way of telling how *many* blacks were effectively transformed into whites. Passing was difficult but not impossible, and it stood as a veiled, unrecognized, and ironic monument to the American ideal of a society open to all comers. But the problem of evidence is insurmountable. The success of the passing mechanism depended upon its operating in silence. Passing was a conspiracy of silence not only for the individual but for a biracial society which had drawn a rigid color line based on visibility. Unless a white man was a white man, the gates were open to endless slander and confusion.

That the existence of such a line in the continental colonies was not predominantly the effect of the English cultural heritage is suggested by even a glance at the English colonies in the Caribbean. The social accommodation of mixed offspring in the islands followed a very different pattern from that on the continent. It was regarded as improper, for example, to work mulattoes in the fields—a fundamental distinction. One observer wrote that mulatto slaves "fetch a lower price than blacks, unless they are tradesmen, because the purchasers cannot employ them in the druggeries to which negroes are put too; the colored [i.e. mulatto] men, are therefore mostly brought up to trades or employed as house slaves, and the women of this description are generally prostitutes." Though the English in the Caribbean thought of their society in terms of white, colored, and black, they employed a complicated battery of names to distinguish persons of various racial mixtures. This terminology was borrowed from the neighboring Spanish, but words are never acquired unless they fulfill a need. While the English settlers on the continent borrowed one Spanish word to describe all mixtures of black and white, the islanders borrowed at least four—*mulatto, sambo, quadroon,* and *mestize*—to describe differing degrees of intermixture.

The connection between the status of mulattoes and the prevailing pattern of miscegenation is obvious. Mulattoes in the West Indies were products of accepted practice, something they assuredly were not in the continental colonies. In the one area, they were the fruits of a desire which society tolerated and almost institutionalized; in the other, they represented an illicit passion which public morality unhesitatingly condemned. On the continent, unlike the West Indies, mulattoes represented a practice about which men could only feel guilty.

The colonist on the American continent, therefore, remained firm in his categorization of mixed-bloods as belonging to the lower caste. It was an unconscious decision dictated perhaps in large part by the weight of Negroes on his community, heavy enough to be a burden, yet not so heavy as to make him abandon all hope of maintaining his own identity, physically and culturally. Interracial propagation was a constant reproach that he was failing to be true to himself. Sexual intimacy strikingly symbolized a union he wished to avoid. If he could not restrain his sexual nature, he could at least reject its fruits and thus solace himself that he had done no harm. Perhaps he sensed as well that continued racial intermixture would eventually undermine the logic of the racial slavery upon which his society was based. For the separation of slaves from free men depended on a clear demarcation of the races, and the presence of mulattoes blurred this essential distinction. Accordingly he made every effort to nullify the effects of racial intermixture. By classifying the mulatto as a Negro he was in effect denying that intermixture had occurred at all.

II

Victorian Images

Nineteenth-century Americans were haunted by the spectre of social chaos engendered by unprecedented change in the nation's economy. After several decades of relative stability, the American economy entered the "take off" phase in the years following 1820. The remainder of the nineteenth century was characterized by sustained and extremely rapid growth. Accompanying this growth was a structural change that featured increasing economic diversification and the gradual shift of the nation's labor force from agriculture to manufacturing and other nonagricultural pursuits.[1]

Although the birth rate declined from the high level of the colonial period, the population roughly doubled every generation during the century. As the population grew, its makeup also changed, as massive waves of immigration brought new ethnic groups into the country. Geographic and social mobility—downward and upward—touched almost everyone. Local studies indicate that nearly three-quarters of the population—North and South, in the emerging cities of the Northeast and in the restless rural counties of the West—changed their residence each decade.[2] As a consequence, "social atomization effected every segment of society," and it seemed to many Americans that "all the recognized values of orderly civilization were gradually being eroded."[3]

Rapid industrialization and increased geographic mobility in the nineteenth century had special implications for American women because they reinforced the social distinctions that had become manifest in the post–Revolutionary War period. In the context of extreme competitiveness and dizzying social change, the Victorian home lost many of its earlier functions and came to serve as a haven of tranquillity and order. "As the larger society lost structural coherence, the family was cut adrift from its old institutional moorings."[4] The roles of husband and wife became more clearly differentiated than ever before, and the size of American families decreased. In the middle class especially, men worked in the productive economy while women ruled the home and served as the custodians of civility and culture. The intimacy of colonial marriage was rent, and a social distance grew up between husbands and wives that at times seemed unbridgable.[5]

Along with the heightened differentiation of male and female spheres, the life styles of middle-class women became increasingly estranged from those of their lower-class sisters. Gerda Lerner focuses upon the ways in which social and economic change in the early nineteenth century affected the status of women of different classes in "The Lady and the Mill Girl." Medicine, law, business, and science—all areas in which women had played at least modest roles in the colonial period—became increasingly professionalized and consequently closed to middle-class women, who were expected to conform to the Victorian model of true womanhood represented by the image of the Lady. At the same time, lower-class women were being forced out of their homes and into the expanding factory system, creating a second social type—the Mill Girl. "In the urbanized and industrialized Northeast the life experience of middle-class women was different in almost every respect from that of lower-class women."[6]

The Victorian idealization of womanhood represented a continuation of an earlier trend, the consequences of which are difficult to weigh. The position of the middle-class woman in the nineteenth century was indeed ambiguous. It typifies the paradoxical role women have played in American history. Women became objects of both adoration and domination. Their moral superiority to the brutish and materialistic male was readily acknowledged, but their sphere of influence was confined to the family and the home. Women were accorded the power of intuition in a world that paid homage to reason; they were given a monopoly on piety, purity, and submissiveness in a society that increasingly trivialized these virtues.[7] Although they gained greater control over their sexual lives, causing the birth rate to decline, women paid for this boon with their own desexualization. The functions of the womb rather than those of the clitoris exemplified female sexuality in the nineteenth century. "Once active sexual desire, and the organ of sexual pleasure, the clitoris, had been all but eradicated from female physiology, the nineteenth century gynecologist proceeded to elevate a woman's reproductive system to a position of biological hegemony."[8]

However, the Victorian image was a malleable one; it could be manipulated to justify often conflicting life styles and be made to serve the interests of both reaction and reform. In "The Female Appendage," Ronald Hogeland shows that this conception of womanhood could accommodate at least four distinct life styles, which he refers to as "Ornamental," "Romanticized," "Evangelical," and "Radical," each generating different forms of political behavior. Hogeland makes clear that each of these life styles was created by men, and he emphasizes that while the "primary accountability for the moral welfare of society" was assigned to women, "the administrative and intellectual reigns of organized religion and politics" remained tightly in the grasp of men.

Nowhere did the contradiction between the image and the reality stand out in starker contrast than in the Southern lady, about whom Anne F. Scott has written so eloquently.[9] In no other section of the country did the "Ornamental" style of womanhood become so much a part of the sustaining myths of the society. In contrast to the image of the somewhat frivolous Southern belle sweeping about the plantation in an imported gown and exuding virtue, charm, and "accomplishment," most Southern ladies assumed many burdensome tasks related to the domestic administration of the plantation system. In her essay, "Women's Perspective on the Patriarchy of the 1850s," Scott supplements her earlier work by showing how the realities of life for the Southern lady conflicted with the "domestic metaphor" that underlay the Southern conception of an organic and patriarchal society. Although there is good reason to doubt that these women coldly resisted the pleasures of the flesh, the ideal of motherhood with its attendant fears of the dangers of pregnancy and childbirth was one of the greatest sources of unhappiness for Southern women. Combined with the gnawing sense of sexual betrayal derived from their knowledge of widespread miscegenation, the condition of Southern women helped to create discontent among "the female portion of the population" within what proslavery propagandist Langdon Cheves predicted would be "the most splendid empire upon which the sun has ever shown."[10] No organized women's movement, however, appeared in the ante-bellum South. When the Southern states seceded, most women gave the rebellion their hearty support, supplying food and clothing for Confederate soldiers, nursing the sick and wounded, and assuming many tasks on the homefront that had formerly been performed by men.[11]

Of course, most women in nineteenth-century America could not afford to aspire to the Victorian image of true womanhood. Recent studies support the slaveholders' contention that the conditions of the free blacks were miserable and indicate that they were plagued by declining economic status and increased family disorganization in the decades preceding the Civil War.[12] But the most obvious contradiction to the stereotype was presented by the nearly two million black women held in bondage within the fifteen slave states of ante-bellum America. The patriarchal image of the contented slave is no more accurate than that of the contented Southern lady serving her appointed master.

In many ways slavery bore more heavily upon women than upon men. The abolitionists—particularly women abolitionists—emphasized the degradation of women and the destruction of the family inherent in the economic and social relations structured by the "peculiar institution." Most scholars have repeated the abolitionists' depiction of slavery, but they have ignored the ways in which their perspective reflected the Victorian image of womanhood.[13] Two themes were prevalent in this indictment, and they have been consistently repeated: slavery destroyed the family through the sale of children and through the refusal to legalize the marriage bond; and slavery encouraged the sexual exploitation of slave women by masters and their white retainers.[14]

Recent studies suggest that claims of the total brutalization of women under slavery have been exaggerated. Resistance took many forms. Family ties among the slaves were far stronger than previous accounts have suggested. Intimate family relationships helped the slave to come to terms with the system. Sales undoubtedly did not break up as many families as the abolitionists believed, although every black woman knew that her "chill'n could be sold away. . . ." Abolitionist views of the sexual exploitation of enslaved black women were warped by the extreme sexual repression within their own lives. However, documentary evidence clearly supports the widespread belief that miscegenation was rampant and a central element of the social reality that characterized and scarred the lives of both black and white women.[15]

In contrast to the most recent works on slavery that generalize about the day-to-day life of the slave, Loren Schweninger's "A Slave Family in the Ante-Bellum South" focuses upon the life of a single slave, Sally, the matriarch of the Thomas-Rapier family. His sensitive portrayal of her life adds a personal dimension to our understanding of what E. Franklin Frazier called "Motherhood in Bondage," and it supports recent studies emphasizing the desire of blacks after the Civil War to establish the legitimacy of their marriages and to provide the necessary basis for a stable family life. Although black men often attempted to emulate the Victorian ideal, black women were forced by necessity to continue to play the important role they assumed under slavery. Until undermined by economic and political discrimination, such attempts to establish stable family ties were surprisingly successful.[16]

Most working women in nineteenth-century America were not black, and the plight of those whom Lerner has associated with the image of the "Mill Girl" was an arduous one. The vast majority of adult women married and continued to work within their homes, meeting the multitude of demands placed upon farm women or attempting to master the fundamentals of "domestic science" detailed in the plethora of manuals for middle-class women appearing on the subject of housekeeping in the mid-nineteenth century.[17] Ironically, as social and economic change created the conditions that generated the cult of domesticity, increasing numbers of women moved out of the home and into the ranks of paid labor. The most common job open to women represented little more than an extension of their former occupational role. Most became domestic servants for the more affluent. Although the majority of working women continued to be domestics at the end of the century, the factory system employed large numbers of women because of their low labor cost and the relative scarcity of male laborers. A handful of errant romantics extolled the "freedom of the factory," but these women were generally secondary earners whose wages supported their families' attempts to attain the minimum necessities of life.

In its inception, the Waltham or "boarding house" system of labor organization comported more closely to the idyllic view of the factory and did not conflict directly with the Victorian conception of true womanhood.[18] In contrast to the Rhode Island or "family" system which, as its name suggests, was based upon the employment of whole families, the key feature of the Waltham system was the exploitation of young women, mostly with rural origins. For relatively short periods of time, they lived in company-owned boarding houses supervised by matronly housemothers. Generally these young women worked in order to send a brother to school or to provide themselves with an adequate trousseau. As the most famous of their number, Lucy Larcom, said in her autobiography, they were "happy in the knowledge that, at the longest, our employment was only to be temporary."[19]

However, reality never conformed completely to the portrait of the Waltham system sketched in the pages of the *Lowell Offering,* a periodical written by mill girls and actively supported by mill owners, the Boston Associates, who wished to popularize a favorable image of their factories. In the two decades before the Civil War that reality was changing and the Waltham system was deteriorating. During these years wages in the textile industry, which had always been low, began to decline relative to wages paid by other jobs employing mostly women. Mill owners successfully resisted employee demands for improved working conditions and shorter hours. More children were drawn into the mills, and native-born women were increasingly replaced by the incoming flood of Irish and other immigrants. A few highly skilled women imported from Scotland were sufficiently well paid to save a portion of their earnings and to use their jobs in the mills to improve their lot,[20] but thousands of unskilled immigrant women endured the long hours and low pay of the New England textile mills and of the sweat shops of New York and Philadelphia. By 1865, New York City alone had nearly 75,000 women workers struggling at the edge of poverty. Consequently, prostitution was extremely widespread.[21]

In "Working Class Women in the Gilded Age," Daniel J. Walkowitz examines a specific group of mid-nineteenth-century mill girls, the cotton textile workers of Cohoes in upstate New York. As elsewhere, the Irish and to a lesser degree the French Canadians were displacing native-born women workers. Walkowitz traces the ways in which work in the mills functioned in the life cycles of women of different ethnic groups and emphasizes the way in which patterns of marriage and family structure varied along ethnic lines. Although mill girls shared in their encounter with the "Dark Satanic Mills," their response to this situation and its effect upon their lives can only be fully understood in relation to the ethnic differences that characterized the society in which they lived and worked.[22]

Throughout the century, a minority of women moved outside the confines of their middle-class homes into the vast array of reform movements that graced the nineteenth-century scene. Early in the century, they became involved in the work of a growing number of benevolent societies, and by the 1840s the outlines of "the woman movement" were clear. American feminism was part of the general ferment of humanitarian reform that appeared in the ante-bellum period. Religious enthusiasm attracted increasing numbers of women to anti-slavery, temperance, pacifism, prison reform, and other causes of these years.[23]

Although women constituted a majority of the supporters of abolition and temperance, they were generally denied leadership positions within these movements and often found men objecting to their activity on the ground that it was inappropriate for women to speak publicly. Even among the radical abolitionists the "woman question" was a source of contention that split the movement.[24]

Criticism of women who would assume "the place and tone of man as a public reformer" prompted Sarah Grimké to write her *Letters on the Equality of the Sexes* in defense of her reform activities. Other women reformers considered separate action to secure civil and political rights equal to those of men. After being barred from taking their seats at the World Anti-Slavery Convention in 1840 simply because of their sex, Lucretia Mott and Elizabeth Cady Stanton moved increasingly toward a more vigorous assertion of women's rights. In 1848 they called together a convention at Seneca Falls, New York, which issued its own declaration of independence proclaiming that "all men and women are created equal." This launched the struggle "to secure to themselves their sacred right to the elective franchise."

Although the Civil War raised feminists' expectations of success in their battle for the vote, the passage of the Fifteenth Amendment granting the right to vote to black men created a crisis in feminist ranks. Women had contributed in many ways to the Northern war effort.[25] Mary Livermore was one of the leaders of the United States Sanitary Commission that employed thousands of women who distributed food and medical supplies; Dorothea Dix served as the superintendent of women nurses for the Army; and Elizabeth Stanton and Susan B. Anthony formed the National Women's Loyal League to support the Thirteenth Amendment that abolished slavery. Because of the work of these women and others such as "Mother" Bickerdyke and Harriet Tubman, feminists assumed that reformers would rally to the cause of woman suffrage. However, most Radical Republicans, who felt that black male suffrage was vital for the freedmen, thought that tying it to woman suffrage would mean inevitable defeat. Although Northern Democrats mocked woman suffrage and tried to use it along with the shibboleth of miscegenation to defeat the Fifteenth Amendment, most feminists refused to sacrifice woman suffrage to the cause of the black male. They consequently broke with those who insisted that it was "the Negro's hour."[26]

Subsequently the suffrage movement split into two groups. The National Woman Suffrage Association, led by Stanton and Anthony, concerned itself with a variety of reform causes and decidedly was the more radical of the two groups. The more conservative American Woman Suffrage Association, headed by Lucy Stone and her husband Henry Blackwell, stuck more closely to the single issue of the vote. In subsequent years, both groups agitated for woman suffrage with little success. As William L. O'Neill shows in "In the Beginning," other issues related to the Beecher–Tilton scandal and Stanton's support of the notorious advocate of free love, Victoria Woodhull, contributed to this rift in the movement and held serious implications for its future. In contrast to historians who have emphasized the importance of economic change and the rise of liberalism and status incongruity in generating "the women's movement" in the nineteenth century, O'Neill relates its emergence to the relatively recent appearance of the "modern conjugal family." Although he probably overemphasizes the conservative nature of feminism, O'Neill makes clear the way in which the feminists' ambivalent attitude toward the Victorian image of true womanhood limited the development of their ideology.[27]

Undoubtedly most women reformers were at best "social feminists" who built their reform activities upon the idea of women's moral superiority, and limited their efforts to reforms such as social purity and temperance, which were designed to relieve women and society of the worst consequences of vulgar masculinity.[28] Even when women did secure the vote, as they did in Wyoming in 1869, it was often the product of social forces over which women in general, and the Eastern feminist movement in particular, had little control. The suffrage victory in Wyoming was the product of an effort to re-establish Eastern ideas of order, refinement, and culture in the West.[29]

Thus even the success of woman suffrage in the western states, which were the first to allow women to vote, reaffirmed the pervasiveness of the Victorian image of woman as the guardian of culture and civilization. Throughout this entire period, most Americans, men and women, treated feminist demands with apathy or disgust. In his book *Sex and Education*, E.M. Clarke argued that college education would "desex" women. Opponents of equal suffrage insisted that it would undermine the family and endanger the entire social order. Women such as Eliza Francis Andrews agreed that a woman's "business is to refine and elevate society . . . her mission is moral rather than intellectual, domestic, rather than political."[30] The feminine intellect was deemed incapable of dealing with civic affairs. Until the twentieth century, the advocates of woman suffrage scored few successes because the opposition of their own sex encouraged the hostility of men.

NOTES

1. The phrase "take off" originated in W.W. Rostow's widely read and widely criticized book, *The Stages of Economic Growth: A Non-Communist Manifesto* (Cambridge: The University Press, 1960). For brief introductions to the economic history of this period, *see* Stuart Bruchey, *The Roots of American Economic*

Growth, 1607–1861: An Essay in Social Causation (New York: Harper & Row, 1965); and Douglas C. North, *Growth and Welfare in the American Past: A New Economic History* (Englewood Cliffs, N.J.: Prentice-Hall, 1966).

2. The findings of these studies are summarized in Stephan Thernstrom, *The Other Bostonians: Poverty and Progress in the American Metropolis, 1880–1970* (Cambridge, Mass.: Harvard University Press, 1973).

3. David Donald, *Lincoln Reconsidered: Essays on the Civil War Era* (New York: Vintage Books, 1961), p. 223. *See also* Rowland Berthoff, *An Unsettled People: Social Order and Disorder in American History* (New York: Harper & Row, 1971).

4. Berthoff, *An Unsettled People*, p. 204. *See also* William E. Bridges, "Family Patterns and Social Values in America, 1825–1875," *American Quarterly* 17 (Spring 1965): 3–11; and Anthony N.B. Garvan, "Effects of Technology on Domestic Life, 1830–1880," in *Technology in Western Civilization*, vol. 1, Melvin Kransberg and Carroll Pursell, Jr., eds. (New York: Oxford University Press, 1967), pp. 546–59.

5. William R. Taylor and Christopher Lasch, "Two 'Kindred Spirits': Sorority and Family in New England, 1839–1846," *New England Quarterly* 36 (March 1963): 23–41.

6. Although Lerner concentrates upon the Northeast and excludes the South from her analysis, an unpublished paper, "The Women of Prince Edward County" by William G. Shade, indicates that even in the Virginia Piedmont a significant number of women worked in the flour mills, tobacco mills, and other manufacturing establishments and lived a life style that little resembled that of the Southern lady.

7. *See* three excellent articles by Barbara Welter: "The Cult of True Womanhood: 1820–1860," *American Quarterly* 18 (Summer 1966): 151–74; "Anti-Intellectualism and the American Woman, 1800–1860," *Mid-America* 48 (October 1966): 258–70; "The Feminization of American Religion: 1800–1860," in *Insights and Parallels: Problems and Issues of American Social History*, William L. O'Neill, ed. (Minneapolis: Burgess Publishing Company, 1973), pp. 305–55.

8. Mary P. Ryan, *Womanhood in America from Colonial Times to the Present* (New York: New Viewpoints, 1975), p. 161. *See also* Ben Barker-Benfield, "The Spermatic Economy: A Nineteenth-Century View of Sexuality," *Feminist Studies* 1 (Summer 1972): 45–74; John S. and Robin M. Haller, *The Physician and Female Sexuality in Nineteenth Century America* (Urbana: University of Illinois Press, 1974); Raymond Lee Muncy, *Sex and Marriage in Utopian Communities: Nineteenth Century America* (Bloomington: University of Indiana Press, 1974); Charles E. Rosenberg, "Sexuality, Class and Role in 19th-Century America," *American Quarterly* 25 (May 1973): 131–53; and Carroll Smith-Rosenberg and Charles Rosenberg, "The Female Animal: Medical and Biological Views of Women in Nineteenth-Century America," *The Journal of American History* 60 (September 1973): 332–56.

9. *The Southern Lady: From Pedestal to Politics, 1830–1930* (Chicago: University of Chicago Press, 1970).

10. Quoted in Rollin G. Osterweis, *Romanticism and Nationalism in the Old South* (New Haven: Yale University Press, 1949), p. 134. The subject of miscegenation is detailed in James Hugo Johnson, *Race Relations in Virginia and Miscegenation in the South, 1776–1860* (Amherst: University of Massachusetts Press, 1970).

11. Scott, *The Southern Lady*, pp. 81–102; H.E. Sterkx, *Partners in Rebellion: Alabama Women in the Civil War* (Teaneck, N.J.: Fairleigh Dickinson University Press, 1970); Bell Irvin Wiley, *Confederate Women* (Westport, Conn.: Greenwood Press, 1975); and Mary Elizabeth Massey, *Bonnet Brigades* (New York: Alfred A. Knopf, 1966).

12. Leon Litwack, *North of Slavery* (Chicago: University of Chicago Press, 1961); Theodore Hershberg, "Free Blacks in Antebellum Philadelphia: A Study of Ex-Slaves, Freeborn, and Socioeconomic Decline," *Journal of Social History* 5 (Winter 1971–72): 183–209; Carl Oblinger, "Alms for Oblivion: The Making of a Black Underclass in Southeastern Pennsylvania, 1780–1860," in *The Ethnic Experience in Pennsylvania,* John F. Bodnar, ed. (Lewisburg: Bucknell University Press, 1973), pp. 94–119; Ira Berlin, *Slaves Without Masters: The Free Negro in the Antebellum South* (New York: Pantheon Books, 1975).

13. Ronald G. Walters has written two articles related to this subject: "The Family and Ante-bellum Reform: An Interpretation," *Societas* 3 (Summer 1973): 223–34; and "The Erotic South: Civilization and Sexuality in American Abolitionism," *American Quarterly* 25 (May 1973): 177–201.

14. The classic study of the subject and one which, while vulnerable to criticism, remains extremely useful is E. Franklin Frazier, *The Negro Family in the United States* (Chicago: University of Chicago Press, 1939). For a recent statement by a black feminist *see* Angela Davis, "Reflections on the Black Woman's Role in the Community of Slaves," *Black Scholar* 3 (December 1971): 3–15. The policy implications of this historical controversy are the subject of Lee Rainwater and William L. Yancey, *The Moynihan Report and the Politics of Controversy* (Cambridge, Mass.: M.I.T. Press, 1967).

15. George P. Rawick, *From Sundown to Sunup* (Westport, Conn.: Greenwood Press, 1972); John W. Blassingame, *The Slave Community: Plantation Life in the Ante-bellum South* (New York: Oxford University Press, 1972); Robert W. Fogel and Stanley L. Engerman, *Time on the Cross: The Economics of American Negro Slavery* (Boston: Little, Brown, 1974); Eugene Genovese, *Roll Jordan Roll: The World the Slaves Made* (New York: Pantheon Books, 1974); Herbert G. Gutman, *Slavery and the Numbers Game: A Critique of "Time on the Cross"* (Urbana: University of Illinois Press, 1975).

16. Robert H. Abzug, "The Black Family During Reconstruction," in *Key Issues in the Afro-American Experience,* Nathan I. Huggins, Martin Kilson, and Daniel M. Fox, eds. (New York: Harcourt Brace Jovanovich, 1971); Herbert G. Gutman, "Le Phenomene Invisible," *Annales: Economies, Societies, Civilisations* (July–October 1972): 1197–1218; Elizabeth H. Pleck, "The Two-Parent Household: Black Family Structure in Late Nineteenth-Century Boston," *Journal of Social History* 6 (Fall 1972): 1–31; C. Peter Ripley, "The Black Family in Transition: Louisiana, 1860–1865," *Journal of Southern History* 41 (August 1975): 369–80.

17. William D. Andrews and Deborah C. Andrews, "Technology and the Housewife in Nineteenth-Century America," *Women's Studies* 2 (Fall 1974): 309–28.

18. Caroline Ware, *Early New England Cotton Manufacture* (Boston: Houghton Mifflin, 1931); Howard M. Gitelman, "The Waltham System and the Coming of the Irish," *Labor History* 8 (Fall 1967): 227–53.

19. *Memories of a New England Girlhood* (Boston: Houghton Mifflin, 1889), p. 157.

20. Ray Ginger, "Labor in a Massachusetts Cotton Mill, 1853–1860," *Business History Review* 28 (March 1954): 67–81.

21. Allan Nevins, *The Emergence of Modern America, 1865–1878* (New York: Macmillan, 1927); David J. Pivar, *Purity Crusade: Sexual Morality and Social Control, 1868–1900* (Westport, Conn.: Greenwood Press, 1973), 30–32; David Kaser, "Nashville's Women of Pleasure in 1860," *Tennessee Historical Quarterly* 23 (December 1964): 379–82; Gutman, *Slavery and the Numbers Game,* pp. 157–62.

22. Cf. Frank L. Mott, "Portrait of an American Mill Town: Demographic Response in Mid-Nineteenth Century Warren, Rhode Island," *Population Studies* 26 (March 1972): 147–57; Virginia Yans-McLaughlin, "Patterns of Work and Family Organization: Buffalo's Italians," *Journal of Interdisciplinary History* 2 (Autumn 1971): 299–314; and Rowland Berthoff, "The Social Order of the Anthracite Region, 1825–1902," *Pennsylvania Magazine of History and Biography* 89 (1965): 261–91.

23. Keith Melder, "Ladies Bountiful: Organized Women's Benevolence in Early 19th-Century America," *New York History* 48 (July 1967): 231–55; Robert Riegel, *American Feminists* (Lawrence: University of Kansas Press, 1963); Alice S. Rossi, "Social Roots of the Woman's Movement in America," in *The Feminist Papers: From Adams to de Beauvoir,* Alice S. Rossi, ed. (New York: Columbia University Press, 1973), pp. 241–81.

24. Gerda Lerner, *The Grimké Sisters from South Carolina: Rebels Against Slavery* (Boston: Houghton Mifflin, 1967); Aileen S. Kraditor, *Means and Ends in American Abolitionism: Garrison and His Critics on Strategy and Tactics, 1834–1850* (New York: Pantheon Books, 1969), pp. 39–77.

25. Massey, *Bonnet Brigades, passim;* Ann Douglas Wood, "The War Within a War: Women Nurses in the Union Army," *Civil War History* 18 (Sept. 1972): 197–212.

26. James McPherson, "Abolitionists, Woman Suffrage, and the Negro, 1865–1869," *Mid-America* 47 (January 1965): 40–47; Willis F. Dunbar and William G. Shade, "The Black Man Gains the Vote: The Centennial of 'Impartial Suffrage' in Michigan," *Michigan History* 56 (Spring 1972): 53–54; Forrest Wood, *Black Scare: The Racist Response to Emancipation and Reconstruction* (Berkeley: University of California Press, 1970).

27. Ellen Du Bois has disputed O'Neill's view in an excellent paper, "The Nineteenth Century Woman Suffrage Movement: Suffrage as a Total Ideology." (Presented to the Organization of American Historians Meeting, 1975.)

28. Carroll Smith-Rosenberg, "Beauty, the Beast and the Militant Woman: A Case Study of Sex Roles and Social Stress in Jacksonian America," *American Quarterly* 23 (October 1971): 562–84; Christopher Lasch, "Emancipated Women," *New York Review of Books* (July 13, 1967): 28–32; and Pivar, *Purity Crusade, passim.*

29. Alan P. Grimes, *The Puritan Ethic and Woman Suffrage* (New York: Oxford University Press, 1967) pp. 3–77; T.A. Larson, "Emancipating the Wests' Dolls, Vassals and Hopeless Drudges: The Origins of Woman Suffrage in the West," in *Essays in Western History in Honor of T.A. Larson,* Roger Daniels, ed. (Laramie: University of Wyoming Publications, 1971).

30. Quoted in Massey, *Bonnet Brigades,* p. 359. Cf. Smith-Rosenberg and Rosenberg, "The Female Animal," *passim.*

7

The Lady and the Mill Girl:
Changes in the Status of Women
in the Age of Jackson

Gerda Lerner

The period 1800–1840 is one in which decisive changes occurred in the status of American women. It has remained surprisingly unexplored. With the exception of a recent, unpublished dissertation by Keith Melder and the distinctive work of Elisabeth Dexter, there is a dearth of descriptive material and an almost total absence of interpretation.[1] Yet the period offers essential clues to an understanding of later institutional developments, particularly the shape and nature of the women's rights movement. This analysis will consider the economic, political and social status of women and examine the changes in each area. It will also attempt an interpretation of the ideological shifts which occurred in American society concerning the "proper" role for women.

Periodization always offers difficulties. It seemed useful here, for purposes of comparison, to group women's status before 1800 roughly under the "colonial" heading and ignore the transitional and possibly

From *American Studies Journal* X (Spring 1969). Reprinted by permission.

Research for this article was facilitated by a research grant provided by Long Island University, Brooklyn, N.Y., which is gratefully acknowledged.

The generalizations in this article are based on extensive research in primary sources, including letters and manuscripts of the following women: Elizabeth Cady Stanton, Susan B. Anthony, Abby Kelley, Lucretia Mott, Lucy Stone, Sarah and Angelina Grimke, Maria Weston Chapman, Lydia Maria Child and Betsey Cowles. Among the organizational records consulted were those of the Boston Female Anti-Slavery Society, the Philadelphia Female Anti-Slavery Society, Anti-Slavery Conventions of American Women, all the Woman's Rights Conventions prior to 1870 and the records of various female charitable organizations.

atypical shifts which occurred during the American Revolution and the early period of nationhood. Also, regional differences were largely ignored. The South was left out of consideration entirely because its industrial development occurred later.

The status of colonial women has been well studied and described and can briefly be summarized for comparison with the later period. Throughout the colonial period there was a marked shortage of women, which varied with the regions and always was greatest in the frontier areas.[2] This (from the point of view of women) favorable sex ratio enhanced their status and position. The Puritan world view regarded idleness as sin; life in an underdeveloped country made it absolutely necessary that each member of the community perform an economic function. Thus work for women, married or single, was not only approved, it was regarded as a civic duty. Puritan town councils expected single girls, widows and unattached women to be self-supporting and for a long time provided needy spinsters with parcels of land. There was no social sanction against married women working; on the contrary, wives were expected to help their husbands in their trade and won social approval for doing extra work in or out of the home. Needy children, girls as well as boys, were indentured or apprenticed and were expected to work for their keep.

The vast majority of women worked within their homes, where their labor produced most articles needed for the family. The entire colonial production of cloth and clothing and partially that of shoes was in the hands of women. In addition to these occupations, women were found in many different kinds of employment. They were butchers, silversmiths, gunsmiths, upholsterers. They ran mills, plantations, tan yards, shipyards and every kind of shop, tavern and boarding house. They were gate keepers, jail keepers, sextons, journalists, printers, "doctoresses," apothecaries, midwives, nurses and teachers. Women acquired their skills the same way as did the men, through apprenticeship training, frequently within their own families.[3]

Absence of a dowry, ease of marriage and remarriage and a more lenient attitude of the law with regard to woman's property rights were manifestations of the improved position of wives in the colonies. Under British common law, marriage destroyed a woman's contractual capacity; she could not sign a contract even with the consent of her husband. But colonial authorities were more lenient toward the wife's property rights by protecting her dower rights in her husband's property, granting her personal clothing and upholding pre-nuptial contracts between husband and wife. In the absence of the husband, colonial courts granted women "femme sole" rights, which enabled them to conduct their husband's business, sign contracts and sue. The relative social freedom of women and the esteem in which they were held was commented upon by most early foreign travelers in America.[4]

But economic, legal and social status tell only part of the story. Colonial society as a whole was hierarchical, and rank and standing in society depended on the position of the men. Women did not play a determining role in the ranking pattern; they took their position in society through the men of their own family or the men they married. In other words, they participated in the hierarchy only as daughters and wives, not as individuals. Similarly, their occupations were, by and large, merely auxiliary, designed to contribute to family income, enhance their husbands' business or continue it in case of widowhood. The self-supporting spinsters were certainly the exception. The underlying assumption of colonial society was that women ought to occupy an inferior and subordinate position. The settlers had brought this assumption with them from Europe; it was reflected in their legal concepts, their willingness to exclude women from political life, their discriminatory educational practices. What is remarkable is the extent to which this felt inferiority of women was constantly challenged and modified under the impact of environment, frontier conditions and a favorable sex ratio.

By 1840 all of American society had changed. The Revolution had substituted an egalitarian ideology for the hierarchical concepts of colonial life. Privilege based on ability rather than inherited status, upward mobility for all groups of society and unlimited opportunities for individual self-fulfillment had become ideological goals, if not always realities. For men, that is; women were, by tacit consensus, excluded from the new democracy. Indeed their actual situation had in many respects deteriorated. While, as wives, they had benefitted from increasing wealth, urbanization and industrialization, their role as economic producers and as political members of society differed sharply from that of men. Women's work outside of the home no longer met with social approval; on the contrary, with two notable exceptions, it was condemned. Many business and professional occupations formerly open to women were now closed, many others restricted as to training and advancement. The entry of large numbers of women into low status, low pay and low skill industrial work had fixed such work by definition as "woman's work." Women's political status, while legally unchanged, had deteriorated relative to the advances made by men. At the same time the genteel lady of fashion had become a model of American femininity and the definition of "woman's proper sphere" seemed narrower and more confined than ever.

Within the scope of this article only a few of these changes can be more fully explained. The professionalization of medicine and its impact on women may serve as a typical example of what occurred in all the professions.

In colonial America there were no medical schools, no medical journals, few hospitals and few laws pertaining to the practice of the healing arts. Clergymen and governors, barbers, quacks, apprentices and women practiced medicine. Most practitioners acquired their credentials by reading Paracelsus and Galen and serving an apprenticeship with an established practitioner. Among the semi-trained "physics," surgeons, and healers, the occasional "doctoress" was fully accepted and frequently well rewarded. County records of all the colonies contain references to the work of the female physicians. There was even a female Army surgeon, a Mrs. Allyn, who served during King Philip's war. Plantation records mention by name several slave women who were granted special privileges because of their useful service as midwives and "doctoresses."[5]

The period of the professionalization of American medicine dates from 1765, when Dr. William Shippen began his lectures on midwifery in Philadelphia. The founding of medical faculties in several colleges, the standardization of training requirements, and the proliferation of medical societies intensified during the last quarter of the eighteenth century. The American Revolution dramatized the need for trained medical personnel, afforded first hand battlefield experience to a number of surgeons and brought increasing numbers of semi-trained practitioners in contact with the handful of European-trained surgeons working in the military hospitals. This was an experience from which women were excluded. The resulting interest in improved medical training, the gradual appearance of graduates of medical colleges and the efforts of medical societies led to licensing legislation. In 1801 Maryland required all medical practitioners to be licensed; in 1806 New York enacted a similar law, providing for an examination before a commission. By the late 1820's all states except three had set up licensing requirements. Since most of these laws stipulated attendance at a medical college as one of the prerequisites for licensing, women were automatically excluded.[6] By the 1830's the few established female practitioners who might have continued their practice in the old ways had probably died out. Whatever vested interest they had had was too weak to assert itself against the new profession.

This process of preemption of knowledge, institutionalization of the profession and legitimation of its claims by law and public acceptance is standard for the professionalization of the sciences, as George Daniels has pointed out.[7] It inevitably results in the elimination of fringe elements from the profession. It is interesting to note that women had been pushed out of the medical profession in sixteenth-century Europe by a similar process.[8] Once the public had come to accept licensing and college training as guarantees of up-to-date practice, the outsider, no matter how well qualified by years of experience, stood no chance in the competition. Women were the casualties of medical professionalization.

In the field of midwifery the results were similar, but the process was more complicated. Women had held a virtual monopoly in the profession in colonial America. In 1646 a man was prosecuted in Maine for practicing as a midwife.[9] There are many records of well trained midwives with diplomas from European institutions working in the colonies. In most of the colonies midwives were licensed, registered and required to pass an examination before a board. When Dr. Shippen announced his pioneering lectures on midwifery, he did it to "combat the widespread popular prejudice against the man-midwife" and because he considered most midwives ignorant and improperly trained.[10]

Yet he invited "those women who love virtue enough, to own their Ignorance, and apply for instruction" to attend his lectures, offering as an inducement the assurance that female pupils would be taught privately. It is not known if any midwives availed themselves of the opportunity.[11]

Technological advances, as well as scientific, worked against the interests of female midwives. In sixteenth-century Europe the invention and use of the obstetrical forceps had for three generations been the well-kept secret of the Chamberlen family and had greatly enhanced their medical practice. Hugh Chamberlen was forced by circumstances to sell the secret to the Medical College in Amsterdam, which in turn transmitted the precious knowledge to licensed physicians only. By the time the use of the instrument became widespread it had become associated with male physicians and midwives. Similarly in America, introduction of the obstetrical forceps was associated with the practice of male midwives and served to their advantage. By the end of the eighteenth century a number of male physicians advertised their practice of midwifery. Shortly thereafter female midwives also resorted to advertising, probably in an effort to meet the competition. By the early nineteenth century male physicians had virtually monopolized the practice of midwifery on the Eastern seaboard. True to the generally delayed economic development in the Western frontier regions, female midwives continued to work on the frontier until a much later period. It is interesting to note that the concepts of "propriety" shifted with the prevalent practice. In seventeenth-century Maine the attempt of a man to act as a midwife was considered outrageous and illegal; in mid-nineteenth century America the suggestion that women should train as midwives and physicians was considered equally outrageous and improper.[12]

Professionalization, similar to that in medicine with the elimination of women from the upgraded profession, occurred in the field of law. Before 1750, when law suits were commonly brought to the courts by the plaintiffs themselves or by deputies without specialized legal training, women as well as men could and did act as "attorneys-in-fact." When the law became a paid profession and trained lawyers took over litigation, women disappeared from the court scene for over a century.[13]

A similar process of shrinking opportunities for women developed in business and in the retail trades. There were fewer female storekeepers and business women in the 1830's than there had been in colonial days. There was also a noticeable shift in the kind of merchandise handled by them. Where previously women could be found running almost every kind of retail shop, after 1830 they were mostly found in businesses which served women only.[14]

The only fields in which professionalization did not result in the elimination of women from the upgraded profession were nursing and teaching. Both were characterized by a severe shortage of labor. Nursing lies outside the field of this inquiry since it did not become an organized profession until after the Civil War. Before then it was regarded peculiarly as a woman's occupation, although some of the hospitals and the Army during wars employed male nurses. These bore the stigma of low skill, low status and low pay. Generally, nursing was regarded as simply an extension of the unpaid services performed by the housewife—a characteristic attitude that haunts the profession to this day.

Education seems, at first glance, to offer an entirely opposite pattern from that of the other professions. In colonial days women had taught "Dame schools" and grade schools during summer sessions. Gradually, as educational opportunities for girls expanded, they advanced just a step ahead of their students. Professionalization of teaching occurred between 1820–1860, a period marked by a sharp increase in the number of women teachers. The spread of female seminaries, academies and normal schools provided new opportunities for the training and employment of female teachers.

This trend which runs counter to that found in the other professions can be accounted for by the fact that women filled a desperate need created by the challenge of the common schools, the ever-increasing size of the student body and the westward growth of the nation. America was committed to educating its children in public schools, but it was insistent on doing so as cheaply as possible. Women were available in great numbers and they were willing to work cheaply. The result was another ideological adaptation: in the very period when the gospel of the home as woman's only proper sphere was preached most loudly, it was discovered that women were the natural teachers of youth, could do the job better than men and were to be preferred for such employment. This was always provided, of course, that they would work at the proper wage differential—30–50% of the wages paid male teachers was considered appropriate. The result was that in 1888 in the country as a whole 63% of all teachers were women, while the figure for the cities only was 90.04%.[15]

It appeared in the teaching field, as it would in industry, that role expectations were adaptable provided the inferior status group filled a social need. The inconsistent and peculiar patterns of employment of black labor in the present-day market bear out the validity of this generalization.

There was another field in which the labor of women was appreciated and which they were urged to enter—industry. From Alexander Hamilton to Matthew Carey and Tench Coxe, advocates of industrialization sang the praises of the working girl and advanced arguments in favor of her employment. The social benefits of female labor particularly stressed were those bestowed upon her family, who now no longer had to support her. Working girls were "thus happily preserved from idleness and its attendant vices and crimes" and the whole community benefitted from their increased purchasing power.[16]

American industrialization, which occurred in an underdeveloped economy with a shortage of labor, depended on the labor of women and children. Men were occupied with agricultural work and were not available or willing to enter the factories. This accounts for the special features of the early development of the New England textile industry: the relatively high wages, the respectability of the job and relatively high status of the mill girls, the patriarchal character of the model factory towns and the temporary mobility of women workers from farm to factory and back again to farm. All this was characteristic only of a limited area and of a period of about two decades. By the late 1830's the romance had worn off; immigration had supplied a strongly competitive, permanent work force willing to work for subsistence wages; early efforts at trade union organization had been shattered and mechanization had turned semiskilled factory labor into unskilled labor. The process led to the replacement of the New England-born farm girls by immigrants in the mills and was accompanied by a loss of status and respectability for female workers.

The lack of organized social services during periods of depression drove ever greater numbers of women into the labor market. At first, inside the factories distinctions between men's and women's jobs were blurred. Men and women were assigned to machinery on the basis of local need. But as more women entered industry the limited number of occupations open to them tended to increase competition among them, thus lowering pay standards. Generally, women regarded their work as temporary and hesitated to invest in apprenticeship training, because they expected to marry and raise families. Thus they remained untrained, casual labor and were soon, by custom, relegated to the lowest paid, least skilled jobs. Long hours, overwork and poor working conditions would characterize women's work in industry for almost a century.[17]

Another result of industrialization was in increasing differences in life styles between women of different classes. When female occupations, such as carding, spinning and weaving, were transferred from home to factory, the poorer women followed their traditional work and became industrial workers. The women of the middle and upper classes could use their newly gained time for leisure pursuits: they became ladies. And a small but significant group among them chose to prepare themselves for professional careers by advanced education. This group would prove to be the most vocal and troublesome in the near future.

As class distinctions sharpened, social attitudes toward women became polarized. The image of "the lady" was elevated to the accepted ideal of femininity toward which all women would strive. In this formulation of values lower class women were simply ignored. The actual lady was, of course, nothing new on the American scene; she had been present ever since colonial days. What was new in the 1830's was the cult of the lady, her elevation to a status symbol. The advancing prosperity of the early nineteenth century made it possible for middle class women to aspire to the status formerly reserved for upper class women. The "cult of true womanhood" of the 1830's became a vehicle for such aspirations. Mass circulation newspapers and magazines made it possible to teach every woman how to elevate the status of her family by setting "proper" standards of behavior, dress and literary tastes. *Godey's Lady's Book* and innumerable gift books and tracts of the period all preach the same gospel of "true womanhood"—piety, purity, domesticity.[18] Those unable to reach the goal of becoming ladies were to be satisfied with the lesser goal—acceptance of their "proper place" in the home.

It is no accident that the slogan "woman's place is in the home" took on a certain aggressiveness and shrillness precisely at the time when increasing numbers of poorer women *left* their homes to become factory workers. Working women were not a fit subject for the concern of publishers and mass media writers. Idleness, once a disgrace in the eyes of society, had become a status symbol. Thorstein Veblen, one of the earliest and sharpest commentators on the subject, observed that it had become almost the sole social function of the lady "to put in evidence her economic unit's ability to pay." She was "a means of conspicuously unproductive expenditure," devoted to displaying her husband's wealth.[19] Just as the cult of white womanhood in the South served to preserve a labor and social system based on race distinctions, so did the cult of the lady in an egalitarian society serve as a means of preserving class distinctions. Where class distinctions were not so great, as on the frontier, the position of women was closer to what it had been in colonial days; their economic contribution was more highly valued, their opportunities were less restricted and their positive participation in community life was taken for granted.

In the urbanized and industrialized Northeast the life experience of middle class women was different in almost every respect from that of the lower class women. But there was one thing the society lady and the mill girl had in common—they were equally disfranchised and isolated from the vital centers of power. Yet the political status of women had not actually deteriorated. With very few exceptions women had neither voted nor stood for office during the colonial period. Yet the spread of the franchise to ever wider groups of white males during the Jacksonian age, the removal of property restrictions, the increasing numbers of immigrants who acquired access to the franchise, made the gap between these new enfranchised voters and the disfranchised women more obvious. Quite naturally, educated and propertied women felt this deprivation more keenly. Their own career expectations had been encouraged by widening educational opportunites; their consciousness of their own abilities and of their potential for power had been enhanced by their activities in the reform movements of the 1830's; the general spirit of upward mobility and venturesome entrepreneurship that pervaded the Jacksonian era was infectious. But in the late 1840's a sense of acute frustration enveloped these educated and highly spirited women. Their rising expectations had met with frustration, their hopes had been shattered; they were bitterly conscious of a relative lowering of status and a loss of position. This sense of frustration led them to action; it was one of the main factors in the rise of the woman's rights movement.[20]

The women, who in 1848 declared boldly and with considerable exaggeration that "the history of mankind is a history of repeated injuries and usurpations on the part of man toward woman, having in direct object the establishment of an absolute tyranny over her," did not speak for the truly exploited and abused working woman.[21] As a matter of fact, they were largely ignorant of her condition and, with the notable exception of Susan B. Anthony, indifferent to her fate. But they judged from the realities of their own life experience. Like most revolutionaries, they were not the most downtrodden but rather the most status deprived group. Their frustrations and traditional isolation from political power funneled their discontent into fairly utopian declarations and immature organizational means. They would learn better in the long, hard decades of practical struggle. Yet it is their initial emphasis on the legal and political "disabilities" of women which has provided the framework for most of the historical work on women. For almost a hundred years sympathetic historians have told the story of women in America from the feminist viewpoint. Their tendency has been to reason from the position of middle class women to a generalization concerning all American women. This distortion has obscured the actual and continuous contributions of women to American life.[22] To avoid such a distortion, any valid generalization concerning American women after the 1830's should reflect a recognition of class stratification.

For lower class women the changes brought by industrialization were actually advantageous, offering income and advancement opportunities, however limited, and a chance for participation in the ranks of organized labor. They, by and large, tended to join men in their struggle for economic advancement and became increasingly concerned with economic gains and protective labor legislation. Middle and upperclass women, on the other hand, reacted to actual and fancied status deprivation by increasing militancy and the formation of organizations for women's rights, by which they meant especially legal and property rights.

The four decades preceding the Seneca Falls Convention were decisive in the history of American women. They brought an actual deterioration in the economic opportunities open to women, a relative deterioration in their political status and a rising level of expectation and subsequent frustration in a privileged elite group of educated women. The ideology still pervasive in our present-day society regarding woman's "proper" role was formed in those decades. Later, under the impact of feminist attacks this ideology would grow defensive and attempt to bolster its claims by appeals to universality and pretentions to a history dating back to antiquity or, at least, to *The Mayflower.* Women, we are told, have always played a restricted and subordinate role in American life. In fact, however, it was in mid-nineteenth-century America that the ideology of "woman's place is in the home" changed from being an accurate description of existing reality into a myth. It became the "feminine mystique"—a longing for a lost, archaic world of agrarian family self-sufficiency, updated by woman's consumer function and the misunderstood dicta of Freudian psychology.

The decades 1800–1840 also provide the clues to an understanding of the institutional shape of the later women's organizations. These would be led by middle class women whose self-image, life experience and ideology had largely been fashioned and influenced by these early, transitional years. The concerns of middle class women—property rights, the franchise and moral uplift—would dominate the women's rights movement. But side by side with it, and at times cooperating with it, would grow a number of organizations serving the needs of working women.

American women were the largest disfranchised group in the nation's history, and they retained this position longer than any other group. Although they found ways of making their influence felt continuously, not only as individuals but as organized groups, power eluded them. The mill girl and the lady, both born in the age of Jackson, would not gain access to power until they learned to cooperate, each for her own separate interests. It would take almost six decades before they would find common ground. The issue around which they finally would unite and push their movement to victory was the "impractical and utopian" demand raised at Seneca Falls—the means to power in American society—female suffrage.

NOTES

1. Keith E. Melder, "The Beginnings of the Women's Rights Movement in the United States: 1800–1840" (Diss. Yale, 1963). Elisabeth A. Dexter, *Colonial Women of Affairs: Women in Business and Professions in America before 1776* (Boston, 1931); *Career Women of America: 1776–1840* (Francestown, N.H., 1950).

2. Herbert Moller, "Sex Composition and Corresponding Culture Patterns of Colonial America," *William and Mary Quarterly*, Ser. 3, II (April, 1945), 113–153.

3. The summary of the status of colonial women is based on the following sources: Mary Benson, *Women in 18th Century America: A Study of Opinion and Social Usage* (New York, 1935); Arthur Calhoun, *A Social History of the American Family*, 3 vols. (Cleveland, 1918); Dexter, *Colonial Women;* Dexter, *Career Women;* Edmund S. Morgan, *Virginians at Home: Family Life in the 18th Century* (Williamsburg, 1952); Julia C. Spruill, *Women's Life and Work in the Southern Colonies* (Chapel Hill, 1938).

4. E. M. Boatwright, "The political and legal status of women in Georgia: 1783–1860," *Georgia Historical Quarterly*, XXV (April, 1941). Richard B. Morris, *Studies in the History of American Law* (New York, 1930), Chap. 3. A summary of travelers' comments on American women may be found in: Jane Mesick, *The English Traveler in America: 1785–1835* (New York, 1922), 83–99.

5. For facts on colonial medicine the following sources were consulted: Wyndham B. Blanton, *Medicine in Virginia*, 3 vols. (Richmond, 1930); N. S. Davis, M.D.,

History of Medical Education and Institutions in the United States. . . . (Chicago, 1851); Dexter, *Career Women;* K. C. Hurd-Mead, M.D., *A History of Women in Medicine: from the earliest Times to the Beginning of the 19th Century* (Haddam, Conn., 1938); Geo. W. Norris, *The Early History of Medicine in Philadelphia* (Philadephia, 1886); Joseph M. Toner, *Contributions to the Annals of Medical Progress in the United States before and during the War of Independence* (Washington, D.C., 1874). The citation regarding Mrs. Allyn is from Hurd-Mead, *Women in Medicine,* 487.

6. Fielding H. Garrison, M.D., *An Introduction to the History of Medicine* (Philadelphia, 1929). For licensing legislation: Davis, 88–103.

7. George Daniels, "The Professionalization of American Science: the emergent period, 1820–1860," paper delivered at the joint session of the History of Science Society and the Society of the History of Technology, San Francisco, December 28, 1965.

8. Hurd-Mead, *Women in Medicine,* 391.

9. *Ibid.,* 486.

10. Betsy E. Corner, *William Shippen Jr.: Pioneer in American Medical Education* (Philadelphia, 1951), 103.

11. *Ibid.*

12. Benjamin Lee Gordon, *Medieval and Renaissance Medicine* (New York, 1959), 689–691. Blanton, *Medicine,* II, 23–24; Hurd-Mead, *Women in Medicine,* 487–88; Annie Nathan Meyer, *Woman's Work in America* (New York, 1891). Harriot K. Hunt, M.D., *Glances and Glimpses or Fifty Years Social including Twenty Years Professional Life* (Boston, 1856), 127–140. Eleanor Flexner, *Century of Struggle: The Woman's Rights Movement in the United States* (Cambridge, Mass., 1959), 115–119.

13. Sophie H. Drinker, "Women Attorneys of Colonial Times," *Maryland Historical Society Bulletin,* LVI, No. 4 (Dec., 1961).

14. Dexter, *Colonial Women,* 34–35, 162–165.

15. Harriet W. Marr, *The Old New England Academies* (New York, 1959), Chap. 8; Thomas Woody, *A History of Women's Education in the United States,* 2 vols. (New York, 1929) H, 100–109, 458–460, 492–493.

16. Matthew Carey, *Essays on Political Economy . . .* (Philadelphia, 1822), 459.

17. The statements on women industrial workers are based on the following sources: Edith Abbot, *Women in Industry* (New York, 1910), 66–80; Edith Abbot, "Harriet Martineau and the Employment of Women in 1836," *Journal of Political Economy,* XIV (Dec., 1906), 614–626; Matthew Carey, *Miscellaneous Essays* (Philadelphia, 1830), 153–203; Helen L. Sumner, *History of Women in Industry in the United States,* in *Report on Condition of Women and Child Wage-Earners in the United States,* 19 vols. (Washington, D.C., 1910), IX. Also: Elizabeth F. Baker, *Technology and Woman's Work* (New York, 1964), Chaps. 1–5.

18. Emily Putnam, *The Lady: Studies of certain significant Phases of her History* (New York, 1910), 319–320. Barbara Welter, "The Cult of True Womanhood: 1820–1860," *American Quarterly,* XVIII, No. 2, Part I (Summer, 1966), 151–174.

19. Veblen generalized from his observations of the society of the Gilded Age and fell into the usual error of simply ignoring the lower class women, whom he dismissed as "drudges . . . fairly content with their lot," but his analysis of women's role in "conspicuous consumption" and of the function of women's fashions is

unsurpassed. For references see: Thorstein Veblen, *The Theory of the Leisure Class* (New York, 1962, first printing, 1899), 70–71, 231–232. Thorstein Veblen, "The Economic Theory of Woman's Dress," *Essays in Our Changing Order* (New York, 1934), 65–77.

20. Like most groups fighting status oppression women formulated a compensatory ideology of female superiority. Norton Mezvinsky has postulated that this was clearly expressed only in 1874; in fact this formulation appeared in the earliest speeches of Elizabeth Cady Stanton and in the speeches and resolutions of the Seneca Falls Conventions and other pre-Civil War woman's rights conventions. Rather than a main motivating force, the idea was a tactical formulation, designed to take advantage of the popularly held male belief in woman's "moral" superiority and to convince reformers that they needed the votes of women. Those middle class feminists who believed in woman's "moral" superiority exploited the concept in order to win their major goal—female equality. For references see: Norton Mezvinsky, "An Idea of Female Superiority," *Midcontinent American Studies Journal*, II, No. I (Spring, 1961), 17–26. E. C. Stanton, S. B. Anthony and M. J. Gage, eds., *A History of Woman Suffrage*, 6 vols. (New York, 1881–1922), I, 72, 479, 522, 529 and *passim*. Alan P. Grimes, *The Puritan Ethic and Woman Suffrage* (New York, 1967), Chaps. 2 and 3.

21. Stanton *et al*, *History of Woman Suffrage*, I, 70.

22. Mary R. Beard, *Woman as Force in History: A Study of Traditions and Realities* (New York, 1946).

8

"The Female Appendage": Feminine Life-Styles in America, 1820-1860

Ronald W. Hogeland

Various keen commentators such as Mary Wollstonecraft, Margaret Fuller and Simone de Beauvoir who have directed their attention to the history of womanhood have correctly observed that men have consistently usurped the initiative in defining the life-styles of the "second sex."[1] For this reason it appears futile to attempt to approach the subject of women—in any age—either by way of a "pots and pans" pseudocultural inquiry,[2] or by means of merely studying atypical women. In the former instance one falls prey to an inclination, which many historians have not avoided, of devaluating the nature of womanhood by making women invisible in a sea of domesticity. It is just because of this attitude that a score of female critics of the American scene have concluded that women have always been "a class outside of history."[3] In the other instance, it appears ineffectual to trace accurately the evolution of the American woman by alluding to nonconventional or "radical" women such as Anne Hutchinson, Mother Ann Lee, Frances Wright, or Elizabeth Cady Stanton. Here the student of history fails to avoid another trap, despite his good intention, of simply underscoring a few women's unconventional practices which are identified (often mistakenly) with feminism. This often subtle (or unconscious) form of ridiculing the atypical woman only reinforces the age-old masculine disposition not to take women seriously.

In either case—by writing as if women were invisible or absurd—the historian has not substantially come to grips with the nature of femi-

From *Civil War History* 17 (June 1971). Reprinted by permission.

ninity. To do this, one must try to relate women as fully human agents who have the capacity to choose meaningful life-styles, to concentrations of power—and hence to men. For what is evident in the American experience, from the colonial period to the present, is that "the male attitude" has been responsible for defining the dimensions of femininity and the roles which the members of the "second sex" were (and are) able to play.[4]

The point of departure for this inquiry has been rather well delineated by Janet James in her fine study, "Changing Ideas about Women in the United States, 1776–1825." James suggests that it was not until the second and third decades of the nineteenth-century that the norm for womanhood was substantially reconstituted. This development in the history of femininity, she correctly contends, received its primary impetus from the evangelical benevolent style which sanctioned certain new functions and activities for women.[5] Prior to these innovations the majority of American women had conformed to a singular mode of life which perhaps can best be equated with the pastoral image of the family portrayed by M. G. St. John de Crevecoeur in his *Letters from an American Farmer.* By the early decades of the nineteenth-century, however, the rural eighteenth-century portrait—in which the woman assumed the role of co-laborer alongside her husband on the farm or in the village store—gave way to fragmented societal functions in which a distinctive division of work was increasingly apparent.[6] This was particularly true for those women who in large numbers identified themselves with the middle and upper classes of American society. There were at least four distinctive life-styles available for these women between 1820 and 1860: "Ornamental," "Romanticized," "Evangelical" and "Radical."

The first pattern of behavior, "Ornamental Womanhood," was undoubtedly the most restrictive and conservative option. It most closely reflected the ideal of genteel white womanhood in the Old South as described by William Taylor and W. J. Cash and as lucidly analyzed by Thomas R. Drew in the *Southern Literary Messenger* in 1835 under the general title, "On the Characteristic Differences between the Sexes, and on the Position and Influence of Woman in Society."[7] This conceptualization of femininity was perpetuated by those men of upper middle class and elite origins who occupied positions of some authority in the towns of New England, in Tidewater Virginia, and in the cities along the Atlantic coast. Their disposition was typified by an Association of Gentlemen—as they referred to themselves—residing chiefly at Princeton, Philadelphia and New York who published the *Princeton Review* between 1829 and 1855.[8]

Sarah Bache Hodge of Princeton, wife of Charles Hodge, the *Review*'s editor, personified the norm for womanhood suggested by the Association. After marrying Hodge in 1822, Sarah, the niece of Dr. Caspar Wistar and the granddaughter of Benjamin Franklin, was quickly transformed from an enthusiastic and imaginative young maiden into a stately and proper wife. The transmutation was primarily achieved by the age-old masculine technique of preempting the woman's energies and time through frequent pregnancies and the consequent caring for children and a large home. This in turn left the woman with little leisure time to intrude upon her husband's professional activities. Charles Hodge pursued his prescribed male role with vigor and with more than moderate success; Sarah bore eight children before her early death in 1849. The record clearly indicates that after some initial vocational interference on the part of Sarah, Hodge was soon able to "bridle her tongue" by redirecting her attention toward motherhood. After the usual mourning period of a year, Charles Hodge married again. Indeed, this was to be expected, for it was imperative that a man of his station have someone to manage his household and tend to the mundane daily domestic tasks in order to liberate him to fulfill his masculine definition in public life.[9]

While marriage freed men to pursue their destiny, it often entrapped women and precluded alternative choices for a life-style. This was very apparent to many a young wife during the first years of marriage when she could recall vividly the freedom she enjoyed as a maiden. Alexis de Tocqueville was one of the many foreign commentators who noted with delight that these young women were "far more the mistresses of their own actions" than their European counterparts.[10] Sarah Bache, before her marriage to Charles Hodge, exemplified this portrait. She was described as "full of imagination, exceedingly enthusiastic, unconscious of self and absorbed in whatever claimed her attention."[11] She informally studied history, philosophy, chemistry and religion; read Shakespeare and Milton; and filled her copy book with poetry and romantic quotations.[12] From all indications her mind was curious, assertive and imaginative. Indeed, while she lived in Philadelphia she was an active member of its "gay society." This is in stark contrast with the image one receives of the docile and prosaic Mrs. Hodge.

Like Charles Hodge, the members of the Association of Gentlemen successfully relegated their women to the periphery of life where they were expected to be ornamental fixtures, supportive of male activity. The correctness of their actions was established through a number of treatises. Such early published public discourses as Samuel Miller's *The*

Appropriate Duty and Ornament of the Female Sex (1808), Ashbel Green's *The Christian Duty of Christian Women* (1825) and Gardiner Spring's *The Excellence and Influence of the Female Character* (1825)—all characteristically delivered to female audiences[13] —clearly illustrate the justification for this masculine temper. For these old-stock gentlemen, who, being educated at Princeton were most often of the Presbyterian persuasion, the norm for womanhood was justified by scriptural precedents, which were summed up by the argument that God created women merely as an afterthought for the benefit of his central creation, man. Thus, the function of woman, aside from perpetuating the race, was to please man. This was best achieved, declared the authors of these discourses, by women freeing men from the mundane tasks of daily existence so that they might engage in the mainstream of public life.[14]

Conversely, women were instructed that it was against their God-given nature to intrude into public affairs. If they insisted upon being involved in some type of activity outside of the home, such as benevolent enterprises, this was to be limited to charities which dealt with widows or orphans, tasks which would not "endanger" their "feminine delicacy and decorum." Samuel Miller, author of *Retrospect of the Eighteenth Century* and later Presbyterian divine at Princeton, echoed the sentiments of both sexes when he concluded that nothing was so unattractive as "masculine females" trying to usurp man's function in society.[15] Any fear within this persuasion that women would "renounce reason" and do so was unfounded. Neither the Association of Gentlemen nor their women were to be initiators of change: men for primarily ideological reasons; women because they were content to be loved, protected and occasionally praised.[16] The life-style of these women was clearly defined, they were to be subordinate to man, objects acted upon rather than self-asserting individuals. For the Association of Gentlemen, as for many American males, womanhood was to be understood as a "given" component of human existence, which by definition needed no elaboration.

The second norm for femininity accessible to women between 1820 and 1860 can most accurately be designated "Romanticized Womanhood," or, as Barbara Welter has characterized it, "the Cult of True Womanhood."[17] The conceptual framework for this feminine attitude was largely developed by those men who were members of the urbane upper-middle-class residing along the Atlantic coast and their counterparts living in the older rural section of the nation. These men were most visible as a group by their association with polite benevolence and, in particular, with the domestic reform movement which began to emerge by the early 1830's.[18] In contrast to what they adjudged to be the "conservative" nature of the Association of Gentlemen, these men conceived of themselves as having a progressive temper. While it appears that like the Association of Gentlemen the "progressive gentlemen" were more often Whigs than Jacksonian Democrats, they did not share Charles Hodge's extreme apprehension about the contemporary political scene, i.e., "a democracy with universal suffrage will soon be worse than an aristocracy with Queen Victoria at the head."[19]

Their moderate inclination was also apparent in their attitude toward "the second sex." Instead of simply insisting that women be segregated from the public arena, these "progressive gentlemen" formulated an elaborate ideology designed to convince women that their domestic role was at the center of meaningful living. This was in contrast, they argued, to man's ephemeral functions at the periphery of human experience. The major means employed to rally women to this point of view was the literature of domestic reform written by old stock clergymen such as Congregationalists John Abbott, Heman Humphrey and Horace Bushnell, and by such women social counselors as Lydia Maria Child, Sarah J. Hale, Catherine Sedgwick and Lydia Sigourney. This literature, aside from its moralistic tone, was permeated with romantic sentiment, particularly those polite writings penned by romanticists like Sedgwick and Sigourney, who had given up writing novels for the opportunity of counselling young mothers.[20]

Mrs. Sigourney's volume, *Letters to Mothers,* exemplifies the pattern of "advice" commonly followed. By their God-given natures women were singularly equipped for the tasks of providing Christian nurture for their children, of managing the domestic realm to complement their husbands' secular pursuits, and of assuring a base for the perpetuation of the moral fabric of the nation. The writers of domestic reform literature consistently made a trilogy of patriotism, Christianity and the mother. Mrs. Sigourney proposed to her readers that motherhood was the highest attainment for a woman since this status was the most influential a person could possess. Who else, she argued, had such a sway over the course of human events?[21] In the same idiom, John Abbott declared: "When our land is filled with virtuous and patriotic mothers, then will it be filled with virtuous and patriotic men. The world's redeeming influence must come from a mother's lips."[22] Women, therefore, were to remain at home and devote themselves wholeheartedly to their domestic duties, not simply because men wanted it so, but because as the only suitable moral agents within society, the very existence of mankind depended upon them.

Essentially the rationales underlying Romanticized Womanhood functioned on two levels. In the most obvious terms, the agitation for women's rights and the emergence of "the public woman" during the first half of the nineteenth-century threatened many men's sense of personal well-being. While this often took the form of warnings about avoidance of marriage and increased divorce, what men feared most was that if women were to choose public life-styles, the preserve of the home as a male sanctuary of rest and peace would be irrevocably lost. In an 1840 address entitled "American Politics" Congregationalist Horace Bushnell of Hartford candidly pleaded,

> Let us have a place of quiet, and some quiet minds which the din of our public war never embroils. Let a little of the sweetness and purity, and, if we can have it, of simple religion of life remain. God made the woman to be a help for man, not to be a wrestler with him.[23]

In more subtle terms, proponents of domestic reform like Bushnell believed that the preservation of woman as "feminine providence" was essential in effectively combating the encroachments of an emerging, urbanizing American society. To revere womanhood was to counter the reality of an anxious, competitive society so well portrayed by Alexis de Tocqueville. Since men could no longer go to nature as readily to be renewed as the nineteenth-century progressed, they sought to establish the home as a sanctuary from the world of motion. For many men the symbols of motherhood and home were necessary substitutes for a lost agrarian society.[24]

As a number of early American feminists such as Lucretia Mott, Elizabeth Cady Stanton and Susan B. Anthony were quick to realize, the subtle psychology of the "progressive gentlemen" was a greater danger to the cause of human equality than the negative stance of Ornamental Womanhood which blatantly insisted that women remain subordinate at home. These advocates of women's rights correctly observed that the constructs for Romanticized Womanhood were either merely rationalizations to justify excluding women from public life or ideological crutches to substantiate masculine priorities.[25] Their anxieties and suspicions were justifiable. Not only were the vast majority of women who rallied to the domestic reform banner convinced that it was a viable alternative to the more conservative view of femininity, but the movement itself diverted many of the most capable female minds from ever considering the harder questions about themselves.[26]

Ironically, what evidence there is of reflective questioning among those who associated themselves with Romanticized Womanhood does not seem to have come from the women, but from their male counterpart. For the man who took this norm for femininity seriously, the resulting conclusion about himself was both unavoidable and disturbing. Having claimed that all virtue, goodness and nonephemeral qualities of life resided with the mother in the home, the introspective male could only logically infer that his own functions were peripheral to the course of significant human events. To be "outside of history" meant in reality to be preoccupied with the essence of what life was all about—beauty, goodness, morality, love. Having shifted the responsibility for the "stuff" of human existence from the public arena to the private realm, men had in effect made themselves nonessential to meaningful living.[27]

A third pattern of behavior available to women in the second quarter of the nineteenth century can be identified directly with the middle-class reformist posture particularly visible in the newly emerging regions of the United States such as western New York, Ohio and Indiana. This norm for femininity might most aptly be described as "Evangelical Womanhood." In contrast to the two preceding feminine stylizations, this disposition was rooted neither in a negative nor positive ideology, but was forged out of practical necessity. In other words, Evangelical Womanhood—described with some skill in terms of *The Burned-Over District* of western New York by Whitney Cross[28] —was a derivative of the reform impulse associated with such figures as Charles Finney, Theodore Weld and Arthur and Lewis Tappan, who believed that reform activities called forth all possible human resources—women's as well as men's. This was especially crucial in the less populated communities of interior America where labor was scarce.[29]

Having assumed that reform was "the order of the day," these evangelicals (who increasingly became known as "Finneyites") actively encouraged women to participate in the causes of antislavery, temperance, education and evangelism which they believed would collectively bring about a "new, more beneficial society." Since these reformers declined to emphasize any intrinsic distinctiveness between the sexes, they were prepared to welcome women to the struggle for moral justice. Women, consequently, were permitted to speak in "mixed assemblies," work with equality alongside of men, and were even employed in the emotional awakening of religion. This was achieved on the most popular level through "Female Benevolent Societies."[30] Here women were allowed to go beyond the genteel norm of "delicacy and decorum," being entreated to do such things as visit the "dens" of prostitution and attempt to "convert their inmates on the spot."[31] Probably the scope and intensity of such activities for women in part accounts for the severity of the attack upon Finney's "new measures" after 1827 by Lyman Beecher and his fellow churchmen of a more conservative temper.

Lydia Andrews Finney, the first wife of the evangelist and educator, Charles Finney, exemplified this feminine life-style. Even before she met her husband in 1821 the young Lydia was active in her local benevolent society in western New York. After her marriage in 1824, Mrs. Finney became deeply involved in her husband's preaching campaigns in the villages and cities of western New York and the Northeast. Her complementary role found its fullest expression as she followed Finney to Oberlin in 1835. Here Lydia closely assisted her husband at the newly founded collegiate institution as an instructor in the "Ladies Department" until her death in 1847. Her correspondence during these twelve years at Oberlin was liberally dotted with letters concerning temperance, antislavery activities and educational reform.[32] In almost every way she—as well as Finney's second wife—was her husband's equal in the task of remaking America over in the evangelical image. Timothy Smith notes that such women, working successfully alongside of their husbands, assisted in undercutting antifeminist objections which attempted to discourage women from participating in activities outside of the home.[33]

Yet, at the heart of this masculine permissive temper at least two factors were at work which expose less than an altruistic male attitude. In the first place, while the evangelical reformers urged women to participate in their endeavors, they consistently refused women any positions of authority. Although women often accounted for the majority of the membership of benevolent societies and a disproportionate number of church members,[34] they were repeatedly told that they were not equipped for leadership roles in the reform movements and were refused the right of pursuing a ministerial education.[35]

The coeducational experiment at Oberlin College provides us with a microcosm of the second, more subtle manipulation of Evangelical Womanhood. While at first glance joint-education of the sexes appears to be for the benefit of both parties equally,[36] upon closer inspection one realizes that the education of young ladies was at best only a secondary aim of the school. In reality, the presence of young maidens at Oberlin was sought for two other reasons. Most obviously, they furnished young men, especially ministerial candidates, with "cultivated" wives by the time of their graduation (or soon after). Charles Finney, president of the college, mirrored this concern in observing that "an unmarried minister is a particular temptation to the other sex" and hence, "ministers need a wife more than other men." In a similar vein one of Finney's contemporaries, Heman Humphrey of Amherst, made a habit of telling his students to "mark out" for themselves one or two promising female companions and later, after completing their education, come back and claim one.[37]

Further, the Oberlin faculty reasoned that the presence of young ladies on campus would save emerging manhood from itself. Too often, they observed, young men in "monastic associations" such as at Princeton and Yale, were soon diverted from their major tasks because of a preoccupation with "a fallacious image of the opposite sex." In such circumstances young men were readily susceptible to "fancies of boyhood images of woman's 'supernatural loveliness' " which obsessed them through "day-dreams and night-dreams." The Oberlin faculty concluded that if young men were confronted daily with the "stark reality" of womanhood, they would be free from any romantic illusions about the nature of the "female character" and would be better able to concentrate upon their studies. In more positive terms, they argued that a "first hand estimate of the female character" would ease sexual frustrations nurtured by young men's "sensual tendencies," and supply healthy and natural associations which would be the foundation for matrimonial bliss.[38] In addition, the presence of young women with their higher degree of personal and social cultivation would transform Oberlin's "careless, rough, abrupt and prankish young men" into mature gentlemen who could more effectively pursue the all important public task of social and religious reform.[39]

That masculine priorities were of first order at Oberlin and among these evangelical reformers was quite clear to Lucy Stone, a graduate of the institution and a feminist. Although she acknowledged that the introduction of coeducation at Oberlin was obviously valuable to the movement for women's rights, because it publicized the fact of men and women working together with equality and propriety, she was quick to agree with its founders' 1836 statement that the education of women was a "female appendage" to the school's major aim.[40]

"Radical Womanhood" was a fourth norm for femininity accessible to middle and upper class American women in the second quarter of the nineteenth century, reaching maturity in the decade immediately preceding the Civil War. It can be accurately designated "radical" in that it encouraged the emergence of "the public woman" in contrast to the three previously discussed feminine life-styles. While Radical Womanhood was rooted in the same masculine assumption about an innate "feminine" character as Romanticized Womanhood, the application of it was different. Rather than confining woman's superior moral energy to the hearth and crib, Radical Womanhood turned it outward toward the public arena.

The men primarily responsible for initiating this feminine stylization were urbane figures residing most often in the cities of the Northeast. A disproportionate number were of the Unitarian persuasion, such as Theodore Parker and Thomas Wentworth Higginson of Boston, who were social and political liberals, as well as religious libertarians. The address of William Furness of Philadelphia, *The Minis-*

try of Women (1842), and that of Samuel May of Syracuse, *The Rights and Conditions of Women* (1845), as well as Parker's *The Public Function of Woman* (1853) and Higginson's *Woman and Her Wishes* (1853), exemplify the male attitude supportive of Radical Womanhood.[41] Since this female life-style can be associated with the more publicized agitation for women's rights in the nineteenth century, only two salient points need to be underscored. In the first place, Radical Womanhood as defined here—prior to the Civil War—should be distinguished from the feminist movement identified with Susan B. Anthony and Elizabeth Cady Stanton which culminated in the founding of the National Woman Suffrage Association in 1868. It was different both in its rejection of the feminists' insistence upon viewing femininity for the most part as environmental, and in its avoidance of the intensity by which these advocates of women's rights pursued their goals. Rather, its temperament was more in concert with the tone of Margaret Fuller's *Woman in the Nineteenth Century* (1845) and with the Grimké sisters' initial interest in women's rights. Later it would find itself more comfortable with the moderate quest for human rights characterized by the activities of Julia Ward Howe, Henry Ward Beecher, Lucy Stone and the Blackwell clan of New England.[42]

Secondly, it is important to observe that this masculine disposition—which sought to confer upon women some measure of equality and power in the public realm—was not unlike the other three male-oriented alternatives regarding its intent. That is, similar to the previous norms for femininity, Radical Womanhood was not conceived of essentially to improve the lot of women, but was implemented for the betterment of men. By turning the rhetoric supportive of Romanticized Womanhood inside-out, the northeastern "liberal" gentlemen were able to affirm with Henry Ward Beecher, in his 1860 tract, *Woman's Influence in Politics,* that "the easiest, the most natural and proper method of introducing reformation into public affairs, is to give woman a co-ordinate influence there." The presence of women in the secular masculine world would transform its preemptory characteristics from greed, malice and avarice to virtue, justice and morality. Since men's natural gifts lay in their ability to make choices in material concerns, but deficient in "heroic justice and disinterested kindness," Beecher explained to his audience, women have been appointed for the "moral refinement of the race." Instead of corrupting the natural goodness of womanhood, the second sex's involvement in profane life would reconstitute men into noble specimens of the human race. In short, Beecher declared, men were "robbing themselves" by prohibiting women from reforming the darker side of "the masculine element."[43]

This is not to say, however, that the advocates of Radical Woman-hood did not have some good intentions in commending this feminine life-style. In the same 1860 address, Beecher noted, as Theodore Parker had discerned seven years before, that just because women lacked power in society at large their influence at home was minimized. Further, he declared, just as Harriet Martineau had asserted, in 1837, that most male attempts to prescribe norms for femininity were merely masculine rationalizations to keep women "in their place," and that it was only arrogance on the part of men to assume that women were always to be an introverted force while men were to personify human activity. From woman's inferior domestic base, Parker deftly argued in 1853, men could readily ignore her or expect her to be content with the primary function of "nursing, cooking and [being] a plaything."[44] This is to say that even the men who appeared most libertarian in their disposition toward women between 1820 and 1860 were afflicted with social myopia. In the final analysis, the concern of the liberal gentlemen to preserve "masculine" priorities eclipsed whatever good intentions they had in commencing feminine stylizations. Like Margaret Fuller, they sacrificed concrete gains for elusive rhetoric about emancipating women in order to bring harmony to the universe.[45]

While shifting primary accountability for the moral welfare of society to women, white middle- and upper-class men in mid-nineteenth-century America increasingly declined the obligation of creating a righteous society. Yet, at the same time, fearing social anarchy and its accompanying threat of sexual anarchy, they tenaciously held on to the administrative and intellectual reins of organized religion and politics. As Donald Meyer has observed, "the nineteenth-century in the United States was a great age for men;" they were in short supply everywhere, particularly after 1830. Ironically, the more men succeeded in the new world of motion, the less women were needed, and the more makework they were given to do.[46] This was especially evident in the plight of middle- and upper-class women between 1820 and 1860, their common experience epitomized by the declaration that women were merely a "female appendage" to the central drama of male activity.

NOTES

1. Mary Wollstonecraft, *Vindication of the Rights of Women* (London, 1792); Margaret Fuller [Ossoli], *Woman in the Nineteenth Century* (Boston, 1845);

Simone de Beauvoir, *The Second Sex,* translated and edited by H. M. Parshley (New York, 1949). Also consult Ernest R. Groves, *The American Woman: the Feminine Side of the Masculine Civilization* (New York, 1942); Edna G. Rostow, "The Best of Both Worlds: Feminism and Femininity," *Yale Review* (Spring, 1962), 384–399; and Betty Friedan's highly popular volume, *The Feminine Mystique* (New York, 1963). The most accessible and scholarly recent bibliographical treatment of the subject of femininity in America is to be teased-out of Andrew Sinclair's *The Emancipation of the American Woman* (New York, 1965), which traces its theme from the colonial period to the present.

2. See David B. Davis' very suggestive "Some Recent Directions in American Cultural History," *American Historical Review* (Feb., 1968), 696–707. I must admit I find myself attracted to "the third level" of investigation which the author notes "is still the most neglected." (704–705).

3. This assertion was underscored afresh by the works of Mary Ellmann, *Thinking About Women* (New York, 1968); Caroline Bird with Sara Welles Briller, *Born Female: The High Cost of Keeping Women Down* (New York, 1968); and Aileen S. Kraditor, who has edited an impressive selection of writings about women, *Up From the Pedestal: Selected Writings in the History of American Feminism* (Chicago, 1968). In the past decade there have been numerous books and articles written about women as a distinctive class. Most of them dealing with American women are broad in their scope and polemical in nature. Hence, they fail to delimit their inquiry historically as both James R. McGovern and Anne F. Scott have illustrated recently can be done successfully: "The American Woman's Pre-World War I Freedom in Manners and Morals," *Journal of American History* (Sept., 1968), 315–333; "The 'New Woman' in the New South," *South Atlantic Quarterly* (Autumn, 1962), 473–483. For the most successful current historiographical treatment of the subject consult Gerda Lerner's "New Approaches to the Study of Women in American History," *Journal of Social History,* (Fall, 1969), 53–62.

4. See, for example, Charles W. Ferguson's occasionally suggestive book, *The Male Attitude* (Boston, 1966). It is interesting to note that the author initially intended to write a book about women—"as a social force"—and concluded with a book about "the male attitude" (pp. 3–4). It is just this kind of inclination on a naive historical level which Mary R. Beard complained about some time ago in *Woman As Force in History: A Study of Traditions and Realities* (New York, 1946), pp. 58–59.

5. Janet Wilson James, "Changing Ideas about Women in the United States, 1776–1825," (Ph.D. dissertation, Harvard University Library, 1954). See ch. 3 and 4.

6. M. G. St. John de Crevecoeur's *Letters From an American Farmer* was published in London in 1782; Janet James has an excellent section on "Colonial Theory and Practice" (ch. 1). For a brief summary on "The Position of American Women up to 1800" consult Eleanor Flexner, *Century of Struggle: the Woman's Rights Movement in the United States* (Cambridge, Massachusetts, 1959), pp. 3–22; for the broader historiographical contours see *The American Woman in Colonial and Revolutionary Times, 1565–1800: A Syllabus with Bibliography* (Philadelphia, 1962) by Eugene A. Leonard, Sophie H. Drinker, and Miriam Y. Holden.

7. William R. Taylor, *Cavalier and Yankee: the Old South and American National Character* (New York, 1961); W. J. Cash, *The Mind of the South* (New York, 1941). Thomas R. Dew wrote three scholarly articles in the *Southern Literary*

Messenger: (May, 1835), 493–512; (July 1835), 621–623; (August, 1835), 672–691.

8. For a general discussion of the place of the members of the Association of Gentlemen and the *Princeton Review* within the Presbyterian establishment see Elwyn A. Smith, *The Presbyterian Ministry in American Culture: A Study in Changing Concepts, 1700–1900* (Philadelphia, 1962).

9. The marriage of Charles and Sarah Hodge is traced rather accurately by their eldest son, Archibald A. Hodge, *The Life of Charles Hodge* (New York, 1880) and substantiated by the letters of Charles Hodge to his wife and his mother collected in the Charles Hodge Papers in the Princeton University Library. For the larger sexual theme see Sidney H. Ditzion, *Marriage, Morals and Sex in America: a History of Ideas* (New York, 1953), pp. 13–68.

10. Alexis de Tocqueville, *Democracy in America,* ed. Phillips Bradley, (New York, 1945); see ch. 9 and 10: "Education of Young Women in the U.S." and "The Young Woman in the Character of a Wife," II, 198–203. Many of America's own "moral stewards" were less delighted with this maiden temper and took great pains to give cautionary counsel, e.g., Jason Whitman, *Young Lady's Aid to Usefulness and Happiness* (Portland, Maine, 1838); see especially ch. 3, "Duty Before Pleasure."

11. "Recollections of Dr. Hugh Hodge," cited in A. A. Hodge, *The Life of Charles Hodge,* pp. 28–29. While Sarah's maiden temper seems to have been admired by Charles' brother, Hugh, Charles was not always happy with his fiancee's independent spirit; see the letters of Hodge to Sarah, reprinted in *Life of Charles Hodge,* pp. 58–60. Similar to Charles Hodge, other members of the Association of Gentlemen, such as Samuel Miller of New York and Joel Hawes of Hartford, took time to educate their young wives as to their proper role. Samuel Miller, *The Life of Samuel Miller* (Philadelphia, 1869), II, 169, 251–263; Edward A. Lawrence, *The Life of the Rev. Joel Hawes* (Hatford, 1871), p. 69.

12. The "List of Books Prepared for Miss Sarah Bache by Samuel Miller (Princeton, September 9, 1818)" and "Poetical Extracts and Quotations by Miss Sarah Bache" are contained in the Charles Hodge Papers.

13. Miller's address was delivered Mar. 13, 1808, "For the Benefit of the Society Instituted in the City of New York for the Relief of Poor Widows with Small Children;" Green's discourse was given before the "Princeton Female Society, for the Support of a Female School in India;" Spring's address was prepared for a similar occasion in New York City.

14. Green, *The Christian Duty of Christian Women,* pp. 9–10. For a clever rebuttal to the biblical justification for the inferior position of women see Sarah Grimké, *The Equality of the Sexes and the Condition of Women* (Boston, 1838), pp. 9–10.

15. Miller, *The Appropriate Duty and Ornament of the Female Sex,* pp. 10–12. Charles Hodge, in like manner, spelled out the implications of the "danger of female emancipation" in his review of *Emancipation in the West Indies,* by Jas. A. Thome and J. Horace Kimball (New York, 1838), *Princeton Review* (Oct., 1838), 602–644. For the limited role these women played in benevolence, see Keith Melder's "Ladies Bountiful: Organized Women's Benevolence in Early 19th-Century America," *New York History* XLVIII, (1967), 231–255.

16. Archibald Alexander, the patriarchial head of the Association of Gentlemen, made some insightful observations about the vested interest women had in preserv-

ing the status quo; see the section entitled "The Necessity of Divine Revelation" (44–45) of his "Lectures Didactic Theology" (no date), Princeton Theological Seminary Library. Mary Elizabeth Massey makes the same kind of observation concerning the majority of nineteenth-century American women prior to the Civil War in *Bonnet Brigades* (New York, 1966), pp. 3–4.

17. Barbara Welter, "The Cult of True Womanhood, 1820–1860," *American Quarterly* XVIII (Summer, 1966), 151–174.

18. Anne L. Kuhn's fine study *The Mother's Role in Childhood Education: New England Concepts, 1830–1860* (New Haven, 1947), provides an introduction to the causes and nature of the domestic reform movement, while Janet James explores its precursors "The Religious Revival and the New Conservatism: Marriage and the Home, 1800–1825," ch. 3 of her dissertation cited above, fn. 5.

19. Charles Hodge to his brother (Hugh Hodge), Aug. 1, 1837, reprinted in A. A. Hodge, *The Life of Charles Hodge*, p. 233.

20. In addition to the work of Anne Kuhn, see James D. Hart's discussion of the domestic novel, *The Popular Book: History of America's Literary Taste* (New York, 1950); Herbert R. Brown, *The Sentimental Novel in America, 1789–1860* (Durham, 1940); Janet James, "The Rise of the Woman Author," ch. 5 and Barbara Cross' erudite chapter, "On Hartford, A Fastidious People," in *Horace Bushnell: Minister to a Changing America* (Chicago, 1958), pp. 31–51. Catherine M. Sedgwick sums up this temperament in her novel *Home* (Boston, 1835), pp. 55–66.

21. Lydia Sigourney, *Letters to Mothers* (New York, 1838), pp. 10–11, 33–36, 162–163, 170. Horace Bushnell reiterates this notion of motherhood in his widely popular book *Views of Christian Nurture* (Hartford, 1848), pp. 61, 173–174.

22. John Abbott, *The Mother at Home, or Principles of Maternal Duty* (Boston, 1835), p. 148; see also pp. 14, 105–108, 147. In addition consult John C. Crandall's comprehensive study "Patriotism and Humanitarian Reform in Children's Literature, 1825–1860," *American Quarterly* (Spring, 1969), 3–22.

23. Horace Bushnell, *The American National Preacher* (December, 1840), p. 199. Also see his later volume aptly entitled *Women's Suffrage: the Reform Against Nature* (New York, 1869).

24. While this *general* theme has been developed by a number of scholars, it is most judiciously analyzed by Leo Marx, *The Machine in the Garden: Technology and the Pastoral Ideal in America* (New York, 1964). For its more particular application regarding women consult Aileen Kraditor's introduction to *Up From the Pedestal* and Donald Meyer's *The Positive Thinkers: A Study of the American Quest for Health, Wealth and Personal Power from Mary Baker Eddy to Norman Vincent Peale* (New York, 1965).

25. One can reconstruct this perspective through a number of books dealing with the feminists: Robert E. Riegel, *American Feminists* (Lawrence, Kansas, 1963); Lois Merk, "Massachusetts and the Woman-Suffrage Movement" (rev. thesis, Radcliffe Library, 1961); Eleanor Flexner, *Century of Struggle*, pp. 23–77; and Andrew Sinclair, *The Emancipation of the American Woman*, pp. 92–101.

26. Catharine Beecher, the eldest daughter of Lyman Beecher, is an excellent example of a capable domestic reform leader who rejected the larger questions about femininity associated with reform movements outside of the home. For a defense of her position, see her volumes, *The Evils Suffered by American Women and Children* (New York, 1846) and *The American Woman's Home, or, Principles*

of Domestic Science (New York, 1861). Barbara M. Cross' introduction to *The Educated Woman in America: Selected Writings* (New York, 1965), pp. 3–15 and Barbara Welter's "The Cult of True Womanhood, 1820–1860," 151–174 make some deft observations about the larger context. Consult Harriet Martineau, *Society in America* (London, 1837) for some of the deeper implications of this feminine dilemma, esp. I, 199–207; III, 106, 109, 145, 238–239, 265–267.

27. Horace Bushnell, a Congregationalist divine of Hartford, Connecticut, typifies this masculine dichotomy. One needs only to look carefully at his correspondence with his wife after 1844 as reprinted in Mary Bushnell Cheney, *Life and Letters of Horace Bushnell* (New York, 1880) to be impressed with Bushnell's sense of doubt about his masculine role.

28. Whitney R. Cross, *The Burned-Over District: the Social and Intellectual History of Enthusiastic Religion in Western New York, 1800–1850* (New York, 1950).

29. For an introduction to this story one must initially look at William G. McLoughlin's lucid introductory chapter to Charles Finney, *Lectures on the Revivals of Religion* (Cambridge, Massachusetts, 1960). More specifically, see Lewis Tappan, *The Life of Arthur Tappan* (New York, 1870); *Letters of Theodore Dwight Weld, Angelina Grimké Weld and Sarah Grimké, 1822–1844* ed. by Gilbert Barnes and Dwight Dumond (New York, 1934), e.g., T. Weld to S. and A. Grimké, Aug. 26, 1837, I, 432; and Gerda Lerner's fine biography, *The Grimké Sisters from South Carolina: Rebels against Slavery* (Boston, 1967).

30. There are numerous references about women's involvement in reform in Finney's *Lectures on Revivals of Religion*, pp. 75, 83, 94–95, 130, 188–189, 241–244, 259–263 and among his remarks in the *Oberlin Evangelist*, Apr. 8, 1840; Sept. 10, 1845; Jan. 21, 1846. His frequent communications with various "female societies" can be noted in his collected papers and letters at Oberlin College Library (OCL); (now also on microfilm); in his *Memoirs* (New York, 1876); and in Whitney Cross, *The Burned-Over District.*

31. *Emancipator*, Dec. 2, 1834. For a detailed narrative of one woman who took Evangelical Womanhood seriously, see Sarah H. Ingraham, *Walks of Usefulness, or, Reminiscences of Mrs. Margaret Prior* (New York, 1844). The larger picture is traced by Robert S. Fletcher, "Female Reformers," *A History of Oberlin College: From its Foundation through the Civil War,* (Oberlin, Ohio, 1943), I, 290–315.

32. Charles Finney reviewed the life of his wife in a letter (Dec. 25, 1847) to the editor of the *Oberlin Evangelist,* Jan. 1848. Lydia Finney's correspondence between 1835 and 1847 is found among her husband's collected papers and letters.

33. Timothy Smith, *Revivalism and Social Reform: American Protestantism on the Eve of the Civil War* (New York, 1957), pp. 82, 144.

34. Typically, 34 of the 43 signatures on a petition extending an invitation to Finney to evangelize their community, were those of women: "Session of the First Presbyterian Church of New Lebanon to Finney, March 5, 1835," (OCL). Surveying the growth of the "Free Church Movement" in 1835, Lewis Tappan observed that two out of three of the newly admitted members were women: Andrew Reed and James Matheson, *A Narrative of the Visit to American Churches by a Deputation Committee from the Congregational Union of England and Wales* (New York, 1835), II, 347. Cedric B. Cowing substantiates a similar picture for many New England churches in the eighteenth century, "Sex and Preaching in the Great Awakening," *American Quarterly* (Fall, 1968), 624–644.

35. Sinclair, *The Emancipation of the American Woman*, pp. 151–159; Emily Louisa (Seely) to Mrs. Lydia Finney, June 12, 1834, Charles Finney Papers (OCL). Elisabeth A. Dexter's *Career Women of America, 1776–1840* (Francestow, N.H., 1950) contains part of the larger story.

36. "Objectives of the College" stated by the Prudential Committee, reprinted in the *Oberlin Evangelist,* Dec. 3, 1851; Charles Finney, "Address before the Graduating Class," *Oberlin Evangelist,* Sept. 10, 1851.

37. James Fairchild was an authoritative spokesman for the Oberlin faculty: *The Joint Education of the Sexes. A Report Presented at a Meeting of the Ohio State Teachers' Association, Sandusky City, July 8* (Oberlin, 1852), pp. 28–33. Charles Finney's quotation is cited in Robert Fletcher, "The Pastoral Theology of Charles G. Finney," *Preceedings of the Ohio Historical Society* (June, 1941), 30; Henry Ward Beecher recorded Humphrey's remark in a letter to Harriet Beecher, Dec. 5, 1831, Beecher Family Papers, Yale University Library.

38. James Fairchild, *Co-education of the Sexes as Pursued in Oberlin College* (Oberlin, 1868), pp. 6, 12–13; and *The Joint Education of the Sexes* (1852), pp. 8–10, 12–18. It is well to note again that Fairchild's observations were not merely his own but were echoed by his associates at Oberlin; Fletcher, "Joint Education of the Sexes," *A History of Oberlin College,* I, 373–385.

39. Fairchild, *Co-education of the Sexes,* pp. 5–8.

40. Lucy Stone, *Woman's Journal* (May 1, 1886), p. 140; Fletcher, *A History of Oberlin College,* I, 290 ff.; Sinclair, *Emancipation of the American Woman,* p. 98; and *Ohio State Archaeological and Historical Quarterly* (July, 1954), 282.

41. Thomas Wentworth Higginson, *Woman and Her Wishes: an Essay, Inscribed to the Massachusetts Constitutional Convention* (Boston, 1853); Theodore Parker, *A Sermon of the Public Function of Woman, Preached at the Music-Hall, Boston, March 27, 1853* (Rochester, 1853): Samuel J. May, *The Rights and Condition of Women, Considered in the Church of the Messiah, November 8, 1846* (Syracuse, 1846); William Furness, *The Ministry of Women* (Philadelphia, 1842). Gordon A. Riegler's *Socialization of the New England Clergy, 1800–1860* (Greenfield, Ohio, 1945) is suggestive for the relationship between the Unitarian persuasion and women's rights, but must be read very critically. For a penetrating study of one of these men consult Tilden G. Edelstein's recent biographical study, *Strange Enthusiasm: A Life of Thomas Wentworth Higginson* (New Haven, 1968).

42. See, for example, Sarah Grimké, *The Equality of the Sexes and the Condition of Women;* Keith Melder, "The Beginnings of the Women's Rights Movement in the United States, 1800–1840" (Ph.D. dissertation, Yale University, 1963). In many ways William E. Channing personifies this temper in his exhortation to women to go beyond her "proper sphere" and get involved in the cause of abolition. *The Works of William E. Channing* (Boston, 1885), p. 844.

43. Henry Ward Beecher, *Woman's Influence in Politics* (New York, 1860), pp. 7–9. Contrast it with Horace Bushnell's *Women's Suffrage: the Reform Against Nature* (New York, 1869) written in the domestic reform idiom.

44. Beecher, *Woman's Influence in Politics,* pp. 12–13; Harriet Martineau, *Society in America,* I, 199–207; Theodore Parker, *The Public Function of Women,* p. 8.

45. Margaret Fuller, *Woman in the Nineteenth Century* (Boston, 1860 ed.) pp. 38, 122, 176.

46. Donald Meyer, *The Positive Thinkers,* pp. 46–49.

9

Women's Perspective on the Patriarchy in the 1850s

Anne Firor Scott

Southern women were scarcely to be seen in the political crisis of the 1850s. Historical works dealing with that crucial decade seldom mention a woman unless it is in a footnote citing a significant letter from a male correspondent. In women's own diaries and letters the burgeoning conflict between the North and South almost never inspired comment before John Brown's raid and rarely even then.

At the same time, women were a crucial part of one southern response to the mounting outside attack on slavery. The response was an ever more vehement elaboration of what has been called the "domestic metaphor," the image of a beautifully articulated, patriarchal society in which every southerner, black or white, male or female, rich or poor, had an appropriate place and was happy in it. "The negro slaves of the South are the happiest, and, in some sense, the freest people in the world," George Fitzhugh wrote, describing the happy plantation on which none were oppressed by care.[1] "Public opinion," he stoutly maintained, "unites with self-interest, domestic affection, and municipal law to protect the slave. The man who maltreats the weak and dependent, who abuses his authority over wife, children, or slaves is universally detested." Slavery, Fitzhugh thought, was an admirable educational system as well as an ideal society.[2]

What Fitzhugh argued in theory many planters tried to make come true in real life. "My people" or "my black and white family" were phrases that rolled easily from their tongues and pens. "I am friend and

From *Journal of American History* 61 (June 1974). Reprinted by permission.

well wisher both for time and eternity to every one of them . . ." a North Carolinian wrote to his slave overseer upon the death of a slave, expressing sorrow that he could not be present for the funeral.[3] This letter was one in a series of fatherly letters to that particular slave, and the writer, a bachelor, offered similar fatherly guidance to his grown sisters, as he doled out their money to them.

Even as planters tried to make the dream come true, they could not hide their fear and doubt. "It gave me much pleasure to see so much interest manifested," one wrote his wife, reporting that the slaves had inquired about her health and welfare, "and I am convinced that much of it was sincere."[4] Quick panic followed rumors of insurrection, and when the war came many planters took the precaution of moving their slaves as Yankee armies approached. For those who enjoy poetic justice there is plenty to be found in the pained comments of loving patriarchs when their most pampered house servants were the first to depart for Yankee camps.

Women, like slaves, were an intrinsic part of the patriarchal dream. If plantation ladies did not support, sustain, and idealize the patriarch, if they did not believe in and help create the happy plantation, which no rational slave would exchange for the jungle of a free society, who would? If women, consciously or unconsciously, undermined the image designed to convince the doubting world that the abolitionists were all wrong, what then?

Some southern men had doubts about women as well as slaves. This is clear in the nearly paranoid reaction of some of them to the pronouncements and behavior of "strong-minded" women in the North. Southern gentlemen hoped very much that no southern lady would think well of such goings-on, but clearly they were not certain.[5] Their fears had some foundation, for in the privacy of their own rooms southern matrons were reading Margaret Fuller, Madame de Stael, and what one of them described as "decided women's rights novels."[6]

Unlike the slaves, southern women did not threaten open revolt, and when the war came they did not run to the Yankees. Instead they were supportive, as they worked to feed and clothe civilians and the army, nurse the sick, run the plantations, supervise the slaves, and pray for victory. Yet even these activities were partly an indirect protest against the limitations of women's role in the patriarchy. Suddenly women were able to do business in their own right, make decisions, write letters to newspaper editors, and in many other ways assert themselves as individual human beings. Many of them obviously enjoyed this new freedom.[7]

Even before the war women were not always as enthusiastic in their support of the patriarchy as slavery's defenders liked to believe. To the assertion that "The slave is held to *involuntary service*," an Alabama minister responded:

> So is the wife. Her relation to her husband, in the immense majority of cases, is made for her, and not by her. And when she makes it for herself, how often, and how soon . . . would she throw off the yoke if she could! O ye wives, I know how superior you are to your husbands in many respects—not only in personal attraction . . . in grace, in refined thought, in passive fortitude, in enduring love, and in a heart to be filled with the spirit of heaven. . . . I know you may surpass him in his own sphere of boasted prudence and worldly wisdom about dollars and cents. Nevertheless, he has authority, from God, to rule over you. You are under service to him. You are bound to obey him in all things. . . . you cannot leave your parlor, nor your bed-chamber, nor your couch, if your husband commands you to stay there![8]

The minister was speaking to a northern audience and intended, no doubt, to convince northern women that they should not waste energy deploring the servitude of the slave since their own was just as bad, but surely this Alabama man shaped his understanding of married life in his home territory.

The minister's perception is supported in a little volume entitled *Tales and Sketches for the Fireside,* written by an Alabama woman for the purpose of glorifying southern life and answering the abolitionists. Woman's influence, she wrote,

> is especially felt in the home circle; she is the weaker, physically, and yet in many other respects the stronger. There is no question of what she can bear, but what she is obliged to bear in her positions as wife and mother, she has her troubles which man, the stronger, can never know. Many annoying things to woman pass unnoticed by those whose thoughts and feelings naturally lead them beyond their homes.

The writer added that since men were so restless, God in his wisdom designed women to be "the most patient and untiring in the performance . . . of duties." Weariness almost leaps from her pages. Not only is she bitter about the burdens of woman's lot, she also feels keenly the one-sidedness of those burdens and the failure of men even to notice.[9]

Personal documents provide even more detailed evidence of female discontent in the South of the 1850s. Unhappiness centered on women's lack of control over many aspects of their own sexual lives and the sexual lives of their husbands, over the institution of slavery which they could not change, and over the inferior status which kept them so powerless.[10]

The most widespread source of discontent, since it affected the majority of married women, was the actuality of the much glorified institution of motherhood. Most women were not able to control their own fertility. The typical planter's wife was married young, to a husband older than herself, and proceeded to bear children for two decades. While conscious family limitation was sometimes practiced in the nineteenth century, effective contraception was not available, and custom, myth, religion, and men operated to prevent limitation. With the existing state of medical knowledge it was realistic to fear childbirth and to expect to lose some children in infancy.[11]

The diary of a Georgia woman shows a typical pattern of childbearing and some reactions to it. Married in 1852 at the age of eighteen to a man of twenty-one, she bore her first child a year later. In the summer of 1855, noting certain telltale symptoms, she wrote "I am again destined to be a mother . . . the knowledge causes no exhilirating feelings . . . [while] suffering almost constantly . . . I cannot view the idea with a great deal of pleasure."[12] The baby was born but died in a few weeks, a circumstance which she prayed would help her live more dutifully in the future. A few months later she was happily planning a trip to the North because "I have no infant and I cannot tell whether next summer I will be so free from care . . . ,"[13] but in four days her dreams of travel vanished abruptly when morning nausea led her to wonder whether she was "in a peculiar situation, a calamity which I would especially dread this summer."[14] Her fears were justified, and she had a miscarriage in August. There was no rest for the weary. By January 1857 she was pregnant again, and on her twenty-fourth birthday in April 1858 she was pregnant for the fifth time in six years, though she had only two living children. Diary volumes for the next two years are missing, but in December 1862 she recorded yet another pregnancy, saying "I am too sick and irritable to regard this circumstance as a blessing *yet awhile*."[15] A year later with the house being painted and all in confusion she jotted the illuminating comment: "I don't wonder that men have studys which . . . I imagine to be only an excuse for making themselves comfortable and being out of the bustle and confusion of . . . housekeeping . . . and children."[16] She also expressed bitter opposition to the practice of sending pregnant slaves to work in the fields. By February 1865, after four years of war, she was writing "unfortunately I have the prospect of adding again to the little members of my household. . . . I am sincerely sorry for it."[17] When the child was born prematurely in June the mother thanked God that it did not live. By 1869, this woman had managed to relegate her husband to a separate bedroom, and, for good measure, she kept the most recent infant in her bed, as effective a means of contraception as she could devise.[18] Later she reflected that she had never "been so opposed to having children as many women I know."[19]

The difference between the male and female angle of vision is illustrated in the life of a South Carolina woman, a niece of James L. Petigru, married to a cousin ten years her senior. She gave birth to six children in the first nine years of her marriage, and her uncle—normally a wise and perceptive human being—wrote to the young woman's mother: "Well done for little Carey! Has she not done her duty . . . two sons and four daughters and only nine years a wife? Why the Queen of England hardly beats her. . . ."[20] If the uncle had had access to the correspondence between "little Carey" and her planter husband he might not have been so quick to congratulate her. It seems likely from the evidence of these letters that her three-month sojourns with her mother in the summers were partly motivated by a desire to prolong the time between babies, but no sooner did her lonesome husband come to visit than she was pregnant again.[21]

This woman had a faithful family doctor who moved into her household when time for her confinement drew near, but even his comforting presence did not prevent her fears of death each time. Mrs. Thomas, writer of the first diary, relied on a slave midwife, her mother, and a town doctor. Both these women loved their children and cared for them, though with ample assistance before the war. Yet each privately insisted that she would have preferred a much longer time between babies. As the Alabama minister quoted earlier suggested, however, a woman could not leave her bedchamber or her couch without her husband's permission.[22]

Women's private feelings about constant childbearing provide one example of unhappiness which was masked by the cheerful plantation image. The behavior of the patriarchs themselves in other realms of sexual life was another source of discontent. The patriarchal ideal which called for pure, gentle, pious women also expected a great deal of men: that they should be strong, chaste, dignified, decisive, and wise. Women who lived in close intimacy with these men were aware of the gap between the cavalier of the image and the husband of the reality, and they were also aware that those who had the greatest power were also—by women's standards—the most sinful. A diarist summarized an afternoon of sewing and conversation in Richmond County, Georgia:

> We were speaking of the virtue of men. I admitted to their general depravity, but considered that there were some noble exceptions, among those I class my own husband. . . .[23]

The entry revealed a certain uneasiness even about the noble exception, since the writer added that if her faith in her husband should be destroyed by experience her happiness on earth would end, and added

"between husband and wife this is (or should be) a forbidden topic."
She was twenty-two.

This notation parallels one in a more familiar dairy. Observing the
goings-on of the low-country aristocracy, Mary Boykin Chesnut wrote:
"Thank God for my country women, but alas for the men! They are
probably no worse than men everywhere, but the lower their mistresses
the more degraded they must be. . . ."[24] Chesnut's comment revealed
the dual nature of male depravity: sexual aberration in general and
crossing the racial barrier in particular. Concern on this topic was an
insistent theme in the writings of southern women and continued to be
so long after emancipation. It may be significant that they did not
blame black women, who might have provided convenient scapegoats.
The blame was squarely placed on men. "You have no confidence in
men," wrote one husband; "to use your own phrase 'we are all hum-
bugs,' " adding that he himself was a great sinner though he did not
specify his sin.[25]

Miscegenation was the fatal flaw in the patriarchal doctrine. While
southern men could defend slavery as "domestic and patriarchal,"
arguing that slaves had "all the family associations, and family pride,
and sympathies of the master," and that the relationship between
master and slave secured obedience "as a sort of filial respect," southern women looked askance at the fact that so many slaves quite literally
owed their masters filial respect.[26] "There is the great point for the
abolitionists . . . ," one wrote.[27] While some southern reviewers blasted
"the fiend in petticoats" who wrote *Uncle Tom's Cabin,* southern
women passed copies of the book from hand to hand.

Impressive evidence of the pervasiveness of interracial sex and its
effects on the minds and spirits of white women, gathered thirty years
ago, has recently found its way into print. James Hugo Johnston
examined 35,000 manuscript petitions to the Virginia legislature.
Among these documents were many divorce petitions in which white
women named slave women as the cause of their distress. In some
petitions wives told the whole story of their marriages, throwing much
light on what could happen to the family in a slave society. One
testified that her husband had repeated connection with many slaves,
another protested several black mistresses who had been placed in her
home and had treated her insolently. Yet another recounted a complicated story in which her brother had tried to force her husband to send
away his black mistress, without success. In several cases the husband's
attention to his mulatto children, sometimes in preference to his
legitimate children, was offered in evidence. The stories run on and on
until one is surfeited with pain and tragedy from the white woman's
point of view, pain which could doubtless be matched from the black

woman's point of view if it had been recorded. Many petitioners candidly described their husbands' long attachment to black mistresses, and their reluctance to give them up. Johnston also adduced evidence of the tortured efforts white men made to provide for their mulatto children, efforts corroborated by Helen Catterall's compilation of legal cases dealing with slavery.[28]

If so much evidence found its way into the official records of the state of Virginia, how much is there yet unexamined in the records of other slave states, and how much more was never recorded because women suffered in silence rather than go against religion, custom, and social approval to sue for divorce by a special act of the legislature? Johnston, from his close acquaintance with the documents, surmised that there must have been many women who calmly or sullenly submitted to becoming "chief slave of the master's harem," a phrase attributed to Dolley Madison.[29]

Even apart from miscegenation, the general sexual freedom society accorded to men was deeply resented by women. A thread of bitterness runs through letters describing marital problems, the usual assumption being that male heartlessness could be expected. The double standard was just one more example of how unfairly the world was organized:

> As far as a womans being forever 'Anathema . . .' in society for the same offence which in a man, very slightly lowers, and in the estimation of some of his own sex rather elevates him. In this I say there appears to be a very very great injustice. I am the greatest possible advocate for womans purity, in word, thought or deed, yet I think if a few of the harangues directed to women were directed in a point where it is more needed the standard of morality might be elevated.[30]

Ten years later the same woman had not changed her mind: "it occurs to me that if virtue be the test to distinguish man from beast the claim of many Southern white men might be questionable. . . ."[31]

In addition to the widely prevailing skepticism with which women viewed the pretensions of their lords and masters (a label often used with a measure of irony), there was widespread discontent with the institution of slavery. "I never met with a lady of southern origin who did not speak of Slavery as a sin and a curse—the burden which oppressed their lives," Harriet Martineau observed in her autobiography.[32]

In Virginia, after the Nat Turner rebellion, twenty-four women joined in a petition to the legislature, noting that though "it be unexampled, in our beloved State, that females should interfere in its political concerns," they were so unhappy about slavery that they were willing to break the tradition. They urged the legislature to find a way to abolish slavery.[33] An overseer of wide experience told Chesnut in 1861 that in all his life he had met only one or two women who were not abolitionists.[34] William Gilmore Simms, reviewing *Uncle Tom's Cabin* in the *Southern Quarterly Review,* made clear his understanding of the opposition to slavery among southern women.[35]

Of course Martineau and the overseer exaggerated to make a point, and the Virginia petitioners were unusual. Women of slaveholding families responded ambiguously to the life imposed on them. Some accepted it without question. Others, complaining of the burden of slavery, nevertheless expected and sometimes got a degree of personal service which would have been inconceivable to women in the free states.[36] It was also true that few were philanthropic enough to give up a large investment for a principle. It is further clear that most southern women accepted, with a few nagging questions, the racial assumptions of their time and place.

Even with these conditions many women of the planter class had strong doubts about either the morality or the expediency of slavery, as the following statements indicate. "Always I felt the moral guilt of it, felt how impossible it must be for an owner of slaves to win his way into Heaven."[37] "But I do not hesitate to say . . . that slavery was a curse to the South—that the time had come in the providence of God to give every human being a chance for liberty and I would as soon hark back to a charnel house for health inspiration as to go to the doctrines of secession, founded on the institution of slavery, to find rules and regulations. . . ."[38] "When the thunderbolt of John Brown's raid broke over Virginia I was inwardly terrified, because I thought it was God's vengeance for the torture of such as Uncle Tom."[39] "I will confess that what troubles me more than anything else is that I am not certain that *Slavery is right.*"[40] "When will it please our God to enfranchise both the holders and the slaves from bondage? It is a stigma, a disgrace to our country. . . ."[41] "In 1864 I read Bishop Hopkins' book on slavery. He took the ground that we had a right to hold the sons of Ham in bondage. . . . Fancy a besotted, grinding, hardfisted slave driver taking up a moral tone as one of God's accredited agents!!"[42]

One doubter suggested that she would happily pay wages to her house servants if her husband would agree, and another thought slaves ought to be permitted to choose their own masters. Still another devoted all her time to teaching slaves to read and write, even though to do so was illegal, and to providing a Sunday school for slave children. [43]

Moral doubts were further complicated by strong personal attachments between white and black women. A South Carolina woman went into mourning in 1857 when her favorite slave died, and her sister wrote that "She loved Rose better than any other human being." [44]

Another member of the same family insisted that her brother and brother-in-law keep promises made to slaves whom she had sold within the family. A Virginia woman, seeking permission to free her slave woman and keep her in the state, contrary to the law, testified to her "strong and lasting attachment to her slave Amanda."[45] Such phrases were not uncommon among southern women.

For every woman who held slavery to be immoral, or who simply loved individual slaves, there were dozens who hated it for practical reasons. "Free at last," cried one white woman when she heard of the Emancipation Proclamation. "If slavery were restored and every Negro on the American continent offered to me," wrote another, "I should spurn them. I should prefer poverty rather than assume again the cares and perplexities of ownership. . . ."[46] Such quotations could be multiplied. They are typified by a diary entry in the fall of 1866 expressing relief "that I had no Negro clothes to cut out this fall O what a burden, like that of Sinbad the Sailor, was the thought of 'Negro clothes to be cut out.' "[47]

Motherhood, happy families, omnipotent men, satisfied slaves—all were essential parts of the image of the organic patriarchy. In none of these areas did the image accurately depict the whole reality.

For women as for the slaves, open revolt was made difficult by many constraints. Though women had complaints, they shared many of the assumptions of men, and, at least intermittently, enjoyed the role and status of the landholding aristocracy. Discontent does not automatically lead to a clear idea of alternatives, and few, if any, southern women in the 1850s had visions of a multiracial society based on freedom, much less equality. Nor did they conceive of fundamental change in the patterns of marriage and family which bound them so tight. Some, to be sure, found widowhood a liberating experience.[48]

The ideology of woman's liberation, which was being worked out in the North by Sarah Grimké, Margaret Fuller, Elizabeth Cady Stanton, and others, had only begun to take shape in the minds of southern women, but signs of change can be found. A letter written from Yazoo, Mississippi, in 1849 to the *Southern Ladies Companion* complained about an article which seemed to imply that only men were part of mankind:

> Woman is not, or ought not to be, either *an article* to be turned to good account by the persons who compose "this life" [men] nor a plaything for their amusement. She ought to be regarded as forming a part of mankind herself. She ought to be regarded as having as much interest or proprietorship in "this life" as anyone else. And the highest compliment to be paid her is that she is useful to herself—that in conjunction with the rest of mankind, in works of virtue, religion and morality, the sum of human

happiness is augmented, the kingdom of the Savior enlarged and the glory of God displayed.[49]

By the 1850s some echoes of the woman's rights debate which had erupted in the North in 1848 began to reach southern ears. A violent attack on the Woman's Rights Convention held in Worcester, Massachusetts, in 1851 appeared in the *Southern Quarterly Review,* written by a distinguished southern woman, Louisa Cheves McCord.[50] A closer look at McCord's own history is instructive with respect to built-in constraints. Daughter of Langdon Cheves, she was outstandingly able both as a writer and as an administrator. Yet she used her ability to defend the whole southern domestic metaphor, including slavery. One has only to imagine her born in Boston instead of Charleston to find in Louisa McCord all the makings of a Margaret Fuller or an Elizabeth Cady Stanton.

What was the significance of this widespread discontent? Public decisions are rooted in private feelings, and the psychological climate in any society is one of the most important things a social or political historian needs to understand. The South by 1860 was in a high state of internal tension, as feelings of guilt and fear of the future mounted. The part played by slaves themselves, as well as by women, in exacerbating these tensions is just now beginning to be examined. Speaking of the American Revolution, Charles Francis Adams once remarked that it "drew its nourishment from the sentiment that pervaded the dwellings of the entire population," and added, "How much this home sentiment did then, and does ever, depend upon the character of the female portion of the people, will be too readily understood by all to require explanation."[51] What Adams called "the home sentiment" was in the South of 1860 an unstable and hence explosive mixture of fear, guilt, anxiety, and discontent with things as they were. How much this stemmed from the unhappiness of "the female portion of the population" is not yet well understood, but it is worth a good deal of study.

NOTES

1. George Fitzhugh, *Cannibals All! or Slaves Without Masters* (Cambridge, Mass., 1960), p. 18.

2. William Pettigrew to Mose, July 12, 1856, Pettigrew Family Papers (Southern Historical Collection, University of North Carolina).

4. Charles Pettigrew to Caroline Pettigrew, Oct. 18, 1857, *ibid.*

5. Anne Firor Scott, *The Southern Lady: From Pedestal to Politics 1830–1930* (Chicago, 1970), 20–21.

6. *Corinne*, Madame de Stael's famous feminist novel, appeared often in lists of books read by southern women. Even Mary Wollstonecraft was not entirely unknown in the South. See William R. Taylor, *Cavalier and Yankee: The Old South and the American National Character* (New York, 1961), 162–67, for discussion of a pervasive malaise among ante bellum southern women.

7. See H. E. Sterkx, *Partners in Rebellion: Alabama Women in the Civil War* (Rutherford, N.J., 1970), for the most recent collection of evidence concerning the extraordinary vigor and range of southern women's activities during the war. It is important to note that this essay does not treat all classes of women. There were eight million southerners in 1860, of whom the largest part were ordinary farmer folk, slaves, and free blacks. This majority was ruled, politically, economically, and socially, by a small top layer, the large and medium-sized plantation owners who had money, or at least credit, slaves, and power. From their ranks came the proslavery philosophers, the mythmakers, the leaders of opinion. From their ranks came the most visible southerners, the minority which the rest saw and heard. It was members of this minority who consciously or unconsciously clung to the idea of the beautiful organic society so well described in George Fitzhugh, *Sociology for the South: or the Failure of Free Society* (Richmond, 1954). It was women of this minority who were called upon to play the appropriate role, to live up to the image of the southern lady. Other women, farmer's wives and daughters and illiterate black women, were part of society and in some inarticulate way doubtless helped to shape it, but historians have just begun to forge tools which may permit an examination of their role. For insights into southern society, see Steven A. Channing, *Crisis of Fear: Secession in South Carolina* (New York, 1970).

8. Fred A. Ross, *Slavery Ordained of God* (Philadelphia, 1859), 54–56.

9. R. M. Ruffin, *Tales and Sketches for the Fireside* (Marion, Ala., 1858).

10. For other sources of women's unhappiness, especially the desire for education, see Scott, *Southern Lady*. This essay concentrates on areas of complaint directly related to the patriarchal myth. Of course the education some women hoped for, had it been available, would have indirectly undermined the patriarchy.

11. See *Annual Report to the Legislature of South Carolina Relating to the Registration of Births, Deaths and Marriages for the Year Ending December 13, 1856* (Columbia, S. C., 1857). Though the report acknowledges grave deficiencies in its fact gathering, this early venture into vital statistics supports generalizations suggested here. For comparative purposes the report includes some statistics from Kentucky which are also supportive. Of the deaths recorded in South Carolina in 1856, nearly one half were children under the age of five and nearly one fourth were children under one year. Of marriages in the same year, 5.7 percent were of men under twenty, while 40.4 percent of the women were under that age. Nearly one half of the men and three fourths of the women who married in 1856 were under twenty-five. One fourth of the men but only 9.4 percent of the women married between the ages of twenty-five and thirty. A cohort analysis of selected groups of southern women patterned on Robert V. Wells' study of Quakers might be useful, if data could be found. See Robert V. Wells, "Demographic Change and the Life Cycle of American Families," *Journal of Interdisciplinary History*, II (Autumn 1971), 273–82. Analysis of the biographical sketches of 150 low-country

planters prepared by Chalmers Gaston Davidson provides further evidence of the age gap between husbands and wives. Davidson's study is based on 440 South Carolinians who had 100 or more slaves on a single estate. (Although fifty of the planters were women—a somewhat startling fact—his information is always about the men these women married.) The majority of the men were one to ten years older than their wives in first marriage. For second marriages the age difference increased, as it did for third and fourth marriages. In cases where the woman was older than her husband (twenty-three in all), the age gap was usually up to five years, though three women were more than ten years older than their husbands. Chalmers Gaston Davidson, *The Last Foray: The South Carolina Planters of 1860: A Sociological Study* (Columbia, S. C., 1971), 170–267.

12. E. G. C. Thomas Diary, June 26, 1855 (Department of Manuscripts, Duke University).

13. *Ibid.*, May 26, 1856.

14. *Ibid.*, June 1, 1856.

15. *Ibid.*, Dec. 1862.

16. *Ibid.*, Dec. 31, 1863.

17. *Ibid.*, Feb. 12, 1865.

18. *Ibid.*, Jan. 29, 1869.

19. *Ibid.*, Nov. 29, 1870.

20. James Petigru Carson, *Life, Letters and Speeches of James Louis Petigru: The Union Man of South Carolina* (Washington, 1920), 441.

21. Letters of Charles and Caroline Pettigrew, 1856–1861, Pettigrew Family Papers.

22. The degree to which maternity shaped women's lives emerges from any random examination of family histories. For example, Charles and Mary Pratt Edmonston of North Carolina had their first child in 1812, their last in 1833. During those twenty-one years Mrs. Edmonston bore eleven children, four of whom died in infancy. Mrs. Andrew McCollum of Louisiana bore ten children between 1840 and 1855, including one set of twins. Three died in infancy. During 180 months of married life, she spent ninety in pregnancy and seventy in nursing babies, since she did not use wet nurses. Thus in all her married life there was one month when she was neither pregnant nor nursing a baby. Margaret Ann Morris Grimball, wife of South Carolinian John B. Grimball, married at twenty and had a child every two years for eighteen years. At seventeen Varina Howell of Mississippi married Jefferson Davis who was thirty-five and a widower. Children were born in 1852, 1855, 1857, 1861, and 1864. Georgian David Crenshaw Barrow married Sarah Pope who bore him nine children in seventeen years, then died. John Crittenden's wife bore seven children in thirteen years. Robert Allston of South Carolina married Adele Petigru, ten years his junior. She bore ten children in seventeen years of whom five lived to maturity. Examples could be multiplied indefinitely, but far more useful would be a careful demographic study of selected southern counties, tidewater and upcountry, to give a firm underpinning to this kind of impressionistic evidence.

23. Thomas Diary, April 12, 1856.

24. Mary Boykin Chesnut, *Diary from Dixie,* Ben Ames Williams, ed. (Boston, 1949), 21–22.

25. Charles Pettigrew to Caroline Pettigrew, July 10, 1856, Pettigrew Family Papers.

26. Quoted in Severn Duvall, *"Uncle Tom's Cabin:* The Sinister Side of the Patriarchy," *New England Quarterly,* XXXVI (March 1963), 7–8. This perceptive article deserves serious attention from social historians.

27. Thomas Diary, Jan. 2, 1858.

28. James Hugo Johnston, *Race Relations in Virginia & Miscegenation in the South 1776–1860* (Amherst, 1970); Helen Tunnicliff Catterall, *Judicial Cases concerning American Slavery and the Negro* (2 vols., Washington, 1926). See also Guion Griffis Johnson, *Ante-Bellum North Carolina: A Social History* (Chapel Hill, 1937), 221, for evidence that cohabitation with a Negro was the second most important cause for divorce in North Carolina.

29. Johnston, *Race Relations in Virginia,* 237.

30. Thomas Diary, Feb. 9, 1858.

31. *Ibid.,* May 7, 1869.

32. Harriet Martineau, *Harriet Martineau's Autobiography: With Memorials by Maria Weston Chapman* (3 vols., London, 1877), II, 21.

33. Augusta County Legislative Petitions, 1825–1833 (Virginia State Library, Richmond).

34. Chesnut, *Diary from Dixie,* 169.

35. William Gilmore Simms, review of *Uncle Tom's Cabin, Southern Quarterly Review,* VIII (July 1853), 216, 233.

36. Their expectations may be illustrated by the E. G. C. Thomas family in its poverty-stricken postwar phase still requiring, so they thought, a person to cook, a person to clean, a person to wash and iron, one to do the chores, and a carriage driver. See Thomas Diary, 1868–1869, as Mrs. Thomas details her search for reliable domestic help among the freed people. One complication was that it was considered unethical to hire fine servants who had once belonged to friends.

37. John Q. Anderson, ed., *Brokenburn: The Journal of Kate Stone 1861–1868* (Baton Rouge, 1955), 8.

38. Rebecca L. Felton, "The Subjection of Women," pamphlet 19, Rebecca L. Felton Papers (Manuscript Division, University of Georgia).

39. Mrs. Burton [Constance Cary] Harrison, *Recollections Grave and Gay* (New York, 1912), 42.

40. Thomas Diary, Sept. 23, 1854.

41. Martha E. Foster Crawford Diary, Feb. 7, 1853, Feb. 3, 1854 (Department of Manuscripts, Duke University).

42. Hope Summerell Chamberlain, *Old Days in Chapel Hill, being the Life and Letters of Cornelia Phillips Spencer* (Chapel Hill, 1926), 93.

43. John Q. Anderson, "Sarah Anne Ellis Dorsey," Edward T. James and others, eds., *Notable American Women 1607–1950: A Biographical Dictionary* (3 vols., Cambridge, Mass., 1971), I, 505–06. There were southern men who opposed slavery, too, but theirs was usually an economic, not a moral critique.

44. Jane P. North to Caroline Pettigrew, Nov. 16, 1857, Pettigrew Family Papers.

45. J. H. Easterby, ed., *The South Carolina Rice Plantation as Revealed in the Papers of Robert F. W. Allston* (Chicago, 1945), 149.

46. Caroline Merrick, *Old Times in Dixie* (New York, 1901), 19. Mary A. H. Gay of Georgia, quoted in Matthew Page Andrews, *Women of the South in Wartime* (Baltimore, 1920), 334.

47. Thomas Diary, Sept. 20, 1866.

48. A study of planter's widows would be interesting. Many of them conducted plantations with considerable success, and as they necessarily came in contact with the outside world in business they began to develop more forceful personalities and interest in politics as well. For example, Jane Petigru North, sister of the famous James L. Petigru, was widowed early and ran one plantation owned by her brother and then another owned by her son-in-law, Charles L. Pettigrew. She did not hesitate to take full responsibility, and like her brother she was an outspoken supporter of the Union down to the moment of secession.

49. *Southern Ladies Companion*, II (1848), 45.

50. [Louisa Cheves McCord] L. S. M., *Southern Quarterly Review*, V (April 1852), 322–41. See also Margaret Farrand Thorp, "Louisa Susannah Cheves McCord," James and others, eds., *Notable American Women*, II, 451–52.

51. Charles Francis Adams, *Letters of Mrs. Adams with an Introductory Memoir by her grandson* (Boston, 1848), xix.

10

A Slave Family
in the Ante Bellum South

Loren Schweninger

Twentieth century scholars of Afro-American history have offered two basically different interpretations concerning the effect of slavery on the black family. In his famous 1932 study *The Negro Family in the United States,* Negro sociologist E. Franklin Frazier asserted that slavery destroyed the black family. Fundamental economic forces and material interests, he said, shattered even the toughest bonds of black familial sentiments and parental love.[1] Supporting Frazier in the 1959 comparative analysis, *Slavery: A Problem in American Intellectual and Institutional Life,* white historian Stanley M. Elkins listed four reasons for the destruction of the black slave family: sexual exploitation, separation, miscegenation, and restrictive legal codes. "The law could permit no aspect of the slave's conjugal state to have an independent legal existence."[2] In an examination of the urban South, historian Richard C. Wade likewise concluded that "For a slave, no matter where he resided, a house was never a home. Families could scarcely exist in bondage. The law recognized no marriage."[3] And Daniel P. Moynihan, in his 1965 report, re-iterated that slavery had an extremely negative effect on the black family.[4]

Recently, three writers have put forth a far more optimistic view of the black family in bondage. Herbert Gutman, Robert Abzug and John Blassingame contend that strong family loyalties developed among slaves. Admitting the obvious institutional barriers, they argue that

From the *Journal of Negro History* 60 (January 1975). Reprinted by permission of The Association for the Study of Afro-American Life and History, Inc.

bondsmen used the family as a shelter against the brutalities of the Southern slave system. "Although it was weak, although it was frequently broken," Professor Blassingame writes in *The Slave Community,* a psychological study of Blacks in bondage, "the family provided an important buffer, a refuge from the rigors of slavery."[5] Thus, though asking the same basic question of the way in which the institution of slavery affected the black family, scholars have advanced two fundamentally different interpretations.

An investigation of one slave family will not end the controversy. In a limited sense it can only tell us about *a* family, and one that was in many respects very fortunate.[6] The members of the Thomas-Rapier slave family received an education; achieved a degree of economic independence; and eventually became free or at least "quasi-free." Moreover, they belonged to extremely permissive and beneficent masters. They lived in an urban environment (as did only 10% of the South's slave population), and hired out, though it was against the law. But, like many other Blacks in the ante bellum South, they too suffered the pains of separation (living in Alabama, Tennessee, and Canada); sexual exploitation (the slave mother bore three sons by three different white men); and the legal denial of the slave family. Yet, in spite of these institutional barriers or perhaps because of them, the members of the Thomas-Rapier family maintained their integrity. Indeed, as seen in a rare collection of slave letters, notes, and autobiographical reminiscences, they preserved a cohesive family unit for three generations. In a larger sense, then, an investigation of one slave family can perhaps shed some light on the family experiences of many slaves in the ante bellum South.

Born in Albemarle County, Virginia, about 1790, the black slave, Sally, grew up on the 1500-acre tobacco plantation of Charles S. Thomas, a friend and neighbor of Thomas Jefferson.[7] At a young age she was sent to the fields. Working from sun-up to sundown, season to season, and year to year, she (along with forty-one other slaves on the "big gang"), prepared beds, planted seeds, transplanted shoots, "wormed and topped" young plants, hung, and then stripped, sorted and bundled the final product. When she was about eighteen, Sally suffered (or accepted) the sexual advances of a white man (probably John Thomas, the owner's eldest son); and in September 1808, she gave birth to a mulatto boy, John. Some years later she gave birth to a second mulatto child, Henry.[8] As Virginia law required that progeny take the status of the mother, both children were born in bondage, but as part of the Thomas Trust Estate, they were protected against sale or separation.[9] Consequently, when one of the heirs of the estate (again probably John) joined the westward movement of slaveholders across the Appalachians into the Cumberland river valley about 1818, Sally, John and Henry were transported to the fast growing town of Nashville, Tennessee.[10]

The city offered many opportunities. With the master's permission, Sally hired out as a cleaning lady, a practice common among urban slaves, and secured an agreement to retain a portion of her earnings. She then rented a two-story frame house on the corner of Deaderick and Cherry Streets in the central business district. Converting the front room into a laundry, and manufacturing her own soap (blending fats, oils, alkali and salt in a small vat in the front room), she established a business of cleaning clothes. She soon built up a thriving trade.[11] At the same time Sally arranged for her eldest son, John, to hire out as a waiter and poll boy to river barge Captain Richard Rapier,[12] who was plying the Cumberland–Tennessee–Mississippi river trade, between Nashville, Florence (Alabama), and New Orleans;[13] and arranged for Henry to hire out as an errand boy to various "white gentlemen" around Nashville. Part of their earnings, along with her own, she saved in a tea cannister, which she hid in the loft, hoping someday to be able to purchase "free papers" for the children. "However, that might cost as much as $2000!" Undeterred, she conscientiously set aside part of her earnings every month, and by early 1826, she had saved over $300.[14]

Though thirty-six years old, Sally was still an attractive woman. In October 1827, in the house on Deaderick Street she gave birth to a third mulatto son, James.[15] The father was the famous ante bellum Judge John Catron, but according to the state law, which, like the law in Virginia, assigned progeny the status of the mother, James was born in bondage. "Now my own father presided over the supreme court of Tennessee [and served as a justice on the United States Supreme Court]," James later recalled, "[but] he had no time to give me a thought. He gave me 25 cents once, [and] if I [were] correctly informed, that is all he ever did for me."[16] With three children, John nineteen, Henry about sixteen, and James, Sally despaired that she might not be able to save enough to free her family.

But her despair soon turned to joy. She received word in 1829 that her eldest son had been emancipated. "I bequeath one thousand dollars to my executors for the purpose of purchasing the freedom of the mulatto boy, John, who now waits on me, and belongs to the Estate of Thomas," Richard Rapier stipulated in his will, and the Alabama General Assembly, the only legal emancipator of slaves in the state, passed a law freeing "a certain male slave by the name of John H. Rapier."[17] Then, she saw an opportunity to free Henry. With the final settlement of the Thomas Estate in 1834, "Sally and the two mulatto

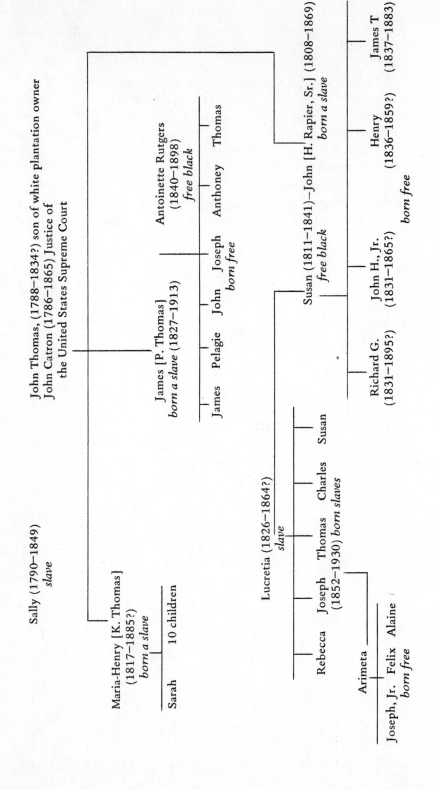

The Genealogy of a Slave Family

boys," reverted to one John Martin, an affable young man who wanted to sell a part of his inheritance for a quick profit. Fearing that her children would be sold "down river to Mississippi," Sally urged Henry to escape. Heeding his mother's advice, Henry fled through upper Tennessee and Kentucky but was captured near Louisville and confined to a guard house. He managed to work off his leg-chains one night, however, steal down to the Ohio River, untie a boat, and drift into the current. "The night was cold," Henry wrote afterwards. "I headed the yawl downstream, sculled over the falls and made for the Indiana shore. There I found a man who freed my hands."[18] Taking the surname Thomas, he travelled to Buffalo, New York, where he opened a barber shop.[19]

Shortly after Henry's escape, Sally went to Ephraim H. Foster, a prominent Tennessee lawyer, and asked for assistance in putting James out of Martin's reach. "Will you talk with him [Martin] and see what he will take for the boy," she asked. "Very well, Aunt Sally," Foster replied, "I will see him and let you know what can be done." A few days later Foster told her that Martin wanted $400. "I have saved only $350," Sally explained, but quickly added: "Now if you, Col. Foster, will pay the fifty and make it four hundred, have the bill of sale made to yourself, you can hold James in trust until I return [the] money. I want you to be his protector." Foster agreed and the bargain was sealed. A short time later, she paid off the debt and received a bill of sale, "free papers," for six-year-old James.[19] Even then, however, he was not free. The law required emancipated Blacks to secure a manumission deed from the county court, and "thereupon immediately leave Tennessee."[20] Thus, despite having "free papers," James was still legally a slave.

But neither the law nor slavery seemed to curtail his activities. As a young boy, he performed a variety of chores for his mother: keeping salt in the hopper for making soap, cutting wood for the fire place, cleaning up around the house, and delivering clothes to customers. He also enrolled in the Nashville school for Blacks. Thomas recalled sitting on splintery benches, in a drafty one-room school house and listening to ill-prepared lessons on such basic subjects as "the fundamentals of reading." In addition, he remembered that the school remained open only a few months each year, the pupils, or "scholars," had to pay a very high $4 tuition fee, and that free Blacks Rufus Conrad, Daniel Watkins and Samuel Lowery taught at the school from time to time. "But often," he said, "there was no school because there was no teacher." In 1836, for instance, a black teacher, described as "a fine scholar," was taken out by whites and whipped nearly to death. "Tennesseans generally opposed educating blacks," he recalled, "they might want the same as whites." But young James had an intense desire to learn and quickly mastered the basics of mathematics, reading and writing.[21]

Having secured a rudimentary education, James hired out as an apprentice barber. Working with bondsman Frank Parrish, who had earlier established a barber shop on Public Square, he quickly learned the trade.[22] "James [is] still with Frank Parrish and has the character of a good barber, So a Gentleman told me," his brother, John Rapier, observed in 1843. "He is well thought of by the Gentlemen. James has manners to please almost anyone who does not let their prejudice go far on account of color."[23] Two years later James was still with Parrish, earned $12 a month, and at the same time had begun violin lessons with one Gordan McGowan. "James will make a man of musick I think. He seems to be very fond of it."[24] Having served a five-year apprenticeship, in 1846, he opened his own barber shop. The nineteen-year-old slave established his shop in the house where he had grown up (and where his mother still operated her cleaning business), at 10 Deaderick Street. The location was ideal. Within a few steps of several banking houses, newspapers, and law firms, as well as the county court house, Market Square, and the Capitol, "the place on Deaderick," he explained, "was convenient to bankers, merchants, lawyers, politicians, and professional men." He counted among his customers six famous Tennesseans: William Carroll, one time governor; E. S. (Squire) Hall, an important businessman; General William Harding, owner of Bellemeade Estate; Ephraim Foster, a Whig political leader; and William G. (Parson) Brownlow, the Civil War governor.[25] Francis Fogg, the well-known Davidson County lawyer, visited the Thomas shop daily. "He returns to us in the evening," Mrs. Fogg noted approvingly, "with face smooth and curls nicely arranged."[26]

While attending to his duties as a barber, James listened attentively to conversations that took place among his customers. "They had time to talk in the barber shop. Nobody seemed in a great hurry. Everything was discussed—social, commercial, political and financial." He remembered conversations about the abolitionists, the advancement of cotton on the Liverpool market, the magnetism and sporting proclivities of Andrew Jackson, plantation acreage along the Mississippi, and fugitive slaves. Once, he recalled being sharply questioned about runaway Blacks. "You have a brother living in Buffalo, New York, I believe," General Harding asked pointedly. "Yes," was the reply. "Well he treated me in a gruff manner. I went to ask him if he knew anything about a boy who ran off from me. I told him I only wanted to see him. I had come to Buffalo for that purpose. I received a very cold and indifferent reply." James could do little but apologize for his brother's "rudeness." Though he usually remained silent when the conversation turned to such controversial issues; at times he ventured an opinion on the slavery question. Once, for example, while shaving a young Virginia lawyer, he defended the Wilmot Proviso, a proposal to prohibit slavery in the newly acquired Mexican territories. "The set back I got caused me to be careful in the future. Among other things he told me I had no right to listen to a gentleman's conversation."[27] Despite such "set backs," James built up a flourishing business. Charging 25 cents for a haircut, 15 cents for a shave, and $1 for occasionally extracting teeth, he operated one of the most prosperous "tonsorial establishments" in Nashville. In the city's first business directory (published in 1853), he advertised in large boldface print: "JAS. THOMAS, BARBER SHOP, 10 Deaderick St."[28]

Meanwhile, Sally's other two children, freedman John H. Rapier and fugitive Henry Thomas, were also prospering as barbers. Rapier opened a shop in Florence, Alabama, soon saved over $500, purchased a white frame house on Court Street in the downtown district, and like James, converted the house into a place of business as well as a residence. In 1831, he married Susan, a free Black from Baltimore, Maryland, and in the next decade the couple had four children: Richard, John Jr., Henry and James.[29] After his wife's death in childbirth at the age of twenty-nine, he purchased a sixteen-year-old slave, Lucretia, and between 1848 and 1861, they had five slave children, the youngest named Susan.[30] During the ante bellum period Rapier acquired real estate holdings in Alabama, the Minnesota Territory, and Canada, purchased valuable railroad stock, and saved $2000 in cash. By 1860, he was one of the wealthiest free Blacks in Alabama, with about $10,000.[31]

Henry Thomas also opened a barber shop. Locating in the basement of Buffalo's elegant hotel Niagara, he too built up a lucrative trade. About 1835, he married a black woman, Maria, and they had eleven children, ten boys and a girl, Sarah.[32] In 1852, to avoid apprehension by slave catchers (who were encouraged by the 1850 Fugitive Slave Law), he moved to the black community of Buxton, Canada West. With resources he had saved as a barber, he purchased one hundred acres of wilderness land, built a log house, cleared the trees, and put in a crop of corn, wheat and barley.[33] "The settlement improves slowly, but prospects are good for its success," he noted in 1856. "The lumber mill is making improvements for the neighborhood. Soon the railroad will pass through. The school is flourishing. I have six acres in wheat and 2 in barley."[34] Thus, using one of the few profitable occupations open to ante bellum Blacks, James, John and Henry were all able to achieve a degree of financial independence.

The members of the slave family were also successful at maintaining close family ties. Though separated by hundreds, even thousands of miles, though forbidden to travel in certain regions, and though denied postal privileges, they kept in close touch. As a slave and also when he was a free Black, John Rapier Sr. frequently visited Nashville. And between 1838 and 1846, he arranged for all four of his children to attend school in the Tennessee capital and to stay with their slave uncle and slave grandmother. "John and James are so [well] pleased with their grandmother [and school], he noted in 1843, "that they do not want to come home, so James writes."[35] A couple of years later he added: "My two sons that are with mother are well when I last hear[d] from them. I entend to go up to Nashville in the course of ten or twelve days and See them all." On that occasion Rapier confessed that he had not been to Tennessee in nearly a year. "I am extremely anxious to See the family again," he said, promising to deliver a letter from his brother, which had been smuggled into the South from the North. After a visit to the Tennessee capital, he wrote to "Brother Henry": "Mother looks as young as she did 8 years ago and works as hard and hardly takes time to talk to you." Forwarding other family news, he said that "Brother James" was doing extremely well as a barber; and of his sons, he proudly observed that Richard wrote in an excellent hand; Henry wanted to continue his education; James read extremely well "for a little boy of his age [6] and training;" and "John has wrote me two letter and writes very plain for a boy of eight, . . . and has as much taste for reading as any child I know off and is very good in arithmetic."[36] Rapier not only journeyed to Tennessee often, but about once a year, he travelled to New York or Canada.[37] After one such sojourn, he expressed concern for Brother Henry's future in the North. "I told him to buy [more] land in that country and to pay the taxes. [But] I am fearful that Brother Henry will come to want in [Canada] as I am of the opinion that [it] is poor farming country."[38] For their parts, Henry and James also expressed a deep concern for the welfare of the slave family. Henry usually concluded his letters with the simple, but significant, line: "All the family is well and wishes to be remembered to you."[39] And James Thomas wrote: "A letter from your hands [John Rapier Jr.] offers me a great deal of pleasure to say nothing of the family news it imparts."[40] It seems that separation, an inherent part of the institution of slavery, had little effect on the spiritual unity of the slave family.

There was also a solidarity among the members of the Rapier family. Deeply concerned about the welfare of his children, John Rapier offered them advice on everything from economic matters to questions of morality: "Settle your debts," "Save your money," "Stay away from liquor," he admonished "The Four Boys." "Stick closer to work and Say nothing and do nothing but what is right and you will do well my sons."[41] In 1845 he wrote Richard, who was attending school in Buffalo and living with Henry Thomas: "Study your books so I can hold you up as an example to your lettle Brothers. You are blessed if you will look at your situation. You have kind relations who are anctious to see you grow up an ornament to society."[42] Perhaps the best expression of the spiritual unity of the Rapier family was written by James Thomas Rapier, James P. Thomas's namesake and one of Sally's twenty-six grandchildren. Also living with fugitive Henry Thomas, and attending school in Buxton, he wrote:

> In our boyhood . . . all four of us boys were together. We all breathed as one. [Now] we are scattered abroad on the face of the Earth. Do you ever expect to see us all together again? I do not. Just look where we are . . . John in [Minnesota]. Myself in the north. Henry and Dick in California. Father in Alabama. Did you ever think how small our family is?[43]

Among the Rapiers, as well as the Thomases, there was an almost religious devotion to the institution of the family.

The ability of the slave family to remain so close seems all the more remarkable in the face of the legal restrictions placed on Blacks. Statutes forbade a free Black from either visiting with slaves, or travelling from one state to another, both on penalty of being sold into slavery. Laws prohibited slaves from owning personal property, renting real estate, earning money, or securing an education. "No person shall hire to any slave," one Tennessee code pronounced, "the time of said slave."[44] Lawmakers prescribed a ten year prison sentence to anyone helping a slave to escape, forging a pass for a slave, harboring a runaway or inciting a Black to defy a white; and laid down the death penalty for Blacks convicted of assaulting or molesting a white woman, maliciously setting fire to a barn, preparing any poison, or conspiring to revolt. "A ring leader or Chief Instigator of any plot to rebel or murder any white," one law stated, "may be lawfully killed [on sight], if it is not practicable, otherwise, to arrest and secure him."[45] Nashville ordinances required free Blacks to pay a capitation (head) tax of $1 or $2, register at the court house, and "carry free papers on their person at all times." Blacks without such papers were to be treated as slaves. Moreover, Negroes were not permitted to walk the streets after dark, enter tippling houses, make weird noises, or gather within the city limits for any purpose, except public worship, and Blacks attending church were to be supervised by whites.[46]

But the slave family disregarded the elaborate code governing Blacks. Sally hired out, earned money, rented a house, and operated a business. "Mother lived so long at the corner of Deaderick and Cherry Streets," James Thomas remarked later, "that the people of Nashville thought she [was free] and owned the property." She moved about the city with little hindrance, boarded her grandchildren as they attended school, and secretly advised Henry to escape to the North.[47] In a similar manner James Thomas hired out, earned money and established a business. He eventually accumulated a large amount of personal property—furniture, mirrors, clothes, and about $1000 in cash, and while still a slave, became the manager of one of the largest barbering establishments in Nashville. He travelled to various parts of the city without a pass, entertained free Blacks in his home, and attended black church meetings. At one such gathering he recalled the black congregation, mostly slaves, singing until 12 o'clock at night. "The owners," he wrote, "seemed to care very little how much religion their servants got. They seemed to encourage it."[48] In much the same way John Rapier and Henry Thomas acquired personal property, hired out, earned as much as $50 a month, and, despite the laws against the movement of Blacks, travelled throughout the South, North, and Canada. Rapier even assisted a slave, Sam Ragland, to escape on one occasion.[49] In short, the slave family was not in the least constrained by the restrictive black codes.

Sally's dream that all of her children secure their freedom finally came true in 1851, when her youngest son, James, asked Ephraim Foster to present a manumission petition to the Davidson County court. The slave and his master appeared at the courthouse in Nashville on March 6. "James has always maintained an exemplary character," Foster told the nine-judge panel hearing the case. "He has been industrious, honest, moral, humble, polite and had conducted himself as to gain the confidence and respect of whites. He is a man of great worth in his place." The testimony of such an eminent Tennessean swayed the magistrates and, after a short deliberation, they ordered "the slave James, otherwise called James [P.] Thomas, emancipated and forever set free." Thomas now addressed the court himself. He requested immunity from the 1831 law requiring manumitted Blacks to leave Tennessee. "I have deported myself in a manner requiring the confidence of whites. I have always earned a good living. I would be greatly damaged having to Start anew in some Strange Country." The judges, after receiving the required $500 good behavior bond, granted the immunity. James P. Thomas thus became the first black man in the county, perhaps the state, under the stringent emigration law of 1831, to gain legally both freedom and residency.[50]

A short time before James gained his freedom, however, Sally died of cholera.[51] A woman of great drive and dedication, she had devoted her life to freeing her children. She had hired out, started a business, and gladly put up her life savings to purchase "free papers" for James. She had also assisted Henry in his quest for freedom. Due in part to her unwavering efforts, the slaves John H. Rapier, Sr., Henry K. Thomas, and James P. Thomas, all gained free status before the Civil War. In addition, the Thomases and Rapiers all found great strength in the slave family. Members of these families were quite successful: John entered politics during Reconstruction; Henry farmed hundreds of acres in Canada; and James acquired property in St. Louis valued at $250,000;[52] while Sarah Thomas became a school teacher, James T. Rapier a Congressman, and John Rapier, Jr. a surgeon, stemmed from the security they found in the slave family.[53] It seems that for the black slave Sally, sexual exploitation, miscegenation, separation, and legal restrictions—the very forces designed, in part, to destroy the black family—gave impetus, *not* to disintegration and disunity, but to an extraordinary feeling of family loyalty, unity, and love. For Sally, her children, and her grandchildren, the slave family was indeed "a refuge from the rigors of slavery."

NOTES

1. E. Franklin Frazier, *The Negro Family in the United States* (Chicago: University of Chicago Press, 1939), pp. 40, 41; "The Negro Slave Family," *Journal of Negro History XV* (April, 1930), pp. 198–259.

2. Stanley M. Elkins, *Slavery: A Problem in American Institutional and Intellectual Life* (Chicago: University of Chicago Press, 1959), pp. 53, 54.

3. Richard C. Wade, *Slavery in the Cities: The South, 1820–1860* (New York: Oxford University Press, 1964), pp. 117–121.

4. Lee Rainwater and William L. Yancey, *The Moynihan Report and the Politics of Controversy* (Cambridge, Massachusetts: The Massachusetts Institute of Technology Press, 1967), pp. 61, 62, 414, 415.

5. Herbert Gutman is working on a book length study of the black family. See: Tamara K. Hareven, editor, *Anonymous Americans: Explorations in Nineteenth-Century Social History* (Englewood Cliffs, N.J.: Prentice-Hall, Inc., 1971), p. 209; Robert H. Abzug, "The Black Family During Reconstruction," in Nathan I. Huggins, Martin Kilson and Daniel M. Fox, *Key Issues in the Afro-American Experience* (New York: Harcourt Brace Jovanovich, Inc., 1971), pp. 26–41; John

W. Blassingame, *The Slave Community: Plantation Life in the Ante-Bellum South* (New York: Oxford University Press, 1971), chapter III.

6. It is not the purpose of this paper to enter the contemporary sociological debate on the origins of the "black matriarchy." As it happened, the central figure in this slave family was a woman. All three of her slave children, however, became dominant fathers, maintaining their marriages for twenty-six, forty-two, and thirty years respectively. In addition, it is not the purpose of this essay to differentiate between the family attitudes of the mother, who remained in bondage, and her children, who eventually gained their freedom. Their family attitudes were for the most part the same.

7. "The Autobiographical Reminiscences of James P. Thomas," Moorland-Spingarn Collection, Howard University, Washington, D.C., [1911], p. 1; hereafter "Thomas Autobiography." In the original manuscript many of the pages are out of place and un-numbered. Thus the page numbers cited are only approximate; Albemarle County Probate Records, Deed Books, Book XXXII (January 2, 1835), p. 89; *ibid.*, Book VI (July 14, 1814), p. 26; *ibid.*, Book IX (November 17, 1825), p. 260; The Genealogy of a Slave Family.

8. "Thomas Autobiography," pp. 2–7; U.S. Census Office, Sixth Census of the United States, "Population Schedules for Lauderdale County, Alabama," Vol. IV, 1840, p. 104.

9. Winthrop Jordan, *White Over Black: American Attitudes Toward the Negro, 1550–1812* (Chapel Hill: University of North Carolina Press, 1968), p. 76; Albemarle County Probate Records, Deed Books, Book XXXII (January 2, 1835), pp. 89, 90.

10. "Thomas Autobiography," pp. 3–6.

11. *Ibid.; The Nashville Business Directory* (Nashville: Printed by John P. Campbell, 1855), *passim;* "Miscellaneous Notes of James P. Thomas," Moorland-Spingarn Collection, Howard University, Washington, D.C., n.p.

12. Richard Rapier, described as "a large fleshy man weighing over 200 pounds," settled in Nashville about 1799. Soon he was transporting large quantities of tobacco to New Orleans and returning with sugar, teas and coffee. In 1806 he formed a "copartnership" with Lemuel T. Turner and James Jackson.

13. Davidson County Probate Records, Minutes, Vol. C. (July 1801), p. 405; *The Tennessee Gazette and Metro District Advertiser Repository*, March 29, 1898; *The Clarion*, September 27, 1808; *The Imperial Review and Cumberland Repository*, May 5, 1808; *The Democratic Clarion and Tennessee Gazette*, May 19, 1812, May 31, 1814.

14. "Thomas Autobiography," chapter 1; "Miscellaneous Notes of James P. Thomas," Moorland-Spingarn Collection, Howard University, Washington, D.C., n.p. (See page 33)

15. "Thomas Autobiography," p. 7.

16. *Ibid.*, chapter 1; *Acts Passed at the First and Second Session of the Nineteenth General Assembly of the State of Tennessee* (Nashville: Allen Hall and A. S. Heiskel, Printers to the State, 1832), pp. 167–170.

17. Lauderdale County Probate Records, Wills, Vol. VI (June 3, 1824), p. 117; *Acts of the Eleventh Annual Session of the General Assembly of the State of Alabama* (Tuscaloosa: McGuire, Henry and Walker, 1830), p. 36; Richard Rapier, Auburn, California, to James P. Thomas, December 14, 1877, Rapier Papers,

Moorland-Spingarn Collection, Howard University, Washington, D.C., hereafter Rapier Papers.

18. "Thomas Autobiography," chapter 1; "Miscellaneous Notes of James P. Thomas," Moorland-Spingarn Collection, Howard University, Washington, D.C., n.p.; John H. Rapier, Sr., Florence, Alabama, to Henry K. Thomas, Buffalo, New York, February 28, 1843, Rapier Papers; A. M. Simmons, Cincinnati, Ohio, to Henry K. Thomas, Buffalo, New York, May 26, 1836, *ibid.; Buffalo City Directory* (Buffalo: Horatio N. Walker, Publisher, 1844), p. 213.

19. "Thomas Autobiography," pp. 1–6.

20. *Acts Passed at the First and Second Session of the Nineteenth General Assembly of the State of Tennessee* (Nashville: Allen Hall and A. S. Heiskel, Printers to the State, 1832), p. 167; Robert William Fogel and Stanley L. Engerman in their statistical study *Time on the Cross: The Economics of American Negro Slavery* (Boston, 1974) also conclude that the slave family was a viable institution, but they, like most historians concerned with the peculiar institution, emphasize the role and attitudes of whites. They suggest that the Negro family survived for three basic reasons: the desire of planters to promote family stability (to increase the output of contented slaves); the extreme reluctance of owners to break up family units; and the Victorian attitudes among the planting class, which made miscegenation extremely rare, resulting in a miniscule percent of mulattoes in the ante bellum South (7.7 in 1850 and 10.4 in 1860). Besides the impressionistic evidence used by the two cliometricians to support their contentions, the dubious relationship between the extent of sexual exploitation and the percent of mulattoes in the South in a given year (which is itself upon question), and the mis-interpretation of the quantified evidence concerning the break up of families on the New Orleans auction block between 1804–1862 (the authors suggest 84 percent of the sales involved unmarried individuals, but failed to reveal that the slave's familial status was generally not recorded), the greatest weakness of the study is the obvious inadequacy of quantification methods in evaluating the slave family. Statistical evidence does not reveal the feelings of interdependence, unity, and cohesiveness that black family members in bondage felt for one another. Robert William Fogel and Stanley L. Engerman, *Time on the Cross: The Economics of American Negro Slavery* (Boston, 1974), pp. 126–144.

21. "Thomas Autobiography," chapters 1, 2; "Miscellaneous Notes of James P. Thomas," Moorland-Spingarn Collection, Howard University, Washington, D.C.; James P. Thomas, Nashville, Tennessee, to John H. Rapier, Jr., St. Paul, Minnesota Territory, October 3, 1856.

22. The Nashville *Republican,* April 21, 1836; The Nashville *Daily Republican Banner,* April 9, 1841; Davidson County Probate Records, Minutes, Book E (October 4, 1853), pp. 563–564. Many times, as in this instance, probate court cases included biographical material about Blacks to illustrate their "good character." Davidson County Probate Records, Wills and Inventories, Vol. 16 (November 28, 1854), pp. 429–430.

23. John H. Rapier, Sr., Florence, Alabama, to Henry K. Thomas, Buffalo, New York, February 28, 1843, Rapier Papers.

24. John H. Rapier, Sr., Florence, Alabama, to Richard Rapier, Buffalo, New York, April 8, 1845, Rapier Papers.

25. "Thomas Autobiography," chapters 1, 2, 3; *The Nashville General Business Directory* (Nashville: The Daily American Book and Job Printing Office, 1853),

1–20; For the early business and financial activities of E. S. Hall in Nashville, see: John Claybrooke Papers, Manuscript Division, State Library and Archives, Nashville, Tennessee; For the activities of the other whites mentioned, see: Philip Hamer, *Tennessee: A History,* Vol. I (New York: American Historical Society, 1935), pp. 282, 370, 381, 475; "Leadership in Nashville: Biographical Sketches of 116 of the Most Prominent Citizens in Nashville," Catherine Pilcher Avery Papers, Manuscript Division, State Library and Archives, Nashville, Tennessee; "Old Days in Nashville, Tennessee: Reminiscences by Jane Thomas," (no relation to James Thomas), reprints from the Nashville *Daily American,* 1895–1896 in Jane Thomas Papers, Manuscript Division, State Library and Archives, Nashville, Tennessee; *The Official Political Manual of the State of Tennessee* (Nashville, Tennessee: Marshall and Bruce, 1890), p. 180.

26. Ellen S. Fogg, Nashville, Tennessee, to E. H. Foster, Louisville, Kentucky, February 15, 1849, Ephraim Foster Papers, Manuscript Division, State Library and Archives, Nashville, Tennessee.

27. "Thomas Autobiography," chapter 2.

28. *Nashville Business Directory* (Nashville: Daily American Book and Job Printing Office, 1853), p. 68.

29. Richard Rapier, Auburn, California, to James P. Thomas, December 14, 1877, Rapier Papers; In this letter Richard, John Rapier's eldest son, refers to his date and place of birth. In the "Diary and Notes of John H. Rapier, Jr.," March 10, 1857, Rapier Papers; John, Rapier's third son, likewise refers to his birth date; U.S. Census Office, Sixth Census of the United States, "Population Schedules for Lauderdale County, Alabama," Vol. IV, (1840), p. 104; James T. Rapier, Florence, Alabama to John H. Rapier, Jr., St. Paul, Minnesota Territory, September 27, 1858, Rapier Papers; "Thomas Autobiography," p. 73; *Alabama State Sentinel,* November 25, 1867; The inscription on Susan Rapier's tombstone reads: "Sacred to the memory of Susan Rapier. Born in Baltimore, Md. 25 of December 1811 departed this life at Florence Alabama 10 of March 1841—also her two infant children Jackson and Alexander—Depart my friends and dry up your tears for I must lie hear [sic] till Christ appears."

30. U.S. Census Bureau, Sixth Census of the United States, Population Schedules for Lauderdale County, Alabama," Vol. IV, (1840), p. 104; United States Census Bureau, Seventh Census of the United States, Populations Schedules for Lauderdale County, Alabama," Vol. I, (1850), p. 293; United States Census Bureau, Eighth Census of the United States, Vol. VI (1860), p. 39.

31. John H. Rapier, Sr., Florence, Alabama, to Richard Rapier, Buffalo, New York, April 8, 1845, Rapier Papers; John H. Rapier, Sr., Florence, Alabama, to John H. Rapier, Jr., St. Paul, Minnesota Territory, September 16, 1857, Rapier Papers; Lauderdale County Probate Records, Wills and Inventories, Vol. B (September 13, 1869), pp. 78–80, Land Deeds, Book II (May 3, 1844), p. 78; Book XVI (August 7, 1858), p. 324; The Florence *Gazette,* March 5, 1862; Loren Schweninger, "John H. Rapier, Sr.: A Slave and Freedman in the Antebellum South," *Civil War History*/Vol. 20, (March 1974), p. 31.

32. A. M. Simmons, Cincinnati, Ohio, to Henry K. Thomas, Buffalo, New York, May 26, 1836, Rapier Papers; *Buffalo City Directory* (Buffalo: Horatio N. Walker, Publisher, 1844), p. 213; John H. Rapier, Sr., Florence, Alabama, to Henry K. Thomas, Buffalo, New York, February 28, 1843, Rapier Papers; "Thomas Autobiography," chapter 1; *Buffalo City Directory* (Buffalo: Jewett, Thomas and Company, Commercial Advertiser Office, 1847–48), p. 158.

33. Henry K. Thomas, Buxton, Canada West, to John H. Rapier, Sr., Florence, Alabama, October 27, 1856, Rapier Papers; James T. Rapier, Buxton, Canada West, to John H. Rapier, Jr., St. Paul, Minnesota Territory, June 26, 1857, Rapier Papers; "Thomas Autobiography," chapter 1.

34. Henry K. Thomas, Buxton, Canada West, to John H. Rapier, Sr., Florence, Alabama, October 27, 1856, Rapier Papers.

35. John H. Rapier, Sr., Florence, Alabama, to Henry K. Thomas, Buffalo, New York, February 28, 1843, Rapier Papers.

36. John H. Rapier, Sr., Florence, Alabama, to Richard Rapier, Buffalo, New York, April 8, 1845, Rapier Papers.

37. "The Autobiography of William King," (1890), p. 255, King Papers, Public Archives of Canada, Ottawa, Ontario; King, who founded Buxton, reminisced about Rapier's frequent visits to Toronto and Buxton during the 1850's; John H. Rapier, Sr., Florence, Alabama, to John H. Rapier, Jr., Minnesota Territory, September 16, 1857, Rapier Papers.

38. John H. Rapier, Sr., Florence, Alabama, to John H. Rapier, Jr., Minnesota Territory, September 15, 1856, Rapier Papers.

39. Henry K. Thomas, Buxton, Canada West, to John H. Rapier, Sr., October 27, 1856, Rapier Papers; March 13, 1857; Henry's only daughter Sarah wrote to John Rapier, Jr.: "Through Papa and James I would like to give you some news ... Mama and Papa are well as is the rest of the family and they sent their compliments. We shall all feel very much pleased if you make a visit to this place." Sarah Thomas, Buxton, Canada West, to John H. Rapier, Jr., Minnesota Territory, March 10, 1857, Rapier Papers.

40. James P. Thomas, St. Louis, Missouri, to John H. Rapier, Jr., Minnesota Territory, June 17, 1858, Rapier Papers.

41. John H. Rapier, Sr., Florence, Alabama to John H. Rapier, Jr., Minnesota Territory, September 15, 1856, Rapier Papers; John H. Rapier, Sr., Florence, Alabama to John H. Rapier, Jr., Benton County, Minnesota Territory, December 13, 1856, Rapier Papers.

42. John H. Rapier, Sr., Florence, Alabama, to Richard Rapier, Buffalo, New York, April 8, 1845, Rapier Papers.

43. James Rapier, Buxton, Canada West to John H. Rapier, Jr., Little Falls, Minnesota Territory, January 27, 1857, Rapier Papers.

44. *Acts Passed at the First Session of the Fourteenth General Assembly of the State of Tennessee* (Knoxville: Heiskell and Brown, Public Printers to the State, 1821), p. 34; *Acts Passed at the Second Session of the Fourteenth General Assembly of the State of Tennessee* (Knoxville: Heiskell and Brown, Printers to the State, 1822), p. 22; *Acts Passed at the First Session of the Fifteenth General Assembly of the State of Tennessee* (Murfreesborough: J. Norvell and G. A. and A. C. Sablett, 1823), p. 76; *Acts Passed at the Extra Session of the Sixteenth General Assembly of the State of Tennessee* (Knoxville: Heiskell and Brown, 1927), 31–33; *Acts Passed at the First and Second Session of the Nineteenth General Assembly of the State of Tennessee* (Nashville: Allen A. Hall and A. S. Heiskell, Printers to the State, 1932), pp. 165–170.

45. *Private Acts Passed at the Called Session of the Nineteenth General Assembly of the State of Tennessee* (Nashville: Allen A. Hall and F. S. Heiskell, Printers, 1832), pp. 5, 6; *Public Acts Passed at the First Session of the Twentieth General Assembly of the State of Tennessee* (Nashville: Allen A. Hall and F. S. Heiskell,

Printers to the State, 1833), pp. 2, 3, 75, 76, 14, 87, 94, 99, 100, 215, 216; *Public Acts Passed at the First Session of the Twenty-first General Assembly of the State of Tennessee* (Nashville: S. Nye and Co., Printers, 1836), pp. 92, 145, 146, 167; *Acts Passed at the First Session of the Twenty-third General Assembly of the State of Tennessee* (Nashville: J. Geo. Harris, Printer to the State, 1840), pp. 82, 83; *Acts Passed by the First Session of the Twenty-fourth General Assembly of the State of Tennessee* (Murfreesborough: Cameron and Company, Printers to the State, 1842), pp. 229, 230; *Acts of the State of Tennessee Passed at the First Session of the Twenty-sixth General Assembly* (Knoxville: James C. Moses, 1846), p. 278; *Acts of the State of Tennessee Passed at the First Session of the Twenty-eighth General Assembly* (Nashville: McKennie and Watterson, Printers to the State, 1850), p. 30; *Acts of the State of Tennessee Passed at the First Session of the Twenty-eighth General Assembly* (Nashville: McKennie and Watterson, Printers to the State, 1850), p. 304; *Acts Passed at the First Session of the Twenty-ninth General Assembly* (Nashville: McKennie Printers, 1852); pp. 120, 521; *Acts of the State of Tennessee Passed at the First Session of the Thirtieth General Assembly* (Nashville: McKennie and Brown, Book and Job Printers, 1854), pp. 121, 122, 157; *Acts of the State of Tennessee Passed at the First Session of the Thirty-first General Assembly* (Nashville: Printed by G. C. Torbett and Company, 1856), pp. 71, 77; William Imes, "The Legal Status of Free Negroes and Slaves in Tennessee," *Journal of Negro History*, IV (July 1919), pp. 260, 261.

46. *Revised Laws of the City of Nashville* (Nashville: Union and American Steam Press, 1854), pp. 147, 154–58; *Revised Laws of the City of Nashville* (Nashville: Harvey M. Watterson Printers, 1850), pp. 124–26; *Acts Passed at the First Session of the Twenty-fifth General Assembly of the State of Tennessee* (Nashville: L. Gifford and E. G. Eastman, Printers, 1844), p. 18.

47. "Thomas Autobiography," chapter 1.

48. *Ibid.;* "Miscellaneous Notes of James P. Thomas," Moorland-Spingarn Collection, Howard University, Washington, D.C., n.d.; James P. Thomas, Louisville, Kentucky, to John H. Rapier, Jr., St. Paul, Minnesota Territory, March 1, 1856, Rapier Papers; James P. Thomas, Nashville, Tennessee, to John H. Rapier, Jr., Minnesota Territory, October 3, 1856, Rapier Papers.

49. Loren Schweninger, "John H. Rapier, Sr.: A Slave and Freedman in the Antebellum South," Vol. 20, *Civil War History* (March 1974), *passim.*

50. "Thomas Autobiography," pp. 1–8; Davidson County Probate Records, Minute Book E (March 6, 1851), pp. 134, 135.

51. "Thomas Autobiography," p. 1; James Thomas said that his mother died in a cholera epidemic in 1850, but it was probably in the spring of 1849, when hundreds of Nashvillians died from the dreaded disease.

52. The Florence *Journal,* September 18, 1869; Assessors Records, City of St. Louis, Plate 1874–1876, number B65, Blk 300, 301, 691; Assessors Records, City of St. Louis, Tax Books for 1871, Book 17 (1871), pp. 20–21; Probate Records of the City of St. Louis, Warranty Deeds, Book 452 (August 13, 1872), pp. 470, 471; "Autobiography of William King," pp. 355–360.

53. James T. Rapier, Montgomery, Alabama, to William King, Buxton, Ontario, July 7, 1872, King Papers; Loren Schweninger, "James Rapier and Reconstruction," (PH.D. dissertation, Chicago, 1972), *passim.*

11

Working-Class Women in the Gilded Age: Factory, Community, and Family Life among Cohoes, New York, Cotton Workers

Daniel J. Walkowitz

In much of the recent work characterized as the "New Urban History," sociologists and historians have focused on the relationship between social mobility and behavior within the nineteenth-century working class.[1] To a large extent this scholarship has tried to grapple with the question often posed by the New Left: "Whatever happened to the revolution?" Two alternative arguments have generally been put forth concerning working-class oppression and united or individual efforts towards social amelioration. In the first case, the oppressed working class organized and struggled—even violently—to gain some affluence and security through the labor movement. In the second case, workers individually achieved some mobility, and consequently little or no united effort was made to win a social revolution.[2] Something, however, of both these views may be correct: workers lived and worked under oppressive conditions, but workers achieved some significant

This is an expanded version of a paper read at the annual meeting of the American Historical Association in Boston, December 30, 1970. Data for the paper were compiled from the United States manuscript census schedules for the city of Cohoes, Albany County, New York: Census Office, 8th Census of Population, 1860; Census Office, 8th Census of Manufactures 1860; Census Office, 10th Census of Population, 1880; and, 10th Census of Manufactures, 1880. Especially helpful also was Arthur Masten, *History of Cohoes, New York, From its Earliest Settlement to the Present Time* (Albany, 1877).

measure of social mobility. Furthermore, considerable violence did occur in labor struggles, but no social revolution occurred.

These seeming paradoxes hinge on the contrast between working-class mobility as it was perceived by the members of the working class themselves and the attempt to make some "objective" assessment of the parameters of that mobility. This essay intends to examine the ways in which the cultural experience of the predominantly immigrant working class might have distorted their view of their social conditions and impaired their ability to focus on the origins of their oppression. Consequently, working-class violence, rather than being directed at the manufacturer, was directed at the ranks of the unemployed ready to claim their jobs. In this way, the working class did not engage in aggressive violence to win a social revolution so much as it fought defensive struggles to protect its modest gains.

Working-class behavior is not merely a response to objective social conditions but is fundamentally shaped by the *perception* of those conditions. Historians have correctly emphasized the poverty and fragility of working-class economic and social existence during the Gilded Age. For instance, a New York State Assembly Committee investigating laboring conditions declared that the testimony of 17 randomly selected employees of the Harmony cotton mills in Cohoes, New York, "very clearly establishes . . . [that] very few families are enabled to save money, while a majority of them barely manage to make both ends meet at the close of the year."[3] But these harsh social realities must be viewed in the context of the expectations—the social dream—and the alternatives open to the working-class community. While violence marked the struggle to control the conditions of industrial life, the equation between poverty and violent social behavior is not precise. The history of the Cohoes cotton worker community is a case in point.

Cohoes, New York, is a small city located eight miles north of Albany on the west bank of the Hudson River at the confluence of that river and the Mohawk River. The cotton mills of Cohoes provided job opportunities in light industry for female laborers, opportunities that helped to create an unusual social community: the mills attracted a high percentage of working women and almost one quarter of the cotton worker families was headed by a woman. Confronted by the values of Puritan America, subjected to the social paternalism of the Harmony Corporation and sensitive to the demands of their own ethnic traditions, these women were immersed in a patriarchal culture. What kind of security and status, then, could Cohoes offer these women and their families? And, equally important, how did security and status function? The history of Cohoes' cotton workers demonstrates that the factory and the community helped both to sustain the mill operatives and to secure some social mobility for them. However, the small degree of status and security they attained did not liberate them from economic and social worries; rather, these modest gains restricted their field of vision and alienated them from their own social reality. It is within this context that we must view labor violence that erupted in Cohoes during the early 1880s.

During the 1870s, in the midst of a national economic storm that produced many financial failures, bitter strikes and violence, the Harmony Mills had offered relative industrial calm—with the not inconsiderable financial security and stability that this represented, especially for the immigrant working-class family. The depression compelled the Harmony Mills to close only one month during that entire decade; and while wages fell, the workers never struck. However, the tone and temper of Cohoes industrial life changed suddenly in 1880. In that year, and in 1882, extended strikes were fought. The strikes and lockouts began usually over further wage reductions, but at their core was a conflict over union recognition and power. These struggles culminated in violent mob scenes where angry women cotton workers and their children confronted imported Swedish "scab" workers and their police bodyguards.

Why was the Cohoes labor movement dormant during the 1870s, and why did disorder and violence erupt after 1880? If as E.P. Thompson suggests,[4] class is a relationship between people, a shared consciousness, what then were the dominant needs and values that influenced working-class behavior? What institutions were most valuable to them? And what effect did the industrial experience have on the position and attitudes of women in nineteenth-century Cohoes? Did it permit them some measure of independence; did it give them some role in community life; did they suffer a loss of status by having to leave the home to work? Central to our concern is the relationship between the factory, the community and the cotton worker and her family.

Since the Industrial Revolution, woman as worker has been seen as a contradiction in terms, as some sort of sin against nature. This attitude underlay the widely held belief that for women to work would, as Richard Ely wrote in 1893, mean "the scattering of the members of the family and the breakdown of the home...."[5] Carroll D. Wright, writing in the Tenth United States Census in 1880 identified the factory as the culprit: "The factory system necessitates the employment of women and children to an injurious extent, and consequently its tendency is to destroy family life and ties and domestic habits, and ultimately the home."[6] Wright's implications were clear: since the factory system removed mother from the home, it destroyed the family; therefore, remove women from the factory and the family would be saved.

Although they have disagreed on the causes, many historians have accepted the view that the working-class family was disorganized. Oscar Handlin has suggested, for example, that the urban industrial slum, "the disorganizing pressure of the environment," and not the factory, weakened the family.[7] In this way, the city, the factory and the immigrant experience, each have received the blame for the disorganization of the working-class family.

The history of the Cohoes, New York, cotton worker community, suggests the need to reconsider the impact of the factory and the city on the lives of the cotton worker and her family. Quite early in its history Cohoes had one distinct feature: by 1860 it had become a company town. Although both wool and cotton mills gave the city its title as the Spindle City, the Harmony Mills Company dominated the city, and by 1864 monopolized the town's cotton industry. But the Harmony Company controlled much more than Cohoes' cotton industry. In association with the wool manufacturers, company officials constituted an interlocking directorate that held virtually every major political and financial post in the city throughout this period.[8] And lastly, the company maintained considerable economic influence over the working-class community. The company built and rented the more than 800 brick tenement houses and five boarding houses that spread over Harmony Hill, the city's first ward where the cotton workers all lived. In addition, Harmony Mill paternalism oversaw the workers' lives from the child's attendance at the Sabbath School to the family's weekly food purchased from the Company Store. Consequently, strike issues included not only wages and hours, but also such complaints as the credit system under which the cotton workers bought their food and the rent deducted from the family's pay.

The cotton mills, led by the Harmony Company, more than kept pace with the growth of the overwhelmingly working-class inhabitants of Cohoes, whose population numbered only 1,850 residents in 1840, 8,800 in 1860 and 19,416 in 1880. Consequently, while approximately one out of every four Cohosiers worked as a cotton hand in 1860, the ratio had risen to almost one in three in 1880. Most important, 60 percent of these cotton workers were women, and in 1860 more than half were immigrant Irish, while in 1880 four out of every five cotton workers were either first or second generation Irish or French-Canadian immigrants.

The experience of Cohoes suggests, however, that the factory and the working-class community play a more ambiguous part in the life of workers and their families than is traditionally thought. The cotton workers organized in response to this corporative omnipresence, and their activities touched all aspects of social life in the Harmony Hill community. The working class organized around the factory. Led by the skilled male spinners and female weavers, cotton workers organized unions which struck and won a wage advance in the Harmony Mills in 1858. During and immediately after the Civil War, the union activity waned, but the cotton workers did participate in the Short Hour Movement, the Workingman's Party and in the Workingman's Cooperative Store. Since working-class culture on Cohoes' Harmony Hill was also ethnic culture, mass strike rallies were addressed in both French and English to help unite the Irish and French Canadians around their common problems and needs. For certain issues involved social conditions which these people experienced together. So, to their laboring, political and ethnic activities must be added their role within the Harmony Hill community. For almost all cotton workers and their families lived on the Hill. There these workers had constructed a full and complex network of fraternal, religious and political clubs and institutions that offered them entertainment, security and some cultural nourishment. Usually several members of each family and occasionally whole families worked in the mills. These workers were not concerned only with narrow economic questions, but saw union activity as vital to the security of their family and community, security some had traveled as much as 3,000 miles to achieve. Thus, we have to view the working-class woman in the full context of her community. But before we can begin to understand behavior within the working-class community, we need to identify the workers and their families and see what changes took place in the Harmony Hill community between 1860 and 1880.

For Lucy Larcom[9] and her fellow workers in the 1830s, the cotton mill might have seemed like a boarding school for young ladies; but in Cohoes in 1857 the image of the factory and the factory girl had drastically changed. In reply to a series of letters from "A Factory Girl" in the local newspaper, a town teacher explains why she held these girls in contempt: "I *do* claim to be superior to the vulgar herd with which our factories are stocked, and I *do* consider them unfit to associate with me, or to move in the same society to which I belong. Such, too, is the sentiment of all 'Upper Tendom.' "[10] For the "elite" of Cohoes society who may well have spent their own girlhood in the mills, factory life had lost status. But it remains to be seen whether it had lost status for the large masses of Cohosiers who now worked in the mills.

The manuscript United States Census of Population for Cohoes in 1860 does not distinguish between cotton and wool workers,[11] but the average textile worker in the town was not a native American by birth.[12] Factory life had become predominantly an immigrant experience. More than one half the employees in 1860 were either Irish immigrants or their children, only one quarter were native Americans, while English and French-Canadian hands each constituted less than one tenth of the workers. The typical cotton worker had more than a single social and cultural identity: this worker was both Irish and female. Moreover, the Harmony Mills cotton hand was most likely an unskilled and unmarried woman between the ages of 15 and 25. Four out of every five Irish women between the ages of 15 and 19 worked in the mills in 1860 (Table 3).

Although fewer women and young men were employed among the other ethnic groups, they followed a common pattern: children entered the mills in their early teens and left increasingly in their twenties. Women then married and men found employment outside the mills. Only English males remained in the mills. Usually married and of middle-age they worked as skilled spinners, weavers, dressers and carders. The husbands of other cotton mill workers found other jobs. Americans established themselves in trades or business outside the factory, while the Irish and French-Canadians became unskilled day laborers on the Erie and Champlain canal network or on the factory maintenance staff.[13]

Thus, even before the Civil War, immigrant Irish families had found work for their children in the Harmony Mills. While the Irish clearly dominated the mills, they were joined by a sizable number of native American workers. Other ethnic groups also moved readily into the mills in numbers equal to their relative share of the city's population. Finally, the factory did not draw mothers away from their families. When they married and began raising families women did not work. Their children worked. The additional income especially from unmarried daughters could be put to good advantage. As Stephan Thernstrom discovered among the Newburyport Irish, income provided by the children enabled the family to gain some small measure of the security Ireland had not afforded—property. Similarly in the Cohoes working-class community of 1860, it was mainly a few families headed by Irish cotton workers who accumulated property: 11 percent of these Irishmen owned property in 1860, compared to only 5.9 percent of the Englishmen, 1.8 percent of the Americans and none of the French Canadians.

Cohoes differed from the early New England textile town. Not only did young immigrant Irishwomen dominate the Cohoes cotton mills in 1860, but also by this time weaving remained the only skilled trade in which women still readily found employment: slightly more than half

TABLE 1 Factory (Textile) Workers (FW) and Ethnicity, 1860, and Cotton Workers (CW) and Ethnicity, 1880

1860*	Male	Female	Total	Percent of Population	FW† (%)
All Textile Workers (Ten and Over)	778 41.4%	1103 58.6%	1881	28.3	100.0
Native American	197 40.2%	293 59.8%	490	22.8	26.0
Irish	377 37.9%	617 62.1%	994	31.6	52.8
English	101 57.7%	74 42.3%	175	30.0	9.3
Fr. Canadian	50 40.3%	74 59.7%	124	26.2	6.5
*1880**					
All Cotton Workers (Ten and Over)	1280 39.5%	1964 60.5%	3244	21.3	100.0
Native American	136 47.9%	148 52.1%	284	9.1	8.8
Irish	514 34.9%	958 66.1%	1472	26.8	45.4
English	151 57.6%	111 42.4%	262	19.2	8.1
Fr. Canadian	435 39.2%	674 60.8%	1109	24.6	34.2

*Manuscript Census of Population data.

†Percentages of ethnic groups do not total 100% because small numbers of Scottish and German workers are omitted.

the Cohoes weavers in 1860 were women. The number of skilled workers distinguished by the census leaves much to be desired. But while the English filled skilled positions in the mills considerably in excess of their relatively small numbers in the town, Irishmen and women held skilled as well as unskilled positions (Table 2). This evidence shows the Irishmen did more than dig ditches and lay railroad track and Irishwomen worked in other than domestic services.[14] While the relative concentration of female English weavers was six times that of the Irish, in Civil War Cohoes, Irishwomen held as many skilled posts as weavers as did workers of American and English extraction. Native Americans still held about one quarter of the jobs, but by 1860 Cohoes' cotton mills had become largely Irish "institutions."

Between 1860 and 1880, Cohoes' Harmony Mills expanded greatly. New hands were needed to operate her spinning mules and looms. But

TABLE 2 Percentage and Relative Concentration* of Skilled and Unskilled Cotton Workers in Ethnic Groups, 1860 and 1880

1860	Unskilled Males	Unskilled Females	Skilled Males	Skilled Females	Spinners (Males)	Dressers Carders (Males)
USA	25.3%	26.5%	2.4%	32.6%	16.6%	46.1%
	80	84	8	103	52	145
IRE	48.4%	55.9%	36.6%	32.6%	25.0%	7.6%
	107	114	81	67	55	17
ENG.	12.9%	6.7%	46.3%	32.6%	50.0%	30.7%
	130	86	468	418	505	310
FR. CAN	6.4%	6.7%	0.0%	0.0%	0.0%	7.6%
	86	97	0	0	0	103
N:	778	1103	41	46	12	13
1880						
USA	10.6%	7.5%	11.1%	2.0%	0.0%	9.0%
	53	37	58	10	0	44
IRE	40.2%	48.8%	44.4%	72.9%	60.0%	54.5%
	117	139	127	200	175	159
ENG	11.8%	5.7%	11.1%	14.5%	33.3%	22.7%
	122	70	117	177	342	233
FR. CAN	34.0%	34.3%	0.0%	4.1%	0.0%	4.5%
	121	114	0	14	0	16
N:	1280	1964	9	48	30	22

*Proportion among gainful workers in all occupations = 100.

how had the characteristics of the average cotton worker and her family changed during these decades? And again, in what ways did these changes reflect the absence of union activity and relative quiescence of the Cohoes' cotton worker then?

During the two decades in question, the most dramatic change in the mill labor force involved the native American and French-Canadian ethnic groups. Whereas one out of every four unskilled textile workers in Cohoes in 1860 had been of native American extraction, and less than one in ten had been of French Canadian origin, by 1880 the percentages were virtually reversed (Table 1). The Harmony Mills population had doubled, but the number of native American workers was almost one half its 1860 figure. The 124 French-Canadian textile workers counted in 1860, for instance, had increased by 1880 ninefold to 1,109 in the cotton mills alone; the number of native Americans dropped 42 percent during this period from 490 to 284. Almost half the workers were still Irish, but better than one in three unskilled cotton hands were of French-Canadian ancestry. Native American and English workers now comprised less than one in ten of each group. Even under the pressure represented by the influx of large numbers of

TABLE 3 Percentage of Cohoes Men and Women of an Age and Ethnic Group Employed as Cohoes Factory (Textile) Workers, 1860

Ethnicity	Age 10–14	15–19	20–29	30–39	40+
American	5.4%	57.2%	34.8%	13.3%	6.9%
Irish	14.7%	81.9%	47.7%	13.7%	6.2%
Females					
English	11.5%	50.8%	31.8%	21.8%	9.2%
French Canadian	11.1%	77.0%	26.0%	12.1%	0.0%
American	6.4%	50.3%	24.9%	13.7%	7.4%
Irish	16.4%	67.6%	29.4%	18.1%	8.8%
Males					
English	3.6%	40.5%	52.1%	44.3%	23.6%
French Canadian	7.8%	58.0%	27.1%	25.0%	10.7%

"cheap" employable French-Canadian immigrant laborers, the Irish found additional employment in the mills. Similarly, the French Canadians found Harmony Hill to be a hospitable textile center. It is true that almost all teenage members of the family had to work for subsistence wages and everyone in the community depended heavily on company paternalism. The Harmony Mills, however, offered these people steady employment, solid brick-construction housing and a steady though meagre income. The French Canadian had found a home and, with friends, had established a community.

Although each ethnic group had distinct work patterns that reflected its separate cultural background, there were similarities among them. Two out of every three cotton workers in 1880 were female. The Irish and French Canadians maintained this ratio, while in contrast, the number of American-born men and women was almost even, and the number of English male workers continued as in 1860 to exceed the number of females in the mills. Native Americans had left the mills: 22.8 percent of the native population age ten and over labored in the textile mills in 1860, but by 1880 the percentage had dropped to 9.1 percent. Otherwise, among each of the three large immigrant ethnic groups—the Irish, French Canadians and English—the percentage of cotton workers remained about one out of every four or five "adults." Finally, as in 1860, the English continued to show a work pattern different from the other groups: the average English cotton hand was more likely to be a married male who was older than was his Irish, French-Canadian or native-American counterpart.

Thus, the typical unskilled cotton hand in 1880 was probably an Irish or French-Canadian woman. Not only was she a young unmarried woman, but the reverse was equally true: if one was a young Irish or

French-Canadian girl growing up in Cohoes, the chance that she once worked, still worked or would shortly work in the Harmony Mills was most probable. It was also likely that she started work in the mills at an earlier age in 1880 than she would have in 1860, especially if she was of French-Canadian extraction (Table 4).

The percentage of workers under twenty remained at about 50 percent in both census years, but the percentage of children under 14 employed tripled between 1860 and 1880 from 7.4 percent of the entire work force in 1860 to 24.1 percent in 1880. And while the increase was more marked among boys than girls, both vastly increased; and children from all ethnic groups worked. The average age of the workers remained fairly constant, at approximately 20. However, the average age of the women *did* vary with ethnicity: for instance, two out of every three female French-Canadian cotton workers were *under* 20, while the same percentage of English were *over* 20. These differences suggest different attitudes toward the child's role in the family and the birth rate among the different ethnic groups. A higher number of English women did not work. The key here is that fewer English children worked. Married Englishwomen did not flock to the mills; rather, they appear to have remained at home and to have kept their daughters home or in school. This decision might have been motivated by a variety of concerns. The desire of the English to educate or protect their daughters, cultural animosities and the fear of loss of status through association with the mass of mostly Irish and French-Canadian cotton workers may serve as explanations. For the Irish and newly arrived French-Canadian family, there was much more to be gained than lost by working in the mills. Children increasingly could and had to work the exhausting 72 hour week under frequently dangerous conditions at absurdly low salaries; but their income enabled mother to stay home with the youngest children. For a young Irish woman or man the mills also offered the prospect of some occupational mobility.

TABLE 4 Percentage of Female Factory (Textile) Workers, 1860, and Cotton Workers, 1880, in Selected Ethnic Groups Who Are under Twenty Years Old

	Age	U.S.A.	Ire.	Eng.	Fr. Can.
1860	0–14	2.7%	7.1%	10.5%	6.4%
	15–19	36.5	48.5	38.2	63.5
	Under 20	39.2	55.6	48.7	69.9
1880	0–14	16.7	15.6	13.5	27.3
	15–19	27.5	32.5	24.3	38.7
	Under 20	44.2	48.1	37.8	66.0

Achievement therefore related to the fortunes of the family. Many Irish appeared to have become skilled weavers and spinners as early as 1860. And by 1880 the Irish filled a majority of the skilled cotton mill positions. Irishwomen comprised 72.9 percent of the female weavers, and their sons and husbands fared equally well. Skilled Irishmen constituted 60 percent of the spinners and 54.5 percent of the dressers, carders and loom harness makers in 1880.

Consequently, while young girls of English and native-American origin may no longer have found factory work desirable, Irish and French-Canadian families wanted and easily obtained employment for their teenage daughters and sons and unmarried young women. So how may we evaluate the economic gains and social mobility experienced by the average cotton worker and her family between 1860 and 1880? High costs and low incomes made steady employment essential, and the Harmony Mills provided it.[15] The hours were long, the work among the whirling machines dangerous, but the Irish family procured work for as many children, relatives and neighbors as might turn up, and gained skilled positions. A few even translated money earned into some small property holdings. In this way, the history of Cohoes' working-class Irish and French Canadians suggests the need to reconsider Thernstrom's conclusion that the nineteenth-century working class did not exhibit the economic and social mobility celebrated in the American success myth.[16]

Thernstrom measured mobility in industrial and economic terms: occupational mobility and change in real estate and personal estate holdings. But these useful indices are too narrow. To grasp more fully the significance and character of social mobility in America, historians need to consider the goals and aspirations of the worker and her family on the one hand, and the form and function of status and power on the other. We can then assess the impact of technology, economic pressures and attitudes toward women. Might it not, for example, be the full realization of a social dream for the cotton worker family, freshly arrived in the new country with memories of famine still vivid, to find ample and steady employment in the mills, to maintain the security of the tenement home and to develop community fellowship? Cohoes' Irish found full employment in the Harmony Mills, and during the 20 years they increasingly dominated the skilled crafts. Life was not easy. But unlike many other factories during the depression, the Harmony Mills continued to provide regular monthly pay checks throughout the 1870s. The Company also maintained some unusually fine living conditions: well constructed apartments, paved streets, even some garbage collection and manicured lawns with room for a small garden. Compared to what one saw and heard of English manufacturing districts, and relative to the sorry conditions that impelled them to leave either Ireland or Quebec, it is easy to understand their desire to defend this small but for them not insignificant measure of security. Moreover, a woman had only to look at her Irish neighbors on the other side of town who worked at more menial service jobs—housekeepers and washerwomen—to recognize her preferred status. As the local newspaper noted, Cohoes' textile mills' employment of women made it "next to impossibility [sic] to get competent, reliable girls, who are willing to do housework at any price." The women had "the feeling that as operatives in the mills they take a higher place in the social scale than is accorded them when they do housework. The fact is, they don't like the idea of being servants, or being treated as such, and unless compelled by lack of the employment of their choice they avoid it with scorn."[17] So by 1880, as far as she was concerned, the cotton worker had achieved some measure of both status and security.

But what impact did the factory have on the cotton worker family? Did the company town tear the family apart? While there were considerable economic strains on the Cohoes cotton worker families, it is significant that working-class marriage patterns strikingly resembled the nonfactory family Richard Sennett described in the middle-class community of Union Park in Chicago during this same period. Except for the important presence of child labor among the working class, there appear to be surprisingly few structural differences between these working-class and middle-class families.

Whatever differences did exist between the marriage patterns of Union Park middle-class families and Cohoes cotton worker families seem to have arisen as much from the various ethnic cultural experiences as from disparities in economic position. For example, the percentage of married workers in the Harmony Mills follows the same pattern found in middle-class Union Park.[18] The average cotton worker couple married only when the husband had reached his early thirties, most likely when he felt somewhat more financially secure (Table 5). For the vast majority of the couples, no wide age difference separated the wife and husband (Table 6). In more than 80 percent of the marriages, the wife was less than ten years younger than the husband. And only Englishwomen married younger men with any frequency. Among 15.6 percent of all couples the wife was older than her husband, but among English couples the percentage was 25.3 percent. Women usually left the mills when they were married to assume the role of wife, mother and homemaker. But what of the relative size of the working-class and middle-class family? Once the family formed, conventional wisdom has it that the working class multiplied while the middle class exercised some reproductive restraint. Quoting Sennett on Union

TABLE 5 Percentage Married Within an Age Group, 1880, Among
Cohoes Cotton Workers and Chicago's Union Park

Age	Workers	Middle Class Union Park Chicago*	Age
15–19	0.8%	3.5%	15–19
20–29	16.2%	20.4%	20–24
		43.0%	25–29
30–39	61.8%	60.3%	30–34
		60.3%	35–39
40–49	74.2%	70.7%	40–44
		72.0%	45–49
50–59	89.3%		

Percentage Married Within an Age Group by Sex and
Ethnicity, 1880, Among Cohoes Cotton Workers

	Age	Ire.	Fr. Can.	Ethnicity Eng.	USA	Total
Females	20–29	8.0%	11.5%	13.0%	25.0%	10.3%
	30–39	44.2%	31.4%	83.3%	17.6%	41.0%
Males	20–29	24.0%	32.3%	39.3%	52.5%	29.1%
	30–39	80.7%	78.5%	91.6%	76.9%	90.6%

*Sennett, Families Against the City, 105.

Park, "A host of sexual taboos and the prohibition of child labor in this middle-class community made abstinence not only possible but a compelling necessity."[19] Cohoes, however, suggests again that the most important variable in terms of family size was ethnicity. The ratio of children under ten to the adult population in each ethnic group in 1860 (the "survival rate") demonstrates that family planning crossed class lines: the English and Irish couples averaged 30 percent and the French Canadians almost 50 percent more children than the couples of native-American extraction.[20] Finally, intermarriage figures between persons of different ethnic background demonstrate further the impact of ethnic culture. Almost 40 percent of the working-class English and native Americans who married wed outside of their own ethnic group. In contrast, French Canadians and Irish almost never married outside their ethnic community.[21] The reasons for this low rate of intermarriage would seem to be twofold: the Catholic injunction against marriage outside the religion, and the exclusiveness of both Canadien and Irish nationalist culture. In sum, working-class marriage patterns shared

TABLE 6   Age Differences Between Husbands and Wifes of Cotton Worker Families, 1880

	Marriages (N)	Wife Older (%)	Husbands 0–9 yr. older (%)	Wife less than 5 yr. older Husbands; 0–9 yr. older (%)
Ir.	303	15.8	69.7	81.6
Fr. Can.	105	11.6	80.0	87.7
U.S.A.	50	12.0	72.0	80.0
Eng.	75	25.3	65.4	82.7
Other	18	16.7	66.6	77.7
Total	601	15.6	71.9	83.0

many of the same concerns for tradition, security and stability as the middle-class marriage. Each ethnic group, however, expressed these concerns in different forms of behavior.

Working-class households on Harmony Hill in 1880 again resembled those in Union Park. As in that middle-class community, working-class Cohosiers predominantly lived in nuclear families. By contemporary standards, however, cotton worker families experienced considerable disorganization. In a culture that celebrated a traditional two-parent family and the guiding role of the father, one-parent families, especially when headed by a woman, were considered incomplete and hence "disorganized." But it is crucial to examine the origins and dimensions of this "disorganization." Three quarters of the Irish and English male- or female-headed households were nuclear families (Table 7). These households, composed of first and second generation immigrants, were nuclear after the 3,000-mile migration. Households headed by native Americans or French Canadians had a percentage of families augmented by both relatives and boarders almost twice that of the other two groups. But it was the high percentage of one-parent families that distinguished the cotton worker family from other working-class and Chicago middle-class families.

One out of every four Cohoes cotton worker families on Harmony Hill was a "broken" family—a family headed by one parent. One-parent Irish families had raised the percentage considerably: 28.8 percent of the Irish families were "broken," compared to only about 14 percent of the families of other ethnic groups. Furthermore, almost all of these "broken" families were female-headed. Thus, almost one-quarter of the Harmony Hill families were headed by a "widow"—a woman whose husband had either left her or died. Family structure among the iron workers of Troy, New York, across the river, suggests that this extra-

TABLE 7 Cotton Worker Household and Family Structure in Cohoes, 1880—Ward One, Harmony Hill

Households	Ire.	Can.	USA	Eng.	Other	Total
Nuclear	323	125	35	63	18	564
	72.7%	67.9%	60.3%	77.8%	81.8%	71.5%
Extended	42	20	6	8	2	78
	9.5%	10.9%	10.3%	9.9%	9.1%	9.9%
Augmented	65	38	15	10	2	130
	14.6%	20.7%	25.9%	12.3%	9.1%	16.5%
Mixed Adult Group* (MAG) & Single	14	1	2	0	0	17
	3.2%	0.5%	3.5%	0.0%	0.0%	2.2%
	444	184	58	81	22	789
*Families***						
Whole	302	157	47	71	17	594
	68.0%	85.3%	81.0%	87.7%	77.3%	75.3%
"Broken"	128	26	9	10	5	178
	28.8%	14.1%	15.5%	12.3%	22.7%	22.6%
Percentage of "broken" families headed by a female	89.8%	88.5%	88.9%	80.0%	80.0%	88.8%
Average No. Cotton Wkers/ Family†	2.75	3.63	1.67	2.04	–	2.79

*The two boarding houses are not included.

**MAG & Singles not included.

†Based on first 250 families enumerated in Ward One.

ordinary rate of family "disorganization" reflected conditions peculiar to the textile industry more than it did the general character of working-class life. Sennett found 10.9 percent of the Union Park families to be without one parent. Troy's iron workers, both skilled and unskilled, lived in "broken" homes to about the same extent.[22]

Differences did occur, however, *between* ethnic groups. In Troy and Cohoes the rate of one-parent Irish families outdistanced the other groups. Combining skilled and unskilled Troy iron workers, approximately 15 percent of the Irish, 6 percent of the English, and 10 percent of the native Americans lived in "broken" homes. Thus working-class and middle-class household and family structure strongly resembled one another: both were nuclear families with two parents. Differences were ethnic and industrial—in our case, especially among the Irish and the cotton industry. Why were so many of the cotton worker families one-parent in structure? Widowed women may have taken their families to Cohoes where their children could find employment in the Harmony Mills' light industry. Almost all the widows were over 40 years old with teenage children, and the cotton mills made it possible for mother to stay home with the youngest children while the older children earned the family's income.

Thus Cohoes' cotton worker families were more "disorganized" than Troy's iron worker families. But the high incidence of nuclear families suggests a problem with the term "disorganization." The term exposes the historical prejudice against the one-parent family and ignores the tensions that may have wracked many two-parent families. In addition, the cotton mill may have provided employment and a financial refuge for the widowed family. Thus Sennett's categories may be inadequate to understand the pressures on the nineteenth-century working-class family. In fact almost nine of every ten non-Irish cotton worker families were two-parent headed. Sennett is correct, however, when he insightfully suggests the importance of the stable family in a changing and complex industrial city. According to Sennett, "The family was enshrined out of a sense of its peril in the city."[23] For Sennett, fear that the stability and security of the family would not be maintained became a "guiding force" in the history of the nineteenth-century American city. The middle class clung to the family as the one stable institution in the midst of a rapidly changing world. Although the pressures on the family were immense, the family did not constitute the workers' single supportive institution. On the contrary, the factory and community also structured their social life. Thus, the working class, and the Irish in particular, made an effort to get their daughters and sons unskilled and skilled jobs in the mills and membership in the network of city fraternal and religious associations.

Why, however, was the Irish family so distinctly scarred? In her pioneering study of working-class Irish in mid-nineteenth-century London, Lynn Lees showed the continued dominance of the nuclear family in the Irish household, noted the similarity between the Irish and the English working-class family and concluded that the Irish had not suffered any unusual breakdown.[24] Lees, however, failed to adequately distinguish between families headed by two parents and those in which only one parent was present. In this regard, we were not told whether or not the Irish in London differed from the English. The evidence in both Troy and Cohoes suggests that the Irish family structure—though not household structure—differed from that of the other major ethnic groups present in these two cities. Statistics compiled by the United States Immigration Commission in 1910 corroborate this evidence: the Commission *Reports* listed 12.4 percent of the immigrant cotton workers born in Ireland as widowed, compared to percentages of 5.9 percent of the French Canadians and 7.1 percent for the English.[25] Significantly, these *Reports* suggested that this difference largely disappeared within one generation. For the second generation immigrant family—the first born in the United States—the percentage of Irish widows more nearly approximates the percentages for the other groups: the percentages for the American-born Irish, English and Canadian respectively are 5.9 percent, 4.8 and 3.8 percent. So, though some of the distinctions between the family structure of the Irish and other ethnic groups appear at face value to have diminished with a generation of acclimation, acculturation and without a 3,000-mile migration, the situation of the immigrant Irish family remains somewhat unique. The fragile Irish family reflected the problems that worried the immigrant in industrial America, i.e., considerable prejudice, high mortality and the intense pressures of industrial capitalism. But the higher number of one-parent Irish families may also have reflected distinct ethnic values. We may offer some preliminary suggestions for this. Peasant, semifeudal Irish cultural traditions celebrated Irish community life and kinship and then were patriarchal. Beyond this, though, the Irish families' willingness to allow young girls out of the home and into the factory during adolescence suggests that the Irish husband subscribed to a set of traditional family values distinctly different from those held by men of Protestant English and American origins. Lastly, the Irish peasants' culture had unregimented preindustrial work rhythms. Adjustment required by factory life, with its highly disciplined work patterns, made the Irish industrial experience disruptive and alienating.[26] Although more work needs to be done in this area, we see the importance of ethnic culture in shaping working-class experience.

What then can we say about the cotton workers and their families, their community and their adjustment to factory life during the Gilded Age? The history of Patrick Dillon and his family illustrates the life of one representative cotton worker family in Cohoes.[27] Patrick Dillon probably left Ireland with his wife Ellen and their six children during the potato famine. They arrived in New York around 1850, and by 1860 had added three more children to their family. At the outbreak of the Civil War the now 11-member family lived in a four- or five-room company tenement at 4 Willow Street in the heart of the Harmony Hill Community. The family had managed to save approximately 300 dollars, but it had not been easy; four members of the family worked full time. Every morning the 45-year-old head of the household left home before six for work as a day laborer. The two eldest sons, Michael and William, age 20 and 18 respectively, answered the call of the Harmony Mills' bell, and walked down the street to the mill for a six-o'clock start, too. And Patrick, the 16-year-old son, joined his father as a day laborer. The father and son possibly worked on one of the canal or railroad labor gangs involved in area construction. They may well, however, have also worked for the Harmony Company—building new tenements or enlarging the newly acquired Ogden Mills. Mother, meanwhile, had her hands full at home. Matthew, age 14, and the 12-year-old twin girls did not yet work and only six-year-old James attended school. In addition, not only was Mrs. Dillon pregnant, but the baby, Bridget, who had only just celebrated her first birthday, and Margaret, age three, must have required considerable attention.

Meanwhile the men came home for lunch on their 40-minute noon break and then returned to the mills. At half past six the bell rang to close the mills for another day. For these 12 hours of work an adult common laborer received $0.75, while a skilled mule spinner received as much as $1.50. Women and especially children who labored in the mills received considerably less: an unskilled "back boy," for example, received $0.30 for his 12-hour day. When the monthly pay day arrived, the tenement house rent of between $5 and $7 was simply deducted from the salary.[28]

What happened to the Dillons during the next two decades? Did the family unit survive intact, did the family remain financially solvent and did they remain to establish themselves within the Cohoes' community? Patrick Dillon, Sr., had died late in the 1860s, but his widow continued to maintain the home on Willow Street. Family economics required that Mrs. Dillon open her small home to another family—John Kanal, his wife and two children—and to a boarder. Of her children, Patrick, Jr., died suddenly in 1870 at the age of 26 (shortly after his marriage) and James died September 15, 1874, at the age of 19—both from causes that are undisclosed. Michael and Matthew reappear periodically in the city directory as operatives in the Harmony Mills. Finally, while the older girls had most likely married, William, the second eldest son 20 years earlier, by 1880 had become head of the family, still located in their Willow Street tenement. The family once again sustained itself without boarders. William Dillon's first wife had died but he had remarried. His second wife, Elizabeth, was 15 years his junior, and was only nine years older than his son Patrick, now 15.[29] William now ran a "saloon" but his three youngest sisters, now 19, 20 and 22 years old, together with Patrick worked in the Harmony Mills, much as the family had for the past 20 years. Over the years the Dillon family had secured a place within the community for its remaining numbers but there had been many deaths in the family and most at relatively young ages.

Work in the mills had hardly changed. Wages for the now ten and a half to 11-hour day had dropped back from the high level maintained between 1867 and 1875 to their 1864 level: for a day's work a common laborer now received $1.12½, a skilled spinner $1.75, and a back boy $0.42. The Harmony Company continued throughout this period to play a central part in the life of the Dillon family: the Willow Street tenement remained a focus for the family, and the mills continuously employed the teenagers and adult Dillons and so helped to sustain the family. In fact, five of the seven members of the family in 1880 worked—four of them in the cotton mills. And, five years later the Dillons evidently felt secure enough to permit young Patrick, now 20 years old, to leave the mills and return to school. While living at home, Patrick Dillon—the grandson of his namesake who arrived in American almost 40 years earlier—had become a "student," with the considerable occupational and social mobility American society afforded the educated man. Though for many of his relatives, mobility had been only from the mills to the grave, young Patrick had achieved an avenue both he and the dominant American culture could celebrate.

Like other families in Cohoes, the lives of the Dillon family extended beyond the factory and was fuller and richer than this industrial portrait suggests. On Cohoes' Harmony Hill, the Irish and French-Canadian cotton workers like the Dillons had established by 1880 a diverse and full community replete with ethnic, religious, social and political club life. There were separate Irish and French Catholic churches; the Irish organized the Fenians and the Land League, and the French formed the St. Jean Baptiste Society; a French newspaper, La Patrie Nouvelle, was begun in the city in 1876; each ethnic group formed benevolent societies; and while Cohoes Irishmen usually voted Democratic, it was not uncommon for French Republican groups to form before the fall elections.

Carl Wittke has emphasized the competition between the Irish and the French Canadians. This competition supposedly stemmed from the French-Canadian support of the Republican Party and their reluctance to organize.[30] There were, however, certain fundamental similarities in their experience as well. Whether the workers were Irish like the Dillons, or French Canadian, both were Catholic, both came to America in search of economic advancement. Both worked side by side in the mills and were neighbors on the Hill. And together both struggled against the manufacturers to preserve their jobs and to control their work conditions. Work for the women and children in the Mills was indeed taxing. But through the depression, families like the Dillons gained some security and status. There were openings in skilled positions and some families had even become property holders. The factory did not provide "pin money," especially in the case of the large number of widowed families. The factory offered women jobs and made it possible to hold the female-headed family together and to maintain a nuclear family. In this way, rather than destroying the family, for the cotton workers, the Harmony Mill helped to sustain it.

In addition, urban Harmony Hill did not necessarily alienate the family. While living conditions left something to be desired, the close relationships and organization of the community also helped sustain the cotton worker family. When the workers went out on strike, the whole city was affected. Community pressure helped to maintain the strike: some businessmen offered discounts and contributions to striking workers; one woman, for instance, complained to the local press that the family above her had been persecuting her family for working, and that the day before she had been hit on the head by a bottle thrown by one of them; various tenants who wanted to work complained of "bulldozing"—intimidation from striking neighbors. But community pressures weakened the strikers, too; many striking weavers would return to Cohoes to work because they and their girls were homesick. As Miss O'Brien wrote from Forestdale, R.I., "This [Forestdale] is a very pretty place, but not like home [Cohoes]."[31]

So, why did violence erupt in Cohoes in the early 1880s? This seemingly optimistic portrait was deceptive. The family, community life and occupational mobility in the factory were enclaves against a threatening and insecure urban industrial life. Cohoes cotton workers lived in poverty. That they could endure three wage reductions during the 1873–1877 depression demonstrates how their depressed lives had lowered their expectations. At least the Harmony Company had not closed. In this way, they felt they had gained some success and had established a home. But they continued to live on the edge of fear—low pay, technological changes in the industry and an always ample supply of surplus labor threatened to destroy the small part of the social dream they had been able to realize. In addition, the increasing competition of industrial capitalism demanded increased production, lower costs and greater efficiency. To secure and maintain their profits the Harmony Mill manufacturers felt it necessary to reduce wages and control all aspects of mill life. Unions stood in their way. When the cotton workers' wages were reduced for the fourth time in seven years, they saw their minimal success, status and security threatened. Central to the struggle was control. At issue were not simply salaries, but the survival of the entire community. When, after six months of strikes, the manufacturers brought in disciplined, Protestant, Swedish immigrant families to replace the strikers, the women and children cotton workers responded directly and vigorously. They gathered at the mill entrances to "greet" the Swedes with stones. Police were brought in to protect the "scabs," and violence ensued. Although the strike was crushed, the working-class community then united and two months later elected the strike leader to the State Assembly.

In conclusion, the behavior of the Cohoes cotton worker community suggests the need to understand the place of ethnic traditions in the context of working-class achievements and perception. Furthermore, we need to reassess the impact of the community and factory on the working-class family. Many working-class cotton mill families *were* broken. Child labor was necessary. Industrial capitalism divested the worker of control over work conditions and threatened the family's quest for social and economic security. Both the factory and the urban experience intensified the problems of adjustment for preindustrial peoples, subjecting them to new and alienating work and to the strange heterogeneity of the city. But it must be remembered that by 1880 both the factory and the community had come to sustain the cotton worker family, and especially the female-headed household, in important ways. Together the mills and community provided another avenue to social fulfillment and achievement for the Irish and French Canadians of Harmony Hill. Thus, ironically, the argument that urged women to be taken out of the factory did much to rob many families of their one vital source of income. For in the textile mills at least, the women who worked not only needed the money desperately, but were usually unmarried adolescents, not mothers. Lastly, the Cohoes cotton worker community illustrates the *embourgeoisement* of the working class; the working class had begun to acquire certain middle-class attitudes about the values of status, security, property and the privatized nuclear family. Thus the final irony of cotton worker mobility: on the road to success, the pressures of industrial capitalism had reduced the cotton worker and her family to perceptual cripples, alienated from and by their own conditions. Cohoes' working class did engage in violence, but the violence was defensive—an attempt to protect their modest social position. There is perhaps no greater testimony to how difficult these people's lives had been, how fragile their economic existence remained and how fearfully they faced the future, than the energetic manner in which the women of Cohoes' Harmony Hill cotton worker community defended and celebrated the modicum of status and security they had achieved. Enmeshed in this difficult, fragile and fearful existence, the working-class dream had become a nightmare.

NOTES

1. See Richard Sennett and Stephan Thernstrom, eds., *Nineteenth-Century Cities: Essays in the New Urban History* (New Haven: 1969).

2. There are, of course, variations on each theme. The first view is widespread in the literature of the labor movement. (One popular refinement of this view emphasizes the considerable oppression of the working class and argues that this suffocated its radicalization.) The second view is expressed by Stephan Thernstrom in the conclusion to his article in a New Left anthology. Stephan Thernstrom, "Urbanization, Migration, and Social Mobility in Late Nineteenth-Century America" in *Towards a New Past: Dissenting Essays in American History,* Barton J. Bernstein, ed. (New York: 1968), 158–75.

3. New York State Bureau of Statistics of Labor, *2nd Annual Report, 1884* Legislative Assembly Document 26 (1882), "Establishing the Fact of the Existence of Child Labor in the State," (Albany: 1885), 112.

4. Edward P. Thompson, *The Making of the English Working Class* (New York: 1963), 9–10.

5. Richard Ely, "Introduction," in Helen S. Campbell, *Women Wage-Earners* (Boston: 1893), n.p.

6. Carroll D. Wright, quoted in Campbell, 90.

7. Oscar Handlin, *The Uprooted* (New York: 1951), 167.

8. The biography of William E. Thorn, the agent and treasurer of the Harmony Company from 1867 to 1910, well exemplifies the social, financial and political institutions that Cohoes textile manufacturers controlled. Thorn was both the son-in-law of Commodore Cornelius Vanderbilt and the nephew of Thomas Garner, the owner of the Harmony Mills. After coming to Cohoes in 1867, Thorn served on the Board of Directors of the Cohoes Company (the water power company), was secretary and treasurer of the Cohoes Gas Light Company (both controlled by the Garner interests), was director and first president of the Manufacturers' Bank of Cohoes and was instrumental in organizing the Cohoes Mechanics' Savings Bank. Finally Thorn was elected mayor of Cohoes in 1878 and 1880 and served as a Republican Presidential elector in 1892. See James H. Manning, *New York State Men* (Albany: 1920).

9. Lucy Larcom, *A New England Girlhood* (New edition, New York: 1961). See Edith Abbott, *Women in Industry: A Study in American Economic History* (New York, 1918), 114–16. Abbott writes of the Lowell, Massachusetts, mills that "all operatives were required to live in the company boarding houses . . . organized to resemble . . . big boarding schools." And, "Lowell had a high reputation for good order, morality, piety, and all that was dear to the old-fashioned New Englander's heart."

10. "A Factory Girl" to the editor, *Cohoes Cataract,* April 18, 1857.

11. One encounters various problems working with census data. In Cohoes all mill hands are simply enumerated in the 1860 Census of Population as "Works in Factory." The Census of Manufactures, however, suggests that the cotton and wool worker situation did not vary much. The statistics from the Census of Population for textile workers closely approximates the Census of Manufactures data for the Harmony and other cotton mills in the city. Therefore, one must interpolate from the former to the latter. In 1880 cotton workers and sections of town are distinguished.

12. Unless otherwise indicated the father's place of birth is used to define ethnicity. Thus a native American is someone whose father was born in the United States.

13. The percentage of Irish and French-Canadian men in their thirties and forties who worked as laborers doubled and tripled respectively the percentage of those in their twenties. The actual number also rose markedly. For example, 49 Irishmen or 17.2 percent of those Irishmen in their twenties were laborers, but among those in their forties the number rose to 95 or 54.3 percent.

14. See Oscar Handlin, *Boston's Immigrants, 1790–1865: A Study in Accultura-tion* (Cambridge, Mass.: 1941), 61–75; Thomas N. Brown, *Irish-American National-ism: 1870–1890* (Phila.: 1966), 18–19; William V. Shannon, *The American Irish* (New York: 1963), 28, 95; Carl Wittke, *The Irish in America* (Baton Rouge, La.: 1956).

15. In 1880, between four and five people worked in the average Irish and French Canadian household respectively; in contrast, only two or three people worked in the average English and American cotton worker household.

16. Stephan Thernstrom, *Poverty and Progress: Social Mobility in a Nineteenth Century City* (Cambridge, Mass.: 1964), 146.

17. *Cohoes Daily News,* May 11, 1881.

18. See Richard Sennett, *Families Against the City: Middle-Class Homes of Indus-trial Chicago, 1872–1890* (Cambridge, Mass.: 1970), 105.

19. Sennett, *Families Against the City,* 118.

20. Comparative birth rates for Cohoes in 1860 can be approximated by compar-ing the ratio between the adult population of each ethnic group and the number of children in that group below a given age. (I have chosen age ten, but the figure can be adjusted easily.) Multiplied by one thousand, the birth rate (actually a "survival rate") per thousand population in 1860 reads:

Native Americans	209
English	263
Irish	277
French Canadians	308

21. Only six of 298 French Canadians in Cohoes Harmony Hill (2.0 percent) married someone from another ethnic group. Forty-two of 596 Irish men or women (7.0 percent) intermarried.

22. Thirteen and eight-tenths percent and 12.2 percent of Troy's skilled and unskilled iron workers respectively lived in one-parent households. See Daniel J. Walkowitz, "Statistics and the Writing of Working-class Culture: The iron workers of Troy, New York, 1860–1880," forthcoming, 1972, in a book edited by Herbert G. Gutman.

23. Sennett, *Families Against the City,* 116–19.

24. Lynn Lees, "Patterns of Lower-class Life: Irish Slum Communities in Nine-teenth-Century London," in *Nineteenth-Century Cities,* 359–85.

25. U.S. Immigration Commission, *Reports of the Immigration Commission to Congress,* 1910, 10, part 3, *Immigrants in Industries,* 154–55.

26. Thompson, 436–44.

27. This biographical sketch is based upon the original federal manuscript census schedules. Most important also was the *Troy Directory, also Cohoes. . . ,* 1867–1885; Masten, *History of Cohoes;* and, Census Office, 10th Census, 1880, *Reports,* 20, "Statistics of Wages. . . ," 361–63.

28. Caroline F. Ware, *The Early New England Cotton Manufacture,* 244, presents a picture of the wage structure in New England cotton towns that is sensitive to the dependence of the employee on meagre wages, the ways in which salary was tied to their total social condition through rent and store pay and the reduced wages of women and children.

29. This 15-year age difference between William Dillon and his second wife reflected the usual pattern. When widowers remarried there is almost always a larger age gap with the second wife than with the first. This suggests something of the poor odds against a widow's remarrying. For an extended discussion of this problem, see William J. Goode, *World Revolution and Family Pattern* (New York: 1963), 318–19.

30. Carl Wittke, *We Who Built America* (New York: 1940), 315–28.

31. *Cohoes Daily News,* August 15, 1882.

12

In the Beginning

William L. O'Neill

All histories of feminism properly begin with the appearance of Mary Wollstonecraft's *A Vindication of the Rights of Women* in 1792. Scattered attempts had been made earlier in both England and North America to secure a redress of feminine grievances, but with little effect. Miss Wollstonecraft's book was, however, both sensational and ineffective. Although widely read, or, at least, commented upon, it met with universal disapprobation. Coming as it did on the heels of Olympe de Gouges' tract *The Declaration of the Rights of Women* (1789) and Thomas Paine's *The Rights of Man* (1791–92) the book was unpleasantly, and correctly, associated in the English mind with revolutionary France. Even had it not been tainted in this fashion, her *Vindication* would still have fallen on deaf or hostile ears. The English-speaking peoples of her day were quite satisfied with their domestic arrangements, and Miss Wollstonecraft's demands seemed to them unsettling, if not actually immoral. In later years prominent feminists were to call the book their Bible. Inferior as it was to the Scriptures in literary power, it obviously possessed a pertinency and vigour insensible to both modern readers and her own contemporaries. This was her tragedy. Had she been born a generation or two later, when numbers of women were beginning to press against the laws and customs that confined them, her life would have been very different; not necessarily happier, but certainly more productive and more obviously relevant to the needs and interests of her sex. Of course the position of women in 1840 was no

From *The Woman Movement: Feminism in the United States and England* (Chicago: Quadrangle Books, 1971). Reprinted by permission of George Allen and Unwin, Ltd.

worse, and in some respects better, than in 1790, but by this time they were becoming conscious of their disabilities and interested in removing them.

No one can speak with certainty of the reasons why women emerged in the early nineteenth century as a distinct interest group. Few areas of human experience have been more neglected by historians than domestic life, and at this stage we can only speculate about it. In the past it was thought that the family had changed little throughout the Christian era until very recent times. The Victorian family was believed to be, therefore, not a modern institution but the most highly developed expression of an ancient way of ordering domestic life. By the same token such developments as woman suffrage, mass divorce, and the employment of women in large numbers could only be understood as radical departures from long-established traditions. The trouble with these assumptions is that they do not explain why a family system which had worked so well for so long suddenly came under attack in the nineteenth century. As a rule two explanations have been offered to account for this. In the first place, it is argued, the libertarian sentiments generated by the Englightenment and the French and American Revolutions gained such force that they came to influence women as well as men. The demand for personal freedom, natural to an egalitarian age, was further stimulated, in the case of women, by an industrial revolution which created jobs for women in great numbers and gave them the opportunities for independence in fact which the rise of liberalism inspired them to demand in principle.

This line of reasoning is plausible enough; it gains strength from the indubitable fact that the first important agitations for women's rights in the 1830s coincided with reform movements in both England and the United States, and came at a time when industrialization was far advanced in one country and well underway in the other. But the problem of timing is more complex than it seems. Why did it take so long for the libertarian sentiments of the Revolution to move American women to action? The first women's rights convention was not held until 1848, nearly three-quarters of a century after the Declaration of Independence was signed. If the prevalence of jobs for women made feminism possible, why were so few leading feminists in both England and America gainfully employed? Middle class women were least affected by the industrial revolution, but they were the backbone of feminism everywhere. I could go on in this vein indefinitely, but the point is obvious. Simply because certain developments take place at approximately the same time, it does not follow that they are causally related. The ideological argument is in some measure self-justifying, but the influence of the industrial revolution cannot similarly be taken for granted.

However, there is another way of explaining the origins of feminism that is suggested by Philippe Ariés' remarkable book *Centuries of Childhood*.[1] This historian and demographer argues, mainly on the basis of French materials, that the history of the family is quite different from what we have thought it to be. In his view the medieval family was large, loose and undemanding. Children were unimportant so long as they were numerous, and all but the poor apprenticed them out at an early age. The family existed chiefly to maintain the continuity of name and property, and its members had relatively few obligations to one another. Men lived in society, not in the family. But, he continues, in the sixteenth century this began to change. Domesticity in the modern sense started to emerge. The family concentrated itself and turned inward, privacy became important, the education of children assumed major proportions, and women acquired a great many new duties and responsibilities. This process, which began with the middle class, was completed in the nineteenth century when all classes developed at least a formal commitment to bourgeois standards of familialism. If Ariés' speculations (and they are rather more than that since he adduces much unconventional evidence to support them) are well-founded, the history of women comes into better focus. Medieval woman enjoyed a considerable freedom. Standards of conduct were broader and more flexible, for noblewomen positions of great authority were not unusual, and even lower class women enjoyed substantial economic opportunities in certain crafts and trades. By the seventeenth century, however, the old ways were being modified. Although some authorities believe that at least a few women voted as late as the eighteenth century in England, and although they were not specifically excluded from the franchise until 1832, the erosion of their legal and political position seems to have begun with the great jurist Sir Edward Coke (1552–1634). In the seventeenth and eighteenth centuries as domestic life became, from the woman's point of view, more demanding and confining, the alternatives to it diminished. They were squeezed out of certain traditional occupations, and by the early nineteenth century women, and especially married women, possessed few legal or political rights of their own.

The merit of this hypothesis is that it enables us to see the organization of the family and the status of women on the eve of the Victorian era as the results of processes that were just culminating, rather than as fixed arrangements of great antiquity. So long as the role of women was assumed to have been stable over long periods of time it was hard to explain why in the early nineteenth century it suddenly became onerous. But when we view the position of women in 1800 or 1825 as one that had only recently been established, then the reaction that in fact took place seems perfectly natural, an appropriate if somewhat overdue response to repressive conditions still, in some instances, being formed. The gap between women's narrowed sphere and men's expanding one appears to have reached its greatest extent at a time when liberal and libertarian ideas were in ascendance. In both England and America the exclusion of women became more obvious as the suffrage was broadened, and more difficult to defend. This was particularly true in the United States, as Harriet Martineau pointed out. 'One of the fundamental principles announced in the Declaration of Independence is, that governments derive their just powers from the consent of the governed. How can the political condition of women be reconciled with this?'[2] Even in England, however, where eligibility was more strictly construed, the disenfranchisement of women was becoming less a matter of course. The very Parliament which in 1832 specifically denied votes to women was also the first to debate the issue. Thus, while thinking to put an end to it, Parliament in fact legitimized votes for women as a serious public question. Congress, by way of contrast, was not to recognize woman suffrage as a matter of legislative concern until almost forty years later.

Despite Parliament's initiative in this respect, the emergence of women proceeded more rapidly in the United States—until the twentieth century at any rate. This fact alone casts doubt on the usual thesis that the emancipation of women was a consequence of industrialization. America was much less developed than England in the 1830s, but even at this early date American women enjoyed certain advantages over their English counterparts. It has always been supposed that the frontier circumstances in which many women lived in the early nineteenth century, and which were part of the ancestral experience of most Americans, improved the status of women. Women were scarce on the frontier, and consequently more valuable. In truth, woman suffrage prevailed first in the raw Western states, and in Wyoming the territorial legislature specifically hoped thereby to encourage the migration of women. The pioneer woman's legendary courage and fortitude gave the lie to those innumerable assumptions about women's inferior physiology and nervous system that justified their civil disabilities. This did not, of course, prevent most men from continuing to cherish their prejudices and admire their own superior physical and mental constitutions.

Probably of greater importance to American women was the tendency toward association that made such a deep impression upon

Tocqueville, and that continues to be so distinctive a feature of American life. In church auxiliaries and missionary societies, and then in philanthropic and charitable bodies, thousands of women found outlets for their altruism and wider fields of enterprise beyond the domestic circle. Barred from the society of men they discovered among themselves talents and resources enough to advance many good causes and perform many good works. By the 1830s there were literally thousands of separate women's groups holding meetings, collecting funds, discussing public issues, and variously improving themselves. In this manner a revolution of rising expectations was launched. The more women did, the more they wished to do, the more they pressed against the barriers that prevented them from exercising their full powers, and the more eager they became to equip themselves for the tasks ahead. An early expression of this desire was a substantial expansion of educational opportunities. In 1821 the first real secondary school for women was founded in Troy, New York. Later Oberlin College became the first institution of higher learning to admit women and in 1841 produced its first woman graduate. By this time American women were not only better organized than their English sisters, but better educated as well, even though the United States was still comparatively poor and underdeveloped.

An important reason for this rising curve of feminine activism was the extraordinary ferment that characterized American society in the 1830s and '40s. Religion, politics, philanthropy, education and, indeed, almost every part of the national life experienced great changes, or attempted changes, for which there were few English counterparts. Orthodox religion was challenged by the great Western revivals, by the emergence of new sects like the Mormons, by a radical Perfectionism that led in some cases to the formation of Utopian communities with bizarre and threatening sexual practices. The most radical European social and political philosophies found institutional expression in hundreds of experiments from Robert Owen's New Harmony to the many Fourierite Phalanxes that sprung up at the end of the period. Prison reform, educational reform, moral reforms of every kind agitated the American conscience and contributed to the happy confusion of those years. Eventually anti-slavery became the most important issue, swallowing up or obscuring many of the others, and finally securing the most durable triumph. Abolitionism was especially important because it became a great field for feminine enterprise. William Lloyd Garrison was a fervent supporter of women's rights, as were other Abolitionist leaders. The two causes were linked by a number of marriages. Elizabeth Cady, who was to become perhaps the greatest single figure in the history of feminism, married Henry B. Stanton, a noted Abolitionist.

Angelina Grimké, who with her sister was the first respectable woman to speak in public (on slavery) married Theodore Weld, a towering figure in the Abolitionist crusade.[3] Lucy Stone married Henry Blackwell without taking his name, and their joint labours on behalf of women's rights and anti-slavery became legendary.

This generalized reform spirit had two important effects on the women's cause. In the first place it created new opportunities for women and a more enterprising spirit. Few reform movements can afford to turn away volunteers, and where the appeal is especially stirring, women as well as men will respond if allowed. Thus, in the 1830s there were perhaps a hundred female anti-slavery societies, and women played some part in most other reforms. By this time women had been organizing long enough so that some precedent existed for this further expansion of their extra-domestic operations. They played a crucial role in the Abolition movement. More than half of the signatures on the great petitions that forced Congress to take up the slavery question were women's. Most of these were obtained by female circulators. Precedent and necessity alike, therefore, compelled doubtful males to swallow their qualms and allow the women a part, however limited, in these activities.

A second and more direct benefit to feminists that stemmed from this yeasty situation was the tendency of one reform to lead to another. Many abolitionists (or temperance workers or whatever) were single issue reformers. Others were capable of embracing a multitude of reforms, their sympathies were generous enough to include an infinite number of exploited or oppressed groups. In a more immediate way female reformers who were not feminists took up the cause as a way of advancing their initial interests. Innumerable women became suffragists because they believed women's votes were essential to their dearest wishes. Others became feminists because they were discriminated against by male reformers. Susan B. Anthony began her public life as a temperance worker, but was driven to feminism by arrogance and male chauvinism.

American feminism in the 1830s and '40s was a slight thing by comparison with later years, but that it existed at all was owing to these two large developments—the organization of women on a local level and the surge of reform that to some degree carried women's rights along with it. English feminism, on the other hand, languished during this period. English women had not yet begun to form associations to any large degree, and the English reform movement was less vigorous and diverse than the American. There were a number of women's groups formed to support the Charter or the Anti-Corn Law League, but neither of these causes was as compelling as the struggle against slavery—itself but one of many movements prodding the American conscience. It is important, however, to bear in mind that the differences were relative rather than absolute. The American feminist movement was in the van, but its actual accomplishments by the middle of the nineteenth century were slight. Feminists supported the expanded educational opportunities afforded to women, but the leaders in this movement were not themselves feminists. Emma Willard and Mary Lyon founded secondary schools mainly to educate future mothers and teachers, while Catherine E. Beecher who helped develop the Normal School (in later years the principal source of public school teachers) became a noted anti-suffragist. Beecher believed that motherhood was woman's chief profession, but since not all women could marry they needed something to fall back on, and teaching seemed to her, as to most people in her day, the most suitable alternative. It was, indeed, a kind of symbolic motherhood and in most respects consistent with the prevailing beliefs about women's role and nature. By the same token, the improvement in women's legal status which began in the 1820s originated in Southern states where feminists had no influence. It seems to have been inspired mainly by the liberal spirit of the times, the progress of equity law, and the desire of male debtors to save their property from seizure.

By mid-century, however, American feminists could point to several achievements that formed the basis for most of their subsequent work. They had begun to make their case known. Although earlier attempts were made, a consistent and effective propaganda did not develop until the 1830s when the Grimké sisters began speaking publicly for anti-slavery and women's rights. The most concrete result of their tours was the publication in 1838 of Sarah Grimké's *Letters on the Equality of the Sexes and the Condition of Women* (Doc. I). First published separately, these letters sought to answer the charges made against the Grimké sisters' public activities by the General Association of Congregational Ministers of Massachusetts. In forceful, lucid terms Miss Grimké made it clear to the ministers that they had no right to fault women for their obvious shortcomings. Man, she observed, 'has done all he could to debase and enslave her mind; now he looks triumphantly on the ruin he has wrought and says, the being he has thus deeply injured is his inferior'. Miss Grimké further demonstrated her own keenness of mind by shrewdly manipulating and commenting upon Biblical texts to demonstrate that Scripture did not authorize women's present status as the ministers had insisted. Soon the sisters were persuaded not to compromise anti-slavery by associating it with women's rights, but the *Letters* remained in circulation, bringing to literate women everywhere fresh arguments and inspiration. Other feminist anti-slavery workers were not so easily convinced that women's rights should give way so completely to anti-slavery. Lucy Stone was willing to give separate addresses on behalf of these two causes, but she refused to give up her feminist propaganda altogether. In 1845 Margaret Fuller published *Woman in the Nineteenth Century*. Although her essay was more confused and pretentious than Grimké's, it reached a wider audience. Her readers doubtlessly found much of her argument nebulous, and she made more concessions to current opinions than radical feminists thought necessary, but in some manner her readers could not escape learning that she believed women could and should do more than law and custom allowed. Together with Mary Wollstonecraft's *Vindication* and Harriet Martineau's influential *Society in America* these works, and other lesser ones, constituted a reasonably substantial base of support for the feminist speakers and writers of the future.

The first organizational fruit of these literary and rhetorical exercises was the calling of a woman's rights convention in Seneca Falls, New York, in 1848. It was a small and provincial affair by later standards. Held in an obscure village which happened to be the home of Elizabeth Cady Stanton, author of the call, and limited to those people in the vicinity who subscribed to the *Seneca County Courier* in which it was published, the meeting (there were no elected delegates) was yet the first of those convocations that eventually played a key role in the struggle for woman suffrage. The group was addressed by, among others, Lucretia Mott, better known at the time than Mrs Stanton, and Frederick Douglass, the leading Negro abolitionist who lived nearby in Rochester. It ended by adopting a Declaration of Principles written by Mrs Stanton and modeled on the Declaration of Independence, that declared the history of mankind to be 'a history of repeated injuries and usurpations on the part of man toward woman, having in direct object the establishment of an absolute tyranny over her' (Doc. 2). The meeting also narrowly passed a resolution calling for woman suffrage. It was thought so dangerous and excessive that Henry Stanton refused to attend the meeting at all on account of it. Even Mrs Mott considered it too far in advance of public opinion. Nonetheless, although the press treated it unkindly for the most part, the convention led to others during the next few years that carried the feminist message to remote parts of the country. There were four in Ohio alone.

At almost the same time the women of England, never too far behind in any case, began to move. In 1848 and 1849 Queen's College and Bedford College were founded to give women a good secondary education. The first suffragist group, the Sheffield Association for Female Franchise, held its inaugural meeting in 1851. In 1855 a Married Women's Property Bill was brought forward and a committee of women created to circulate petitions on its behalf. The Bill failed to pass, but in 1857 a Marriage and Divorce Bill which met the most urgent needs of married women did become law. In 1859 the Society for the Employment of Women was organized and the following year it was affiliated with the National Association for the Promotion of Social Science. Soon the Educated Woman's Emigration Society was born. Also in the 1850s Louisa Twining founded a Workhouse Visiting Society which brought middle class women into contact with the frequently appalling character of these institutions, and inspired the campagin for female Poor Law Guardians. At the end of the decade the *Englishwoman's Journal* came into being. Thus, by 1860 Englishwomen in some numbers were engaged in roughly the same kinds of activities as their American sisters: on the one hand those broadly charitable, philanthropic, educational and reformist enterprises in which men and women had an equal interest but that women were only just becoming active in, and on the other hand the more strictly defined efforts designed to improve their status which were symbolized by woman suffrage.

At this point the United States suffered a war that affected American women in several ways. All American reformers, feminists among them, have traditionally been handicapped by the regional character of government in the United States. The great variety of governmental units, their differing powers and laws, and the inability or unwillingness of Congress (especially in the nineteenth century) to legislate in a host of areas, force American reformers to organize locally if they are to be effective. Until 1860 the woman movement had been largely provincial, a matter of scattered groups and individuals addressing themselves to local questions. But the Civil War gave them a common tragic experience. Moreover, Union women in particular had unknowingly prepared themselves for a part in the national drama. Having become accustomed in some measure to confront public questions and to organize for specific purposes they were able to respond quickly when war broke out, and to deal with one another on a national scale.[4] The Sanitary Commission and other relief agencies, although in the main controlled by men, gave large numbers of women public work to do. Thousands served as nurses. Daring individuals such as Clara Barton, Mary Livermore and Louisa May Alcott, not to mention the eccentric few who became spies, soldiers and the like, distinguished themselves. On the ideological front Elizabeth Cady Stanton and Susan B. Anthony formed the National Woman's Loyal League to inspire patriotism, support the Thirteenth Amendment, and secure for women an honourable role in the war effort. Most importantly, perhaps, the war gave Union women a heroic myth that echoed down the generations. No single woman achieved the reputation of a Florence Nightingale—the honours were spread among many notable women—but this helped to universalize the experience. It also had the effect, from a feminist point of view, of giving women a claim on the nation. One great woman might well be ignored, but a heroic generation was something else again.

The chief consequence of the war was not, therefore, an actual revolutionizing of the status of women—some new jobs came their way, although the best of these were lost after the war as often as not—but a change in their self-image and expectations. In particular it persuaded the most ardent that their war services entitled them to vote. This conviction was further stimulated by the rush of events that led to Constitutional amendments guaranteeing the political and civil rights of ex-slaves. Feminists were buoyed up by the libertarian spirit of the moment. Having helped to crush the great evil of slavery, they found it easy to think that the lesser evil of sex discrimination would be similarly dealt with. Moreover, as their heated debates on the question amply demonstrated, most of the radical feminists, for all their genuinely liberal sentiments, could not believe that men would humiliate them by enfranchising black males while leaving white women beyond the pale. It soon became clear, however, that Northern politicians intended to do just that. Their best friends, men such as Wendell Phillips and William Lloyd Garrison, assured the feminists that not only would Congress refuse to give women the vote, but that any attempt to secure such a Bill would jeopardize black suffrage. 'This is the Negro's hour', they were told repeatedly; women would just have to wait their turn (Doc. 5).

This situation placed insupportable strains on what could now properly be called the woman suffrage movement. Since the call had gone out in 1848, woman suffrage had progressed from being an unthinkable idea to becoming merely unlikely. This was sufficient gain to hearten moderate suffragists, but it was not enough for the radicals. The gap between these two factions, one based in New York and led by Susan B. Anthony and Elizabeth Cady Stanton, and the other centred in Boston where women like Julia Ward Howe and Lucy Stone were supported by a cadre of male allies, grew steadily wider. Not only did they disagree over the wisdom of striking for immediate enfranchisement, but on the relationship between woman suffrage and other liberal causes. In 1868 the Stanton-Anthony wing began publishing a weekly journal called *The Revolution* (Doc. 6). Its primary function was to agitate for women's rights, but it also endorsed a host of other causes, some of which were extremely controversial. The Boston group preferred a conservative policy of working exclusively for women's legal and political rights. Moreover, they disapproved of *The Revolution*'s financial sponsor, a mentally unbalanced, morally unsound speculator named George Train whose Fenian sympathies soon landed him in an English jail. His defects, and his racial prejudices, were outweighed by his virtues, so far as the Stantonites were concerned. These consisted mainly of an enthusiasm for women suffrage and a willingness to give them complete editorial freedom. In return he asked only that the paper carry news of his dubious financial schemes. Soon *The Revolution* was cheerfully flailing away at marriage, the currency, the law, customs, morals, labour practices, and everything else that Mrs Stanton considered in need of reformation.

Two years later it was bankrupt, Susan B. Anthony as publisher was saddled with debts that were to burden her for a decade, and two entirely separate, largely hostile, woman suffrage organizations had come into being. In 1868 the New Yorkers formed their National Woman Suffrage Association. The next year Boston organized its American Woman Suffrage Association. Efforts to reunite the two wings of the suffrage movement were frustrated by the differences in principle and tactics responsible for the rift, personality clashes between the leaders of each bloc, and the Boston group's reluctance to become associated with New York's more radical and dangerous enterprises. Chief among these was the reform of marriage.

Before the war a sort of underground agitation had been conducted against marriage on a variety of fronts (Doc. 3). Perfectionists like John Humphrey Noyes regarded it as fundamentally immortal, a source of rivalry, jealousy and possessiveness, a mechanism for dividing mankind, a human perversion of the natural order. At Oneida and elsewhere marriage was, in fact, done away with. Other groups like the Shakers had discarded not only marriage but sexual intercourse as well. Some feminists were attracted by these approaches, both because marriage laws seemed to them so discriminatory that women could find true equality only outside of them, and for the very practical reason that marriage and motherhood made it all but impossible for most women to function in an extra-domestic capacity. Angelina Grimké's marriage to Theodore Weld ended her public career, even though Weld himself was sympathetic to it. Elizabeth Cady Stanton's five children prevented her playing a very active role in the movement until late middle age. She always said that her real life began at fifty when her children no longer needed her. Lucy Stone was spared these complications only because she had but one child.

In the largest sense feminists were quite right to think that marriage sharply limited their prospects. Experience has demonstrated that the formal barriers to women's full emancipation—votelessness, educational and occupational discriminations and the like—are less serious and more susceptible to change than the domestic, institutional and social customs that keep women in the home (Doc. 4). As long as women are mainly responsible for child-rearing, and for managing homes with continually rising standards of living entailing higher and higher levels of performance, they cannot be expected to play as active a part in the world as men do (Doc. 9). Broadly speaking there are only two ways that women's domestic and maternal obligations can be made compatible with their public aspirations. One way is to erect an effective welfare state on the Swedish model which guarantees that children of working mothers will be well cared for, offers paid maternity leaves, and in every manner possible gives women equal employment opportunities with men. The other way is to alter the institution of marriage itself. The welfare state was not a real possibility in nineteenth century America. Therefore, far-sighted women were led inevitably to speculate on the means by which marriage could be altered to permit the widest use of their talents.

The handful of women who reached this point were, however, faced with two all but unanswerable questions. What was to replace orthodox marriage? How could the transition to a higher form of union be made socially acceptable? The first question was answerable in principle. John Humphrey Noyes had succeeded, admittedly under unique and probably unduplicatable conditions, in abolishing marriage and raising women to a state of absolute equality with men. However, Noyes had not only a kind of genius, but possessed charismatic powers enjoyed by few others. In addition his system rested on religious convictions of limited appeal. The Mormons had moved beyond monogamy, and while polygamy was in one sense a reactionary marital system, in theory there was no reason why it could not lead to a new division of labour by which some wives could shoulder the entire domestic burden to free others for outside work. However, Mormons were everywhere hated and despised, largely because of polygamy. Thus, while serious feminists knew that alternatives existed, none of them were able to devise an acceptable variation on traditional monogamy. Their writings are full of elusive hints on the subject, but nothing more than that.

The problem of devising alternatives, however sticky, was nothing compared with the task of making such alternatives acceptable to public opinion. The Victorians were obsessed with family life. If Ariés is correct, the nineteenth century was the first in which every class, from top to bottom, was expected to observe bourgeois family norms. The universalization of these standards having just been effected, the Victorians had no intention of permitting any relapse into the bad old ways. In America this determination reached its peak in the post-Civil War era. Not that earlier generations had welcomed novel opinions on the subject of marriage. Still, it was possible even into the 1860s to propagate the varieties of free love through the United States mails, and there was plenty of room in an underpopulated country for Shakers, Mormons, Perfectionists and the like to experiment. In 1873 the Comstock Act was passed, denying the mails to 'obscene literature'. It ended the dissemination not only of radical literature on marriage and the family, but of birth control information and related matter as well. Thus the act was not only a symbol of the hardening public temper, but, together with the state and local statutes modelled on it, the chief instrument by which public opinion was put into effect.

The high Victorian era was, therefore, the worst possible time for feminists to cast doubt on the perfection of America's domestic arrangements and marital customs. The Stanton–Anthony group did so in two ways. They attempted to criticize the existing order in their own right, and they became involved with a group of notorious free lovers of whom Victoria Woodhull was most conspicuous. Mrs Stanton was a persistent advocate of liberalized divorce laws. In principle divorce and marriage were entirely compatible; indeed, I have argued elsewhere that divorce was an essential feature of the marital system which had become general in the nineteenth century.[5] However, at the time divorce was considered the chief threat to marriage as an institution, and by supporting it Mrs Stanton put her reputation in jeopardy. Although by no means a believer in free love, she was actually something of a skeptic on the marriage question. In private she condemned it as 'opposed to all God's laws'. *The Revolution* abounded with intimations to this effect, the plainest statement being made by one of her followers who cautioned women not to expect too much from the ballot.

> 'Woman's chief discontent is not with her political, but with her social, and particularly her marital bondage. The solemn and profound question of marriage . . . is of more vital consequence to woman's welfare, reaches down to a deeper depth in woman's heart, and more thoroughly constitutes the core of the woman's movement, than any such superficial and fragmentary question as woman's suffrage.'

Even such delicately phrased remarks compromised the movement, but the Woodhull affair was nearly fatal to it. Victoria Woodhull had arrived in New York in 1868 with her sister Tennessee Claflin. The beautiful and raffish pair attracted the attention of Commodore Vanderbilt, whose taste in women was almost his only engaging quality, and with his support they became stock brokers and editors. Although their business was more sensational than profitable, their magazine, *Woodhull and Claflin's Weekly*, initially attracted some favourable comment.

It was a lively and interesting journal that promoted all manner of causes from Marxism (which the sisters completely misunderstood) to spiritualism. Their intellectual mentor was a curious figure named Stephen Pearl Andrews. Best known for his advocacy of free love, he had also devised a synthetic universal language (Alwato) and discovered the key to all knowledge (Universology). Mrs. Woodhull rapidly won a commanding position among the New York suffragists and scored a great coup when in 1871 she persuaded the House Judiciary Committee to hold hearings on a proposed constitutional amendment to give women the vote. This was the first time Congress formally recognized woman suffrage as an issue, and Mrs Woodhull further enhanced her stature by testifying to good effect before the sub-committee. Mrs Stanton was charmed, and even the more reserved Susan B. Anthony recognized her gifts.

Unfortunately for the cause Victoria Woodhull was nothing less than a human time-bomb. Sensual, reckless, mentally unstable at the least, she was attracted to bizarre fads and cults into which she poured her immense, volatile energies. Always promiscuous, under the guidance of Stephen Pearl Andrews she moved closer and closer to declaring in principle what she had already put into practice. On November 20, 1871 she announced her belief in free love from the stage of Steinway Hall in New York City. Open season was immediately declared on her. Denounced by press and pulpit, turned out by landlords, excoriated by all the organs of respectable society, Mrs Woodhull became increasingly irrational. After threatening to carry 'the war into Africa' she finally struck back at her critics by telling all she knew of the Beecher–Tilton affair. Her choice of targets left something to be desired. Henry Ward Beecher was not only the most famous preacher of the day, but a good friend of woman suffrage. Elizabeth Tilton was the wife of Mrs Woodhull's principal champion, Theodore Tilton, a liberal editor who had written a biographical sketch of her and was the only man in New York with the courage to chair her Steinway Hall meeting. When Mrs Woodhull revealed that Beecher and Mrs Tilton had been lovers she embarrassed her friends, not her enemies. She was angry with Beecher for having criticized her spiritualist activities, but she professed only to disapprove of his hypocrisy. She insisted that he too was a believer in free love, and only his fears kept him from saying so in public. Apparently she had no grievances against Tilton who was not only a friend, but possibly also a lover.

The consequences of her exposé were entire predictable. Tilton sued Beecher. Beecher denied everything and, although probably guilty, was essentially acquitted by both the courts and public opinion. Tilton fled the country a broken man, and before long the Claflin sisters were compelled by an indignant populace to follow him. They landed on their feet, however. Settling in England, they waged skilful campaigns against their own reputations. Both succeeded in marrying men of money and position and lived out the balance of their long lives in, for the most part, respectable obscurity.

Their former friends in America did not fare so well. The Stanton–Anthony group was smeared and ridiculed, both because of its association with the Claflins and because several of its members had played minor roles in the Beecher–Tilton affair. For years a taint of free love clung to woman suffrage, embarrassing its partisans and, most importantly, inspiring in them a profound revulsion against everything unorthodox. In the course of rehabilitating itself the National Woman Suffrage Association adopted the policies of compromise and expedience that already dominated the American Woman Suffrage Association. Increasingly the National focused on the comparatively safe legal and political problems that it had once scorned the American for failing to see beyond. Soon only personal animosities separated the two. By 1890 these had sufficiently abated, so that the woman suffrage movement could be reunited in the cumbersomely titled National American Woman Suffrage Association, hereafter to be known as the NAWSA.

The Woodhull affair, therefore, despite its grotesque and accidental features, marked a decisive turning point in the history of American feminism. Until it happened, a small but important group of suffragists were prepared to think deeply and radically about the position of women. It is true that they had had but small success, yet their minds were open to the possibility that the entire domestic system would have to be restructured as a pre-condition for sexual equality. This was the central insight of early American feminism, and the losing of it crippled the movement intellectually. Of course the period running roughly from 1860 to 1890 was so hostile to radical speculations on marriage and the family that feminists would have had to be more discreet in any event. But the Woodhull affair did not simply inspire caution, it literally destroyed the possibility that feminism would be able to generate a body of theory adequate to its later needs. This was to become evident after 1920 when, having won the vote, feminists were confronted with all those problems that had been suppressed in its favour so long before.

As the American feminist movement became more conservative and respectable it also became more like its English counterpart. Serious English feminists seem not to have been tempted by the dangerous speculations which nearly ruined the Stantonites in America. Although English suffragists began to coalesce at approximately the same time as the Americans, they operated in an entirely different atmosphere.

Woman suffrage in America was stimulated by the reforming spirit of the 1830s and '40s. In England these years were less expansive and optimistic. England was faced with the consequences of industrialization earlier than America, and the English mood in the thirties and forties was nervous and defensive—in some respects like the American atmosphere a generation later. In the 1850s, with the Corn Law struggle resolved, Chartism disposed of, and a period of great prosperity beginning, the English temper mellowed. Thus, while the woman suffrage movement got under way in both countries during the same decade, their respective heritages were quite different. The first generation of American feminists matured in a buoyant era that was already passing away when they began to agitate. This was not without its advantages, but it did not equip them to withstand the challenges presented by the more conservative age to come. English feminists, having passed through a less sanguine time, were not disposed to take chances or flirt with radical notions in the American manner. Thus, woman suffrage in England from its inception enjoyed all the orthodoxy and respectability which a generation of American suffragists laboured to secure.

Oddly enough, however, woman suffrage in both countries peaked out at almost exactly the same time. In America the extension of male suffrage in the 1860s stimulated woman suffragists, and in England the Reform Bill of 1867 had a similar effect. Talk of expanding the suffrage always encouraged English feminists to think that they might be included too, but in this instance they had additional reasons for hope. In 1865 John Stuart Mill was elected to Parliament, even though he was an open advocate of woman suffrage. The next year Disraeli announced his belief in votes for women. Thus encouraged, women suffragists collected 1,500 signatures for a petition that was presented to Mill in June 1866. In October Miss Lydia Becker founded the first durable suffragist organization, the Manchester Women's Suffrage Committee. In 1867 Mill introduced a women's suffrage amendment to the Representation of the People Bill which secured 74 aye votes as against 194 notes. This was a respectable showing and encouraged feminists to think that some kind of women's suffrage might be obtained in the very near future. Under the leadership of Miss Becker the tempo picked up. In 1868 the first public meeting on behalf of the cause was held in Manchester, and Miss Becker was among the speakers. She was the first Englishwoman to speak in public for woman suffrage, but other meetings were soon held and other women followed her example. In 1869 Lady Amberley, whose husband had voted in Parliament for Mill's amendment, caused a sensation by addressing a suffrage meeting in Stroud. In 1870 Jacob Bright introduced a Suffrage Bill in Parliament that passed its first reading and was only defeated on the second. This proved to be the early suffrage movement's high water mark.

The chief reason for the failure of women's suffrage after the 1870s would seem to have been simply that it was much in advance of its time. To get so far as a second reading in Parliament within five years of their first spokesman's election was a remarkable accomplishment for the suffragists. The American movement, although older, larger, and better organized was in the nineteenth century[6] never able to get its Bills out of committee. But these initial gains were misleading. Apparently they were easy to get because the public did not at first take woman suffrage seriously. Some thought, no doubt, that after the Court of Common Pleas ruled in 1868 that women were ineligible to vote, ancient precedents not withstanding, the suffragists would give up. When, instead, they increased their efforts and began to speak publicly on their own behalf resistance increased. Lady Amberley's appearance in Stroud provoked Queen Victoria to say privately that the noble suffragist ought to be horsewhipped. Henceforth her influence was exercised to dissuade women from pursuing what the Queen called, in a letter not then made public, 'a mad, wicked folly'. Gladstone threw his great weight against Parliamentary suffrage and although a Bill was brought in and debated every year in the 1870s except 1874, none passed the first reading after 1870. In the 1880s the matter came to a division only once, when a small majority was secured in 1886. This did not happen again until 1897.

In both countries, therefore, the development of woman suffrage followed similar lines. From small beginnings in the 1850s unique events led to high hopes and intense efforts in the late '60s and early '70s. Failure in both countries led to a long period of organizing and agitation at a lower level of intensity and under discouraging circumstances. These naturally had the effect of keeping woman suffrage alive (sometimes only just) and gradually conditioning the public mind for its eventual acceptance. In England Parliament remained the chief theatre of war. Having been induced in 1869 to extend the municipal franchise to women ratepayers, and in 1870 to allow women to vote for and serve on the School Boards brought into existence by the Education Act, it had at least established a means by which women could acquire political experience and render some public service during the long years when they vainly sought the right to do for the nation what they were beginning to do for their communities.

Because in America the States could establish their own voting requirements, suffragists turned to them once it became clear that Congress was not to be moved. Until the turn of the century, their most important work was done on the state and local level. Some good resulted. In 1869, Wyoming became the first territory to give women the vote, and in 1890 the first state. This was a source of considerable satisfaction to its several thousand female residents. In the next ten years the women of Colorado, Utah and Idaho were similarly blessed. On the whole, the attempts to secure woman suffrage by amending state constitutions were more exhausting and hardly more productive than efforts to amend the Federal Constitution. In both countries, therefore, the political situation of women was about the same. Large numbers of English women acquired a very limited vote in the nineteenth century, while a small number of American women were fully enfranchised.

The most significant difference to emerge in this period was that while American suffragists remained obdurately non-partisan, female auxiliaries to the major parties were formed in England—the Primrose League in 1885 and the Women's Liberal Federation a bit later. The relationship of the parties to women's suffrage was, however, a complicated one. Liberals nominally favoured votes for women, but in an age when the suffrage was based on property it was believed that female voters, because they would be propertied, would naturally incline towards the Conservative Party. Conservatives, on the other hand, while they stood to benefit by an accession of female voters, were resolutely opposed to women's suffrage in principle. Thus, the suffragist's ideological allies were reluctant to assist them for very practical reasons, while those who had practical grounds for supporting them were ideologically unable to do so. In America, where universal male suffrage already obtained, enfranchised women were not expected to alter the political balance, American politicians were consequently free to indulge their prejudices (or principles, as the case may be), and so neither party gave suffragists any reason to abandon their neutrality.

In summary, then, while the history of woman suffrage in England and America followed roughly parallel lines during the nineteenth century, the two feminist movements were at one time quite different. Both came in the end to look much alike, yet at first the Americans were not only more colourful and electric, but capable of entertaining more radical speculations than their English sisters. The suppression of these qualities after 1870 was a crucial event in the history of Anglo-American feminism. Respectability was won at the expense of intellectual adventurousness. Possibility gave way to propriety. A mental calcification set in that prevented suffragists in both countries from taking advanage of the opportunities that matured in the next century.

NOTES

1. Philippe Ariès, *Centuries of Childhood: A Social History of Family Life* (New York, 1962).

2. Harriet Martineau, *Society in America,* (London, 1837), i, 107.

3. Frances Wright was actually the first woman to speak regularly in public, but although wonderful she was not respectable. The Grimke sisters came from a wealthy Southern family and their public work was conducted under impeccable circumstances.

4. These remarks do not apply to Southern women who participated in public affairs on a very small scale, even during the war. However, they did suffer in the end much more than Northern women. This had the peculiar effect of giving their daughters a legendary background equal to that of Northern women. Their shared misconceptions about the past made possible the reconciliation of Northern and Southern women at the century's end.

5. William L. O'Neill, *Divorce in the Progressive Era,* (New Haven, 1967).

6. The two situations were not exactly comparable. Since Congress votes on a Bill only once, many Bills that in Parliament would get a first or second reading never reach the floor. Congress was even more careful about amendments to the Constitution, which had then to be passed by two-thirds of the states.

III

The Progressive Impulse

Throughout the latter part of the nineteenth century and into the twentieth, urbanization and industrialization proceeded at an ever-increasing pace. Women followed the general migration pattern from country to city, from farm to factory. At all levels, women were breaking out of the confines of the home and entering the public arena. For new immigrants and for lower-class women in general, this process brought their dubious emancipation of domestic service, the sweat shop, and the shirtwaist factory. For their wealthier sisters, increased leisure time and education enabled more women to enter the professions and to invest their energies in the cause of social justice. Women became a major element in the Progressive reform coalition, creating a growing tangle of organizations that confronted a wide range of social ills from pornography and prostitution to world peace.

The latter part of the nineteenth century witnessed major changes in thought and behavior that ushered in an era of reform. Nearly all elements of the Victorian intellectual synthesis were subjected to scathing criticism by the new generation of "reform Darwinists," whose social thought emphasized "coming to grips with life, experience, process, growth, context and function."[1] Their emphasis on the economic context of social behavior and their optimistic belief in the possibility of "social engineering" in the interest of a more equitable social order promised immense benefits to women. Although these thinkers failed to seriously confront many aspects of the nineteenth-century definition of a woman, they challenged the sanctity of social and economic institutions that confined women to "their proper sphere." In "Loving Courtship or the Marriage Market?" Sondra R. Herman compares the traditional nineteenth-century view of marriage with the anxious orthodoxy of the social purity movement and the critical analyses of five leading "reform Darwinists," including Charlotte Perkins Gilman, the era's most interesting feminist.[2] At the heart of Gilman's brilliant polemic, *Women and Economics,* which emphasized the economic basis of women's subordination to men, was a radical assault on the inequalities and inefficiencies of contemporary marriage. She agreed with radical men like Edward Bellamy and Lester Frank Ward that only a fundamental alteration of the economic specialization of the sexes could produce a reorientation of the relationship between husband and wife to make true social progress possible.

At the same time that radical critics were challenging the sanctity of traditional marriage, major shifts were occurring in sexual and marital practices.[3] Urban conditions, including the shrinking dimensions of the household, the growing autonomy of middle-class women created by expanded educational opportunities, and increased employment of women outside the home, produced new patterns of behavior. A startling upturn in the rates of illegitimacy and premarital intercourse, which had been falling throughout the nineteenth century, indicated increased sexual activity. Although marriage and childbirth continued to characterize the average woman's life, in the final two decades of the nineteenth century larger numbers of women chose not to marry than at any other time in American history. Those who did were, on the average, older when they decided to marry, and a greater percentage of married women chose to not have children. More startling to contemporaries, however, was the rapid increase in the number of women who sought release from unfortunate liaisons through divorce.[4] As the percentage of women marrying returned to "normal" after the turn of the century, the United States had the anomolous distinction of having both marriage and divorce rates which ranked among the highest in the world.

Expanded opportunities for education drew middle-class women out of the home and into some professions. Under the leadership of Emma Willard and Catherine Beecher, secondary education was increasingly opened to women before the Civil War.[5] In 1837 Mary Lyon founded Mount Holyoke Female Seminary, which set an example for the rapid expansion of women's colleges after the war; in 1865, Vassar was established; Smith and Wellesley in 1875; and Bryn Mawr in 1885. Coeducation on the college level emerged first in the Midwest when Oberlin College in Ohio opened its doors to women in the 1830s.[6]

After the Civil War, a growing number of state universities followed Oberlin's example. By the end of the century, over 5,000 women were graduating yearly from the nation's colleges, and the majority moved into the labor force. The number of women doctors increased as medical education (in sexually segregated classes) became available to more women. Through the dogged efforts of women such as Myra Bradwell and Belva Lockwood, who ran for president in 1884 and 1888, resistance to women in the legal profession was gradually eroded. However, most women were excluded from these professions and confined to teaching, nursing, and library work, occupations characterized by low status and low pay.[7] However, this unique group, whom Vida D. Scudder termed "the first generation of College Women," provided the nucleus for the contemporary outpouring of reform.[8]

Horrified by multiplying slums, contaminated food and water, and unhealthy conditions under which the poor, and particularly poor women, labored, they devoted themselves to serving others in missions overseas and in settlement houses of the urban ghettos.[9] The activities of Lillian Wald and Jane Addams are well known, but the women's organizations that appeared in increasing numbers after 1890 were more typical of the Progressive era. These organizations, which often shared members and sometimes worked together, ranged from the numerous women's clubs that focused on civic improvement—loosely united after 1901 under the aegis of the General Federation of Women's Clubs (GFWC)—to older political groups like the Women's Christian Temperance Union (WCTU).[10] As women who wished to reform the social order increasingly felt their disfranchisement a great handicap, woman suffrage became the focus of the women's movement. In "The 'New Woman' in the New South," Anne Firor Scott traces the expanding Progressive impulse in the South. Beginning with the WCTU, Southern women gradually moved into a succession of community activities and finally joined the quest for the vote.

In 1890 the warring factions of the suffrage movement made peace and banded together in the National American Woman Suffrage Association under the presidency of Elizabeth Cady Stanton. From 1890 to 1910, the new organization continued to follow the strategy of securing woman suffrage on a state-by-state basis. Although they had remarkable success in opening school board and municipal elections to women, only a handful of states provided for equal suffrage.[11]

The new century ushered in a new generation of suffrage leaders represented by Dr. Anna Howard Shaw[12] and Carrie Chapman Catt who led the NAWSA to its final victory. However, it was not until 1910 that any major strides were made. In quick succession, four more far western states along with Kansas and Illinois gave women the vote; in

1912, the Progressive Party included a woman suffrage plank in its plat-form. Although they failed in each, suffragists waged major campaigns in the populous states of the Midwest and East during 1915, and results indicated their possibility of future success was excellent.

At about the same time, the campaign for an amendment to the Constitution was revived through the vigorous action of Alice Paul, a young Quaker woman who had been deeply influenced by her work with the English militants.[13] On returning to the United States, she organized the Congressional Union, that was at first affiliated with the NAWSA, but which eventually became the basis for the independent Woman's Party. Until 1917 the two groups maintained an uneasy alli-ance. Under the direction of Catt, NAWSA swelled to nearly two million members and concentrated on the enactment and ratification of the Nineteenth Amendment.

It does not diminish the achievement of Catt to argue that the final success of woman suffrage depended not only upon a few heroic national leaders, but also upon the vigorous activity of the rank and file who struggled within the complex web of state politics. In "Leadership and Tactics in the American Suffrage Movement" Sharon Hartman Strom focuses on the struggle for the vote in Massachusetts and the relationship between feminism and Progressivism. Strom explains how the suffrage movement, which seemed to have been stymied by a defeat in the Massachusetts referendum of 1895, was revitalized after the turn of the century and grew in power until it swept the ratification of the Nineteenth Amendment before it. She emphasizes the impor-tance of the relation of the rank and file to other Progressive reforms and of the suffragists' incorporation of some of the radical tactics employed by their English sisters. Strom's study is detailed and com-plex; it shows once again the problems that ethnicity, religion, and class posed to the unity of the women's movement. She highlights to a greater extent than any previous scholar the intricate political maneuv-ering between suffragists and Progressives, which led to the final success of the suffrage amendment.[14]

Ironically the Nineteenth Amendment was finally recommended by President Woodrow Wilson as a war measure—in response to the whole-hearted support of World War I rendered by American women.[15] Women had traditionally made up a sizable element of the American peace movement, and at first organizations such as NAWSA joined with the radical Woman's Peace Party to oppose American entrance into the war. But once war was declared, the majority of women supported the administration. Anna Howard Shaw, former president of NAWSA, served as head of the National Women's Committee of the Council of National Defense during the war. Although she had little effect on the government, NAWSA worked through state and local branches, rolling bandages for the Red Cross and providing food and clothing for the soldiers. Many other women took over men's jobs in factories and the civil service and worked in Europe with the U.S. Army Corps of Nurses, the Red Cross, and the Salvation Army. Such activities drew wide praise and contributed positively to the attainment of suffrage.

By 1920 women reformers had reason to be proud of their accomplishments and to be optimistic about the future. The two major reforms for which women organized and worked during the nineteenth century had been achieved with the enactment of the constitutional amendments providing for prohibition and woman suffrage. Organized women had played an important role in securing protective legislation for child labor, pure foods and drugs, and conservation. They also influenced Progressive measures in two other traditional areas of women's interest—reform of divorce laws and the curbing of prostitution.[16] This impressive body of legislative success in the interest of women has led one scholar to term the Progressive era "the greatest age in the history of American women."[17] However, the achievement of these reforms was not without cost to the women's movement.

Although the conditions of children and working women were ameliorated through the work of women such as Mary "Mother" Jones and Florence Kelley, the executive secretary of the National Consumers' League, and by Elizabeth Gurley Flynn and Rose Schneiderman who worked in the interest of the working classes, women workers remained generally unorganized.[18] During the nineteenth century, women's protests against low wages and horrid working conditions seldom provided the basis for long-term organization. Attempts to organize working women by the Daughters of St. Crispin and later by the Knights of Labor failed; the American Federation of Labor vacillated and was generally unsympathetic to the problem.[19] Feminism and labor radicalism never joined, and working-class women contributed little to Progressive reform.

Although the percentage of women in industry gradually declined, the number of working women increased with each census. By 1900 working women represented 20 percent of the total female population over sixteen years of age. For the most part, they remained domestics or farm workers, and many still labored in the textile mills. However, new white-collar jobs, such as telephone and telegraph operators and secretaries, employed increasing numbers of women. The lot of most working women was a hard one that improved little until the enactment of Progressive reforms setting minimum wages and controlling hours and conditions of labor. In 1910 the Bureau of Labor reported that most working women were "paid very low wages—wages in many cases inadequate to supply a reasonable standard of living for women dependent upon their own earnings for support."[21]

Only a few women in select areas, such as the garment industry, moved into the labor movement. After 1903 the Women's Trade Union League, organized by Mary Kenny O'Sullivan, attempted with limited success to bring women into the trade-union movement.[22] The idea behind the WTUL was to join working-class women and their middle-class female "allies" in a single organization to improve the wages and working conditions of laboring women. Nancy Schrom Dye illustrates some of the problems within the New York WTUL in her essay, "Creating a Feminist Alliance." Class and ethnic differences among these women undermined a sense of sorority. The League also failed to develop "an analysis which came to terms with both facets of women workers' situation, which synthesized class and gender into a meaningful explanation."

In the face of adversity, the WTUL did score a few modest successes. They gave crucial support to the New York shirtwaist makers' strikes of 1909–1910, and were primarily responsible for the establishment of the Women in Industry Division of the Department of Labor during World War I, which eventually became the Woman's Bureau under the direction of Mary Anderson in 1920. The career of the WTUL illustrates both the immense problems involved in organizing women due to the opposition of male workers and the limitations of the women's movement of the Progressive era. As so often in the American past, differences between women had a greater impact on their behavior than the common problems that they faced because of their sex.

Aside from class and ethnic divisions within the movement, feminism was plagued by ideological inconsistencies. In the 1890s the basis of the suffrage argument shifted from natural rights to expediency. Suffragists increasingly related other reform measures to their demand for the vote. They insisted that a purification of the political process would follow the entrance of women into the polling place.[23] Alice Stone Blackwell, the activist daughter of Lucy Stone, believed that "in the main suffrage and prohibition have the same friends and the same enemies" and urged clergymen to support suffrage because it would augment the power of the churches in "the warfare against the liquor traffic, and the white slave traffic, child labor, impure food, and many other existing evils. . . ."[24]

In "Women Reformers and American Culture, 1870–1930," Jill Conway emphasizes the importance for the ideological development of feminism of the failure of reformers to question basic aspects of traditional sexual stereotypes and their emphasis on the distinctive moral qualities of women. Women like Jane Addams and Lillian Wald "worked within the tradition which saw women as civilizing and moralizing forces within the society." They conceived of women as temperamentally suited to the task of social housekeeping. Because women alone possessed the virtues extolled in Victorian sexual stereotypes, Addams and Wald urged women to move out of the home into efforts for social justice and the reform of politics. Even Charlotte Gilman, who questioned almost every aspect of the subordination of women, believed that motherhood was the biological destiny of women and that women were by nature more peaceful, even tempered, and less competitive than men. The success of the major progressive reforms was based upon "not the image of women as equals . . . but the image of women as victims."[25]

As success became a possibility, the increasing concern for tactics undermined the idealism of the movement.[26] In order to gain the unity necessary for effective political pressure, the major women's organizations had to disavow their more militant elements, such as Alice Paul's Women's Party, and ignore the needs and desires of black women. Blacks were involved in the Progressive movement; Ida B. Wells-Barnett led the crusade against lynching, and Mary Church Terrill organized the National Association of Colored Women. A few white women took a special interest in racial equality; Mary White Ovington was one of the founders of the National Association for the Advancement of Colored People.[27] But for the most part, the interests of black women were sacrificed to attain Southern support. The GFWC and the WCTU were built upon sectional reconciliation and were strong in the South, but even NAWSA, whose roots stretched back into the abolitionist movement, tolerated racist arguments and gave in to the racist demands of its Southern members.

NOTES

1. Morton White, *Social Thought in America: The Revolt Against Formalism* (Boston: Beacon Press, 1957), p. 13. The term "reform Darwinists" is from Eric Goldman, *Rendezvous with Destiny: A History of Modern American Reform* (New York: Alfred A. Knopf, 1952).

2. On Charlotte Gilman, *see* Carl N. Degler, "Charlotte Perkins Gilman on the Theory and Practice of Feminism," *American Quarterly* 8 (Spring 1956): 21–39,

and Degler, "Introduction to the Torchbook Edition," of Charlotte Perkins Gilman, *Women and Economics* (New York: Harper & Row, 1966).

3. *See* Daniel Scott Smith, "Family Limitation, Sexual Control and Domestic Feminism in Victorian America," in *Clio's Consciousness Raised,* Mary Hartman and Lois W. Banner, eds. (New York: Harper & Row, 1974); *idem,* "The Dating of the American Sexual Revolution: Evidence and Interpretation," in *The American Family in Social-Historical Perspective,* Michael Gordon, ed. (New York: St. Martin's Press, 1973), pp. 321–35; and Smith and Michael S. Hindus, "Premarital Pregnancy in America 1640–1971: An Overview and Interpretation," *The Journal of Interdisciplinary History* 5 (Spring 1975): 537–70. Although women's sexual behavior during these years is a subject still open to much debate, two sources are: Katharine Bement Davis, *Factors in the Sex Life of Twenty-Two Hundred Women* (New York: Harper and Brothers Publishers, 1929), and Carl N. Degler, "What Ought To Be and What Was: Women's Sexuality in the Nineteenth Century," *American Historical Review* 79 (December 1974): 1467–90.

4. On this debate, *see* William L. O'Neill, *Divorce in the Progressive Era* (New Haven: Yale University Press, 1967). Most Americans, including many Progressives, resisted the changing morality of the day, as can be seen in Nathan G. Hale, Jr., *Freud and the Americans: The Beginnings of Psychoanalysis in the United States* (New York: Oxford University Press, 1971).

5. On women's education, *see* Merle Curti, *Social Ideas of American Educators* (Totowa, N.J.: Littlefield Adams, 1959), pp. 169–93; and Mabel Newcomer, *A Century of Higher Education for American Women* (New York: Harper and Brothers, 1959).

6. Ronald W. Hogeland, "Coeducation of the Sexes at Oberlin: A Study of Social Ideas in Mid-Nineteenth Century America," *Journal of Social History* 6 (Winter 1972–73): 160–76.

7. Dee Garrison, "The Tender Technicians: The Feminization of Public Librarianship, 1876–1905," *Journal of Social History* (Winter 1972–73): 131–59. Cf. Margaret W. Rossiter, "Women Scientists in America Before 1920," *American Scientist,* 62 (May–June 1974): 312–23.

8. Quoted in Arthur Mann, *Yankee Reformers in the Urban Age* (Cambridge, Mass.: Harvard University Press, 1954), p. 201. This includes an excellent essay on Dr. Scudder and her environment.

9. Robert H. Bremner, *From the Depths: The Discovery of Poverty in the United States* (New York: New York University Press, 1956); Allan F. Davis, *Spearheads For Reform: The Social Settlements and the Progressive Movement, 1890–1914* (New York: Oxford University Press, 1967); Davis, *American Heroine: The Life and Legend of Jane Addams* (New York: Oxford University Press, 1973).

10. William L. O'Neill, *Everyone Was Brave: A History of Feminism in America* (Chicago: Quadrangle Books, 1971), pp. 77–106.

11. Aileen S. Kraditor, *The Ideas of the Woman Suffrage Movement, 1890–1920* (New York: Columbia University Press, 1965) remains the best general study. It should be supplemented by Louise R. Noun's *Strong-Minded Women: The Emergence of the Woman-Suffrage Movement in Iowa* (Ames: Iowa State University Press, 1970).

12. James McGovern, "Anna Howard Shaw: New Approaches to Feminism" *Journal of Social History* 3 (Winter 1969–70). This exceptional essay is best understood

when compared with McGovern's other essay, "David Graham Phillips and the Virility Impulse of Progressives," *New England Quarterly* (Sept. 1966): 334–55.

13. Brief comparisons of the two movements are presented in William L. O'Neill, *The Woman Movement: Feminism in the United States and England* (London: George Allen and Unwin, Ltd., 1969); and James L. and Sheila M. Cooper, *The Roots of American Feminist Thought* (Boston: Allyn and Bacon, 1973).

14. The most interesting attempt to study the political activities of any large number of women during these years is Richard Jensen's, "Family, Career, and Reform: Women Leaders of the Progressive Era," in *The American Family*, Gordon, ed., pp. 267–80.

15. On women and World War I, *see* Walter I. Trattner, "Julia Grace Wales and the Wisconsin Plan for Peace," *Wisconsin Magazine of History* 44 (Spring 1961): 203–13; Allan F. Davis, "Welfare, Reform and World War I," *American Quarterly* 19 (Fall 1967): 516–33; O'Neill, *Everyone Was Brave*, pp. 169–222; J. Stanley Lemons, *The Woman Citizen: Social Feminism in the 1920s* (Urbana: University of Illinois Press, 1973), pp. 3–40; and June Sochen, *The New Woman: Feminism in Greenwich Village, 1910–1920* (New York: Quadrangle Books, 1972).

16. Roy Lubove, "The Progressives and the Prostitute," *The Historian* 25 (May 1962): 308–30; Egal Feldman, "Prostitution, the Alien Woman and the Progressive Imagination, 1910–1915," *American Quarterly* 19 (Summer 1967): 192–206.

17. William L. O'Neill, *The Progressive Years: American Comes of Age* (New York: Dodd, Mead and Company, 1975), pp. 85–86.

18. C.K. McFarland, "Crusade for Child Laborers: 'Mother' Jones and the March of the Mill Children," *Pennsylvania History* 38 (July 1971): 283–96; Dale Fetherling, *Mother Jones: The Miners' Angel* (Carbondale: Southern Illinois University Press, 1974).

19. James J. Kenneally, "Women and Trade Unions, 1870–1920: The Quandary of the Reformer," *Labor History* 14 (Winter 1973): 42–55.

20. The limitations of the socialists are discussed in Mari Jo Buhle, "Women and the Socialist Party, 1901–1914," *Radical America* 4 (February 1970): 36–55.

21. Quoted in Harold Underwood Faulkner, *The Quest For Social Justice, 1898–1914* (New York: Macmillan Company, 1931), p. 154.

22. Cf. Allan F. Davis, "The WTUL, Origins and Organization," *Labor History* 5 (Winter 1964): 3–17; William H. Chafe, *The American Woman: Her Changing Social, Economic and Political Role, 1920–1970* (New York: Oxford University Press, 1972), pp. 66–88.

23. Kraditor, *Ideas of the Woman Suffrage Movement*, pp. 38–64; Alan P. Grimes, *The Puritan Ethic and Woman Suffrage* (New York: Oxford University Press, 1967), pp. 78–144.

24. Quoted in Kraditor, *Ideas of the Woman Suffrage Movement*, pp. 47–48. Cf. Ross Evans Paulson, *Women's Suffrage and Prohibition: A Comparative Study of Equality and Social Control* (Glenview, Ill.: Scott Foresman, 1973).

25. Christopher Lasch, "Divorce and the Family in America," *Atlantic* (November 1966), p. 59.

26. Kraditor, *Ideas of the Woman Suffrage Movement*, pp. 105–84; Christopher Lasch, *The Agony of the American Left* (New York: Alfred A. Knopf, 1969), pp. 23–27.

27. Cf. Gilbert Osofsky, *Harlem: The Making of a Ghetto* (New York: Harper & Row, 1966); Alan Spear, *Black Chicago: The Making of a Ghetto, 1890–1920* (Chicago: University of Chicago Press, 1967); Seth M. Scheiner, *Negro Mecca: A History of the Negro in New York City, 1865–1920* (New York: New York University Press, 1965); Scheiner, "President Theodore Roosevelt and the Negro, 1901–1908," *Journal of Negro History* 47 (July 1962): 169–82; and August Meier, *Negro Thought In America, 1880–1915* (Ann Arbor: University of Michigan Press, 1966).

13

Loving Courtship
or the Marriage Market?
The Ideal and Its Critics, 1871-1911

Sondra R. Herman

During the last three decades of the 19th century and the first of the 20th, American feminists generally avoided discussion of marital and sexual issues. Fearful of disgracing the movement with scandal, particularly after the Victoria Woodhull affair, and sharing the sexually repressive standards of the age, feminists increasingly turned their attention to the suffrage and the supposed benefits it would bring all of society.

Yet in these same decades of repression a debate *did* arise over marital questions. If the implications of sexuality could not be considered freely, neither could the subject of marriage be avoided. More women were going to work; more were seeking a college education, particularly after the 1890s. More couples were moving to the city. Defenders of traditional marriage promulgated the old ideals of female domesticity, submissiveness and sexual purity in the face of what they thought were some dangerous trends. Critics of American marriage found that male domination, female uselessness and economic depen-

From the *American Quarterly* 25 (May 1973). Copyright © 1973 by the Trustees of the University of Pennsylvania. Reprinted by permission.

A revised version of this paper was presented at the meeting of the Organization of American Historians, April 1972.

The author would like to thank all of the following individuals for helpful comments on an earlier version of this paper, although none should be associated with the positions I have taken in it: Carl N. Degler, Samuel Haber, Anne Sherrill, Carroll Smith-Rosenberg, Warren I. Susman.

dency had distorted marital happiness. Both groups concentrated their attention on the processes of courtship, for here they perceived the sex roles they were either defending or challenging took on most obvious forms.

The debate centered on a peculiar question: Was American courtship a process of practical love-seeking or was it a marriage market? Since we have no evidence that American marriages were in fact marriages of convenience in the 1880s and 1890s any more than earlier, the critics' charge of materialism seemed in large measure a weapon in the battle for female independence. The defense of courtship as love-seeking similarly was part of an effort to keep women at home in an age known for the restlessness of its females.

Both defenders and critics realized that their evaluation of marriage was connected to their evaluations of the whole social order. In general the defenders of traditional marriage implied that America offered opportunity enough for men and contentment for wives if they would only be supportive. The critics of American marriage, at least the five treated here—Edward Bellamy, Lester Frank Ward, Charlotte Perkins Gilman, Thorstein Veblen and Theodore Dreiser—attacked traditional marriage as part of the general injustice of American society. Thus while the debate could not before 1910 take direct sexual terms, it took a social form—defense of or attack upon the social status quo.

The defenders of the status quo were most often Protestant, especially evangelical clergy, conservative women, and doctors who wrote books offering the most traditional marital advice. The critics were intellectuals who refused to acknowledge religious authority and who openly challenged the ideal of fixed sex roles contained in such works. Only toward the end of the era, after 1910 or so, did an actual rebellion against repressive notions of sexuality begin. The debate in the eighties and nineties, while occasionally hinting at discontent with sexual standards, focused on proper sex roles and on woman's economic dependency.

Writers of the marriage manuals frequently asserted that indissoluble matrimony was the foundation of the whole social order. It was a "duty binding upon all well-equipped people who cannot show some larger obligation that is inconsistent with this."[1] It was, first, essential to complete the humanity of each man and woman. The two sexes, more different from one another than alike, needed to enter a human trinity—man, woman, child, so that each could become more truly a self. Celibacy not only meant incompletion, it threatened a sinful life, especially for men. Marriage was essential, secondly, to fulfill the social obligation of parenthood.[2] Sex was an expression of love but essential for reproduction only.

Like the Puritan clergy generations earlier, the marital advisers of the late 19th century assumed that it was completely within the partners' capabilities to make or unmake their marriage. Marital happiness became a duty to be performed not only for the husband and wife's own benefit, but for the sake of the children and society.

Critics of American marriage, on the other hand, believed that marital happiness was deeply influenced by social conditions outside of marriage. They implied by the term "marriage market" that materialistic motives were necessarily present in most marriage choices. Young ladies presented themselves as merchandise for eager young men to marry. The girls, being dependent, had to do so in order to survive. Secondly, the term "market" suggested a terrible impersonality in the exchange of love for support. The harshness of the business world was invading the home itself. Home was no longer a refuge from the cold world, but rather its extension. To correct these conditions, the critics argued, a new social ethic was needed—more independence for women, more freedom to marry outside of one's class, more freedom to reject marriage altogether.

The audience for these strictures was an urban middle class who may have found marital choice freer and more difficult than ever before.[3] The sheer population of neighborhoods, the increasing opportunities for men and women to meet at work, made it virtually impossible for parents to know all the eligibles from whom a son or daughter would make a choice. Some resource had to replace the valuable gossip of the small town. The marriage advice books flowed into the gap. Some of these works, particularly those of doctors promising postnuptial sexual advice, as well as advice as to marital choice, were quite popular. *The Physical Life of Woman* by Dr. George Napheys sold 150,000 copies in its original 1869 edition and was reprinted in 1888. Others appeared to be collections of sermons circulating little further than the clergyman's parish, but clerical works sometimes ran to later editions as well.[4]

The marital advice books attempted to erect barriers against changing values. They cautioned against neglect of the church and against extravagant, worldly women. They upheld static definitions of role, relating these to the protection of the American home from declining moral standards. The major responsibility for creating a moral society, by building the foundations at home, lay with the wife. Unlike the critics, the nuptial guides viewed woman as relatively influential because they valued her role as moral guardian. Home was to provide a haven of tenderness in the cold world, and woman, by nature more emotional than man, was the source of that warmth. Her husband's success and therefore the economic well-being of the family, her children's character, and therefore the moral future of the republic, depended critically upon her patient strength. She, more than anyone else, upheld the ideals of sexual purity and family devotion.[5]

Given such conditions the ministers and doctors wrote fairly uniform descriptions of the good wife, and they castigated behavior that did not conform with their ideals. Men were advised to seek both character and performance in a wife. The prospective bride had to show she could become a thrifty, meticulous housekeeper. But prevalent female extravagance in dress made this requirement difficult to meet. The writers feared that idle wives who ministered only to their husbands' sensual needs were on the increase. Their families were not large enough to occupy them.[6] A wife, secondly, had to identify her future with her husband's completely, listen sympathetically to his plans and comfort him when they failed. And sympathy was needed by the husband. "I counsel the wife to remember in what a severe and terrific battle of life her husband is engaged," preached the Reverend DeWitt Talmage in 1886.[7] The independent college graduate, more in evidence in the next decade, evidently had to learn this submissive, traditional role. Above all, the wife had to be trustworthy, which meant both that she could be her husband's confidante, and that she was sexually pure. No hint of sexual interest should ever touch her manner or conversation. Her reputation, more than her husband's, became the reputation of the entire family. For the most part, the marriage advisers believed that this requirement would be easier to meet than the others. Most asserted or implied that woman's sexual drive was much weaker than man's, although some doctors emphasized that it was not absent altogether.[8] The fulfillment of these feminine ideals—tenderness, chastity, homemaking skills—came with maternity. The requirements of motherhood pervaded the advice literature which was often anti-birth-control literature as well.

Similarly, the prospective husband was regarded in his role as paterfamilias. If a woman's duty was to comfort and serve, a man's was to love and protect. Assuming that man's "animal nature" was much stronger than woman's (yet necessary for the propagation of the race), the doctors and clergy issued stern warnings about the average masculine morality. Women might exercise a softening influence, but they could never reform fundamental wrongs. The girls should avoid men much older than themselves, licentious men, drunkards, gamblers, cold-hearted tyrants, those whose work took them away from home frequently and "despisers of the Christian religion."[9] Of all the post-nuptial failings, man's overabsorption in his business and in the attractions of hotel life were believed most common. Marriage advisers warned wives to stay neat and attractive.[10]

The wife's choice of a husband (but interestingly, not the husband's choice of a wife) was deemed fatal. Presumably the clergy's opposition to divorce would equalize the seriousness of choosing. It did not. Some writers acknowledged that a man could always escape to his club, but a woman had no escape. Was this an implied acknowledgment of the double standard? It is hard to say, for other advisers cautioned men against "lascivious actions which are a drain upon the whole system" and asked them to come to the marriage bed as virginal as their brides.[11]

One factor that increased the dangers of poor choice by the woman, her economic dependence, a major concern of critics, was rarely mentioned by the guides. They may have taken the husband's provider role for granted. Yet this avoidance of any discussion of money appeared to be related to the estimate of woman's weaker sex drive. When a man sought a girl he was following a powerful instinct. The girl, on the other hand, could judge a suitor more rationally.[12] Thus the clergymen avoided any statement implying ecclesiastical approval of women coldly evaluating prospective husbands in terms of earning power.

Having presented marriage as a sacred institution, and home as a refuge from the world's commercialism, the advisers could hardly allow commercial standards of judgment about marriage. To have acknowledged materialistic motives on a general scale would have been to admit precisely what the critics implied—the obligation to Christianize the social order, an order that had so corrupted matrimony. The marital advisers acted on the contrary assumption: the traditional marital relationship was pure. It did not need woman's economic independence to cure its materialism. On the contrary, when marriage was delayed in order to acquire the money for a respectable "establishment," it was the sinner's corruption not society's. Woman's worship of fashion, man's "absurd social ambition," were individual evils, not symptoms of social disorder.[13]

After cautioning their readers about financial extravagance, the preachers presumed to tell lovers how to judge love. Their intentions were clear—to discourage matches of sudden passion and deceptive romance. Sudden falling in love they believed a myth fostered by too much novel reading. A marriage based upon passion was as dangerous as an overcalculating one. Instead, men and women should grow in love, that is, make reasonable and practical choices based upon secure knowledge of one another's characters. Above all, it was important to distinguish passion from love. The first was easily satiated and carnal, but love was at least partially spiritual and entirely unselfish, reasonable and tender. It could pass certain tests which lovers should make before they married. It had the constancy required for indissoluble marriage

Loving Courtship or the Marriage Market?   237

and responsible parenthood.[14] By emphasizing love's reasonableness, the nuptial counselors gave hardly any hint of the mysterious process by which men and women discovered their mutuality, nor of the possibilities of tragic choices. If one was sensible, the endings were happy. Love, true tender love, was essential to marriage. It was the greatest guarantee of marital and social stability.

Frequently, objections to romantic love merged with objections to marriage across class lines. Harmonious differences in temperament were considered healthy, but not marked differences in status. Cultural incompatibility would destroy such a marriage which might have been motivated by social climbing on the part of the poorer partner. As they feared such class mixtures (and certainly racial and religious mixtures were beyond the pale), so the advisers feared the drowning of an educated, Protestant, older American population in a sea of ignorant, immigrant poor. The urging of practical, compatible marriages sometimes took place in this context.[15]

In spite of the pleas for class compatibility, the Cinderella ideal remained as popular as ever in short stories and plays. Writers usually sought a formula to prove that Cinderella was not a fortune-hunter. In one of the longest-run productions on the New York stage and on the road, Steel McKaye's *Hazel Kirke* (1880), the lovely, submissive miller's daughter fell in love with a titled Englishman, quite unaware of his position. When the inevitable obstacles arose in the form of previously promised marriages of convenience, the hero sacrificed fortune and position to keep Hazel—thereby equalizing their social positions. In most short stories, however, in the women's mass circulation magazines of the first decade of the 20th century, the fortune, hidden during courtship, was revealed and kept at the end as a reward for true love.[16] Although the fiction upheld the Cinderella ideal and the marriage manuals cautioned against it, together they constituted a success literature. Both declared that chastity and virtuous courtship would win rewards—both spiritual and practical.

It is difficult to know just how seriously readers took the advice to marry within their class. Some middle-class families, perhaps chiefly those in the upper middle class, found that neighborhood acquaintance alone was not enough to maintain the lines. When Ethel Sturgis, daughter of the President of the Chicago, Northwestern Bank, became engaged to Francis Dummer, Vice President of the same bank in 1888, she wrote, "I almost tremble to think if love and duty had not coincided, what a struggle our two lives would have been." Ethel's father and Francis' sister had, however, pointed out the virtues of Ethel and Francis to each other.[17] In contrast, when a niece of the famous Doctors Blackwell, Elizabeth and Emily, pursued a young farmer in

Martha's Vineyard, the family placed every possible obstacle in the way of this "common" marriage. In spite of their niece's behavior the aunts assumed a lower moral standard went with the lower class.[18]

In this assumption, the Blackwells reflected an undercurrent of anxiety that ran through some of the purity campaigns of the 1890s and 1900s. The purity crusaders were a diverse group of women, doctors, prohibitionists, later progressives who launched a series of campaigns against prostitution and lax age-of-consent laws. They certainly wanted a single standard of sexual morality—but not only for both sexes, but for all classes as well. They resented society's "heartless discriminations in favor of the rich and the influential."[19] As Benjamin Flower, editor of the *Arena,* a vehicle for the movement, observed: "The immorality and degradation of rapid life among the mushroom aristocracy is matched by the grosser manifestations of immorality in the social cellar . . . [and] the great middle class absorbs the contagion from above and below."[20]

The purity advocates warned against social climbing in marriage, believing that ambitious marriages increased extramarital temptations. Avaricious parents led innocent sons and daughters into such marriages while corrupt churchmen ignored the social consequences.[21] As Nathan G. Hale has pointed out, the purity campaigns for sex education, their muckraking against white slavery, the whole drive for a break in the wall of silence they claimed protected vice, had very different results than they envisioned. The campaigns undermined the old repressive standards.[22] In spite of this contrast in effects, the campaigners upheld the same values as those of the churchmen whose protection of virtue they considered so inadequate. Their ideals remained: chastity, female domesticity, rational love and class compatibility.

The purity campaigners' emphasis upon the social injustices which they thought imperiled the home was one indication among many that Americans were, by the 1880s, more receptive to more radical analyses of their society. No stronger weapon existed in the radical armory than the charge that even the home, the supposed haven of warmth and love, was corrupted by materialism. All of the five critics—Bellamy, Ward, Gilman, Veblen and Dreiser—had reason to challenge the alliance of church, home and business. Edward Bellamy and Lester Frank Ward, for example, had early experienced crises of belief which left them with the idea that the church's repressive sexual standards and the guilt they induced were themselves a source of evil.[23] Economic insecurity had scarred the childhoods of Charlotte Perkins Gilman and Theodore Dreiser. Mrs. Gilman's father had deserted a family of four, offering only occasional financial, and no psychological support. Charlotte, seeing her mother's submissive suffering, could never play the traditional female role. Theodore Dreiser's family disintegrated altogether under the combined disasters of his father's obsessive moralism and frequent unemployment. Thorstein Veblen appeared to have learned his skepticism early by contrasting the life of the hard-working Norwegian American farmers with that of the Yankee middle class. By the time he attended Carleton College, he was a full-fledged rebel.[24] In various ways, then, these critics' early experiences led them to reject the conservative success ethos that shaped traditional marital standards.

Edward Bellamy, whose utopian novel, *Looking Backward* (1888) appealed both to intellectuals and to the general public as a solution to the ills of monopolistic capitalism, did not revolt against his own closely knit family, but first against the remnants of Calvinist dogma which crushed the individual conscience. The destructive sense of guilt, the haunting Nemesis of an evil fate, he considered more psychologically damaging than any evil deed. By the 1870s his vaguely transcendental Religion of Solidarity replaced the old religion and provided the philosophical ground of his utopia, being at once impersonal and social.[25]

While he was in his twenties, in the midst of this religious crisis, Bellamy *had* entertained profound doubts about marriage. Avoiding it himself, he argued that marriage became the grave of the creative man who had to prostitute his talents in order to support dependents. In an unpublished novel, *Eliot Carson,* he toyed with the monastic solution for artists. This could hardly answer for all of society. Bellamy himself finally found it unsatisfactory and married late in his thirties.[26] Yet the question remained: How could men have love and a home without the imprisoning economic dependency of women?

Only when Bellamy turned from his fiction of individual psychological transformation to his utopia of revolutionary social transformation did he find the answer. In *Looking Backward,* the hero Julian awoke in the year 2000 to find a society in which both men and women worked for the state until their forties, and all received state support throughout their lifetimes. Men had the delights of domesticity without its restrictive burdens; women, having simpler homes (and with much of the traditional domestic labor performed publicly), had the interest of working in the world. The price, unfortunately, was considerable regimentation, but Bellamy did not think this an obstacle.[27] Society was rid of inhumane poverty and inequality.

The economic equality of the year 2000 utterly destroyed the marriage market. Men and women married for love alone; there could be no other reasons. Class distinctions in marriage were gone as were the classes themselves. Bellamy believed that such a free marriage system had tremendous genetic implications: "For the first time in human history, the principle of sexual selection with the tendency to preserve and transmit the better types of the race . . . has unhindered operation. The necessity of poverty, the need of having a home, no longer tempt women to accept as fathers of their children men whom they can neither love nor respect. . . . The gifts of the person, mind, and disposition . . . are sure of transmission to posterity."[28]

Thus did Bellamy affirm one of the strongest values of the radical critics of American marriage—the goal of an improved future generation. This goal, which was also implicit in the marital guidebooks' concern for proper parenthood, took a different form in the critics' analysis. They thought about the development of future generations more in post-Darwinian terms. Bellamy had even for a time entertained the idea of stirpiculture.[29] The guides believed that a marriage system which preserved class divisions, and in which the educated produced more children than the poor and uneducated, promised the best future. The critics believed that a class society, and a society of economically dependent women, harmed the future generation. They valued instead what Veblen called the parental bent—concern not just for one's own children, but for all children and for their future.

Bellamy relied upon "nationalism" to destroy the marriage market and he claimed it would end such accompanying evils as female triviality, hypocrisy (induced by 19th century courtship) and the double standard. This last reflected sexual economics more than sexual morality. It protected the purity of dependent married women at a horrible cost in prostitution. Since true ethical behavior could originate only with free choice, and since neither prostitutes nor chaste women were free, true sexual morality could begin only when women were economically independent of men. Such free women could frankly confess their love to men. No longer compelled to please the average man, in order to catch a husband, each woman could develop her own interests and talents. Women would no longer pass on their "mental and moral slavery" to their offspring.[30]

In thus simplifying the problem in economic terms, Bellamy was deferring to the popular, sexually repressive opinion of his day. His brother Charles had offered in a utopian novel, *An Experiment in Marriage* (1889), solutions Edward eschewed—virtually complete communal living, easy divorce and frequent remarriage. Only this system preserved the freshness of love.[31] With his brother's ideals of frank courtship and female equality Edward agreed. But divorce he could not endorse publicly, and he certainly had reservations about the sensuality favored in *An Experiment in Marriage*. Under "nationalism" he suggested the sexual drive would be not more intense but more diffuse, "like light that passes through a prism . . . refracted into many shades and hues."[32] In place of the free divorce system he created in the story "To Whom This May Come" a society of mind readers who recognized their true loves at once (vitiating the need for sensual experimentation). And these mind readers' unions were, of course, more spiritual than passionate, affirming the Bellamy ideal of love—moderate rapture. Since men would not have to support women in the socialist state, intense passion would not be needed to induce marriage. As family relationships declined in intensity, everyone would be "a thousandfold more than now occupied with nature and the next steps of the race."[33]

Like Bellamy, Lester Frank Ward and Charlotte Perkins Gilman attacked the exaggerated sexual differentiation of lives in late 19th century America. While Ward deplored sexual repression, Mrs. Gilman, who had paid the high price of nervous depression, divorce and separation from her daughter to attain autonomy, felt that American marriages *over-emphasized* sensuality. She was never able to accept the freer standards of the war years. In the early seventies Ward launched attacks upon the church, whose doctrines of female submission and indissoluble marriage he held directly responsible for prostitution.[34] Yet he left off his attack as he turned his attention to evolutionary theory and only took up the defense of freer sexual expression in 1903. In the 1890s then both Ward and Gilman criticized American marriage in the only "acceptable" way it could be criticized—by challenging traditional notions of the female role.

Both asserted that female inferiority was not inherent, but developed in the processes of the marriage market. Both extended the discussion to include a naturalistic consideration of the mate-selection process. Ward outlined a woman-centered theory of evolution indicating how the female of the species had abandoned an initially superior status. In all subhuman species, he noted, it was the female, not the male, who transmitted the characteristics of the race. She selected the males with whom to mate. Eventually, however, the females began to select not only the strongest, but the most intelligent mates. At that point, just as primitive man evolved, a crucial transformation took place. The men perceived that it was easier to seize females for mating than to contest for their favors with stronger males, allowing the female to choose the victor. This seizure and rape process, male-dominated mate selection, was the germ of marriage. And men continued to dominate the marriage market until modern times.[35]

Charlotte Perkins Gilman added that this male domination of the market bred a race of frail, backward women. Men chose such women for wives, so the smarter, stronger ones did not reproduce their own kind. But there was an even more crucial reason for female inferiority. Once man had conquered woman and enslaved her, she could no longer hunt for her own food, or provide for her own young as female animals did. Man stood between woman and the challenging environment of the economic world. Women, thus, developed largely through their relationships with men. They developed those traits needed to catch a husband: conformity, flirtatiousness, sexual exaggeration and passivity.[36] Marriageable women, as much as prostitutes, were utterly dependent upon men and in essence sold themselves. "When we confront this fact boldly . . . in the open market of vice, we are sick with horror. When we see the same economic relation made permanent, established by law . . . sanctified by religion, covered with flowers and accumulated sentiment, we think it innocent, lovely, and right. The transient trade we think evil, the bargain for life we think good."[37]

Both Ward and Gilman saw signs, however, that the age of the marriage market was passing. As societies became more complex and more highly civilized, the most fastidious individuals, Ward believed, had difficulty choosing a mate, and tended to decline marriage altogether. This, and the burden of economically unproductive women, made the goal of one indissoluble marriage for each impossible of realization.[38]

Ward asserted that by the end of the 19th century male-dominated selection was fortunately declining. If men continued to select women for their frail, ephemeral beauty, the race would eventually be extinct. But modern men were selecting women for their mental and moral strengths as well as for beauty. By this process they happily increased female influence. More and more *mutual* selection took place. Ward identified this mutual selection with romantic love. Unlike most nuptial guides, he cherished and celebrated romance as not only beautiful for individuals, but beneficial for society. It was the highest form of man's noblest natural instinct—sexual love. When men and women fell in love, they advanced both the race and the civilization. By choosing mates of contrasting temperament and build, they acted out of a natural wisdom to produce well-balanced offspring. Thus the only sound eugenics was obedience to the law of love.[39] Ward, arguing in evolutionary terms, was using a powerful weapon against "practical" marriage advice.

Moreover, romantic love aided civilization just because it rarely ran smooth. For each couple it meant working, struggling, long denial. Out of this yearning struggle came man's deepest inspirations to create in the arts and sciences. And the struggle, unstable in itself, ended in fulfillment, with the onset of calm conjugal love. Society's standards, therefore, should not be sexually repressive. Love was a "higher law" that should prevail over social conventions. Free divorce should be allowed so that marriages contracted out of unromantic motives, loveless, practical marriages could be ended for the sake of romance and the next generation.[40] This combination of romantic idealism and evolutionary science constituted Ward's plea for greater sexual freedom.

Mrs. Gilman was distinctly less enthusiastic about sexual freedom, although she too wanted love unshackled from economic marriage. Her own experiences, her early allegiance to Bellamy's socialism, led her to emphasize the collective life of modern society which she wished women to enter. In her famous *Women and Economics* (1898) she demonstrated that the individualism of the marital relation contradicted and distorted economic relations which tended to collectivity as industries modernized. Man's selfishness for "the sake of the family" was no more reasonable in a cooperative world than woman's isolation at home or overspecialization as to sex. The traditional roles had to and would decay for the world's benefit. Already a complex economy was drawing women out of the home, ending their alienation from creative labor. Primitive household labor was becoming obsolete. Woman's very restlessness in the domestic role indicated a new social consciousness.[41]

Woman's economic independence would not threaten marriage itself, but would end the male-dominated marriage market. Marriage would no longer be a "sexuo-economic" relationship. Women would choose husbands, sublimating immediate sexual attractiveness to the demands of "right parentage." At the same time, female influence would counteract the aggressive tendencies of the man-made world with the values of "peaceful, helpful interservice." A new social environment, reinforcing industrial efficiency, would prevail, making the egalitarian changes in the marriage relationship permanent.[42]

Although he was less hopeful than Mrs. Gilman, Thorstein Veblen made a very similar identification between the peaceful primitive matriarchy of the past and a possible future industrial republic. Like Ward and Gilman he looked backward in order to criticize the present and reconstruct the future. His anthropological economics was so implicitly subversive that readers could only regard their own mores as vestiges of barbarism. In all the Veblenian lexicon the most barbaric institution of all was the patriarchal marriage.

The patriarchy originated when primitive tribes acquired an excess of goods and encountered hostile tribes. Seizing the conquered tribes' goods and women, they eventually made war a way of life. In the transformation into a barbaric society, private ownership, slavery and patriarchal marriage originated. Because only wives and slaves worked, labor was judged irksome. The patriarch displayed his wives as possessions, and he owned the products of their labor. Riches and status came together. "The ownership and control of women is gratifying evidence of prowess and high standing."[43]

When Veblen extended this argument into a work both popular and scholarly, *The Theory of the Leisure Class* (1899), he forged a weapon of considerable power against traditional sex roles. For in stating that the middle-class wife functioned only to display luxury and idleness as proof of her husband's social standing, he touched an area as sensitive with the conservative preachers as with the radical critics. America's traditional values could not encompass idleness or uselessness and Veblen knew this. Moreover, he answered a hopeful strain of the 1890s by stating that in spite of the interference of barbaric capitalism, the processes of modern technology would destroy the patriarchal marriage and allow a reemergence of "the most ancient habits of thought of the race."[44]

Veblen's economics implied goals very similar to those of Bellamy's utopia, Gilman's feminist analysis and Ward's naturalistic sociology. All viewed marriage as an institution distorted by late 19th century capitalistic culture. In its distorted form, in its competitive materialism, it was an impediment to a cooperative future. While the writers of marriage manuals viewed marriage as a sacred absolute, the critics thought it had the tinges of a modern slavery. Nevertheless, they too suggested an ideal marriage at the end of evolutionary change—a relationship personal yet more responsive to community needs, romantic because freed from the man's one-sided economic dominance and responsibilities. In place of the guides' values—home, purity, social order—they cherished woman's economic independence, creative and cooperative labor, romantic love and the parental bent. They grounded these values in a naturalistic Weltanschauung rather than in a traditionally Protestant one.

Only when the repressive sexual ethic met a direct challenge, however, would the revolt against the older morality be launched. Of course, changing behavior itself was such a challenge. But ideologically the challenge, out of a naturalistic framework, was issued by a "new man" with no loyalty to the older, small-town America, to its code or its optimism. Theodore Dreiser confronted the sexual code by depicting directly its everyday violations. His first two novels, *Sister Carrie* (1900) and *Jennie Gerhardt* (1911) grew out of his sister's experiences with the civilized morality. In those works, as in his others, Dreiser painted Americans as they actually stood—unprotected in the lonely urban world. His newspaper experience had told him a great deal about the city's real values in contrast to the small-town pieties.[45] But Dreiser's first lessons began at home.

After witnessing repeated contradictions between the standard 19th century moral conventions and his sisters' escape from poverty through illicit affairs, between his father's gloomy prudery and the life of pleasure his brother, songwriter Paul Dresser, led, Theodore compounded his own naturalistic religion to replace his father's Catholicism. He came to believe that sexual love, infused with the love of natural beauty, was *the* experience initiating men and women into nature's truth. Change was the law of life, and any static institutions or ideals of respectability had to be cast aside if they stood in the way of sheer survival.[46]

In *Sister Carrie* the heroine adapted to the urban world, first by a simple, hardly considered abandonment of virginity, then by a determined struggle and finally by developing into an actress. In choosing to become Drouet's mistress, rather than remain a cold, poorly paid, worn factory-hand, Carrie was taking the first step toward survival and success, rather than toward the traditional downfall and ruin. Her second lover, Hurstwood, destroyed himself not by stealing money or committing adultery, but in a futile effort to retain his middle-class respectability.[47] Carrie knew how to fight; Hurstwood gave up. That was all. Their sexual behavior brought neither punishment nor reward. That was what was most devastating about Dreiser's portraits—his refusal to pass any condemning judgments. Carrie trading her body outside of marriage appeared not a whit more materialistic than Hurstwood's wife trading within marriage, and offering her daughter Jessica in the marriage market.

In *Jennie Gerhardt* (1911) Dreiser drew the contrast between "the grasping legality of established matrimony" and the free flow of love most clearly. Jennie was that most ancient of literary heroines, the woman in love. Full of passionate tenderness, she seemed at one with nature itself. Lester Kane, her lover, heir to a manufacturing fortune, shared a passionate communion with Jennie. But he knew he need never marry her. She was a lower-class girl and marriage was a very practical arrangement. He had hoped to escape it altogether. When business interests and his family dictated otherwise, Kane left Jennie to marry an attractive, rich widow with whom he shared social and intellectual interests. Thus Dreiser portrayed man in the natural world of feeling, a world of great depth, and yet bound to the world of convention, if unable to pay the price of defiance. The conventional world upheld that static institution—marriage—and reversed the natural value of passionate love. That was reason enough for Dreiser's contempt for convention. Jennie, alone, having lost social acceptance, her love and her child, triumphed by sheer affirmation of natural love.[48]

By the time Dreiser wrote this defiance of the marriage market, the age of new sexual standards was beginning. *Jennie Gerhardt* was a critical and popular success. Although his subsequent struggle with *The Genius* (1915) indicated that Comstockery did not die all at once, the tide had turned. Perhaps for this very reason the revolt of the 1880s and 1890s seemed excessive to the new age. Dreiser's attack upon marriage, and especially upon the class divisions marriage upheld, was not repeated, although studies confirmed that Americans continued to marry those of similar wealth and status.[49] To the postwar generation there would be something anachronistic about Gilman's feminism, although American women had not achieved anything approaching her ideal of economic independence.

Above all, the critics' implicit association between marital discontent and the inequalities of late 19th century society seemed too radical for the war and postwar generations. Did social institutions require a thoroughgoing transformation for men and women to enjoy a healthier, franker relationship? In the age of Freud the younger generation doubted it. The double standard was withering, but women were receptive to a new ideology of domesticity. Yet the radicals of the 1880s and 1890s *did* connect social transformation with true freedom for romantic love. The sexually repressive standards of Gilman and Bellamy were distinctly Victorian. But in their attacks upon the home, upon women's economic dependency and upon exaggerated sexual differentiation of roles, the critics appear to speak more to our own generation than they did to the generations that directly succeeded them.

NOTES

1. Delos S. Wilcox, *Ethical Marriage: A Discussion of the Relation of Sex from the Standpoint of Social Duty* (Ann Arbor: Wood-Allen, 1900), p. 10; see also John L. Brandt, *Marriage and the Home* (Chicago: Laird & Lee, 1892), pp. 21–22, 57.

2. Caroline Corbin, *A Woman's Philosophy of Love* (Boston: Lee, Shepard, 1893), p. 13; Minot Judson Savage, *Man, Woman, and Child* (Boston: George Ellis, 1884), pp. 64, 136–37; George McLean, *The Curtain Lifted: Hidden Secrets Revealed* (Chicago: Lewis, 1887), pp. 165–67; James Reed, *Man and Woman: Equal but Unlike* (Boston: Nichols & Noyes, 1870), *passim;* Samuel R. Wells, *Wedlock* (New York: S. R. Wells, 1871), pp. 24–25; William H. Holcombe, *The Sexes Here and Hereafter* (Philadelphia: Lippincott, 1869), p. 166; and George H. Napheys, M.D., *The Physical Life of Woman* (Philadelphia: David McKay, 1888), pp. 57–58.

3. The author is indebted to Prof. Samuel Haber of the University of California, Berkeley for this observation and for pointing out that the very existence of many choices may have popularized the phrase "marriage market."

4. Napheys, *Physical Life,* preface, p. vii. Other doctor works include Henry Hanchett, *Sexual Health* (New York: Charles Harlburt, 1887); Henry Guernsey, *Plain Talks on Avoided Subjects* (Philadelphia: F. A. Davis, 1882); and H. S.

Pomeroy, *The Ethics of Marriage* (New York: Funk & Wagnalls, 1888), commended as an anti-birth-control work in Brevard Sinclair, *The Crowning Sin of the Age* (Boston: H. L. Hastings, 1892), p. 15, and in *Journal of the American Medical Association,* 2 (1888), 309–11. Clerical works or limited edition collections of sermons used as brides' books include: S. D. & Mary Kilgore Gordon, *Quiet Talks on Home Ideals* (New York: Fleming Revell, 1909); Robert F. Horton, *On the Art of Living Together* (New York: Dodd Mead, 1896); and F. B. Meyer, *Lovers Always* (New York: Fleming Revell, 1899). Examples of second editions in marital guidebooks are: Wells, *Wedlock* (c. 1869, 1871 ed.); Mrs. E. B. Duffy, *The Relations of the Sexes* (New York: M. L. Holbrook, c. 1876, 1889 ed.); and James R. Miller, D.D., *The Wedded Life* (Presbyterian Board of Publication of Philadelphia, c. 1886, 1894 ed.).

5. Brandt, *Marriage and Home,* pp. 51, 210; Wells, *Wedlock,* p. 173; and Savage, *Man, Woman, and Child,* pp. 33, 37. The same assumptions cropped up in personal correspondence concerning courtships and betrothal. For example, when Austin Baldwin of Savannah became engaged to Louise Maynard of Massachusetts, Baldwin's brother wrote: "It is . . . not the man that makes his wife, but the wife that more often makes the man and I hope my new sister will prove a good advisor and helpmate. . . . If Lou is as good as she is handsome . . . you may date your success in life from the time you were married." T. J. Baldwin to A. Baldwin, May 15, 1872, Baldwin Family Papers, Schlesinger Archives, Radcliffe College. Similarly, Emily Blackwell wrote her sister Elizabeth: "I felt a great deal depended upon the woman he married. If she had been a girl whose ambition was for society . . . it would have spoiled him. Frances will be ambitious for him to choose a worthwhile career, and will support him in any serious work. I believe she will be an excellent influence in his life." Nov. 6, 1904, Blackwell Family Papers, Schlesinger Archives, Radcliffe College.

6. Cortland Myers, *The Lost Wedding Ring* (New York: Funk & Wagnalls, 1902), pp. 100–2; Elizabeth Blackwell, *Counsel to Parents on the Moral Education of their Children* (New York: Brentano, 1883), p. 75; Charles Frederick Goss, *Husband, Wife and Home* (Philadelphia: Vir Publishing, 1905), pp. 33–34; Brandt, *Marriage,* pp. 70–71, 81–85, 85–88; and Miller, *Wedded Life,* pp. 65–67.

7. *The Marriage Ring: A Series of Discourses in Brooklyn Tabernacle* (New York: Funk & Wagnalls, 1886), p. 62. See also Savage, *Man, Woman, and Child,* p. 38; and Miller, *Wedded Life,* pp. 20–21.

8. Napheys, *Physical Life,* pp. 96, 102; Hanchett, *Sexual Health,* p. 37; Brandt, *Marriage,* pp. 80–81.

9. Talmage, *Marriage Ring,* pp. 24–25, 28–29; M. Salmonsen, *From the Marriage License Window* (Chicago: John Anderson, 1887), pp. 100, 103; Savage, *Man, Woman, and Child,* pp. 13–21; and Miller, *Wedded Life,* pp. 31–39, 42–49, 52–54 detail the masculine ideal.

10. Goss, *Husband, Wife, Homes,* pp. 50, 66–68; and Talmage, *Marriage Ring,* pp. 62–64, 66.

11. Guernsey, *Plain Talks,* p. 36; Brandt, *Marriage,* p. 111; Talmage, *Marriage Ring,* pp. 24–25; Myers, *Wedding Ring,* p. 84.

12. Frank N. Hagar, *The American Family: A Sociological Problem* (New York: University Publishing Soc., 1905), pp. 44–45.

13. McLean, *Curtain Lifted,* pp. 161–62; Kate Gannett Wells, "Why More Men Do

Not Marry," *North American Review*, 165 (July 1897), 124; George Shinn, *Friendly Talks About Marriage* (Boston: Jos. Knight, c. 1897), pp. 56–57.

14. Anthony W. Thorald, *On Marriage* (New York: Dodd Mead, 1896), p. 16; Pomeroy, *Ethics of Marriage*, p. 51; Sarah Grand, "Marriage Questions in Fiction: The Standpoint of a Typical Modern Woman," *Living Age*, 217 (Apr. 1898), 73; Corbin, *Woman's Philosophy*, pp. 38–41; Mary Wood-Allen, M.D., *What a Young Woman Ought to Know* (Philadelphia: Vir Publishing, 1893), pp. 200–4; Brandt, *Marriage*, pp. 41–42; and Wells, *Wedlock*, pp. 51–52.

15. Wilcox, *Ethical Marriage*, pp. 25–28; Thorold, *Marriage*, p. 25; Myers, *Wedding Ring*, p. 7; McLean, *Curtain Lifted*, pp. 161–62; Shinn, *Friendly Talks About Marriage*, pp. 31–32; Hagar, *American Family*, pp. 73–74; Sinclair, *Crowning Sin*, pp. 13, 17–18; and Wells, *Wedlock*, pp. 45, 47, 49.

16. Arthur Hobson Quinn, ed., *Representative American Plays* (New York: Appleton-Century, 1930) pp. 435–36, 439–40, 451, 453, 457, 465, 470; and Donald Makosky, "The Portrayal of Women in Wide Circulation Magazine Short Stories, 1905–1955," Diss. University of Pennsylvania 1966, pp. 139–40.

17. Ethel Sturgis to Francis Dummer, June 11, 1888. See also Dummer to Sturgis, Mar. 6, 1888; Mrs. Sturgis to F. Dummer, June 12, 1888; Katherine Dummer to Ethel Sturgis, June 12, 1888; and Katherine Dummer to Francis Dummer, June 12, 1888, Sturgis-Dummer Family Papers, Schlesinger Archives, Radcliffe College.

18. Emily Blackwell to Elizabeth Blackwell, Aug. 13, 1881, Oct. 2, 1881. For a contrasting view within the family see Alice Stone Blackwell to Kitty Barry Blackwell, July 23, 1882, Aug. 27, 1882, Blackwell Family Papers, Schlesinger Archives, Radcliffe College. The marriage took place nevertheless.

19. J. Bellanger, "Sexual Purity and the Double Standard," *Arena*, 11 (Feb. 1895), 373.

20. "Social Conditions as Feeders of Immorality," *Arena*, 11 (Feb. 1895), 410–11. For the way in which the purity movement shifted from an ecclesiastical to a scientific rationale for its positions, see David J. Pivar, "The New Abolitionism: The Quest for Social Purity, 1876–1900," Diss. University of Pennsylvania 1965.

21. Helen Gardiner, *Is This Your Son My Lord?* (Boston: Arena Publishing, 1890), *passim*.

22. *Freud and the Americans: The Beginnings of Psychoanalysis in the United States, 1876–1917* (New York: Oxford Univ. Press, 1971), pp. 252–54.

23. Joseph Schiffman, "Editor's Introduction," *Edward Bellamy: Selected Writings on Religion and Society* (New York: Liberal Arts Press, 1955), pp. xii–iii; Bellamy, *Dr. Heidenhoff's Process* (New York: c. 1880, Ams. Press, 1969), pp. 119–20, 138–39; Ward, "Revealed Religion and Human Progress," from *Iconoclast*, i (Nov. 1, 1870); *Glimpses of the Cosmos* (New York: Putnam, 1918), 1: 91–95; and "The Social Evil," *Iconoclast*, 2 (Aug. 1871), *Glimpses*, 1: 238–41.

24. Carl N. Degler, "Introduction to the Torchbook Edition," Gilman, *Woman and Economics* (New York: Harper & Row, 1966), pp. ix–x; Robert H. Elias, *Theodore Dreiser, Apostle of Nature* (Ithaca: Cornell Univ. Press, 1970), pp. 6, 11–13; and Henry Steele Commager, *The American Mind: An Interpretation of American Thought and Character Since the 1880's* (New Haven: Yale Univ. Press, 1959), pp. 238–39.

25. "The Religion of Solidarity" (1874) in Schiffman, *Bellamy, Religion and*

Society, pp. 15–17; Arthur E. Morgan, *Edward Bellamy* (New York: Columbia Univ. Press, 1955), p. 138.

26. Sylvia E. Bowman, *The Year 2000: A Critical Biography of Edward Bellamy* (New York: Bookman Associates, 1959), pp. 69–70, 279; and Morgan, *Edward Bellamy*, p. 55.

27. *New Nation*, 1 (Mar. 14, 1891), 110; (Apr. 4, 1891), 159.

28. *Looking Backward 2000–1887* (New York: Random House, n.d.), p. 218.

29. "Stirpiculture," *Springfield Daily Union* (Oct. 2, 1875), p. 4. The term, used by John Humphrey Noyes of the Oneida Community and briefly practiced there, meant arranged marriages to bring out the genetic strengths of the partners—the breeding of children. At the same time Bellamy was supporting "common-sense" in marriage which he occasionally identified with "like marrying like" in terms somewhat similar to those of the guides. He thought that marked class differences were accompanied by cultural differences, but he did not raise the objections of fortune hunting, etc. See "Literary Notices," *Springfield Daily Union* (Jan. 30, 1875), p. 6; and (Feb. 6, 1875), p. 6. *Looking Backward* then meant a considerable change in outlook.

30. *Equality*, 10th ed. (New York: Appleton, 1909), pp. 135–38, 140–41.

31. *An Experiment in Marriage: A Romance* (Albany: Albany Book, 1889), pp. 17, 24–25, 96–102, 116–17.

32. *New Nation*, 1 (1891), 298.

33. *The Blindman's World and Other Stories* (New York: Garrett, 1968), pp. 405–6, 408–9; papers B 2-7-10,11 quoted in Arthur E. Morgan, *The Philosophy of Edward Bellamy* (New York: Kings Crown, 1945), pp. 76–77. Bellamy's distrust of passion came early and remained with him; see Morgan, *Bellamy* (biography), p. 81.

34. "Revealed Religion and Human Progress" and "The Social Evil."

35. "Our Better Halves," *Forum*, 6 (Nov. 1888), 266–75: Speech Before the Six O'Clock Club, May 24, 1888, *Glimpses*, 4: 129: and *Dynamic Sociology* (New York: Appleton, 1883), 1: 617, 648.

36. *Our Androcentric Culture or the Man-Made World*, as serialized in *Forerunner*, 1 (Nov. 1909), 23–25; *Women and Economics*, pp. 61–63, 86–88.

37. *Women and Economics*, pp. 63–64.

38. *Dynamic Sociology*, 1: 624–26.

39. *Pure Sociology* (New York: Macmillan, 1903), pp. 381, 384, 398–99. In spite of Ward's appreciation for the importance of the sexual drive, Harriet Stanton Blatch thought he underestimated female sexuality, and even the "pretty clear physiological aim" of those mothers whom the world thought mercenary in pushing their daughters into the marriage market. Blatch to Ward, June 31, 1903, Sept. 2, 1903, Ward Collection, Brown University.

40. *Pure Sociology*, p. 398 n.; pp. 401–3.

41. *Woman and Economics*, pp. 105–7, 143, 154–57, 160; see also "All the World to Her," *Independent*, 55 (July 9, 1903), 1614 for the effects of woman receiving the world through her husband, and her overconcentration upon him.

42. "Man Made World," *Forerunner*, 1 (Dec. 1910), 22–24; (Dec. 1909), 14.

43. "The Barbarian Status of Women," *American Journal of Sociology*, 4 (Jan.

1899), 510; see also pp. 503–4 and "The Beginnings of Ownership" (Nov. 1898), pp. 364–65.

44. "Barbarian Status," p. 514. For Veblen's discussion of feminine beauty and dress in this regard see *The Theory of the Leisure Class* (New York: Modern Library, 1934), pp. 146–48, 179–82.

45. Dreiser, *Dawn* (New York: Liveright, 1931), pp. 173, 264; *A Book About Myself* (London: Constable, 1939), pp. 65–67, 70, 480, 488–89; Malcolm Cowley, "Sister Carrie Her Fall and Rise," *The Stature of Theodore Dreiser,* eds. Alfred Kazin and Charles Shapiro (Bloomington: Indiana Univ. Press, 1965), p. 174.

46. Maxwell Geismar, *Rebels and Ancestors: The American Novel, 1890–1915* (Boston: Houghton Mifflin, 1953), p. 291; John McAleer, *Theodore Dreiser: An Introduction and an Interpretation* (New York: Holt, Rinehart & Winston, 1968), pp. 34–35.

47. *Sister Carrie* (New York: New American Library, 1961), pp. 56, 61–62, 75–76, 84–88, 258, 267, 270–72, 315, 330–31, 421–22, 462.

48. *Jennie Gerhardt: A Novel* (New York: Harper, 1911), pp. 18, 128, 130, 215, 238, 313, 317, 322.

49. August Hollingshead, "Cultural Factors in Selection of Marriage Mates," in Marvin Sussman, ed., *Sourcebook in Marriage and the Family* (Cambridge: Riverside Press, 1955), pp. 43–50; and Richard Centers, "Occupational Endogamy in Marital Selection," ibid., pp. 56–61.

14

The "New Woman" in the New South

Anne Firor Scott

In 1884 a distinguished lady in New Orleans was made chairman of a committee of the New Orleans Education Society. When she came to make the report of her committee, over which she had labored long, the Society decreed that it must be read for her by one of the male members. The lady resigned in protest—but even her protest required male co-operation: "I requested my husband," she recorded, "to cease paying my dues!" Here, in miniature, was the "woman problem" as it began to take shape in the post-Civil War South.

Northern women had begun in the 1830's to raise their voices against legal and social discrimination, to protest the lack of equal educational and professional opportunity. In the South the institution of chivalry had held firm. It seems to have been characterized by a widespread legal and theoretical acceptance of the premise that woman was an inferior creature and a widespread practical expectation that she would perform as a superior one. The acceptable goals for southern women were to please their husbands and to please God, and to this end they were supposed to be beautiful, mildly literate, gracious, hardworking, and church going. "Woman's sphere," as they called it, was well marked out. This description applies to the minority of women who belonged to the pace-setting plantation families. For the rest, our information is small, but such as we have indicates that they worked hard and knew their place.

Testimony is unanimous that slavery did not make for leisure as far as plantation mistresses were concerned. They carried large responsibili-

From *South Atlantic Quarterly* 65 (Autumn 1962): 473–83. Reprinted with permission of Duke University Press.

ties and did as well much physical work. Open protest against their disabilities was infrequent, and genuine rebels such as the Grimké sisters found it necessary to leave the South altogether.

Then came the war. Southern women were thrust into new public and private responsibilities, ranging from running whole plantations to providing food, clothing, bandages, and nursing care for the Confederate army. With the men away "woman's sphere" suddenly became very elastic. If the fire-eaters had foreseen this particular consequence, perhaps they would have been less eager for secession—for as far as women were concerned Pandora's box was opened. Reconstruction offered other challenges, including for many the necessity of making one's way in a world in which women outnumbered men. With the whole South to rebuild, every pair of hands was needed, and while the legend of the southern lady was tended along with other more or less accurate legends of the old South, the lady herself had not much time for acting her prescribed role. In addition, the whole structure of women's lives was being changed by the multiplication of factory-made products which lightened domestic burdens immeasurably. The single invention of the sewing machine was an immense emancipation of mothers. For southern women there was an additional emancipation in the freeing of the slaves. Nearly all who recorded their opinions rejoiced that slavery was ended.

The culture pattern, of course, remained strong and was faithfully reflected by the law. In some southern states a married woman could not make a will, collect her own wages, or claim possession of any property, real or personal. Guardianship rights were often vested wholly in the husband. In 1879 Louisiana women were outraged when a generous bequest by a woman to an orphan asylum was lost because all the witnesses to the will were women. They were, declared the Chief Justice of the North Carolina Supreme Court, "slaves of despots."

There was plenty of evidence that any change would be difficult. A traveling organizer for the national woman's suffrage organization found her way to Mississippi and found discouragement on every hand. In some towns she was not permitted to lecture on suffrage at all, and had to content herself with a discourse on "Literature and Modern Tendencies" into which she bootlegged as much talk of the forbidden subject as she dared. "Death and education have much to do to redeem the southland," she concluded. A prominent Baptist minister declared that a woman who went into politics "violated the womanly instinct and defied God's law as certainly as did the painted woman who walks the streets and invites the noonday sun to witness her shame." The University of Georgia trustees found a petition for the admission of women so unfitting that they agreed to expunge all mention of it from the record. In Louisville, Henry Watterson announced that votes for women would imperil the whole human species.

The contrary forces stirred up by the war, reinforced by material and intellectual influences from the north, would not have an easy time. They were too strong, however, to be downed. The end of slavery and intellectual and material influences from the North were catalytic forces. They could not have had a significant influence without a corresponding change in the way southern women were viewing the world. Here and there such a change was taking place. In Kentucky in 1874, a twenty-five-year-old daughter of the Clay family recorded her "rebelliousness to the inequality set between men and women in this world" and decided that God had called her to help further Women's Rights. In North Carolina, a busy planter's wife, with a house full of children, was writing that "the greatest need in the world is educated, vigorous and unhampered womanhood. . . ." In Mississippi, a planter's daughter, forbidden by her father to undertake a career, felt "a constant and unceasing rebellion" at "the injustice that had always been heaped upon my sex." Another Mississippi woman mocked the favorite male palliative for discontented women—"the hand that rocks the cradle is the hand that rules the world"—as nonsense, saying that if men did not respect women, children would not either.

These were the women who now began to emerge as leaders in the southern version of what was inelegantly called the Woman Movement. Most of them were women of such impeccable family that they could, as it were, afford to be radical. They were generally in outward appearance the very model of Southern Ladies, described by their contemporaries as beautiful, charming, poised, intelligent, and brave. They were educated women, and not solely because they had been to school. All were voracious readers and writers. A long intimacy with the English classics had produced in them a pungent English style. Many were married and had children. They were women with enough energy to travel outside the South, who very early established contact with women leaders in other parts of the country, as well as with each other. They listened to and were influenced by Frances Willard, Susan B. Anthony, Elizabeth Cady Stanton, and later Anna Howard Shaw and Carrie Chapman Catt. All of them were deeply religious. Perhaps most significant, all were women of talent who had at some time in their lives felt that their talents might well be wasted for lack of opportunity to use them. As one of them put it: ". . . of all the unhappy sights the most pitiable is that of a human life, rich in possibilities and strong with divine yearnings for better things than it has known, atrophying in the prison house of blind and palsied custom."

Leaders are indispensable, but to produce a major social change many ordinary people must also be involved. In the face of the strong cultural pattern with its narrowly defined role for women, how could anything in the way of a following emerge? Not for southern women was any such blatant call to action as the "Declaration of Rights" flung to the shocked world by the Woman's Rights Convention at Seneca Falls in 1848. On the contrary, to the eye of the casual observer the southern home and fireside seemed as safe from radical modernism and the dangerous "new woman" in the eighties as it had been in the forties.

An acute observer, however, might have been led to look closely at such respectable and safe groups as the women's missionary societies of the various churches. It was here that many women first had a taste of running their own affairs. The minister who had opposed the organization of a separate prayer meeting on the grounds that if they were alone "who knows what the women will pray for?" was perhaps more prescient than he seemed. For it was in precisely such groups that the intense soul searching which had characterized southern religion before the War began to be transformed into a demand for social reform. In what was euphemistically called "home and foreign mission work" women encountered the disinherited of the post-war world, and began to question the political and social arrangements which permitted them to exist. In these church societies, natural leaders had a chance to lead, to learn to stand on their feet and make speeches, to keep records, and to organize. Yet because they were doing "church work," it was all very respectable and the most suspicious husband or father could hardly forbid attendance.

Equally respectable—for what could be more proper than a concern for Christianity and temperance?—was the Woman's Christian Temperance Union. Yet no group did more to subvert the traditional role of women, or to implant in its southern members a sort of unselfconscious radicalism which would have turned the conservative southern male speechless if he had taken the trouble to listen to what the ladies were saying. Between efforts to secure prohibition laws, the women of the WCTU worked in various southern states for prison reform, child labor regulation, shorter hours of labor, compulsory education—and cheered Frances Willard to the echo when she announced that the industrial revolution must be made to benefit the average working man and added "If to teach this is to be socialist, then so let it be."

Part of the influence of the WCTU in the lives of emerging southern women came from the quality of its national leader. Frances Willard was one of the most magnetic personalities of the nineteenth century and her tours of the South, during which she expounded a comprehensive program for reform (for which, one is tempted to think, demon rum was only a respectable front), were vastly influential. "For the local and denominational" one southern woman wrote, "she substituted the vision of humanity." "The W.C.T.U.," said another, "was the generous liberator, the joyous iconoclast, the discoverer, the developer of southern women."

The woman who penned this flowery description of the WCTU spoke from personal experience. Belle Kearney had been born into an aristocratic Mississippi family which had been so impoverished by the war that for a time she and her mother did sewing for their former slaves. She yearned for education, but the idea of a girl working her way through school was so foreign to her father's view of life that it was never even discussed. Over his vigorous protests she opened a school in her bedroom, and attained thereby her first small measure of independence. Public opinion and family pressure were so strong, however, that she succumbed to the accepted pattern, hating herself for her weakness and abhorring the way her time was spent. Then came Frances Willard, whose ability to identify potential leaders was considerable. Before long "Miss Belle" was organizing the WCTU in Mississippi, and from her success in this endeavor she moved easily into the national suffrage movement. When women were finally enfranchised, she crowned her career by being elected first woman senator in the Mississippi legislature. "The Woman's Christian Temperance Union," she recorded in her autobiography, "was the golden key that unlocked the prison doors of pent-up possibilities."

Hard upon the heels of the missionary societies and the WCTU came the women's clubs. This movement, which began spontaneously in many parts of the country, mushroomed in the south in the eighties after the pioneer organization in New Orleans announced its purpose to assist "the intellectual growth and spiritual ambition of the community." Literary societies, Browning and Shakespeare clubs, Daughters of the American Revolution, and village improvement societies began to dot the landscape. Some began wholly as cultural groups—what husband could object to the ladies gathering to read Shakespeare or study Dante? And how was he to know if they moved along to John Stuart Mill's "On the Subjugation of Women" or read Margaret Fuller or discussed, as the Portias in New Orleans were wont to do, the problems of organized labor?

As every authoritarian regime knows, association can be a dangerous thing. From discussion it is only a few steps to action, and by 1900 the list of things that women's clubs were doing or trying to do in the South was staggering. They organized libraries; expanded schools;

tackled adult illiteracy; organized settlement houses; fought child labor; supported sanitary laws, juvenile courts, pure water, modern sewage systems; planted trees; and helped girls to go to college. Doubtless many of these groups would have inspired the pen of an earlier Helen Hokinson, but it is impossible to overlook their record of achievement or the spirit in which they began to attack the problems with which their native region was so plentifully supplied. One has only to read their diaries and scrapbooks to catch a sense of the seriousness of purpose and the broad ambitions which motivated these women.

In North Carolina, Governor Elias Carr appointed a personal friend, Mrs. Sallie Southall Cotten, to be North Carolina Lady Manager for the Chicago World's Fair of 1893. Mrs. Cotten had lived a quiet life as a planter's wife, raising six children, and spending most of her spare time reading and thinking, thinking especially about the need for better educated and more independent women. The World's Fair responsibility took her to Chicago, where she met outstanding women from all over the country. It also took her over the whole state of North Carolina from New Bern to Asheville, and in many towns she found small clubs working away at village improvement or self-improvement. She came back after the Fair determined to unite the women of North Carolina in their efforts, and by strenuous personal effort managed to bring the local groups into a state-wide federation, which she then proceeded to lead into one battle after another for the improvement of North Carolina.

In the nature of things it would not be long before such groups began to have political significance. It is rare to find these women speculating upon any philosophical analysis of the proper relationship of government to the people. But in a pragmatic way they discovered more and more that the things they wanted to accomplish could only be accomplished through political action.

As a lobbyist, the southern lady turned new woman proved herself ingenious. The principle enunciated by one Arkansas lady, "If you don't make a friend at least don't leave an enemy," might have stood for most of these women as they journeyed to city council and state legislature armed with facts and figures to be presented with quiet dignity. "An unpleasant aggressiveness will doubtless be expected from us," a Mississippi leader told her group. "Let us endeavor to disappoint such expectations and spend the year in learning what to do and how to do it." One indignant Alabama legislator announced that the ladies had "apparently hypnotized some members of the Senate."

Occasionally more direct methods were possible, as when Miss Kate Gordon of New Orleans discovered that taxpaying women could vote in New Orleans when a question of taxes was involved. New Orleans suffered from a shortage of good water—the poorer people relied entirely upon cisterns—and an absence of a municipal sewage system. Wakened to their danger by a yellow fever epidemic, more farsighted members of the community were anxious to acquire both a water system and a sewage system, but the weight of opinion appeared to be of the "what was good enough for father is good enough for me" variety. Then Miss Gordon, with the Equal Rights Association (a pioneer woman's club) behind her, undertook to ferret out and register every woman taxpayer. The proposition to raise twenty million dollars for sewage and drainage passed handily.

It was experiences such as these, added to many others when women could *not* vote and felt the consequences, rather than an abstract belief in "women's rights," which was the real impetus behind the suffrage movement in the South. Miss Jean Gordon, a sister of the redoubtable Kate, put the case pungently in recording her battle for a Louisiana child labor law:

> The much boasted influence of the wife over the husband in matters political is one of the many theories which melt before the sun of experience. The wife of every representative present was heartily in sympathy with the child labor bill, but when the roll was called the husbands answered "no" and in that moment were sown the seeds of a belief in the potency of the ballot beyond that of woman's influence.

In 1910 Miss Mary Partridge of Alabama recorded a similar experience. "After seeing the defeat of the constitutional amendment for prohibition despite the earnest but ineffectual effort of women who beseiged the polls," she decided the time was ripe for a suffrage organization. She walked out of the hall and began organizing. Seven years later she counted eighty-seven suffrage societies in her state, and remarked that she had also converted thirty-two newspapers.

A year later Patty Blackburn Semple of Kentucky made the same point in a speech to the National American Woman Suffrage Association:

> Last year an appeal came to the Woman's Club—to the women of Louisville—to take our schools out of politics. It was a gigantic fight but we won. As the climax of our struggle we spent the greater part of election day at the polls and I think at the close of that day every one of us had exhausted all the joys of "indirect influence," which is supposed to satisfy the craving of every female heart. Our club will be twenty-one years old in November, and we want to vote!

By 1910 the woman movement in the South was moving out into the open. The missionary societies and the women's clubs, the Browning groups and the village improvement societies had laid the ground-work, and had afforded an essential period of security during which leaders were developed and followers gathered. Now the time had come to throw down the gauntlet and wage an open battle for suffrage, and for equality in the eyes of the law.

The dividing lines were not those of sex. In many states able and progressive-minded men took an equal part; Desha Breckenridge in Kentucky, Luke Lea in Tennessee, Walter Clark and Josephus Daniels in North Carolina were among the best known champions of women's rights, and in every state there were public men and newspapermen supporting the movement. On the other hand, multitudes of southern women were afraid of change and believed emancipation of women to be a threat to the stability of the home. The "new women" were asking not only rights, but responsibilities, and there were plenty of women who found the older system perfectly comfortable and satisfactory. Others were sympathetic in their hearts, but had not the courage to do battle with public opinion or to face ridicule.

From 1912 onward southern newspapers were publicly rubbing their eyes in astonishment at some of the accomplishments of the women's groups. Women were credited with "the improvement of health; the betterment of morals, the modernizing of education and the humanizing of penology." "Persistence is what carries them along," wrote another editor. "These women will secure every one of the things demanded in their program and will be no fifty years about it, either ... their aims can no more be resisted than the tides. We believe they are really unconscious of their tremendous power to affect condi-tions. ..." "Woman's day has arrived," said another, "never to depart. From the back seat of obscurity she has stepped ... to the front rank of world activities ... and the world is going to be a happier and brighter place because of her coming."

In spite of such recognition, and in spite of a steady increase in the number of converts to the suffrage cause, the cultural pattern in the South remained the most rigid in any part of the country. In 1918 the seventy-year-old national battle to persuade Congress to initiate a constitutional amendment for woman suffrage was finally won, and the amendment sent to the states for ratification. In every southern state there was a battle royal. The victorious opposition in North Carolina even sent reinforcements to Tennessee to encourage the opponents there. Only Tennessee of the states of the former Confederacy formed part of the required three-fourths of the states who ratified the amend-ment.

Despite the recalcitrance of southern legislatures, there were—thanks to the developments which have been related here—plenty of southern women ready to take advantage of suffrage when it came. Not only Miss Kearney, but Mrs. Nellie Nugent Somerville was soon sitting in the Mississippi legislature. In Georgia the ladies reported that they hardly recognized their hitherto hostile and chilly legislators who now suddenly found they had plenty of time to listen to their women constituents. In many states the suffrage groups were promptly converted to Leagues of Women Voters to finish the battle, as Carrie Chapman Catt put it, and to educate other women to their responsibilities.

The achievement of suffrage was symbolic and important, but it was only part of the larger story of the transformation, in the years after 1865, of the southern lady into the "new woman." Like the lady, the new woman represented only a small minority of all women in the South. Unlike the lady she did not become the universal ideal. At her best, she maintained the graciousness and charm which had been the sound part of the chivalric ideal, and without losing her feminity or abandoning her responsibility for the propagation of the species, became an important force in public as well as in private life.[1] She made it possible for the young women who came after her to begin at once to develop whatever talent they might have, without having first to fight a long battle for the right to education and opportunity.

This change was brought about by the unremitting efforts of a few women who longed for a chance to develop as individual and independent human beings, and who felt a responsibility for improving the quality of the larger society in which their children would grow up. For themselves and to some degree for the society at large they evolved a new conception of the proper role of women. Their efforts were reinforced by a changing economy, by the influence of the modern world, and by what that first woman's club in New Orleans in 1884 had rightly called "the irresistible spirit of the age."

In an environment basically hostile, southern women had taken on various protective colorations in their initial efforts to develop independence and maturity. In the name of temperance, or Shakespeare, or the church, they had resolutely set out to work, for themselves and for their communities. In many cases they were led into a pragmatic radicalism and had tackled problems which, had they been more sophisticated, might well have frightened them.

This analysis ends, except for an occasional glance ahead, in 1920. Whether southern women with the long-sought nineteenth amendment in their hands would live up to the promise of their accomplishments when they had no vote is another tale, for another time.

NOTE

1. In introducing Mrs. Cotten in 1913, the president of the North Carolina Federation of Women's Clubs made this point: ". . . probably the ideal woman is the one who combines all the graces of the golden days gone by with the highest type of the woman of the present time. She has caught step with the broadening and mighty influences which characterize her age. . . . Such a woman we have with us tonight."

15

Leadership and Tactics
in the American Woman Suffrage Movement:
A New Perspective from Massachusetts

Sharon Hartman Strom

In the fall of 1915 Massachusetts voters defeated an amendment to the state constitution granting women the suffrage by a margin of 132,000 votes. Suffrage workers predicted that defeat because they knew Massachusetts had long been the center of popular and well-organized resistance to votes for women. Yet in 1919, when the Congress of the United States passed the Nineteenth Amendment and sent it to the states for ratification, Massachusetts was the eighth state to ratify, a month after the amendment left Washington. Massachusetts may have been the eastern locus of anti-suffrage sentiment, but it was also the home of a dynamic and politically sophisticated state suffrage movement. Determined women suffragists had gained enough experience by 1919 to crown ten years of innovative and aggressive political agitation with victory.

The history of the woman suffrage movement has traditionally focused on a group of titanic figures: the pioneers, Elizabeth Cady Stanton, Susan B. Anthony, and Lucy Stone; the inspirational leader of the middle years, Anna Howard Shaw; and the great organizer of the final drive for the federal amendment between 1914 and 1920, Carrie Chapman Catt. Accounts by contemporary chroniclers and autobiographies of leaders of the movement are in large part responsible for this focus on a few personalities,[1] and most recent historians have largely

From the *Journal of American History* 62 (September 1975). Reprinted by permission.

taken these uncritical assessments on faith. While historians of other social movements have begun to move away from reliance on such egocentric sources and conclusions, historians of the suffrage movement give the impression that the success of the cause resulted from the drive and determination of these gifted women, especially in the last campaigns for a federal amendment.[2]

Even the most recent histories convey the feeling that the mass of the American movement was curiously isolated from any contact with its foreign counterparts. Although women in both England and America were fighting for the suffrage at the same time and shared a common ideological heritage, surprisingly few women in the American movement seem to be responsible for the adoption of English militant suffragist tactics.[3] Again, a few unusual individuals account for whatever English influence was felt in America: Harriot Stanton Blatch, daughter of the invincible Stanton, and Alice Paul, militant leader of the Woman's party, both of whom spent time working in the English movement and tried to adapt English tactics to the American scene.[4]

The history of the woman suffrage movement in Massachusetts between 1901 and 1919, however, indicates that these assumptions may be incorrect. Although studies of other states' suffrage movements will be required to substantiate these new hypotheses completely, the evidence from Massachusetts shows that extensive changes both within the rank and file of the movement and in the wider arena of social reform, not the aggressive leadership of a few personalities, were responsible for a highly mobilized and efficient organization in the years before World War I. Massachusetts sources also indicate that large numbers of ordinary American women suffragists enthusiastically supported their militant English sisters and consciously adapted militant suffragist tactics to the work in America several years before Paul arrived in Washington.

Massachusetts women have long been downgraded in analyses of the national movement. As the nineteenth-century headquarters of the American Woman Suffrage Association, the more conservative of the national organizations, Boston is usually characterized as the capital of stuffy feminism.[5] New York, the home of the founders of the more radical National Woman Suffrage Association, is usually credited with having produced most of the innovative tactics and aggressive leaders. Stanton and Susan B. Anthony were far more catholic in their reform interests and consistently feminist than Stone and Henry Blackwell. By 1890, however, when the two groups merged to become the National American Woman Suffrage Association (NAWSA), most women in the suffrage movement neither knew nor cared about the original quarrel between the two organizations. In fact, there is every reason to believe that, while the New York movement produced the precinct organization method and such personalities as Blatch and Catt, the woman's movement in Massachusetts was an equally rich source of tactics and workers for the final battle.

The fight in Massachusetts for an amendment to the state constitution granting women the vote in the late-nineteenth century was largely an exercise in futility. The road to final adoption was difficult; passage required a two thirds vote in both houses of two sucessive legislatures, as well as approval by referendum. Before 1880, the suffragists followed a well-established routine. Every year they presented petitions to the state legislature, and then eloquent proponents of woman suffrage testified at the subsequent public hearing in the State House, hoping both to convince legislators and obtain publicity. They also sought endorsement of the suffrage by reformers, editors, politicians, and educators, and, whenever they were invited, spoke in churches and lecture halls. They also organized suffrage societies. But after fifteen years of such work, there was still no evidence that the state legislature would enact a suffrage amendment—the yearly hearings had become a barely noticed ritual.[6]

In 1879 suffragists thought they had made a breakthrough. With the temporary support of the Republicans, who controlled the state, they secured the right for women to vote for and serve on their local school committees. Republicans supported school suffrage partly in recognition of the stake women had in the education of their children, but mostly in the hope that middle-class females would help to combat the growing voting power of Catholic immigrant and working-class men in local communities. The School Suffrage Law was possible because bills regarding local elections required only a simple majority in the state legislature. The state constitution, in effect, specified male voters for state offices.

Members of the Massachusetts Woman Suffrage Association (MWSA) immediately moved to take advantage of their 1879 victory and this constitutional exception. They began to work for an additional form of partial suffrage, the municipal vote, and played down their demands for an amendment to the state constitution, which would give women the same voting rights as men.[7] This change of emphasis from their traditional argument to a more "expedient" one led suffragists to imply that voting women in the cities could clean up urban politics, combat boss rule, and restore the municipal order upset by industrialization and immigration.[8] However, the new strategy of the state suffrage organization proved to be a disaster. MWSA found itself not only again allied with the Woman's Christian Temperance Union but also with the virulently anti-Catholic Loyal Women of America.[9] Even this approach failed to reclaim Republican support. The municipal bill passed in the Massachusetts lower house in 1894 but was defeated in the state senate. Abandoned by the Republicans, suffragists also found their campaign had elicited the strongest statewide anti-suffrage movement in the country, whose leaders now maneuvered to get rid of the municipal voting issue once and for all by proposing a mock referendum in the election of 1895. Women eligible to vote for their school committees were asked to participate. Ignoring the fact that women who voted in the referendum overwhelmingly voted "yes," the antis gloated over the poor turnout; only 4 percent of the eligible female voters went to the polls. For years Massachusetts suffragists had to combat the anti-suffrage position that women should not be given the vote because they did not want it anyway.

With Stone's death in 1893 seeming to foreshadow a general dampening of enthusiasm, the suffrage movement in Massachusetts entered a period of steady decline.[10] Ninety local leagues had been organized in 1889; only twenty-six remained in 1895.[11] Yet by 1908, though there had been no apparent significant change in leadership, the Massachusetts Woman Suffrage Association was among the largest in the country.[12]

Many factors account for the resurgence of the suffrage movement in Massachusetts. The lessons learned in the municipal suffrage referendum of 1895 about the specific nature of Massachusetts politics, general social changes which occurred during the Progressive era, and changes among women, especially those in the upper class, were the most important. One of the effects of urbanization and industrialization in America in the late-nineteenth century was a frantic growth in organizations which for many people took the place of the extended family, the church, and the rural village.[13] The concomitant move of middle- and upper-class women into a limited participation in public life and the professions, especially teaching and social work, gave them new skills and self-confidence. In reform circles, these new talents allowed women to move away from their reliance on male reformers, who had always been somewhat dubious allies, and to create their own organizations.[14]

In Massachusetts these trends were well on their way by the time of the municipal suffrage debacle in 1895. That referendum convinced women suffrage workers that they should concentrate entirely on reaching women, who, they decided, must never again be accused of indifference to their own rights and needs. They also learned that their arguments should be as universal as possible, or combined with specific ones for every special interest group in the state, since arraying themselves against so many power blocs had led to defeat. But the crucial point is that, once having made these decisions, Massachusetts suffragists could act on them because of the proliferation of organizations for women at the turn of the century.

There were three important organizations in Massachusetts that worked in concert with dozens of others to promote the suffrage after 1900: MWSA; the College Equal Suffrage League (CESL); and the Boston Equal Suffrage Association for Good Government (BESAGG). This group of organizations provided the impetus for the resurgence of the woman's vote question. The smallest and most specialized of them, BESAGG, was probably the most important. Founded in 1901, BESAGG was initially a civic organization with committees on the schools, sanitation, temperance, vice reform, peace, and the suffrage. By 1904, however, suffrage work dominated its activities.[15] Three of the founders of BESAGG—Pauline Agassiz Shaw, Mary Hutcheson Page, and Maud Wood Park—are typical of the kind of women who reinvigorated the Massachusetts movement and then worked in the national campaign during its final years.[16] They were well-educated, confident, independent, and determined to become first-class citizens. In 1900 they needed a small organization in which to discuss new ideas, unencumbered by the stodgy membership of MWSA and its older, more conservative leaders—Julia Ward Howe and Mary A. Livermore—who were still using all the old tactics.

The first president of BESAGG, Pauline Agassiz Shaw, was the daughter of world-renowned Harvard professor Louis Agassiz and wife of Quincy A. Shaw, owner of the fabulous Calumet and Hecla mines. The most powerful supporter of suffrage in Massachusetts, Pauline Agassiz Shaw moved in the state's most élite circles of education and wealth. She preferred to work behind the scenes and left decision-making and public speaking to friends like Mary Hutcheson Page and Maud Wood Park. Her money kept BESAGG financially sound, and more than once saved the *Woman's Journal* from ceasing publication. It was rumored upon her death in 1917 that she had donated millions to Boston schools and reform groups.[17]

Perhaps it is because she was so adept at manipulating people and at backstage politics that Mary Hutcheson Page's contributions have been overlooked. Born in 1860 to a family of bankers, she was orphaned at the age of sixteen, left "comfortably off" and almost entirely on her own. Unhappy with her traditional finishing school education, she sought tutoring in mathematics and then enrolled in Massachusetts Institute of Technology as a special student. In 1890 she married George Hyde Page, son of James Page, the headmaster of Dwight School. Despite her four young children, but with the hearty endorsement of her husband, she worked in the suffrage movement all through the 1890s. At first she helped to organize a special "Committee of Work" in Massachusetts to raise money for Catt's Colorado campaign. But she soon turned her hand to work closer to home. BESAGG was born in her Committee of Work in 1901, and it was she who convinced Pauline Agassiz Shaw to become its first president. Her fund-raising abilities and powers of persuasion were legendary within the movement. She raised thousands of dollars through her social contacts and had a special genius for finding the right person to do the right job. Convinced, for instance, that Alice Stone Blackwell was an ineffective chairman of the Executive Board of MWSA, she quietly convinced Alice Stone Blackwell in 1901 to step down and be replaced by her personal choice, Maud Wood Park.[18]

In 1895, the year of the municipal suffrage referendum in Massachusetts, Maud Wood had enrolled in Radcliffe, where the faculty was solidly opposed to suffrage for women, and where there were almost no suffragists among her fellow students. In her senior year she was invited to speak at the annual MWSA dinner because she was one of the few college women interested in suffrage. After her marriage in 1898 to Charles Park, an architect in sympathy with the suffrage cause, she became a devoted worker. In 1900, searching for inspiration, she visited NAWSA's convention in Washington. She came away appalled. The meeting was held in the basement of a church and attended by an audience of about 100 middle-aged and elderly women. The first speaker presented a state report from Missouri in rhyme. Convinced something must be done to attract younger, especially educated, women, Maud Wood Park and a college friend, Inez Haynes, decided that spring to form a new organization, a College Equal Suffrage League. Based at first in Boston, CESL was ingeniously designed to interest two groups of women in suffrage. College alumnae were to form chapters in CESL and then were charged with organizing women currently attending their alma maters. In 1901, Maud Wood Park strengthened her suffrage ties by becoming chairwoman of the Executive Board of MWSA, and by founding BESAGG with Mary Hutcheson Page.[19]

CESL mushroomed in Massachusetts among the numerous new college women graduates, and in 1904 Maud Wood Park was invited by Blatch and Caroline Lexow to set up college leagues in New York State. In 1906 NAWSA asked her to organize leagues throughout the country. Pauline Agassiz Shaw missed her so much that she volunteered to pay her salary for five years if she would return to New England and work full time. Maud Wood Park promised to return eventually, but in the meantime continued to travel; and in 1908 along with M. Carey Thomas, president of Bryn Mawr, formed a national CESL, complete with an executive council. The older and more prestigious Thomas was made president of the league and perhaps partly out of resentment Maud Wood Park, now widowed, took temporary leave of suffrage work in 1909 to embark on a tour to study women throughout the world, predictably financed by Pauline Agassiz Shaw. Although Maud Wood Park was out of the country during the summers of 1909 and 1910, when new tactics were introduced, she had been instrumental in laying the organizational groundwork and returned to Massachusetts for full-time work in 1911.[20]

While women like Mary Hutcheson Page and Maud Wood Park formed new organizations, they also sought to strengthen old ones. By 1901 they held powerful positions in MWSA and had begun vigorous new recruitment activities. They contacted women in all the religious denominations and teachers' societies, sent speakers to chapters of the Massachusetts Federation of Women's Clubs, and set up booths at agricultural and county fairs.[21] MWSA and CESL also quickly moved to take advantage of the arrival in Boston in 1903 of the Women's Trade Union League (WTUL), hoping to strengthen ties with the American Federation of Labor and convert more working women to suffrage. Unions and suffrage groups exchanged speakers and held joint meetings.[22] By 1909 Mary Hutcheson Page reported that 235 unions had endorsed woman suffrage.[23]

For the first time since the Civil War the wealthy and college-educated women who made up the suffrage movement found themselves allied with large and potentially powerful segments of the population. Organized labor, consumers, ethnic groups, and progressive reformers were all, like the suffragists, on the outside looking in at the entrenched Republican establishment and the interests it represented. In Massachusetts this establishment had conspired to defeat all of the truly "modern" measures such as factory regulations, child labor laws, temperance, and the suffrage.[24] Most WTUL women were suffragists, and most suffrage workers were genuinely concerned about the plight of working women.[25] Each group needed the others' support to obtain the legislation they wanted; organized labor could reasonably expect that once women had the vote they would help elect progressive candidates pledged to support regulatory factory legislation. To convince the unions of their potential support, suffragist speakers emphasized what the ballot would do for working women. The alliance between organized labor and suffrage organizations was a long-lived and amicable one. The zeal with which Massachusetts women pursued the friendship indicates they were aware of the important role labor would play in the fight for suffrage.[26]

By 1907 the success of the Massachusetts women in rebuilding the suffrage movement had brought them to the point where they were restless. The movement seemed to have reached a hiatus, in which the convinced reinforced their own convictions. The method of reaching women through the endorsements of prominent citizens, labor leaders, and civic-minded organizations seemed to have reached maximum efficiency. Maud Wood Park, on tour for CESL in 1907, expressed these dissatisfactions to Mary Hutcheson Page from San Francisco:

> You know how we are hampered because we are thought to be merely suffragists, how we can seem to go just so far and no farther. For example, when I want to speak to an audience of college girls it's almost impossible to get them together unless someone of great influence works up the meeting. We rarely get a chance to be heard by uninterested persons. . . .[27]

Maud Wood Park was struggling here to articulate two questions asked more and more frequently by members of the Massachusetts suffrage movement. The first was how the suffragists could gain attention strictly on their own. The second was how they could expand their realm of agitation so as to draw in the uninformed citizen. For ultimately, woman suffrage would have to run the gauntlet of popular opinion before the Massachusetts state constitution could be amended.

The answers to these questions were not always self-evident. For the most part these upper- and middle-class women did not expect suffrage to lead to any fundamental change in woman's special function as wife, mother, and civilizer. To think of themselves as political agitators meant calling into question the whole notion of special spheres of female activity, which was especially prevalent in their age.[28] Once given an inkling of how to overcome these obstacles, however, Massachusetts women did so with remarkably little hesitation.

The hint came not from American leadership or from a more dynamic state suffrage movement but from England. British suffragists had been using more aggressive tactics than their American counterparts for some time, largely as a result of women's involvement with the anti-corn law agitation. Even the more conservative constitutionalist suffrage societies in England considered public speaking and barnstorming campaigns legitimate realms of activity for respectable women.[29] Precisely for this reason, however, these activities failed to stir up much interest or notice. The militant groups, of which Emmeline G. Pankhurst's Women's Social and Political Union (WSPU) was the most famous, sought public attention when they introduced more dramatic tactics: interruptions of political meetings; partisan campaigns in by-elections; and enormous processions through the streets of London, culminating in demonstrations at Westminster. The militants, who were quickly labeled "Suffragettes," got what they bargained for and more;

they were in the headlines for years. Police usually turned the processions into ugly riots, and many women were injured and arrested; a few were killed.[30]

Women in America did not evidently become aware of tactics used for some time by English suffragists until the English militants made them famous on both sides of the Atlantic. Not surprisingly, Mary Hutcheson Page was one of the first Massachusetts women to develop contacts with the militants. In 1908 she initiated a correspondence with Emmeline Pethick-Lawrence, subscribed to the militant paper, *Votes for Women,* and began work on an article concerning the English militant suffragists, which appeared in *Colliers* in 1909.[31] Her attitudes toward the English movement were largely the same as those that were to be expressed by most Massachusetts women over the next few years. She explained that English women had been using constitutional methods for years and had never been taken seriously by any government in power. The women were simply forced to take more aggressive steps, none of them illegal, to make their point. For this they had been beaten, arrested, and imprisoned. She was obviously impressed with the respectable origins of the militants, so much like her own, and found them convincing proof of the sincerity and legitimacy of their motives. She portrayed Pankhurst as a fearless heroine, devoted to the suffrage and the cause of working women. "The suffragettes," she explained, "prefer to go to prison rather than politically recant their dearest convictions; namely, the right to demand the vote in a way that they consider necessary and legal."[32] The cause also received sympathetic treatment in the *Woman's Journal.*[33]

The difficulty for the Massachusetts suffragists lay in deciding what lessons could legitimately be drawn from the English experience. Most important, they had to consider the ways in which the methods used to gain the suffrage in Massachusetts were bound to be different from those employed in England. Pressuring the majority government into supporting the suffrage was only one step in most American states, since constitutional amendments would ultimately have to be approved by the voters.[34] The suffrage movement in America had to gain the spotlight without alienating the voting public. The Massachusetts suffrage organizations, while openly sympathetic with the plight of the English militant suffragists, were more interested in finding out about less defiant tactics that could, nonetheless, bring American women publicity. Some discussion of English tactics, including the open-air meeting, took place at a MWSA meeting in October 1908.[35]

The open-air meeting was perfectly suited to the requirements of the Massachusetts suffragists. It was a dramatic new tactic, for unlike their English sisters American women had typically spoken at only carefully prearranged indoor meetings.[36] It was well-suited to the need the women felt to reach a wider range of people on their own. Moreover, it could be defended as a relatively conservative tactic, since even the constitutional societies in England had long used it. Two English suffrage workers visited Boston during the winter of 1908–1909 and became much-sought-after speakers on the subject of their open-air speaking tours.[37] The result was that in the spring and summer of 1909 a virtual revolution in suffragist tactics took place in Massachusetts. Most of them were consciously adopted from the English movement. One suffragist succinctly summarized the new strategy when she told her colleagues that opposition to suffrage was not the major difficulty in winning the vote:

> We are handicapped by indifference and its resulting ignorance . . . we have got to prove our case, not to a small body of lawmakers, but to a large body of the people, those who elect the lawmakers, and to prove it to them we must make them listen. . . . If they are uninterested it is because you have not made the subject interesting. Make it so. Make it picturesque. This is what the English women have accomplished. Then when you have made it picturesque there is one other step; make it easy . . . you must go to him [the voter].[38]

The first steps taken were naturally a bit tentative and timid, for these suffrage workers were about to do something quite novel for women of their rank and class: they were going to speak, not to prearranged audiences with guaranteed manners, but to whatever assortment of listeners might appear, including the possibly rude or hostile. On May 7 in a meeting of MWSA Mary Hutcheson Page proposed that a storefront in downtown Boston be rented for propaganda work. MWSA, in cooperation with BESAGG, opened a suffrage shop in Tremont Street in late May. Speeches were given there every day at noon.[39] On May 29 the Woman's Journal reported that even the New England Woman Suffrage Association was discussing English tactics and concluded that although "it would not be useful in America to smash windows or interrupt public speakers . . . most of the other methods of propaganda work invented in England could be well employed here."[40]

By June more vigorous plans were under way. Again, MWSA and BESAGG cooperated by forming a special joint Votes for Women Committee, headed by Mary Hutcheson Page, which would operate outside both organizations, probably to avoid identifying the more radical tactics with either organization.[41] She promptly sought the best person for the job of directing the first open-air meetings. Her choice, Susan Walker Fitzgerald, the daughter of Admiral John G. Walker, and wife of a wealthy, Harvard-trained lawyer, had majored in political science and history at Bryn Mawr and after her graduation in 1893 had done social work on the West Side of New York. A colleague of Ernest Poole, Robert Hunter, and Lillian Wald, she had served as a truant officer and settlement worker before coming to Boston in 1907.[42]

The women chose the quiet village green of Bedford for their first open-air talk.[43] On June 5 it rained, but on June 12 they held "that first painful meeting" with an audience of about 100. Although they tried to prearrange times and places at first, they soon learned "the only thing to do was to reach a town, take possession of the busiest spot and begin to talk."[44] Under the guidance of Fitzgerald, a small corps of women speakers toured the smaller towns, villages, and vacation spots of Massachusetts during the summers of 1909 and 1910 in automobiles, trolley cars, and trains, outfitted with banners, leaflets, petitions, and "Votes for Women" buttons.[45] One of the travellers delightfully described the routine:

> Picture our party unloading from a street-car in the central square of some little country town. . . . Then we make for the nearest drug store, deposit all our luggage in one corner, and to compensate for its storage all of us are in duty bound to buy sodas. . . . While we drink, the drug clerk is crossexamined as to where the best audience can be collected, time of trolleys, hotel for the night, factories and mills in town, number of employees, men or women, union or non-union, what they manufacture, and a few dozen other similar things. Meanwhile, if the town is large enough for us to require a permit to speak, Mrs. Fitzgerald has interviewed the police. Then our leaflets are unpacked, our flag erected, we borrow a Moxie box from the obliging drug clerk and proceed to the busiest corner of the town square. Our chief mounts the box, the banner over her shoulder, and starts talking to the air, three assorted dogs, six kids, and the two loafers in front of the grocery store just over the way. The rest of us give handbills to all the passers-by and the nearby stores. Within ten minutes our audience has increased from twenty-five to five hundred, according to the time and place. We speak in turn for an hour or more, answer questions, sell buttons, and circulate the petition. Then we leave, generally in undignified haste, to catch our car for the next meeting.[46]

The success of the new tactics was indisputable. The suffragists made converts in their open-air meetings but, more important, gained wide coverage in the newspapers. All summer, reporters and photographers followed them around, delighted with the drama of giving some of Boston's élite families prominent news coverage.[47] As the women steadily became more experienced and accomplished, they tried to invade at least two towns a day and worked six days a week.

Although several dozen women became veteran crowd-handlers, two in particular caught the attention of the press. Florence Luscomb, a 1909 graduate from Massachusetts Institute of Technology in architecture, slim and delicately beautiful, was an aggressive and always self-confident speaker. Her mother, Hannah Knox Luscomb, had long been a suffrage worker and had used her private income to help finance the movement.[48] Margaret Foley may have been the only speaker in the first tours with a working-class background. She grew up in Irish Roxbury, worked in a hat factory, joined the hat-trimmers union, and was eventually put on the local board of WTUL. She was certainly the most colorful of the speakers, for as the Boston *Transcript* rhapsodized, "she stands five feet eight and weighs in at one hundred and forty, but she can easily manage seven feet, turn her brown hair to flame, descend like a mountain of brick and extend her mellifluous accent to megaphonics."[49] Some of the women visited factories and spoke at noon to the workers. Florence Luscomb thought those meetings were especially challenging but claimed the mill audiences were "ready to be entertained," and "often sympathetic in advance."[50] Suffrage workers also distributed thousands of leaflets and gave dozens of speeches at county fairs, sent Margaret Foley up in a balloon, put a float in the Waltham Fourth of July parade, and persuaded the manager of a circus to drape his elephant with a Votes for Women sign.[51]

At home, in the Boston headquarters, the response of most suffrage workers was wholly supportive. The patriarch of the New England movement, Henry Blackwell, heartily endorsed the open-air meetings in the *Woman's Journal,* often combining his kudos with admiration for the English militant suffragists.[52] He died in September 1909, but his daughter, Alice Stone Blackwell, the chief editor of the *Woman's Journal,* was even more enthusiastic about new tactics than her father, and tenaciously defended the Pankhursts through some of their most difficult moments in 1909 and 1910.[53] Noting that English women sold suffrage newspapers on the street, she suggested the same might be done in Boston; and in November 1909, Florence Luscomb and Mabel Ewell entered the ranks of the Boston "newsies," most of whom were working-class boys.[54] This tactic also received much attention in the press and got suffragists, probably for the first time, out onto the streets of Boston.[55]

When Pankhurst visited the city in October, she received a tumultuous greeting from Boston women; and the entire issue of October 16 of the *Woman's Journal* was devoted to the English woman suffrage cause. The first suffrage parade in Boston carried Pankhurst from South Station to Boylston Street suffrage headquarters. More than 2000 people heard the English leader at Tremont Theatre, where she was introduced by Fitzgerald. She stayed in the home of Mary Hutcheson Page. Her visit to the city was capped by a luncheon at the Vendome, where Alice Stone Blackwell compared her to Stone, Henry Blackwell, and the other great reformers.[56]

In December, Foley and Gertrude Cliff invaded the floor of the Boston Stock Exchange and Chamber of Commerce and distributed leaflets advertising the visit of Ethel Snowden, then second in command of WSPU.[57] The total hegemony of the younger generation of more militant Massachusetts women was fittingly symbolized by the appearance of Julia Ward Howe, the most ancient and respectable of all New England feminists, on the same platform with Snowden, who, according to the Boston *Herald,* said that classes or sexes with no redress had eventually to resort to violence.[58]

By 1910, enthusiasm for English tactics was so widespread among Massachusetts suffragists that perhaps the greatest danger to the vitality of their movement lay in losing a feel for what might be appropriate in America and in underestimating their abilities. A more practical atmosphere settled over the Massachusetts movement after the summer of 1911, when two of the most popular open-air speakers in the recent campaigns, Foley and Florence Luscomb, went to the convention of the International Woman Suffrage Alliance in Stockholm. In fact, the main purpose of their trip abroad was to study the English suffrage movement. They spent over a month in London, interviewing leaders of all the suffrage societies, attending meetings, marching in parades, attending demonstrations, visiting Parliament, and selling newspapers.

Florence Luscomb, who kept a detailed diary of what she saw and heard, was obviously in sympathy with the militants and carefully recorded all their tactics and lines of argument that might be useful in America. She was particularly taken with the militant campaigns in by-elections to defeat candidates publically opposed to suffrage. However, she found the English suffrage movement to be more complicated than she had believed. Accustomed to a close alliance between trade union women and suffragists, she was disturbed to learn that many English labor leaders distrusted the Pankhursts and other aristocratic militant suffrage leaders because they were willing to work for a limited franchise for women and ignore the question of universal suffrage for adults. The most militant suffragists were not, evidently, the most radical.[59] In general she came away feeling grateful for American institutions and democratic principles, which, she felt, would make suffrage easier to obtain in America than in England. She was also convinced that American women suffragists were at least as competent as their English counterparts, and she wrote her mother:

> Understand, I am not for a moment disparaging the splendid enthusiasm of the WSPU. . . . But with the exception of Mrs. Pankhurst I did not find

many of their speakers or workers superior ... their methods, ingenuity, etc., seem no better than our own, when we really set about it. ... I am coming home more encouraged and pleased with our work than ever.[60]

Foley's new inspiration and self-confidence were also immediately apparent. In the fall of 1911 she set out on a personal campaign to initiate in Massachusetts the English technique of quizzing politicians on their suffrage views at public rallies. She and a group of fellow "hecklers," as they were dubbed in the newspapers, set off by automobile to pursue the Republican campaign through the Berkshires. They were followed by newspaper reporters who gleefully reported the politicos' unsuccessful attempts to escape. She also invaded Tammany Hall, where Congressman James M. Curley and other Democrats recognized her right to speak and gave at least tacit support to woman suffrage.[61] The heckling campaign, although not an official activity of MWSA or BESAGG, was clearly a precursor of future developments.

In 1911 and 1912 the national suffrage movement was at a crossroads over the issue of participation in political campaigns. For years the policy of NAWSA had been one of absolute neutrality. At the national convention in 1912 a major controversy would explode over the party affiliations of several members. After an emotional debate the convention voted to allow its officers to work for the political parties of their choice.[62] For years Henry Blackwell had advocated fierce opposition to anti-suffrage candidates, a form of political partisanship which ultimately would be adopted in the last stages of the federal amendment drive.[63] The successful use of the tactic in England helped to revive interest in it in Massachusetts and in 1909 Alice Stone Blackwell editorialized on its merits in the *Woman's Journal*.[64] Such exhortations could seriously be considered by 1911 because women suffragists in the state were now clearly a significant political force. Morever, the policy was well suited to politics in Massachusetts, where the suffrage issue cut across party lines. Although the entrenched Republicans were the most obvious enemies of the cause, the suffragists skillfully refused to ally with the Progressive, Democratic or Socialist parties except on specific issues, in order to avoid being identified with any potential losers. They concentrated instead on identifying specific enemies, supporting friends, and educating the public on the suffrage issue.

By the summer of 1911 they were ready to overcome the largest center of indifference to suffrage in their state, the city of Boston. The method for reaching city voters and potential women supporters was consciously borrowed from the suffrage workers in New York City who had suggested using the precinct organization method to mobilize city residents for the suffrage cause.[65] In Boston each voter was identified from the registration lists. A suffrage worker visited each voter's residence in the hope of enlisting the women of the house in a new Woman Suffrage party, for which no dues were required. Suffrage literature was also distributed for the voting men. Rallies were held on street corners or party headquarters in every ward of the city, with speeches by women in whichever languages predominated.[66] The door-to-door canvassing was probably the final baptism of fire for the elegant Bostonian suffragists. As the state chairman of ward organization reported after a trial effort in 1910:

> It took some sense of duty, some devotion to our cause, to push us up the dim . . . staircase, to knock at any one of the several non-committal doors on the first shabby landing. Probably the woman who answered knew no English, and stared uncomprehendingly. No matter—you did as well as you could, the children, who have learned English, helped; the Yiddish and Italian flyers helped; and best of all the women, as soon as they knew what it was all about, proved so kindly, so approachable, so open-minded and responsive . . . that whatever the future may hold . . . the pilgrimage through Ward 8 proved of the deepest interest and meaning.[67]

In 1912 suffragists in Massachusetts demonstrated their new political power. They defeated Roger Woolcott, an old enemy, who as chairman of the state senate's Constitutional Amendments Committee, had blocked suffrage bills. In the same year the Progressive party endorsed suffrage, and the Progressive members of the state legislature, supported by pro-suffrage lobbyists, defeated conservative attempts to force another referendum. In coalition with Progressive elements suffragists defeated Levi Greenwood, president of the state senate, in 1913, although his district had been a Republican stronghold for years. By 1914 woman suffrage was supported by the Socialists, the Progressives, the Democrats, the State Federation of Labor, and the new Democratic governor of Massachusetts, David Walsh. In 1914 and 1915 the amendment easily passed both houses of the legislature and was on its way to the voters.[68]

Suffragists in Massachusetts expected to lose the referendum battle and did, but when the federal amendment was passed by Congress in 1919, they quickly remobilized for the ratification drive. Calling on the coalition that had put the state amendment through in 1914 and 1915, they defeated a move by their opponents which would have submitted the amendment to referendum. They collected 135,000 petition signatures in two weeks, and spent an "eleventh hour" session with the chairman of the Federal Relations Committee arguing the legal aspects of ratification. The committee produced a favorable report on the floor of the house, and on June 25 ratification carried by a vote of 185 ayes to 47 noes. There were only five votes against the measure in the senate.[69]

The woman suffrage workers of Massachusetts had, by 1919, transformed a dormant, unimaginative state society of suffragists into a network of aggressive organizations, which mobilized thousands of women, many of them young, in suffrage work and a unique political movement. Their energy and success were stimulated by their own self-confidence, talents, rising aspirations, the example of their English sisters, and the assistance given them by organized labor and other progressive elements in Massachusetts. Their history should remind scholars that while national leaders are important, the rank and file of any movement can be more significant.

NOTES

1. The most widely used original accounts of the suffrage movement are Carrie Chapman Catt and Nettie Rogers Shuler, *Woman Suffrage and Politics: The Inner Story of the Suffrage Movement* (Seattle, 1926); Ida Husted Harper, *The Life and Work of Susan B. Anthony* (3 vols., Indianapolis, 1893–1908); Anna Howard Shaw, *The Story of a Pioneer* (New York, 1915); Elizabeth Cady Stanton, *Eighty Years and More 1815–1897: Reminiscences* (New York, 1898); Elizabeth Cady Stanton, Susan B. Anthony, Matilda Joslyn Gage, and Ida Husted Harper, eds., *The History of Woman Suffrage* (6 vols., Rochester, 1899–1922).

2. Eleanor Flexner, *Century of Struggle: The Woman's Rights Movement in the United States* (New York, 1970), 236; Aileen S. Kraditor, *The Ideas of the Woman Suffrage Movement, 1890–1920* (New York, 1965), 9; William L. O'Neill, *The Woman Movement: Feminism in the United States and England* (London, 1969), 73–78. Alan P. Grimes nearly goes to the other extreme by suggesting that the success of the suffrage movement was due, especially in the West, not so much to the work of suffragists as to generally conservative and irrational social forces which viewed woman suffrage as a means of gaining social control. Alan P. Grimes, *The Puritan Ethic and Woman Suffrage* (New York, 1967).

3. For an analysis of the origins of English and American feminism, see James L. Cooper and Sheila M. Cooper, *The Roots of American Feminist Thought* (Boston, 1973), and O'Neill, *Woman Movement.*

4. Flexner, *Century of Struggle,* 249–53, 263; William L. O'Neill, *Everyone Was Brave: A History of Feminism in America* (Chicago, 1971), 126–27.

5. For example, see Flexner, *Century of Struggle,* 216. The bias in the original sources toward New York may possibly be attributed to several factors: New York women wrote almost all of the published autobiographies; the state of Massachusetts was so notorious among suffragists for its anti-suffrage movement that the hundreds of suffrage activists were often forgotten; New York won a popular

referendum for woman suffrage in 1917 while Massachusetts lost one in 1915, leading to the possible but not necessarily logical conclusion that Massachusetts had a weaker suffrage organization; the official history of the movement was edited by New York women, except Ida Husted Harper, who was a devoted biographer and companion of Susan B. Anthony and enthusiastic champion of Carrie Chapman Catt. Whether in a moment of pique or forgetfulness, Harper managed to avoid including Massachusetts in the index of Volume V of the *History of Woman Suffrage;* sixteen states, including New York, had entries.

6. For a history of the Massachusetts suffrage movement in the nineteenth century, see Lois Bannister Merk's, "Massachusetts and the Woman Suffrage Movement" (doctoral dissertation, Northeastern University, 1961). See also Arthur Mann, *Yankee Reformers in the Urban Age* (Cambridge, Mass., 1954), 205–16.

7. Merk, "Massachusetts and the Woman Suffrage Movement," 58–64.

8. For a discussion of the differences between the "justice" and "expediency" arguments, see Kraditor, *Ideas of the Woman Suffrage Movement,* 43–74.

9. Lois Bannister Merk, "Boston's Historic Public School Crisis," *New England Quarterly,* 31 (June 1958), 172–99.

10. Maud Wood Park, "Massachusetts Woman Suffrage Association: Introductory Notes," June 1943, Woman's Rights Collection (Schlesinger Library, Radcliffe College).

11. *Ibid.;* Merk, "Massachusetts and the Woman Suffrage Movement," 330.

12. NAWSA reported in 1908 that Massachusetts was second only to New York in membership: New York had 27,476; Massachusetts had 19,197; and Illinois had 10,080. *Proceedings of the Annual Convention of the National American Woman Suffrage Association* (Warren, Ohio, 1908), 21–22.

13. See Robert H. Wiebe, *The Search for Order, 1877–1920* (New York, 1967), 111–32, 165.

14. O'Neill, *Everyone Was Brave,* 77–106; Mann, *Yankee Reformers in the Urban Age,* 201–04.

15. *First Report of the Boston Equal Suffrage Association for Good Government, 1901–1903* (Boston, 1903); Maud Wood Park, "Boston Equal Suffrage Association for Good Government. (1901–1907) Introductory Note," Woman's Rights Collection.

16. Mary Hutcheson Page retired from the suffrage movement in 1918 and Pauline Agassiz Shaw died in 1917. Maud Wood Park, as chairwoman of the Congressional Committee of NAWSA from 1917 to 1920, was responsible for directing the work of getting the federal amendment through Congress. For her experiences in Washington, see Maud Wood Park, *Front Door Lobby,* Edna Lamprey Stantial, ed. (Boston, 1960).

17. Edward T. James, Janet Wilson James, and Paul S. Boyer, eds., *Notable American Women, 1607–1950: A Biographical Dictionary* (3 vols., Cambridge, Mass., 1971), III, 278–80; Harper, ed., *History of Woman Suffrage,* V, 337; Boston *Transcript,* Feb. 10, 1917.

18. Katherine Page Hersey, "Mary Hutcheson Page," May 1943, Maud Wood Park, "Mary Hutcheson Page," April 1943, Anthony to Mary H. Page, March 15, 1899, Page Scrapbook, Woman's Rights Collection. See also, National American Woman Suffrage Association, *Victory How Women Won It: A Centennial Symposium, 1840–1940* (New York, 1940), 76. Carrie Chapman Catt knew of Mary Hutcheson

Page's abilities: "*Now*, you are the great persuader . . . I've heard how you go in and camp before your object of entreaty and just smile until she does just what you want." Carrie C. Catt to Mary H. Page, Aug. 12, 1905, Page Scrapbook, Woman's Rights Collection.

19. Lois Bannister Merk, "The Early Career of Maud Wood Park," *Radcliffe Quarterly*, 32 (May 1948), 10–17; Maud Wood Park, "Supplementary Notes," Jan. 1943, and "College Equal Suffrage League Introductory Notes," Dec. 1942, Woman's Rights Collection; "Constitution of the College Equal Suffrage League," May 24, 1905, *ibid.*

20. Park, "College Equal Suffrage League Introductory Notes," Dec. 1942; Park, "College Equal Suffrage League Supplementary Notes," Jan., 1943, Woman's Rights Collection; Pauline A. Shaw to Maud W. Park, April 10, 1907 (copy), *ibid.*

21. Merk, "Massachusetts and Woman Suffrage," 340–56.

22. College Equal Suffrage League, *Minutes*, 1 (Dec. 5, 1906), 64–65, Woman's Rights Collection; Massachusetts Woman Suffrage Association, *Records*, 2 (June 1, 1906 and Oct. 28, 1908), 221, 302, *ibid.*

23. Massachusetts Woman Suffrage Association, *Records*, 2 (Oct. 22, 1909), 348, *ibid.*

24. Whether there was a progressive movement in Massachusetts is debatable. Richard M. Abrams believes the state, with a few exceptions, woman suffrage among them, had enacted most progressive reforms by 1900. He says that Republican leaders, who controlled the government, were "conservative," and when a successful challenge came to their rule, it came from Irish-Americans, not progressives. Since Abrams confines his discussion of woman suffrage to one footnote and excludes women as a political force entirely, his book cannot be considered a comprehensive political study of the period or of the progressive movement in Massachusetts. Richard M. Abrams, *Conservatism in a Progressive Era: Massachusetts Politics 1900–1912* (Cambridge, Mass., 1964). That ethnic leaders in Massachusetts might also be labeled progressives is explored by John D. Buenker, "The Mahatma and Progressive Reform: Martin Lomasney as Lawmaker, 1911–1917," *New England Quarterly*, 44 (Sept. 1971), 397–419.

25. The Women's Trade Union League was organized in Boston, in 1903 at a regular convention of AFL. Although Chicagoans soon dominated the national organization, there was a very strong league in Boston that supported striking women, agitated for labor legislation, organized women workers, and supported feminist causes. Gladys Boone, *The Women's Trade Union Leagues in Great Britain and the United States of America* (New York, 1968).

26. For example, see two accounts of speeches given by Florence Luscomb. Bangor (Maine) *Daily News*, April 22, 1909; Richmond (Virginia) *News Leader*, Oct. 4, 1910. The Woman's Rights Collection has a large number of newspaper clippings and suffrage fliers which attest that women suffragists consistently tried to appeal to labor. See also, Merk, "Massachusetts and Woman Suffrage," 269–74.

27. Maud W. Park to Mary H. Page, Nov. 25, 1907 (copy), Woman's Rights Collection.

28. Aileen S. Kraditor, *Up from the Pedestal: Selected Writings in the History of American Feminism* (Chicago, 1968), 7–13.

29. Constance Rover, *Women's Suffrage and Party Politics in Britain 1866–1914* (London and Toronto, 1967), 61.

30. *Ibid.*, 72–101. See also E. Sylvia Pankhurst, *The Suffragette: The History of the Women's Militant Suffrage Movement 1905–1910* (London, 1911); E. Sylvia Pankhurst, *The Life of Emmeline Pankhurst: The Suffragette Struggle for Women's Citizenship* (New York, 1969).

31. Emmeline Pethick-Lawrence to Mary H. Page, Sept. 16, Nov. 12, 1908, Page Scrapbook, Woman's Rights Collection.

32. Mary Hutcheson Page, "Mr. Asquith's Prisoners," *Colliers*, 43 (May 15, 1909), 17. See also, Mary Hutcheson Page, "Letter to the Editor," Boston *Herald*, March 23, 1909.

33. For example, see "The Struggle in England," *Woman's Journal*, 39 (Oct. 31, 1908), 174; "Events in England," *ibid.*, 39 (Nov. 7, 1908), 178; "An American in England," *ibid.*, 40 (Aug. 14, 1909), 130.

34. Harper succinctly made this point in 1907: "In the United States there are forty-five Parliaments to be reckoned with, and that is only the beginning; for, when a majority of their members have been enlisted, they can only submit the question to the electors. It encounters then such a conglomerate mass of voters as exists nowhere else on the face of the earth, and it is doubtful if under such similar conditions women could get the franchise in any country on the globe." Ida Husted Harper, "Woman Suffrage Throughout the World," *North American Review*, 186 (Sept. 1907), 70.

35. Massachusetts Woman Suffrage Association, *Records*, 2 (Oct. 28, 1908), 303–04, Woman's Rights Collection.

36. There were probably many exceptions to this general rule. The chairwoman of the Meetings Committee of MWSA reported in 1908 that as many as 1000 people a day had been spoken to by suffragists at local fairs that summer and fall. *Ibid.*, 304. The first open-air meetings in Boston took place by accident outside the state house because everyone present could not fit into the building. Boston *Herald*, Feb. 24, 1909.

37. *Woman's Journal*, 40 (Jan. 2, 1909), 3; *ibid.*, 40 (Feb. 20, 1909), 29; *ibid.*, 40 (March 6, 1909) 35.

38. Florence H. Luscomb, "Our Open-Air Campaign," circa 1909, p. 1, Woman's Rights Collection.

39. Massachusetts Woman Suffrage Association, *Records*, 2 (May 7, 1909), 327, *ibid.*; *Woman's Journal*, 40 (May 29, 1909), 86.

40. *Woman's Journal*, 40 (May 29, 1909), 85.

41. Massachusetts Woman Suffrage Association, *Records*, 2 (June 4, 1909), 335, Woman's Rights Collection; *Fifth Report of the Boston Equal Suffrage Association for Good Government, 1908–1910* (Boston, 1910), 9.

42. "Mrs. Susan W. Fitzgerald," *Woman's Journal*, 41 (Feb. 5, 1910), 21. Susan Walker Fitzgerald served as recording secretary for NAWSA from 1912 to 1915. Another original participant in the Massachusetts open-air meetings, Katherine Dexter McCormick, was treasurer of NAWSA in 1913 and 1914, and first vice-president from 1915 to 1920.

43. The question of which group or individual gave the first open-air meeting in the United States remains in doubt. Scholars have generally accepted the contention of Harriot Stanton Blatch that she pioneered the technique in America, but she admits that her first attempt, a trolley car campaign along the Erie Canal in May 1908, was a dismal failure. See Harriot Stanton Blatch and Alma Lutz, *Challenging*

Years: the Memoirs of Harriot Stanton Blatch (New York, 1940), 107. Winifred Cooley, who reported on the use of such tactics in New York City, claimed a group called the Suffragettes, led by Lydia K. Commander, gave the first open-air meetings in New York City during the winter of 1907–1908. Winifred Cooley, "Suffragists and 'Suffragettes' a Record of Actual Achievement," *World To-Day*, 15 (Oct. 1908), 1066–71. Two English suffrage workers instigated a parade followed by an open-air meeting in Boone, Iowa, in 1908. Louise R. Noun, *Strong-Minded Women: The Emergence of the Woman Suffrage Movement in Iowa* (Ames, 1969), 246. Harriot Stanton Blatch's trolley tour was routinely reported in the *Woman's Journal*, 39 (June 13, 1908), 95, with no editorial comment. The crucial point here is that Massachusetts women were convinced that they had adopted the technique from England, not from New York. Certainly the Massachusetts women were the first moderate organization with a statewide membership to use the tactic systematically and consistently. See Florence H. Luscomb, "Brief Biographical Sketch," 1945, pp. 1–3, Woman's Rights Collection; interview with Florence Luscomb, Nov. 6, 1972, Oral History Project of Rhode Island (University of Rhode Island).

44. *Fifth Report of the Boston Equal Suffrage Association for Good Government*, 9.

45. For a description of the tours, see *ibid.*; Luscomb, "Our Open-Air Campaign"; *Woman's Journal*, 40 (Aug. 28, 1909), 138–39; *Proceedings of the Annual Convention of the National American Woman Suffrage Association* (New York, 1910), 118–19.

46. Luscomb, "Our Open-Air Campaign," 4–5.

47. "Annual Report of the Massachusetts Woman Suffrage Association," *Minutes*, 2 (Oct. 22, 1909), 343, Woman's Rights Collection.

48. Interview with Florence Luscomb, July 18, 19, 1972, Oral History Project of Rhode Island; Luscomb, "Brief Biographical Sketch," 1–2.

49. Clipping, circa 1911, Woman's Rights Collection.

50. Luscomb, "Our Open-Air Campaign," 5.

51. Interview with Florence Luscomb, Nov. 6, 1972, Oral History Project of Rhode Island; Luscomb, "Brief Biographical Sketch," 2–4.

52. For example, see "Open-Air Meetings," *Woman's Journal*, 40 (Aug. 14, 1909), 130; "Contrasting Methods," *ibid.*, 40 (Sept. 11, 1909), 146. Meanwhile the open-air technique had captured the interest of women all over the country. At the 1910 NAWSA convention in Washington, D.C., two Massachusetts women were asked to participate in a symposium presided over by Blatch on open-air meetings and help give a "practical demonstration." Mary Hutcheson Page was asked to lead a meeting on "Practical Methods of Work." When the state of California voted in favor of suffrage for women in 1911, workers there enthusiastically reaffirmed that open-air meetings and publicity in the papers were a crucial factor in their success. By 1911 Anna Howard Shaw endorsed open-air campaigns in her presidential address to the convention and in 1912 the tactic was officially introduced on the national level at a huge rally in Independence Square in Philadelphia. See Harper, ed., *History of Woman Suffrage*, V, 286, 317, 333; *Proceedings of the Annual Convention of the National American Woman Suffrage Association* (New York, 1911), 100–07.

53. "Mrs. Pankhurst's Methods," *Woman's Journal*, 40 (Oct. 23, 1909), 170; "Militant Moods," *ibid.*, 40 (Oct. 30, 1909), 174.

54. "Sell the Woman's Journal," *ibid.*, 40 (Sept. 25, 1909), 154.

55. "Selling the Woman's Journal," *ibid.*, 40 (Nov. 13, 1909), 183; "Selling the Woman's Journal," *ibid.*, 40 (Nov. 20, 1909), 186.

56. "Mrs. Pankhurst in Boston," *ibid.*, 40 (Oct. 30, 1909), 174.

57. "The climax of the excitement came when Miss Gertrude Cliff . . . was gently but firmly escorted from the center of the wheat pit." Boston *American*, Dec. 13, 1909.

58. Boston *Herald*, Dec. 15, 1909.

59. This diary is in the possession of Florence Luscomb.

60. Florence H. Luscomb to Hannah K. Luscomb, June 4, 1911, *ibid.*; Boston *Globe*, April 6, 1911.

61. Boston *Globe*, Sept. 9, 1911; Boston *Herald*, Sept. 16, 1911; Boston *Globe*, Sept. 26, Oct. 10, 1911. The Woman's Rights Collection has a large number of clippings about Margaret Foley's "heckling" in the fall of 1911. See also Harper, ed., *History of Woman Suffrage*, VI, 296.

62. *Ibid.*, V, 342.

63. "Militant Woman Suffrage," *Woman's Journal*, 40 (Feb. 20, 1909), 30; Merk, "Massachusetts and Woman Suffrage," 100. After a federal amendment granting woman suffrage was defeated in the United States Senate in 1918 by two votes, NAWSA decided to work for the defeat of one incumbent senator from each party up for election that year. Senators John Weeks of Massachusetts and Willard Saulsbury of Delaware were defeated. See Flexner, *Century of Struggle*, 310–11.

64. "Non-Partisan Influence," *Woman's Journal*, 40 (Sept. 25, 1909), 154.

65. Ronald Schaffer, "The New York City Woman Suffrage Party, 1909–1919," *New York History*, 43 (July 1962), 268–87.

66. *Sixth Report of the Boston Equal Suffrage Association for Good Government, 1910–1912* (Boston, 1912), 14–16.

67. *Quarterly Report of the Massachusetts Woman Suffrage Association*, June 1910 (Boston, 1910), 14. Ward 8 was the political domain of city boss Martin Lomasney. Although he remained opposed to woman suffrage, he gave the suffragists some assistance in their campaign in his district, perhaps one of the best indications of the political power of the suffrage movement in Massachusetts by 1910. For Lomasney's views on suffrage, see Buenker, "The Mahatma and Progressive Reform," 409–10, 412.

68. For a discussion by Alice Stone Blackwell of this sequence of events, see Harper, ed., *History of Woman Suffrage*, VI, 296–99. See also Luscomb, "Brief Biographical Sketch," 5.

69. Harper, ed., *History of Woman Suffrage*, VI, 301–02; interview with Florence Luscomb, Aug. 27, 1973, Oral History Project of Rhode Island.

16

Creating a Feminist Alliance:
Sisterhood and Class Conflict
in the New York
Women's Trade Union League, 1903-1914

Nancy Schrom Dye

A "small band of enthusiasts who believed that the nonindustrial person could be of service to her industrial sister in helping her find her way through the chaos of industry"[1] formed the Women's Trade Union League of New York late in 1903. The organization's members—a unique coalition of women workers and wealthy women disenchanted with conventional philanthropic and social reform activities—dedicated themselves to improving female laborers' working conditions and their status in the labor movement.

The women who formed the core of the New York Women's Trade Union League's membership were both trade unionists and feminists. As unionists, they worked to integrate women into the mainstream of the American labor movement. As feminists, they tried to make the early twentieth-century women's movement relevant to working women's concerns. To these ends, the WTUL attempted to serve as a link between women workers and the labor movement and as a focal point for unorganized women interested in unionism. The League agitated among unorganized women workers in an effort to educate women to the importance of unionization. In addition, the organization made concerted efforts to change male trade unionists' negative attitudes

From *Feminist Studies* 2 (1975). Reprinted by permission of the publisher, *Feminist Studies*, 417 Riverside Drive, New York, N.Y. 10025.

This paper was originally presented at the Conference on Class and Ethnicity in Women's History, SUNY—Binghamton, September 1974.

toward women. The WTUL offered assistance to municipal labor organizations and often aided local unions during strikes. League members also worked as organizers and helped establish several dozen unions of unskilled and semiskilled women workers in New York City. Most notably, the New York League played an important role in building the shirtwaist makers' union (International Ladies' Garment Workers' Union Local 25) and the white goods workers' union (International Ladies' Garment Workers' Union Local 62). In a later period of its history, particularly during the 1910s and 1920s, the New York League abandoned its singleminded emphasis on union organizing in order to concentrate most of its efforts on the campaigns for woman suffrage and women's protective labor legislation.[2]

Women came to the League from a variety of backgrounds. Many members were young working women who learned of the WTUL through their unions or through League publicity campaigns. Other members were wealthy women. Often college-educated, allies, as upper-class members were called, usually came to the League with experience in charity organizations, social reform societies, or social settlements. The New York City Consumers' League, the working girls' clubs, and the Workingwomen's Society were among the groups dedicated to improving the women's position in the labor force. Such organizations as the Municipal League and the Young Women's Christian Association occasionally conducted investigations of women's working and living conditions. Residents of the city's settlement houses frequently took an interest in working women and in the rapidly growing trade union movement.

The WTUL, however, differed from these organizations in two important respects. First, the League stressed the importance of actual union organizing efforts rather than such customary reform activities as social investigations. Many women joined the League precisely because they were discouraged by the slow approach of social reform organizations or by the elitism of traditional charity work. As Gertrude Barnum, a leading upper-class member in the League's early years, explained,

> I myself have graduated from the Settlement into the trade union. As I became more familiar with the conditions around me, I began to feel that while the Settlement was undoubtedly doing a great deal to make the lives of working people less grim and hard, the work was not fundamental. It introduced into their lives books and flowers and music, and it gave them a place to meet and see their friends or leave their babies when they went out to work, but it did not raise their wages or shorten their hours. It began to dawn on me, therefore, that it would be more practical to turn our energies toward raising wages and shortening hours.[3]

Second, the Women's Trade Union League stressed the importance of cross-class cooperation between upper-class and working-class women, and it was the only early twentieth-century women's organization that attempted to build such an egalitarian, cross-class alliance into its organizational structure. New York League membership was open to any individual who professed her allegiance to the American Federation of Labor and who indicated her willingness to work to unionize New York's women workers. League members stressed that allies as well as workers could be dedicated trade unionists and effective labor organizers.

Examining the day-to-day relationships WTUL members established among themselves and studying the alignments on policy issues makes it possible to observe the dynamics of cross-class cooperation and conflict. Two questions are of particular importance: How successful was the League in establishing an egalitarian, cross-class alliance? What were the sources of conflict within the organization that undermined the alliance?

The success of the New York Women's Trade Union League depended upon maintaining harmony and a sense of purpose within its coalition of workers and allies. The individuals who founded the League did not expect the coalition's stability to be a problem. The first WTUL members—most of whom were settlement residents and social reformers—apparently anticipated few difficulties in relating to one another: women could, they believed, surmount social and ethnic differences and unite on the basis of their common femininity. In this respect, the Women's Trade Union League was typical of the early twentieth-century women's movement. A conviction that women could relate to one another across class lines in the spirit of sisterhood and an emphasis on the special qualities that women shared linked many League members to the larger feminist movement. One of the major ideological strains in American feminism at the turn of the century was that women were different, emotionally and culturally, from men. Unlike mid-nineteenth-century feminists who had inveighed against the notion of a separate sphere for women and who had argued that both sexes shared a common humanity, early twentieth-century feminists, suffragists, and social reformers stressed the importance of sex differences. As WTUL member Rheta Childe Dorr expressed this philosophy,

> Women now form a new social group, separate, and to a degree homogeneous. Already they have evolved a group opinion and a group ideal. . . . Society will soon be compelled to make a serious survey of the opinions and the ideals of women. As far as these have found collective expressions, it is evident that they differ very radically from the accepted opinions and ideals of men. . . . It is inevitable that this should be so.[4]

League members, like other feminists in the early twentieth century, were often vague when they tried to define women's sisterhood. They usually used the term to convey the idea that social class was less important than gender for understanding a woman's status. The primary social dichotomy was a sex distinction rooted in differences between women and men, not classes. Women, some League members argued, shared distinct emotional qualities: they were more gentle and moral than men, more sensitive and responsive to human needs. League members also argued that women, regardless of class, could empathize with one another because they belonged to an oppressed social group.[5] This belief in sisterhood provided the ideological impetus for the League's formation and helps explain why many women joined the organization.

In certain basic respects, members found that their ideal of sisterhood could be realized. As an organization in which both upper-class and working-class women played important roles, and in which working-class and upper-class women could gain knowledge and confidence from one another, the WTUL remained viable for several decades. And it is possible to document many examples of close personal and working relationships within the League that transcended class lines.

In many other respects, however, WTUL members discovered that it was considerably easier to make verbal assertions of sisterhood than it was to put the ideal into practice. In contrast to the League's public affirmation of sorority, the organization's internal affairs were rarely harmonious. Beyond a basic commitment to unionizing women workers and to the American Federation of Labor, there was little upon which women in the League could agree. Far from behaving in sisterly fashion in their day-to-day affairs, members were often at odds with one another over League objectives and policies: Who should be allowed to join the organization? How much money and energy should the League commit to labor organization, to educational activities, to suffrage agitation? Should the League support protective legislation for women? Personal animosity and rancor accompanied debates over WTUL priorities. Leading members frequently submitted resignations or threatened to resign. They wrote angry letters denouncing one another or defending themselves against others' attacks. In short, WTUL women were a contentious lot. "If we have failed in what might be our greatest usefulness to the workers," Leonora O'Reilly, a leading working-class member, concluded wearily in 1914, "it is just in proportion as we have exhausted the energy of our friends and ourselves . . . in periodical tiffs and skermishes [sic]."[6]

What accounted for the high level of animosity within the New York WTUL? It is tempting to single out class conflict as a blanket explanation for the League's factionalism, policy disputes, and difficult personal relationships. Without doubt, class conflict was a reality within the League and a factor which undercut members' attempts to create an egalitarian alliance. Allies and workers came to the organization with different conceptions of social class, different attitudes toward work, and, of course, radically different social, educational, and cultural backgrounds. The ideal of sisterhood notwithstanding, difficulties and misunderstandings between women from different social backgrounds were inevitable. Yet class conflict in and of itself is not an adequate explanation for the controversies that regularly shook the organization. Indeed, social relationships among League members sometimes tended to mitigate serious class conflict. More important, there were no simple class alignments on League issues. Clearly, factors in addition to class conflict were involved.

The women who made up the organization were never able to reconcile their dedication to women as an oppressed minority within the work force and their commitment to the labor movement as a whole. Belief in sisterhood, League members discovered, was not always compatible with a belief in the importance of class solidarity. In other words, League members were unable to develop a satisfactory solution to the problem of women's dual exploitation: were women workers oppressed because they were workers or because they were female? In effect, many controversies which characterized the organization were in large part a reflection of the League's struggle to synthesize feminism and unionism—a struggle that had personal as well as ideological ramifications for many WTUL members.[7]

Although differences in members' social backgrounds did not fully account for the conflicts within the League, they were an important contributing factor. In the organization's first years, from late 1903 through 1906, allies much more readily than working women joined the WTUL. During these years, when the League rarely had more than fifty members, upper-class women dominated the organization numerically. Although the League's first president was a working woman—Margaret Daly, a United Garment Workers organizer—she remained in the League for only a short time. She was succeeded by Margaret Dreier, an ally. With the exception of Daly, all of the WTUL's officers and a small majority of the executive board members were allies. References can be found to young working women who joined the League between 1903 and 1907, but their role in the organization was shadowy—few remained in the League for more than a year or took a vocal role in the organization's activities.[8]

To stem the tide of young college graduates and settlement residents who flocked to the League in its first years, Gertrude Barnum, an ally herself, suggested that the WTUL impose a quota system to limit the number of upper-class members and that prospective allies be required to endorse the principle of the closed shop as a measure of their commitment to the labor movement. The League did not implement either of these policies. The organization's major provision to guard against upper-class domination was contained in its constitution, which stipulated that working women were to hold the majority of executive board positions. In addition, positions of leadership on organizing committees were sometimes reserved for working women. Such safeguards, however, could not change the fact that in the first years allies dominated the organization numerically. Although no one questioned the desirability of large numbers of working-class members, the first members had difficulty recruiting them.

By 1907, the League had established itself and had begun to come to the attention of young working women through its organizing efforts and its support of labor activities. More workers joined the organization. Three of the League's five officers in 1907 were working women, as was a clear majority of the executive board. After the 1909 general shirtwaist strike, in which the WTUL played a central role, workers joined the League in greater numbers than at any time previously. The year after the strike, eight of the ten executive board members were working women. For the rest of the period under consideration, the League's total membership was several hundred individuals, and working women and allies were numerically balanced.[9]

Numerical equality, however, could not solve the more serious problem of upper-class cultural domination—a problem that was always with the WTUL. Most upper-class members were seemingly unconscious of the genteel atmosphere that permeated the League, despite its unpretentious headquarters in dingy Lower East Side flats. Allies apparently saw nothing incongruous about juxtaposing "interpretive dance recitals" with shop meetings or inviting women to stop by for an afternoon of "drinking tea and discussing unionism." For working women, however, the League had an aristocratic air about it. For example, Rose Schneiderman, a young Jewish capmaker who had grown up on the Lower East Side, recalled her amazement when she attended her first League meeting and watched the participants dance the Virginia Reel. She, like many workers, had to overcome initial reluctance to join an organization with so many wealthy, college-educated women. On a personal level, the League's gentility undermined workers' self-confidence and made them feel awkward; on an ideological level, the organization's aristocratic character was foreign and often suspect. "Contact with the Lady does harm in the long run," Leonora O'Reilly declared at one point. "It gives the wrong standard."[10]

Ideally, allies were to extirpate from themselves any trace of the "Lady with something to give to her sisters."[11] They were to make way for working-class members to take the initiative in labor affairs. In short, they were to learn about trade unionism, labor organizing, and working conditions from the women who had first hand experience in such matters. Despite the emphasis on egalitarian relationships between working-class and upper-class members, however, allies often took the lead in day-to-day affairs. In part, this might be explained by the fact that upper-class members had the advantages of good education and financial independence. Then, too, allies were, on the average, ten years older than working-class members, and their age may have given them additional confidence and authority in the League.[12]

The patronizing attitudes of certain allies toward working-class members were evident in the WTUL's educational work. Upper-class members occasionally assumed the self-appointed task of discovering and developing natural leaders among New York City working women. As Mary Beard confided to another League member, "It has been my dream to develop young women to be a help in the awakening of their class. . . ."[13] One young WTUL organizer recorded in her monthly work report that her scheduled activities included writing lessons. ". . . Miss Scott felt that I ought to practice my writing as I would have to do a great deal of it in the future. I put in several days at nothing else but writing. I had two lessons with Mrs. Charles Beard."[14] Instead of working-class members teaching allies to relate to women workers and to be effective organizers, the opposite was sometimes the case.

Such attitudes did not go ignored or uncriticized. Leonora O'Reilly, a working woman with long experience as a garment trades organizer and labor speaker and one of the original members of the League, was particularly vocal in expressing her dislike of college women who came to the labor movement with lofty ideals of feminism and solidarity but who knew nothing about the realities of labor organizing or of working for a living. She was determined that working-class members should not be intimidated by upper-class women's academic and financial advantages. More specifically, she carried on a running campaign against Laura Elliot, an older ally who joined the League in 1910. Elliot offered League members courses in singing, elocution, and art history; she organized a League chorus and took groups of young women workers to museums and concerts. Most members apparently regarded Elliot as an eccentric but harmless individual and paid her little mind. O'Reilly, however, found her ideas pernicious enough to attack. She harangued Elliot about her condescending attempts to save working women by filling them with useless and pretentious notions of culture.

Elliot was hurt and confused by O'Reilly's anger, but insisted that she had a contribution to make to the League.

> You cannot push me out and you cannot make me afraid of any working girl sisters or render me self-conscious before them, I refuse to be afraid to take them to the Metropolitan Museum and teach them and help them. . . . I feel no fear in putting my side of the proposition up to any working girl. I'm not afraid to tell her that I have something to bring her and I'm never afraid that she will misunderstand or resent what I say. She needs my present help just as the whole race needs her uprising. . . .[15]

Workers sometimes asserted that allies, despite good intentions, did not know how to appeal to working women: their experiences and backgrounds were simply too different from those of their constituents to bridge the gap. Pauline Newman, a young Jewish immigrant who joined the League during the 1909 shirtwaist strike, summarized her impressions of upper-class limitations in both the League and the suffrage campaign in her remark: "the 'cultured' ladies may be very sincere . . . I don't doubt their sincereity [sic] but because their views are narrow and their knowledge of social conditions limited, they cannot do as well as some of us can."[16]

Workers' frustration with the well-intentioned but sometimes inept efforts of their affluent colleagues was understandable. Allies, as the executive board admitted at one point, could be "trying."[17] Upper-class members were sometimes responsible for decisions which exasperated working women. On at least one occasion, for example, League officers scheduled a conference on Yom Kippur, despite Jewish members' protestations. In the League's book of English lessons, *New World Lessons for Old World People*, references to Jewish working girls going to church slipped by uncorrected. Only one League ally is known to have studied Yiddish. Some allies held stereotypic conceptions of immigrant women. Jewish women were often described as "dark-eyed," "studious," and "revolutionary" in League literature. Italians were usually "docile," "fun-loving," "submissive," and "superstitious."[18]

Overt class and ethnic conflict in the WTUL reached its peak during a 1914 presidential contest between Rose Schneiderman and Melinda Scott. At the time of the election, Rose Schneiderman was the WTUL's East Side or Jewish organizer. Scott, a skilled hat trimmer and president of an independent union in her trade, served as the League's organizer of American-born women in the neckwear and dressmaking industries. Although both candidates were workers, they represented widely divergent approaches to the problems of organizing women. Schneiderman had always emphasized the importance of reaching immigrant women. Scott was pessimistic about organizing immigrants and advocated a policy of concentrating on American-born workers. Thus, the election involved League attitudes and policies toward immigrants. Nevertheless, support for the two candidates divided along class lines: allies backed Scott while working women voted for Schneiderman.[19] When Scott won by four votes, Pauline Newman related the details to Schneiderman.

> Your vote, with the exception of three or four was a real trade Union vote. On the other hand, the vote for Linda was purely a vote of the social workers. People who have not been near the League for four or five years, came to vote . . . but they could not get the girls from the Union to vote against you. . . . So you see, that nothing was left undone by them to line up a vote for Linda on the ground that you were a socialist, a Jewes [sic] and one interested in suffrage.[20]

Part of the difficulty underlying clashes between allies and workers lay in the fact that the two groups had different conceptions of class. The importance of class differences was usually far more obvious to working women than it was to allies. Upper-class members were not as acutely aware of class antagonism within the League and often downplayed the importance of social background. Many were confused by the emphasis workers placed on class differences. As Laura Elliot wrote to Leonora O'Reilly, "Before I was unconscious about this class and that class and this stupid difference and that stupid difference. Girls were just girls to me, and now you people are putting all sorts of ideas in my head and making me timid and self-conscious."[21]

Many allies believed that with great effort an individual could transcend her social background. Social class was flexible, not immutable. When allies talked of transcending their backgrounds, they were referring to young women from wealthy families who became self-sufficient and who could relate to workers without self-consciousness. Helen Marot, an ally who came from a comfortably affluent Philadelphia family regarded herself as a worker because she worked as the League's secretary and supported herself on her earnings. In similar fashion, Violet Pike, a young woman who joined the League shortly after her graduation from Vassar in 1907, was included among the working women on the executive board because she performed some clerical duties and joined the Bookkeepers, Stenographers, and Accountants' union.[22] Maud Younger, a wealthy ally, was listed on the League's masthead as a representative of the Waitresses' Union because she conducted an investigation of waitresses' working conditions and attended meetings of the union. In a sense, these women were workers, and they were proud of being self-supporting and resisted being categorized in their fathers' class.

Allies and workers came to the League with different conceptions of work as well. Upper-class members frequently had romanticized views of poverty and often regarded self-sufficiency as a kind of luxury. Work meant liberation from the confines of proper femininity. This attitude contributed to allies' naivete concerning the role of work in the lives of female wage-earners. Because they idealized work and equated it with economic and emotional self-sufficiency, many allies never seemed to come to terms with the fact that most women were not independent laborers but part of a family economic unit in which work did not usually connote independent economic status.[23] "Thank God working girls have a chance to be themselves because they earn their own wage and nobody owns them," one typical League article began. "I am pretty sure you are somebody, because you are self-support-ing."[24]

That the New York League was characterized by personal, cultural and political strife there can be no doubt. But Pauline Newman's 1914 depiction of an organization sharply divided between "social workers" and "trade unionists" was overdrawn and simplistic. Although it is easy to document class conflict, it is also possible to document experiences that mitigated serious, sustained conflict between upper-class and work-ing-class women. There were cohesive factors as well as divisive ten-dencies that operated within the League and enabled the organization to function.

League members' personal relationships with one another con-stituted one factor that undercut the class conflict inherent in the organization. Sisterhood sometimes became a tangible reality in friend-ships. Mary Dreier, the WTUL's president from 1907 through 1914, and Leonora O'Reilly, for example, maintained a warm personal relation-ship for many years that survived numerous political and cultural differences between the two women. "You say you wonder whether I would always trust you," Dreier wrote O'Reilly after some disagree-ment over League policy.

> There doesn't even seem to be such a word as trust necessary between thee and me. . . . I might not always understand, as you might not always understand my activities—but as to doubting your integrity of soul, or the assurance on which trust is built seems as impossible to me as walking on a sunbeam into the heart of the sun for any of us humans—a strange and beautiful mixture of personal and impersonal is my relationship to you and I love you.[25]

Such relationships were not uncommon among League women. Some, like that of Dreier and O'Reilly, cut across class lines. Other close friendships were established between women of the same social back-ground.

It is not surprising that such relationships were common among League members. For many WTUL women, the organization was a full-time commitment, a way of life. Then, too, that League members should form their closest emotional ties with other women is not surprising in light of the social conventions that governed personal relationships in the pre-Freudian culture of the early twentieth century. Emotional attachments between individuals of the same sex were not viewed with the same suspicion that would characterize a later period. Intense relationships involving open expressions of tenderness and affection were accepted as natural.[26]

Then, too, the longer a working woman spent in the League, the more she had in common with an upper-class ally. Both groups of women were atypical in early twentieth-century American society: the majority were single at ages when most women were married, they prided themselves on being independent and self-supporting, and they lived in a gynaecentric environment in which other women were their closest companions, their working colleagues, and their sources of emotional support. Only an extremely mechanistic definition of social class could fail to take into account that these women shared many important life experiences.

Finally, class conflict is not an adequate explanation for the dis-agreements within the organization for the simple reason that a member's social background did not dictate her stand on League policies. On every important issue, alignments were unclear. Suffrage, traditionally regarded as a middle-class issue, was an important priority for many working-class members. Rose Schneiderman and Pauline Newman were the first members to devote themselves full-time to the suffrage campaign. Ally Helen Marot, on the other hand, resisted the League's growing emphasis on the importance of the vote. Protective labor legislation, an issue that was enormously important in the League's history during the 1910s and 1920s, was a more controversial issue than woman suffrage, but on that issue as well, there were no clear class alignments. Allies and workers could be found on both sides of the question. In short, one cannot argue that only upper-class League members supported such reform issues as protective legislation while only workers supported labor policies such as direct organizing. There is no evidence to support the view that working women saw the League as a labor union and allies viewed it as a social reform organization. Rather, it is clear that factors in addition to class conflict played a role in creating the controversies in which League members found them-selves embroiled.[27]

League members, regardless of class background, viewed the WTUL both as a women's organization and as a labor organization. Therein lay the second and perhaps more pervasive source of discord. Members had difficulty reconciling their commitment to organized labor with their commitment to the women's movement. They could not agree on a solution to the problem of women workers' dual exploitation or find a way to reconcile their belief in sisterhood with their belief in the importance of working-class solidarity. If a woman dedicated herself to working for protective legislation or for suffrage, or if she advocated separate unions for women workers, she opened herself to the charge of dividing the working class. If, on the other hand, she stayed away from women's issues entirely, she was guilty of ignoring women's special problems in the work force. This dilemma was real, and neither the League nor the individuals in it fully resolved the question.

Some members felt strongly that dedication to the labor movement should override the League's feminist leanings. In their analysis, the problems of women workers were bound up inextricably with the problems of working men. Class, not gender, was the main concern. True, they said, women suffered discrimination in the labor movement, but such opposition was not insurmountable.

Other members found their primary orientation in the women's movement. Or, as happened more frequently, women first attempted to cooperate with organized labor but ultimately despaired of changing male unionists' attitudes. They dismissed the labor movement and turned to suffrage and protective legislation as ways to ameliorate women workers' conditions.

Helen Marot, the League's secretary and an organizer, epitomized the first, or "woman as worker" position. Although she was never an industrial worker, she never wavered from her conviction that the WTUL should be committed to organized labor as a whole and not to women as a separate group. Female workers, she emphasized, should be regarded as inseparable from male workers: to think otherwise was to impede class solidarity and to denigrate women's capabilities. Throughout her career in the League and in her book, *American Labor Unions*, Marot vigorously opposed any policy that smacked of caste-consciousness. She emphasized that women were difficult to organize because they were unskilled, not because they were female. She was vehement in her opposition to the minimum wage for women, despite the fact that the measure eventually won the approval of many working-class League members. "If women need state protection on the ground that they do not organize as men do," she told the New York State Factory Investigating Commission, "then also do the mass of unskilled, unorganized men who do not appreciate or take advantage of organization. . . . The reasons for trade unionists to oppose State interference in wage rates apply to women workers as they do to men."[28]

Harriot Stanton Blatch, a well-known suffragist, represented the other strain of the WTUL. Unlike Marot, her interest in women workers derived from her involvement in the women's movement, not from a concern with industrial problems. Unions for women were only one aspect of a multifaceted campaign for women's rights, not an end in themselves. For Blatch, any class-related issue was secondary to the vote. In part, expedient 'considerations motivated her participation in the League: she realized that working women's support was vital for the ultimate success of the suffrage movement, and the League offered an avenue by which to reach them. On another level, however, Blatch was convinced that political equality was a prerequisite for any other improvement in women's status. Thus, only when women could vote would they command the respect of the labor movement. And only with suffrage would women develop the confidence to fight for indus-trial equality. "I have . . . [been] working with the Women's Trade Union League and attending meetings of the women's locals on the E. Side," Blatch wrote Gompers in 1905. "Those young women need stirring up, need independence, and some fight instilled into them. . . . I am understanding of all that the vote would mean to them—[it] would help in the trade union work as nothing else could."[29]

Marot and Blatch were sure of their objectives and their ideological orientation. The problem of women's dual status was not so clearcut for the majority of League members, however. For working-class mem-bers, the problems posed by the WTUL's dual commitment to its constituents as women and as workers were particularly vexing. For them, the matter was not only a theoretical and political issue, but frequently a personal dilemma as well. On the one hand, workers identified with their class background. They came to the League with experience in organizing activities and committed to trade unionism. On the other hand, they, like allies, were also feminists. Although workers were less likely than allies to come to the WTUL with an interest in the women's movement and probably became acquainted with the ideas of organized feminism and with the goals of the women's movement through their relationships with allies, most became dedi-cated feminists. More important, by comparing their experiences in the League with their role in trade unions they often came to a realization that the WTUL offered more opportunities for women to fill autono-mous, responsible positions than male-dominated unions did.

Leonora O'Reilly's career in the League provides a good example of working-women's difficulties. Her commitment to the League was al-ways ambivalent. She was faced with what she regarded as a conflict between her class background and her work in a women's organization. This was aggravated by her conviction that any serious attempt to organize working women had to be a feminist as well as a labor effort. An outspoken feminist herself, she recognized the need for an organization such as the League to devote special attention to women. She knew from her own experience as a United Garment Workers' organizer that women could count on little assistance from male unions. For all that, O'Reilly never came to terms with her ambivalence. She vacillated between urging the League to refrain from interfering in union affairs and stressing that the League should implement its policies in an autonomous fashion.[30] Sometimes she exalted the ability of women to fend for themselves in the work force, independent of men. ". . . I want to say to my sisters," she once declared to a WTUL convention, "for mercy's sake, let's be glad if the men don't help us!"[31] From her days in the Working-women's Society in the 1890s, O'Reilly had stressed the importance of sisterhood. She was a dedicated suffragist. On a number of occasions she spoke of "women's real togetherness." "Personally," she wrote, "I suffer torture dividing the woman's movement into the Industrial Group and all the other groups. Women real women anywhere and everywhere are what we must nourish and cherish."[32] Yet at other times, O'Reilly denounced the League as an elitist organization that had no real concern for working-class people. "The League ought to die," she reportedly said at one point, "the sooner the better." [33] Her two resignations from the WTUL in 1905 and in 1914 indicated her continual difficulty in resolving the conflict. In both instances she emphasized that working women would have to organize themselves.[34]

Rose Schneiderman and Pauline Newman exhibited similar confusion and ambivalence about their role as working women in the League. On the one hand, they identified with the East Side immigrant working-class community in which they had grown up. On the other, they regarded themselves as feminists devoted to women's issues. Like O'Reilly, they frequently experienced enough conflict to consider resigning from the League.[35]

Both women were torn between working in the WTUL and devoting themselves to the East Side Jewish labor movement. Yet to work as an organizer for a Jewish union or for the International Ladies' Garment Workers' Union, as both women discovered, was often an isolated and lonely experience. If the WTUL was not sufficiently interested in the progress of the working class and did not sufficiently appreciate efforts and ability to reach immigrant women, the Jewish labor organizations ignored the special problems of women altogether and discriminated against the small number of women organizers. Newman, after several years of unhappy and unrewarding work as an ILGWU organizer concluded that League work was more desirable than she had thought originally: ". . . remember Rose that no matter how much you are with the Jewish people, you are still more with the people of the League and that is a relieff. [sic]"[36] It seems clear, therefore, that working women could compare the League favorably with trade unions. The WTUL offered women organizers considerably more autonomy and responsibility than unions did. What was more, the League provided the company of women who shared interests and experiences.

Still, both Schneiderman and Newman continually had difficulty reconciling the women's movement and the labor movement. On occasion, both women denounced the superficial efforts of upper-class philanthropists and reformers to improve industrial conditions. Yet they were the first WTUL members to work as full-time suffrage agitators. Later in the League's history, both were vocal supporters of women's protective legislation, especially of minimum wage statutes and maternity insurance, despite the fact that the labor movement frowned upon the principle of protective legislation in general and upon the minimum wage in particular. During Rose Schneiderman's presidency in the 1920s, the WTUL devoted itself almost exclusively to legislative activity.

The difficulties these women faced were not uncommon. Most League members experienced some conflict between feminism and unionism. The organization's policies also reflected this: during the first decade of its history, from 1903 to 1914, the WTUL downplayed women's special problems in the work force and concentrated on integrating women into the labor movement as workers, while during a later period its members worked hard to implement demands that were relevant only to women workers: suffrage and protective legislation. For League members, explanations for the oppression of working women were always couched in "either/or" terms: either a working woman was exploited as a worker or she suffered as a woman. What the League needed was an analysis which came to terms with both facets of women workers' situation. That analysis was never realized, and the League remained split. Caught between two alternatives, League members frequently were unable to define their purpose or their role.

In short, the Women's Trade Union League had only limited success in achieving its goal of an egalitarian cross-class alliance. Although the League went further than any other women's organization in establishing sustained relations with working women and in grappling with the problems a feminist alliance posed, its internal affairs were rarely harmonious. In part, the organization's difficulties can be attributed to conflict between allies and workers. Both groups' problems in resolving the WTUL's dual commitment to the labor movement and the women's movement also contributed to the difficulties in establishing a cross-class alliance.

NOTES

1. Mary Dreier, "Expansion Through Agitation and Education," *Life and Labor* 11 (June 1921): 163.

2. The New York Women's Trade Union League was an autonomous organization, but it was closely related to a larger body, the National Women's Trade Union League of America. The same individuals founded both organizations in late 1903.

3. *Weekly Bulletin of the Clothing Trades,* March 24, 1905, p. 2.

4. Rheta Childe Dorr, *What Eight Million Women Want* (Boston: Small, Maynard, 1910), p. 5. For a good discussion of the changes in American feminist ideology from the mid-nineteenth century to the early twentieth century, see Aileen Kraditor, *The Ideas of the Woman Suffrage Movement* (New York: Columbia University Press, 1965), Chapter 3.

5. See, for example, Gertrude Barnum, "The Modern Society Woman," *Ladies' Garment Worker* 2 (June 1911): 8. "All women before the laws of the country . . . are of equal rank or lack of rank, being classed without exception with children, idiots, and criminals. With a common sense of injustice, feminine descendents of Patrick Henry, Tom Paine, and Thomas Jefferson ignore social differences and march shoulder to shoulder in campaigns to secure their 'inalienable rights'—to secure the fullest possible social equality with man."

6. Leonora O'Reilly to the executive board, Women's Trade Union League of New York, January 14, 1914, Women's Trade Union League of New York Papers, New York State Labor Library, New York, New York (hereafter cited as WTUL of NY papers).

7. Some historians who have dealt briefly with the Women's Trade Union League have interpreted the discord within the organization and the shift from labor organizing to legislative activity as the result of class conflict between allies, or social reformers, and working women. William Chafe argues, for example, "Reformers viewed the WTUL's primary function as educational, and believed that the interests of the workers could best be served by investigating industrial conditions, securing legislative action, and building public support for the principle of trade unionism. Female unionists, on the other hand, insisted that organizing women and strengthening existing unions represented the League's principal purpose. One group perceived the WTUL as primarily an instrument of social uplift, the other as an agency for labor organization" (Chafe, *The American Woman, Her Changing Social, Economic, and Political Roles, 1920–1970* (New York: Oxford University Press, 1972), p. 71.

8. The New York League was never a large organization. Although it counted several hundred women among its dues-paying members in the years after 1907, few of these individuals played active roles in the League's day-to-day work. In the years from 1903 to 1914, about twenty women formed a core group of members. These women made League policies, served as League officers, organizers, and speakers, and set League priorities. Although the composition of this core group changed from year to year, most of these members devoted most of their time to the organization for at least several years. Using the lists of executive board members, officers, and committee members that are extant, it is possible to reach some conclusions about the changing class composition of the core membership

group. This discussion on membership is based on a more complete treatment in my doctoral dissertation, "The Women's Trade Union League of New York, 1903–1920," (University of Wisconsin, Madison, Wisconsin, 1974).

9. Women's Trade Union League of New York, *Annual Reports, 1909–1910* to *1913–1914.* For a more detailed discussion of membership, see Dye, "The Women's Trade Union League of New York, 1903–1920."

10. Letter to Leonora O'Reilly, 1908. O'Reilly's statement is in the form of a note written to herself on the back of the letter. Leonora O'Reilly Papers, Schlesinger Library, Cambridge, Massachusetts (hereafter cited as Leonora O'Reilly Papers).

11. William English Walling to Leonora O'Reilly, December 1903 (O'Reilly's handwritten note on the back of the letter), Leonora O'Reilly Papers.

12. This statement is based on the compilation of biographical information on the WTUL's core membership group. For more complete information, see Dye, "The Women's Trade Union League of New York."

13. Mary Beard to Leonora O'Reilly, July 21, 1912, Leonora O'Reilly Papers.

14. Report of the Organizer, October, 1915, Women's Trade Union League of New York, WTUL of NY Papers.

15. Laura Elliot to Leonora O'Reilly, March 1911, Leonora O'Reilly Papers.

16. Pauline Newman to Rose Schneiderman, July 16, 1912, Rose Schneiderman Papers, Tamiment Institute, New York University, New York, N.Y. (hereafter cited as Rose Schneiderman Papers).

17. Minutes, Executive Board, Women's Trade Union League of New York, January 25, 1906, WTUL of NY Papers.

18. See, for example, Violet Pike, *New World Lessons for Old World People* (New York: Women's Trade Union League of New York, 1912); Gertrude Barnum, "A Story with a Moral," *Weekly Bulletin of the Clothing Trades,* November 20, 1908, p. 6; Gertrude Barnum, "At the Shirtwaist Factory, A Story," *Ladies' Garment Worker,* 1 (June 1910): 4.

19. Pauline Newman recorded her impressions of the election in three letters to Rose Schneiderman. Pauline Newman to Rose Schneiderman, 1914, Rose Schneiderman Papers.

20. Ibid.

21. Laura Elliot to Leonora O'Reilly, March 1911, Leonora O'Reilly Papers.

22. Women's Trade Union League of New York, *Annual Reports, 1910–1911, 1911–1912.* In both years, Pike is listed as a union representative for the Book-keepers, Steographers, and Accountants' Union.

23. U. S. Congress, Senate, *Report on Condition of Woman and Child Wage-Earners in the United States,* "Wage-Earning Women in Stores and Factories," S. Doc. 645, 61st Cong., 2d sess., 1910, 5: 18, 25, 144. Senate investigators pointed out that New York City had the smallest proportion of self-supporting women of all the major cities investigated.

24. Gertrude Barnum, "Women Workers," *Weekly Bulletin of The Clothing Trades,* July 13, 1906, p. 8.

25. Mary Dreier to Leonora O'Reilly, June 19, 1908, Leonora O'Reilly Papers.

26. Other historical studies have touched upon this phenomenon. See, for example, Christopher Lasch and William Taylor, "Two Kindred Spirits," *New England Quarterly* 36 (Winter 1963): 23–41.

27. This interpretation differs from brief accounts of the WTUL in other works. See, for example, Kraditor, *Ideas of the Woman Suffrage Movement,* Chapter 6, and Chafe, *American Woman,* Chapter 3.

28. New York, Factory Investigating Commission, *Fourth Report of the New York State Factory Investigating Commission, 1915* 1: 774; Helen Marot, *American Labor Unions, By a Member* (New York: Henry Holt, 1915), Chapter 5.

29. Harriot Stanton Blatch to Samuel Gompers, December 30, 1905, American Federation of Labor Papers, Wisconsin State Historical Society, Madison, Wisconsin; Harriot Stanton Blatch, *Challenging Years* (New York: Putnam, 1940).

30. See, for example, Leonora O'Reilly to executive board, Women's Trade Union League of New York, January 14, 1914, WTUL of NY Papers.

31. National Women's Trade Union League, *Proceedings of the Second Biennial Convention, 1909,* p. 26.

32. Leonora O'Reilly to Mary Hay, December 29, 1917, Leonora O'Reilly Papers.

33. Leonora O'Reilly's statement was quoted in a letter from Pauline Newman to Rose Schneiderman, 1914, Rose Schneiderman Papers. Newman wrote, "Mrs. Robins wanted Nora [Leonora O'Reilly] to tell her what she thought of the candidats [sic] but Nora said that, 'this you will never know, but I can tell you what I think of the League, it ought to die, and the sooner the better.''

34. Minutes, Special Meeting, Executive Board, Women's Trade Union League of New York, November 19, 1915, WTUL of NY Papers.

35. See, for example, Pauline Newman to Rose Schneiderman, February 22, 1912, Rose Schneiderman Papers.

36. Pauline Newman to Rose Schneiderman, April 17, 1911, Rose Schneiderman Papers.

17

Women Reformers
and American Culture, 1870-1930

Jill Conway

The history of American feminism has an Alice in Wonderland quality. The story of the achievement of legal and institutional liberties for women in America must be accompanied by an account of their loss of psychological autonomy and social segregation. The historian of American feminism must write a double narrative in which something more than the reversals of Looking-Glass Land must be advanced. The historian must relate the outward story of a successful agitation to some causal analysis of why this agitation first for legal rights, then for access to higher education, then for the franchise and for liberation from a traditional Christian view of marriage had so little influence on actual behavior. For there is no escaping the fact that in the very decade of the twenties when the franchise was secured and when a liberal view of marriage ties had finally gained public acceptance that the vast majority of American women began to find social activism unattractive and to return to an ethic of domesticity as romantic and suffocating as any code of the high Victorian era. In fact the stereotype of femininity which became dominant in the popular culture of the thirties differed little from the stereotype of the Victorian lady except that the twentieth-century American woman had physical appetites which dictated that she could only know fulfillment by experiencing maternity and joyfully adapting to the exclusively feminine world of suburbia.[1]

To some historians and social analysts this paradox has seemed so puzzling that nothing short of a plot theory of history can explain this sudden alteration in what appeared to be the direction of social change. Betty Friedan, for instance, feels that the triumph of domesticity can only be accounted for by the recognition by capitalists that women could best serve the economy of abundance as passive consumers.[2] Yet her diagnosis does not take into account the fact that before the thirties women made the role of consumer an important one for social criticism through the organization of the National Consumers' League, a body which pioneered in legal and political campaigns in favor of state and federal welfare legislation. As the history of the League ably demonstrated between 1899, the year of its foundation, and the beginning of the New Deal welfare programs, consumers need not be passive victims of the capitalist system.

More recently historians of feminism have seen an underlying continuity behind the appearance of change in the social position of American women. Both Aileen Kraditor and William O'Neill have concluded that the remarkable stability of the bourgeois family in the twentieth century was the social fact which led to the frustration of all aspirations for change in the role and status of women.[3] Thus the reformers who made divorce and birth control acceptable in the early decades of the twentieth century put emphasis on the need to strengthen the family in a secular society. Both divorce and limitation of family size finally won popular acceptance when they were advocated as reforms which would allow the bourgeois family the flexibility necessary to survive the pressures of an upwardly mobile urban society rather than as reforms which would permit real changes in sexual behavior.[4] In the light of the evidence of historical demography we see the logic working for this kind of reform to preserve the family. Demographic study indicates that the duration of marriage unions was actually lengthening in the twentieth century as compared with earlier centuries such as the seventeenth, customarily regarded as a period of family stability. In fact, increased life expectancy in the twentieth century meant that fewer marriage partnerships were terminated after a short period by death; consequently, the sanctioning of divorce became a social necessity. There is thus no contradiction between the development of liberal attitudes toward the dissolution of marriage and the renewed stress on the value of maternity and domesticity for women. Divorce and birth control, both reforms which could have been advocated in terms opposed to female domesticity, actually won acceptance as measures to preserve the family and along with it female domesticity.

While historians are correct in emphasizing these underlying continuities in the history of American feminism between the Civil War and the 1930s, it is misleading to do so without drawing attention to the fact that women activists of the period represented a real change in feminine behavior. The failure of feminists to understand the significance of the intense social activism of women reformers during these years indicates that new ways of behaving do not necessarily evoke any new view of the female temperament. Though women of the stature of Jane Addams and Lillian Wald were actually wielding national power and influencing the decisions of the White House, neither they nor any of their contemporaries thought about adjusting the image of the female to this position of command. This failure to see women's activism for what it was, a real departure from women's traditional domesticity, indicates the controlling power of the stereotype of the female temperament which continued unaltered from the 1870s to the 1930s. Acquiescence in this control was indeed the major weakness in the ideology of feminism for the stereotype of the female personality was an essentially conservative one although women reformers coupled it with social innovation and occasionally with trenchant social criticism.

We see the controlling power of the stereotype of the female temperament most clearly in the thought of Jane Addams and Lillian Wald.[5] Both women were aggressive public campaigners who relished a good political fight and who hungered after power. Yet they claimed to be reformers in the name of specialized feminine perceptions of social injustice. These specialized perceptions came from women's innate passivity and from women's ability to empathize with the weak and dependent. Like all reformers with a program for action, Jane Addams and Lillian Wald believed they had found a social group who would bring a new, just social order into being, but theirs was a group defined by sex rather than by class. Lacking a clear class consciousness, they expected a sex group to be agents of social change because of the unique qualities with which they believed the feminine temperament was endowed. Because of these qualities women were capable of direct, intuitive awareness of social injustice exactly in the style of the abolitionists who had been fired for the antislavery crusade through direct intuitive perception of social sin. Just what it was in the psyche of a Jane Addams or a Lillian Wald which would permit empathy with the weak and dependent remains shrouded in mystery for the most assiduous biographer. Both women gave evidence from an early age of the capacity to create and dominate large organizations, and they moved naturally into a position of leadership in any area of reform which they took up, whether it be settlement work, child welfare legislation or the international peace movement.

Even though Jane Addams and Lillian Wald could not recognize their drive to power, their adoption of feminine intuition as a style of reform by which to come to grips with the problems of industrial cities is a puzzling choice. One expects tough-minded economic analysis from critics of industrial society. However, middle-class women reformers of their generation needed to find a basis for criticizing an exploitive economic system in which women of their class played no active part. It was for this reason that they were obliged to make such claims for the intuitive social power of the female temperament. They were encouraged in these claims by the dominant biological view of social evolution which did place great emphasis upon the evolutionary significance of biologically determined male and female temperaments. However, to base one's social criticism upon the idea that feminine intuition could both diagnose and direct social change was to tie one's identity as a social critic to acquiescence in the traditional stereotype of women. Further, to the extent that such women succeeded in gaining popular acceptance as reformers they were lending strength to the stereotype and helping to prepare the ground for the acceptance of another view of sexually specialized intellect, the neo-Freudian, romantic and conservative one, which began to gain acceptance in American culture in the twenties and the thirties.

In my study of American women who were both feminists and social critics in the post-Civil War era, two clearly distinct social types have emerged. The first is a borrowing from European culture, the type of the sage or prophetess who claimed access to hidden wisdom by virtue of feminine insights. The second is the type of the professional expert or the scientist, a social identity highly esteemed in American culture but sexually neutral. Jane Addams represents the best example of the Victorian sage to be found in American culture during her active public career from the 1890s to the 1930s. Florence Kelley, the organizer of the National Consumers' League and a kind of composite Sidney and Beatrice Webb for American industrial society, represents one of the best examples of the professional expert who took on the role of the social engineer. What is interesting about the two types is that the sage had great resonance for American popular culture and was celebrated in endless biographies, memoirs and eulogistic sketches.[6] Women who took on that role became great public figures, culture heroines known in households throughout the nation. But the woman as expert did not captivate the popular imagination and did not become a model of feminine excellence beyond a small circle of highly educated women of a single generation. Julia Lathrop, who was the pioneer strategist of the mental health movement, the innovator responsible for the juvenile court movement and the head of the first Federal Child Welfare Bureau which became the model for many New Deal welfare agencies, simply did not excite the faintest ripple of public attention during a lifetime exactly contemporaneous with Jane

Addams. Indeed this remarkable woman remained so anonymous despite a lifetime devoted to public service that Jane Addams wrote a biography of her so that she could serve as a model for future generations of American women.[7] The biography was little read and could not serve its purpose because Jane Addams lost the substance of this consummate political strategist's life in describing the empathetic and unaggressive woman heroine which the stereotype of female excellence required. Similarly Florence Kelley's biographer, Josephine Goldmark, was unable to preserve for future generations any of the fiery personality of this powerhouse of a woman.[8] The surface account of her lifetime devoted to the welfare of the industrial working class was accurately recorded. But the volcanic personality whose rages were so monumental that she could stamp out of a White House conference slamming the door in the face of Theodore Roosevelt is lost. Since women were supposed to be gentle, none of Mrs. Kelley's passion could come through the uncharacteristic calm imposed by her biographer. Thus the achievements of the experts were lost to subsequent generations and the significance of their actual behavior was completely misunderstood.

What survived for popular consumption was the woman reformer as sage and prophetess, the social type of which Jane Addams is the perfect exemplar. This survival led to an unfortunate association of critical perceptions of society with unquestioning acceptance of traditional views of the female psyche. It is the development of this type which we must understand if we want to comprehend how radical discontent could be expended in every social direction except the one which required questioning the stereotype of women.

The path to Jane Addams' identity as a sage lay through the experience of higher education and the recognition that she had access to learning of a scale and quality not available to preceding generations. The Addams family was involved in the abolition movement and important in local Republican politics and through these concerns became committed to equality with men in women's legal rights and educational opportunities. Daughters of the Addams family thus inherited a family tradition of reform without the corresponding obligation to business success which was imposed by such families on their sons. However, the standard curriculum for women's colleges like Rockford Seminary which Jane Addams attended entirely neglected the question of relevance for future vocational or intellectual purposes. Jane Addams was exposed at Rockford to the standard Victorian literary culture together with a high saturation of Protestant Christianity since the seminary's founder hoped to raise up a race of Christian women who could civilize the West.

The result of rigorous training in moral and aesthetic concerns was considerable disorientation when Jane Addams left college and began to try to define some social role in which her education could be put to use. Not only did her education fail to relate her in any significant way to the occupational structure of society, it had also trained her to be a moral agent in a society which expected middle-class women to be passive spectators and consumers. Two possible responses to this situation seem to have attracted the post-Civil War generation of college-educated women. The first was to withdraw to graduate study and acquire a respectable social role through professional training. Graduate school offered both escape from the family and the opportunity to enter a neutral social territory where the traditional rigidity of the American division of labor between men and women had not had time to establish itself. Those of an intellectual bent for graduate work seem to have found this adaptation a satisfactory one. It was the path to the social type of the woman expert. However, for those to whom graduate school was merely a strategy to escape from family discipline, only the second response was possible. Self-deception about an intellectual or professional career culminated in the standard Victorian ailment of emotional prostration. A minor illness took Jane Addams out of the Women's Medical College in Philadelphia in 1882 and kept her an invalid for over twelve months. Travel was of course the major therapy for such persistent nervous and emotional ailments, and it was while visiting London that Jane Addams began to develop the first signs of a nagging social conscience. In England the stereotypes of nativism could not inhibit perception of the sufferings of the London poor. The faces which stared back at the visitor to London's East End were not the faces of degenerate Irish or Poles, but English faces which could arouse the racially selective democratic feelings of young native Americans as no other sight could.[9]

Travel next suggested the idea of expatriation and the refinement of a literary education through involvement in European aristocratic culture. For a woman who had been trained to see herself as an heir to the abolitionist tradition of moral fervor, however, there could be no more than temporary dabbling in the expatriate life. Once she had recognized her common human ties with the urban poor, it was only a matter of time before she put the two styles of life together by visiting an immigrant ghetto in Chicago and espousing the lot of the common man now seen as the logical object of reforming zeal which an earlier generation had directed toward the Negro.

The consequences of the life style which Jane Addams pioneered and other educated women emulated are well known. In New York and Chicago, women were the first founders of settlement houses. They also were preponderant among settlement residents in Philadelphia, Boston and Cleveland. The initial impulse for this kind of feminine migration to the slums was not identification with the working class, as in the European settlement movement, but the recognition that there was a social cure for the neurotic ills of privileged young women in America because their ailments were socially induced. As Jane Addams and Ellen Starr put it when they were looking for a house in an immigrant ward of Chicago in 1889: moving to the ghetto was ". . . more for the benefit of the people who do it than for the other class. . . . Nervous people do not crave rest but activity of a certain kind."[10] By definition "nervous people" in need of releasing activity in American society were not men but women. Men were also discarded as irrelevant in the planning of Hull-House and other women's settlements because they were thought of as "less Christian" in spirit than women and motivated to action entirely by commercial rewards. It was thus as a consequence of an accurate perception of the problems of educated women in American society that middle-class women were brought into contact with the social problems of urban-industrial America. They were on location, settled and ready to become involved in urban problems just before the great depression of 1893–94 struck. Living in an urban slum that winter was the searing, unforgettable confrontation with social injustice which turned all of them into real critics of American society and obliterated their earlier concern with personal adjustment. But in forgetting the reasons for their presence in the urban slums women began to equate their recognition of social problems with special qualities of feminine insight. In *Democracy and Social Ethics* for instance, the work which was the most popular of Jane Addams' early writings on social problems, the culture of poverty is seen through the eyes of a middle-class woman visitor and the perception of the way American society exploited immigrants is made a feminine one. Exploiters are masculine and those who can see the true vision of a democratic society are women.[11]

Quite apart from the process of social selection which took women reformers to the city, there were good intellectual grounds for ascribing special qualities to the female intellect. These were to be found in the current interpretation of the significance of sex differences in the evolution of society. Jane Addams' papers show that she derived her views on this subject from three supposedly unimpeachable sources. She read Herbert Spencer's *Study of Sociology* of 1873 early in her career and accepted from it Spencer's view that the female psyche and mind were of special significance in the evolutionary process because of the innate feminine capacity to empathize with the weak. Once she had met Lester Ward at Hull-House in the decade of the 1890s, she accepted

Ward's assumption that the female was the prototype of the human being and the most highly evolved of the two sexes. In 1900 she met the Scottish biologist and sociologist Patrick Geddes whose *The Evolution of Sex* of 1889 was the major work in English by a biologist of repute on the evolutionary significance of sex differences. Geddes believed that from the smallest single-celled organism to man sex differences were tied to differences in cell metabolism which made female organisms passive and nurturing and male organisms warlike and aggressive. After she met Geddes, she added a natural bent of pacifism to women's special capacity for social insight and played her role as sage with confidence that it conformed to everything current biology and sociology had to say about the place of women in society.[12]

While she held to this traditional picture of women, however, Jane Addams had by 1900 arrived at some fundamental criticisms of American society. She recognized that political institutions which conformed to the classical theory of democracy were incapable of creating the kind of social equality which was central to the American democratic belief. She was convinced that traditional Puritan individualism was no guide to morality in an urban-industrial society. She saw that every social and political institution in America needed radical change if immigrants and workers were to participate in political decisions and receive the benefits of the American industrial economy to the same degree that native Americans did. She thought the family should be modified so that its members could not settle into a private domesticity which made them blind to social suffering outside the family circle; church and charitable institutions needed to be pried loose from adherence to the old Puritan economic ethic and negative morality; business corporations and trade unions needed to be less concerned with productivity and material rewards and more aware of human values; political parties needed to be reformed so that they could become more responsive to the needs and concerns of the urban immigrant. The tendency to violence in American life which she saw as the heritage of the need to coerce a slave population in the South must be eradicated if the divisions in industrial society were not to lead to class warfare. As a diagnosis of American social ills, this was not unimpressive. It was free from the usual Progressive concern with institutionalizing middle-class values. It was future oriented, ready to accept radical change and optimistic about the potential of the American city to become a genuinely creative, pluralistic community.[13]

One can say that important elements of radical discontent are present in this social criticism—an accurate diagnosis of the present and a creative, dynamizing view of the future. Contemporaries certainly thought so. In 1902 when Jane Addams published *Democracy and*

Social Ethics, the work that contained the major themes of her social criticism up to 1900, her mail ranged from appreciative notes from John Dewey and William James calling it "one of the great books of our time" to emotional letters from college students who said they found reading the book a religious experience which liberated them to be moral beings for the first time.[14]

What *Democracy and Social Ethics* lacked was a realistic perception of the social group who would be agents of desirable social change. To Jane Addams and women reformers of her generation, it seemed perfectly clear that women were the only people in America capable of bringing about a new order in which democracy would find social as well as political expression. As an organized force in politics, they would moralize and socialize a state which Jane Addams recognized was at present organized to protect and promote the interests of businessmen. Of even greater importance, women would be able to solve the problems of city government because the efficient management of urban affairs involved generalizing the skills of housekeeping which were exclusively feminine skills.

This celebration of women as makers of the future democratic society was a position from which there was no retreating as the suffrage agitation mounted. Indeed after 1900 the only modification of this feminist creed which Jane Addams made was to celebrate women's unique capacities for internationalism and the mediation of war. The woman as diplomat could settle the problems of world order as well as those of urban government. Such delusions are comic, but they are also very significant when entertained by minds with the range and scope for social analysis which Jane Addams certainly had.

They point to a predicament which was almost universal for middle-class American women of Jane Addams' generation. Intellectually they had to work within the tradition which saw women as civilizing and moralizing forces in society, a tradition given spurious scientific authority in evolutionary social thought. Yet within American society there was no naturally occurring social milieu in which these assumptions about the exclusive attributes of women could be seen for what they were. Women had to create the very institutions which were their vehicle for departure from middle-class feminine life, and in doing so they naturally duplicated existing assumptions about the sexes and their roles. Beatrice Webb remarked after visiting Hull-House that "the residents consist, in the main, of strong-minded energetic women, bustling about their various enterprises and professions, interspersed with earnest-faced self-subordinating and mild-mannered men who slide from room to room apologetically."[15] Since Beatrice Webb knew this model well in herself and Sidney, it is highly probable that the perception was accurate. In settlement houses women could find endless opportunities for social action but no way out of the prevailing romantic stereotypes of men and women as social beings. As social workers struggling to solve the problems of the poor in American cities, women met mostly businessmen–philanthropists and clergymen with wide social concerns. The businessmen could be disregarded as tainted by acquisitiveness and the profits of commercial exploitation. The clergymen were representatives of a religious tradition which had failed to recognize the superior moral qualities of women. Such men could not be accepted as moral or intellectual equals no matter how readily they wrote checks or served on community charities for they were distrusted as agents of a society which subordinated women for economic or religious purposes. Yet without seeing men and women as moral equals, women reformers could find no way out of the traditional stereotype of the female temperament; and they could not see themselves as they really were, notably aggressive, hard-working, independent, pragmatic and rational in every good cause but that of feminism.

The consequence of this failure to question traditional views of femininity meant that the genuine changes in behavior and the impact of women's social criticism were short-lived. On the other hand, the national eminence of the woman reformer as sage merely strengthened sterile romanticism in popular attitudes to women. In this way a generation of women who lived as rebels against middle-class mores was finally imprisoned by them. We see the limitations imposed by this imprisonment in the absence of thought about or concern for sexual liberty in the lives of two women reformers of national eminence always in search of social issues to explore. For them rejection of Victorian bourgeois and economic values was never accompanied by questioning of Victorian sexual stereotypes.

Nothing is more pathetic than the shocked incomprehension of Jane Addams and Lillian Wald when faced with a popularized version of Freudian thought towards the close of their lives. Each in writing the concluding chapters of her memoirs towards the end of the decade of the twenties tried to grapple with the problem of explaining how their intuitive female sage could be distinguished from Freud's irrational woman whose destiny is shaped by her biological nature.[16] They were powerless to deal with the assertion that their long careers as social reformers were merely evidence of failures in sexual adjustment because they had always accepted the romantic view of women as passive and irrational. This acceptance left them with no recourse when they were told their careers of activism represented deviance; for in terms of the stereotype of femininity which they had always accepted, they had been deviant. They had adopted a feminist ideology and a public identity which gave the widest possible currency to a modernized version of the romantic woman. They had acted very differently but had never understood the significance of the difference, much less reflected upon it until it was too late. Quite unwittingly they had helped to prepare a cultural climate ideally suited to the reception of Freudian ideas. Had they ever reflected on the significance of their behavior it is possible that with their superb talents for publicity and popular writing they could have dramatized some other model of feminine excellence besides the gentle, intuitive woman. Certainly they could have brought in question the negative image of the career woman emerging in the mass media of the thirties. As it was they were silent, and the mass media were left free to begin the commercial exploitation of the romantic female without a murmur of dissent from two women who had used the identity of the romantic sage for far more elevated social purposes.

NOTES

1. On this point see Andrew Sinclair, *The Better Half: The Emancipation of American Women* (New York, 1965).

2. Betty Friedan, *The Feminine Mystique* (New York, 1963).

3. See Aileen S. Kraditor, *Up From the Pedestal* (Chicago, 1968), and William L. O'Neill, *Divorce in the Progressive Era* (New Haven, 1967), and *Everyone was Brave: The Rise and Fall of Feminism in America* (Chicago, 1969).

4. See David M. Kennedy, *Birth Control in America: The Career of Margaret Sanger* (New Haven, 1970).

5. Jane Addams' thought on women's role as reformers is most readily available in her *Democracy and Social Ethics* (New York, 1902), *Newer Ideals of Peace* (New York, 1907), *The Long Road of Woman's Memory* (New York, 1916), and *Peace and Bread in Time of War* (New York, 1922). Her two volumes of autobiography are mostly concerned with the question of women's social role. See *Twenty Years at Hull House* (New York, 1910) and *The Second Twenty Years at Hull House* (New York, 1930). Lillian Wald's ideas on women's place in society are only available in print in her two volumes of autobiography, *The House on Henry Street* (New York, 1915), and *Windows on Henry Street* (Boston, 1934). Her speeches and addresses in the Lillian Wald Papers, New York Public Library are a valuable manuscript source for her thought on this question.

6. Winifred E. Wise, *Jane Addams of Hull House: A Biography* (New York, 1935), and R. L. Duffus, *Lillian Wald* (New York, 1953) are examples of the eulogistic biography.

7. Jane Addams, *My Friend Julia Lathrop* (New York, 1935).

8. Josephine Goldmark, *Impatient Crusader,* (University of Illinois Press, Urbana, 1953). See also Dorothy Blumberg, *Florence Kelley: The Making of a Social Pioneer* (New York, 1966).

9. My attention has been drawn to this by Allen F. Davis in his *Spearheads for Reform: The Social Settlements and the Progressive Movement, 1890–1914* (New York, 1967). See also Jane Addams, *Twenty Years at Hull-House,* 66–70.

10. Ellen G. Starr to Sarah A. Haldeman, Chicago, Feb. 23, 1889, Ellen G. Starr Papers, Sophia Smith Collection, Smith College Library.

11. See Jane Addams, *Democracy and Social Ethics,* 13–70, 137–77.

12. Herbert Spencer, *The Study of Sociology* (New York, 1873); Patrick Geddes and J. Arthur Thompson, *The Evolution of Sex* (London, 1889).

13. *Democracy and Social Ethics* was the first systematic statement of her social criticism. It drew on essays and speeches written entirely in the decade of the 1890s.

14. See William James to Jane Addams, New Hampshire, Sept. 17, 1902; Elizabeth D. Stebbins to Jane Addams, New York, July 18, 1909, both letters in the Jane Addams Correspondence, Swarthmore College Peace Collection.

15. *Beatrice Webb's American Diary* (ed. D.A. Shannon, Madison, 1963), 108.

16. See Jane Addams, *Second Twenty Years at Hull House,* 196–99; also Jane Addams, "A Feminist Physician Speaks," a review of *Modern Woman and Sex* by Rachelle S. Yarros, M.D., *Survey,* LXX, 2, (Feb., 1934), 59. See Lillian D. Wald, *Windows on Henry Street,* 5–11, 322.

IV

The Illusion of Equality

The paradox of women's position in American society became profoundly evident in the twentieth century. The suffrage victory in 1920, increased numbers of women in industry, and women's new sexual freedom enhanced their status. Yet the promise of emancipation has remained largely unfulfilled. As Max Lerner wrote in the 1950s, "In theory, in law, and to a great extent in fact, the American woman has the freedom to compete with men on equal terms: but psychically and socially she is caught in a society still dominated by masculine power and standards."[1] Women found that gaining the vote did not ensure an effective bloc of women voters, armed with the power and determination to champion women's interests. In spite of new job opportunities for women, employers maintained differences in men's and women's salaries. By the mid-1960s, radicals commonly referred to the "illusion" of equality, and a new generation of feminists boldly attacked what they termed the "sexist" attitudes that have remained the last barrier to women's emancipation.

The many women's organizations that had been active during the Progressive era continued the struggle for reform during the 1920s. The General Federation of Women's Clubs (GFWC), National Consumers League (NCL), and National Women's Trade Union League (NWTUL) joined with the League of Women Voters (LWV), which carried on the work of the National American Woman Suffrage Association, to bring pressure on the Congress and the state legislatures in relation to a wide range of matters of concern to women. In 1920, they established the Women's Joint Congressional Committee (WJCC) "as a clearing house for the federal legislative efforts of the affiliated organizations."[2] The most conspicuous success of the WJCC was the short-lived Sheppard–Towner bill, designed to ensure protection to mothers and children through federal aid to maternal and health care programs. Both the NCL, under the direction of Florence Kelley, and the NWTUL continued their campaign in the interest of working women throughout the decade. Little tangible success marked their efforts until the economic crisis of the 1930s generated social legislation on behalf of workers in general. As Clarke A. Chambers makes clear in "The Campaign For Women's Rights," such activity typified the way in which organized women carried on the Progressive spirit in the 1920s, and it kept alive reform issues that became part of the New Deal agenda.

Toward the end of the 1920s, these efforts began to wane. Women's ranks were divided by the issue of an equal rights amendment, which became the sole focus of the Woman's Party. Although the League of Women Voters carried on a widespread effort in the states against discriminatory legislation, its leaders—like those of the NCL and the NWTUL—believed that the amendment would endanger legislation protecting women workers, which they had struggled so vigorously to see implemented.[3] Aside from internal division, the conservative mood of the decade sapped the strength of women's organizations. Membership in the LWV never reached that of the NAWSA, and it began to drop sharply after 1924. The preoccupation with a constitutional amendment prohibiting child labor strained the resources of the NCL. The GFWC grew increasingly conservative, and the work of the WJCC succumbed to the charge of Communist influence, something that plagued women's efforts throughout the 1920s.[4]

The focus on women in the 1920s shifted greatly in ways which feminists of the time deplored. The changes in social life and behavior that characterized the decade—the oft-noted "revolution in manners and morals"—shifted emphasis toward the individual and away from the society, from a concern for social justice to one glorifying individual gratification. This represented a major shift in the history of women in American life. Trends in illegitimacy and premarital intercourse at the turn of the century signaled the change in behavior.[5] By the 1920s the alteration of sexual norms was clearly apparent.[6] The decade witnessed not only a new emphasis upon sexuality which permeated popular culture, but also the emergence of women's demands for equality of sexual pleasure, both inside and outside of marriage. In "The American Woman's Pre-World War I Freedom in Manners and Morals," James R. McGovern discusses the nature of these changes and presents clear evidence that a radical shift in sexual behavior and attitudes appeared among urban Americans well before the end of the Great War.

The "new woman" who emerged in the 1920s was neither the creation of the prewar feminists nor their successors, who remained active during the decade. She was a product of the new moral climate accentuated by post-war prosperity. The stylish Gibson Girl of the 1890s gave way to the flapper who seemed the very essence of modernity. With her bobbed hair and short skirts, she represented a direct challenge to traditional conceptions of the ideal woman. Relating boyishness to female sexuality she threatened traditional sex roles.[7] Although homosexuality did assume faddish proportions among bohemians during the 1920s, the androgenous flapper was in fact a monument to heterosexuality.

Most women were neither bohemians nor flappers, but in the 1920s they were enthralled with the technological magic represented by the nation's number-one glamour industry, the motion pictures.[8] The media increasingly created idols for young women, and the movies assumed tremendous importance.[9] The sweet innocents portrayed by Mary Pickford continued to be screened, but increasingly the sexually explicit "vamp" dominated the silver screen. In "Projection of a New Womanhood," Mary P. Ryan shows the ways in which the young movie industry vividly exploited "the flapper's personality complete with her characteristic gestures, energy, and activism." Such films reflected the times and gave role models to young women. They became the most consistent purveyors of the flapper image and the idea of woman as a sexual predator.

Stripped of its traditional functions, the twentieth-century family became primarily concerned with serving the personalities of its members. Its main function was psychological. "Marriage was in a sense displacing the family itself; a husband and wife now referred colloquially to their 'marriage', implying not so much a fixed social institution as a special arrangement between two people who had 'fallen in love.' "[10] Held together solely by the tenuous bonds of personal relationships, marriages dissolved with increasing rapidity. Divorces, which had reached 100,000 per year in 1914, passed the 200,000 mark by 1929.[11] Many women with a degree of economic independence were unwilling to tolerate unhappy marriages. At the same time, the decline in the birth rate indicated that couples deliberately chose to limit their families in order to maintain their standard of living. Children were no longer an economic asset as they were in the nineteenth century; rather, they had become a liability.

The emphasis on personal fulfillment that emerged in the 1920s altered the ideals and aspirations of American women. The hard times of the Great Depression dampened the divorce rate as couples chose security above personal happiness and a confused society tried to reaffirm traditional sex roles in the face of economic crisis and war.[12] In the decade after World War II, prosperity made large families possible, and women accepted the cult of domesticity—"the feminine mystique"—which idealized the affluent suburban housewife devoted to home and family. *The Ideal Marriage,* which appeared in the United States in 1931, charted the course to sexual bliss; the emphasis on home economics and the "scientific" home rationalized domestic drudgery. Personal fulfillment escaped women during these years, just as political power had remained beyond their grasp since the 1920s. The suburban wife was sexually discontented.[13] Her role as housewife expanded in the consumption-oriented society of the 1950s, and the number of hours spent doing housework and related tasks actually increased for unemployed women.[14]

In the late 1950s this picture began to change. Sexual norms became increasingly permissive and alternative modes of child raising and marital relations gained popularity. In the early 1970s, a best-selling book touted the psychological benefits of "open marriage," which stripped marital relationships of the burdensome responsibilities of the past. The new moral climate of the 1960s not only permitted, but almost demanded, explicit self-analysis and open discussion of sexual matters. This climate led two sociologists to comment: "If there has been a sexual revolution . . . it is in terms of frankness about sex and the freedom to discuss it."[15]

There can be no doubt, however, that behavior was also changing. Aided by "the pill," introduced in 1961, and by liberalized abortion statutes following the Supreme Court decision in the early 1970s, the birth rate plummeted to the point at which the population is barely replenishing itself.[16] Although marriage has been more popular than ever in American history, there has also been an increasing number of single women. The age of first marriage has gone up, and the divorce rate has reached staggering proportions. In the first six months of 1970, new divorces exceeded the number granted during the previous decade; in some jurisdictions, such as Marin County, California, they outnumbered legal marriages. At the same time, sexual activity of women has increased and has become more varied and more pleasurable. Studies conducted in the early 1970s indicate that "Today's teenagers from 15 to 19 are at least twice as likely to have had coital experience as the Kinsey women born during the 1920s."[17] Marital sex has become more satisfying for women, and the traditional gulf between the premarital and extramarital experiences of men and women has closed dramatically.[18]

The changes in attitudes and behavior in recent years have been of immense importance to American women since they indicate the downfall of the hypocritical double standard and a more equitable distribution of power in sexual and marital relationships. It is easy to overemphasize the "sexual revolution" and place excessive importance on its more bizarre elements, which are in some ways detrimental to the interest of women.[19] Donald E. Carns focuses on the relationship between altered behavior and traditional values in "Identity, Deviance and Change in Conventional Settings: The Case of the 'Sexual Revolution.'" In contrast to others who have written on this subject,[20] Carns is primarily concerned with the development of sexual identity in adolescent women. Carns sees the experience of men and women converging with little actual increase in promiscuity. Women clearly no longer value virginity as they once did. Premarital sexual relations are associated with the experimental tenor of this era and are followed by "a kind of *latency* period" in the mid-teens. The most common post-adolescent sexual behavior involves relationships that generally take the form of trial marriages, in which sexual activity is associated with affection and the expectation of marriage.

From 1920 until the present the most important change in the lives of American women has been in the area of employment. It has produced widespread social and political consequences.[21] Although the percentage of working women has risen continuously throughout the twentieth century, most women have been segregated in low-paying and routine "women's jobs." New Deal legislation provided further protection for women in the areas of hours and wages, but both the National Industrial Recovery Act and the Fair Labor Standards Act tolerated wage differentials and set minimums for women at lower rates than those for men.

After 1939, wartime production drew thirteen million women into the ranks of labor, and for the first time married women exceeded single women in the working population. Although industry dropped one out of every four women employed at the end of the war, the number of working women has grown yearly since 1947; in 1970, women constituted 40 percent of the American labor force. As one might have suspected from the war experience, the greatest post-war increase in employment occurred among married women and the age distribution of women workers shifted dramatically.

Even though they have played an increasingly important role in the American economy, women continue to be plagued by unequal pay and job segregation. It was not until the 1960s that they were able to force government action on these problems. Although competition from women as a cheap labor source generated solid support for equal pay from the union movement by the 1940s, legislation on this subject failed in 1945 and again in 1947. Women's continuing concern with the issue of equal pay led to the Women's Bureau Conference on Equal Pay and to the inclusion of the demand in the Republican and Democratic platforms of the early 1950s. However, little was done until President John F. Kennedy appointed the Commission on the Status of Women in 1961. The Commission's report focused attention on the problem of equal pay and recommended reform in the areas of job discrimination, federal social security insurance, tax law, and federal and state labor law regulating hours, wages, and night work. The Commission also concerned itself with other differences in the treatment of men and women, and with services provided for women in education, counseling, job training, and day care centers. Although this report led to the passage of the Equal Pay Act in 1963 and the addition of Title VII to the Civil Rights Act of 1964 (prohibiting employment discrimination by the federal government), a careful student of the matter could argue that "the sexual division of labor is so nearly complete that it is difficult to find comparable jobs of the two sexes to make a definitive study [of wage discrimination]."[22]

The sexual division of labor remains the crucial economic problem facing women today and accounts for the eagerness with which most women activists have embraced the Equal Rights Amendment (ERA). However, in "The Paradox of Progress" William H. Chafe emphasizes the social and political consequences of changes that have taken place in the economic role of American women in the past half-century. Focusing upon the dialectic between behavioral and attitudinal shifts that comprises the process of social change, Chafe argues that World War II proved to be a crucial watershed in the history of American women because it precipitated a rapid increase in the number of married women employed in the economy and a radical upward shift in the average age of employed women. Once established, this pattern affected all of the crucial relationships in women's lives and undermined traditional attitudes toward sex roles. Ironically, the decade of the 1950s created the seedbed for the flowering of feminism in the 1960s. "Perhaps," Chafe writes, "the most important pre-condition for the revival of feminism . . . was the amount of change which had already occurred in women's lives."

The rebirth of feminism in the 1960s remains the most enduring and ultimately most radical of the by-products of that much-disturbed decade.[23] Explanation of this phenomenon is at once simple and complex. Few would deny that women are discriminated against in most salient aspects of American life; however, the historian must explain why long-term conditions generated a specific set of responses among certain groups of people at the precise time when they were able to erect the structural apparatus of a social movement. Even Chafe's explanation seems exceedingly abstract and fails to account for the grievances specific to groups of women who actually constructed the women's liberation movement.

Although it has gained support from women in all segments of the society, the women's liberation movement emerged from professionally active upper-middle-class women who, during the mid-1960s, found themselves under a form of intense psychological strain that has been termed "relative depravation."[24] Such women did not perceive their situation in actual terms; they perceived it relative to the situation of men of their class whose career patterns they used to evaluate their own lives. The conditions of the 1960s encouraged professional women with long-term political commitments and aspiring professional women in college, who were disillusioned in very special ways by the student civil rights and peace movements, to generate a revival of feminism. Contemporary feminism differs in many ways from its nineteenth-century predecessor. At times, it seems to lack the necessary coherence to be considered a social movement. But the popularity of traditional women's issues today is immense. Although the majority of American women refuse to accept the direction of the movement, few could be called anti-feminist, and a growing majority favor all efforts to enhance women's status in American society.[25]

The feminist movement split asunder on the rock of racial prejudice in the early part of this century, and the relation of black women to the contemporary movement remains a problem. Although they tend to be more favorable than white women to the leading feminist issues, particularly in the economic realm, black women face role conflicts that whites have been able to transcend.[26] Focusing primarily on the struggle for racial dignity, black women have consciously accepted traditional supportive roles in the interest of reversing the history of pathological destruction that white racism has brought down upon black men. Black women have thus for the most part thrown in their lot with the efforts to enhance the status of black men, and they have viewed with suspicion feminist efforts that seemed inimical to this goal. To a large degree, black women have remained outside the movement, a fact which Pauli Murray, a black civil rights lawyer, successful academician, and one of the founders of the National Organization for Women (NOW), deplores. Murray contends that the issue is one of human rights—women must "transcend the racial barrier" and form an alliance beginning with educated, middle-class women of both races.

According to Jean E. Friedman's analysis of the movement in "Contemporary Feminism: Theories and Practice," there are presently three major groups of feminists: privatists, who hope to achieve solutions within the context of their personal lives; moderates, who actively work toward political and legal changes; and radicals, who have reintroduced consideration of basic questions concerning sex and the social order.[27] The radicals have been heavily influenced by Marxist writings and to Friedman seem to be moving toward a truly feminist ideology. However, Friedman believes that today the most pressing need for women is that they understand the nature of their traditional roles and the ways in which those roles have hindered self-realization. American women must comprehend the paradoxical nature of their existence in a society in which equality remains an illusion.

NOTES

1. Max Lerner, *America as a Civilization* (New York: Simon and Schuster, 1957), p. 604.

2. Dorothy E. Johnson, "Organized Women as Lobbyists in the 1920's," *Capitol Studies* 1 (Spring 1972): 43.

3. J. Stanley Lemons, *The Woman Citizen: Social Feminism in the 1920s* (Urbana: University of Illinois Press, 1973), studies these conflicts in great detail. Cf. William L. O'Neill, *Everyone Was Brave: A History of Feminism in America* (Chicago: Quadrangle Books, 1971); and William H. Chafe, *The American Woman: Her Changing Social, Economic and Political Role* (New York: Oxford University Press, 1972).

4. It should not be forgotten that the critics of women reformers during the 1920s were often women, such as those of the National Association of the Daughters of the American Revolution and the Woman Patriot Publishing Company, which grew out of the National Association Opposed to Woman Suffrage.

5. Daniel Scott Smith, "The Dating of the American Sexual Revolution: Evidence and Interpretation," in *The American Family in Social Historical Perspective,* Michael Gordon, ed. (New York: St. Martin's Press, 1973), pp. 321–35.

6. David Kennedy, *Birth Control in America: The Career of Margaret Sanger* (New Haven: Yale University Press, 1970). Although Freud was commonly referred to in popular literature, the actual effect of *his* psychological ideas was limited. *See* Geoffrey H. Steere, "Freudianism and Child-Rearing in the Twenties," *American Quarterly* 20 (Winter 1968): 759–65.

7. Kenneth A. Yellis, "Prosperity's Child: Some Thoughts on the Flapper," *American Quarterly* 21 (Spring 1969): 44–64.

8. Molly Haskell, *From Reverence to Rape: The Treatment of Women in the Movies* (New York: Holt, Rinehart and Winston, 1973).

9. Leo Lowenthal, "Biographies in Popular Magazines," in *Radio Research, 1942–43,* Paul F. Lazarsfeld and Frank N. Stanton, eds. (New York: Duell, Sloan and Pearce, 1944), pp. 507–48, and Fred I. Greenstein "New Light on Changing

American Values: A Forgotten Body of Survey Data," *Social Forces* 42 (May 1964): 441–50, both show the increased importance of movie stars to children.

10. Rowland Berthoff, *An Unsettled People: Social Order and Disorder in American History* (New York: Harper & Row, 1971), p. 403. *See also* William Ogburn and Clark Tibbitts, "The Family and Its Functions," *Recent Social Trends in the United States,* vol. 1 (New York: McGraw-Hill, 1933), pp. 661–79; John Sirjamaki, *The American Family in the Twentieth Century* (Cambridge, Mass.: Harvard University Press, 1953); William J. Goode, *World Revolution and Family Patterns* (Glencoe, Ill.: Free Press, 1963).

11. William E. Leuchtenburg, *The Perils of Prosperity, 1914–32* (Chicago: The University of Chicago Press, 1958), p. 162.

12. *See* Caroline Bird, *The Invisible Scar* (New York: David McKay Co., 1966); Peter Gariel Filenre, *Him/Her/Self: Sex Roles in Modern America* (New York: Harcourt Brace Jovanovich, 1975); and Warren Susman, ed., *Culture and Commitment 1929–1945* (New York: George Braziller, 1973).

13. Lerner, *America as a Civilization,* pp. 609–10.

14. Joann Vanek, "Time Spent in Housework," *Scientific American* 231 (Nov. 1974); Ruth Schwartz Cowan, "A Case Study of Technological and Social Change: The Washing Machine and the Working Wife," in *Clio's Consciousness Raised,* Mary Hartman and Lois W. Banner, eds. (New York: Harper & Row, 1974), pp. 245–53; Cowan, "Household Technology and Social Change: A Case Study of Technological Determinism," *Technology and Culture,* forthcoming; John Kenneth Galbraith, *Economics and the Public Purpose* (Boston: Houghton Mifflin, 1973).

15. Edwin O. Smigel and Rita Seiden, "The Decline and Fall of the Double Standard," *The Annals* 376 (March 1968): 7–17.

16. A valuable fund of information on changes in all aspects of women's lives is provided by Abbott L. Ferriss, *Indicators of Trends in the Status of American Women* (New York: Russell Sage Foundation, 1971).

17. Smith, "The Dating of the American Sexual Revolution," p. 329.

18. Morton Hunt, *Sexual Behavior in the 1970s* (New York: Playboy Press, 1974). On married women's sexual satisfaction, the evidence is mixed. Clearly, intercourse is more prolonged and sexual techniques are more varied than thirty years ago, and, consequently, orgasm is experienced more often. At the same time, women seem to be telling investigators that they would like to have sexual relations more often than they are presently having them, in contrast to the responses of women previously studied.

19. Anselma Dell'Olio, "The Sexual Revolution Wasn't Our War" in *The First Ms. Reader,* Francine Klagsbrun, ed. (New York: Warner Communications Co., 1973), raises some interesting questions. Most studies also show "swingers" (of both sexes) to be "largely politically conservative, homebodies with few outside interests, middle income with middle education and technical occupations in large corporations." (James R. McIntosh, *Perspectives on Marginality: Understanding Deviance* [Boston: Allyn and Bacon, 1974], p. 66.)

20. *See* three excellent works by Ira L. Reiss: *The Social Context of Premarital Sexual Permissiveness* (New York: Holt, Rinehart and Winston, 1967); "How and Why America's Sex Standards are Changing," *Trans-Action* 5 (March 1968): 26–32; and *Heterosexual Relationships: Inside and Outside of Marriage* (Morristown, N.J.: General Learning Press, 1973).

21. This is most fully detailed in Chafe, *The American Woman*. *See also* Robert W. Smuts, *Women and Work in America* (New York: Columbia University Press, 1959); and Robert O. Blood, "Long Range Causes and Consequences of the Employment of Married Women," *Journal of Marriage and the Family* 27 (February 1965): 43–47.

22. Carl Degler, "Revolution Without Ideology: The Changing Place of Women in America," *Daedalus* (Spring 1964): 403. *See also* Edward Gross, "Plus Ca Change . . . The Sexual Structure of Occupations Over Time," *Social Problems* 16 (Fall 1968): 198–208; Caroline Bird, *Born Female: The High Cost of Keeping Women Down* (New York: David McKay, 1968).

23. Cf. Filene, *Him/Her/Self*, pp. 203–40; Gerda Lerner, "The Feminists: A Second Look," *Columbia Forum* 13 (Fall 1970); Judith Hole and Ellen Levine, *Rebirth of Feminism* (New York: Quadrangle Books, 1971).

24. Jo Freeman, *The Politics of Women's Liberation* (New York: David McKay Co., 1975).

25. Jessie Bernard, *Women, Wives, Mothers: Values and Opinions* (Chicago: Aldine Publishing Co., 1975), summarizes the most recent research on these matters.

26. Cf. Linda J.M. LaRue, "Black Liberation and Women's Lib," *Trans-Action* 8 (Nov.–Dec. 1970): 59–64; Cellestine Ware, *Woman Power: The Movement For Women's Liberation* (New York: Tower Publications, 1970); Cellestine Ware, "The Black Family and Feminism: A Conversation with Eleanor Holmes Norton," in *The First Ms. Reader*, Klagsbrun, ed., pp. 36–41; and Catharine Stimpson, "Thy Neighbors Wife, Thy Neighbors Servants: Women's Liberation and Black Civil Rights," in *Woman in a Sexist Society: Studies in Power and Powerlessness*, Vivian Gornick and Barbara Moran, eds. (New York: Basic Books, 1971).

27. A useful anthology sampling mainly radical feminist views is *Sisterhood Is Powerful*, Robin Morgan, ed. (New York: Vintage Books, 1970).

18

The Campaign
for Women's Rights in the 1920's

Clarke A. Chambers

The children of the nation were always the special concern of humanitarian reformers in the 1920's. Especially were the children of the poor the object of programs aimed at liberation from premature and excessive labor, at the enlargement of opportunity through educational, recreational, and welfare measures. If efforts had often been thwarted, the results of reform activity were nevertheless substantial. If the decade had proved uncongenial to statutory regulation, at least the advances in other areas gave cause for authentic satisfaction.

The hope that another disadvantaged group in the population—working women—could win the protection of the state against unreasonable exploitation proved less valid. Two lines of ameliorative action had taken form during the Progressive Era. One pointed toward the organization of women workers into labor unions in order that they might gain, through union, the strength to bargain collectively with employers. It was for this end that the Women's Trade Union League, with the nominal and rhetorical support of the AFL, strove with zeal if not with very large success. The second path led toward legislation, particularly at the state level of government, which would set standards of maximum hours, minimum wages, and decent conditions for women employees. Here notable advances had been won during the culminating

From *Seedtime of Reform: American Social Service and Social Action, 1918–1933*
(Minneapolis: University of Minnesota Press, 1963), pp. 61–83. Copyright © 1963 by the
University of Minnesota. Reprinted by permission.

years of the Progressive Era just before the nation's entrance into the Great War.

The regulation of hours and conditions had come first, the Supreme Court in the classic *Muller* v. *Oregon* case in 1908 upholding such legislation as an entirely reasonable exercise of the state's police power to promote the health, morality, and welfare of the community. Minimum-wage legislation came a bit later, but in the five years before America went to war, eleven states invoked the power to set a floor under wages earned by women. The argument that women, as mothers of the race, required the special protection of the community acting through government presumably applied as logically to the one area, minimum wages, as to the other, maximum hours. The Supreme Court did not see the parallel quite as clearly as the reformers did, but in 1917—as noted earlier—it had sustained by a tie vote an affirmative ruling of the Oregon Supreme Court. Following this *Stettler* v. *O'Hara* decision, three other states, Puerto Rico, and the federal Congress acting for the District of Columbia had established special commissions with the power to set minimum-wage levels in accordance with subjective criteria of health and morality.

Wartime demands had brought tens of thousands of women into the labor force, where they enjoyed relatively high wages and augmented opportunity, if never equal pay for equal work with men, or equal opportunity to enter certain crafts and trades, restricted to men as often by custom and prejudice as by physical requirements. The Woman in Industry Service had proved competent, however, in winning for women special positions of economic influence not previously enjoyed. Women continued, in the postwar decade, to join the labor force, often to supplement the husband's income when it was insufficient to support the family at a decent level, until 1929 over ten million women were gainfully employed where but eight million so labored at the end of the war. The ratio of working women to all women of working age in the nation remained roughly constant—approximately one to five.

With a total labor force pushing fifty million by the end of the decade, women constituted approximately one-fifth of all those employed. Millions of girls and married women worked in the service trades, of course, as waitresses or hotel domestics or telephone operators, as stenographers and as retail clerks; millions more were employed in textile mills, in the garment trades, and on the assembly lines of light industries, many of them, like the household appliance industries, new in the 1920s. The proportion of women working in a particular area of the economy changed but slightly within the decade: about a third of all working women were employed in domestic or personal service, a quarter in manufacturing, a fifth in agriculture, and a tenth in trade and transportation.

Motives for entering the labor force remained much as they had been before the war—to earn at least partial financial independence, to escape from household drudgery, to save up a little extra money before marriage, to find companionship and a more satisfying career than housewifery or spinsterhood offered, and above all necessity. Careful studies of the female working force made during the 1920's indicated that most women sought gainful employment outside the home because they had no alternative—they had to find a job or be thrown onto charity. Many working women were widows or victims of desertion; others were wives of chronically sick or unemployed husbands, or were married to men who could not command wages sufficiently high to supply the family's basic needs. The old notion that women worked for "pin money" was dispelled by studies that proved that most working women earned "the whole or a necessary part of the family income." In any case there was no wage differential between those who worked for the "extras" of life and those who drudged from sheer necessity. A very substantial number were not only wives but mothers of young children as well, driven out of the home into the labor market by the pressures of existence. One analysis, made in mid-decade at the very peak of prosperity, concluded that "the mother works because she has to work, and unless some other method of raising the family income is devised she is in industry to stay."[1] Another study of 728 working mothers in Philadelphia, made by Gwendolyn S. Hughes under the auspices of the Seybert Institution and the graduate department of Bryn Mawr College, indicated that 89 per cent worked from economic necessity—some to meet emergencies, sickness, or unemployment; more to meet regular household expenses.[2]

Although the Women's Trade Union League continued to seek better conditions for women workers through unionization and stepped up these organizational efforts toward the end of the decade, many reformers drew the lesson from long and often humiliating experience that only the rigid enforcement of regulative legislation could be counted on to alleviate the grievances which sprang from the excessive exploitation of the labor of women. Women workers for the most part were lacking in skill; they had few resources to fall back upon other than their availability for cheap labor; the organization of women into trade unions was "a slow and arduous process requiring long periods of time."[3] Frances Perkins added the salient observation, derived from hard factual analysis of female labor in the state of New York, that nearly three-quarters of all women factory workers were employed in plants with fewer than fifty workers; in these small plants the unionization of employees, never easy, was particularly difficult; and management in these small factories could rarely afford the luxury of enlightened or "scientific" policies.[4]

Some studies stressed the objective causes of exploitation and proposed specific remedies; other surveys stressed the subjective costs paid by working women and ultimately by society itself. Those who strained, day after day, month after month, on the assembly line or in sweated industries, before the loom or the sewing machine, could best testify as to what the pace of machine labor involved. Asked by the instructor of a course in remedial English, established by the Women's Trade Union League for immigrant working girls, to write compositions on their factory experience, the class responded with essays later compiled and edited for publication. Complaining of constant fatigue and depression, the girls noted that even the machines on which they toiled were rested and oiled; why, then, could not the same concern be shown for the health and vigor of the workers, whose energies were sapped often beyond repair. From experience they had learned the costs in health and character that excessive hours of labor under conditions of the stretchout and speedup exacted. From their evening classes, apparently, they had picked up a bit of basic economics as well. Maximum-hour legislation, they argued, would spread employment; minimum-wage legislation would increase purchasing power; enlarged leisure and purchasing power would promote sound prosperity throughout the entire economy. Rarely was the pragmatic argument for maximum hours, minimum wages, and full employment put more cogently in that decade.[5]

Confident that their cause was just and that their arguments were irrefutable, encouraged by the sense of organic community which the war had fostered, the reformers set out to consolidate their gains and advance into new frontiers of social action. The immediate goals were the achievement for women workers of an eight-hour day and a forty-eight-hour week, one day of rest in seven, and a prohibition on night work in every state in the Union. Massachusetts led the way with the passage of a forty-eight-hour bill in April 1919. Exemptions there were—of chambermaids, stenographers, and domestic servants—but the Consumers' League and the Women's Trade Union League were generally pleased. Their pleasure was short-lived. The pattern in New York soon proved different.

In New York, the Women's Joint Legislative Conference was able to win a nine-hour day and a fifty-four-hour week for a limited number of women workers in 1919, but subsequent attempts to broaden the coverage and to reduce the maxima were blocked by the Republican-dominated State Assembly. Probably in no other state was there quite such a vigorous proponent of protective labor legislation as Governor Alfred E. Smith, but neither his endorsement nor favorable action by the State Senate was ever sufficient to override the negative of the lower house. Up to Albany from New York City the women went to lobby, only to be rebuffed by arguments of the conservative speaker of the Assembly, Thaddeus Sweet, and others that labor legislation would increase costs and drive industry from the state. Florence Kelley might argue that the "orderly processes of the law" were to be preferred to "clumsy, costly, painful" strikes, but few seemed to fear that the alternative of direct action would be resorted to. "More leisure and more money women must have unless the public health and morals are to suffer irreparably," she protested; but the times seemed prosperous, and to the comfortable and complacent an enlargement of government power appeared not only inappropriate, but downright wicked.[6] Moreover, was not the liberty of employer and employee to bargain and make contracts a sacred freedom? Far from winning new gains, the reform groups had to throw all their resources into a struggle to block repeal of the prohibition on night work in some industries. Distraught and giddy from months of frustrating toil, the WTUL solemnly recorded in the minutes of the executive board, toward the end of the session in 1921, a bit of doggerel which labeled their foes as "tools" and "fools," as "bad" and "mad":

> They're overfed,
> And anti-red,
> And rave around like loons.
> They wave the flag,
> And chew the rag,
> But all of them are prunes,
> Prunes, prunes!
> Yes, all of them are prunes![7]

In 1924, Molly Dewson, formerly of the Consumers' League but now civic secretary of the Women's City Club of New York (whose vice president was Eleanor Roosevelt), carried through a survey of women workers to test their attitudes toward maximum-hour regulations. She reported her findings to bureaus of the state government and to the legislature—a substantial majority of working women desired a forty-eight-hour week, even if a cut in weekly income were involved. A bill put forward in 1926 was set aside and a study of the issue proposed in its place. When the special Industrial Survey Commission reported back, its recommendations included not only a forty-eight-hour week, but minimum wages and equal pay for equal work as well. With these recommendations before it, the state legislature reduced the maximum from fifty-four hours to fifty-one and adjourned.[8]

New York, not Massachusetts, set the pace for the nation. Here and there, partial gains were achieved. As often as not the gains were illusory or temporary as in Minnesota, for example, where a fifty-four-hour law was set aside by the State Supreme Court on a technicality; efforts to amend the bill to make it constitutional were unavailing. Over and over legislative committees and governors, ladies' clubs and associations of social workers were told that "Physical debility follows fatigue. Laxity of moral fibre follows physical debility."[9] But the nation's attention was focused on other issues; the nation's energies were consumed by other affairs. From the end of the war to the election of 1932, only two states added maximum-hour legislation where none existed before; substantial improvements of the regulations were won in twelve of the forty states which had statutes on the books by 1918.

At mid-decade, a special subcommittee of the WTUL, charged with re-evaluating the league's entire legislative program, acknowledged broad and increasing "dissatisfaction with legislation for women as a means to the end for which the Women's Trade Union League" was organized. Political action had become a "slow and painful process" of achieving reform. Perhaps it was time to consolidate forces and place emphasis again on the league's alternative line of action—the organization of women into unions. The board, after prolonged and bitter debate, finally accepted the recommendation to close its Chicago office and invest legislative moneys in one central office in the nation's capital, and acted at the same time to reopen the unionization campaign;[10] this activity will be traced in a later chapter.

If the women's reform associations had been able to hold the line on maximum-hour legislation and win a few slight gains from time to time, no such good fortune attended the parallel movement for minimum-wage statutes. The Consumers' League, the Trade Union League, and the American Association for Labor Legislation had seized the initiative during the years preceding America's entrance in World War I in coordinating the drive for state minimum-wage legislation. They had joined to persuade Massachusetts, in 1912, and eight more states the following year to establish minimum-wage commissions, with permissive rather than mandatory authority. By 1918, eleven states plus the District of Columbia and by 1923 fifteen states in all had regulations of some sort. There the matter rested. That moderate but nonetheless significant benefits had derived from this body of legislation the reform groups knew. The procedures of enforcement were often clumsy and rested as frequently upon the sanction of good will and enlightened public opinion as upon the coercive power of the state; but levels of wages for women had generally been raised, and the minima had not become maxima as some trade union spokesmen had feared. Ten years of experience, it was believed, gave ample evidence that higher wages had a clear bearing on health, moral decency, and industrial efficiency. Furthermore, it was argued, the extension of the principle was justified on the premise that employers properly should bear the costs that society otherwise had to assume in the form of charitable relief to those who broke down from ill health, fatigue, and insufficient income. The minimum wage was a means to prevent the delinquency and disease which, if unprevented, society would have to cure. To the employers it was said that regulations lessened labor turnover, increased worker morale and efficiency; no one, save the marginal, unscrupulous, and unfair producer, had anything to lose.

There was, of course, overt opposition to the extension of minimum-wage regulations. A move in Ohio by the Council of Women and Children in Industry (composed of representatives of the Consumers' League, the Women's Trade Union League, the Urban League, the YWCA, and the WCTU) was successfully blocked by the Ohio Manufacturers' Association. More often, however, the drive for minimum wages was diverted or stopped by apathy and unconcern, and by a widespread feeling that such legislation was of doubtful constitutionality. The Supreme Court of the state of Oregon had upheld minimum-wage legislation in two parallel cases, back in 1914, on the ground that the wages of women workers were a legitimate concern of the state in seeking to improve the health, morals, and general welfare of the community. But the tie vote by which the United States Supreme Court in 1917 sustained the Oregon decision certainly was no ringing mandate to encourage other states to act.

Then, in 1921, the constitutionality of the District of Columbia's minimum-wage act was challenged. The Consumers' League rushed to the defense. Molly Dewson was retained to prepare the factual material for the case, while Felix Frankfurter volunteered his services as counsel. Florence Kelley sensed at once that the crucial battle was at hand. Dropping everything else for the moment, she threw herself into the task of finding the money to underwrite the legal and research costs and to publicize the cause. There is "Merry Hell in general," wrote Mrs. Kelley to Adolf Berle, Jr., describing the office of the Consumers' League as the brief was finally being assembled. "Even Felix up in Cambridge is jumping high jumps twice daily," she added in a postscript.[11] In November 1922 the District Court of Appeals, by a vote of two to one, found the law null and void. The *Adkins* case was taken on appeal at once to the Supreme Court. But Florence Kelley was not hopeful. "There is no short road to Justice and Mercy in this Republic," she wrote dejectedly to an old friend.[12]

Mrs. Kelley's forebodings proved accurate. By five to three (Justice Brandeis again abstaining), the highest tribunal knocked down the District's act, sounding the "death knell" (as Felix Frankfurter said later in life) for all kinds of social legislation and inhibiting the launching of new welfare experiments.[13] Frankfurter had argued that the statute Congress had passed, sitting as the "state legislature" for the District of Columbia, fell well within the boundary of what was reasonable; it was not "arbitrary, wanton, or spoilative." That wages for women workers were considered to have a clear bearing upon health and morality was evidenced by many regulations of several states and by the action of nearly every industrial nation.

To George Sutherland, who had been recently added to the Supreme Court by President Harding, it was not all that clear. Drawing upon the ancient and honorable tenets of nineteenth-century individualism, Sutherland announced for the majority its conviction that minimum-wage legislation constituted arbitrary interference of the state in the private affairs of citizens competent to use their inviolable liberties in such ways as to promote the well-being and progress of society. The freedom of employers and employees to make a contract clearly was covered by the due process clause of the Fifth Amendment. As for the unanimous decision of the court in the Oregon case, the premises on which it rested no longer applied, for women, he argued, had gained a kind of equality with men that rendered special legislative protection for women obsolete. He cited the Nineteenth Amendment as proof that differences in civil status between men and women had reached the "vanishing point." The law was, in light of these historic changes, "a naked, arbitrary exercise of power."

To William Howard Taft, new chief justice, Sutherland's logic was deficient. "The Nineteenth Amendment did not change the physical strength or limitations of women upon which the decision in *Muller* v. *Oregon* rests," he wrote in dissent. Oliver Wendell Holmes, Jr., made a more elaborate attack upon the majority decision. "Freedom of contract" was nowhere to be found in the Constitution. The state had for generations legitimately restricted individual freedom; if legislatures deemed it essential that the government set minimum wages as well as maximum hours, the courts were obliged to accept their judgment as reasonable unless there were overwhelming evidence to the contrary. "It will need more than the Nineteenth Amendment to convince me that there are no differences between men and women or that legislation cannot take those differences into account." Irony and indignation availeth not; Sutherland spoke for the majority of five, and that was that.[14] Mary Dewson, who had labored for months on the case, recalled later in life the bitter conclusion of her legal comrade, Felix Frankfurter: "Molly, you must learn that if the U.S. Supreme Court says a red rose is green, it is green. That's final."[15]

John Kirby, in a cartoon for the *New York World,* depicted a gracious Justice Sutherland handing a scroll to a shabbily-dressed and dejected woman worker and saying: "This decision affirms your constitutional right to starve." Other comments were no more subtle. Even the usually mild-mannered and courtly Mr. Gompers announced that the court had "usurped" authority nowhere granted to it in the Constitution, and concluded that the "brutality of the majority decision can beget nothing but wrath." A more careful critic, Henry R. Seager, noted that five men had overridden three other justices, majorities of two houses of Congress and thirteen state legislatures, thirteen governors, the President of the United States, and many previous courts. It was left to the good gray feminist, Florence Kelley, to comment that not a single woman had participated in the judicial process at any point. Francis Bowes Sayre concluded that the traditional judicial practice of finding in favor of a law in the absence of substantial legal doubt had been violated by the majority. The decision, he said, indicated that the Supreme Court was arrogating to itself a veto power not unlike that exercised by a House of Lords. Governor Louis F. Hart of the state of Washington labeled the decision as infamous as the Dred Scott ruling and stated categorically that any business that could not pay a decent wage was not a desirable business. Governor Walter M. Pierce from Oregon (home of so many pioneer measures of social legislation) was more temperate, but perhaps more to the point: "It is neither humane nor wise socially to allow the untrained to become public charges or worse through lack of a living wage. It is detrimental to the future of individuals as well as the nation to permit child labor under improper conditions. Since the untrained and young cannot hope to stand up under the competition and demands of industry, only government had so far been able to afford them protection." Father John A. Ryan, one of the very first propagandists for the living wage principle, particularly in its application to women workers, blamed the court's ruling upon the persistence of nineteenth-century utilitarianism with its extravagant insistence upon the individual's freedom to do what he wished as long as the freedom of other autonomous individuals was not thereby limited; that such a philosophy was irrelevant in an industrial era, that its capricious application led to inhumane practices, was clear to him as to many others.[16]

Florence Kelley had been through enough battles to know that verbal protest alone was never sufficient to carry the day: the heavier artillery of action would have to be unloosed. Invitations were sent to reform association leaders and to state officials to confer jointly on how best to meet the emergency. On 20 April 1923—Felix Frankfurter and Florence Kelley taking the lead—the delegates gathered in New York City to deliberate upon strategy. Jesse C. Adkins, chairman of the District of Columbia Minimum Wage Board, was there; so were representatives of law-enforcement agencies in this area of social legislation from Wisconsin, Washington, North Dakota, Minnesota, Massachusetts, and New York. Representatives were sent by all the major reform associations—the Consumers' League, of course, the Women's Trade Union League, the League of Women Voters, the National Catholic Welfare Association and the National Council of Catholic Women, the Child Labor Committee, the American Association for Labor Legislation, and the WCTU. The chief of the Women's Bureau, Mary Anderson, arrived; so too did Mary Van Kleeck, now with the Russell Sage Foundation; and Paul Kellogg of the *Survey*.

Felix Frankfurter led the discussion. There was little hope that the court would reverse itself in the near future, he observed. Justice Brandeis' vote could be counted on, of course, in cases on which he would not feel obliged to abstain; but otherwise the lines were drawn rather sharply for the moment. Sutherland was clearly hopeless; and as for Justice Butler, "He is a farmer, and spent from twenty to thirty years of his life in working up a practice [in law]. This is very confining and limited." His major recommendation, therefore, was to revise state minimum-wage legislation along the permissive lines of Massachusetts' law rather than try to incorporate mandatory provisions. In the meantime, he reminded the.conference, the court had acted on the District of Columbia statute and nothing else. The "continued aggressive enforcement" of all state laws was absolutely essential. The court had always recognized local differences and until it specifically rejected state laws, the presumption that they were constitutional stood. The analysis and the conclusions were generally shared by the other delegates. F. A. Duxbury, chairman of Minnesota's Industrial Commission, resented, however, what seemed to him slurs on the integrity of Sutherland and Butler; respect for the law and for the courts was called for, even by those who could not agree with the decision. Father Ryan, who had joined Frankfurter in chiding Sutherland and Butler, replied that he had intended no disrespect, that he had merely wished to point out that the five justices were living in the eighteenth century. If any feelings were hurt, he was sorry but he felt it was hardly appropriate for him, above all others, to concur in any notion of judicial infallibility.

Out of the conference came no formal resolution, but only a general agreement. State laws should be enforced with vigor, as always. The suggestion that New York press for a permissive law, on the Massachusetts model, was endorsed. Further study of the economic and legal aspects of the decision would be made, and at once.[17]

Not satisfied with the inconclusive results of the April meeting, the WTUL called one of its own in mid-May, on the eve of the annual Conference of Social Work. Many of the groups represented at the April gathering sent delegates to this one as well. Mary Anderson set a tone of objective analysis, presenting evidence of the disparity in bargaining power that women workers suffered under, of the sub-standard wages that existed in states and in industries not covered by wage minima, and of the obvious relation between decent wages and community health. The presentation was forceful, if objective, but added little to the conclusions stated so cogently, although with so little practical effect, by Frankfurter and Dewson in the Adkins case. Dean Acheson was present to offer advice similar to Frankfurter's several weeks earlier—the states should continue to enforce their own minimum-wage laws; all interested groups should work unceasingly for a redefinition of due process of law along lines that would permit and encourage a reasonable extension of the state's police power. Other delegates were less patient. To wait for the Supreme Court to change its mind on what constituted reasonable regulations and proper procedures was to postpone indefinitely the enforcement of sound measures. Why not amend the Constitution, asked Molly Dewson, to authorize federal regulation of women's wages? Why so delimited a proposal, replied Maud Swartz for the Trade Union League? Why not work for an amendment which would grant broad powers to regulate conditions of labor, of men workers as of women? Elisabeth Christman and Rose Schneiderman, on the other hand, despairing of both judicial self-reform and the amendment procedure, demanded an energetic campaign to organize women into unions as the only valid course. Still others suggested that perhaps the time had come to limit the powers of the high tribunal to review both state and federal legislation.[18]

Divided counsel merely deepened the sense of demoralization. More than two decades of crusading had taught the reformers how to lobby, how to get around recalcitrant employers, how to by-pass stubborn legislative committees, how to stir up public support, how to argue the rule of reason before reasonable courts. It had not taught them how to react to hostile court decisions from which there was no appeal. For the moment they had lost both momentum and equilibrium. John R. Commons, accepting election as president of the Consumers' League in the autumn of 1923, summed it up exactly: "You find yourselves baffled and your work, at least an essential part of it, brought to a standstill by the recent adverse decisions of the Supreme Court" bearing upon child-labor and minimum-wage legislation.[19] Florence Kelley put it more picturesquely: "Truly we are like a semi-paralyzed centipede with its legs all moving at different rates of speed, if at all, and how few legs moving!"[20] In the middle years of the decade, she fell into the closing salutation when writing to intimate friends "Yours, *still* hopefully." But throughout 1923 and 1924, and on into 1925 when the child-labor amendment failed to win ratification, there was little cause for hopefulness. Reporting to the Board of Directors of the Consumers' League in October 1923, Jeanette Rankin, field secretary for the league in Illinois, reported that the "total legislative harvest" for that year was "a law adopting a state flower!"[21] And two years later, with reform still in eclipse, a Seattle lawyer confessed his discouragement to Mrs. Kelley: "the tide is running out now and all we can do is hold fast to our moorings until the tide turns."[22]

Mrs. Kelley was not about to accept the Supreme Court's negative actions as final and irrevocable. Other obstacles had yielded; the court could be circumvented or brought to its senses. The task was clear—to modernize the eighteenth-century Constitution in such ways as to make it possible to meet the new industrial demands of an urban civilization. Until the Constitution was transformed, and until the "court that interprets the Constitution" was modernized, it was "purely academic" to discuss industrial legislation.[23] The goal was clear enough, but not the means. Some advised an amendment authorizing Congress to reenact by a two-thirds majority any federal statute found to be unconstitutional by the court. Others would require a two-thirds majority of the court to rule a state or federal legislative enactment null and void. (At various times the ante was raised to seven and eight judges, until finally a unanimous court was suggested.) A more widely favored proposal was to grant to Congress, by the amendment procedure, broad authority to act in the large arena of social legislation. The legalists tended to prefer persuading the courts, by trying one case after another, to adopt a more permissive attitude toward legislative experiments; judicial self-restraint, not coercive action against the court, was the more efficacious path, they insisted. A few hardy souls suggested enlarging the court to fifteen members, or eighteen; but with Harding and then Coolidge in the White House, what a later generation would know as "packing" the court did not win wide support among reformers who were disrespectful enough of the court as then constituted but were not foolhardy. Whatever means were explored, even Florence Kelley knew they were "far easier to name than to draft."[24]

For a while Mrs. Kelley leaned toward an amendment requiring a seven to two majority to find state and federal legislation unconstitutional, but her closest legal adviser, Felix Frankfurter, would have none of it. "The 7 to 2 proposal will not come off," he advised, "and at the rate at which the Sutherlands and the Butlers are being appointed to the Court, it wouldn't do any good if it did."[25] This proposal might have the backing of Senator Borah and Father Ryan, but it was "utterly hopeless" to expect that either a bill or an amendment so providing could ever be passed. It was unwise, in any case, to seek such a deceptively simple "mechanical remedy" for a complex legal dilemma. The point rather, Frankfurter continued, was to improve the quality of the court itself.[26] Roscoe Pound concurred. The amendment procedure was clumsy; "legislative revision of judicial action" was inadvisable. Ultimately the only proper means of securing the court's approval for social and industrial legislation, without jeopardizing other rights, was to persuade the justices to make a broader and more flexible interpretation of the due process of law provision and the police power. He recommended popular agitation for court reform, however, as one way to bring about "a better judicial frame of mind."[27] Zechariah Chafee added one final caveat—reformers should not forget, in their desire to limit property rights, that legislative bodies often limit personal rights; if a seven to two majority were required to set aside a law, a minority of three could block the unconstitutionality of laws subversive of civil rights.[28]

Agreement upon a single viable course of action was not to be had. The inadvisability of restricting the court's powers came to be abundantly evident. To wait for the court to change its mind seemed futile. In the meantime, as Florence Kelley noted, women and children remained exposed to exploitative actions of unscrupulous employers.[29] A move to win agreement on a strategy of assault upon the court, in July 1924, was abortive.[30] Reformers by that time were focusing their energies upon the child-labor amendment and upon La Follette's crusade for the presidency. The court issue was relevant enough, there was just no way to bring the court to its senses without jeopardizing the equilibrium of government and the security of individual rights. Another battle had been lost, but not before the need for judicial self-restraint had been recognized by this handful of rebels. Almost every legal and political argument of the great court fight in 1937 was anticipated back in 1923 and 1924. Ultimately the issue was resolved as Frankfurter, Pound, Chafee, Freund, and Acheson had recommended—not by statute, not by amendment, but by the addition of new personnel to the court dedicated to a broader interpretation of social welfare and willing to accept legislative action as legitimate unless obviously unconstitutional beyond all reasonable doubt. The frontal assault upon the wisdom—and even, at times, the integrity—of the court may have helped to clarify the issues and thus served to prepare the way for the constitutional revolution that began in 1937.

As for practical and immediate achievements, there were few. The court continued on its path, undeflected by the feeble efforts of the critics. "Don't hurry away from the scene of battle," pleaded Florence Kelley to Molly Dewson in 1924. "So long as there is a *glimmering* chance of usefulness, that's the place to be."[31] Three years later, Mrs. Kelley confided to John R. Commons that their function should be study, research, publicity until the times should change: "Keeping the light on is probably the best contribution that we can make where there is now Stygian darkness."[32]

The candle was kept lit, and was set upon a hill. It was no floodlight or searchlight as long as the mood of normalcy prevailed, but it burned persistently. The motto of the Consumers' League continued to be implemented—"Investigate, Record, Agitate." Throughout the remainder of the decade, the league regularly remained in touch with state officials desirous of enforcing industrial minima. Effective regulation, however, all but collapsed. The voluntary, permissive arrangement in Massachusetts won partial advances for limited numbers of women workers but never more than that. And, at that, Massachusetts led the nation. Arizona's law was struck down by the Supreme Court in 1925, Arkansas' in 1927; local courts followed suit in Kansas and Puerto Rico; in Texas and Nebraska the laws were repealed; in Minnesota the attorney general ruled that its law was no longer enforceable. As late as June 1936, the United States Supreme Court in *Morehead* v. *Tipaldo* ruled that the *Adkins* decision was still controlling, this in negation of a 1933 New York State fair-wage law. Not until 1937 was the *Adkins* rule explicitly overridden.

Just as the Children's Bureau under Julia Lathrop and Grace Abbott was the coordinating agency of federal government in the field of child welfare, so the Women's Bureau under Mary Anderson played a similar role in parallel fields. Its central commitment was to the national community's obligation through government to protect the women of the land for the general good of society. With no regulatory laws to administer, it relied entirely upon "fact finding and fact furnishing" to achieve its ends. "Every movement making for reform needs a reservoir of reliable data upon which to draw and by which to be guided," an official publication of the Women's Bureau declared.[33] Through research and publication, speeches and reports, and sponsorship of conferences, and through cooperation with state labor bureaus and with voluntary associations, its influence was extended to every section of the nation. When the occasion demanded, it could call out a host of allies: the Women's Trade Union League, the Consumers' League, the League of Women Voters, the WCTU, the YWCA, the PTA, the General Federation of Women's Clubs, the American Association of University Women, church and labor union groups. These associations had been formed into a loose alliance in the Women's Joint Congressional Committee, the clearinghouse and coordinating federation which crusaded for maternal and infant health programs, the regulation of child labor, adequate appropriations for the Children's and Women's bureaus, welfare legislation for the District of Columbia, social hygiene, and public health. Mrs. Maud Wood Park, president of the League of Women Voters from 1920 to 1924 and Belle Sherwin, its president from 1924 to 1934, were among the committee's most effective and loyal leaders, but every other member group could also be counted upon to work with Grace Abbott and Mary Anderson within government for common objectives.

Of the making of committees, of course, there was no end; and committee meetings and resolutions can never be taken for effective action. With the best of intentions, women reformers often assembled determined to strike a blow for welfare only to play out a ritualistic role of protest. One woman reformer, long active in the WTUL, once wrote to a friend about the quality of committee work and rhetoric: "I was trying to *show* a dear old Boston lady how a rich man's *do-nothing* son was a worse tramp than the *other* tramps—'Oh Mrs. Faxon, I don't believe you mean that.'—'Yes, I do.'—'O,' she says, 'I've heard people talk on committees like that!'—Now my family says whenever I *get to* talking—'Now don't talk like a committee!' "[34]

There was a good deal of committee talk in the 1920's, particularly when the National Woman's party, a stridently feminist group that had fought for the Nineteenth Amendment, proposed still another amendment to the federal Constitution designed to remove all legal discriminations relating to sex. The proposed amendment took several forms during the decade, but the intent of its original phrasing persisted: "Men and women shall have equal rights throughout the United States and every place subject to its jurisdiction." Put forward by ladies drawn primarily from the wealthy and professional classes, the proposed amendment was viewed at once by a vast majority of women reformers as a measure subversive of all protective and welfare legislation. Florence Kelley, herself a suffragette and feminist, would have nothing to do with a measure that proposed to establish complete "legal equality of the sexes," when it was clear, on the face of it, that because of the special sexual functions of women they could not be afforded absolute equality of treatment without placing in jeopardy their hard-won legal right to special protection.[35] It would be "insanity," she wrote to Newton Baker, to follow the lead of Alice Paul and the Woman's party down a path that would utterly destroy maximum hours and minimum wages, mothers' pensions, and maternity insurance.[36] The proposal, moreover, was legally ambiguous: no one was really against "equal rights," Mary Anderson later recalled of the struggle, but what did "equal" mean and what really constituted "rights"?[37] For a generation women had benefitted from legislation designed to protect them from "untrammeled exploitation," wrote Dean Acheson to Ethel Smith. "All this, to my mind, is now threatened by this sweeping prohibition of unnamed inequalities and disabilities." The courts were likely to rule, he warned, "that this new-won equality guarantees to women all the intolerable and antisocial conditions which their brothers in industry now enjoy."[38] What of the status of laws of desertion and nonsupport, queried Florence Kelley? What of the rules of illegitimacy, seduction, and rape? What of conscription in time of war? "Will husbands need to continue to support their wives?"[39] A special conference of women's groups, in early December 1921, arranged by Florence Kelley, concluded with Alice Paul's announcement that despite the fears of the reformers that, even if the amendment did not pass Congress, its agitation would imperil the whole movement for social legislation, the Woman's party was determined to press for its enactment and ratification.

From this point forward the dispute became increasingly embittered. Alice Hamilton set down her indignation in a draft letter to one of the "equal rights" proponents: "I could not help comparing you as you sat there, sheltered, safe, beautifully guarded against even the ugliness of life, with the women for whom you demand 'freedom of contract.' " Laundry workers, textile workers, "The great army of waitresses and hotel chambermaids, unorganized, utterly ignorant of ways of making their grievances known, working long hours and living wretchedly" would be left unprotected if the amendment carried. A sweeping amendment was not the proper means for removing the discriminations and legal disabilities of sex.[40] The main business of the Women's Industrial Conference, called by the Women's Bureau in January 1923, was interrupted by altercations over the amendment; the conference in January of 1926 was all but broken up by this hotly disputed issue. Sarah Conboy of the AFL fired a parting shot by publicly expressing her wish that the Woman's party ladies might be afforded the opportunity of working in mine and factory so they could learn first hand the problems of working women. Mabel Leslie reported to the Trade Union League that the Woman's party members were "merely theoretical ultra-feminists who [did] not have to work for a living."[41]

The squabble was of no particular significance—the proposed amendment never had a chance of serious consideration—except that it illustrates the kind of irrelevant wrangle which so often engaged the social reformers during the twenties. Their energies were often dissipated in countering charges of radicalism and subversion, and in this instance charges of antifeminism. The thousands of reform-hours consumed in fruitless and rancorous debate with the Woman's party represented time the reformers would have preferred to invest in other pursuits. Year after year, Mary Anderson recorded bitterly in her reminiscences, reform associations "had to lay aside the work they were doing to improve conditions for women and spend their time combating the equal rights amendment."[42]

Less spectacular but of surpassing significance was the workers' educational movement which was so often linked to the reform activities of women's associations in these years. The WTUL had pioneered during the years before the war in training potential trade union leaders in a program that Margaret Dreier Robins inaugurated in Chicago. Arrangements had been made for young working women to enroll as special students at Northwestern University and in the Chicago School of Civics and Philanthropy. Of the forty working girls from seventeen different trades who enjoyed formal course work from 1913 until the program was discontinued in 1926, nearly three-quarters remained active in trade union leadership, a record which the league took as justification of the time and money it had invested in the enterprise. The difficulty of integrating young working women, who were so often of recent immigrant origin and who so rarely had formal educational training, into university classes (even when conducted by such sympathetic professors as Paul Douglas) tended to vitiate the experiment, however, and this particular form of workers' education was never widely adopted.

Established in April of 1921, the Workers' Educational Bureau set out to stimulate and coordinate educational efforts of all sorts. Chaired by James H. Maurer, a functionary of the Socialist party and president of the Pennsylvania Federation of Labor, the bureau drew as well upon the diverse talents of such typical reform leaders as Fannia M. Cohn, of the International Ladies' Garment Workers' Union and the Trade Union League; John Brophy of the United Mine Workers and Abraham Epstein, then secretary of the labor education committee of the Pennsylvania Federation of Labor. Through the Workers' Educational Bureau and through the Brookwood Labor College which it helped to sponsor, the promotion of the ideas of industrial unionism and of political action by labor was achieved. Generally "leftist" in its leanings, the Brookwood Labor College, directed by A. J. Muste, trained a number of young trade union officials who would later contribute substantially to the formation of the CIO.

The major effort for the education of women workers came at the Bryn Mawr summer school, opened first in 1921 on the instigation of Mary Anderson, Hilda Smith, and Dr. M. Carey Thomas, president of the college. Hilda Smith, who later headed up workers' education in the WPA, was named the summer school's director. Raised in a devout Episcopalian household, Hilda Smith turned very early in her life to a career of social service. A graduate of Bryn Mawr in 1910, she had worked summers in settlement camps and had gone on to do casework with the Girls' Friendly Society and to take courses at the New York School of Philanthropy before returning to her alma mater as dean of the college in 1919. Under Miss Smith's direction from 1921 to 1934, the Bryn Mawr School for Working Women drew its students from the trade union movement, from local units of the WTUL and, in the South where trade unionism was unknown, from the YWCA. Here the students received courses in economics, government, the history of the labor movement, remedial social legislation, the causes and cures of unemployment, trade union procedures, public speaking, and composition. That the sessions offered a lively opportunity for curious young women is attested to by the mixture of ethnic and religious groups that composed the student body and by the excellence of its faculty which included outstanding experts like Paul Douglas, Alice Henry, Broadus Mitchell, Carter Goodrich, Colston Warne, Mark Starr, and Stephen Raushenbush. Dedicated to such objectives as widening the influence of the trade union movement, training the students in "clear thinking," stimulating in them "an active and continued interest in the problems of [the] economic order," and promoting "the coming social reconstruction," the Bryn Mawr school made a major contribution to the elaboration of concepts and leadership in the social reform movement.[43] The school had immediate practical consequences as was evidenced by the successful move on the part of the students to organize college employees and to win for them an eight-hour day not only during the summer session but during the regular academic year as well.[44]

The significance of the Bryn Mawr School for Working Women and similar programs conducted at Barnard (1927–1934), the Vineyard Shore School for Women Workers in Industry (1929–1934), and the Brookwood Labor College is difficult to measure. It is fair to suggest, however, that they kept alive a commitment to trade union activity;

they trained many young men and women who were to become union and political leaders of some note during the depression decade; they kindled the aspirations of many young people in times of moral slump; they kept open the path of purposeful social change. Eleanor Roosevelt summed it up at a banquet honoring Dr. M. Carey Thomas, whose initiative had been crucial in the establishment of the Bryn Mawr school: If the New Deal were to win through to higher levels of life, the people must participate intelligently and constructively in social affairs. It was to this end that worker education had been directed, she said, toward giving "people the tools so that they [could] work out their own salvation wisely and well."[45] In so doing the workers' education movement contributed to the larger movement for reform.

Together, proponents of industrial minima, particularly for women and children, enlarged the rationale for legislative action, until by the end of the decade the philosophy of New Deal action in this arena had been elaborated in nearly every detail. Research notes of John R. Commons, made sometime in the mid-1920's, included an observation of Lord Northington's: "Necessitous men are not, truly speaking, free men, but, to answer to present exigency, will submit to any terms that the crafty may impose upon them."[46] The idea could hardly claim originality, but in the United States it did not, until the interwar era, receive much notice or elaboration. It came to be basic to every consideration by liberals whose central commitment was still to the enlargement of individual opportunity and freedom. Necessitous men, insecure men, men made anxious by low wages, uncertain employment, long hours at labor, and arbitrary industrial discipline were truly not free men. The establishment of industrial minima, of measures of social security broadly conceived, it followed, was essential to human liberty.

On the heels of this simple conclusion came another axiom—society, through government, had an obligation to force industry to bear its just burden of responsibility for community welfare. If industry paid substandard wages, argued Ethel M. Johnson in 1927, society would somehow in some way have to make up the difference. It might be through "hospitals and dispensaries to care for women who are broken down in health because they did not earn enough to permit them sufficient wholesome food and suitable living arrangements." Or it might be through charitable relief. A minimum wage assessed the burden upon industry where it belonged.[47] If floors under wages could be set by law or administrative ruling as a proper charge against industry, then it could be left to collective bargaining by unions to win living wages above that level.[48] Unless workers, particularly women workers, enjoyed these minimum guarantees, they could not build up reserves for sickness or unemployment. A woman employed at "oppressive" levels, below the minimum, thereby became a "liability rather than an asset to the community," and a burden upon society.[49]

Over and over the point was hammered home—industrial minima were required not alone as humanitarian considerations or as charity but as measures essential to the over-all long-run efficiency of industry, to community health and welfare, and to social stability and orderly progress. The New York Consumers' League offered as its slogan for 1927 "Social Justice Is the Best Safeguard against Social Disorder"; while Florence Kelley, commenting on the violent textile strikes of 1929, insisted that the only alternative to industrial disorder and social strife was "peaceful progress" through legislation.[50]

It was perhaps Newton Baker who best summarized the need for social action to remedy the grievances associated with intense industrialization. Given the growing impersonality of all society, the sanctions of civilization were not as easily applied as once they were. The role of voluntary associations, such as the Consumers' League, was to "investigate, record, agitate" in order that men of good will might act with the knowledge of the consequences of their behavior, while the law coerced the "recalcitrants." The league and its allies could show the way for society to accomplish "on a large and collective scale, in a collective way, that which we so delighted to do as individuals under simpler conditions."[51]

The New Deal drew heavily and specifically upon these concepts, which had grown out of progressivism and had been tempered in the 1920's. The depression afforded the occasion for their implementation, because economic crisis overrode most other considerations in 1933. The National Recovery Administration prohibited child labor, and encouraged codes of labor standards governing hours, wages, and conditions for both women and men workers. When the NRA was broken, the industrial minima were rewritten in the Fair Labor Standards Act of 1938; and this time the Supreme Court concurred. The contribution of liberal reform in the 1920's had been to keep alive the progressive objectives, and then to modify them, extend them, and elaborate a rationale which, under the pressure of emergency, was incorporated as part of the New Deal consensus and program.

NOTES

1. Helen Glenn Tyson, "Mothers Who Earn," *Survey*, 67:5 (1 December 1926), pp. 275–279.

2. Nelle Swartz, review of *Mothers in Industry*, in *Survey*, 67:6 (15 December 1926), pp. 400–401.

3. Resolution in *Proceedings* (1924), pp. 336–337, WTUL, Box 15.

4. Frances Perkins, "Do Women in Industry Need Special Protection? Yes," *Survey*, 55:10 (15 February 1926), pp. 529–531.

5. Monthly Labor Bulletin of Massachusetts WTUL (January 1928), in WTUL Local Bulletins (Radcliffe), Box 1. Box 3, in same collection, contains comments of factory girls to an investigator of the Connecticut Consumers' League.

6. Florence Kelley, "The Inescapable Dilemma," *Survey*, 41:25 (22 March 1919), p. 885.

7. Executive Board of the New York WTUL, Minutes (6 June 1921), in WTUL (Radcliffe), Box 2.

8. The stories in Massachusetts and New York may be traced in WTUL, Box 15; NCL, Box 20; Dewson Papers (F. D. R. Library), Box 17.

9. Dr. George W. Webster quoted in "The Woman's Work Day," *Survey*, 46:4 (23 April 1921), p. 121.

10. Report of Rose Schneiderman, Julia S. O'Connor, and Matilda Lindsay (8 November 1925), WTUL, Box 3.

11. Florence Kelley to Adolf A. Berle, Jr. (31 January 1923), NCL, Box 8.

12. Florence Kelley to Mildred Chadsey (8 March 1923), NCL, Box 11.

13. Felix Frankfurter, *Felix Frankfurter Reminisces* (New York: Reynal, 1960), pp. 101–104.

14. Felix Frankfurter and Mary R. Dewson, *District of Columbia Minimum Wage Cases* (New York: Steinberg, 1923); *Adkins* v. *Children's Hospital*, 261 U.S. 525 (1923).

15. Mary R. Dewson to Isador Lubin (April 1957), Dewson Papers (F. D. R. Library), General Correspondence, Box 18.

16. "The Minimum Wage—What Next?" *Survey*, 50:4 (15 May 1923), pp. 215–222, 256–258, 263; Francis B. Sayres, "The Minimum Wage Decision," *Survey*, 50:3 (1 May 1923), pp. 150–151, 164, 172; Florence Kelley to Mrs. John Blair (1 May 1923), NCL, Box 10.

17. Typescript of Stenographic Report of Minimum Wage Conference (20 April 1923), NCL, Box 10.

18. Mimeographed Report on Conference in Tilton Papers, Box 3; Press Releases, WTUL, Box 25; Correspondence, WTUL, Box 2; Florence Kelley to Edward P. Costigan (31 May 1923), NCL, Box 10.

19. John R. Commons, Notes for Speech (9 November 1923), NCL, Box 8.

20. Florence Kelley to Amy G. Maher (17 March 1923), NCL, Box 11.

21. Jeanette Rankin, Report to Executive Board (25 October 1923), NCL, Box 8.

22. James A. Haight to Florence Kelley (19 December 1925), NCL, Box 11.

23. "Highlights of a Speech Made by Florence Kelley in 1923," in Massachusetts Consumers' League (Radcliffe), Drawer 1.

24. Florence Kelley to Board of Directors (12 June 1923), NCL, Box 11.

25. Felix Frankfurter to Florence Kelley (19 October 1923), NCL, Box 10.

26. Felix Frankfurter to Florence Kelley (25 October 1925), NCL, Box 10.

27. Roscoe Pound to Florence Kelley (22 October 1923), NCL, Box 10.

28. Zechariah Chafee to John R. Commons (1 April 1924), NCL, Box 11. See also Florence Kelley's correspondence, 1923–1924, with Charles Beard, Ernst Freund, Charles Warren, Ethel Smith, Newton D. Baker, Edward P. Costigan, NCL, Boxes 10 and 11.

29. Florence Kelley to Felix Frankfurter (25 June 1924), NCL, Box 11.

30. Correspondence in regard to conference (1 July 1924) that broke up with no agreement having been reached, NCL, Box 11.

31. Florence Kelley to "Dear Sister Dewson" (8 April 1924), NCL, Box 8.

32. Florence Kelley to John R. Commons (13 April 1927), NCL, Box 8.

33. Women's Bureau, *Fact Finding with the Women's Bureau* (Bulletin 84, 1931).

34. Mrs. Peake Faxon[?] to Leonora O'Reilly (no date, c. 1919), O'Reilly Papers (Radcliffe), Box 7.

35. Florence Kelley, "The New Woman's Party," *Survey*, 45:23 (5 March 1921), pp. 827–828.

36. Florence Kelley to Newton D. Baker (3 June 1921), NCL, Box 13.

37. Mary Anderson, *Woman at Work: The Autobiography of Mary Anderson as Told to Mary N. Winslow* (Minneapolis: University of Minnesota Press, 1951), Chapter 16.

38. A carbon copy of Dean Acheson's letter to Ethel M. Smith (8 September 1921) found its way into the files of the NCL, Box 13.

39. Florence Kelley to Mrs. C. J. Evans (16 December 1921), NCL, Box 13.

40. Alice Hamilton, draft of letter to Mrs. Hooker (16 January 1922), Hamilton Papers, Box 1. There is no evidence that the letter was ever sent, but it reflects the feelings of the amendment's opponents.

41. Mabel Leslie to Maud Swartz (4 May 1926), WTUL, Box 3.

42. Mary Anderson, *Woman at Work,* pp. 171–172.

43. Quotation from official statement of the Bryn Mawr School for Working Women (1921 and 1923), in Hilda Smith, *Women Workers at the Bryn Mawr Summer School* (New York: American Association for Adult Education, 1927), p. 7. Papers, bulletins, reports, memoranda of the school, 1921–1933, may be found in Smith Papers, Boxes 2, 3, and 16.

44. Mary Anderson, *Woman at Work,* Chapter 25.

45. Eleanor Roosevelt, Address (24 October 1933), quoted in Hilda Smith, "Autobiography," Smith Papers, Box 16.

46. Research folder on Minimum-Wage Legislation, Commons Papers, Box 9.

47. Ethel M. Johnson, "Fourteen Years of Minimum Wage in Massachusetts" (Typescript, 1927), WTUL (Radcliffe), Box 3.

48. Elizabeth Brandeis to Florence Kelley (20 June 1929), NCL, Box 10.

49. "What Girls Live On and How," *Survey,* 64:6 (15 June 1930), p. 277.

50. Leaflet of New York Consumers' League (1927) in Dewson Papers (Radcliffe), Box 2; Florence Kelley, Report to Board of Directors (27 September 1929), NCL, Box 8.

51. Newton D. Baker, Preface to Maud Nathan, *Story of an Epoch-Making Movement* (Garden City, N.Y.: Doubleday, 1926), pp. xii–xiv.

19

The American Woman's
Pre-World War I Freedom
in Manners and Morals

James R. McGovern

The Twenties have been alternately praised or blamed for almost everything and its opposite;[1] but most historians hold, whether to praise or to condemn, that this decade launched the revolution in manners and morals through which we are still moving today. This judgment seems to be part of an even more inclusive one in American historiography to exceptionalize the Twenties. No other decade has invited such titles of historical caricature as *The Jazz Age, This Was Normalcy, Fantastic Interim,* or *The Perils of Prosperity.* Richard Hofstadter's classic, *The Age of Reform,* subtly reinforces this view by seeing the Twenties as "Entr'acte," an interim between two periods of reform, the Progressive era and the New Deal, which themselves display discontinuity.[2]

Revisionism, in the form of a developmental interpretation of the relationship between the Progressive era and the Twenties, has been gaining strong support in recent years. De-emphasizing the disruptive impact of World War I, Henry F. May asked whether the 1920s could be understood fully "without giving more attention to the old regime."[3] He declared that "Immediately prewar America must be newly explored," especially "its inarticulate assumptions—assumptions in such areas as morality, politics, class and race relations, popular art

From the *Journal of American History* 55 (September 1968): 315–33. Reprinted by permission.

and literature, and family life."[4] May pursued his inquiry in *The End of American Innocence* and showed that for the purposes of intellectual history, at least, the Twenties were not as significant as the preceding decade.[5] Political historians have been reassessing the relationship of the Progressive era to the Twenties as well. Arthur Link has demonstrated that progressivism survived World War I,[6] and J. Joseph Huthmacher has established continuity between progressivism and the New Deal in the immigrant's steadfast devotion to the ameliorative powers of the government.[7] Together with May's analysis, their writings suggest that the 1920s are much more the result of earlier intrinsic social changes than either the sudden, supposedly traumatic experiences of the war or unique developments in the Twenties. Since this assertion is certain to encounter the formidable claims that the 1920s, at least in manners and morals, amounted to a revolution, its viability can be tested by questioning if the American woman's "emancipation" in manners and morals occurred even earlier than World War I.

Even a casual exploration of the popular literature of the Progressive era reveals that Americans then described and understood themselves to be undergoing significant changes in morals. "Sex o'clock in America" struck in 1913,[8] about the same time as "The Repeal of Reticence."[9] One contemporary writer saw Americans as liberated from the strictures of "Victorianism," now an epithet deserving criticism, and exulted, "Heaven defend us from a return to the prudery of the Victorian regime!"[10] Conditions were such that another commentator asked self-consciously, "Are We Immoral?"[11] And still another feared that the present "vice not often matched since [the time of] the Protestant Reformation" might invite a return to Puritanism.[12] Yet, historians have not carefully investigated the possibility that the true beginnings of America's "New Freedom" in morals occurred prior to 1920.[13] The most extensive, analytical writing on the subject of changing manners and morals is found in Federick L. Allen's *Only Yesterday* (1931), William Leuchtenburg's *The Perils of Prosperity* (1958), May's *The End of American Innocence* (1959), and George Mowry's *The Urban Nation* (1965).

Allen and Leuchtenburg apply almost identical sharp-break interpretations, respectively entitling chapters "The Revolution in Manners and Morals" and "The Revolution in Morals."[14] Both catalogue the same types of criteria for judgment. The flapper, as the "new woman" was called, was a creature of the 1920s. She smoked, drank, worked, and played side by side with men. She became preoccupied with sex—shocking and simultaneously unshockable. She danced close, became freer with her favors, kept her own latchkey, wore scantier attire which emphasized her boyish, athletic form, just as she used makeup and bobbed and dyed her hair. She and her comradely beau tried to abolish time and succeeded, at least to the extent that the elders asked to join the revelry. Although there were occasional "advance signals" of "rebellion" before the war, it was not until the 1920s that the code of woman's innocence and ignorance crumbled.

May, who comes closest to an understanding of the moral permissiveness before the 1920s, describes in general terms such phenomena of the Progressive era as the "Dance Craze," birth control, the impact of the movies, and the "white-slave panic."[15] He focuses on the intellectuals, however, and therefore overlooks the depth of these and similar social movements. This causes him to view them as mere "Cracks in the Surface" of an essentially conservative society. He quotes approvingly of the distinction made by the *Nation* "between the fluttering tastes of the half-baked intellectuals, attracted by all these things, and the surviving soundness of the great majority."[16] His treatment also ignores one of the most significant areas of changing manners and morals as they affected the American woman: the decided shift in her sex role and identification in the direction of more masculine norms. Again, *The End of American Innocence* does not convincingly relate these changes to the growth of the cities. Perhaps these limitations explain Mowry's preference for a "sharp-break" interpretation, although he wrote seven years after May.

Mowry, who acknowledges especial indebtedness to Leuchtenburg,[17] is emphatic about the "startling" changes in manners and morals in the 1920s.[18] He highlights "the new woman of the twenties"[19] whose "modern feminine morality and attitudes toward the institution of marriage date from the twenties."[20] Mowry concedes to the libidos of progressives only the exceptional goings-on in Greenwich Village society.

These hypotheses, excluding May's, hold that the flapper appeared in the postwar period mainly because American women en masse then first enjoyed considerable social and economic freedom. They also emphasize the effect of World War I on morals.[21] By inference, of course, the Progressive era did not provide a suitable matrix. But an investigation of this period establishes that women had become sufficiently active and socially independent to prefigure the "emancipation" of the 1920s.

A significant deterioration of external controls over morality had occurred before 1920. One of the consequences of working and living conditions in the cities, especially as these affected women, was that Americans of the period 1900–1920 had experienced a vast dissolution of moral authority, which formerly had centered in the family and the small community. The traditional "straight and narrow" could not serve the choices and opportunities of city life.[22] As against primary controls and contacts based on face-to-face association where the norms of family, church, and small community, usually reinforcing each other, could be internalized, the city made for a type of "individualization" through its distant, casual, specialized, and transient clusters of secondary associations.[23] The individual came to determine his own behavioral norms.

The "home is in peril" became a fact of sociological literature as early as 1904.[24] One of the most serious signs of its peril was the increasing inability of parents to influence their children in the delicate areas of propriety and morals.[25] The car, already numerous enough to affect dating and premarital patterns,[26] the phone coming to be used for purposes of romantic accommodation,[27] and the variety of partners at the office or the factory,[28] all together assured unparalleled privacy and permissiveness between the sexes.

Individualization of members served to disrupt confidence between generations of the family, if not to threaten parents with the role of anachronistic irrelevance. Dorothy Dix observed in 1913 that there had been "so many changes in the conditions of life and point of view in the last twenty years that the parent of today is absolutely unfitted to decide the problems of life for the young man and woman of today. This is particularly the case with women because the whole economic and social position of women has been revolutionized since mother was a girl."[29] Magazine articles lamented "The Passing of the Home Daughter" who preferred the blessed anonymity of the city to "dying of asphyxiation at home!"[30] The same phenomenon helps to explain the popularity in this period of such standardized mothers as Dorothy Dix, Beatrice Fairfax, and Emily Post, each of whom was besieged with queries on the respective rights of mothers and daughters.

Woman's individualization resulted mainly because, whether single or married, gainfully employed or not, she spent more time outside her home. Evidence demonstrates that the so-called job and kitchen revolutions were already in advanced stages by 1910. The great leap forward in women's participation in economic life came between 1900 and 1910; the percentage of women who were employed changed only slightly from 1910 to 1930. A comparison of the percentages of gainfully employed women aged 16 to 44 between 1890 and 1930 shows that they comprised 21.7 percent of Americans employed in 1890, 23.5 percent in 1900, 28.1 percent in 1910, 28.3 percent in 1920, and 29.7 percent in 1930.[31] While occupational activity for women appears to stagnate from 1910 to 1920, in reality a considerable restructuring occurred with women leaving roles as domestics and assuming positions affording more personal independence as clerks and stenographers.[32]

Married women, especially those in the upper and middle classes, enjoyed commensurate opportunities. Experts in household management advised women to rid themselves of the maid and turn to appliances as the "maid of all service."[33] Statistics on money expended on those industries which reduced home labor for the wife suggest that women in middle-income families gained considerable leisure after 1914.[34] This idea is also corroborated from other sources,[35] especially from the tone and content of advertising in popular magazines when they are compared with advertising at the turn of the century. Generally speaking, women depicted in advertising in or about 1900 are well rounded, have gentle, motherly expressions, soft billowy hair, and delicate hands. They are either sitting down or standing motionless; their facial expressions are immobile as are their corseted figures.[36] After 1910, they are depicted as more active figures with more of their activity taking place outside their homes.[37] One woman tells another over the phone: "Yes[,] drive over right away—I'll be ready. My housework! Oh, that's all done. How do I do it? I just let electricity do my work nowadays."[38] Vacuum cleaners permitted the housewife to "Push the Button—and Enjoy the Springtime!"[39] Van Camp's "Pork and Beans" promised to save her "100 hours yearly,"[40] and Campbell's soups encouraged, "Get some fun out of life," since it was unnecessary to let the "three-meals-a-day problem tie you down to constant drudgery."[41] Wizard Polish, Minute Tapioca, and Minute Gelatine also offered the same promise. The advertising image of women became more natural, even nonchalant. A lady entertaining a friend remarks: "I don't have to hurry nowadays. I have a Florence Automatic Oil Stove in my kitchen."[42] It had become "so *very* easy" to wax the floors that well-dressed women could manage them.[43] And they enjoyed a round of social activities driving the family car.[44]

It was in this setting that the flapper appeared along with her older married sister who sought to imitate her. No one at the office or in the next block cared much about their morals as long as the one was efficient and the other paid her bills on time. And given the fact that both these women had more leisure and wished "to participate in what men call 'the game of life' " rather than accept "the mere humdrum of household duties,"[45] it is little wonder that contemporaries rightly assessed the danger of the situation for traditional morals by 1910.

The ensuing decade was marked by the development of a revolution in manners and morals; its chief embodiment was the flapper who was urban based and came primarily from the middle and upper classes.

Young—whether in fact or fancy—assertive, and independent, she experimented with intimate dancing, permissive favors, and casual courtships or affairs. She joined men as comrades, and the differences in behavior of the sexes were narrowed. She became in fact in some degree desexualized. She might ask herself, "Am I Not a Boy? Yes, I Am—Not."[46] Her speech, her interest in thrills and excitement, her dress and hair, her more aggressive sexuality, even perhaps her elaborate beautification, which was a statement of intentions, all point to this. Women, whether single or married, became at once more attractive and freer in their morals and paradoxically less feminine. Indeed, the term sexual revolution as applied to the Progressive era means reversal in the traditional role of women just as it describes a pronounced familiarity of the sexes.

The unmarried woman after 1910 was living in the "Day of the Girl."[47] Dorothy Dix described "the type of girl that the modern young man falls for" in 1915 as a "husky young woman who can play golf all day and dance all night, and drive a motor car, and give first aid to the injured if anybody gets hurt, and who is in no more danger of swooning than he is."[48] Little wonder she was celebrated in song as "A Dangerous Girl"; the lyrics of one of the popular songs for 1916 read, "You dare me, you scare me, and still I like you more each day. But you're the kind that will charm; and then do harm; you've got a dangerous way."[49] The "most popular art print . . . ever issued" by *Puck* depicts a made-up young lady puckering her lips and saying "Take It From Me!"[50] The American girl of 1900 was not described in similar terms. The lovely and gracious Gibson Girl was too idealized to be real.[51] And when young lovers trysted in advertising, they met at Horlick's Malted Milk Bar; he with his guitar, and she with her parasol.[52] Beatrice Fairfax could still reply archaically about the need for "maidenly reserve" to such queries as those on the proprieties of men staring at women on the streets.[53] And the *Wellesley College News* in 1902 reported that students were not permitted to have a Junior Prom because it would be an occasion for meeting "promiscuous men," although the college sanctioned "girl dances."[54]

The girls, however, dispensed with "maidenly reserve." In 1910, Margaret Deland, the novelist, could announce a "Change in the Feminine Ideal."

> This young person . . . with surprisingly bad manners—has gone to college, and when she graduates she is going to earn her own living . . . she won't go to church; she has views upon marriage and the birth-rate, and she utters them calmly, while her mother blushes with embarrassment; she occupies herself, passionately, with everything except the things that used to occupy the minds of girls.[55]

Many young women carried their own latchkeys.[56] Meanwhile, as Dorothy Dix noted, it had become "literally true that the average father does not know, by name or sight, the young man who visits his daughter and who takes her out to places of amusement."[57] She was distressed over the widespread use by young people of the car which she called the "devil's wagon."[58] Another writer asked: "Where Is Your Daughter This Afternoon?" "Are you sure that she is not being drawn into the whirling vortex of afternoon 'trots' . . . ?"[59] Polly, Cliff Sterrett's remarkable comic-strip, modern girl from *Polly and Her Pals,* washed dishes under the shower and dried them with an electric fan; and while her mother tried hard to domesticate her, Polly wondered, "Gee Whiz! I wish I knew what made my nose shine!"[60]

Since young women were working side by side with men and recreating more freely and intimately with them, it was inevitable that they behave like men. Older people sometimes carped that growing familiarity meant that romance was dead[61] or that "nowadays brides hardly blush, much less faint."[62] And Beatrice Fairfax asked, "Has Sweet Sixteen Vanished?"[63] But some observers were encouraged to note that as girls' ways approximated men's, the sexes were, at least, more comradely.[64] The modern unmarried woman had become a "Diana, Hunting in the Open."[65] Dorothy Dix reported that "nice girls, good girls, girls in good positions in society—frankly take the initiative in furthering an acquaintance with any man who happens to strike their fancy." The new ideal in feminine figure, dress, and hair styles was all semi-masculine. The "1914 Girl" with her "slim hips and boy-carriage" was a "slim, boylike creature."[66] The "new figure is Amazonian, rather than Miloan. It is boyish rather than womanly. It is strong rather than soft."[67] Her dress styles, meanwhile, de-emphasized both hips and bust while they permitted the large waist. The boyish coiffure began in 1912 when young women began to tuck-under their hair with a ribbon;[68] and by 1913–1914, Newport ladies, actresses like Pauline Frederick, then said to be the prettiest girl in America, and the willowy, popular dancer Irene Castle were wearing short hair.[69] By 1915, the *Ladies Home Journal* featured women with short hair on its covers, and even the pure type of woman who advertised Ivory Soap appeared to be shorn.[70]

The unmarried flapper was a determined pleasure-seeker whom novelist Owen Johnson described collectively as "determined to liberate their lives and claim the same rights of judgment as their brothers."[71] The product of a "feminine revolution startling in the shock of its abruptness," she was living in the city independently of her family. Johnson noted: "She is sure of one life only and that one she passionately desires. She wants to live that life to its fullest. . . . She wants adventure. She wants excitement and mystery. She wants to see, to know, to experience. . . ." She expressed both a "passionate revolt against the commonplace" and a "scorn of conventions." Johnson's heroine in *The Salamander,* Doré Baxter, embodied his views. Her carefree motto is reminiscent of Fitzgerald's flappers of the Twenties: " 'How do I know what I'll do to-morrow?' "[72] Her nightly prayer, the modest " 'O Lord! give me everything I want!' "[73] Love was her "supreme law of conduct,"[74] and she, like the literary flappers of the Twenties, feared "thirty as a sort of sepulcher, an end of all things!" [75] Johnson believed that all young women in all sections of the country had "a little touch of the Salamander," each alike being impelled by "an impetuous frenzy . . . to sample each new excitement," both the "safe and the dangerous."[76] Girls "seemed determined to have their fling like men," the novelist Gertrude Atherton noted in *Current Opinion,* "and some of the stories [about them] made even my sophisticated hair crackle at the roots. . . ."[77] Beatrice Fairfax deplored the trends, especially the fact that "Making love lightly, boldly and promiscuously seems to be part of our social structure."[78] Young men and women kissed though they did not intend to marry.[79] And kissing was shading into spooning (" 'To Spoon' or 'Not to Spoon' Seems to Be the Burning Question with Modern Young America")[80] and even "petting," which was modish among the collegiate set.[81] In fact, excerpts from the diary of a co-ed written before World War I suggest that experimentation was virtually complete within her peer group. She discussed her "adventures" with other college girls. "We were healthy animals and we were demanding our rights to spring's awakening." As for men, she wrote, "I played square with the men. I always told them I was not out to pin them down to marriage, but that this intimacy was pleasant and I wanted it as much as they did. We indulged in sex talk, birth control. . . . We thought too much about it."[82]

One of the most interesting developments in changing sexual behavior which characterized these years was the blurring of age lines between young and middle-aged women in silhouette, dress, and cosmetics.[83] A fashion commentator warned matrons, "This is the day of the figure. . . . The face alone, no matter how pretty, counts for nothing unless the body is as straight and yielding as every young girl's."[84] With only slight variations, the optimum style for women's dress between 1908 and 1918 was a modified sheath, straight up and down and clinging.[85] How different from the styles of the high-busted, broad-hipped mother of the race of 1904 for whom Ella Wheeler Wilcox, the journalist and poet, advised the use of veils because "the slightest approach to masculinity in woman's attire is always unlovely and disappointing."[86]

The sloughing off of numerous undergarments and loosening of others underscored women's quickening activity and increasingly self-reliant morals. Clinging dresses and their "accompanying lack of under-garments" eliminated, according to the president of the New York Cotton Exchange, "at least twelve yards of finished goods for each adult female inhabitant."[87] Corset makers were forced to make adjust-ments too and use more supple materials.[88] Nevertheless, their sales declined.[89]

The American woman of 1910, in contrast with her sister of 1900, avidly cultivated beauty of face and form. In fact, the first American woman whose photographs and advertising image we can clearly recog-nize as belonging to our times lived between 1910 and 1920. "Now-adays," the speaker for a woman's club declared in 1916, "only the very poor or the extremely careless are old or ugly. You can go to a beauty shop and choose the kind of beauty you will have."[90] Beauti-fication included the use of powder, rouge, lipstick, eyelash and eye-brow stain. Advertising was now manipulating such images for face powder as "Mother tried it and decided to keep it for herself,"[91] or "You can have beautiful Eyebrows and Eyelashes. . . . Society women and actresses get them by using Lash-Brow-Ine."[92] Nearly every one of the numerous advertisements for cosmetics promised some variation of "How to Become Beautiful, Fascinating, Attractive."[93]

In her dress as well as her use of cosmetics, the American woman gave evidence that she had abandoned passivity. An unprecedented public display of the female figure characterized the period.[94] Limbs now became legs and more of them showed after 1910, although they were less revealing than the promising hosiery advertisements. Rolled down hose first appeared in 1917.[95] Dresses for opera and restaurant were deeply cut in front and back, and not even the rumor that Mrs. John Jacob Astor had suffered a chest cold as a result of wearing deep decolleté[96] deterred their wearers. As for gowns, "Fashion says—Evening gowns must be sleeveless. . . . afternoon gowns are made with semi-transparent yokes and sleeves."[97] Undoubtedly, this vogue for transparent blouses and dresses[98] caused the editor of the *Unpopular Review* to declare: "At no time and place under Christianity, except the most corrupt periods in France. . . . certainly never before in America, has woman's form been so freely displayed in society and on the street."[99]

In addition to following the example of young women in dress and beautification, middle-aged women, especially those from the middle and upper classes, were espousing their permissive manners and mor-als.[100] Smoking and, to a lesser extent, drinking in public were becom-ing fashionable for married women of the upper class and were making headway at other class levels.[101] As early as 1910, a prominent clubwoman stated: "It has become a well-established habit for women to drink cocktails. It is thought the smart thing to do."[102] Even before Gertrude Atherton described in the novel *Black Oxen* the phenomenon of the middle-aged women who sought to be attractive to younger men, supposedly typifying the 1920s,[103] it was evident in the play "Years of Discretion." Written by Frederic Hatton and Fanny Locke Hatton, and staged by Belasco, the play was "welcomed cordially both in New York and Chicago" in 1912. It featured a widowed mother forty-eight years of age, who announces, "I intend to look under forty—lots under. I have never attracted men, but I know I can."[104] Again, "I mean to have a wonderful time. To have all sorts and kinds of experience. I intend to love and be loved, to lie and cheat."[105] Dorothy Dix was dismayed over "the interest that women . . . have in what we are pleased to euphoniously term the 'erotic.' " She continued, "I'll bet there are not ten thousand women in the whole United States who couldn't get one hundred in an examination of the life and habits of Evelyn Nesbitt and Harry Thaw. . . ."[106] Married women among the fashionable set held the great parties, at times scandalous ones which made the 1920s seem staid by comparison.[107] They hired the Negro orchestras at Newport and performed and sometimes invented the daring dances.[108] They conscientiously practiced birth control, as did women of other classes.[109] And they initiated divorce proceedings, secure in the knowledge that many of their best friends had done the same thing.

Perhaps the best insights on the mores and morals of this group are to be found in the writings of the contemporary, realistic novelist, Robert Herrick.[110] Herrick derived his heroines from "the higher income groups, the wealthy, upper middle, and professional classes among which he preferred to move."[111] His heroines resemble literary flappers of the 1920s in their repudiation of childbearing. "It takes a year out of a woman's life, of course, no matter how she is situated," they say, or, "Cows do that."[112] Since their lives were seldom more than a meaningless round of social experiences, relieved principally by romantic literature, many of them either contemplated or consented to infidelity. Thus Margaret Pole confesses to her friend, Conny Woodyard, " I'd like to lie out on the beach and forget children and servants and husbands, and stop wondering what life is. Yes, I'd like a vacation— in the Windward Islands, with somebody who understood.' 'To wit, a man!' added Conny. 'Yes, a man! But only for the trip.' "[113] They came finally to live for love in a manner that is startlingly reminiscent of some of the famous literary women of the Twenties.[114]

Insights regarding the attitudes of married women from the urban lower middle class can be found in the diary of Ruth Vail Randall, who lived in Chicago from 1911 to the date of her suicide, March 6, 1920.[115] A document of urban sociology, the diary transcends mere personal experience and becomes a commentary on group behavior of the times. Mrs. Randall was reared in a family that owned a grocery store, was graduated from high school in Chicago, and was married at twenty to Norman B. Randall, then twenty-one. She worked after marriage in a department store and later for a brief period as a model. She looked to marriage, especially its romance, as the supreme fulfillment of her life and was bitterly disappointed with her husband. She began to turn to other men whom she met at work or places of recreation, and her husband left her. Fearing that her lover would leave her eventually as well, she killed him and herself.

The diary focuses on those conditions which made the revolution in morals a reality. The young couple lived anonymously in a highly mobile neighborhood where their morals were of their own making. Mrs. Randall did not want children; she aborted their only child. [116] She was also averse to the reserved "womanly" role, which her husband insisted that she assume.[117] She complained, "Why cannot a woman do all man does?"[118] She wished that men and women were more alike in their social roles.[119] She repudiated involvement in her home, resolved to exploit equally every privilege which her husband assumed, drank, flirted, and lived promiscuously. Telephones and cars made her extramarital liaisons possible. Even before her divorce, she found another companion; flouting convention, she wrote, "He and I have entered a marriage pact according to our own ideas."[120] Throughout her diary she entertained enormous, almost magical, expectations of love. She complained that her lovers no more than her husband provided what she craved—tenderness and companionship. Disillusionment with one of them caused her to cry out, "I am miserable. I have the utmost contempt for myself. But the lake is near and soon it will be warm. Oh, God to rest in your arms. To rest—and to have peace."[121]

That America was experiencing a major upheaval in morals during the Progressive era is nowhere better ascertained than in the comprehensive efforts by civic officials and censorial citizens to control them. Disapproval extended not only to such well-known staples as alcohol, divorce, and prostitution, but also to dancing, woman's dress, cabarets, theaters and movies, and birth control. "Mrs. Warren's Profession" was withdrawn from the New York stage in 1905 after a one night performance, the manager of the theater later being charged with offending public decency.[122] When a grand jury in New York condemned the "turkey trot and kindred dances" as "indecent," the judge who accepted the presentment noted that "Rome's downfall was due to the degenerate nature of its dancers, and I only hope that we will not suffer the same result."[123]   Public dancing was henceforth to be licensed. Mayor John Fitzgerald personally assisted the morals campaign in Boston by ordering the removal from a store of an objectionable picture which portrayed a "show-girl" with her legs crossed.[124]   Meanwhile, the "X-Ray Skirt" was outlawed in Portland, Oregon, and Los Angeles;[125]   and the police chief of Louisville, Kentucky, ordered the arrest of a number of women appearing on the streets with slit skirts.[126]   Witnessing to a general fear that the spreading knowledge of contraception might bring on sexual license, the federal and several state governments enacted sumptuary legislation.[127]   And in two celebrated incidents, the offenders, Van K. Allison (1916) in Boston and Margaret Sanger (1917) in New York, were prosecuted and sent to jail.[128]

Public officials were apprehensive about the sweeping influence of the movies on the masses, "at once their book, their drama, their art. To some it has become society, school, and even church."[129]   They proceeded to set up boards of censorship with powers to review and condemn movies in four states: Pennsylvania (1911), Ohio (1913), Maryland (1916), and Kansas (1917), and in numerous cities beginning with Chicago in 1907.[130]   The Pennsylvania board, for example, prohibited pictures which displayed nudity, prolonged passion, women drinking and smoking, and infidelity. It protected Pennsylvanians from such films produced between 1915 and 1918 as "What Every Girl Should Know," "A Factory Magdalene," and "Damaged Goodness."[131]

Such determination proved unavailing, however, even as the regulatory strictures were being applied. According to one critic the "sex drama" using "plain, blunt language" had become "a commonplace" of the theater after 1910 and gave the "tender passion rather the worst for it in recent years."[132]   Vice films packed them in every night, especially after the smashing success of "Traffic in Souls," which reportedly grossed $450,000.[133]   In Boston the anti-vice campaign itself languished because there was no means of controlling "the kitchenette-apartment section." "In these apartment houses, there are hundreds of women who live as they please and who entertain as they will." [134] Mayor Fitzgerald's "show-girl," evicted from her saucy perch, gained more notoriety when she appeared in a Boston newspaper the following day.[135]   Even Anthony Comstock, that indefatigable guardian of public morals, had probably come to look a bit like a comic character living beyond his times.[136]

When Mrs. Sanger was arrested for propagating birth control information in 1917, she confidently stated, "I have nothing to fear. . . . Regardless of the outcome I shall continue my work, supported by thousands of men and women throughout the country."[137] Her assurance was well founded. Three years earlier her supporters had founded a National Birth Control League; and in 1919, this organization opened its first public clinic.[138] But most encouraging for Mrs. Sanger was the impressive testimony that many Americans were now practicing or interested in birth control.[139] When Paul B. Blanchard, pastor of the Maverick Congregational Church in East Boston, protested the arrest of Van K. Allison, he charged, "If the truth were made public and the laws which prevent the spreading of even oral information about birth control were strictly enforced how very few of the married society leaders, judges, doctors, ministers, and businessmen would be outside the prison dock!"[140]

The foregoing demonstrates that a major shift in American manners and morals occurred in the Progressive era, especially after 1910. Changes at this time, though developing out of still earlier conditions, represented such visible departures from the past and were so commonly practiced as to warrant calling them revolutionary. Too often scholars have emphasized the Twenties as the period of significant transition and World War I as a major cause of the phenomenon. Americans of the 1920s, fresh from the innovative wartime atmosphere, undoubtedly quickened and deepened the revolution. Women from smaller cities and towns contested what was familiar terrain to an already seasoned cadre of urban women and a formidable group of defectors. Both in their rhetoric and their practices, apparent even before the war, the earlier group had provided the shibboleths for the 1920s; they first asked, "What are Patterns for?" The revolution in manners and morals was, of course, but an integral part of numerous, contemporary, political and social movements to free the individual by reordering society. Obviously, the Progressive era, more than the 1920s, represents the substantial beginnings of contemporary American civilization.

The revolution in manners and morals, particularly as it affected women, took the twofold form of more permissive sexuality and diminished femininity. Women from the upper classes participated earlier, as is evidenced by their introductory exhibition of fashions, hair styles, dances, cosmetics, smoking, and drinking. Realistic novels concerned with marriage suggest that they entertained ideas of promiscuity and even infidelity before women of the lower classes. Yet the cardinal condition of change was not sophistication but urban living and the freedom it conferred. As technology and economic progress narrowed the gap between the classes, middle-class women and even those below were free to do many of the same things almost at the same time. Above all, the revolution in manners and morals after 1910 demonstrates that sexual freedom and the twentieth-century American city go together.

NOTES

1. Henry F. May, "Shifting Perspectives on the 1920's," *Mississippi Valley Historical Review*, XLIII (Dec. 1956), 405–27.

2. Richard Hofstadter, *The Age of Reform: From Bryan to F. D. R.* (New York, 1955), 282–301.

3. May, "Shifting Perspectives on the 1920's," 426. See also Henry F. May, "The Rebellion of the Intellectuals, 1912–1917," *American Quarterly*, VIII (Summer 1956), 115, wherein May describes 1912–1917 as a "pre-revolutionary or early revolutionary period."

4. May, "Shifting Perspectives on the 1920's," 427.

5. Henry F. May, *The End of American Innocence: A Study of the First Years of Our Own Time, 1912–1917* (New York, 1959).

6. Arthur S. Link, "What Happened to the Progressive Movement in the 1920's?" *American Historical Review*, LXIV (July 1959), 833–51.

7. J. Joseph Huthmacher, "Urban Liberalism and the Age of Reform," *Mississippi Valley Historical Review*, XLIX (Sept. 1962), 231–41. Other political and economic historians concur on a developmental interpretation. Gerald D. Nash, *State Government and Economic Development: A History of Administrative Policies in California, 1849–1933* (Berkeley, 1964), 250, 291, 326, views the period 1900–1933 as a unit because it was characterized by notable coordination and centralization of authority by agencies of state government in California. Donald C. Swain, *Federal Conservation Policy, 1921–1933* (Berkeley, 1963), 6, sees the national conservation program making continuous advances through the 1920s based upon beginnings in the Progressive period.

8. "Sex O'clock in America," *Current Opinion*, LV (Aug. 1913), 113–14. The anonymous author borrowed the phrase from William M. Reedy, editor of the St. Louis *Mirror*.

9. Agnes Repplier, "The Repeal of Reticence," *Atlantic Monthly*, CXIII (March 1914), 297–304, objected to the "obsession of sex which has set us all a-babbling about matters once excluded from the amenities of conversation" (p. 298). Articles on birth control, prostitution, divorce, and sexual morals between 1910 and 1914 were cumulatively more numerous per thousand among articles indexed in the *Reader's Guide to Periodical Literature* than for either 1919 to 1924 or 1925 to 1928. Hornell Hart, "Changing Social Attitudes and Interests," *Recent Social Trends in the United States: Report of the President's Research Committee on Social Trends* (2 vols., New York, 1933), I, 414.

10. H. W. Boynton, "Ideas, Sex, and the Novel," *Dial*, LX (April 13, 1916), 361. In Robert W. Chambers, *The Restless Sex* (New York, 1918), 143, the heroine remarks, "What was all wrong in our Victorian mothers' days is all right now."

11. Arthur Pollock, "Are We Immoral?" *Forum*, LI (Jan. 1914), 52. Pollock remarks that "in our literature and in our life to-day sex is paramount."

12. "Will Puritanism Return?" *Independent*, 77 (March 23, 1914), 397.

13. Mark Sullivan, *Our Times: The War Begins* (New York, 1932), 165–93, states in colorful and impressionistic terms that significant changes in moral attitudes had taken place in the Progressive era. He attributes much of this to the influence of Freud, Shaw, and Omar Khayyám. Preston William Slosson, *The Great Crusade and After: 1914–1928* (New York, 1930), describes the period 1914–1928 as a unit, but his material dealing with morals centers on the 1920s. For example, there are only five footnotes based on materials written between 1914 and 1919 in his chapter, "The American Woman Wins Equality," 130–61. Samuel Eliot Morison makes brief mention of a "revolution in sexual morals" before 1920 in *The Oxford History of the American People* (New York, 1965), 906–08.

14. Frederick Lewis Allen, *Only Yesterday: An Informal History of the Nineteen-Twenties* (New York, 1931), 88–122; William E. Leuchtenburg, *The Perils of Prosperity: 1914–32* (Chicago, 1958), 158–77.

15. May, *The End of American Innocence*, 334–47, is lightly documented; there are only twelve footnotes to support his discussion of these and similar developments.

16. *Ibid.*, 347. May's view of women's changing attitudes is contradicted by Margaret Deland: "Of course there were women a generation ago, as in all generations, who asserted themselves; but they were practically 'sports.' Now, the simple, honest woman . . . the good wife, the good mother—is evolving ideals which are changing her life, and the lives of those people about her." Margaret Deland, "The Change in the Feminine Ideal," *Atlantic Monthly*, CV (March 1910), 291.

17. George E. Mowry, *The Urban Nation: 1920–1960* (New York, 1965), 250.

18. *Ibid.*, 23.

19. *Ibid.*

20. *Ibid.*, 24.

21. "By 1930 more than ten million women held jobs. Nothing did more to emancipate them." Leuchtenburg, *Perils of Prosperity*, 160. See also Allen, *Only Yesterday*, 95–98. For estimates of the effects of World War I on morals, see Leuchtenburg, *Perils of Prosperity*, 172–73; Allen, *Only Yesterday*, 94; Mowry, *Urban Nation*, 24.

22. Population in urban territory comprised only about 28 percent of the total American population in 1880; but by 1920, approximately 52 percent were living there. Department of Commerce, Bureau of the Census, *Historical Statistics of the United States, Colonial Times to 1957* (Washington, 1960), 14.

23. Scott Nearing and Nellie M. S. Nearing, *Woman and Social Progress* (New York, 1912), 137–41. The Nearings wrote: "The freedom which American Women have gained through recent social changes and the significance of their consequent choice, constitutes one of the profoundest and at the same time one of the most inscrutable problems in American life" (p. 138). William I. Thomas, *The Unadjusted Girl: With Cases and Standpoint for Behavior Analysis* (Boston, 1923), 86. Ernest R. Mowrer, *Family Disorganization* (Chicago, 1927), 6–8. Mowrer attributes "Family Disorganization" to the "conditions of city life" which resulted in a "rebellion against the old ideals of family life. . . ."

24. George Elliott Howard, "Social Control and the Functions of the Family," Howard J. Rogers, ed. *Congress of Arts and Sciences: Universal Exposition, St. Louis, 1904* (8 vols., Boston, 1906), VII, 702.

25. Louise Collier Willcox, "Our Supervised Morals," *North American Review,* CXCVIII (Nov. 1913), 708, observes: "The time is past when parents supervised the morals of their children. . . "

26. There was a surprisingly large number of cars sold and used in America between 1910 and 1920. Approximately 40 percent as many cars were produced each year between 1915 and 1917 as were manufactured between 1925 and 1927. *Facts and Figures of the Automobile Industry* (New York, 1929), 6, 22. There were approximately 7,500,000 cars registered in 1919. "Existing Surfaced Mileage Total" on a scale of 1,000 miles was 204 in 1910, 332 in 1918, 521 in 1925, and 694 in 1930. *Historical Statistics of the United States,* 458. Newspapers reported the impact of the automobile on dating and elopements. For a moralistic reaction to the phenomenon, see Dorothy Dix, Boston *American,* Sept. 5, 1912. For an enthusiast of "mobile privacy" in this period, see F. Scott Fitzgerald, "Echoes of the Jazz Age," *Scribner's Magazine,* XC (Nov. 1931), 460. Fitzgerald wrote: "As far back as 1915 the unchaperoned young people of the smaller cities had discovered the mobile privacy of that automobile given to young Bill at sixteen to make him 'self-reliant.' "

27. Dorothy Dix, "A Modern Diana," Boston *American,* April 7, 1910.

28. Beatrice Fairfax, *ibid.,* May 28, 1908; Dorothy Dix, *ibid.,* Sept. 9, 1912.

29. *Ibid.,* Aug. 21, 1913.

30. Marion Harland, "The Passing of the Home Daughter," *Independent,* LXXI (July 13, 1911), 90.

31. Sophonisba P. Breckinridge, *Women in the Twentieth Century: A Study of Their Political, Social and Economic Activities* (New York, 1933), 112. Overall percentages of women gainfully employed rose from 19 percent of the total work force in 1890 to 20.6 percent in 1900, 24.3 percent in 1910, 24 percent in 1920, and 25.3 percent in 1930. *Ibid.,* 108.

32. While the number of women who worked as domestics declined after 1910, large numbers of women were employed for the first time as clerks and stenographers. In fact, more women were employed in both these occupations between 1910 and 1920 than between 1920 and 1930. *Ibid.,* 129, 177.

33. Martha Bensley Bruere and Robert W. Bruere, *Increasing Home Efficiency* (New York, 1914), 236–41.

34.

	Total Amount Expended in Millions of Dollars				
Item	1909	1914	1919	1923	1929
(a) canned fruits and vegetables	162	254	575	625	930
(b) cleaning and polishing preparations	6	9	27	35	46
(c) electricity in household operation	83	132	265	389	615.5
(d) mechanical appliances (refrigerators, sewing machines, washers, cooking)	152	175	419	535	804.1

TABLE—*Continued*

Item	1909	1914	1919	1923	1929
Percentage of expenditures on household equipment to total expenditures	9.9%	9.2%	10.3%	11.6%	13.2%

(a-b) is found in William H. Lough, *High-Level Consumption: Its Behavior; Its Consequences* (New York, 1935), 236, 241. These figures are tabulated in millions of dollars for 1935. Items (c-d) and the percentage of expenditure on household equipment to total expenditures were taken from James Dewhurst, *America's Needs and Resources: A New Survey* (New York, 1955), 702, 704, 180.

35. Realistic novelists note the leisure of the middle-class women. David Graham Phillips, *The Hungry Heart* (New York, 1909) and *Old Wives for New* (New York, 1908); Robert Herrick, *Together* (New York, 1908), especially 515–17.

36. For example, see *Cosmopolitan,* XXXV (May-Oct. 1903); *Ladies Home Journal,* XXI (Dec. 1903–May 1904). A notable exception showing a woman riding a bicycle may be found in *ibid.* (April 1904), 39.

37. *Ladies Home Journal,* XXXIV (May 1917), for example, shows a woman entertaining stylish women friends (34, 89, 92), driving the car or on an automobile trip (36–37, 74), economizing on time spent in housework (42), the object of "outdoor girl" ads (78), beautifying at a social affair or appearing very chic (102, 106). Perhaps the best illustration for woman's activity in advertisements was employed in *Ladies Home Journal* by Williams Talc Powder. It read, "After the game, the ride, the swim, the brisk walk, or a day at the sea-shore, turn for comfort to Williams Talc Powder." *Ibid.,* XXXIV (July 1917), 74.

38. *Collier's,* 56 (Nov. 27, 1915), 4.

39. *Cosmopolitan,* LIX (June 1915), advertising section, 50.

40. *Collier's,* 56 (Sept. 25, 1915), 22.

41. *Ibid.* (Nov. 27, 1915), 25.

42. *Ladies Home Journal,* XXXV (April 1918), 58.

43. *Ibid.,* 57.

44. *Ibid.,* XXXIII (Jan. 1916), 46–47. Women drove their friends and families about in their cars. *Ibid.,* XXXII (July 1915), 34–35; (Aug. 1915), 38–39; (Oct. 1915), 86; XXXIII (Nov. 1916), 71.

45. Susanne Wilcox, "The Unrest of Modern Women," *Independent,* LXVII (July 8, 1909), 63.

46. Nell Brinkley, a nationally syndicated cartoonist and commentator on women's activities, asked this question of one of her young women. Boston *American,* July 14, 1913.

47. Nell Brinkley coined the phrase. *Ibid.,* Nov. 14, 1916.

48. *Ibid.,* May 4, 1915. See also *Ladies Home Journal,* XXXII (July 1915), which depicts a young woman driving a speedboat while her boyfriend sits next to her.

49. Boston *American,* Oct. 1, 1916.

50. *Collier's,* 56 (March 4, 1916), 38.

51. Emma B. Kaufman, "The Education of a Debutante," *Cosmopolitan*, XXXV (Sept. 1903), 499–508.

52. *Cosmopolitan*, XXXIX (Oct. 1905).

53. "Girls, Don't Allow Men to be Familiar," Boston *American*, June 17, 1904; *ibid.*, July 15, 1905.

54. *Wellesley College News*, Feb. 20, 1902. Wellesley relented on "men dances" in 1913.

55. Deland, "The Change in the Feminine Ideal," 291.

56. *Ibid.*, 289.

57. Boston *American*, May 6, 1910.

58. *Ibid.*, Sept. 5, 1912.

59. Ethel Watts Mumford, "Where Is Your Daughter This Afternoon?" *Harper's Weekly*, LVIII (Jan. 17, 1914), 28.

60. Boston *American*, Sept. 5, 1916; *ibid.*, Jan. 4, 1914.

61. Alice Duer Miller. "The New Dances and the Younger Generation," *Harper's Bazaar*, XLVI (May 1912), 250.

62. Deland, "Change in the Feminine Ideal," 293.

63. Boston *American*, March 24, 1916. In a letter to the editor of the New York *Times*, one critic of the "women of New York" complained that they seemed to be part of a "new race" or even a "super-sex." He waxed poetic: "Sweet seventeen is rouge-pot mad, And hobbles to her tasks blase, . . . Where are the girls of yesterday?" New York *Times*, July 20, 1914.

64. Miller, "New Dances and the Younger Generation," 250. According to Helen Rowland, the woman was "no longer Man's plaything, but his playmate. . . ." Helen Rowland, "The Emancipation of 'the Rib,' *Delineator*, LXXVII (March 1911), 233.

65. Boston *American*, April 7, 1910.

66. *Ibid.*, March 20, 1914.

67. *Ibid.*, June 11, 1916.

68. *Ibid.*, Nov. 27, Dec. 8, 1912.

69. On Newport and Boston society women see *ibid.*, July 6, 27, Aug. 10, 24, 1913. Pauline Frederick's picture may be found in *ibid.*, Aug. 2, 1913. For Irene Castle, see Mr. and Mrs. Vernon Castle, *Modern Dancing* (New York, 1914), 98, 105.

70. *Ladies Home Journal*, XXXII (July and Sept. 1915); *ibid.* (Nov. 1915), 8.

71. Owen Johnson, *The Salamander* (Indianapolis, 1914), Foreword, n.p.

72. *Ibid.*, 9.

73. *Ibid.*, 129.

74. *Ibid.*, 66.

75. *Ibid.*, 61.

76. *Ibid.*, Foreword, n.p. Chamber's young heroine Stephanie Cleland in *The Restless Sex*, 191, practiced trial marriage in order to learn by experience. See also Phillips, *Hungry Heart*, 166–80; Terry Ramsaye, *A Million And One Nights: A History of the Motion Picture* (2 vols., New York, 1926), II, 702–04.

77. "Mrs. Atherton Tells of Her 'Perch of the Devil,' " *Current Opinion*, LVII (Nov. 1914), 349.

78. Boston *American*, Feb. 8, 1917.

79. The "kiss of friendship" criticized by Fairfax had become a major issue of her mail by 1913. See, for example, *ibid.*, July 5, 1913. Girls shocked her with inquiries as to whether it was permissible to "soul kiss" on a first date. *Ibid.*, Feb. 13, 1914. An engaged girl asked whether it would be all right to kiss men other than her fiance. *Ibid.*, May 2, 1916.

80. *Ibid.*, Feb. 8, 1917.

81. Fitzgerald, "Echoes of the Jazz Age," 460.

82. Thomas, *Unadjusted Girl*, 95.

83. "Today in the world of fashion, all women are young, and they grow more so all the time." Doeuilet, "When All The World Looks Young," *Delineator*, LXXXIII (Aug. 1913), 20. Advertisements used flattery or played up the value of youth for women and warned that they might age unless certain products were used. *Cosmopolitan*, LIX (Nov. 1915), 112; *ibid.* (July 1915), 81; *Ladies Home Journal*, XXXII (Nov. 1915), 65; *Cosmopolitan*, LIX (Oct. 1915), 57.

84. Eleanor Chalmers, "Facts and Figures," *Delineator*, LXXXIV (April 1914), 38.

85. Boston *American*, March 20, 1910; *Delineator*, LXXXIX (Oct. 1916), 66.

86. Boston *American*, March 28, 1904.

87. New York *Tribune*, April 4, 1912; Eleanor Chalmers, "You and Your Sewing," *Delineator*, LXXXIII (Aug. 1913), 33.

88. Eleanor Chalmers, *Delineator*, LXXIV (April 1914), 38. The sense of relief these changes brought is amusingly described in Dorothy A. Plum, comp., *The Magnificent Enterprise: A Chronicle of Vassar College* (Poughkeepsie, 1961), 43–44.

89. Percival White, "Figuring Us Out," *North American Review*, CCXXVII (Jan. 1929), 69.

90. Boston *American*, Dec. 10, 1916.

91. *Delineator*, LXXXV (July 1914), 55.

92. Boston *American*, Sept. 3, 1916.

93. *Cosmopolitan*, LIX (July 1915).

94. An editorial declared that women's dresses in 1913 had approached "the danger line of indecency about as closely as they could." New York *Times*, July 6, 1914.

95. *Ladies Home Journal*, XXXIV (Oct. 1917), 98.

96. Boston *American*, June 8, 1907. "The conventions of evening dress have changed radically in the last four or five years. Not so very long ago a high-necked gown was considered *au fait* for all evening functions except formal dinners and the opera. Nowadays, well-dressed women wear decolleté dresses even for home dinners, and semi-decolleté gowns for restaurants and theaters." *Delineator*, LXXV (Jan. 1910), 60.

97. *Cosmopolitan*, LIX (July 1915).

98. *Ladies Home Journal*, XXXII (Oct. 1915), 108; *ibid.*, XXXIII (Oct. 1916), 82; *ibid.*, XXXIII (Nov. 1916), 78–79; *ibid.*, XXXIV (Jan. 1917), 53.

99. "The Cult of St. Vitus," *Unpopular Review*, III (Jan.-March 1915), 94.

100. Boston *American*, July 6, 1912. Dix noted "flirtatious" middle-aged women were "aping the airs and graces of the debutante" and "trying to act kittenish" with men.

101. *Ibid.*, Dec. 6, 10, 1912. Anita Stewart, a movie star who wrote "Talks to Girls," though personally opposed to smoking, admitted that "lots of my friends smoke" and "they are nice girls too." *Ibid.*, Dec. 14, 1915. In 1916, the Boston *American* titled a column on a page devoted to women's interests "To Smoke or Not to Smoke." *Ibid.*, April 12, 1916. The *Harvard Lampoon*, LXXI (June 20, 1916), 376, spoofed women smoking: it carried a heading "Roman Society Women Agree to Give Up Smoking" and a commentary below, "Oh, Nero, how times have changed!"

102. Boston *American*, March 7, 1910.

103. Leuchtenburg, *Perils of Prosperity*, 174–75.

104. " 'Years of Discretion'—A Play of Cupid at Fifty," *Current Opinion*, LIV (Feb. 1913), 116.

105. *Ibid.*, 117.

106. Boston *American*, April 10, 1908. Evelyn Nesbitt, the wife of Harry Thaw, was romantically involved with architect Stanford White, whom Thaw shot to death.

107. *Ibid.*, Aug. 25, Sept. 1, 1912.

108. Most of the dances which became very popular after 1910, such as the Turkey Trot, the Bunny Hug, and the Grizzly Bear, afforded a maximum of motion in a minimum of space. The Chicken Flip was invented by a Boston society woman. *Ibid.*, Nov. 11, 1912. See also "New Reflections on The Dancing Mania," *Current Opinion*, LV (Oct. 1913), 262.

109. Louis I. Dublin, "Birth Control," *Social Hygiene*, VI (Jan. 1920), 6.

110. Alfred Kazin, "Three Pioneer Realists," *Saturday Review of Literature*, XX (July 8, 1939), 15. Herrick's biographer, Blake Nevius, declares, "It can be argued that Herrick is the most comprehensive and reliable social historian in American fiction to appear in the interregnum between Howells and the writers of the Twenties. . . ." Blake Nevius, *Robert Herrick: The Development of a Novelist* (Berkeley, 1962), Preface.

111. Nevius, *Robert Herrick*, 177.

112. Herrick, *Together*, 91, 392.

113. *Ibid.*, 263, 250–51, 320–24.

114. Herrick describes the temperament of the modern woman as one of "mistress rather than the wife. . . . 'I shall be a person with a soul of my own. To have me man must win me not once, but daily.' " *Ibid.*, 516. The last sentence above nearly duplicates Rosalind's statement to her beau in *This Side of Paradise*, "I have to be won all over again every time you see me." F. Scott Fitzgerald, *This Side of Paradise* (New York, 1920), 194.

115. Chicago *Herald and Examiner*, March 10–17, 1920.

116. *Ibid.*, March 10, 1920.

117. *Ibid.*, March 11, 1920.

118. *Ibid.*

119. *Ibid.*, March 11, 12, 1920.

120. *Ibid.*, March 13, 14, 1920.

121. *Ibid.*, March 15, 1920.

122. New York *Tribune*, Nov. 1, 1905.

123. New York *Times,* May 28, 1913.

124. *Ibid.,* Dec. 20, 1912.

125. *Ibid.,* Aug. 20, 23, 1913.

126. *Ibid.,* June 29, 1913.

127. Carol Flora Brooks, "The Early History of the Anti-Contraceptive Laws in Massachusetts and Connecticut," *American Quarterly,* XVIII (Spring 1966), 3–23; George E. Worthington, "Statutory Restrictions on Birth Control," *Journal of Social Hygiene,* IX (Nov. 1923), 458–65.

128. Boston *American,* July 14, 21, 1916; New York *Times,* Feb. 6, 1917.

129. *Report of the Pennsylvania Board of Censors,* June 1, 1915 to Dec. 1, 1915 (Harrisburg, 1916), 6.

130. Ellis Paxson Oberholtzer, *The Morals of the Movie* (Philadelphia, 1922), 115–23.

131. *Report of the Pennsylvania State Board of Censors,* 1915, pp. 14–15; *ibid.,* 1916, pp. 24–25; *ibid.,* 1917, pp. 8–9.

132. Boston *American,* Aug. 10, 1913.

133. Ramsaye, *A Million and One Nights,* II, 617.

134. Boston *American,* July 7, 1917.

135. *Ibid.,* Dec. 20, 1912.

136. Heywood Broun, *Anthony Comstock: Roundsman of the Lord* (New York, 1927); Mary Alden Hopkins, "Birth Control and Public Morals: An Interview with Anthony Comstock," *Harper's Weekly,* LX (May 22, 1915), 489–90.

137. Boston *American,* Jan. 4, 1917.

138. Norman E. Himes, "Birth Control in Historical and Clinical Perspective," *Annals of the American Academy of Political and Social Sciences,* 160 (March 1932), 53.

139. Dublin, "Birth Control," 6.

140. Boston *American,* July 16, 1916. According to International News Service, "Mrs. Rose Pastor Stokes was literally mobbed by an eager crowd in Carnegie Hall when she offered, in defiance of the police, to distribute printed slips bearing a formula for birth control." *Ibid.,* May 6, 1916.

20

The Projection of a New Womanhood:
The Movie Moderns in the 1920's

Mary P. Ryan

The ideal of femininity was changing so dramatically around the third decade of the twentieth century that contemporaries began to speak of an entirely "new woman." In 1925 the mothers of Middletown recognized the transformation in their own daughters: "Girls aren't so modest nowadays; they dress differently," "Girls are more aggressive today. They call the boys up to try to make dates with them as they never would have when I was a girl." "When I was a girl, a girl who painted was a bad girl—now look at the daughters of our best families."[1] Historians have called attention to the same transformation of the female image in popular literature, advertising, and the graphic arts, underway even before World War I.[2] Historians have not been as diligent, however, in culling another rich body of imagery regarding the new woman—the moving pictures, which vividly record the full flavor of the flapper's personality, complete with her characteristic gestures, energy, and activism. Although many of these early films have been destroyed, enough remain from which to piece together a schematic moving portrait of the new woman.

Careful analysis of popular movies, furthermore, offers the historian access to the dream-life of past generations, male and female. By the 1920's, movie making had become a smoothly functioning industry, capitalized at over one billion dollars and tooled for the mass production and distribution of fantasies. The output of the major studios (Paramount, Fox, MGM, Universal, Warner Brothers) was manufactured

This article appears by permission of the author.

by an army of directors, technicians, writers, and businessmen, all working under the imperative of pleasing an audience that numbered as many as 100 million viewers a week, gathered together in over 18,000 theatres all across America.[3] The understandable result of this collective process was a standardized product that could be simply classified by such formulas as the adventure story, western, comedy, and love story. The success of each popular genre depended upon striking a responsive cord in the mass audience, reaching some common denominator in the experience, hopes, and fears of Americans. This juncture of dream and reality on the silver screen provides the historian a multidimensional cultural document.

Cinema also provides an ideal vantage point from which to observe the making of the new woman. Screen femininity in the twenties was often the creation of woman scenarists, like Bess Meredyth, Anita Loos, Frances Marion, Jeanie MacPherson, and June Mathis,[4] who worked in teams and at a frantic pace to construct captivating images and compelling plots. Their formulaic stories reached an audience which included millions of women often in their formative years. One survey concluded that females between the ages of 8 and nineteen attended the movies an average of 46 times a year[5] in the twenties.

Perhaps the crucial link in this female cultural chain was the star. Well before the studios were willing to identify their actresses by name, the mails were flooded with chatty letters to familiar screen personalities. When Universal revealed the "biograph girl" to be Florence Lawrence, this first starlet was immediately mobbed in St. Louis, hounded by fans begging her autograph and ravaging her clothing.[6] The star was a unique cultural phenomenon, an actress whose personal style enlivened a multiplicity of familiar but fictional roles, blending the real with the imaginary in one glamourous individual. She was, as Stanley Cavell phrases it, an "individuality" that "projects particular ways of inhabiting a social role."[7] By the 1920's national surveys revealed that movie stars had replaced political, business, and artistic leaders as the favorite role models of American youth.[8] In the twenties, the female social role was projected on the screen by such personalities as Madge Bellamy, Clara Bow, Joan Crawford and Gloria Swanson, all vivid embodiments of the new womanhood, known to contemporaries as "the moderns."

By the mid-twenties the sweet heroines of the late Victorian age had been totally banished from the screen by these new women. The cinematic staples of the pre-war era, both the one-reelers that stocked the nickelodeons in working-class neighborhoods and the prestigious features directed by D.W. Griffith, featured actresses like Lillian Gish and Mary Pickford who reveled in motherly sacrifice, sexual purity and shy submission. Another woman who enacted such parts, Linda Arvidson Griffith, described her typical roles as "the peasant, washwoman and tenement lady" staunchly protecting her babes from starvation, and her virginity from despoilment by rich and vulgar villains. When Mrs. Griffith wrote her memoirs in 1925, however, she woefully acknowledged that such true womanhood was regarded as old-fashioned and had been replaced by an antagonistic set of mores: "We were dealing in things vital in our American life and not one bit interested in close-ups of empty-headed little ingenues with adenoids, bedroom windows, manhandling of young girls, fast sets, perfumed bathrooms or nude youths heaving their muscles."[9] Such permissiveness in the display of the female body and the treatment of sexual themes was the most obvious hallmark of the new woman.

Nonetheless, early cinema had not been as asexual as Arvidson liked to remember. One of the first scandals of the screen was the 1896 "Anatomy of a Kiss" which drew out that intimate act to a full 42 frames. As the medium advanced from merely photographing natural phenomena to full-fledged story-telling, sex became a favorite theme, albeit veiled in moralistic condemnations of the villainous roué and the hapless prostitute. It was in the hey day of Griffith, in fact, that female sexuality struck its most aggressive pose in the screen antics of Theda Bara—"The wickedest face in the world, dark, brooding, beautiful and heartless"—luring unfortunate males to self-destruction. Theda Bara made no less than 40 films on the torrid vamp theme in the three years after her first appearance in the 1915 film *A Fool There Was.*[10]

Although the vamp was too extreme a caricature to endure, she had cleared the air of the dangerous vapors of female passion and cleared the way for a more respectable brand of sex appeal. The arrival of the new woman on the screen was clearly apparent by 1919 when she intruded into the wholesomely titled film made by the most Victorian of directors, Griffith's *True Heart Susie.* The heroine, played by Lillian Gish, radiated 19th-century womanhood as she worked, sacrificed, and waited in the blush of innocence for the boy next door. Yet True Heart Susie was a much beleaguered heroine in 1919. In fact she temporarily lost her hero to a member of the fast set, whose city ways included a painted face, short clinging skirts, and a wiggling walk that the camera followed with delight. Even True Heart Susie was momentarily tempted to powder her face with corn starch and hitch up her skirt. The contrived nature of the plot also illustrated the obsolescence of Victorian values. The old virtues did not triumph until Susie's rival had been exposed as a bad cook, sloppy housewife, an unfaithful wife, and then died of pneumonia. The last shot of the film underscored the nostalgia for the old morality and the old code of femininity: as the reunited couple walked into the sunset their images faded into a photograph from their rural childhood.[11]

The backward-looking ethic of *True Heart Susie* becomes even more distinct when the film is compared with the box-office sensation of 1919. It was in that year that Cecil B. De Mille, in collaboration with screenwriter Jeanie MacPherson, transposed the *Admirable Chrichton* into a film entitled *Male and Female.* Under De Mille's direction the play became little more than a sexual display whose centerpiece was the female body. The movie audience was invited to share the hero's fantasy of sexual domination, to gaze upon Gloria Swanson's naked thighs and surging breasts in the frenzy of a shipwreck and watch in amazement as the star gingerly steps into the bath.[12] *Male and Female* grossed the extraordinary amount of one and one-quarter billion dollars, and ensured that sex appeal would become a favorite movie theme. Partial female nudity, excused by the bath or draped only in lingerie became a staple of cinema in the decade to come. De Mille was its undisputed master: "He made of the bathroom a delightful resort . . . a mystic shrine to Venus and sometimes to Apollo. . . . Underclothes became visions of translucent promise."[13] Most every star who came to popularity in the twenties played a lingerie scene, which placed her in a languorous pose with soft, body-hugging silk around her torso. Clara Bow played the familiar lingerie salesgirl in *It* (1927); critics raved about Bebe Daniels' "negligible negligee" in *Stranded in Paris* (1926); *Bertha the Sewing Machine Girl* (1926) was described by William Fox Productions as "A Love and Lingerie Edition of the Great Melodrama"; and Joan Crawford modeled lingerie with matchless sensuality in *Our Blushing Brides* (1930).[14]

The exposure of the star's limbs was but one harbinger of the new woman. The women in lingerie were more than mannequins. They were the personification of the "moderns," females whose whole projected personalities had a new vitality and aura. Whether they played the upper-class flapper as did Gloria Swanson and Norma Talmadge, or the working girls characteristic of Clara Bow and Madge Bellamy, the same spirit surrounded them.[15] The new movie woman exuded above all a sense of physical freedom—unrestrained movement, confident gait, abounding energy—the antithesis of the controlled, quiet, tight-kneed poses of Griffith's heroines. These women moved confidently into a once male world. With a dashing spontaneity they rushed onto dance floors, leapt into swimming pools, and accepted any dare—to drink, to sport, to strip as Bow did in *Saturday Night Kid* (1929). They entered the world of work and college as well as the social circle, dashing down the city streets to offices, shops and classrooms with aplomb and self-assurance. They were an ambitious group, determined to use their bodily charms to make their way in the world.

The Hollywood ingenues enthusiastically embraced the remodeled image of women and imbued their new roles with a spirit of independence. Joan Crawford's scintillating Charleston sequence in *Our Dancing Daughters* (1928) is a case in point. Although the editor cut periodically to lustful male faces, the camera emphasized Crawford's gusto and liveliness, rather than eroticism. When the dancing Crawford ripped off her skirt, it was as if to remove a constricting garment, to facilitate freedom of movement and release of energy, not to entice male admirers. Her Charleston consisted not of bumps and grinds, but of jumps and starts at a frantic pace. Her sheer vitality and self-confidence were at the forefront.[16] In the role of "Dangerous Diana" Crawford upheld the new standard of movie virtue. In contrast, it was the "evil women" of *Our Dancing Daughters* who portrayed shy innocence, a mere ruse to captivate an old-fashioned hero.

The type of sex appeal labeled *It* by Elinor Glyn and presented on film by Clara Bow in 1927 had a similarly wholesome cast. Bow rendered this trait of the new woman as spirited bravado; she seduced her prey at an amusement park and captured her man in the course of a boyish prance through the fun house. The essence of Bow's screen presence was recognized by contemporary critics. Agreeing that Clara Bow had "it," or "good old-fashioned sex appeal," one reviewer described her as "an amusing little person, a slam-bang kid, full of vitality and an easy, none too subtle appeal."[17] The movie moderns did indeed project more of the aura of the slam-bang kid than that of the femme fatale or the vamp. It was her mischievous vivacity that most emphatically eclipsed the old woman.

Yet the stars vitality only embellished a rigidifying set of movie stereotypes; the twenties' films gave precise details on how to become *correctly* modern. Gloria Swanson performed the requisite transformation in *Why Change Your Wife* (1920). In one extravagant gesture she tore off her old garb, draped herself in plumes and lamé, and realigned her shapely form in a stylized seductive posture. The popular stars of the twenties excelled in such movements and poses, the hands placed low on the hip, the jaunt in the walk, the cock of the head that made the new woman a lively reality. The education in the mannerism of the flapper was undertaken with special self-awareness by a shopgirl named Nora (Madge Bellamy) in *Ankles Preferred* (1926). The portion of her anatomy mentioned in the title propelled the plot and mesmerized the camera. Nora regarded the first compliment to her ankles as a lecherous insult. When she retired to her apartment, however, she gazed at her legs with a new interest and pride. Her narcissism reached its fullest development in a situation common to many movies of the era, the heroine's first modeling experience. Goaded on by two lascivious old shopkeepers, Nora tried out a sexy strut, a self-caressing gesture and a heightened hemline. Once this modern style of self-projection had been acquired, Nora's bosses put her to work seducing first the male customers and then a business tycoon from whom they sought financial assistance.[18] This objectification of the female before male admirers was lodged deep in the scenario of the flapper film, and was depicted with entrancing finesse by movie moderns.

These cinematic personalities are more than an historical depository of female images. In the twenties they served as a means of propagating new values and translating popular images into social behavior. As a consequence the movie moderns claim a part in the making of modern womanhood with all the sex roles and sexual stereotyping it entailed. Their initial function was simply didactic and instructional, to train the female audience in fashionable femininity. The movies of the silent era were inherently stereotypical, relying on extravagant images, bold-faced titles and enthralling musical accompaniment. Thus, they were particularly suited to shaping women's aspirations in a uniform direction. Many of the first cinematic lessons were very rudimentary. DeMille's *Why Change Your Wife,* made in 1920, was a simple parable admonishing women to discard the remnants of Victorian womanhood and embrace the flapper model. The audience assimilated this advice through the example of Elizabeth Gordon, played by Gloria Swanson, who at the beginning of the film was a staid, bespectacled wife who reads books on "How to Improve Your Mind" and listens to classical music. The error of her ways was proclaimed by her husband's grimaces at her glasses and chaste attire, and his vulnerability to the wiles of a new woman armed with perfume, short skirts and a panoply of gadgets designed to entrap men. When Robert Gordon divorced his wife to marry this coquette, the first Mrs. Gordon vowed to cling to the old ways, to devote herself to charity, claiming she "hates men and clothes." Upon overhearing a conversation that attributed her divorce to her matronly attire, however, Elizabeth made an abrupt about-face: she exclaimed that she would go the limit to regain her spouse and ordered a "sleeveless, backless, transparent, indecent" wardrobe. The heroine, of course, succeeded in regaining her husband, and their second wedding night found her thoroughly remodeled, dressed in an inanely fashionable gown and dancing a foxtrot.[19] By the mid-twenties, this scene of female transformation had been replayed so many times that one reviewer could write of *His Secretary* (1926): "so cliched and worn was it all we finally fell from our seat suffering from some ancient atavistic complaint that the ennui of this theme always rouses in us."[20] The point had been made over and over again: to win husband and happiness, women must join the competition on equal terms with the American flapper.

Such basic lessons were not lost on the movie audience. Studies of female movie-goers, financed by the Payne Fund and conducted between 1929 and 1933 revealed that young women paid close attention to the star's appearance and behavior. Of a Joan Crawford film, one girl said, "I watch every little detail, of how she's dressed, and her make-up, and also her hair." Another surmised, "I'll bet every girl wishes she was the Greta Garbo type. I tried to imitate her walk, she walks so easy as if she had springs on her feet." This young woman's attempt to mimic Garbo succeeded only in provoking laughter, a fate that also befell a black girl enamored of Clara Bow. "After seeing her picture (*It*) I immediately went home to take stock of my personal charms before my vanity mirror and after carefully surveying myself from all angles I turned away with a sigh, thinking that I may as well want to be Mr. Lon Chaney. I would be just as successful." Such an observation suggests the active, often good-humored ways in which young women might interpret the movie message.[21]

Young moviegoers of the twenties were educated in other, more personal matters, as well. One college girl told the Payne Fund interviewers that "movies are a liberal education in the art of making love." She went on to recount such specific benefits of this cinematic education as learning "how two screen lovers manage their arms when they are embracing; there is a definite technique; one arm over, the other under." This young woman was grateful to the movies for providing a remedial education in a subject avoided by her straitlaced parents, while another found cinematic instructions in love-making "more suggestive and effective than I could possibly find in any book by say Elinor Glyn on 'How to Hold Your Man.'" The adolescent girls who flocked to the movies each week were getting their sex education through the prism of the Hollywood clinch, a training which culminated in erotic awareness if not in actual necking parties. The magic of the movies brought one teenager a rich fantasy life: "Buddy Rogers and Rudy Valentino have kissed me oodles of times but they don't know it, God bless 'em!" Whatever the behavioral consequences of this education, its cultural impact cannot be denied. Movies were handmaidens to the modern preoccupation with intimate heterosexual relations. Moving pictures were clearly more effective than static literary images in detailing the active components of flapper sexuality. One sixteen-year-old girl came to these apt historical conclusions: "No wonder girls of older days, before the movies, were so modest and bashful. They never saw Clara Bow and William Haines. . . .if we did not see such examples in the movies, where would we get the idea of being 'hot'? We wouldn't."[22]

It would be very difficult, on the other hand, for a movie-going girl to receive the idea that sexual promiscuity was an approved form of behavior in the nineteen-twenties. The movie heroine was always chaste at heart. Whatever extremes of brash free-living Bow or Crawford might portray, they preserved their virginity until marriage. Likewise, infidelity among the upper classes, so often sanctioned in the films of Cecil B. DeMille, was prescribed only as a means of retrieving a lost spouse or enlivening a spiceless marriage. Sex in the films of the twenties existed as a readiness to display physical attractions, not as a willingness to give in to the yearnings of the flesh; it heightened sexual awareness without promising ultimate gratification.

Sexiness was in fact associated more with apparel, make-up, and perfume than with the body itself. While movie morality kept sexuality within traditional bounds, materialistic desires were given bountiful gratification in the cinema of the twenties. Hollywood fed consumer lusts through its stock of production values—epitomized by the spend-thrift DeMille who surrounded his heroines with furs, jewels, modish clothes, and modern household artifacts. Fashion shows and tours of modern homes and apartments became staples of the new woman's movie world. In the 1920's, whole films were devoted to the new joys and pitfalls of consumption with titles like *Charge It, Ladies Must Dress, Gimme.*[23] Thirty-eight films detailed the career of the fashion model, another convenient method of inculcating consumerism. The expansion of the consumer sector of the American economy in the twenties called for an accelerated tempo of shopping and the movies provided incentives and instruction for yet another updated female role.

Movies offered to the women of the twenties, and reveal to historians, something more dynamic than packaged instructions about the new femininity and new female roles. The object of the Hollywood craftsman was to arrange images into engrossing stories. To the movie audience, gathered together in darkness and anonymity, the moving picture offered a vicarious dream life. This cinematic experience has been aptly defined by Raymond Durgnat: "For the masses the cinema is dreams and nightmares, or it is nothing. It is an alternative experience freed from the tyranny of the 'old devil consequences'; from the limitation of having only one life to live. One's favored films are one's unlived lives, one's hopes, fear, libido."[24] Movie fantasies are nonetheless inextricably intertwined with the realities of the age in which they are produced. Films, after all, as Stanley Cavell has pointed out, are composed of photographs, images that reproduce the world outside the theatre. Moreover the basic events presented in contemporary dramas are at least conceivable, perhaps even probable, in the lives of viewers. This evocative mixture of reality and dream, furthermore, is concocted by an industry whose imperative is box office profits. The popular film formula is constructed around the aspirations and anxieties of the contemporary audience. The relation of the world on the screen and American realities has been elegantly described by Barbara Deming. After viewing up to one-fourth of Hollywood's productions between 1942 and 1948, Deming reached this conclusion: "The heros and heroines who are most popular at any particular period are precisely those who, with a certain added style, with a certain distinction, act out the predicament in which we all find ourselves—a predicament from which the movie-dream then cunningly extricates us. But the . . . movie-goer . . . need never admit what that condition really is from which he is being vicariously relieved."[25]

The historian's task, given this interpretation of film culture, is to identify the predicaments which underlie the popular film, to analyze the condition from which the viewer is "being vicariously relieved." In the case of the woman's film, the superficial problem is quite obvious: to win and keep a husband's love, and to secure the social and economic status which accompanies marriage. The Payne Fund survey of movie themes between 1920 and 1933 found the most common plot theme to be winning the loved one. Through six decades of cinema history the problems of the unmarried woman and the neglected wife have been "resolved" in thousands of happy endings, enacted by characters from every walk in life and every social station. One variation on this theme was particularly germane to the twenties, however, and deserves special attention: the predicament of the working girl.

In point of fact the work force had been a familiar environment for young women well before 1920. The rate of female employment skyrocketed in the teens and increased at only a moderate rate, if at all, between 1920 and 1930 when over ten million women were at work outside the home. Most of these women, like their impersonators on the screen, were under thirty years of age and single. The employed women of the twenties were apt to congregate in a relatively new segment of the work force, deserting factories and domestic service to take up white-collar employment. The number of female clerks had increased almost 300 percent between 1910 and 1920; the number of stenographers and typists more than doubled, making women the majority in those occupations.[26] These facts were also reflected in the films of the era. In the twenties the American Film Institute Catalog listed only four films made about factory workers, while only 46 concerned housemaids, most of them in minor roles. On the other hand the catalog lists 49 sales clerks, 28 stenographers, and no less than 114 secretaries who appeared on the screen between 1921 and 1930.[27] On occasion, the films detailed this historical progression in female work roles. For example, *Bertha The Sewing Machine Girl* (1926) carried the heroine from her factory job, to the role of telephone operator, then model, then fashion designer.[28] The movie camera tended to skirt the mundane aspects of white-collar work, preferring to dwell on the glamor of a setting full of consumer goods, entertainment, and eligible men, all of which the young woman could pursue without parental interference. The demand of the economy for women's labor in this job sector, as well as women's responsiveness to this need, was nonetheless very real. By 1925, 34 percent of high school girls in Middletown, for example, aspired to be clerical workers.[29] Fan magazines took pains to associate movie stars with these prosaic roles, pointing out that Joan Crawford was once a shop girl in Kansas City; that Janet Gaynor clerked in a shoe store; and that Frances Marion earned $25 a week as a stenographer before she became a star, then screen writer.[30] Early films no doubt facilitated the transformation of the female work force, reflecting, endorsing, and legitimizing women's assumption of new roles.

By the late twenties, Hollywood seemed to take the work experience of young females for granted. No longer bothering to issue tantalizing invitations to enter the work force, they planted heroines firmly behind desks and counters. At this point, the focus of the film shifted to grappling with the specific complaints of working women. In fact several films began with a sharp critique of the routine and rigid nature of the work situation. The opening shot in *Ankles Preferred* featured Madge Bellamy at a department store counter, annoyed at the customers, bored with her work, and anxiously gazing at the clock. The monotony of woman's work was emphatically underlined by the superimposition of a clock upon Bellamy's forelorn countenance, followed by her jubilation at closing time. The clock motif appeared again in *Our Blushing Brides*. This 1930 film opened with a close-up of the time clock as a long line of workers, mostly female, filed into a department store. Throughout the film the alarm clock stood as the exasperating symbol of work which the women dreamed of throwing out the window forever. The regimentation associated with the conscription of women into the modern work force was presented in other ways as well. The assembly line nature of work in these white-collar occupations was painstakingly delineated in *Our Blushing Brides.* In the opening sequence the camera panned across a massive, dreary locker room as hundreds of women scurried past. They amassed behind the mirror until a clamorous bell sent them rushing to their assigned places at the consumer counter. Once in their stations, the mechanical and impersonal nature of sales work is underscored by the supervisors; one girl was addressed only as number 36, another as number 42.[31] In this department store film and in secretarial films like *Soft Living* (1928), special care was taken to show the working girls laboriously filling out forms and adding up columns of numbers. The movies took cognizance of the discipline imposed by the modern work place, a regimen which the women of the twentieth century rarely escaped by retaining a life-long place in the home.

The work world so bleakly pictured in these films also encroached upon the private lives of the female characters. It established their tedious weekday schedule, composed of a frantic struggle on the subway, hasty meals, and shattered nerves. The homes which these women entered at the end of a work day were a tribute to their meager earnings on the job. The movie set included a carefully constructed working girls' apartment: cramped quarters, shabby furnishings, a tiny table where the roommates took their frugal meals. Silent filmmakers did not hesitate to insert titles expressing the girls' complaints about these conditions, the implicit lot of their sex and class. In fact they frequently used an intertitle to announce the specific wage rate for female labor, usually between twenty-five and thirty-five dollars a week. Once the essential features of woman's work had been established, the thrust of the heroine's dream was obvious—escape.

Impermanence was built into the work situation of these screen heroines. The cheerful camaraderie and spunky optimism characteristic of the working-girl flapper stemmed from the assumption that her job tenure would be brief. The avenue of escape was predictable enough: matrimony. Yet there were a variety of ways to secure a husband while on the job. The bluntest technique was the aggressive use of sexual attractions as employed by the ubiquitous gold digger. No less than 34 films were made on this theme between 1921 and 1930.[32] The most famous movie in this genre, *Gentlemen Prefer Blondes* (1928) written by Anita Loos, approvingly recounted the heavy-handed tactics of Lorelei Lee, who entrapped America's richest bachelor.[33] *Soft Living,* made the same year, traced gold digging directly to the plight of the working girl. The heroine, played by Madge Bellamy, was secretary to an attorney specializing in divorce cases. She embarked upon her hunt for a millionaire after comparing her weekly salary of $35 to the thousands in alimony carted away each week by a deft gold digger. Her original intention was to remain a "kissless bride," file for divorce on trumped-up charges, and retire on her alimony. The typical sexual shyness beneath the flapper exterior was revealed on the heroine's honeymoon when she cowered in the upper berth of the train to avoid viewing a pajama-clad husband. In the end, love triumphed over avarice, and the secretary and millionaire settled into a bone fide love nest. Nonetheless, the fantasy was clear, the secretary had won her millionaire; in the parlance of the day she had "slapped a trap on a sucker's bank roll."[34]

More typically the working girl of the twenties' cinema won her retirement through the promptings of love and trusting submission to her man. Charm, poise, virtue and the advantage of close proximity to eligible men were ingredients in the scenario that captured many a wealthy mate. Secretaries were particularly successful in this regard, placed as they were in close association with their boss. But salesgirls did equally well despite the odds against their meeting millionaires across department store counters. Joan Crawford achieved this success in *Our Blushing Brides,* proving her worth by rejecting the owner's son as an illegitimate lover, later to win him as her spouse. Other working women found rich men in the most unlikely places. The character in the title role of *Five and Ten Cent Annie* (1928) married a street cleaner who conveniently inherited a fortune. A theatre cashier came upon her affluent husband at the box office in *The Girl in the Glass Cage* (1929).[35]

The working girl's fantasy as manufactured by Hollywood was not always this extravagant. In numerous movies of the twenties, heroines found their happy ending in the arms of a man of their own class. A subway guard was the perfect match for both *The Girl From Woolworth's* (1929) and *Sub Way Sadie* (1926).[36] Such alliances were often formed after females had given up their daydreams of independent success, be it as showgirls or department store buyers. The homely solution to this variety of working girl drama was epitomized by *Ankles Preferred.* Madge Bellamy's success in the retail trade took her into the company of many wealthy men, all of whom wanted only the pleasures of her body. Disillusioned by status climbing of this sort Bellamy turned her attention to a more trustworthy young man, who shared her own social world, the lower-class boarding house. Clara Bow illustrated the same sensible solution in *Kid Boots* (1926). She chose as her spouse a humble tailor played by Eddie Cantor, convinced, as a title clearly announced, that unlike many foolish females she craved a man who was "just reliable." The climax of this picture also conveyed the boyish *joie de vivre* with which these marriages were forged. Bow recited her marriage vows to Cantor at the end of a comic chase, attired in disheveled pants and running behind a speeding automobile containing the judge.[37] The role pattern which the movie moderns embraced so ebulliently was mundane reality to millions of American women, the youthful female labor force that retired en masse upon marriage henceforth to rest, however insecurely or impecuniously, on the income of their mates.

The magic of these movies, and their meaning to the historian, lie as much in the anxieties which precede the domestic denouement as in the happy ending itself. Movie fantasies have a double-edged quality, are both "dreams and nightmares" as Raymond Durgnat puts it. At times the nightmares constitute the direct and central themes of the movies; more often, particularly in women's films, fearful visions provide the cutting edge of the romance itself. Imbedded in the images and plots of the movie moderns are a prevalent set of tensions, unfulfilled promises, and unhappy endings for minor characters. These tragic subplots provided the essential dramatic tension in the films of the twenties. Many women lost out in the marriage competition, and not even the most optimistic melodrama tied up every female character in a neat wedding knot. In most working girl stories at least one of the roommates was required to function as a negative example for the audience. In *Our Blushing Brides* the gold digger Frankie was punished for her mercenary sexuality by the discovery that her hard-won husband was a gambler whose expensive gifts were quickly confiscated by the police. A second roommate, a naive and trusting sort named Connie, was deceived into the unsavory position of a kept woman, only to have her concubine marry one of his own class. In this film the odds were two to one against a successful marital alliance. The third roommate, Jerry, played by Joan Crawford, succeeded only because she was painfully cautious in bestowing her love. In fact, the disastrous fate which befell Connie was in many ways the emotional pivot of *Our Blushing Brides.* The forsaken woman happened to turn on the radio to hear an on-the-scene report of her lover's engagement party. Her lost love and lost status were detailed simultaneously in a merciless account of what the fashionable entourage was wearing on this occasion. The finale laced suspense with maudlin sentimentality as the prostrate Connie swallowed poison amid intercuts to her speeding rescuers, while the radio blared cruelly away in the background. This death scene was prolonged to full melodramatic length as the evil male was carted against his will to Connie's bedside, allowing her to die with her romantic illusions intact. This bittersweet story was designed by Bess Meredyth, a woman who created hundreds of such dream portraits. The successful formula, steeped in a pessimistic female consciousness and a cynical view of men, exposed the underside of modern romances. Might not this movie cliché suggest that some women secretly yearned to escape the whole tortuous labyrinth of the sexual marketplace?

Another empathic ploy of these films preyed on the apprehension that marriage itself does not put an end to woman's anxiety. In fact in the twenties almost 300 films were made on the theme of infidelity. [38] In addition to their titillating value these movies harped upon the insecurity of the married woman, inevitably aging and losing her girlish charms within a world constantly replenished by a stream of attractive flappers. Over and over again wives were charged with rejuvenating their appearance in order to retrieve husbands from flirts and gold diggers. One woman's success on the marriage market was all too often another's failure. A dowdy wife was poor competition for the young workers who shared her husband's store or office. The anxieties of upper class wives were endlessly exploited by DeMille, and by the mid-twenties even Theda Bara was placed in the predicament of the shunned wife (*Unchastened Woman*, 1925).[39] Alternately, the older woman was made the object of ridicule. In *Ankles Preferred*, for example, the wives of the shopkeepers were introduced into scenes by their ankles—fleshy, drooping, with sagging stockings—clearly identified as dinosaurs in the modern movie era. On the other hand a few films of the twenties recognized, in a roundabout fashion, that the married woman might be discontented with her role, as well as fearful of losing her husband. One remarkable film, *Dancing Mothers* (1926), ended as the wife defiantly leaves home. Two films of 1922, *The Real Adventure* and *A Woman's Woman*, portrayed older women whose boredom with housework and lack of appreciation from their husbands drove them into business. Although their successful careers culminated either in marital disaster or restoration to the fireside, these themes suggested to at least a few movie-goers the further problems that lay beyond the happy ending.[40]

These dark shadows were further accentuated by the characterization of male-female relations throughout these films. In most movies the male characters were very limply drawn; their chief role was to express, often in a puppylike fashion, the love sickness inspired by the heroines, some of whom overtly manipulated them into marriage. Seen through the woman's eyes, moreover, the movie male was often the object of distrust, even disgust. As Gloria Swanson set out on a second courtship of her ex-husband, her underlying view of the opposite sex was baldly announced in the title: "The more I see of men the better I like dogs." In the course of her uneven courtship in *Our Blushing Brides,* Joan Crawford displayed deep-seated cynicism about men, which she repeatedly pounded home to her roommates. This attitude was expressed to her prospective spouse in the most virulent attacks on his manhood. When she labeled his sweet-talk "ridiculous rubber-stamped lines," he responded: "When it comes to the matter in question I don't trust any modern girl." On their next encounter, when the boss's son intruded upon her in her underwear, she hurled further insults at his masculine ego, saying he wasn't "man enough" to take advantage of the situation, and that it made her "deathly ill" to have him touch her. Crawford's working girl also takes this opportunity to allude to the contradictions of class as well as sex: "I suppose your position entitles you to these little privileges." All in all the animosities in the courtship process cast considerable doubt on the quality of male and female relations after the happy ending.

The relations between female characters were also distorted by the new sexual mores. The sisterly solace associated with Victorian womanhood lingered on in many of these films, as working girls and roommates freely embraced to express sympathy and share joys. Yet the divisions between women were subtly and not so subtly indicated. The fragility of sisterhood was a movie cliché often expressed in a shot of a lonely girl in an empty apartment on evenings when her roommates had dates. The most heart-felt sympathy between women, furthermore, arose to salve the wounds inflicted by males. Female friendship appeared as a supportive by-product of heterosexual relations, not as a primary female bond. The fragmenting effect of the preoccupation with personal attractiveness was symbolized in another recurrent movie image, that of females gathered together before a mirror, obsessed with their own images and oblivious to one another. The conversations that ensued often bordered on the vicious, replete with snide attacks on one another's appearance or reputation. Then, of course, cinema delighted in portraying the most extreme negation of female friendship, the vitriolic "cat fight." This movie cliché was perfected by 1920 when the female rivals in *Why Change Your Wife* scratched, kicked, and threatened to throw acid in each other's faces, par for the course in movie man-hunting.

The melodrama's happy ending could not entirely efface all these peripheral failures and inherent contradictions. As Stanley Cavell observed in another connection, "The walk into the sunset is a dying star; they live happily ever after—as long as they keep walking."[41] The audience that emerged from the darkened theatre in the twenties, to gaze upon mundane reality and perhaps their own quite ordinary mates, might feel a disquieting let-down. The thrills of the film had been built on the activism and gay abandon of the flapper figure, a style that hardly jibes with the unacknowledged denouement into a world of dishes and diapers. At best the female viewer would return to the security of her work-a-day womanhood, content with only a brief relief and catharsis to be renewed in a week or so at the movies. Yet it is unlikely that modern maidens and dancing daughters, the Clara Bow's and Joan Crawford's, could survive unchanged in such a humdrum atmosphere.

As the reality of modern womanhood eclipsed the initial optimism of the flapper era, these dreams themselves came to seem extravagant, even dangerous, too hedonistic for women returned home and fighting off a depression to boot. Accordingly, the star of the flapper declined precipitiously in the thirties. Its demise was already apparent in *Our Blushing Brides* (1930), the last in a series of Joan Crawford vehicles which included *Our Dancing Daughters* and *Our Modern Maidens.* At the outset of this film, Crawford's effervescence had been reduced to a sparkle in her eye and a spring in her step as she entered the department store. Back home in her sparsely furnished apartment she battered the high hopes of her roommates by calling attention to the chill reality of the working girl's predicament, a stance that she commended because "at least it's real." The stoical Jerry (Crawford) then spent the bulk of the movie ministering to disasters bred by the recklessness of the film's flappers. She became progressively more ridden with cares, looking more like a beaten-down worker than a dashing modern. Jerry's ultimate rescue from work and spinsterhood came suddenly and improbably. Her triumph was rent by contradictions. Her engagement to the boss's son was announced by an act of male possessiveness, her fiancé's genial threat to beat up a male caller. This announcement, furthermore, was made in her lover's hideaway, the scene of his previous seductions and a ferocious argument with the heroine, who is now attired in a costume she once modeled while an employee of her husband-to-be. This is a rather tawdry fantasy—that the working woman can win by marriage the very commodities and privileges that were expropriated from her labor. The screenwriters were making a telling if subtle point about modern womanhood.

Clara Bow exited from the twenties in an equally somber fashion. The thirties found her a box office wash-out attempting a come-back in abysmal roles like that of Nasa in *Call Her Savage.* Although Bow retained her characteristic volatility, it was given a completely different interpretation in this film of 1932. Her devilish pranks lost their gaiety, were judged symptomatic of uncontrollable wildness in her temperament which persisted despite her longing "to be like other girls." The exuberant charms that once won the screen heroine an ideal mate now invited bad matches, broken hearts, alcoholism and loneliness. The flapper had become perverse by 1932, and had to be explained away. Hollywood devised an uncanny solution, tracing Nasa's abnormality to heredity, the fact that she was indeed a savage, descended from an Indian.[42] Such was the ignoble end of the "it girl" as the zesty young actresses of the twenties went the way of the Charleston and the hip flask into a soberer and still unliberated era.

Very few of the stars of the twenties weathered the fashions in womanhood that followed. One sturdy actress fought her way through the Hollywood jungle for forty years only to secure less than savory female roles. She was, of course, Joan Crawford. In 1959 after a series of movies in which she played neurotic, lonely women, Crawford found herself back in the world of the working girl in a film entitled *The Best of Everything*.[43] In many ways the plot of this film replicated the working girl's formula of the twenties. The setting moved to the typing pool and editorial offices of a publishing firm, but the drama was familiar: three young women searching for an honorable escape from the workforce through matrimony. Crawford, however, was too old, too hardened by some 51 years experience of womanhood to have a central role in this plot. As Amanda Farrow she stood on the sidelines, admonishing women against the careerism which made of her a bitter, nasty, carping boss, left only a sterile relationship with a married man. Ironically, however, the very devastation of this woman's life entitled her to some stature and legitimacy in the business world. Crawford made one last-ditch attempt to reform, giving up her lucrative job for marriage in hopes that home life would "soften" her frustrated personality. Yet her marriage was casually allowed to fail. When Amanda returned to her editor's job it was with a new equanimity. In a genuinely warm gesture she extended her businesswoman's hand to the female work force, represented here by the central female character (played by Hope Lange) who we are led to believe will give up her career for marriage and launch another generation on a familiar "happy ending." Yet Joan Crawford's role bespoke another reality of womanhood in the 1950's. Her fans from the twenties had most likely returned to the labor force after a career of homemaking. The typical working woman was no longer an ingenue but a middleaged, married woman—who, unlike Amanda Farrow, could secure only low-paying clerical and retail jobs. The aging of the new woman left at least this fanciful imprint on the screen.[44]

This modern adjustment of woman's roles was insinuated into the minds of millions of movie-goers beginning in the 1920's. But statistics concerning female employment and marriage rates hardly require this kind of confirmation. The fantasies which movies wove around common female experiences contain richer historical meaning. The movie-goer did not merely travel through a remote fantasy land but briefly inhabited a well-contrived make-believe role. In the case of the movie moderns, that role was a glamorous rendition of the social options open to women. Those vicarious lives could channel female expectations in a socially acceptable direction and then reconcile women to their lot, providing both relief and reinforcement in the guise of routine entertainment. The twenties marked the solidification of a new pattern of female roles characterized by a dynamic equilibrium between work, home, and consumer activities. The movies not only fixed these new priorities in the American woman's mind, but simultaneously prepared her for the discontinuities of a woman's life as she traversed the facile transformations of the typical scenario. The movies, particularly in periods like the twenties when female roles were undergoing a major remodeling, constituted a powerful cultural force, shaping individual choices within the boundaries of social and economic possibilities, thus assisting in the creation of a new womanhood. The movie moderns project the historical reality of the American woman's dream.

NOTES

1. Robert S. and Helen Merrell Lynd (New York, 1929) p. 140.
2. Kenneth A. Yellis "Prosperity's Child: Some Thoughts on the Flapper" *American Quarterly*, XXI (Spring, 1969), pp. 44–64; James R. McGovern, "The American Woman's Pre-World War I Freedom in Manners and Moral," *Journal of American History*, LV (September 1968), 315–333.
3. Kenneth MacGowan, *Behind the Screen* (New York, 1965), 256.
4. Lewis Jacobs, *The Rise of the American Film, A Critical History* (New York, 1949), 328–329; MacGowan, 264.
5. Henry James Forman, *Our Movie-Made Children* (New York, 1933), chapter I.
6. Jacobs, 86–87.
7. Stanley Cavell, *The World Viewed: Reflections on the Ontology of Film* (New York, 1971), 33.
8. Fred I. Greenstein, "New Light on Changing American Values: A Forgotten Body of Survey Data," *Social Forces*, XLII (1964), 441–450.
9. Linda Arvidson Griffith, *When the Movies Were Young* (New York, 1969), 198.
10. Marjorie Rosen, *Popcorn Venus, Women, Movies and the American Dream* (New York, 1973), 59–67; Jacobs, 267.
11. *True Heart Susie*, directed by D.W. Griffith, 1919, Film Department, Museum of Modern Art (hereafter MOMA).
12. *Male and Female*, directed by Cecil B. DeMille, 1919, MOMA.
13. Benjamin B. Hampton, *History of the American Film Industry* (New York, 1970), 249; MacGowan, 261–2.
14. Clipping File, MOMA, under *Bertha the Sewing Machine Girl*, title index.
15. Molly Haskell, *From Reverence to Rape: The Treatment of Women in the Movies*, (New York, 1973), 75–82.

16. *Our Dancing Daughters*, MGM, directed by Harry Beaumont, 1928, "The Charleston Episode" MOMA.

17. Clipping file, MOMA, under *It*, title index.

18. *Ankles Preferred*, Fox, directed by J.G. Blystone, 1919, MOMA.

19. *Why Change Your Wife*, directed by Cecil B. DeMille, 1920, MOMA.

20. Clipping File, MOMA, under *His Secretary*, title index.

21. Forman, 141, 145, 225.

22. *Ibid.*, 151, 154, 167.

23. Jacobs, 407.

24. Raymond Durgnat, *Films and Feelings* (Cambridge, Mass., 1967), 135.

25. Barbara Deming, *Running Away from Myself: A Dream Portrait of America Drawn from the Films of the Forties* (New York, 1969), 2.

26. William Chafe, *The American Woman, Her Changing Social, Economic and Political Role 1920–1970* (New York, 1972), 48–50; Joseph A. Hill, *Women in Gainful Occupations, 1870–1920* (Washington, 1929), 42–47.

27. *The American Film Institute Catalog, Feature Films, 1921–1930*, Vol. F2 (New York 1971), 1523, 1545, 1615, 1619, 1631.

28. *AFI Catalog*, 51.

29. Lynd and Lynd, 50.

30. Margaret Thorp, *America at the Movies* (Arno Reprint, 1970 original, New Haven, 1939), 100.

31. *Our Blushing Brides*, MGM directed by Harry Beaumont, 1930, distributed by Films Incorporated.

32. *AFI Indexes*, 1538.

33. *AFI Catalog*, 285.

34. *Soft Living*, Fox, directed by James Tinley, 1928, MOMA.

35. *AFI Catalog*, 249, 292.

36. *Ibid.*, 291, 775.

37. *Kid Boots*, Paramount, directed by Frank Tuttle, 1926, MOMA.

38. *AFI Indexes*, 1549–1551.

39. *AFI Catalog*, 842.

40. *Ibid.*, 636, 992–993.

41. Cavell, 49.

42. *Call Her Savage*, Fox, directed by John Francis Dillon, 1932, MOMA.

43. *The Best of Everything*, Twentieth Century Fox, Directed by Jean Negulesco, 1959, distributed by Films Incorporated.

44. *See* Valerie Kincade Oppenheimer, The Female Labor Force in the United States (Berkeley, 1970).

21

The Paradox of Progress

William H. Chafe

Although historians have largely neglected the role of women in America's past, few groups in the population merit closer study as a barometer of how American society operates. Not only do women comprise a majority of the population, but gender—together with race and class—serves as one of the principal reference points around which American society is organized. The sociologist Peter Berger has observed that "identity is socially bestowed, socially sanctioned and socially transformed," and gender has been one of the enduring foundations on which social identity has rested. It has provided the basis for dividing up the labor of life ("breadwinning" versus "homemaking"), it has been central to the delineation of roles and authority in the family, and it has served as the source for two powerful cultural stereotypes—"masculine" and "feminine." Any change in the nature of male and female roles thus automatically affects the home, the economy, the school, and perhaps above all, the definition of who we are as human beings.[1]

When the nation entered the Depression decade of the 1930s, few people anticipated any major shift in the status of American women. Although the Nineteenth Amendment had enfranchised women in 1920, the ensuing years witnessed none of the revolutionary changes predicted by either proponents or detractors of the suffrage campaign. Many women who were eligible to vote did not register, and those women who did go to the polls generally cast their ballots for the same candidates as their husbands and fathers. The suffragists had optimist-

From *Paths to the Present,* James T. Patterson, ed. (Minneapolis: Burgess Publishing Co., 1975), pp. 8–24. Reprinted by permission.

ically assumed that women would think, act, and vote together as an independent "bloc," but that assumption underestimated the depth and pervasiveness of traditional ideas on woman's "place." Most Americans had grown up believing that within the family fathers and husbands exercised ultimate authority, particularly regarding issues of a "worldly" nature. Thus it seemed perfectly natural that women should follow the lead of men in political or other nondomestic affairs.[2]

Ratification of the suffrage amendment also failed to produce any significant change in the economic opportunities or activities of women. Although the absolute *number* of women in the labor force increased as the population grew, the *proportion* of women at work shifted very little and in 1940 was approximately the same (25 percent) as it had been in 1910. In addition, women made few inroads into the occupational area of greatest interest to feminists—business and the professions. Three out of four new career women in the 1920s and 1930s went into teaching or nursing (already defined as "women's work"), and the percentage of women in male-dominated professions such as law or medicine either remained constant or declined (as late as the 1940s most medical schools had a 5 percent quota on female admissions).[3]

Here too, the principal reason for the absence of change was the persistence of social norms which prescribed separate and segregated spheres of activities for men and women. Since women were expected to make marriage their career, few businessmen showed any interest in training them for management positions. "The highest profession a woman can engage in," one executive wrote, "is that of a charming wife and wise mother." For most people the idea of combining marriage *and* a career was too radical to consider, first because such a notion flew in the face of prevailing beliefs about a woman's primary responsibility, and second because it required a restructuring of the family, with men assuming some of the tasks of cooking, child-care, and homemaking. In light of such a situation, Margaret Mead observed, a woman with career ambitions had to make a choice between irreconcilable alternatives. She could either be "a woman and therefore less an achieving individual, or an achieving individual and therefore less a woman." If she chose the second alternative, she took the risk of losing any opportunity to be "a loved object, the kind of girl whom men will woo and boast of, toast and marry." It was not surprising, then, that most women traveled the prescribed path and decided not to pursue careers, or continue work after marriage.[4]

If anything, the experience of the Depression decade accentuated the difficulty of altering the status of women. Although the Depression encouraged innovations in politics and social welfare policy, it also seemed to have a chastening effect on cultural values, calling people back to the tried and true verities of family, hearth, and home. Nowhere was this better illustrated than in attitudes toward women. Labor, business, and government undertook a concerted campaign to discourage women from taking jobs, especially married women whose employment might deprive an able-bodied man of a job to support his family. At the same time, women's magazines celebrated the virtues of homemaking and lambasted those women who sought careers or employment. "No matter how successful," one article declared, "the office woman. . . . is a transplanted posey. . . . Just as a rose comes to its fullest beauty in its own appropriate soil, so does a home woman come to her fairest blooming when her roots are stuck deep in the daily and hourly affairs of her own most dearly beloved." Perhaps most important, the American people seemed to agree. When the pollster George Gallup asked whether wives should work if their husbands were employed, 82 percent said no, including more than 75 percent of the women.[5]

The eruption of World War II made the first significant dent in this pattern. The national emergency caused new industries to develop and new jobs to open up, providing an opportunity for women, like other excluded groups, to improve their economic position. Almost overnight, the woman munition worker became an accepted part of the labor force. In one California aircraft plant, 13,000 men and no women had been employed in the fall of 1941. A year later there were 13,000 women and 11,000 men. The same story was repeated throughout the nation. The New York Central Railroad doubled the number of its female employees, assigning them to grease and oil locomotives, load baggage, and work on section gangs. Elsewhere, women riveted gun emplacements, welded hatches, took the place of lumberjacks in downing huge redwoods, became precision toolmakers, and ran giant overhead cranes. Hardly a job existed which women did not perform.

The statistics of female employment suggest the dimensions of the change. Between 1941 and 1945 6.5 million women took jobs, increasing the size of the female labor force by 57 percent. At the end of 1940 approximately 25 percent of all women were gainfully employed; four years later the figure had soared to 36 percent—an increase greater than that of the previous forty years combined. Perhaps most important from a social point of view, the largest number of new workers were married and middle-aged. Prior to 1940 young and single women had made up the vast majority of the female labor force. During the war, in contrast, 75 percent of the new workers were married, and within four years the number of wives in the labor force had doubled. Although some of the new labor recruits were newlyweds who might have been expected to work in any event, the majority listed themselves as former housewives and many, including 60 percent of those hired by the War Department, had children of school and preschool age. By the time victory was achieved, it was just as likely that a wife over forty would be employed as a single woman under twenty-five. The urgency of defeating the Axis powers had swept away, temporarily at least, one of America's entrenched customs.[6]

If women took jobs in unprecedented numbers, however, there was little evidence of a parallel shift in attitudes toward equality between the sexes. Women were consistently excluded from top policy-making committees concerned with running the war, and from higher-level management and executive positions. In addition, the war had only a minimal effect on the traditional disparity between men's and women's wages. Although the War Manpower Commission announced a firm policy of equal pay for equal work, enforcement was spotty, and employers continued to pay women less than men simply by changing the description of the job from "heavy" to "light." As a result, a woman inspector in one plant earned 55 cents an hour while her male counterpart was paid $1.20.[7]

The issue of establishing day care centers provided the most revealing example of enduring attitudes. If women were to be equals with men in the labor market, they required some relief from the burden of sole responsibility for homemaking and child-rearing. Government reports showed a direct correlation between female absenteeism and the need to stay at home and care for youngsters, and newspapers were full of stories of children being exiled to neighborhood movie houses while their parents worked. Yet for many Americans, there was no more sacred obligation than that of a woman to rear her children on a full-time basis. "Now, as in peacetime," the Children's Bureau declared, "a mother's primary duty is to her home and children. This duty is one she cannot lay aside, no matter what the emergency." As a result of the profound value conflict over the issue, a federal day care program was at first postponed, then prevented from becoming fully effective.[8]

The staying power of traditional values received vigorous confirmation in the postwar years. Despite effusive expressions of gratitude for women's contribution to the war effort, many Americans believed that women should return to their rightful place in the home as soon as the war had ended. In one of the most popular treatises of the postwar years, Ferdinand Lundberg and Marynia Farnham argued that female employment was a feminist conspiracy to seduce women into betraying their biological destiny. The independent woman, they claimed, was a "contradiction in terms." Women were born to be soft, nurturant, and dependent on men; motherhood represented the true goal of female life. Sounding the same theme, Agnes Meyer wrote in the *Atlantic* that though women had many careers, "they have only one vocation—motherhood." The task of modern women, she concluded, was to "boldly announce that no job is more exacting, more necessary, or more rewarding than that of housewife and mother." Most Americans seemed to agree. A series of public opinion polls taken in the postwar years showed that a large majority of people continued to subscribe to the idea of a sharp division of labor between the sexes, with husbands making the "big" decisions and wives caring for the home.[9]

In fact, the situation was more complicated than either public opinion polls or magazine rhetoric seemed to indicate. It was one thing to focus renewed attention on traditional values, and quite another to eradicate the impact of four years of experience. As observers noted at the time, women had discovered something new about themselves in the course of the war, and many were unwilling to give up that discovery just because the war had ended. Although most of the women workers viewed their employment as temporary when the war began, a Women's Bureau survey disclosed that by war's end, 75 percent wished to remain in the labor force. "War jobs have uncovered unsuspected abilities in American women," one worker commented. "Why lose all these abilities because of a belief that 'a woman's place is in the home'? For some it is, for others not."[10]

The prospect of a job appealed particularly to those women over thirty-five. According to the 1940 Census, the average woman married at age twenty-one and sent her last child off to school when she was thirty-five. With the children out of the house most of the day, many middle-aged women were free to join, or remain in, the labor force. Economic interest in augmenting family income was matched by personal interest in pursuing new activities. Many women workers relished the recognition and sense of accomplishment associated with a job. Work in a factory or office might not seem that much more exciting or fulfilling than washing dishes or cleaning floors, but it had the advantage of providing social companionship, a tangible reward in the form of a paycheck, and contact with the "outside" world.

To a surprising extent, these women succeeded in their desire to remain in the job market. Although the number of women workers declined temporarily in the period immediately after the war, female employment figures showed a sharp upturn beginning in 1947, and by 1950 had once again reached wartime peaks. By 1960 the number of women workers was growing at a rate four times faster than that of men, and 40 percent of all women over sixteen were in the labor force compared to 25 percent in 1940. More important, the women who spearheaded the change were from the same groups that had first gone to work in the war. By 1970, 45 percent of the nation's wives were employed (compared to 11.5 percent in 1930 and 15 percent in 1940), and the 1970 figure included 51 percent of all mothers with children aged six to seventeen. In addition, the economic background of the women workers had shifted significantly. During the 1930s employment of married women had been limited almost exclusively to families with poverty level incomes. By 1970, in contrast, 60 percent of all families with an income of more than $10,000 had wives who worked. In short, the whole pattern of female employment had been reversed. Through legitimizing employment for the average wife and making it a matter of patriotic necessity, the war had initiated a dramatic alteration in the behavior of women and had permanently changed the day-to-day content of their lives.[11]

But if the "objective" conditions of female employment changed so much, why did attitudes toward equality not follow suit? Why, if so many wives and mothers were holding jobs, was there so little protest about continued low pay and discrimination? Why, above all, did the woman's movement not revive in the forties or fifties instead of developing only in the late sixties? Such questions have no easy answers, but to the extent that an explanation is possible, it has to do with the context of the times. The prospect for value changes in any period depends on the frame of reference of the participants, their awareness of the possibility or need for action, and the dominant influences at work in shaping the society. When the appropriate conditions are present, change can be explosive. When they are not present, change can take on the character of an underground fire—important in the long run but for the moment beneath the surface. The latter description fits the situation of women in the forties and fifties and a consideration of the context in which their employment increased during these years is crucial to an understanding of the relationship between behavior and attitudes.

To begin with, most women in the forties and fifties lacked the frame of reference from which to challenge prevailing attitudes on sex roles. Although many women worked, the assumptions about male and female spheres of responsibility were so deeply engrained that to question them amounted to heresy. If social values are to be changed, there must be a critical mass of protestors who can provide an alternative ideology and mobilize opposition toward traditional points of view. In the postwar period, that protest group did not exist. Feminists at the time simply had no popular support and were generally viewed as a group of cranky women who constituted a "lunatic fringe." The Women's Bureau probably represented the views of the majority of the population in 1945 when it described feminists as "a small but militant group of leisure class women [giving vent] to their resentment at not having been born men."[12]

In such a situation, it was not surprising that most women workers exhibited little feminist consciousness. Most had taken jobs because of the benefits associated with employment, not out of a desire to compete with men or prove their equality. When a pattern of discrimination is so pervasive that it is viewed as part of the rules of the game, few individuals will have the wherewithal to protest. It takes time and an appropriate set of social conditions before a basis for ideological protest can develop. With their experience in World War II, women had gone through the first stage of a monumental change. But it would be unrealistic to think that they could move immediately into a posture of feminist rebellion without a series of intervening stages. New perceptions had to evolve; new ideas had to gain currency. And both depended to some extent on the dominant influences at work in the immediate environment.

The second reason for the persistence of traditional attitudes was that women's employment expanded under conditions which emphasized women's role as "helpmates." The continued entry of women into the labor force was directly related to skyrocketing inflation and the pent-up desire of millions of families to achieve a higher living standard. In many instances, husbands and wives could not build new homes, buy new appliances, or purchase new cars on one income alone, and the impulse not to be left behind in the race for affluence offered a convenient rationale for women to remain in the labor force. Men who might oppose in theory the idea of married women holding jobs were willing to have their own wives go to work to help the family achieve its middle-class aspirations. But under such circumstances, the wife who held a job was playing a supportive role, not striking out on her own as an "independent" woman. The distinction was crucial. If women had been taking jobs because of a desire to prove their equality with men, their employment would probably have encountered bitter resistance. In contrast, the fact that they were thought to be only "helping out" made it possible for their efforts to receive social sanction as a fulfillment of their traditional family role.

To say that attitudes did not change, however, did not mean that behavior was without important long-range effects. Indeed, the growing employment of women offers an excellent example of the way in which changes in behavior can pave the way for subsequent changes in attitudes. As more and more wives joined the labor force after 1940, the sexual segregation of roles and responsibilities within the family gradually gave way to greater sharing. Sociological surveys showed that wherever wives held jobs, husbands performed more household tasks, especially in the areas of child care, cleaning, and shopping. In addition, power relationships between men and women underwent some change. Women who worked exercised considerably more influence on "major" economic decisions than wives who did not work. In no instance did the changes result in total equality, nor were they ideologically inspired; but sociologists unanimously concluded that women's employment played a key role in modifying the traditional distribution of tasks and authority within the family.[13]

Similarly, the presence of an employed mother exercised a substantial impact on the socialization patterns of children. Young boys and girls who were raised in households where both parents worked grew up with the expectation that women—as well as men—would play active roles in the outside world. A number of surveys of children in elementary and junior high school showed that daughters of working mothers planned to work themselves after marriage, and the same studies suggested that young girls were more likely to name their mother as the person they most admired if she worked than if she did not work. At the same time, it appeared that these daughters developed a revised idea of what it meant to be born female. On a series of personality tests, daughters of working mothers scored lower on scales of traditional femininity and agreed that both men and women should enjoy a variety of work, household, and recreational experiences. Thus if behavioral change did not itself produce a challenge to traditional attitudes, it set in motion a process which prepared a foundation for such a challenge.[14]

All that was required to complete the process was the development of an appropriate context, and in the early 1960s that context began to emerge. After eight years of consolidation and consensus in national politics during the Eisenhower administration, a new mood of criticism and reform started to surface in the nation. Sparked by the demands of black Americans for full equality, public leaders focused new attention on a whole variety of problems which had been festering for years. Poverty, racial injustice, and sex discrimination had a lengthy history in America, but awareness of them crystallized in a climate which emphasized the need for activism to eradicate the nation's ills. Once the process of protest had begun, it generated a momentum of its own, spreading to groups which previously had been quiescent.

Again, the experience of women dramatized the process of change. Just as World War II had served as a catalyst to behavioral change among women, the ferment of the sixties served as a catalyst to ideological change. The first major sign of the impending drive for women's liberation appeared with the publication in 1963 of Betty Friedan's best-selling *The Feminine Mystique*. Writing with eloquence and passion, Friedan traced the origins of women's oppression to a social system which persistently denied women the opportunity to develop their talents as individual human beings. "The core of the problem of women today," she wrote, "is not sexual but a problem of identity—a stunting or evasion of growth. . . ." Friedan pointed out that while men had abundant opportunities to test their mettle, women saw their entire lives circumscribed by the condition of their birth and were told repeatedly "that they could desire no greater destiny than to glory in their own femininity." If a woman had aspirations for a career, she was urged instead to find a full measure of satisfaction in the role of housewife and mother. Magazines insisted that there was no other route to happiness; consumer industries glorified her life as homemaker; and psychologists warned her that if she left her position in the home, the whole society would be endangered. The result was that she was imprisoned in a "comfortable concentration camp," prevented from discovering who she really *was* by a society which told her only what she *could be*. Although Friedan's assessment contained little that had not been said before by other feminists, her book spoke to millions of women in a fresh way, driving home the message that what had previously been perceived as only a personal problem was in fact a *woman* problem, shared by others and rooted in a set of social attitudes that required change if a better life was to be achieved.[15]

A second—and equally important—influence feeding the woman's movement came from the burgeoning drive for civil rights. Although it was true that blacks and women had strikingly different problems, they suffered from modes of oppression which in some ways were similar. For women as well as blacks, the denial of equality occurred through the assignment of separate and unequal roles. Both were taught to "keep their place," and were excluded from social and economic opportunities on the grounds that assertive behavior was deviant. The principal theme of the civil rights movement was the immorality of treating any human being as less equal than another on the basis of a physical characteristic, and that theme spoke as much to the condition of women as to that of blacks. In its tactics, its message, and its moral fervor, the civil rights movement provided inspiration and an organizational model for the activities of women.

Just as significant, the civil rights movement exposed many women to the direct experience of sex discrimination. Younger activists in particular found that they frequently were treated as servants whose chief function was to be sex partners for male leaders. ("The place of women in the movement," Stokely Carmichael said, "is prone.") Instead of having an equal voice in policy-making, women were relegated to tasks such as making coffee or sweeping floors. Faced with such discrimination, some female activists concluded that they had to free *themselves* before they could work effectively for the freedom of others. The same women became the principal leaders of the younger, more radical segment of women's liberation, taking the organizing skills and ideological fervor which they had learned in the fight for blacks and applying them to the struggle for women.[16]

Perhaps the most important precondition for the revival of feminism, however, was the amount of change which had already occurred in women's lives. As long as the overwhelming majority of women remained in the home, there was no frame of reference from which to question the status quo. Woman's "place" was a fact as well as an idea. With the changes which began in World War II, on the other hand, reality ceased to conform to attitudes. The march of events had already delivered a fatal blow to conventional ideas on woman's place, thereby creating a condition which made feminist arguments both timely and relevant. The experience of *some* change gave millions of women the perspective which allowed them to hear the feminists call for more change. Thus if the women who took jobs during the forties did not themselves mount an ideological assault on the status quo, they prepared a foundation which enabled the subsequent generation to take up the battle for a change in attitudes and ideas.

With the convergence of these forces, the drive for women's liberation surged to national prominence in the late sixties. Like all social movements, the quest for sex equality assumed a variety of political and ideological forms. The more moderate activists found an organizational shelter in the National Organization of Women (NOW), formed in 1966 by Betty Friedan to spearhead the drive for legal and economic reforms. The younger, more radical segment of the movement took root in female cadres of student organizations like SDS and SNCC. Beginning with "consciousness-raising" sessions in which women discussed the common problems they had encountered on the basis of their sex, these more radical activists quickly developed a loose coalition of small cell groups which advocated a revolutionary transformation of society based upon a change in the status of women. Whatever their particular ideological stance, however, all feminists were united in demanding an end to class treatment, to the idea that women—as women—should automatically be expected to take minutes at meetings, get lower pay than men, wash dishes, get up with the baby at night, or place their aspirations behind those of their husbands. Within months, the movement had become a national sensation, its advocates storming professional meetings to demand equal employment opportunities, boycotting the Miss America contest to protest the treatment of women as sex objects, and demonstrating before state legislatures for the repeal of abortion laws. By 1970 the movement was one of the media's biggest news items, rivaling student demonstrations, inflation, and the war in Vietnam for public attention.[17]

The image projected by the mass media told only part of the story, however. While network television and national news magazines focused on splashy demonstrations or the movement's attitude toward lesbianism, women in countless towns and cities were organizing in small groups to consider the reality of discrimination in their own lives and devise a strategy to combat it. Although they never comprised more than a small minority in any community, such women engaged in a remarkable variety of activities and made up in impact what they lacked in numbers. Some joined local NOW chapters and pressured merchants and employers to stop treating women differently from men. Others organized for political action, published children's books which eliminated invidious sexual stereotypes, started abortion and birth control clinics, or established day care centers. Some observers criticized the movement for its lack of focus and organization, but its alleged weaknesses were actually the source of its greatest strength. By not becoming attached to a single issue or piece of legislation, the movement avoided the danger of rising or falling with one victory or defeat. And by emphasizing decentralization and diversity, it gave maximum leeway to the energies and interests of the local women who constituted its lifeblood.

Almost inevitably, the women's movement provoked hostility and controversy. Particularly in its more radical manifestations, it represented an effort to alter the nature of the family, to change the way in which children were raised, and to overthrow conventional attitudes concerning who should hold which jobs. Furthermore, at its foundation the movement was calling for men and women to fashion a new definition of human identity—one which no longer would rely on cultural preconceptions of masculinity and femininity. In the context of such ideas, it was not surprising that a large number of people reacted to the movement with dismay and anger. Many men felt that their authority, their strength, their whole self-image had come under attack. And many women, who had devoted their lives to fulfilling the culturally sanctioned role of homemaker, believed that the movement was judging and indicting them as failures.

The astonishing thing was that in the face of powerful opposition, a considerable change in attitudes did take place. Although opinion surveys in the early seventies showed that many women continued to harbor antagonism toward the movement *per se* ("it's too extreme," "it goes overboard"), the same women in a majority of cases endorsed positive action on feminist issues such as day care centers, repeal of abortion laws, equal career opportunities for women, and a greater sharing of household tasks. Whatever the acceptability of the movement as a movement, its message and ideas seemed to be filtering through. Younger women in particular gave evidence of standing up for their rights. Many women students declared that they were just as committed to careers as men, and announced that they intended to incorporate marriage into their overall work pattern rather than make it the chief end of their existence.[18]

The ultimate test of the movement's impact, of course, was whether the attitudes it espoused had any effect on the behavior of women. Here, the evidence suggested at least some correlation between the campaign to change values and the way in which women conducted their lives. In a survey of women students at a large urban university, two sociologists found that behavior and attitudes toward premarital sex changed significantly in the years after 1965. Prior to that time, rates of premarital intercourse conformed to the pattern established in the 1920s, with engaged women having the highest frequency of premarital sex. After 1965, in contrast, a major increase occurred in the number of women having intercourse while in a "dating" or "going steady" relationship. The same survey showed a sharp drop in guilt feelings related to sexual experience as compared to a similar study done in 1958. Marriage statistics too showed a substantial shift during the 1960s. By 1971 more than half of all women 20 years of age were single in contrast to only one-third in 1960, and the number of unmarried women in the 20–24 age bracket had climbed from 28 percent in 1960 to 37 percent a decade later.[19] If the number of female applicants for graduate study was any indicator, it would seem that some of these single women were postponing marriage in order to pursue a career. Although such developments did not necessarily reflect the overt influence of women's liberation, there seemed to be a common thread uniting the feminists' call for increased autonomy among women, and the growing tendency of younger women to seek professional training and exhibit greater independence in their approach to sex and marriage.

The change in women's roles had perhaps its greatest potential impact in the field of population growth, or demography. Beginning in the 1920s the birth rate went into a gradual decline, reaching a nadir in the midst of the Depression. Although demographers at the time predicted a continued low birth rate, the end of World War II produced a massive upsurge of births which lasted through the late fifties. There then ensued another downturn which in 1967 resulted in a birth rate of 17.9 live births per 1000 persons compared to 27.2 a decade earlier. Some experts believed that the shifts were strictly a function of the economy, with affluence explaining the "Baby Boom" in the fifties. But prosperity had also been cited as a rationale for the *declining* birth rate of the twenties, thereby calling into question its validity as a primary determinant. Others attributed the "Baby Bust" of the sixties to the development of oral contraceptives. But this explanation too had shortcomings. The "pill" had not been available during the low birth period of the thirties, and the decline in birth rate during the sixties had begun three years before the pill was marketed.

A somewhat more persuasive explanation traced the changes in the birth rate to a combination of previous demographic trends and economic developments. According to this analysis, the "Baby Boom" started when young couples began to have families which they had deferred during the war, and continued as the generation born in the twenties and thirties came of age in the midst of an expanding job market. Due to affluence, it was easy for such people to marry early and contemplate large families. By the 1960s, in contrast, a crowded labor market, unsettled social conditions, and the expense of raising families put a damper on the birth rate. Demographers confidently predicted, however, that the "Baby Boom" of the fifties would have an echo effect in the late sixties and seventies, when the children born twenty years earlier began to reproduce. The only problem with this theory was that it failed to anticipate—or explain—the continued decline of the birth rate after 1970. Rather than rising, the birth rate reached an all-time low in 1972 and 1973, achieving the reproduction level required for Zero Population Growth.[20]

Perhaps the best approach to the trends of the sixties and seventies is to see the birth rate as a product of economic and social forces interacting with cultural values. Clearly, it would be a mistake to discount the impact of economic conditions. Concern about the ability to provide for children frequently enters into the decision to limit the size of a family, especially in a time of recession. Similarly, the accessibility of contraceptives provides the means for implementing a decision after it is made. But a crucial variable which demographers have underestimated is the influence of cultural values. Seen in this light, the declining birth rate of the sixties and seventies can be traced to the "multiplier effect" of changing values and economic conditions. During the sixties, women married later, delayed the birth of their first child, and bore their last child at an earlier age. Whether as cause or effect, this trend coincided with many women finding careers and interests outside of the home. The rewards of having a job and extra money tended to emphasize the advantages of a small family and the freedom to travel, entertain, or pursue individual interests. This pattern, in turn, was reinforced during the late sixties by the ideology of feminism and the ecology movement. Two Gallup polls in 1967 and 1971 sharply revealed this shift in values. The earlier survey showed that 34 percent of women in the prime child-bearing years anticipated having four or more children. By 1971, in contrast, the figure had dropped to 15 percent. In the absence of more persuasive explanations, it would appear that female employment and changing attitudes toward the role of women played major parts in confounding the predictions of population experts and producing the low birth rates of the early seventies.[21] The ramifications of these forces—if they continue—promise to have a profound effect not only on the size of the family but, more important, on the roles of men and women within the home.

In the end, of course, the historian's judgment on change depends on the vantage point which he or she adopts. From one point of view, it can be argued that little progress has been made toward sex equality. Great problems remain, particularly in cultural assumptions about woman's "place." Yet, on balance, the trends in employment, marriage patterns, attitudes toward sex and careers, and the birth rate suggest that the world of women has altered greatly since 1930. As the nation entered the mid-seventies, it seemed that for the first time in thirty years, behavior and attitudes were reinforcing each other; and the direction of events indicated that changes in the family, the economy, and women's definition of themselves would continue to be dominant themes in the social history of modern America.

NOTES

1. Peter Berger, "Social Roles: Society in Man," in Dennis H. Wrong and Harry L. Grace, eds. *Readings in Introductory Sociology* (New York, 1967). For a much more detailed discussion of the material covered in this section, see William H. Chafe, *The American Woman: Her Changing Social, Economic and Political Roles, 1920–1970* (New York, 1972).

2. Emily Newell Blair, "Are Women a Failure in Politics?" *Harpers* CLI (October 1925), pp. 513–22; Stuart H. Rice and Malcolm Willey, "American Women's Ineffective Use of the Vote," *Current History* XX (July 1924), pp. 641–47; Seymour M. Lipset, *Political Man* (New York, 1963), pp. 209–11, 217, 221–23.

3. Janet Hooks, "Women's Occupations Through Seven Decades," *Women's Bureau Bulletin* No. 232 (Washington, D.C., 1951), p. 34; Willystine Goodsell, "The Educational Opportunities of American Women, Theoretical and Actual," *Annals* of the American Academy of Political and Social Science CXLIII (May 1929); Florence Lowther and Helen Downes, "Women in Medicine," *Journal of the American Medical Association,* October 13, 1945.

4. *Independent Woman* VI (October 1922); Mabel Lee, "The Dilemma of the Educated Woman," *Atlantic Monthly* CXLVI (November 1930), pp. 590–95; Margaret Mead, "Sex and Achievement," *Forum* XCIV (November 1935), pp. 301–3.

5. Claire Wallas Callahan, "A Woman With Two Jobs," *Ladies Home Journal* XLVII (October 1930), p. 114; "America Speaks, The National Weekly Poll of Public Opinion," November 15, 1936.

6. Katherine Glover, *Women at Work in Wartime* (Washington, D.C., 1943); "Women in Steel," *Life,* August 9, 1943; Eva Lapin, *Mothers in Overalls* (New York, 1943); "Changes in Women's Employment During the War," *Women's Bureau Bulletin* No. 20 (Washington, 1944); International Labor Organization, *The War and Women's Employment* (Montreal, 1946). See also Chafe, *American Woman,* pp. 135–50.

7. Florence Cadman, "Womanpower 4 F," *Independent Woman* XXII (September 1943); Women's Advisory Committee Archives, National Archives, Boxes 133–135; International Labor Organization, *The War and Women's Employment,* p. 221; Women's Bureau memorandum, October 9, 1945, folder entitled "Equal Pay–General," Women's Bureau Archives, Federal Record Center, Suitland, Maryland.

8. Helen Baker, *Women in War Industries* (Princeton, 1942); "Women Drop Out," *Business Week,* August 21, 1943; "More Child Care," *Business Week,* August 26, 1944; G. T. Allen, "Eight Hour Orphans," *Saturday Evening Post,* October 10, 1942; Katherine Lemoof, "The Children's Bureau Program for the Care of Children of Working Mothers," in Women's Bureau Archives.

9. Ferdinand Lundberg and Marynia Farnham, *Modern Woman, The Lost Sex* (New York, 1947); Agnes Meyer, "Women Aren't Men," *Atlantic* CLXXXVI (August 1950); Hadley Cantril, *Public Opinion, 1935–1946* (Princeton, 1951), p. 1047, The *Fortune* Survey, *Fortune* XXXIV (August and September 1946).

10. "Women Workers in Ten Production Areas and Their Postwar Employment Plans," *Women's Bureau Bulletin* No. 209 (Washington, D.C., 1946), p. 5; "Give Back Their Jobs," *Woman's Home Companion* LXX (October 1943), pp. 5–7.

11. National Manpower Council, *Womanpower* (New York, 1955); Elizabeth Baker, *Technology and Women's Work* (New York, 1964), vii; National Manpower Council, *Work in the Lives of Married Women* (New York, 1957), pp. 17, 72; *New York Times,* October 10, 1970; Elizabeth Waldman, "Changes in the Labor Force Activity of Women," *Monthly Labor Review* XCIII (June 1970).

12. Women's Bureau Memorandum, August 22, 1945, Women's Bureau Archives.

13. Mildred Weil, "An Analysis of the Factors Influencing Married Women's Actual or Planned Work Participation," *American Sociological Review* XVI (January 1951), pp. 91–96; Lois Hoffman, "Parental Power Relations and the Division of Household Tasks," in F. Ivan Nye and Lois Wladis Hoffman, eds. *The Employed Mother in America* (Chicago, 1963), pp. 215–30; Robert Blood, "The Husband-Wife Relationship," in Nye and Hoffman, pp. 282–305; Robert Hamblin and Robert Blood, "The Effect of the Wife's Employment on the Family Power Structure," *Social Forces* XXXVI (May 1958), pp. 347–52; David Heer, "Dominance and the Working Wife," *Social Forces* XXXVI (May 1958), pp. 341–47.

14. Ruth E. Hartley, "Children's Concepts of Male and Female Roles," *Merrill-Palmer Quarterly* VI (January 1959–60), pp. 83–91; Selma M. Matthews, "The Effect of Mothers' Out-of-Home Employment Upon Children's Ideas and Atti-

tudes," *Journal of Applied Psychology* XVIII (February 1954), pp. 116–36; Elizabeth Douvan, "Employment and the Adolescent," in Nye and Hoffman, pp. 142–64; Lois Hoffman, "Effects on Children: Summary and Discussion," in Nye and Hoffman, pp. 196–202.

15. Betty Friedan, *The Feminine Mystique* (New York, 1963), especially pp. 11, 69, 271–98.

16. Susan Brownmiller, "Sisterhood Is Powerful," *New York Times Magazine,* March 15, 1970; Allan Matusow, "From Civil Rights to Black Power: The Case of SNCC, 1960–1966," in Barton Bernstein and Allan Matusow, eds. *Twentieth Century America* (New York, 1969); Richard Gillam, "White Racism in the Civil Rights Movement," *Yale Review* LXII (Summer 1973), pp. 520–43.

17. Susan Brownmiller, "Sisterhood Is Powerful"; "Women's Lib: The War on Sexism," *Newsweek,* March 23, 1970; Robin Morgan, ed. *Sisterhood Is Powerful* (New York, 1970); *Notes From the Second Year* (New York, 1970).

18. *The Gallup Opinion Index,* September 1970, Report No. 63; Louis Harris and Associates, "The 1972 Virginia Slims American Woman's Opinion Poll: A Survey of the Attitudes of Women on Their Roles in Politics and the Economy"; Amy Hogue, "Women at Duke: Their Attitudes and Aspirations," unpublished honors paper, 1973; Adeline Levine and Janice Crumrine, "Women and the Fear of Success: A Problem in Replication," paper presented at the American Sociological Association Meeting, August 1973; *New York Times,* March 24, 1972.

19. Robert K. Bell and Jay B. Clarke, "Pre-marital Sexual Experience Among Coeds, 1958 and 1968," *Journal of Marriage and the Family* XXXII (February 1970), pp. 81–84; New York *Times,* November 5, 1971; "Birth Dearth," *Christian Century,* November 24, 1971.

20. Paul Woodring, "There'll Be Fewer Little Noses," *Saturday Review,* March 18, 1967; "End of Baby Boom," *Science Digest,* September 1967; "Falling Birthrate," *Scientific American,* April 1968; "Z.P.G.," *Scientific American,* April 1971; Lawrence A. Mayer, "Why the U.S. Population Isn't Exploding," *Fortune,* April 1967; "Levelling Off," *Scientific American,* February 1973; "The Surprising Decline in the Birth Rate," *Business Week,* June 3, 1972; Herman Miller, *Rich Man Poor Man,* p. 236; Conrad Taueber, "Population Trends and Characteristics," in Sheldon and Moore, pp. 27–76.

21. *New York Times,* February 21, 1972.

22

Identity, Deviance, and Change in Conventional Settings: The Case of "Sexual Revolution"

Donald E. Carns

I

No one is overly surprised by the assertion that, historically and across cultures, different standards have existed for the sexual behavior of men as opposed to women. In one particular area—that of sex before marriage—the term *double sexual standard* has been coined to capture the essence of the very different cultural expectations for men and women.

Probably because this terminology is so readily available to social scientists, mental health practitioners, moralists, and journalists, changes in female sexual behavior over the past few decades have been heralded (or denounced) as a "sexual revolution," a profound change in *both* our cultural expectations concerning a female's premarital sexuality *and* a significant increase in the amount of coital activity by women before they enter into legal marriages. The two together form a "revolution," it is said, because older, more conventional standards for the premarital sexual behavior of women have crumbled, and no particular standards have emerged to take their place. Patterns of premarital sexual behavior are variously viewed as inchoate, immoral, liberating,

From James R. McIntosh, ed., *Perspectives on Marginality: Understanding Deviance* (Boston: Allyn and Bacon, 1974). Article reprinted by permission of the author.

To a limited degree, data gathered under the auspices of PHS grant HD were used in the preparation of this paper.

promiscuous, permissive, long overdue ("with affection"), egocentric, irresponsible, drug-induced, or whatever, depending upon what commentator one is reading.

But there is another and even more basic element in what we could consider a revolution in female sexuality, that of the *sexual identity* of premarital women. This identity is forged as much from available cultural materials (the "double standard" or the "sexual revolution") as it is from significant experiences and, most of all, from the legitimations which women use to justify their acts to themselves and others. Further, legitimations are essentially systems of ideas which have various cultural supports—that is, they are more or less acceptable in given social settings. This further implies, then, that a woman, contemplating premarital coitus (or already having coitus), is faced with some array of *models* by which she must evaluate herself and by means of which she will explain and justify herself to people who matter to her: peers, parents, and significant "others."

In this paper we shall first examine the evidence for a "revolution" in sexual *behavior* before marriage: that is, has there been some profound shift toward greater amounts of premarital coital involvement on the part of women? We shall then relate this to the meaning of *gender* socialization—male and female—and the double sexual standard. At this point we shall look at some up-to-date evidence bearing on sexual behavior *and* on the question of the double standard: in other words, how do women *handle* the fact of premarital sexual involvement especially when contrasted with their male counterparts. We shall conclude with a discussion of the different paths women use to reach their first coital experience and the ways in which young females can now evaluate themselves and relate to others.

A final note before we get started. The idea of deviance is always relative to general standards as well as to those standards and expectations ("norms") which are applicable to given individuals in specific role situations. A great deal of deviance literature deals with either very dramatic or highly esoteric kinds of human social behavior: murder, robbery, gang violence, homosexuality, transvestism, heroin addiction, and the like. But we are all faced with the problem of conformity and, correspondingly deviance. This is especially critical in areas such as we are discussing—"normal" heterosexual behavior—and during an era that is witnessing rapid cultural and social change. By examining the *scripts* which people follow in their interactions with others and by which they evaluate themselves, feeling guilty or satisfied as the case may be, we should be able to understand better the nature of standards, their relationship to individual identity, and the impact of change in sex role models. It may not be either arcane or dramatic, but it is a subject basic to us all, and therefore it is fundamental to an understanding of social deviance and identity formation and change.

II

One of the more compelling statistics from the Kinsey study of females (1953) was that two variables accounted for more of the variance in premarital sexual involvement than any others: religious devoutness and, especially, decade of birth. In other words, the younger the female, the more likely it was that she would engage in premarital coitus, especially if she were among the less "devout" (Kinsey operationally defined "devoutness" as how frequently the respondent attended church services). Thus, if we simply extend Kinsey's finding into the more recent past—say for the twenty years since publication of his study of females—we should expect younger women today to be more sexually active before marriage than were their mothers, who in turn (according to Kinsey's data) were more active than *their* mothers, and so forth.

It is difficult if not impossible to compare statistics from current research with those gathered by Kinsey due to many problems, not the least of which is the rather unusual sampling techniques used by the Kinsey group for both their original reports (1948; 1953). However, two recent studies have gathered data at two different points in time— the first in the late 1950s and the second ten years later—in order to establish trends in premarital sexual behavior among women. Both studies are narrow in their focus: they deal with cases interviewed on college campuses, and the samples are not true national samples of American college undergraduates (Christensen and Gregg, 1970; Bell and Chaskes, 1970).[1] In both studies there is evidence that women are more sexually involved than statistically comparable women were ten years ago. Male experience is seen as stable over the ten years, and with increases in female involvement with intercourse before marriage obviously *convergence* between men and women seems to be occurring.

But gross increases in behavior are not enough to speak of a revolution in premarital sexuality. To be sure, women (in this case, female undergraduates) may be experiencing intercourse before marriage to a greater degree than comparable girls were ten years ago, and by implication, far more than were their mothers of a generation ago, but we need additional ingredients for our revolution: some evidence of profound shifts in the *sexual selves* of women away from traditional bases of legitimation and toward some new basis.

But this requires some explanation. The double sexual standard, as noted before, has apparently existed for millennia. Exodus 22:16–17 contains a strong statement of *women as property* (or more precisely, chattel), not to be sullied by sexual contacts before going on the bridal market, for their worth would be reduced accordingly. Other instances of different sexual standards for men and women exist throughout the Bible. Similarly, other ancient codes—Hammurabi's Code, the Law of Eshunna, the Middle Assyrian Laws—were worded in such a way as to suggest that men and women were expected to respond to quite different sexual norms (Pritchard, 1950). This double standard would seem to be an integral part of the Judaeo-Christian tradition (Kinsey, 1948: 322; Reiss, 1967), and there is some evidence that such a difference exists and has existed in other, non-Western societies (Blumberg, Carns, and Winch, 1970), although Murdock (1949: 264–265) reaches a somewhat different conclusion.

In our society over the past century, men have lived under a premarital sexual code which, with some variance, *prescribed* sexual intercourse for them.[2] In identity terms, this frequently translated into a social imperative; a budding adolescent, full of sexual fantasies and masturbating as frequently as he could manage, was *constrained* to seek sexual experience *and* feed the knowledge of it back to his same-age, same-sex peers. By experiencing sex and selectively broadcasting his involvement in it, he built an identity which was integral with his on-going adolescence. Failure in the sexual arena meant at least partial failure in the group, which suggests that many males, in the absence of actual experience, have created fictive sexual selves to be *au courant* with both general cultural prescriptions and the expectations of their homosocial peers. And with insufficient experience, they have embellished their sexual exploits following scripts supplied by pornography, novels, Hollywood, and most of all, their own rich imaginations.[3]

But women have been in a different position. For them premarital sexual involvement, except under rigidly specified circumstances, has been *proscribed,* that is, the opposite of cultural *prescription* for males. The female's problem, then, is not the embellishment of experience but the justification of involvement, and she has traditionally done this by employing the rhetoric of love and marriage: that is, romanticism and the reality principle of approaching legal family formation. In this way, if she talked at all of her sexual exploits, she probably imbedded them in a context of love and approaching marriage; whether she talked or not, and that is not so critical at this point, she certainly used such legitimations to herself and, in that way, created self-justifications. Indeed, by contrast to the male, her embellishments or fictive creations centered on the *context* of the *relationship* and not on the nature of the sexual action. As we shall see, both the nature of the romantic content and the reality principle centering on legal marriage have changed to a certain degree, but it is this raw material which women have used to create their post-adolescent sexual identities in the past, and in all likelihood at present and into the future. On this point, see the excellent essay by William Simon and John H. Gagnon (1969) which contrasts male and female sexual socialization after puberty. It offers a strong argument against (or supplementing) the orthodox Freudian view that experiences in early childhood have a determining, rather than mere potentiating, influence on adult sexual character.[4]

III

Using data from a 1967 study of college and university undergraduates, conducted on a nation-wide scale by the Institute for Sex Research of Indiana University, we can gain a clearer picture of differences between males and females.[5] First, and not surprisingly, more men than women at any given age report premarital coital experience, and—more to the point—males first experience coitus at earlier ages, have intercourse with more partners, and do so in generally more casual relationships. Looking only at undergraduates who report coital experience, and isolating the first coital encounter itself, it is significant that more men than women talk to someone else "immediately" or within one month than do women; indeed over a quarter of the undergraduate women never talked of their sexual experiences until the time of the interview. When women do talk to someone, it is generally to only one or two other people, and most likely to same-sex peers: presumably room-mates, close friends, and the like.

Men, on the other hand, when they do talk tend to socialize their sexual experiences to several other same-sex peers indicating, therefore, that they are gaining something from making their experiences public. By implication, too, if a woman engages in sexual intercourse before marriage on a casual basis—dating, "pick-up," and the like—she is *ipso facto* creating a semi-public sexual status for herself, for, chances are, her male partner will talk of the event with his peers. If it is a safe assumption that the identity of the female is part of this discussion—and one would assume that it is, for this should be part of the male's "payoff" among his peers—then the woman has acquired a reputation to some degree.[6] If she has sex with two or more males and if they talk of their experiences, and if their friends in turn talk to others, her newly acquired sexual status is spreading at something approaching a logarithmic rate.

Referring back to the Simon-Gagnon model of post-adolescent psychosexual development, one of the key assumptions is that males first learn to be sexual, then with progressing age learn to imbed these impulses in socially and culturally meaningful settings: i.e., "relationships" which have some probability of being relatively permanent. Women, on the other hand, first learn to relate—that is, create relationships with males on both the fantasy level and in actual practice—and then learn to be sexual within such contexts.[7] Simon and Gagnon cite evidence from the Kinsey studies, for example, which clearly shows that males, on the average, begin to masturbate soon after puberty and—middle-class males, at least—continue this activity to some extent until well into marriage. Women, by contrast, typically do not initiate masturbation until after some significant amount of socio-sexual experience—for example, genital petting or intercourse—if they ever masturbate at all.

Data from the 1967 study tend to bear out this interpretation. It is especially noteworthy that the older the male, the less likely he is to socialize his first coital experience to his peers, and, correspondingly, the more intense the emotions involved in the first relationship in which he had coitus, the less likely he is to share knowledge of his experiences. Thus, the male in this post-adolescent period—the college years—appears to be learning to appreciate the social and emotional meaning of the relationship and to protect it from public knowledge.

The female, one would presume, could or would socialize her first coital encounter to her same-sex peers as a function of *her* definition of the situation—i.e., *if* the relationship had some enduring quality and was defined by her as "loving" and/or had some kind of future—*and* if she could legitimately claim some kind of reality to her definition of the situation. This latter point would include the appropriateness of her behavior in terms of the characteristics of her first sexual partner—was he an appropriate kind of person to marry?—and whether she was in even remotely a position to claim that marriage was impending. Among working-class youths who have little thought or hope of attending college, the female can readily justify her acts on both these bases, especially that of her impending marriage, which, statistically speaking, will come earlier in her life than for her middle-class female counterpart. The latter, however, must accomplish some verbal gymnastics to convince her friends—or closest friend or roommate—and herself that she is in a position to marry in the relatively near future *unless* she is nearing graduation from college *or* she does not plan to finish.

IV

Obviously changes are taking place, for women are first experiencing coitus at earlier ages and presumably are able to justify such behavior. If we are not to completely throw out our assumptions about psychosexual development in adolescent and post-adolescent women, and especially about the tradition-based legitimations for their premarital sexual involvement, we must say something about what is happening to cultural expectations.

If we imagine a continuum of emotional involvement which logically ranges from little or no commitment at the one end to full romantic love *cum* marriage at the other, according to Ira Reiss (1967), somewhere in the middle we would find the shift we are looking for. The traditional female could legitimate her sexual activity before marriage in only one way: there was an impending marriage in sight. This implied, then, that she was at least engaged to her partner before having intercourse with him, and, most likely, the engagement had been formalized with the cultural accoutrements of attachment: diamond rings, announcements, marriage dates, and the like. This was, for her, the reality principle we mentioned earlier, and if one goes far enough back to, say, the Victorian period in England, on the Continent, and in this country, little romanticism attended the mating process itself—i.e., there was a maximum separation between legal relationships and feeling states (Winch, 1971: 526).

From all that has been happening in this country in recent years, we should suspect that, in general, institutional expectations and the symbols of institutional conformance have become seriously delegitimized among the young. Girls still participate in rituals surrounding engagement and marriage, for example, but we suspect they do so with far less wide-eyed wonder when compared with the past. And much of the apparent conformance which remains—especially among college youth—is a function of felt duty for the older generation and their ways of creating social legitimacy for the family.

If this assumption is valid,[8] then strictly speaking legal marriage need not be an expected outcome of relationships "with affection" at college, and the affectional state alone should be enough to legitimize premarital sexual involvement. Such, as I read it, is the crux of Reiss's argument.

What is particularly noteworthy about this argument, however, is *not* that legal marriage itself is becoming delegitimized, for it is not—equal proportions of every age cohort are still marrying as they once did—but that for the college-attending population, legal marriages are delayed somewhat, and consensual unions (or consensually based households) are much more common than they once were. This suggests, then, that Reiss's concept of "permissiveness with affection," which he used to describe the basis of legitimacy for premarital coital involvement by modern coeds, is correct enough to characterize the women in the 1967 study. For most of them, premarital intercourse was not casually experienced nor was it necessarily put into the context of marriage. Most of them insisted upon *some* commitment both from themselves and from their partner, even if this meant only affectional relationship.[9] Permissiveness maybe, but promiscuity rarely.

V

However, 1967 was only one year in a fast-changing sexual scene in the United States, especially on college campuses, but also in the society at large. Data from that one year can offer us a photograph of one point in the change process, but not a film of such changes. Therefore, we can do one of the following two things. We can compare 1967 with previous data, and project changes into the future—say for the current year—assuming that change is constant and that the general tendency is for male and female sexuality to converge both in expectations and actual behavior. Or we can look at some more recent data and, in conjunction with what we already know or suspect, evaluate Reiss's findings as well as our own.

It happens that investigators at Johns Hopkins University recently completed a national study of premarital females, pre-college, college-attending, and non-college attending. From sketchy reports on that study—gleaned primarily from *Time* Magazine[10]—the most remarkable thing appears to be the general prevalence of premarital coitus among women in the sample, even among those as young as the sophomore year in high school. Proportions of experienced women at each age before marriage were considerably higher than those in previously known studies: e.g., 21 percent at age 16 and 46 percent at age 19. However, some part of this increase is undoubtedly due to the social class variable: that is, non-college bound females marry younger, possibly experience coitus at a younger age, and their representation in this sample would accordingly increase the overall incidence percentages.[11]

Even more striking than the prevalence figures, however, were those of incidence. We are using the two terms—incidence and prevalence—in much the same way they are used in epidemiological research in medicine or psychiatry. Prevalence refers to the proportion of some population that has ever experienced a particular symptom (in this case, ever had sexual intercourse). Incidence, on the other hand, refers to the proportion in the population who, at any given point in time, are experiencing the symptom. As you can well imagine, incidence is usually far lower than prevalence for any given phenomenon.

Now, in the Hopkins study, despite the quite high prevalence figures of premarital coital experience, a relatively low proportion of experienced females at each age reported that they had had sexual intercourse in the month preceding the interview data: 40 percent had none at all, and of the remainder, 70 percent had had coitus no more than twice. The image one receives from the *Time* article, then, is of a large number of high school and college-age (but not necessarily college-attending) females who have once or a few times experienced sexual intercourse and then, for whatever reason, are no longer indulging.

VI

This strongly suggests, as a consequence, that some additional variable should be introduced into our reasoning about the legitimations which women use to justify to themselves and to others their experience with sex before marriage, and more specifically with sexual intercourse. Obviously, if the prevalence figures from the Hopkins study can be taken seriously (and we have no reason to doubt the adequacy of the study's sampling or interviewing techniques), then even the "permissiveness with affection" argument must go by the wayside. In order to incorporate these data into our thinking, we probably have a choice of two lines of argument.

First, somehow the meaning of "affection" may have become so diluted that modern women, in contradistinction to their earlier counterparts, are capable of falling into and out of love with alacrity and ease, and can use the very temporary nature of their emotional bondings to justify the degree of sexual involvement with their partners. In short, no stable anchors now exist by which others and the female in question can (or will) evaluate the plausibility of the emotional relationship and/or its somewhat truncated future. In such a system, *rhetoric without reality* would have become the order of things such that, by the merest uttering of certain words to some other person or by using them within the confines of one's own imagination, any sexual act including intercourse would become legitimate.

Before we dismiss this line of argument out of hand, consider that it is the logical end point of a continuum which had at its beginning the strong probability of fairly immediate family formation ("engagement") and in which, near some mid-point, could be found Reiss's permissiveness with affection. We have, thus, begun to characterize one end of our previously mentioned continuum of emotional involvement, and we have retained the defining element of the continuum: at least there remains the rhetoric of romantic love to legitimize sexual involvements although, as noted, little reality of permanence may be likely. Somewhere between this end point of the continuum and Reiss's permissiveness with affection we would find consensual unions, for these represent, in one sense, the retention of *relationships* but the delegitimization of legal marriage, at least until some later time in the age/maturation cycle. Or we could argue the other way around that Reiss's proposition represents a less conservative basis for legitimation of sexual intercourse than do consensual household unions (consensual marriage, "living together," and the like). Using this latter reasoning, thus:

Legal[12] Marriage (1)	Legal Marriage (2)	Consensual Marriage (3)	"Relationship" (4)	Uncontextualized (5)
Little affection	Affection	Affection	Affection	Affection rhetoric

Since the left-hand end of the continuum represents an historical reality more so than any current or recent state of affairs, then speaking historically *affection* describes a curvilinear function with the declining degree of contextualization which accompanies first coital involvement on the part of females before marriage.[13] In other words, for the past hundred years or so, less and less contextualization has been required to induce a woman to have her first experience with premarital sexual intercourse. For some portion of that time, more and more affection was demanded of the relationship, presumably (following the reasoning in this paper) to justify—or legitimize—her sexual involvement. But in the latter phase, such "affection" begins to have less and less reality and, as noted before, takes on a "purely" rhetorical character. In this sense, rhetoric—as an institutionally based set of ideas by which given acts are made legitimate—is all, or nearly all, that remains of the once imperative institutional structure[14] which provided the context within which first sexual encounters were embedded and made legitimate.

This could lead us to conclude, as did the staff writers of *Time,* that *virginity,* as a socio-sexual status, is "outmoded" (*Time*'s phrase: p. 69). Put in terms we are using in this paper, it has become less *legitimate* to maintain a sexual status of *virgin* but, on the other hand, there appears to be little evidence that *promiscuity* is rampant. The 1967 data, those of Christensen and Gregg and Bell and Chuaskes, and those from the Zelnik and Kantner study do not suggest that women are experiencing coitus with multiple partners or are doing so with anything approaching lusty abandon. It is significant, by the way, that 60 percent of the non-virgins in the Hopkins sample had experienced intercourse with only one male, and most importantly, fully half of that number reported that they planned to marry that man.

And recall, we are talking only of prevalence, not incidence. In short, this reasoning concerns only the first encounter with sexual intercourse, and we still have other findings from the Hopkins study to contend with, especially those which deal with the relatively low levels of sexual activity over the period of the month preceding the interview.

VII

And so, on to our second hypothesis. We should like to suggest that two very different standards now exist for, on the one hand, first coital encounters and, on the other, subsequent heavy involvement with intercourse before marriage. In other words, one kind of reasoning would pertain to data on prevalence while a quite different basis of legitimacy may exist for incidence.

By proposing this, we raise a whole new set of problems, but we solve some existing ones. For one thing, this second line of reasoning— or hypothesis—is based upon certain assumptions about what is happening in the American culture in general, and especially among the belief systems of the young. For one thing, *experimentalism,* as a mode of thought, has become very nearly institutionalized among the young such that, as with any institutionalized pattern, it carries with it given expectations. We believe that the young expect to be experimental, to at least try new things before accepting or rejecting them, and this is particularly pertinent to those behaviors proscribed by adults: pre-marital sexual behavior, use of marijuana—in certain circumstances— harder drugs, alcohol consumption, and the like.[15]

If we are correct in positing an experimental mode among the young, this fact would account for much of the reported incidence among sample subjects in the Johns Hopkins study. And, correspondingly, the very low proportion of females who reported a high incidence of sexual intercourse over the month preceding the interview would also bolster this interpretation. For experimental—curiosity-based or defiant—behavior would seem to be short-run at best.

If one is speaking of first coitus, a few encounters, with one or at the most two males, should be sufficient to satisfy one curiosity, answer experimental questions, and/or support the logic of youthful protest against existing, and frequently illogical, adult sexual standards.

Let us for a moment return to the Simon-Gagnon (1969) model of adolescent psycho-sexual development for more insight into this experimental phase. If their reasoning is correct, and females first learn to relate and then to be sexual, this newer wave of experimenting females is clearly violating the model sequences which Simon and Gagnon suggest. If their reasoning is valid, we should not expect to find that these experimenting and very young females (say, 15 to 18 using the Hopkins data) particularly enjoy the sexual acts per se. Enjoyment of sex for the modal female should be a function of two interrelated conditions: familiarity with and acceptance of the partner—i.e., the socio-cultural context of the act—and practice or experience with sex, its techniques, and, most especially, experience with feeling sexual, with possessing and accepting a sexual side of oneself.[16] As we have reasoned, such experimental acts are imbedded in only the most sketchy of relationships, bearing as they do more rhetorical reality than actual probability of surviving the day or few days of the first sexual encounter.

There is, however, no particular reason why we should reject Reiss's proposition about permissiveness with affection as a legitimation for subsequent premarital intercourse—"subsequent" referring, of course, to sexual involvement by women at a slightly later stage in the age/maturation cycle. Our mythical female has experimented, satisfied her curiosity, and if our reasoning is correct, has found sex to be wanting. But two, three, or more years later she is at college, and permissiveness with affection should take the form of ever-increasing levels of sexual involvement. And it is the nature of sexuality, and the norms which govern it within relationships with some meaning to the actors, that each new behavior tried is a threshold, not to be retreated from. Indeed, our female who has experimented at an earlier age and is no longer a virgin, technically and anatomically speaking, should more readily reinitiate sexual intercourse within whatever loving relationships she finds herself in at college. In a sense we are implicitly proposing a kind of *latency* period between adolescent experimentation and post-adolescent permissiveness with affection.

For some women such a latent period may be exceedingly short, or even non-existent. Especially for women who are not college bound and who, on the average, marry earlier, the second period may follow hard on the heels of the first or, indeed, overlap it.[17] For others a great deal of time may elapse, and it may not be until after college, when they are singles in the work world, that they begin to blossom sexually. For some few, and we have no way of knowing how many, the initial experimental phase, if it occurred, may have been traumatic, and subsequent romantic involvements either may not be accompanied with sexual intimacy or their level of sexual performance may be handicapped.

VIII

It is not necessary for us to choose between these two hypotheses for they compliment each other. We can permit ourselves to retain Reiss's permissiveness with affection notion while, at the same time, suggesting that more and more women are now experimenting with coitus, especially at younger ages. And it is entirely likely, although we have no evidence of this, that *some* of the rhetoric of romanticism but little of the reality of enduring relationships is used by these young experimenters, a reminder of our cultural past when such legitimations were indispensable if a woman wished to legitimize her sexual involvement to herself and others. But the burden of our argument has been that experimentation itself—as new experience, curiosity, rebellion—has become a more and more legitimate reason for engaging in intercourse before marriage. It probably has been so for some time, but the age at which intercourse is appropriate or feasible has been dropping, and the heretofore strict cultural insistence upon female virginity has begun to slip.

Most certainly we can move easily to the position that when *relationships* do occur that contain sexual intimacy, the older legitimation of impending legal matrimony need not, in many cases, any longer pertain and that consensual rather than legal unions are increasingly occurring and are becoming more legitimate. These latter contain many of the characteristics of legal mating except that they are not accompanied by the varied symbols—engagement, wedding, gifts, public recognition—of the institution of marriage. But these relationships are clandestine only to the eyes of the older generation, or at least may go uncelebrated by parents and family; among same-age peers they carry a legitimacy of their own, in some respects as sanctioned and accepted as the older, legal variety.

1. There is a considerable amount of controversy over the meaning of such changes. For a summary of the debate, see Cannon and Long (1971).

2. As we shall see later, this statement is intended to represent the middle-class and working-class urban mode. Considerably different prescriptions and proscriptions obviously exist for males who grow up in more traditional sub-cultures, especially the very religious. See Carns (1970a; 1970b).

3. Put differently, Alexander Portnoy may be much more archetypical than many of us would care to admit.

4. We shall have occasion to return to the Simon-Gagnon argument at a later point in this paper. For similar views, see Ehrmann (1959: 169) and Winch (1971: Chap. 19). For the contrasting Freudian view, see Freud (1962: II), and for a critique of the Freudian position on infantile sexuality, Chodoff (1966).

5. For a fuller discussion of sampling techniques used and questions asked, see Carns (1970a: Chap. 2). A total of 1177 men and women were interviewed at twelve colleges and universities.

6. And, needless to say, it is the kind of reputation that she will have difficulty managing.

7. Actually, the double standard implies that these are precisely the strategies used by each sex in the dating-rating-mating process. In the words of Ehrmann: "More males than females want sexual gratification first and then an intimacy relation, whereas more females than males want an intimacy relation first and then sexual gratification." (1959: 169).

8. A disclaimer: for every political radical at Berkeley, there are undoubtedly five or ten highly conforming business and engineering majors. Similarly, for every youth who attends any college, there are many more who do not attend but who enter the working world at or around age eighteen. Thus, our comments about the delegitimization of certain cultural practices is intended to portray, at best, a trend, and may only reflect what part we, as blind Indians, happen to touch on the elephant.

9. Whether a woman defines a relationship as "contextualized," i.e., affectional, loving, or likely leading to marriage, and then experiences intercourse with her partner, or whether she first slips progressively into greater levels of sexual intimacy and then contextualizes her acts, is unknown. It is likely that some kind of interactional model is the most appropriate: increases in sexual intimacy demand an escalation of the relationship which, in turn, justifies further sexual intimacy, and so forth. On this point, see footnote 16 below.

10. *Time* (May 22, 1972: 69–70). The investigators were Melvin Zelnik and John Kantner.

11. Another significant factor is the racial variable. Even when controlling social class and age, black women were more experienced than whites.

12. The horizontal line represents the continuum we propose. Above the line we find the nature of the relationship in which coital involvement is legitimate. Below the line are affection or love states. Thus, in (1) we find legal marriage but with little affection, the middle-class, urban Victorian phenomenon. In (2) we find legal marriage with affection. In (3) consensual marriages with affection. (4) is Reiss's

category of permissiveness with affection, or some variant of it. (5) contains the word "uncontextualized," and this refers to an almost total lack of a relationship between coital partners, in this case the first coital experience for the female, while at the same time the vocabulary of motives may include some rhetorical expressions of affection. As we shall see, even the latter need not be present in an "experimental" setting, i.e., when the legitimation for coital entry exists within a generally (or subculturally) approved norm of "doing your thing" or "checking it out for yourself."

13. Put differently, if the nature of the relationship occupies the abscissa in Cartesian space, and along the ordinate we have the degree of affection, then the function should describe a reverse-U in shape.

14. Centering on the institution of the family and marriage, of course.

15. As evidence for our hypothesis that a great deal of youthful sexuality is legitimized by an "experimental" ethic, it would be seductive to cite the apparent great increase in the use of birth control practices by young females. In fact one commentator (Winch, 1971) suggests that fear of pregnancy was the primary restraining force for the older, premarital abstinence ethic. However, from the *Time* report, such an interpretation is not tenable, for most of the experienced women in the sample *were not using birth control techniques.* One possible interpretation for this fact, especially in light of our reasoning to this point, is that use of the pill, for example, presumes a self-conscious sexual motivation on the part of the female. In other words, in order for a woman to go on the pill, she must have a sexual self-conception, and this is simply not probable until a woman has entered a reasonably intimate, socio-emotional relationship with a male. If this reasoning seems invalid, we suggest that you interview 10 or so college coeds, preferably freshmen, who are using birth control pills. In our experience, 2 or 3 will be self-consciously sexual in their motivations, while the remainder will cite reasons ranging from "they regulate my period" to "they clear up my complexion."

16. Parallels between experimental sex and experimental drug use are too close to ignore. See Becker (1963: Chap. 3). This is particularly interesting if one can equate the experience of turning on to marijuana to the phenomenon of incipient sexual arousal in females. If so, Becker's words (1963: 42) would apply equally to a woman's first and subsequent encounter with intercourse: "Instead of the deviant motives leading to the deviant behavior, it is the other way around; the deviant behavior in time produces the deviant motivation. Vague impulses and desires—in this case, probably most frequently a curiosity about the kind of experience the drug will produce—are transformed into definite patterns of action through the social interpretation of a physical experience which is in itself ambiguous." Among the young, and especially those in college, it is still probably more legitimate to be a non-virgin in the marijuana sense than in the sexual. But more to the point, Becker's comments about marijuana indoctrination and appreciation apply especially to later, more committed sexual relationships. The contrast with men, as per the Simon-Gagnon (1969) argument mentioned earlier, is striking.

17. For these women, we should return to the Hopkins data and their finding that about half of the females who had had sexual intercourse with only one man intended to marry that person. One would suppose, then, that these women will indeed marry earlier and that the first sexual encounter was motivated more by emotional embeddedness than by curiosity, or at least by both. Lacking access to the Hopkins data, we can only suggest that if this were true, it should manifest

itself in higher *incidence* figures (intercourse in the month preceding the interview) for this sub-sample when compared with other females in the sample.

REFERENCES

Becker, Howard S. *Outsiders: Studies in the Sociology of Deviance*. New York: Free Press, 1963.

Bell, Robert R. and Jay B. Chaskes. "Premarital Sexual Experience Among Coeds, 1958 and 1968." *Journal of Marriage and the Family*, 32 (1970): 81–84.

Blumberg, Rae, Donald E. Carns, and Robert F. Winch. "High Gods, Virgin Brides, and Societal Complexity." Paper read before the annual meetings of the American Sociological Association, 1970.

Cannon, Kenneth L. and Richard Long. "Premarital Sexual Behavior in the Sixties." *Journal of Marriage and the Family*, 33 (1971): 36–49.

Carns, Donald E. *Religiosity, Premarital Sexuality and the American College Student*. Bloomington: Indiana University (unpublished thesis), 1970a.

_____. "Religiosity and the Double Sexual Standard." Paper read before the annual meetings of the Midwest Sociological Society, 1970b.

Chodoff, P. "Critique of Freud's Theory of Infantile Sexuality." *American Journal of Psychiatry*, 123 (1966): 507–518.

Christensen, Harold T. and Christina F. Gregg. "Changing Sex Norms in America and Scandinavia." *Journal of Marriage and the Family*, 32 (1970): 616–627.

Ehrmann, Winston. *Premarital Dating Behavior*. New York: Holt, Rinehart and Winston, 1959.

Freud, Sigmund. *Three Contributions to the Theory of Sex*. New York: E. P. Dutton, 1962. (Originally published in 1905 in Germany by Deuticke.)

Kinsey, Alfred et al. *Sexual Behavior in the Human Male*. Philadelphia: Saunders, 1948.

_____. *Sexual Behavior in the Human Female*. Philadelphia: Saunders, 1953.

Murdock, George P. *Social Structure*. New York: Macmillan, 1949.

Pritchard, J. B., ed. *Eastern Texts Relating to the Old Testament*. Princeton, N.J.: Princeton University Press, 1950.

Reiss, Ira. *The Social Context of Premarital Sexual Permissiveness*. New York: Holt, Rinehart and Winston, 1967.

Simon, William and John H. Gagnon. "On Psychosexual Development." *Handbook of Socialization Theory and Research* (ed. by David A. Goslin). Chicago: Rand McNally, 1969, pp. 733–752.

Winch, Robert F. *The Modern Family*. 3rd edition. New York: Holt, Rinehart and Winston, 1971.

23

The Liberation of Black Women

Pauli Murray

Black women, historically, have been doubly victimized by the twin immoralities of Jim Crow and Jane Crow. Jane Crow refers to the entire range of assumptions, attitudes, stereotypes, customs, and arrangements which have robbed women of a positive self-concept and prevented them from participating fully in society as equals with men. Traditionally, racism and sexism in the United States have shared some common origins, displayed similar manifestations, reinforced one another, and are so deeply intertwined in the country's institutions that the successful outcome of the struggle against racism will depend in large part upon the simultaneous elimination of all discrimination based upon sex. Black women, faced with these dual barriers, have often found that sex bias is more formidable than racial bias. If anyone should ask a Negro woman in America what has been her greatest achievement, her honest answer would be, "I survived!"

Negro women have endured their double burden with remarkable strength and fortitude. With dignity they have shared with black men a partnership as members of am embattled group excluded from the normal protections of the society and engaged in a struggle for survival during nearly four centuries of a barbarous slave trade, two centuries of chattel slavery, and a century or more of illusive citizenship. Throughout this struggle, into which has been poured most of the resources and much of the genius of successive generations of American Negroes, these women have often carried a disproportionate share of responsi-

From *Voice of the New Feminism*, Mary Lou Thompson, ed. (Boston: Beacon Press, 1970), pp. 88–102. Reprinted by permission.

bility for the black family as they strove to keep its integrity intact against a host of indignities to which it has been subjected. Black women have not only stood shoulder to shoulder with black men in every phase of the struggle, but they have often continued to stand firmly when their men were destroyed by it. Few Blacks are unfamiliar with that heroic, if formidable, figure exhorting her children and grandchildren to overcome every obstacle and humiliation and to "Be somebody!"

In the battle for survival, Negro women developed a tradition of independence and self-reliance, characteristics which according to the late Dr. E. Franklin Frazier, Negro sociologist, have "provided generally a pattern of equalitarian relationship between men and women in America." The historical factors which have fostered the black women's feeling of independence have been the economic necessity to earn a living to help support their families—if indeed they were not the sole breadwinners—and the need for the black community to draw heavily upon the resources of all of its members in order to survive.

Yet these survival values have often been distorted, and the qualities of strength and independence observable in many Negro women have been stereotyped as "female dominance" attributed to the "matriarchal" character of the Negro family developed during slavery and its aftermath. The popular conception is that because society has emasculated the black male, he has been unable to assume his economic role as head of the household and the black woman's earning power has placed her in a dominant position. The black militant's cry for the retrieval of black manhood suggests an acceptance of this stereotype, an association of masculinity with male dominance and a tendency to treat the values of self-reliance and independence as purely masculine traits. Thus, while Blacks generally have recognized the fusion of white supremacy and male dominance (note the popular expressions "The Man" and "Mr. Charlie"), male spokesmen for Negro rights have sometimes pandered to sexism in their fight against racism. When nationally known civil rights leader James Farmer ran for Congress against Mrs. Shirley Chisholm in 1968, his campaign literature stressed the need for a "strong male image" and a "man's voice" in Washington.

If idealized values of masculinity and femininity are used as criteria, it would be hard to say whether the experience of slavery subjected the black male to any greater loss of his manhood than the black female of her womanhood. The chasm between the slave woman and her white counterpart (whose own enslavement was masked by her position as a symbol of high virtue and an object of chivalry) was as impassable as the gulf between the male slave and his arrogant white master. If black males suffered from real and psychological castration, black females bore the burden of real or psychological rape. Both situations involved the negation of the individual's personal integrity and attacked the foundations of one's sense of personal worth.

The history of slavery suggests that black men and women shared a rough equality of hardship and degradation. While the black woman's position as sex object and breeder may have given her temporarily greater leverage in dealing with her white master than the black male enjoyed, in the long run it denied her a positive image of herself. On the other hand, the very nature of slavery foreclosed certain conditions experienced by white women. The black woman had few expectations of economic dependence upon the male or of derivative status through marriage. She emerged from slavery without the illusions of a specially protected position as a woman or the possibilities of a parasitic existence as a woman. As Dr. Frazier observed, "Neither economic necessity nor tradition has instilled in her the spirit of subordination to masculine authority. Emancipation only tended to confirm in many cases the spirit of self-sufficiency which slavery had taught."

Throughout the history of Black America, its women have been in the forefront of the struggle for human rights. A century ago Harriet Tubman and Sojourner Truth were titans of the Abolitionist movement. In the 1890's Ida B. Wells-Barnett carried on a one-woman crusade against lynching. Mary McLeod Bethune and Mary Church Terrell symbolize the stalwart woman leaders of the first half of the twentieth century. At the age of ninety, Mrs. Terrell successfully challenged segregation in public places in the nation's capital through a Supreme Court decision in 1953.

In contemporary times we have Rosa Parks setting off the mass struggle for civil rights in the South by refusing to move to the back of the bus in Montgomery in 1955; Daisy Bates guiding the Little Rock Nine through a series of school desegregation crises in 1957–59; Gloria Richardson facing down the National Guard in Cambridge, Maryland, in the early sixties; or Coretta Scott King picking up the fallen standard of her slain husband to continue the fight. Not only these and many other women whose names are well known have given this great human effort its peculiar vitality, but also women in many communities whose names will never be known have revealed the courage and strength of the black woman in America. They are the mothers who stood in schoolyards of the South with their children, many times alone. One cannot help asking: "Would the black struggle have come this far without the indomitable determination of its women?"

Now that some attention is finally given to the place of the Negro in American history, how much do we hear of the role of the Negro woman? Of the many books published on the Negro experience and the

Black Revolution in recent times, to date not one has concerned itself with the struggles of black women and their contributions to history. Of approximately 800 full-length articles published in the *Journal of Negro History* since its inception in 1916, only six have dealt directly with the Negro woman. Only two have considered Negro women as a group: Carter G. Woodson's "The Negro Washerwoman: A Vanishing Figure" (14 *JNH*, 1930) and Jessie W. Pankhurst's "The Role of the Black Mammy in the Plantation Household" (28 *JNH*, 1938).

This historical neglect continues into the present. A significant feature of the civil rights revolution of the 1950's and 1960's was its inclusiveness born of the broad participation of men, women, and children without regard to age and sex. As indicated, school children often led by their mothers in the 1950's won world-wide acclaim for their courage in desegregating the schools. A black child can have no finer heritage to give a sense of "somebodiness" than the knowledge of having personally been part of the great sweep of history. (An older generation, for example, takes pride in the use of the term "Negro," having been part of a seventy-five-year effort to dignify the term by capitalizing it. Now some black militants with a woeful lack of historical perspective have allied themselves symbolically with white racists by downgrading the term to lower case again.) Yet, despite the crucial role which Negro women have played in the struggle, in the great mass of magazine and newspaper print expended on the racial crisis, the aspirations of the black community have been articulated almost exclusively by black males. There has been very little public discussion of the problems, objectives, or concerns of black women.

Reading through much of the current literature on the Black Revolution, one is left with the impression that for all the rhetoric about self-determination, the main thrust of black militancy is a bid of black males to share power with white males in a continuing patriarchal society in which both black and white females are relegated to a secondary status. For example, *Ebony* magazine published a special issue on the Negro woman in 1966. Some of the articles attempted to delineate the contributions of Negro women as heroines in the civil rights battle in Dixie, in the building of the New South, in the arts and professions, and as intellectuals. The editors, however, felt it necessary to include a full-page editorial to counter the possible effect of the articles by women contributors. After paying tribute to the Negro woman's contributions in the past, the editorial reminded *Ebony*'s readers that "the past is behind us," that "the immediate goal of the Negro woman today should be the establishment of a strong family unit in which the father is the dominant person," and that the Negro woman would do well to follow the example of the Jewish mother "who pushed her husband to success, educated her male children first and engineered good marriages for her daughters.'' The editors also declared that the career woman "should be willing to postpone her aspirations until her children, too, are old enough to be on their own," and, as if the point had not been made clear enough, suggested that if "the woman should, by any chance, make more money than her husband, the marriage could be in real trouble."

While not as blatantly Victorian as *Ebony,* other writers on black militancy have shown only slightly less myopia. In *Black Power and Urban Crisis,* Dr. Nathan Wright, Chairman of the 1967 National Black Power Conference, made only three brief references to women: "the employment of female skills," "the beauty of black women," and housewives. His constant reference to Black Power was in terms of black males and black manhood. He appeared to be wholly unaware of the parallel struggles of women and youth for inclusion in decision-making, for when he dealt with the reallocation of power, he noted that "the churches and housewives of America" are the most readily influential groups which can aid in this process.

In *Black Rage,* psychiatrists Greer and Cobbs devote a chapter to achieving womanhood. While they sympathetically describe the traumatic experience of self-deprecation which a black woman undergoes in a society in which the dominant standard of beauty is "the blond, blue-eyed, white-skinned girl with regular features," and make a telling point about the burden of the stereotype that Negro women are available to white men, they do not get beyond a framework in which the Negro woman is seen as a sex object. Emphasizing her concern with "feminine narcissism" and the need to be "lovable" and "attractive," they conclude: "Under the sign of discouragement and rejection which governs so much of her physical operation, she is inclined to organize her personal ambitions in terms of her achievements serving to compensate for other losses and hurts." Nowhere do the authors suggest that Negro women, like women generally, might be motivated to achieve as *persons.* Implied throughout the discussion is the sexuality of Negro females.

The ultimate expression of this bias is the statement attributed to a black militant male leader: "The position of the black woman should be prone." Thus, there appears to be a distinctly conservative and backward-looking view in much of what black males write today about black women, and many black women have been led to believe that the restoration of the black male to his lost manhood must take precedence over the claims of black women to egalitarian status. Consequently, there has been a tendency to acquiesce without vigorous protest to policies which emphasize the "underemployment" of the black male in relation to the black female and which encourage the upgrading and education of black male youth while all but ignoring the educational and training needs of black female youth, although the highest rates of unemployment today are among black female teenagers. A parallel tendency to concentrate on career and training opportunities primarily for black males is evident in government and industry.

As this article goes to press, further confirmation of a patriarchal view on the part of organizations dominated by black males is found in the BLACK DECLARATION OF INDEPENDENCE published as a full-page advertisement in *The New York Times* on July 3, 1970. Signed by members of the National Committee of Black Churchmen and presuming to speak "By Order and on Behalf of Black People," this document ignores both the personhood and the contributions of black women to the cause of human rights. The drafters show a shocking insensitivity to the revitalized women's rights/women's liberation movement which is beginning to capture the front pages of national newspapers and the mass media. It evidences a parochialism which has hardly moved beyond the eighteenth century in its thinking about women. Not only does it paraphrase the 1776 Declaration about the equality of "all Men" with a noticeable lack of imagination, but it also declares itself "in the Name of our good People and our own Black Heroes." Then follows a list of black males prominent in the historical struggle for liberation. The names of Harriet Tubman, Sojourner Truth, Mary McLeod Bethune, or Daisy Bates, or any other black women are conspicuous by their absence. If black male leaders of the Christian faith—who concededly have suffered much through denigration of their personhood and who are committed to the equality of all in the eyes of God—are callous to the indivisibility of human rights, who is to remember?

In the larger society, of course, black and white women share the common burden of discrimination based upon sex. The parallels between racism and sexism have been distinctive features of American society, and the movements to eliminate these two evils have often been allied and sometimes had interchangeable leadership. The beginnings of a women's rights movement in this country is linked with the Abolitionist movement. In 1840, William Lloyd Garrison and Charles Remond, the latter a Negro, refused to be seated as delegates to the World Anti-Slavery Convention in London when they learned that women members of the American delegation had been excluded because of their sex and could sit only in the balcony and observe the proceedings. The seed of the Seneca Falls Convention of 1848, which marked the formal beginning of the women's rights struggle in the United States, was planted at that London conference. Frederick Douglass attended the Seneca Falls Convention and rigorously supported Elizabeth Cady Stanton's daring resolution on woman's suffrage. Except for a temporary defection during the controversy over adding "sex" to the Fifteenth Amendment, Douglass remained a staunch advocate of women's rights until his death in 1895. Sojourner Truth and other black women were also active in the movement for women's rights, as indicated earlier.

Despite the common interests of black and white women, however, the dichotomy of a racially segregated society which has become increasingly polarized has prevented them from cementing a natural alliance. Communication and the cooperation have been hesitant, limited, and formal. In the past Negro women have tended to identify discrimination against them as primarily racial and have accorded high priority to the struggle for Negro rights. They have had little time or energy for consideration of women's rights. And, until recent years, their egalitarian position in the struggle seemed to justify such preoccupation.

As the drive for black empowerment continues, however, black women are becoming increasingly aware of a new development which creates for them a dilemma of competing identities and priorities. On the one hand, as Dr. Jeanne Noble has observed, "establishing 'black manhood' became a prime goal of black revolution," and black women began to realize "that black men wanted to determine the policy and progress of black people without female participation in decisionmaking and leadership positions." On the other hand, a rising movement for women's liberation is challenging the concept of male dominance which the Black Revolution appears to have embraced. Confronted with the multiple barriers of poverty, race, and sex, the quandary of black women is how best to distribute their energies among these issues and what strategies to pursue which will minimize conflicting interests and objectives.

Cognizant of the similarities between paternalism and racial arrogance, black women are nevertheless handicapped by the continuing stereotype of the black "matriarchy" and the demand that black women now step back and push black men into positions of leadership. They are made to feel disloyal to racial interests if they insist upon women's rights. Moreover, to the extent that racial polarization often accompanies the thrust for Black Power, black women find it increasingly difficult to make common cause with white women. These developments raise several questions. Are black women gaining or losing in the drive toward human rights? As the movement for women's liberation becomes increasingly a force to be reckoned with, are black women to take a backward step and sacrifice their egalitarian tradition?

What are the alternatives to matriarchal dominance on the one hand or male supremacy on the other?

Much has been written in the past about the matriarchal character of Negro family life, the relatively favored position of Negro women, and the tensions and difficulties growing out of the assumptions that they are better educated and more able to obtain employment than Negro males. These assumptions require closer examination. It is true that according to reports of the Bureau of the Census, in March 1968 an estimated 278,000 nonwhite women had completed four or more years of college—86,000 more than male college graduates in the nonwhite population (Negro women constitute 93 per cent of all nonwhite women), and that in March 1966 the median years of school completed by Negro females (10.1) was slightly higher than that for Negro males (9.4). It should be borne in mind that this is not unique to the black community. In the white population as well, females exceed males in median years of school completed (12.2 to 12.0) and do not begin to lag behind males until the college years. The significant fact is that the percentage of both sexes in the Negro population eighteen years of age and over in 1966 who had completed four years of college was roughly equivalent (males: 2.2 per cent; females: 2.3 per cent). When graduate training is taken into account, the proportion of Negro males with five or more years of college training (3.3 per cent) moved ahead of the Negro females (3.2 per cent). Moreover, 1966 figures show that a larger proportion of Negro males (63 per cent) than Negro females (57 per cent) was enrolled in school and that this superiority continued into college enrollments (males: 5 per cent; females 4 per cent). These 1966 figures reflect a concerted effort to broaden educational opportunities for Negro males manifested in recruitment policies and scholarship programs made available primarily to Negro male students. Though later statistics are not now available, this trend appears to have accelerated each year.

The assumption that Negro women have more education than Negro men also overlooks the possibility that the greater number of college-trained Negro women may correspond to the larger number of Negro women in the population. Of enormous importance to a consideration of Negro family life and the relation between the sexes is the startling fact of the excess of females over males. The Bureau of the Census estimated that in July 1968 there were 688,000 more Negro females than Negro males. Although census officials attribute this disparity to errors in counting a "floating" Negro male population, this excess has appeared in steadily increasing numbers in every census since 1860, but has received little analysis beyond periodic comment. Over the past century the reported ratio of black males to black females has decreased. In 1966, there were less than 94 black males to every 100 females.

The numerical imbalance between the sexes in the black population is more dramatic than in any other group in the United States. Within the white population the excess of women shows up in the middle or later years. In the black population, however, the sex imbalance is present in every age group over fourteen and is greatest during the age when most marriages occur. In the twenty-five to forty-four age group, the percentage of males within the black population drops to 86.9 as compared to 96.9 for white males.

It is now generally known that females tend to be constitutionally stronger than males, that male babies are more fragile than female babies, that boys are harder to rear than girls, that the male death rate is slightly higher and life expectancy for males is shorter than that of females. Add to these general factors the special hardships to which the Negro minority is exposed—poverty, crowded living conditions, poor health, marginal jobs, and minimum protection against hazards of accident and illness—and it becomes apparent that there is much in the American environment that is particularly hostile to the survival of the black male. But even if we discount these factors and accept the theory that the sex ratio is the result of errors in census counting, it is difficult to avoid the conclusion that a large number of black males have so few stable ties that they are not included as functioning units of the society. In either case formidable pressures are created for black women.

The explosive social implications of an excess of more than half a million black girls and women over fourteen years of age are obvious in a society in which the mass media intensify notions of glamour and expectations of romantic love and marriage, while at the same time there are many barriers against interracial marriages. When such marriages do take place they are more likely to involve black males and white females, which tends to aggravate the issue. (No value judgment about interracial marriages is implied here. I am merely trying to describe a social dilemma.) The problem of an excess female population is a familiar one in countries which have experienced heavy male casualties during wars, but an excess female ethnic minority as an enclave within a larger population raises important social issues. To what extent are the tensions and conflicts traditionally associated with the matriarchal framework of Negro family life in reality due to this imbalance and the pressures it generates? Does this excess explain the active competition between Negro professional men and women seeking employment in markets which have limited or excluded Negroes? And does this competition intensify the stereotype of the matriarchal society and female dominance? What relationship is there between the high rate of illegitimacy among black women and the population figures we have described?

These figures suggest that the Negro woman's fate in the United States, while inextricably bound with that of the Negro male in one sense, transcends the issue of Negro rights. Equal opportunity for her must mean equal opportunity to compete for jobs and to find a mate in the total society. For as long as she is confined to an area in which she must compete fiercely for a mate, she will remain the object of sexual exploitation and the victim of all the social evils which such exploitation involves.

When we compare the position of the black woman to that of the white woman, we find that she remains single more often, bears more children, is in the labor market longer and in greater proportion, has less education, earns less, is widowed earlier, and carries a relatively heavier economic responsibility as family head than her white counterpart.

In 1966, black women represented one of every seven women workers, although Negroes generally constitute only 11 per cent of the total population in the United States. Of the 3,105,000 black women eighteen years of age and over who were in the labor force, however, nearly half (48.2 per cent) were either single, widowed, divorced, separated from their husbands, or their husbands were absent for other reasons, as compared with 31.8 per cent of white women in similar circumstances. Moreover, six of every ten black women were in household employment or other service jobs. Conversely, while 58.8 per cent of all women workers held white collar positions, only 23.2 per cent of black women held such jobs.

As working wives, black women contribute a higher proportion to family income than do white women. Among nonwhite wives in 1965, 58 per cent contributed to 20 per cent or more of the total family income, 43 per cent contributed 30 per cent or more and 27 per cent contributed 40 per cent or more. The comparable percentages for white wives were 56 per cent, 40 per cent, and 24 per cent respectively.

Black working mothers are more heavily represented in the labor force than white mothers. In March 1966, nonwhite working mothers with children under eighteen years of age represented 48 per cent of all nonwhite mothers with children this age as compared with 35 per cent of white working mothers. Nonwhite working mothers also represented four of every ten of all nonwhite mothers of children under six years of age. Of the 12,300,000 children under fourteen years of age in February 1965 whose mothers worked, only 2 per cent were provided group care in day-care centers. Adequate child care is an urgent need for working mothers generally, but it has particular significance for the high proportion of black working mothers of young children.

Black women also carry heavy responsibilities as family heads. In 1966, one-fourth of all black families were headed by a woman as compared with less than one-tenth of all white families. The economic disabilities of women generally are aggravated in the case of black women. Moreover, while all families headed by women are more vulnerable to poverty than husband–wife families, the black woman family head is doubly victimized. For example, the median wage or salary income of all women workers who were employed full time the year round in 1967 was only 58 per cent of that of all male workers, and the median earnings of white females was less than that of black males. The median wage of nonwhite women workers, however, was $3,268, or only 71 per cent of the median income of white women workers. In 1965, one-third of all families headed by women lived in poverty, but 62 per cent of the 1,132,000 nonwhite families with a female head were poor.

A significant factor in the low economic and social status of black women is their concentration at the bottom rung of the employment ladder. More than one-third of all nonwhite working women are employed as private household workers. The median wages of women private household workers who were employed full time the year round in 1968 was only $1,701. Furthermore, these workers are not covered by the Federal minimum wage and hours law and are generally excluded from state wage and hours laws, unemployment compensation, and workmen's compensation.

The black woman is triply handicapped. She is heavily represented in nonunion employment and thus has few of the benefits to be derived from labor organization or social legislation. She is further victimized by discrimination because of race and sex. Although she has made great strides in recent decades in closing the educational gap, she still suffers from inadequate education and training. In 1966, only 71.1 per cent of all Negro women had completed eight grades of elementary school compared to 88 per cent of all white women. Only one-third (33.2 per cent) of all Negro women had completed high school as compared with more than one-half of all white women (56.3). More than twice as many white women, proportionally, have completed college (7.2 per cent) as black women (3.2 per cent).

The notion of the favored economic position of the black female in relation to the black male is a myth. The 1966, median earnings of full-time year-round nonwhite female workers was only 65 per cent of that of nonwhite males. The unemployment rate for adult nonwhite women (6.6) was higher than for their male counterparts (4.9). Among nonwhite teenagers, the unemployment rate for girls was 31.1 as compared with 21.2 for boys.

In the face of their multiple disadvantages, it seems clear that black women can neither postpone nor subordinate the fight against sex discrimination to the Black Revolution. Many of them must expect to be self-supporting and perhaps to support others for a considerable period or for life. In these circumstances, while efforts to raise educational and employment levels for black males will ease some of the economic and social burdens now carried by many black women, for a large and apparently growing minority these burdens will continue. As a matter of sheer survival black women have no alternative but to insist upon equal opportunities without regard to sex in training, education, and employment. Given their heavy family responsibilities, the outlook for their children will be bleak indeed unless they are encouraged in every way to develop their potential skills and earning power.

Because black women have an equal stake in women's liberation and black liberation, they are key figures at the juncture of these two movements. White women feminists are their natural allies in both causes. Their own liberation is linked with the issues which are stirring women today: adequate income maintenance and the elimination of poverty, repeal or reform of abortion laws, a national system of child-care centers, extension of labor standards to workers now excluded, cash maternity benefits as part of a system of social insurance, and the removal of all sex barriers to educational and employment opportunities at all levels. Black women have a special stake in the revolt against the treatment of women primarily as sex objects, for their own history has left them with the scars of the most brutal and degrading aspects of sexual exploitation.

The middle-class Negro woman is strategically placed by virtue of her tradition of independence and her long experience in civil rights and can play a creative role in strengthening the alliance between the Black Revolution and Women's Liberation. Her advantages of training and her values make it possible for her to communicate with her white counterparts, interpret the deepest feelings within the black community, and cooperate with white women on the basis of mutual concerns as women. The possibility of productive interchange between black and white women is greatly facilitated by the absence of power relationships which separate black and white males as antagonists. By asserting a leadership role in the growing feminist movement, the black woman can help to keep it allied to the objectives of black liberation while simultaneously advancing the interests of all women.

The lesson of history that all human rights are indivisible and that the failure to adhere to this principle jeopardizes the rights of all is particularly applicable here. A built-in hazard of an aggressive ethnocentric movement which disregards the interests of other disadvantaged groups is that it will become parochial and ultimately self-defeating in the face of hostile reactions, dwindling allies, and mounting frustrations. As Dr. Caroline F. Ware has pointed out, perhaps the most essential instrument for combating the divisive effects of a black-only movement is the voice of black women insisting upon the unity of civil rights of women and Negroes as well as other minorities and excluded groups. Only a broad movement for human rights can prevent the Black Revolution from becoming isolated and can insure its ultimate success.

Beyond all the present conflict lies the important task of reconciliation of the races in America on the basis of genuine equality and human dignity. A powerful force in bringing about this result can be generated through the process of black and white women working together to achieve their common humanity.

24

Contemporary Feminism:
Theories and Practice

Jean E. Friedman

The 1960s witnessed a revival of feminism with the Women's Liberation movement. Cynics considered the movement a creation of the media, because the women's early protests, "bra-burning"[1] and the crowning of a sheep at Atlantic City's Miss America Pageant, had all the elements of theater. Too much emphasis has been placed on the sensational and peripheral aspects of the women's movement. As a result, ridicule detracted from the most substantial issue of the movement—the question of women's identity.

The concept of identity has such broad and indeterminate meaning in both popular and scientific usage that perhaps we can speak only of a few of its "dimensions" as they relate to women.[2] Simone De Beauvoir in *The Second Sex*[3] wrote that throughout history the clearest identity has been male. Women as a sex never claimed an historic role; civilization as we know it is man-made. Even the universal term for all human beings is *man*. Why? Because, De Beauvoir says, men defined themselves as Self, the Absolute, and relegated women to the status of "Other" or Object, a referent incidental to the Self. Similarly, Vivian Gornick, a freelance writer and frequent contributer to the *Village Voice* considers woman an "outsider," an object onto whom man projects his fears and fantasies. Woman as seducer and goddess is, "steeped in sex, drugged on sex, defined by sex, *but never actually realized through sex.*"[4] It is evident that Gornick touched upon the primal antagonism to the Women's Liberation movement—the deep-seated fear that women's fully developed identity would unleash the supposed, terribly destructive forces of her sexuality.[5] To men who reason this way, Gornick passionately argues, women could not be real; only the "idea" of woman is real to them. Gornick, like De Beauvoir, suggests that women have been defined by others and concludes that the psychic effect of this lack of self-definition is that today women cannot take themselves seriously. The solution as Gornick sees it lies in "responsibility." Like the blacks, barred from assuming the responsibility of "serious" work (problem solving), and thus deprived of a sense of self, women through their relegation to the routine and monotonous household tasks, have been cut off from both "serious" work and the realization of their own womanhood.[6] De Beauvoir and Gornick typify the general focus of contemporary feminist thought.

The three main groups within the movement—privatists, reformers and radicals—respond to the problem of identity with differing programmatic alternatives. Privatists probably make up the bulk of the movement but generally are not members of any organized group. They prefer to operate within the confines of their families and concentrate upon a highly individual development of their own identity. The reformers are the white middle class and professional women who responded to Betty Friedan's *The Feminine Mystique*, a study which examined the restlessness of educated suburban wives whose only measure of personal fulfillment was through their children and husbands. It was from this group that Friedan recruited a base for NOW (National Organization for Women). Founded in 1966, NOW has worked for equal opportunity in business and professional jobs and in education. NOW women tend to emphasize the social aspect of identity. The individual woman identifies with the organization, its principles and her work for NOW. Radical women, angry when they were treated as second class citizens in the New Left movement, became more militant. By encouraging women to talk to each other radical groups hope to build some thoughtful awareness of what sexual roles are and how they affect women's lives. Radicals view revolutionary change as the only recourse. The emphasis upon individual identity more often than not leads to a social or revolutionary purpose in radical groups.

The theories of each feminist group become clearer upon closer examination. For Jane Gallion privatism has meaning in that each woman must face herself and have the courage to grow up. Gallion claims liberation of oppressed womankind is valueless unless directed to the fulfillment of individual needs and potential. In her witty and insightful book, *The Woman as Nigger,* Gallion contends women have been sold an adulterated product—themselves. To understand themselves women must cut through artificial media and advertising images. The lie is that women are liberated; the truth is women dare not ask for freedom. So women live the lie exchanging overt for covert bondage. In an ironic and biting play on women's submission Gallion thanked society for her privileges:

> Thank you for giving me a cigarette of my own. Thank you for giving me a thousand red buttons to push. Thank you for giving me Section IV of the newspaper. Thank you, thank you, thank you. . . .
> Thank you for giving me money instead of love. Thank you for telling me that when I am good. . . . I am masculine, that I think like a man.
> Thank you for making my greatest expectation my subjugation, body and soul and spirit, to any man alive, if he will only notice me.
> Thank you for allowing me to serve you.[7]

In the battle of the sexes Gallion encourages women to take the first step and try to understand male fears. She views women's subjugation as a projection of male insecurities—fears of sexual inadequacy, of growing old, of losing power. Understand these anxieties, she urges, and then like Nora in Ibsen's *A Doll's House,* say no to being used. Gallion's is a personal solution. Liberation begins, she says, when the men in your life know that you are no longer a servant.

Caroline Hennessey, a more militant privatist, believes in the efficacy of individual guerrilla action that would break patterns of docility and submission; individual employees can sabotage business by causing slowdowns, cutting efficiency, misfiling documents. Personal commitment will then lead to broader involvement—groups of women banded together to pressure schools, universities, or businesses that discriminate, but in Hennessey's alternative rests basically upon her faith in individual action or commitment.[8]

Privatism is characteristic of some movement organizations as well. Suburban women, who meet in various Women's Liberation groups, have a tendency to concentrate on problems of their individual identities and needs. Painful transitions to personal autonomy challenge traditional sex roles, but discussion rarely goes beyond informal, unstructured rap sessions. For many privatists the group sessions provide an escape from anomie. For others, invigorated marital relations have allowed them to adapt to their lives.[9]

Much of the initial political drive of the women's movement was supplied by *The Feminine Mystique,* the publication of which raised feminist expectations. Betty Friedan cut through the accepted notion that women had a certain "nature" which predetermined their role. The argument is a variation on the conservative theme that "whatever is, is natural," a proposition designed to set limits on highly variable human personality. The feminine mystique defined femininity solely in terms of the housewife—mother role, "the mistake, says the mystique, the root of women's troubles in the past is that women envied men . . . instead of accepting their own nature, which can find fulfillment only in sexual passivity, male domination and nurturing maternal love."[10] Denied access to personal satisfaction in careers outside the home women found they had "no image of themselves" and were vulnerable, Friedan says, to "public images" manipulated by Madison Avenue, "Freudian" psychologists, "functional" behavioral scientists, and "sex-directed" educators.

Freud's tentative theories about women supported much of the feminine myth. Friedan challenged Freudian assumptions of women's biological inferiority and attacked his concept of "penis envy" which she described as particularly degrading to women. The motivation which Freud claimed led, "in normal femininity, to the wish for the penis of her husband, a wish that is never really fulfilled until she possesses a penis through giving birth to a son,"[11] Friedan explained, is understood by some modern behavioral analysts as simply a manifestation in the human personality of the need to grow and develop an ego. Freud's theory was culturally determined according to Friedan; he had simply rationalized Victorian ethos which glorified women's servility. He directed his efforts toward maintaining the status quo, helping men and women adjust to their roles in society.

For Friedan, Margaret Mead represented the prime "functionalist," another progenitor of the feminine mystique. In her early study, *Sex and Temperament in the South Seas,* Friedan noted that Mead found variety as characteristic of sexual patterns, reasoning from this that masculinity or femininity cannot be regarded as derived from sex. But as her work progressed she considered differentiation as universal and interference in the cultural definition disastrous. Therefore, she supported the traditional sexual roles of wife and mother so prevalent in Western society. Friedan wryly noted Mead's personal life-pattern deviated from the norm, and that she created a significant body of work in a man's world.

Finally, college and university educators, who have viewed women as totally sexual beings and taught them to adjust to motherhood as their sole function, have been equally important in prepetuating the feminine mystique. Friedan maintained greater concern was given to women's biological functioning than to cultivating their creative abilities. The mystique was further reinforced by advertisers in the media who exploited housewives in order to guarantee the most lucrative market-products for home. Producers and advertisers displaced women's feeling of "emptiness" by crowding the home with the latest household gimmicks.

In the years following the publication of *The Feminine Mystique* important issues of concern to women were being debated in Congress and the courts. An amendment to the Civil Rights Act of 1964 prohibiting employment discrimination on the basis of sex was proposed jokingly by southern congressman Howard W. Smith in order to defeat the bill. When the act passed, there was a question whether Title VII which banned sex discrimination would ever be enforced. It became evident to Betty Friedan and others concerned that without pressure from organized women's groups attempts to counter discrimination would be largely ineffectual. It was this realization that prompted the founding of NOW in 1966.[12]

NOW is in the women's rights tradition by virtue of its leadership principles, organization, and its political-legal reform strategy. The businesslike structure of NOW attempts to obtain for women "a truly equal partnership with men." A social consciousness very much in the Liberal–Progressive tradition, NOW believes its legal and political reforms will find a response in the government. NOW has claimed some victories, such as an amendment of the president's executive order to prohibit job discrimination by the government and its contractors and subcontractors. In addition, the Equal Employment Opportunity Commission ruled sex-segregated "help-wanted-male" and "help-wanted-female" advertisements violated Title VII. Currently, NOW is campaigning for the repeal of abortion laws in line with its belief in the right of women to control their own bodies. NOW has also been active in the campaign for passage of the Equal Rights Amendment, first proposed by Alice Paul in 1923. It provides that "equality of rights under the law shall not be denied or abridged by the United States or by any state on account of sex." The amendment will affect marriage and employment laws in some forty states. Directly related to the ERA is the campaign to establish child care centers by law "on the same basis as parks, libraries and public schools."[13]

NOW insists that it is "an action organization" and holds to the belief that feminism cannot be defined until it has been realized through action. NOW seeks to multiply the options for women by securing greater opportunity in "church, state, college, or office" and providing upward mobility for women who although they are 40 percent or more of the labor force, occupy routine or undesirable positions. Work is institutionalized according to sex roles with women occupying the supportive positions. Women are nurses rather than doctors, and secretaries not executives. Paralleling the division in work is the differentiation in salaries. The reasoning behind these discrepancies is that it is assumed a woman's salary is supplementary; furthermore, she is not expected to remain permanently on the job. A study made in 1967 revealed the contrary. Over 60 per cent of women worked because of economic necessity; either they or their husbands earned less than $5,000 a year. Women's full-time employment contributed 35 percent to 40 percent of the family income while part-time employment allowed for 15 percent to 20 percent of the combined income. With regard to turnover and absenteeism, Caroline Bird argued that that is related to job and not sex.[14] "Equal pay for equal work" is one of NOW's primary demands.

Friedan insists her views and those of NOW are realistic; that revolutionaries talk in terms of visionary abstractions. Retaining a liberal's optimism, Friedan believes institutions will change and that decisions concerning sex and children will be much more responsible and rational, because they will be controlled by both men and women. Manless revolution is nonsense, a "cop-out" when a majority of women want children. However, Friedan does argue that "revolutionary" concepts in education are needed to develop women's potential. Sweden is her idea of utopia. The government subsidizes equality of the sexes; boys and girls take cooking and shop; in the universities dormitories are integrated sexually. Swedish husbands and wives adjust their work schedules to share household duties; the adjustment is temporary pending the establishment of government supported day care centers.[15] Friedan supports evolutionary change that would benefit, rather than disrupt, the system.

Reform is unacceptable to radical women for whom the only alternative is a fundamentally altered society. Sexual roles institutionalized in family, state, and church can be transformed only by overthrowing present institutions. The radicals object to the idea of an "equal partnership with men," because it implies partnership in a system in which social institutions have been constructed by the traditionally dominant groups.[16]

The problem of instituting a new society has created something of an ideological crisis in radical feminist ranks. New Left experience found Marxism useful only in a limited sense. Radical women activists are struggling to construct an ideology capable of competing with established political systems. In classical Marxism the modes of production determine social, cultural, and intellectual structures. History is a struggle between economic classes—those who own the means of production and those who do not, bourgeoise and proletariat, master and slave, exploiter and exploited. Engels theorized women were the first exploited class; "within the family . . . [the husband] is the bourgeoisie and the wife . . . the proletariat."[17] To feminists the problem with Marx and Engels is that they discuss women primarily in relation to questions of family and private property; in fact, they define the patriarchial family as a means of controlling property. Juliett Mitchell, a Marxist, has observed, "The liberation of women remains a normative ideal, an adjunct to socialist theory, not structurally integrated into it."[18]

Lenin regarded "the emancipation of women" as a bourgeois ruse. The woman question was part of the social working class question, the proletarian class struggle, and above all, the revolution. The great revolutionary chided Clara Zetkin, leader of the international women's communist movement, because she allowed sex and marriage problems to be discussed in meetings of women workers. He argued that such questions were not private matters since marriages involved children and the future of the community. Lenin's myopia can be attributed to his assumption that full equality was a working principle within the party even though he recognized that there were "philistines" indifferent to their wives' double burden of housework and "productive labor." Liberation in socialist terms has meant simply full participation in production.[19]

Influenced by the New Left, most radical feminists have ceased to accept orthodox Marxism. They no longer believe that economic determinism is the most significant factor of women's oppression. Celestine Ware notes that the difficulty of socialist theory is that it "would emancipate women in order to acquire a larger work force and not aid in their self-actualization."[20] The development of the radical idea of self-actualization as a revolutionary principle grew directly out of women's experience in the New Left. Radical women, activists in the Civil Rights movement, SNCC, and SDS resented being relegated to the routine jobs while the men assumed decision-making positions inside and outside the organization. Most striking to activist women was the elitism displayed by radical men. Bullying tactics, the "I am more revolutionary than you" ploy, and accusations of "sloppy thinking" effectively stymied women "socialized to fear aggression [and] who tend[ed] to lack experience in articulating abstract concepts."[21] Radical men pontificating the orthodox line insisted that the woman question was part of the "social, working class question." As far as radical women were concerned the movement had left them; the "philistines" were not to be persuaded. Some women did remain in the New Left movement. Radical feminists refer to them as "politicos," those who tend to see "feminism as only tangential to 'real' radical politics instead of directly radical in itself."[22]

The radical women who split from the New Left were forced to reevaluate Marx in feminist terms. Roxanne Dunbar in her essay, "Female Liberation as the Basis for Social Revolution," argued that the women's movement contains revolutionary potential because women developed as a separate caste. She claims that although women have shared in the predominate male culture, they have had a separate experience. Woman's special capacity for reproduction forced her into a sedentary life where she developed a community based upon cooperation. With the overthrow of woman's primitive communist society, women were subjugated in a lower caste. Caste is assigned from birth by physical characteristics and unlike economic class a woman cannot escape from it. "It means," Dunbar explains, "that whatever traits [are] associated with the lower caste will be devalued in the society or will be mystified in some way."[23] The caste system rooted in the patriarchal family will be destroyed, Dunbar explains, only when a cooperative society is created.

For Dunbar, women must lead the revolution and use feminist principles to reorganize society. She never identifies the feminist principles that will replace established ones. Marx identified women's oppression as part of proletarian class oppression. Dunbar claims that because women have had a separate experience they exist as a caste apart from the proletariat. To exploit the revolutionary potential of class and caste, radicals must relate to both working class and women's experience. Dunbar believes that the woman revolution will precede social revolution.

A similar but less orthodox position is taken by Ti-Grace Atkinson.[24] She argues that biological and sociological functions of child bearing and child rearing determined women's class status. This role reduced women to the "functional" rather than human level. Atkinson, however, is best known as a proponent of the "new politics" of egalitarianism within the movement. As president of the New York chapter of NOW in 1968, Atkinson and the by-laws committee proposed executive rotation to facilitate a more equitable power distribution and counteract government by a few. This issue split the movement. Betty Friedan, then national president of the organization, earnestly promoted her case, "I want to get women into positions of power." Friedan's statement provoked Atkinson to reply, "We want to destroy the positions of power . . . not get into those positions."[25]

Atkinson's group (later called the Feminists) broke from NOW to initiate a more radical feminism dedicated to the "annihilation of sex roles" and the elimination of the politics of domination. The Feminists instituted the lot method of leadership. The principle justification for the measure is that "all women are capable . . . of leadership"; Feminists refused to duplicate the male power hierarchy which implies domination of those below them in the structure.[26]

The egalitarian principle is exemplified by the way Atkinson and the Feminists use consciousness-raising. Women meet in small unstructured groups and examine the lives of group members. The object of these sessions is to relate individual problems to the pattern of discrimination which society perpetuates. In the process women attempt to construct political issues from the problems discussed, and promote self-awareness and a sense of solidarity.[27] Through consciousness-raising, radical groups such as the Redstockings, WITCH, and the New York Radical Feminists offer critiques of sexist society and, in the case of the NYRF, have begun to construct an ideology that deals with the reconstruction of women's roles.

The Redstockings, an offshoot of New York Radical Women, abandoned New Left activism for consciousness-raising. The Redstockings reject all ideologies as male rationales, and insist that only out of their own experience can they reveal sexism in our society. The group supports any action for liberation regardless of its sponsor. Similarly, WITCH (Women's International Terrorist Conspiracy from Hell), engages in consciousness-raising and in a bizarre guerilla theater type of action. WITCH organized the famous protest against the Miss America Pageant indicting society's commercialization of feminine beauty.[28]

The New York Radical Feminists is an amalgam of former members of the Feminists and Redstockings. The NYRF responds to political issues connected with the family, motherhood, marriage, sexual intercourse, and love. On the subject of love NYRF declared, "in the context of an oppressive male–female relationship, [love] becomes an *emotional* cement to justify the dominant-submissive relationship." From this perspective the aim of the NYRF is to break the pattern of the sexual role system and "develop a new dialectic of sex class." [29] Shulamith Firestone, one of the founders of the NYRF, elaborated the ideology of the group in *The Dialectic of Sex: The Case for Feminist Revolution.*[30]

Firestone, a utopian feminist, adapted Marx to her own radical analysis. *The Dialectic of Sex* is a theory of class conflict which Firestone traces to the differing biological functions of the sexes and the domination of one sex by the other. A caste system of discrimination, she argues, became institutionalized in the family by the division of labor. Women's oppression in the family can then be traced to her child-bearing capacity, economic dependence, the segregation of the sexes within the family, and sexual repression.

To eliminate this class oppression, Firestone says women must revolt and seize both the means of production and the means of artificial reproduction in order to restore the ownership of their own bodies. The goal of Firestone's feminist revolution is abolition of not only male class privileges, but sexual distinction itself and its mythic embodiment in the incest taboo. The consequence of this would be a reversion to a more "natural" state of polymorphous perversity in which sexual relations between all persons regardless of age, sex, or familial relationship would be legitimatized. Firestone is convinced that sexual repression learned in the family is the basis of all "political, ideological, and economic" oppression. With artificial reproduction children would be born independently of the sexes and reared communally in licenced households; the family system would cease to exist. In this utopia of "cybernetic socialism," machines would eliminate the wage system, the foundation for class oppression.

Love and motherhood have different connotations for Firestone than for the more moderate members of the movement. Romantic love, according to her, is the "pivot of woman's oppression" because the woman is trapped in a one-sided political situation in which the male absorbs her "emotional strength" with no return commitment. The "sexual revolution" to Firestone is nothing but a complete capitulation to the male will. In reconsidering the hallowed institution of motherhood, the author insists that since "pregnancy is barbaric" and "childbirth hurts," there should be no conflict in introducing artificial reproduction, especially if the system is administered humanely without sinister motives of racial or intellectual control.

Firestone's utopian scheme is, at best, an optimistic statement that envisions a time when relationships between the sexes cease to be political and equality is substituted for domination. In contrast, Valerie Solanas' SCUM (Society for Cutting Up Men) Manifesto, which circulated underground in women's liberation circles for several years, is a dark vision of a society without men. Her piercing manifesto expresses neurotic hostility against the male domination of society. Just hours before Robert Kennedy's assassination, Valerie shot artist Andy Warhol because, she said, "he had too much control over my life."[31] Her acute sensibility to women's role as sexual object has led her to resist male domination and submission to the traditional female role through asexuality. "You've got to go through a lot of sex to get to anti-sex" [32] says Solanas, insisting that "sex is the refuge of the mindless"[33] —the refuge of those who indulge in the male "culture." In Solanas' revolution, women will refuse to act out their customary role, remaining cool, cerebral, and asexual. Solanas presents the eternal female dilemma: defined in unrealistic sexual terms, the woman becomes obsessed by sex and must either transcend it or cease to live.[34] In SCUM's mirror view of male–female relationships the images are reversed:

> The male is psychically passive. He hates his passivity so he projects it onto women . . . Being an incomplete female, the male spends his life attempting to complete himself to become female. He attempts to do this . . . by claiming as his own all female characteristics—emotional strength and independence, forcefulness, dynamism, decisiveness, coolness, objectivity, assertiveness, courage . . . and projecting onto women all male traits— vanity, frivolity, triviality, weakness, etc. It should be said, though, that the male has one glaring area of superiority over the female—public

relations. (He has done a brilliant job of convincing millions of women that men are women and women are men.)[35]

It is intriguing to observe that in the *SCUM Manifesto,* the most radical and extreme statement in the woman's movement, the concepts of male and female follow traditional stereotypes. The "psychic" division between the sexes remains passive–aggressive, and passive tendencies are regarded as inferior. To refute the proposition that women are inferior because they are passive, Solanas simply reverses the usual sexual attributes. In a sense her dilemma is an historic feminist one.

Much of the confusion that plagues feminist thought can be attributed to what historian David Potter termed the "dualism" with regard to women's roles. Accepting the traditional role of wife and mother, women allowed for the corollary assumption that they were best suited for that role by their "natural" traits of docility and maternity. Feminists are then trapped in reconciling "a new condition with an old one, to hold in balance the principle of equality, which denies a difference [between the sexes] and the practice of wifehood which recognizes a difference in the roles of men and women."[36] Both moderates and radicals within the movement have given attention to the problem of the family as a barrier to liberation. Their proposed solutions reveal the main reason why the two strands of feminism are antagonistic. The reformers are reluctant to tamper with the nuclear family. Child care centers and repeal of abortion laws are their methods for relieving the strains upon the women within the family. Radicals prefer to consider basic structural changes in the social order that would eliminate the family, claiming that its power structure serves as the basis of all hierarchies of dominance.

It is true that the family pattern has changed. In our agrarian past the family was a coordinated economic unit which provided an array of functions from education to recreation. The urban nuclear family, however, is chiefly an agent of socialization. It is not inconceivable, therefore, that day care centers and nurseries will cooperate in performing residual family duties just as schools have shared in socialization. In addition, communal living and collective child rearing are providing possible alternatives to the nuclear family pattern. However, indications are that mixed communes do not in themselves liberate either sex from their customary roles.[37] What is evident in the evolution of the family is that changes have been made in response to economic and social conditions rather than to the demands of any group. This may account for the movement's lack of success in instituting either reforms or radical change in the family structure.

In attempting to understand contemporary feminism, one might conclude that there is no movement. Confusion on this point is understandable in light of the multiplicity of groups and conflicts among self-proclaimed feminists. More to the point, however, most observers do not grasp the multifarious nature of feminist activism. Most social movements have used political means to change the order of things. The main goal of nineteenth century feminism was suffrage. Today the women's movement continues to be political. Disparate groups such as the American Home Economics Association joined with radical feminists, NOW, and the National Women's Political Caucus in carrying the Equal Rights Amendment through the House and Senate. State ratification is now in order. Although opposition has recently stiffened and two states have attempted to rescind earlier votes in favor of the ERA, close cooperation of various groups at the local level has won ratification in thirty-five of the necessary thirty-seven states. The NWPC, which has channeled considerable energy in traditional political avenues, is not an independent "women's party" but a bi-partisan pressure group designed to support women candidates. Recently, they have organized state and regional caucuses to encourage women to stand as delegates to the Democratic and Republican National Conventions. In addition, the Caucus campaigned for national day care legislation which President Nixon ultimately vetoed.[38]

While certain women's groups today are involved in traditional political ventures, an important element of the Women's Liberation movement has always emphasized consciousness-raising as preliminary to social action. At this level the direction of the movement is inward, toward self-actualization. Until a majority of women develop a critical attitude toward the society which discriminates against them, political success will be elusive. Whether the movement's political caucus is successful or not, the problem of reaching the vast woman population remains. There's always that "doubt," the nameless fear that keeps women from approaching a solution. M. Carey Thomas talked about that private anguish in 1908, "The passionate desire of women of my generation for higher education was accompanied throughout its course by the awful doubt, felt by women themselves as well as by men, as to whether women as a sex were physically and mentally fit for it." [39] That sense of inferiority socialized deep in the female psyche prevents a'l kinds of action, collective and private. Miriam Allen de Ford in a searching article, "Women Against Themselves," noted that women obligingly assume secondary roles, preferring to deal with men "by indirection, evasion, subterfuge, by the 'power behind the throne syndrome,' " but by so doing De Ford contends women exhibit "the classical symptom of self-hatred."[40] It is these self-destructive tendencies which divide women among themselves and form the main resistance to the woman's movement. The political success of the movement is wholly dependent upon the individual woman's attitude and her refusal to play her traditional role. As Mary Anne Krupsack told the 1975 Philadephia meeting of N.O.W.:

> We will never fulfill the American dream until the images in the minds of women, as well as the minds of men, are allowed to share in the dream.[41]

NOTES

1. A municipal fire ordinance prevented any burning demonstration by the women. "Bra-burning" never took place at Atlantic City.

2. Erik H. Erikson, *Identity, Youth and Crisis* (New York: W. W. Norton, 1968), 19–22.

3. New York: Alfred A. Knopf, 1953.

4. "Woman as Outsider," in Vivian Gornick and Barbara K. Moran, eds., *Woman in Sexist Society* (New York: Basic Books, 1971).

5. For a discussion of the range of male fears see "Are American Men Afraid of Women?" *Sexual Behavior*, I (May, 1971), 34–36.

6. "Women's Liberation, The Next Great Movement in History Is Theirs," *The Village Voice*, November 27, 1969. Reprints available from KNOW, Inc., Pittsburgh, Pennsylvania.

7. *The Woman as Nigger* (Canoga Park, California: Weiss, Day & Lord, 1970), 78–79.

8 *The Strategy of Sexual Struggle* (New York: Lancer Books, 1971).

9. *The New York Times*, April 7, 1971, p. c–28.

10. New York: W. W. Norton, copyright © 1963 by Betty Friedan.

11. *Ibid.*, 106.

12. Julie Ellis, *Revolt of the Second Sex* (New York: Lancer Books, 1970), 22.

13. Gornick, "Women's Liberation. . . ."

14. Caroline Bird with Sara Welles Briller, *Born Female: The High Cost of Keeping Women Down* (New York: David McKay, 1968), 81–84; Marlene Dixon, "Why Women's Liberation," in Thomas R. Frazier, ed., *Underside of American History* (New York: Harcourt Brace Jovanovich, 1971), 326.

15. "Our Revolution Is Unique," in Mary Lou Thompson, ed., *Voices of the New Feminism* (Boston: Beacon Press, 1970), 37– 42.

16. Alice S. Rossi, "The Beginnings of Ideology," in Thompson, *Voices of the New Feminism*, 72.

17. *The Origin of the Family, Private Property and the State* (New York: International Publishers, 1942), 65–66.

18. "Women, the Longest Revolution," *New Left Review* (November/December 1966). Reprint available from the New England Free Press, Boston, Massachusetts. See quote p. 5.

19. Clara Zetkin, "My Recollections of Lenin," in *The Emancipation of Women* (New York: International Publishers, 1934), 97–123. See also Juliet Mitchell, "Women, the Longest Revolution," *New Left Review* (November/December 1966), *passim*.

20. *Woman Power: The Movement for Women's Liberation* (New York: Tower Publications, 1970), 101.

21. Kathy McAfee and Myrna Wood, "Bread and Roses," in Leslie B. Tanner, ed., *Voices from Women's Liberation* (New York: New American Library, 1971), 425; see also Marge Piercy, "The Grand Coolie Damn" in Robin Morgan, ed., *Sisterhood Is Powerful* (New York: Random House, 1970), 421–438.

22. Shulamith Firestone, *The Dialectic of Sex: The Case for Feminist Revolution* (New York: Bantam Books, 1970), 33.

23. In *Sisterhood . . .*, 482.

24. "Radical Feminism," in Shulamith Firestone and Anne Koedt, eds., *Notes from the Second Year: Women's Liberation* (New York, 1970), 32–37.

25. Ware, *Woman Power . . .*, 25.

26. Unfortunately, the Feminists rigidified their system and imposed penalties on those who missed meetings or opposed the will of the group. One-third of the membership was limited to married women or women living with men. Heterosexual relations were considered exploitative. The authoritarianism and separatism of Atkinson and her supporters destroyed the Feminists. See Ware, *Woman Power . . .*, 27–32.

27. Ware, *Woman Power . . .*, 109–110.

28. Gornick, "Woman's Liberation. . . ."

29. Ware, *Woman Power . . .*, 60, 61.

30. New York: William Morrow, 1970.

31. Ellis, *Revolt . . .*, 138.

32. New York: Olympia Press, 1967, 32.

33. *Ibid.*, 30.

34. Gornick, "Woman as Outsider," 68.

35. Solanas, *SCUM*, 5–6.

36. David Potter, "American Women and the American Character," in John A. Hague, ed., *American Character and Culture* (DeLand, Fla.: Everett Edwards Press, 1964), 82.

37. See Joseph J. Downing, "The Tribal Family and the Society of Awakening," in Herbert A. Otto, ed., *The Family in Search of a Future* (New York: Appleton-Century-Crofts, 1970), 123; Herbert A. Otto, "Communes: The Alternative Life-Style," *Saturday Review* (April 24, 1971), 20.

38. Gloria Steinem, "What Nixon Doesn't Know About Women," *New York*, IV (July 26, 1971), 8–9.

39. "Present Tendencies in Women's College and University Education," quotation reprinted by permission of Quadrangle Books from *Up From the Pedestal*, edited by Aileen S. Kraditor, copyright © 1968 by Aileen S. Kraditor.

40. In *The Humanist*, XXXI (January/February 1971), 8–9.

41. Quoted in *Allentown Morning Call*, Oct. 25, 1975.

Bibliography

HISTORIOGRAPHY

Freedman, Estelle B. "The New Woman: Changing Views of Women in the 1920s." *Journal of American History* 61 (September 1974): 372–93.

Gordon, Ann D.; Buhle, Mari Jo; and Schrom, Nancy E. "Women in American Society: An Historical Contribution." *Radical America* 5 (1971): 3–66.

Gordon, Linda; Pleck, Elizabeth; Hunt, Persis; Scott, Marcia; and Ziegler, Rochelle. "A Review of Sexism in American Historical Writing." *Women's Studies* 1 (1972): 133–58.

Kruppa, Patricia S. "The American Woman and the Male Historian." *Social Science Quarterly* 55 (December 1974): 605–14.

Lerner, Gerda. "New Approaches to the Study of Women in American History." *Journal of Social History* 3 (Fall 1959): 53–62.

_____. "Women's Rights and American Feminism," *The American Scholar* 40 (Spring 1971): 235–48.

Potter, David. "American Women and the American Character." In John A. Hague, ed. *American Character and Culture: Some Twentieth Century Perspectives.* Deland, Florida: Everett Edwards Press, 1964. Pp. 65–84.

Watkins, Bari. "Women and History." In *Women on Campus: The Unfinished Liberation.* New Rochelle, N.Y.: Change Magazine, 1975. Pp. 95–101.

Zangrando, Joanna Schneider. "Women in the Archives: An Historian's View of the Liberation of Clio." *American Archivist* 36 (April 1972): 203–14.

_____. "Women's Studies in the United States: Approaching Reality." *American Studies International* 14 (Autumn 1975): 15–36.

GENERAL HISTORIES

Banner, Lois. *Women in Modern America*. Englewood Cliffs, N.J.: Prentice-Hall 1975.

Flexner, Eleanor. *Century of Struggle: The Women's Rights Movement in the United States*. Cambridge: Harvard University Press, 1975.

Lerner, Gerda. *The Woman in American History*. Reading, Mass.: Addison-Wesley, 1971.

Riegel, Robert E. *American Women: A Story of Social Change*. Teaneck, N.J.: Fairleigh Dickinson Press, 1970.

Ryan, Mary P. *Womanhood in America From Colonial Times to the Present*. New York: New Viewpoints, 1975.

Sinclair, Andrew. *The Better Half*. New York: Harper & Row, 1965.

Smith, Page. *Daughters of the Promised Land*. Boston: Little, Brown and Co., 1970.

Sochen, June. *Herstory: A Woman's View of American History*. New York: Alfred Publishing Co., 1974.

_____. *Movers and Shakers: American Women Thinkers and Activists 1900–1970*. New York: Quadrangle Books, 1973.

ANTHOLOGIES

Cott, Nancy F., ed. *Root of Bitterness: Documents of the Social History of American Women*. New York: E.P. Dutton and Co., 1972.

Cooper, James L. and Cooper, Sheila M., eds. *The Roots of American Feminist Thought*. Boston: Allyn and Bacon, 1973.

Kraditor, Aileen, ed. *Up From the Pedestal: Selected Writings in the History of American Feminism*. Chicago: Quadrangle Books, 1968.

Lerner, Gerda, ed. *Black Women in White America*. New York: Pantheon Books, 1972.

Martin, Wendy, ed. *The American Sisterhood*. New York: Harper & Row, 1972.

Parker, Gail, ed. *The Oven Birds: American Women on Womanhood, 1820–1920*. Garden City, N.Y.: Doubleday, 1972.

Rossi, Alice S., ed. *The Feminist Papers: From Adams to de Beauvoir*. New York: Columbia University Press, 1973.

Schneir, Miriam, ed. *Feminism: The Essential Historical Writings*. New York: Random House, 1973.

Scott, Anne F., ed. *The American Woman: Who Was She?* Englewood Cliffs, N.J.: Prentice-Hall, 1972.

Sochen, June, ed. *The New Feminism in Twentieth Century America*. Lexington, Mass: D.C. Heath and Company, 1971.